AF754574

MAX-PLANCK-GESELLSCHAFT

Universität Augsburg University

TECHNISCHE UNIVERSITÄT MÜNCHEN

THE GEORGE WASHINGTON UNIVERSITY

WASHINGTON, DC

**MIPLC Studies**

Edited by

Prof. Dr. Christoph Ann, LL.M. (Duke Univ.)
TUM School of Management

Prof. Robert Brauneis
The George Washington University Law School

Prof. Dr. Josef Drexl, LL.M. (Berkeley)
Max Planck Institute for Innovation and Competition

Prof. Dr. Michael Kort
University of Augsburg

Prof. Dr. Thomas M.J. Möllers
University of Augsburg

Prof. Dr. Dres. h.c. Joseph Straus
Max Planck Institute for Innovation and Competition

Volume 39

Teresa Trallero Ocaña

# The Notion of Secrecy

## A Balanced Approach in the Light of the Trade Secrets Directive

Nomos

MIPLC Munich Intellectual Property Law Center
Augsburg München Washington DC

This publication was supported by the Max Planck Society.

**The Deutsche Nationalbibliothek** lists this publication in the Deutsche Nationalbibliografie; detailed bibliographic data are available on the Internet at http://dnb.d-nb.de

a.t.: München, LMU, Diss., 2020

ISBN 978-3-8487-7146-2 (Print)
978-3-7489-1197-5 (ePDF)

**British Library Cataloguing-in-Publication Data**
A catalogue record for this book is available from the British Library.

ISBN 978-3-8487-7146-2 (Print)
978-3-7489-1197-5 (ePDF)

**Library of Congress Cataloging-in-Publication Data**
Trallero Ocaña, Teresa
The Notion of Secrecy
A Balanced Approach in the Light of the Trade Secrets Directive
Teresa Trallero Ocaña
640 pp.
Includes bibliographic references.

ISBN 978-3-8487-7146-2 (Print)
978-3-7489-1197-5(ePDF)

1st Edition 2021

© Teresa Trallero Ocaña

Published by
Nomos Verlagsgesellschaft mbH & Co. KG
Waldseestraße 3–5 | 76530 Baden-Baden
www.nomos.de

Production of the printed version:
Nomos Verlagsgesellschaft mbH & Co. KG
Waldseestraße 3–5 | 76530 Baden-Baden

ISBN 978-3-8487-7146-2 (Print)
ISBN 978-3-7489-1197-5 (ePDF)
DOI https://doi.org/10.5771/9783748911975

Onlineversion
Nomos eLibrary

This work is licensed under a Creative Commons Attribution – Non Commercial – No Derivations 4.0 International License.

# Acknowledgements

I would like to thank my supervisor Professor Annette Kur for her support during the completion of the dissertation and her valuable academic guidance. I would also like to express my gratitude to Professor Ansgar Ohly for providing the Zweitgutachten.

After graduating from the Munich Intellectual Property Law Center (MIPLC), I was fortunate to be accepted as a doctoral student by the Max Planck Institute for Innovation and Competition, to which I owe not only the financial support, but also the possibility of conducting research in the most stimulating academic environment.

I am particularly grateful to Seth Ericsson, Margit Hinkel and Ulrike Stubenvoll for their support throughout this long journey and making the MIPLC my family far away from home.

I would not have been able to complete this work without the support of so many friends and colleagues, but among them I would especially like to mention my good friend Marisa for her constant encouragement.

Special thanks go to Fabian for everything.

Most importantly, I would like to thank my mother Maite, my sister Anna, and my grandparents Manuel and María Teresa. This dissertation is dedicated to them.

# Table of Contents

# Abbreviations

| | |
|---|---|
| AIA | America Invents Act |
| BAG | Bundesarbeitsgericht or Federal Labour Court |
| BC | Berne Convention |
| BGB | Bürgerliches Gesetzbuch |
| BGH | Bundesgerichtshof or Federal Supreme Court |
| BKartA | Bundeskartellamt |
| BverGe | Bundesverfassungsgerichtentscheidungen |
| CCZ | Corporate Compliance Zeitschrift |
| CFI | Court of First Instance |
| ChFREU | Charter of Fundamental Rights of the EU |
| CJEU | Court of Justice of the European Union |
| Commission | The European Commission |
| CR | Computer und Recht |
| DPMA | German Patent and Trade Mark Office |
| DSU | Dispute Settlement Understanding |
| DTSA | Defend Trade Secrets Act of 2016 |
| e.g. (from Latin *exempli gratia*) | For example |
| EC | European Community |
| EC Treaty | The Treaty Establishing the European Community |
| ECHR | European Convention of Human Rights |
| ECJ | European Court of Justice |
| ECR | European Court Reports |
| ECS | European Copyright Society |
| ECtHR | European Court of Human Rights |
| ed/eds | Editor/Editors |
| EIPR | European Intellectual Property Review |
| EJIL | European Journal of International Law |
| EPC | European Patent Convention |
| EPO | European Patent Office |
| EU | European Union |

| | |
|---|---|
| EUTMR | European Union Trade Mark Regulation |
| FTC | Federal Trade Commission |
| GATT | General Agreement on Tariffs and Trade |
| GCEU | General Court of the European Union |
| GG | Grundgesetz für die Bundesrepublik Deutschland |
| GRUR | Gewerblicher Rechtsschutz und Urheberrecht |
| GRUR Int | Gewerblicher Rechtsschutz und Urheberrecht/Internationaler Teil |
| HGB | Handelsgesetzbuch |
| HRA | Human Rights Act |
| i.e. (from Latin *id est*) | That is to say |
| IDEA | IDEA: The Intellectual Property Law Review |
| IIC | International Review of Intellectual Property and Competition Law |
| IoT | Internet of Things |
| IP | Intellectual Property |
| IPQ | Intellectual Property Quarterley |
| IPR(s) | Intellectual Property Right(s) |
| JEP | Journal of Economic Perspectives |
| JIPITEC | Journal of Intellectual Property, Information Technology and Electronic Commerce Law |
| JIPLP | Journal of Intellectual Property Law and Practice |
| JuS | Juristische Schulung |
| LJ | Law Journal |
| LQR | Law Quarterly Review |
| LR | Law Review |
| MCAD | Misleading and Comparative Advertisement Directive |
| NAFTA | North American Free Trade Agreement |
| NDA | Non-disclosure agreement |
| NZA | Neue Zeitschrift für Arbeitsrecht |
| NZA-RR | Neue Zeitschrift für Arbeitsrecht -Rechtsprechungs-Report Arbeitsrecht |
| para(s) | Paragraph(s) |
| PC | Paris Convention |
| R&D | Research and Development |

| | |
|---|---|
| R&DBER | Research and Development Block Exemption Regulation |
| SC | Supreme Court |
| TEU | The Treaty of the European Union |
| TFEU | The Treaty on the Functioning of the European Union |
| TMD | Trade Mark Directive |
| TMR | Trade Mark Review |
| TRIPs | Trade-Related Aspects of Intellectual Property Rights |
| TSD | Trade Secrets Directive |
| TTBER | Technology Transfer Block Exemption Regulation |
| UK | United Kingdom |
| U.S. | United States of America |
| UN | United Nations |
| UTSA | Uniform Trade Secrets Act |
| UWG | Gesetz gegen den unlauteren Wettbewerb |
| VCLT | Vienna Convention on the Law of Treaties |
| VPN | Virtual Private Networks |
| WHO | World Health Organisation |
| WIPO | World Intellectual Property Organization |
| WRP | Wettbewerb in Recht und Praxis |
| WTO | World Trade Organisation |

# Introduction

> In this regard I should like to recount an anecdote that is so beautiful that one trembles at the thought that it might be true. It gathers into a single figure all constraints of discourse: those which limit its powers, those which master its aleatory appearances, and those which carry out the selection among speaking subjects. At the beginning of the seventeenth century, the Shogun heard tell that Europeans' superiority in matters of navigation, commerce, politics, and military skill was due to their knowledge of mathematics. He desired to get hold of such precious knowledge. As he had been told of an English sailor who possessed the secret of these miraculous discourses, he summoned him to his place and kept him there. Alone with him, he took lessons. He learned mathematics. He retained power, and lived to a great old age. It was not until the nineteenth century that there were Japanese mathematicians. But the anecdote does not stop there: it has a European side too. The story has it that this English sailor, Will Adams, was an autodidact, a carpenter who had learnt geometry in the course of working in a shipyard. Should we see this story as the expression of one of the great myths of European culture? The universal communication of knowledge and the infinite free exchange of discourses in Europe, against the monopolised and secret Oriental tyranny?[1]

The theme that underlies the passage reproduced above is the relationship between power and knowledge. By learning mathematics, the Shogun aspired to achieve the same level of dominance as the Europeans in strategic matters such as navigation, commerce, politics and military skills. Indeed, the knowledge he acquired from the English sailor allowed him to have a long and prosperous reign. Foucault's short story ultimately tells us that knowledge defines and confers power upon those who possess it. By the same token, the rhetorical questions posed at the end of the passage highlight the dichotomy between the exchange of information, which has dominated occidental discourses, and the exclusivity conferred by secrecy, which has prevailed in oriental traditions. Such a tension is a recurring one

1 Michel Foucault, 'The Order of Discourse' 52, 62 in Robert Young (ed), *Untying the Text: A Post-Structuralist Reader* (1st edn, Routledge & Kegan Paul 1981).

in the field of intellectual property, where policy makers strive to find the most appropriate balance between the access to and sharing of information and the necessary exclusivity to incentivise creation and innovation.

This conflict is even more present in the realm of trade secrets, where the holder of commercial secret information may use it in the market exclusively for as long as it remains concealed from competitors. Remarkably, unlike IPRs, trade secrets afford protection to their holders without the need to meet any qualitative threshold and without imposing any disclosure obligations or time restrictions. This explains why trade secrets are often identified as one of the preferred forms of appropriating returns from innovation and creative activities. Following Foucault's example, trade secrets confer a competitive advantage and market power upon their holders, without participating in the trade-off imposed by the general IPR framework. As a result, the coexistence of trade secrets with traditional IPRs is not a peaceful one, as in some instances they serve contradictory objectives.

In the digital age, information has become an increasingly valuable, but at the same time vulnerable commodity. In effect, in the knowledge economy, companies operate globally and outsource their research and manufacturing activities to other countries in search of cost-optimisation and the best qualified human capital.[2] In such a globalised context, the strategic role that trade secrets play in the economy of the Single Market and the scattered legal framework across EU jurisdictions prompted the EU Commission to harmonise this field of law, which led to the adoption of the Trade Secrets Directive (TSD),[3] that should have been implemented in all 28 EU Member States before 9 June 2018. This dissertation looks into the fundamentals of the law of trade secrecy in the wake of the Directive. In particular, it aims at studying the cornerstone of trade secret protection: the secrecy requirement.

---

2 Anselm Kamperman Sanders, 'The Actio Servi Corrupti' from the Roman Empire to the Globalised Economy' 3, 4 in Christopher Heath and Anselm Kamperman Sanders (eds), *Employees, Trade Secrets and Restrictive Covenants* (Wolter Kluwer 2016).

3 Directive (EU) 2016/943 of 8 June 2016 on the protection of undisclosed know-how and business information (trade secrets) against their unlawful acquisition, use and disclosure [2016] OJ L157/1 (Trade Secrets Directive, TSD).

## *§ 1 Object, scope and structure of the research*

The primary aim of this thesis is to analyse the conditions under which information loses its secret nature, enters the public domain and is then free for competitors to use, taking into account the legal framework created by the TSD. Indeed, the requirements for the protection of formal IPRs such as copyright or patents have been the object of academic study for years. However little attention has been paid to the requirements of the protection of trade secrets and the policy implications of defining them in a narrower or broader sense.

In the light of the above, the following research questions guide the dissertation. First, the thesis examines whether the protection of trade secrets is justified by the mere fact of them being unknown to competitors on the basis of utilitarian and deontological arguments. Secondly, it delves into the relationship between formal IPRs and trade secrets in order to investigate whether the latter should be conceptualised as falling within the realm of IPRs or unfair competition rules. Next, it analyses how the secrecy requirement has been construed in Germany and England up two now. These jurisdictions represent two of the most effective models for the protection of trade secrets in the EU before the harmonisation. Based on this comparative study, the thesis enquires whether there is common ground that would allow for further harmonisation of such a requirement in view of the challenges raised by the advent of new technologies and the harmonisation goals pursued by the Directive. Thereafter, taking the perfume industry as a study case, the dissertation interrogates the strategic importance of secrecy as a means of appropriating returns from innovation as opposed to formal IPRs and the impact of new technologies in the lead time conferred by secrecy. Ultimately, the thesis aims at proposing a legal solution with regard to the optimal scope of protection conferred by secrecy.

With a view to providing answers to the previous research questions, the following structure has been implemented.

Chapter 1 discusses the rationales underlying trade secrets protection. Against this background, deontological and utilitarian arguments are analysed. Then, the interplay between trade secrets and other IPRs (i.e. patents, trade marks, copyright and the sui generis database right) is examined for the appraisal of the functionality of secrecy. Lastly, the chapter discusses the hybrid legal nature of trade secrets, which are bound to sit between the realms of traditional IPRs and unfair competition rules.

Chapter 2 surveys the international legal framework for trade secrets protection. A two-fold approach is adopted. First, the minimum standards set forth by Article 39 of the Agreement on Trade-Related Aspects of Intellectual Property Rights[4] are studied in connection to Article 10bis of the Paris Convention[5]. Next, the U.S. regime upon which the relevant TRIPs provisions on undisclosed information were modelled is analysed. In both instances particular emphasis is placed on the study of the definition of trade secrets and how the secrecy requirement is construed in the relevant treaties, statutes and case law.

Chapter 3 identifies six pre-eminent models in the protection of trade secrets among the 28 EU jurisdictions before the implementation of the TSD. The method of comparative law is applied to study two of them: the German jurisdiction and the English system under the breach of confidence action. Again, both legal systems are closely examined with a view to obtaining a better understanding of the relevant liability conduct in order to assess when information enters the public domain. Then, the emerging harmonised framework created by the TSD is critically analysed. To that end, first the legal basis to harmonise trade secrets protection across the EU are surveyed. Next, the relevant types of lawful and infringing conduct and the limitations to the rights conferred under the TSD are studied. Finally, some remarks on the enforcement provisions and their importance in keeping information undisclosed are presented.

Chapter 4 maps out the notion of secrecy considering the harmonisation goals laid down in the TSD. To this end, first the requirements of protection of trade secrets are analysed from a comparative law perspective (England and Germany). Drawing on this analysis, a number of interpretative principles regarding the understanding of the concept of secrecy (or to be more precise, the circumstances under which it is lost) and its interplay with other IPRs normative standards are provided with a view to ensuring a uniform appraisal by national courts after the implementation of the TSD. Finally, the chapter concludes by examining the applicability of the trade secrets liability regime to Big Data sets and proposes an analytical framework to that end.

Chapter 5 delves into the relation between perfumes and trade secrets. For the purposes of the present research, the fragrance industry is used as a

4 Agreement on Trade-Related Aspects of Intellectual Property Rights (TRIPs) (adopted 15 April 1994) (Annex 1C to the Agreement establishing the World Trade Organization), 1869 UNTS 183.

5 Paris Convention for the Protection of Industrial Property (adopted 29 March 1883, as revised at Stockholm on 14 July 1967 and as amended on 28 September 1979) 21 UST 1583, 828 UNTS 305 (PC).

study case to outline the main difficulties in keeping business information undisclosed. This sector was selected based on the possibility of conducting qualitative empirical research with a major undertaking, but also due to the relevance of trade secrets in appropriating returns from innovation in the manufacturing and commercialisation stages. The first part of the chapter examines the relationship between perfumes and IPRs (copyright, trade mark, unfair competition and patents) and the central role that trade secrets play in ensuring the competitiveness of the firms in this sector. Finally, the major risks faced by fragrance and scent manufacturers in concealing valuable commercial information are identified.

Finally, chapter 6 studies the external and internal spheres of secrecy and their limitations in order to propose a balanced legal solution to regarding the understanding of secrecy.

## *§ 2 Research methodology*

To answer the research questions described above, two combined methodologies are followed. In the first place, the method of comparative law is applied to study the legal mechanisms for the protection of trade secrets in England and Germany before the implementation of the Directive. The main points of comparison are the concept of trade secret and the requirements for protection followed in each jurisdiction and the main features of the regimes in place to achieve trade secrets protection. This research is conducted with reference to the main statutory provisions, but also the relevant case law, legal scholarly works and a number of studies and reports.

To further understand the challenges that stakeholders face in keeping their valuable information secret, qualitative empirical research has been conducted with regard to the perfume industry. This sector is used as an example case to illustrate the increasing difficulties in maintaining secrecy and the strategic importance of trade secrets in certain industries. Hence, a perfumist and the head of IP of a multinational perfume company have been interviewed and the methodology of qualitative content analysis is used to analyse the interviews.[6] The main outcome of the interviews is presented in chapter 5 and a transcript of the interviews is included in Annex 1 and Annex 2.

---

6 Philipp Mayring, 'Qualitative content analysis' 266-269 in Uwe Flick, Ernst von Kardoff and Ines Steinke (eds), *A companion to qualitative research* (Sage 2004).

The manuscript of this dissertation was concluded on 27 May 2018. Since its completion, the UK has passed the Trade Secrets Regulations 2018, which implement the TSD. Similarly, Germany has adopted the Gesetz zum Schutz von Geschäftsgeheimnissen vom 18. April 2019 (BGBl. I S. 466). The amendments introduced by the legislation implementing the TSD fall outside the temporal scope examined in this dissertation and therefore, no specific reference is made to them.

# Chapter 1. Concept, justifications and legal nature of trade secrets

## *§ 1 The significance and concept of trade secrets*

On an abstract level, the intrinsic significance of trade secrets revolves around two conflicting forces: the principles of openness, freedom of discourse and communications, which clash with the principles of privacy, secrecy and a restrictive flow of information.[7] Such a tension also reflects the dichotomy between the intellectual commons movement and the increasing commodification of intellectual creations.[8] The former aims at fostering open innovation and knowledge dissemination and opposes overpowering proprietary systems. In such a context, the interest of firms in keeping their valuable information secret conflicts with the public interest in securing a certain degree of openness and free circulation of information in the markets, both of which are essential in democratic societies that operate under free market principles.[9]

Despite the economic and social importance of trade secrets, there is no universally accepted definition of the concept. At the international level, much common ground is provided by Article 39(2) TRIPs, which has laid down minimum standards of protection to be implemented by all WTO Member States. Pursuant to this provision, to merit protection "undisclosed information" needs to be secret, derive economic value from its secret nature and be subject to reasonable steps under the circumstances to keep it secret. Yet, on the basis of this three-pronged approach, which has also been included in the TSD as the foundation to conceptualise trade secrets, WTO Member States, including some EU jurisdictions, have developed different definitions, some of which include additional requirements.[10] The requirements of protection and the subject matter covered by

---

7 William van Caenegem, *Trade Secrets and Intellectual Property* (Kluwer Law International 2014) 11.

8 William van Caenegem 2014 (n 7) 11; Yochai Benkler, 'Free As the Air to Common Use: First Amendment Constraints on Enclosure of the Public Domain' [1997] 74 NYULR 354, 355.

9 William van Caenegem 2014 (n 7) 11.

10 Recital 6 TSD.

the notion of trade secrets constitute the study of chapter 2 (from the perspective of the TRIPs Agreement and the U.S. jurisdiction) and chapter 4 (from the perspective of the English and German jurisdictions, and the harmonised framework created by the TSD).

For clarity, it should be noted that throughout the thesis, unless specified otherwise, the term "undisclosed information" is used as a synonym for trade secrets, as defined in Article 39 TRIPs. In the same vein, "confidential information" is deployed as an alternative expression to "secret" or "concealed information", i.e. information that is not generally known (and that does not necessarily confer a competitive advantage upon its holder). Yet, in the context of the English jurisdiction, this expression should be understood as referring solely to information covered by the breach of confidence action. Likewise, unless stated otherwise, "know-how" is used exclusively in the sense laid down in Article 1(i) TTBER, that is, to refer to a specific type of non-patentable technical trade secret resulting from experience and testing.[11]

## *§ 2 The problematic justifications underlying trade secrets protection*

Market economies operate under the principles of (typically) unrestricted competition and the free circulation of goods and information in order to enhance consumer welfare. However, at first glance, trade secrets protection seems to contravene this proposition, as protection is afforded to information for the mere fact of keeping it undisclosed to competitors. In this context, it appears that the study of the optimal scope of secrecy should first start by considering the rationales underlying the protection of valuable secret information.

Indeed, the underpinning policy justifications for the protection of trade secrets remain to a large extent unexplored, if compared to other IPRs such

11 Article 1(1)(g) of Commission Regulation (EU) No 316/2014 of 21 March on the application of Article 101 (3) of the Treaty on the Functioning of the European Union to categories of technology transfer agreements [2014] OJ L93/17 (TTBER): "know-how' means a package of practical information, resulting from experience and testing, which is: (i) secret, that is to say, not generally known or easily accessible, (ii) substantial, that is to say, significant and useful for the production of the contract products, and (iii) identified, that is to say, described in a sufficiently comprehensive manner so as to make it possible to verify that it fulfils the criteria of secrecy and substantiality".

as patents and copyright.[12] Legal scholars and industry representatives usually resort to the argument that trade secrets should be protected because they are economically valuable and thus constitute relevant assets for their holders.[13] However, such an approach conflicts with most of the policy justifications upon which the intellectual property system is built, where providing incentives to create or innovate through exclusivity is weighed against the welfare effects triggered by the disclosure of information.[14]

Against this background, a number of grounds have been put forward to explain the need to protect secret information,[15] although in Europe the theoretical foundations have garnered less scholarly discussion than in the U.S. Nonetheless, a comprehensive inquiry into the underlying justifications appears to be of paramount importance considering the TSD. If the EU Member States are to embark on the complex task of harmonising their legal systems (in this case, as regards trade secrets) they should do so on the basis of solid and coherent grounds.[16]

In line with the above, this section surveys the most relevant policy arguments that have been invoked by legal scholars and case law, following the traditional classification of justifications for intellectual property: deontological and utilitarian.[17] The former are linked to the concept of fairness

12 Robert G. Bone, 'A New Look at Trade Secret Law: Doctrine in Search of Justification' [1998] 86 California LR 241, 245 refers to a "normative vacuum that continues to remain unfulfilled".

13 Ansgar Ohly, 'Harmonising the Protection of Trade Secrets' 2, 35 in Jacques de Werra (ed), *La protection des secrets d'affaires* (Schulthess 2013).

14 For a more detailed account of the underpinning policy justifications to IPRs see Justin Hughes, 'The Philosophy of Intellectual Property' [1988] 77 George Mason LJ 287; for an overall assessment of trade secrets vis-à-vis IPRs see chapter 1 § 3 A) below.

15 Some of the most influential scholarly works concerning the justification of trade secrets are Robert G. Bone, 'A New Look at Trade Secret Law: Doctrine in Search of Justification' [1998] 86 California LR 241; Robert G. Bone, 'Trade Secrecy, Innovation and the Requirement of Reasonable Secrecy Precautions' 46 in Rochelle C. Dreyfuss and Katherine J. Strandburg (eds), *The Law and Theory of Trade Secrecy: A Handbook of Contemporary Research* (Edward Elgar 2011); Robert G. Bone, 'The Still Shaky Foundations of Trade Secret Law' [2014] 92 Texa s LR 1803; Mark A. Lemley, 'The Surprising Virtues of Treating Trade Secrets as IP Rights' [2008] 61 Stanford LR 311; Michael Risch, 'Why Do We Have Trade Secrets?' [2007] 11 Marquette IPLR 1.

16 Ansgar Ohly 2013 (n 13) 36 highlighting the importance of finding a solid theoretical justification, particularly after the creation of the still contested sui generis right by the Directive 96/9 on the legal protection of databases [1996] OJ L77/20 (Database Directive).

17 Ansgar Ohly 2013 (n 13) 36.

and encompass the need to maintain commercial morality, labour value theories, and veil-of-ignorance arguments.[18] From a utilitarian perspective, it has been suggested that affording protection to secret information generates incentives to innovate and to disclose, reduces investment in protective measures and ultimately protects business privacy.[19] More generally, it has been argued that trade secrets law serves as a complement to the patent system. Each of these policy justifications is analysed in turn, with the exception of the complementary theory, which is examined in § 3 A), where the interplay between patents and trade secrets is studied.

18 Pursuant to the Stanford Encyclopaedia of Philosophy "Deontological theories (…), hold that some choices cannot be justified by their effects— that no matter how morally good their consequences, some choices are morally forbidden" <http://plato.stanford.edu/entries/ethics-deontological/#DeoThe> accessed 15 September 2018; Immanuel Kant, *Groundwork for the Metaphysics of Morals* (first published 1785, CUP 2011), probably the most prominent among the deontological philosophers, regarded that good will was central to any moral choice. As applied to the realm of IPRs, it is held that these are granted based on the principle of justice in one's intellectual creations and against free riders.

19 Utilitarism holds that the morally right action is the one that yields the most good. One of classical exponents of this normative ethics approach was Jeremy Bentham; see Stanford Encyclopedia of Philosophy <http://plato.stanford.edu/entries/utilitarianism-history/#JerBen> accessed 15 September 2018; Jeremy Bentham, *An Introduction to the Principles of Morals and Legislation* (first published 1781, Batoche Books 2000) Chapter I.II regarded the principle of utility as "that principle which approves or disapproves of every action whatsoever. According to the tendency it appears to have to augment or diminish the happiness of the party whose interest is in question: or, what is the same thing in other words to promote or to oppose that happiness. I say of every action whatsoever, and therefore not only of every action of a private individual, but of every measure of government". As applied to IPRs, utilitarism suggests that granting an exclusive right to exploit an intangible good stimulates the development of socially valuable inventions or creations and is essential to avoid the market failure inherent to their exploitation; see further Jeanne C. Former, 'Expressive Incentives in Intellectual Property' [2012] 98 Virginia LR 1745, 1751.

## A) Deontological arguments

### I. Commercial ethics

One of the most widely accepted theories underlying trade secrets legislation is that it is necessary in order to maintain "the standard of commercial ethics".[20]

This argument stems from a general moral principle according to which "reaping without sowing" is unfair.[21] It is unethical for a business to acquire the information of another by unfair means and thus be unjustly enriched.[22] At first glance, this justification seems very appealing. Behaviours that contravene generally accepted ethical codes or customs appear immediately morally reprehensible.[23] Notwithstanding this, upon a closer look the contours of the "standard of commercial ethics" seem intrinsically open-ended.[24] As noted by Jacob J "what one man calls 'unfair' another calls 'fair.'"[25] However, flexibility and a certain degree of uncertainty are typical characteristics of any unfair competition law regime[26] and this has not prevented the development of unfair competition legislation in most continental European jurisdictions, especially vis-à-vis intellectual property law.[27]

---

20 In the words of the U.S. Supreme Court in *Kewanee Oil Co. v. Bicron Co.*, 416 U.S. 470, 481 (1974): "The maintenance of standards of commercial ethics and the encouragement of invention are the broadly stated policies behind trade secret law".

21 This principle was most notably applied by the U.S. Supreme Court in *INS v. Associated Press*, 248 U.S. 215 (1918); Ansgar Ohly 2013 (n 13) 35.

22 Tanya Aplin and others, *Gurry on Breach of Confidence* (2nd edn, OUP 2012) para 3.20.

23 Notwithstanding this, Michael Risch 2007 (n 15) 36-37 considers that this is a "populist justification" rooted in the fact that people do not like bad actions; the opposite view is purported by Michael Spence, *Intellectual Property* (OUP 2007) 62.

24 Vincent Chiappetta, 'Myth, Chameleon or Intellectual Property Olympian?' [1999] 8 George Mason LR 69, 90.

25 *L'Oréal SA v Bellure NV* [2007] EWCA Civ 968 (CA), [139].

26 Ansgar Ohly, 'Unfair Competition', *Max Planck Encyclopaedia of European Private Law* (OUP 2012) 1172.

27 Annette Kur, 'What to Protect, and How? Unfair Competition, Intellectual Property, or Protection Sui Generis' 11, 14 in Nari Lee and others (eds), *Intellectual Property, Unfair Competition and Publicity* (Edward 2014); conversely, on the UK's approach to unfair competition Tanya Aplin and others 2012 (n 22) para 3.27 highlight that: "The first problem (...) is the problem of legal knowledge: how

Likewise, some purport that trade secret legislation could be used for the purposes of enforcing morality in the marketplace, i.e. to enforce industry norms. This hypothesis has been challenged essentially for two reasons. First, there is no empirical evidence that shows that generally accepted norms for a given industry regulating when the acquisition, use and disclosure of secret valuable information from a competitor should be deemed lawful exist. Second, even if they did exist, the extent to which judicial enforcement would increase the already high litigation costs and undermine the equilibrium upon which any tacit norm is built is unclear.[28]

In view of the foregoing, it is submitted that on the basis of commercial ethics only certain types of behaviour such as the breach of a confidential relationship, the theft of a secret or fraud can be proscribed. The inherent vagueness attached to the commercial ethics justification does not provide solutions for more controversial issues, such as the limits of reverse engineering and obligations after termination of an employment relationship.[29]

## II. Labour value theory

The labour value justification draws from John Locke's theory of property and in essence submits that those who create value should own the products of their work.[30] As regards trade secrets, this is understood as meaning

does the law know what is to count as ethically appropriate or inappropriate commercial behaviour? It is this problem that has informed the refusal of the English Courts to sanction 'unfair' competition as a cause of action in English law"; similarly, Anselm Kamperman Sanders, *Unfair Competition Law* (1st edn, OUP 1997) 78 noting that "Reasons for the absence of a law of unfair competition in common law systems lie mostly in the fact that the judges are of the opinion that general principles are not suited for regulation of the market-place. This is because the criteria for the assessment of what is unfair behaviour in the market-place are thought to be ambiguous".

28 Robert G. Bone 1998 (n 15) 294-296.

29 This argument is raised by Ansgar Ohly 2013 (n 13) 36.

30 John Locke, *The Selected Political Writings of John Locke* (Paul E. Sigmund ed, Norton& Company 2005) 28-29: "Whatsoever then he removes out of the state that nature hath provided and left it in, he hath mixed his labour with, and joined to it something that is his own, and thereby makes it property (...) For this labour being the unquestionable property of the labourer, no man but he can have a right to what that is once joined to, a least where there is enough , and as good, left in common for others".

that the person who creates information has a right in such information and against third parties.[31]

However, following this natural law argument as a guiding principle does not offer a convincing ground to justify two of the essential features of trade secret protection, namely (i) the secret nature of information and (ii) the fact that protection is only envisaged against misappropriation.[32] Under the labour value theory even non-secret information can be protected, so long as it is the result of one's effort.[33] Similarly, information should be afforded protection against appropriation as such, irrespective of the means used. This may lead to the overprotection of information, one of the aspects that has garnered more criticism when applying the Lockean theory of property to trade secrets. Furthermore, it does not provide solid grounds to justify the exceptions and limitations to trade secrets protection, which are central to the interplay with the intellectual property system.

### III. Contractarian theory

The contractarian argument results from applying the hypothetical bargaining model created by Rawls in *A Theory of Justice* with the purpose of finding a solid explanation for trade secrets protection. Rawls' theory is based on the decision-making process that occurs in a social contract under the so-called "veil of ignorance". This is a hypothetical state of nature under which rational individuals decide on the distribution of rights without knowing which position they will ultimately occupy in a society (their wealth, social status, level of intelligence and the like), as well as the particular circumstances of that society (economic and political), the so-called

---

31 As stressed by Justin Hughes (n 14) 306: "There is a very simple reason why the legal doctrines of unfair competition and trade secret protection are inherently orientated toward the value-added theory: they are court-created doctrines and people rarely go to court unless something of valuable is at stake. When intellectual property is created more systematically, such as through legislation, the resulting property doctrines seem less singularly oriented toward rewarding social value"; but see also Michel Risch 2007 (n 15) 29: "An initial criticism of this theory is that Locke was dealing with real property and not intellectual property, which can be 'possessed' by two people at the same time".

32 Robert G. Bone 2014 (n 15) 1824.

33 Robert G. Bone 2014 (n 15) 1825; contrary Eric R. Claeys, 'Private Law Theory and Corrective Justice in Trade Secrecy' [2011] 4 J of Tort Law 1, 33 arguing that the secrecy requirement signals the information as his own.

"original position".[34] Against this background, Rawls propounds that individuals will make choices following the maximin rule, that is, they "are to adopt the alternative the worst outcome of which is superior to the worst outcome of the others".[35] This will ensure that even if individuals turn out to be in the worst position in society, they will not be in need.[36]

As applied to the trade secrets scenario, under the veil of ignorance companies will agree to provide at least some level of trade secrets protection in order to reduce the negative outcome resulting from an eventual loss of confidential information.[37] On the same ground, it has been suggested that industry members would ex ante accept reverse engineering due to the expected gains stemming from product improvements.[38] Notwithstanding this, as with most contractarian arguments, it has been fiercely criticised, due to the fact that there is no solid reason to believe that firms would accept the terms of the agreement in the real world.[39]

### B) Utilitarian arguments

#### I. Incentives to innovate

The most frequently cited economic argument to justify trade secrets protection, which is also invoked in connection to formal IPRs, submits that it generates incentives to innovate.[40]

---

34 John Rawls, *A Theory of Justice* (OUP 1972) 136-142.

35 John Rawls, *A Theory of Justice* (OUP 1972) 152-153.

36 Ultimately, Rawls advocates in favour of a redistribution of wealth as part of the concept of justice; see Michael Risch 2007 (n 15) 35.

37 See Kim Lane Scheppele, *Legal Secrets: Equality and Efficiency in the Common Law* (The University of Chicago Press 1992) 76-83.

38 William Landes and Richard Posner, *The Economic Structure of Intellectual Property Law* (Belknap Press 2003) 370.

39 Robert G. Bone 1998 (n 15) 292-293; Michael Risch 2007 (n 15) 35 holds a different view and argues that this justification is useful from a normative perspective and notes that even an efficient analysis cannot predict if one rule or another will turn out to be more efficient under all circumstances.

40 Innovation is understood as creation of inventions, but also other types of information that do not meet inventive standards. For the purposes of the present research, the definition of Innovation provided by Schumpeter will be followed as per Jon Sundbo, *The Theory of Innovation: Entrepreneurs, Technology and Strategy* (Edward Elgar 2009) 20: "Schumpeter defines innovation as one or more of the following events:
1. Introduction of a new product or a new product quality.

Economists consider that information falls within the category of "public goods", namely those goods whose "use by one person does not preclude use by another person and does not cost additional resources, except the small cost of distributing them".[41] As a result, information is defined as non-rival because it can be consumed by an individual without limiting its availability to others.[42] Another essential characteristic is that it is non-exclusive, meaning that it is very difficult to prevent unauthorised individuals from making use of it once it is created. Indeed, the development of information can be very costly; yet its acquisition and use by third parties can be carried out at a very low incremental cost. This has a two-fold effect: acquirers save the costs of generating the data and at the same time the competitive advantage conferred by the information on its creator disappears. As a result, acquirers may compete at a much lower price. This may ultimately lead to a market failure, if there are no incentives to create the information because the creator cannot recoup the investment made in its development.[43]

It is against this backdrop that trade secrets law provides the owner of new and valuable information the right to restrict others from using it.[44] Consequently, he can obtain supracompetitive profits from the information, both as regards technical and commercial secrets and in terms of re-

2. Introduction of a new production method. This need not be a new scientific invention. It may consist of a new way of treating a product commercially.
3. The opening up of a new market.
4. The opening up of a new source of raw materials, or semimanufacturers regardless of whether the source has existed before.
5. The creation of a new organizational structure in industry, for example by creating or breaking down a monopoly situation".

41 Suzanne Scotchmer, *Innovation and Incentives* (1st edn, The MIT Press 2004) 311.

42 Yochai Benkler, *The Wealth of Networks* (Yale University Press 2006) 35; as opposed to that, apples are rival goods.

43 Vincent Chiappetta 1999 (n 24) 86; Suzanne Scotchmer 2004 (n 41) 31; also Harold Demsetz, 'The Private Production of Public Goods' [1970] 13 Journal of Law and Economics 293, 300-306 and Wendy J. Gordon, 'On Owning Information: Intellectual Property and the Restitutionary Impulse' [1992] 78 Vanderbilt LR 149, where she provides an overview of the conditions that may lead to a market failure in the appropriation of intellectual goods and concludes that there is a need for intellectual property protection.

44 Jonathan R. Chally, 'The Law of Trade Secrets: Toward a More Efficient Approach' [2004] 57 Vanderbilt LR 1269, 1280: "Trade secret law enhances exclusivity and thereby increases innovation by supplanting the precautions that an innovator must take to guard the secrecy of her information".

covering his investment.[45] In this scenario, there would be no market failure, as the holder would internalise the benefits of innovation and would be able to recoup the investment made in the creation of the information.[46] However, the rights in a trade secret are not absolute; protection is only envisaged against misappropriation.[47]

The incentives to innovate argument was most prominently raised by the U.S. Supreme Court in its landmark decision *Kewanee Oil Co. v. Bicron Co.*, where it was noted that "trade secret law will encourage invention in areas where patent law does not reach, and will prompt the independent innovator to proceed with the discovery of his invention".[48]

Notwithstanding the aforementioned, in recent years, a number of scholars have cast doubt on the extent to which trade secrets law in fact creates incentives to innovate and create.[49] It cannot be ensured that the

---

45 See Mark A. Lemley 2008 (n 15) 330; the TSD also echoes this argument in Recital 1, where it is stated that "By protecting such a wide range of know-how and commercial information, whether as a complement or as an alternative to intellectual property right, trade secrets allow the creator to derive profit from his/her creation and innovations and therefore are particularly important for research and development and innovative performance".

46 David D. William M. Landes and Richard A. Posner, 'Some Economics of Trade Secret Law' [1991] 5 JEP 61, 64 noting that trade secret law provides means of internalizing the benefits of innovation; similarly, Jerome H. Reichman, 'How trade secrecy law generates a natural semicommons of innovative know-how' 185, 188 in Rochelle C. Dreyfuss and Katherine J. Strandburg (eds), *The law and theory of trade secrecy* (Edward Elgar 2011) purports that the law of trade secrets encourage investment in innovative activities: "the conduct-based liability rules of trade secrecy law were the primary vehicle for stimulating investment in innovative enterprise after the industrial revolution. This conclusion follows because most innovation consists of cumulative and sequential applications of know-how to industry by routine engineers at work on common technical trajectories. Given relatively high standards of non-obviousness in patent law, as well as the possibilities for inventing around patents once issued, most commercial ventures depend on the conduct-based liability rules of trade secrecy law (and other unfair competition laws, as well as trade mark law) for opportunities to recoup their investment in R&D".

47 See Mark A. Lemley 2008 (n 15) 329-330.

48 *Kewanee Oil Co. v. Bicron Corp.*, 416 U.S. 470, 481-482 (1974).

49 See Michael Risch 2007 (n 15) 26 noting that the creation of incentives to innovate "is only a very minor justification of trade secret law".

information protected is innovative, as it merits protection for the mere fact of being secret.[50]

From an economic perspective, Bone argues that the objective of protecting information is to distribute it widely, so long as such information is still created. He further notes that secrecy generates high costs, but these have been overlooked by most of the existing literature.[51] In his cost-benefit analysis, two different scenarios are considered: (i) incentives as regards patentable inventions that most likely will not be reinvented during the patent term, and (ii) non-patentable inventions that are difficult to invent around.

In the first case, choosing secrecy over patent protection may lead to a wasteful duplication of efforts, as trade secrets law does not prevent independent discovery by competitors. Furthermore, this may have an adverse effect on cumulative innovation.[52] As noted by Beier and Straus, "the greatest danger of keeping an invention secret lies in the fact that the inventor cannot be fertile in its own field as the mother of new inventions".[53] In effect, innovation nowadays is to a large extent cumulative; every innovator uses prior discoveries or developments as a basis for further innovation.[54] Hence, in most cases, the benefit of a given innovation lies in the boost it gives to subsequent innovators.[55] If the holder of innovative information conceals it as a trade secret, later innovators will not be able to use it for their own innovations.

In the case of non-patentable inventions, Bone purports that trade secrets law only creates ex ante incentives to innovate if they are "moderately" difficult to reverse engineer. If the secret can be unveiled with little effort it only merits very weak protection, as it will most likely not be considered secret. At the other end of the spectrum, inventions that are very

50 Josef Drexl, 'Refusal to grant access to trade secrets as an abuse of market dominance'165, 181-182 in Steven Anderman and Ariel Ezrachi (eds), *Intellectual Property and Competition Law* (OUP 2011).

51 Robert G. Bone 1998 (n 15) 266; Michael Abramowicz and John F. Duffy, 'Intellectual Property for Market Experimentation' [2008] 83 NYULR 337, 391.

52 William Landes and Richard Posner 2003 (n 38) 357 note that in this case, applying for a patent may enable the competitor to invent around of instruct him on how to infringe. The relationship between patents and trade secrets is discussed in detail in chapter 1 § 3 A) I.

53 Friederich-Karl Beier and Josef Straus, 'The Patent System and Its Informational Function' [1977] IIC 387, 397.

54 Cumulativeness is central in technological fields such as biotechnology, computer hardware and computer software.

55 Suzanne Scotchmer 2004 (n 41) 127.

difficult to reverse engineer or reinvent are likely to be deemed inventive and thus patent law would provide greater incentives than trade secrecy law.[56] On this specific point he disagrees with Landes and Posner, who consider that allowing for trade secret protection proves that the patent system was wrong and consequenlty the holder can achieve a level of exclusivity similar to the one provided by patent rights.[57]

In a similar vein, Chiappetta submits that there are two major shortcomings to the encouragement of innovation theory. In the first place, he argues that this guiding principle alone does not provide solid grounds to establish the rights conferred by a trade secret and the equally important limitations to those rights, such as reverse engineering and independent creation. Next, he is of the opinion that the grant of IPRs is largely based on the presumption that they will provide incentives to create and that applying the same foundation to justify trade secrets protection may "conflict, duplicate or absorb" the incentives provided by patent and copyright law.[58]

Against this background, Risch further suggests that formal IPRs, such as patents and copyright, confer a period of exclusivity to allow the holder to recoup the cost of the creation. However, he convincingly argues that this rationale does not apply in the case of trade secrets protection: in the absence of self-help measures, if a company cannot keep valuable information concealed from third parties, trade secrets laws will not provide additional incentives to maintain the confidentiality of the said information.[59]

In the light of the foregoing criticism, it has been suggested that the protection of trade secrets is to be understood as a social subsidy to encourage market experimentation, rather than as an incentive to innovate. Such an approach underscores that trade secrets laws, as opposed to patent laws, also afford protection to non-technological information produced during the ordinary course of business. Consequently, the main purpose of trade secrets law would not be to foster the creation of information, but rather to foster the development of business activities as such. Under this theory, by protecting business data that can be kept undisclosed, the entry of competitors would be deterred and the profits of the first comers would increase accordingly. This is likely to generate stronger incentives for com-

56 Robert G. Bone 1998 (n 15) 266-270.
57 William Landes and Richard Posner 2003 (n 38) 358-359.
58 Vincent Chiappetta 1999 (n 24) 88.
59 Michael Risch 2007 (n 15) 27.

panies to carry out market experiments that create data, irrespective of their inventive or original nature.[60]

Bearing the above analysis in mind, it can be concluded that trade secrets protection does provide certain incentives to create new information of both a commercial and technical nature. It protects factual secrecy over the information concerned until it becomes generally known, thus allowing the creator to internalise the benefits of innovation. It is also a useful means to encourage market experimentation and the development of business. The most salient problem in this context is reconciling these incentives with the ones created by other IPRs (more notably patent law), and avoiding tensions with the former. This can best be achieved through the establishment of clear and solid exceptions and limitations to the rights in a trade secret, such as reverse engineering, independent discovery or even a public interest defence, such as the one implemented in England under the breach of confidence action.[61]

## II. Incentives to disclose

One of the soundest policies that explains trade secrets law is that it creates incentives to disclose by reducing transaction costs. The efficient exploitation of secret information requires that the holders are able to pass on information to other parties, with some certainty that they will not reveal it or use it against their interests. This applies not only within the internal sphere of a company (employees), but also in relation to third parties (suppliers of materials, prospective company partners, clients or licensees).[62]

Even though at first glance this may seem counterintuitive, trade secrets protection provides a partial solution to the so-called "Arrow's Information Paradox", which is best explained with an example, such as the nego-

---

60 Michael Abramowicz and John F. Duffy 2008 (n 51) 391 the authors nevertheless conclude that "on our theory, trade secret law may be overinclusive -it protects copycat businesses too- but in general, innovators are the businesses that have the most information worth protecting".

61 This topic will be elaborated further in chapter 6 below.

62 Aurea Sunol, 'Trade Secrets vs Skill and knowledge' 197, 198-199 in Fabrizio Cafaggi and others (eds), *The Organizational Contract, From Exchange to Long-term network Cooperation in European Contract Law* (Ashgate 2013).

tiation of a licensing agreement.[63] In this case, the commercial exploitation of information requires that any potential licensee, prior to concluding the agreement, gains full knowledge of the information object of the contract. However, such a disclosure implies that the licensee acquires the information in question without cost and to the detriment of the licensor. In view of this, the licensor will be reluctant to engage in negotiations unless the licensee agrees not to use such information in the event that no contract is concluded. Under such an agreement the licensee could be precluded from using the information even if he developed it independently or through reverse engineering. Therefore, transaction costs increase and licensing becomes more difficult.[64] In order to solve the Information Paradox, trade secrets provide a legal right to prevent third parties from using and disclosing information revealed in confidence during the course of precontractual negotiations.[65] As a result, the holder of information will be more willing to share it, thus facilitating the conclusion of licensing agreements (or any other commercial transactions) and ultimately the exploitation of knowledge.[66]

This argument has been strongly criticised because it does not contemplate a number of parameters. In particular, it has been suggested that the limited disclosure achieved through a licensing agreement or other transactions is not the kind of disclosure that intellectual property law aims at promoting.[67] For instance, in patent law the grant of an exclusive right is conditioned upon the publication of the relevant technology in the patent specification. This allows competitors to invent around and avoid the duplication of research,[68] thus fostering competition in the market and incentivising the creation of new products. In the words of the U.S. Supreme Court:

---

63 Kenneth J. Arrow, 'Allocation of Resources for invention' 609, 615 in Universities-National Bureau Committee for Economic Research and Committee on Economic Growth of the Social Science Research Council (ed), *The Rate and Direction of Inventive Activity: Economic and Social Factors* (Princeton University Press 1962): "There is a fundamental paradox in the determination of demand for information; its value for the purchaser is not known until he has the information, but then he has in effect acquired it without cost"; Josef Drexl 2011 (n 50) 181-182.

64 Robert G. Bone 1998 (n 15) 280.

65 Mark A. Lemley 2008 (n 15) 336.

66 James Pooley, *Trade Secrets* (Law Journal Press 2002) § 1.02[5]1-12

67 Robert G. Bone 1998 (n 15) 280.

68 William Landes and Richard Posner 2003 (n 38) 357.

> Patents are not given as favours (…) but are meant to encourage invention by rewarding the inventor with the right, limited to a term of years fixed by the patent, to exclude others from the use of his invention.[69]

The disclosure of the technical teachings of a patent is of paramount importance for technological, economic and social development.[70] As a matter of principle, this function is undermined by the law of trade secrecy, due to the fact that information may never become generally known. As a whole, there is social value in the general dissemination of information that is not fulfilled in the case of licensing agreements (or any other commercial transaction), where information is only disclosed to the other parties to the negotiation. In the same vein, it has been argued that the Arrow Paradox could be solved by the operation of contract law, without the need to resort to specific legislation.[71]

To be sure, it is undeniable that trade secrets laws incentivise some level of secrecy, as protection is only afforded to information that is not generally known. However, considering the previous analysis, there are solid grounds to argue that they also help to lower the transaction costs associated with the commercial exploitation of confidential information, which despite not fulfilling the patent system's underlying information function in the broadest sense, is also desirable in order to enhance cooperation between market participants and facilitate organisation within a company.

### III. Limit to the arms race

Even more convincing is the theory that trade secrets protection helps to decrease the economic investment in the factual protection of secret information. Trade secrets law serves as an alternative to measures that undertakings would otherwise have to adopt for the purposes of ensuring confi-

---

69 *Sears Roebuck&Co. v. Stiffel Co.*, 376 U.S. 225, 229-230 (1964).

70 Friedrich-Karl Beier, 'Die Bedeutung des Patentsystems für den technischen, wirtschaftlichen und sozialen Fortschritt' [1979] GRUR Int 227, 234: "Wichtig ist aber vor allem die Erkenntnis, daß die Verbreitung technischer Kenntnisse durch die Ausschließlichkeit des Patentrechts nicht etwa gehemmt, sondern im Gegenteil entscheidend *gefördert* wird. Man sollte an sich meinen, die optimale Form der Verbreitung und Anwendung technischen Wissens bestehe darin, es jedermann, z. B. durch Veröffentlichung in Fachzeitschriften, kostenlos zur Verfügung zu stellen".

71 Robert G. Bone 2014 (n 15) 1818.

dentiality (self-help measures).[72] If no such thing as the law of trade secrets existed, holders of information would spend large sums of money protecting their secrets (both through physical measures and additional remuneration for employees to keep the business's secrets or not leave the company). In turn, appropriators would increase the amount spent to acquire them. This would lead to a so-called "arms race" without social value.[73]

This is best illustrated with a real example. An undertaking with two manufacturing facilities, one located in the United States and the other in China, equipped the latter with very sophisticated technology in order to prevent trade secrets misappropriation (fingerprint scanners, almost no Internet access, physical security, etc.), whereas in the one located in the United States only standard efficient measures were implemented. The difference in the self-help measures adopted was triggered by the fact that the trade secret holder did not rely on the possibility of enforcing trade secrets protection in China.[74]

In view of these conflicting interests, the law of trade secrets strikes a balance between the wish to acquire a competitor's information and the need to protect one's own information. This is achieved by prohibiting only the costliest means of acquiring a secret, thus preventing holders from being forced to implement equally expensive and non-efficient protective measures.[75] The resources saved both by the holder of the information and the alleged misappropriator can be invested in a more productive way.[76] In order to achieve such a balance, trade secret holders are only required to implement "reasonable steps under the circumstances".[77]

Although convincing, this justification has been challenged by commentators in the U.S. on the basis of the following four arguments: in the first place, the detection of misappropriation conduct in practice can be very

---

72 Mark A. Lemley 2008 (n 15) 332.

73 Michael Risch 2007 (n 15) 43-44; similarly, Mark A. Lemley 2008 (n 15) 334 noting that evidence shows that overinvestment in secrecy is a problem in countries like Brazil or Mexico where trade secret protection and enforcement are not efficient.

74 This case is reported by Michael Risch 2007 (n 15) 44.

75 William Landes and Richard Posner 2003 (n 38) 364, 365; Peter S. Menell and Suzanne Scotchmer, 'Intellectual Property' 1473, 1479 in A. Mitchell Polinsky and Steven Shave (eds), *Handbook of Law and Economics*, vol 2 (Elsevier 2007).

76 William Landes and Richard Posner 2003 (n 38) 371: "Obtaining a trade secret by force or fraud ... should be punishable because of the heavy costs that would be incurred in self-help remedies against such incursions if they were lawful and the damage to the incentive to invent that would be produced".

77 See Article 39(2)(c) TRIPs.

costly.[78] Similarly, bringing lawsuits is also usually very expensive for most trade secret holders, as they bear the burden of proof.[79] Likewise, the extent to which rules that try to prevent arms races will merely result in the efforts being directed elsewhere (namely, costly litigation or more sophisticated technology to acquire the secret) is unclear.[80] Finally, it should be borne in mind that not all arms races are wasteful. The law should not prevent those (unusual) ones that yield spill-over benefits that would not have been achieved otherwise.[81] Ultimately, the persuasiveness of this argument should be based upon a comparison of the costs in a legal system where no trade secrets protection is envisaged and the social cost incurred where such protection is foreseen.[82]

## IV. The privacy rationale

Trade secrets protection has often been justified on the basis of business privacy.[83] This approach has both a deontological and utilitarian dimen-

78 James Pooley and others, 'Understanding the Economic Espionage Act of 1996' [1997] 5 Texas IPLJ 177, 224: "Information loss is inherently difficult to detect, since the original property remains intact, apparently untouched".

79 Robert G. Bone 2014 (n 15) 1816.

80 Douglas Gary Lichtman, 'How the Law Responds to Self-Help' (2004) John M. Olin Program in Law and economics Working Paper 232, 31 <http://www.law.uchicago.edu/Lawecon/index.html> accessed 15 September 2018.

81 Douglas Gary Lichtman 2004 (n 80) 32 arguing that the race on distribution of online materials protected under copyright law has yielded substantial progression on Internet based technologies.

82 Tanya Aplin and others 2012 (n 22) para 3.16.

83 The U.S. Supreme Court adopted a similar position in three of its landmark decisions on trade secret protection. In *E.I. DuPont de Nemours&Co. v. Cristopher*, 447 431 F.2d 1012, 1016 (5th Cir. 1970) the Court noted that "Our tolerance of the espionage game must cease when the protections required to prevent another's spying cost so much that the spirit of inventiveness is dampened. Commercial privacy must be protected from espionage which could not have been reasonably anticipated or prevented"; some years later, when ruling on the potential preemption of state trade secret law by federal patent law, the Court stressed in *Kewanee Oil Co. v. Bicron Corp.*, 416 U.S. 470, 487 (1974) that "A most fundamental right, that of privacy, is threatened when industrial espionage is condoned or is made profitable; the state interest in denying profit to such illegal ventures is unchallengeable; finally, the Supreme Court restated that privacy was one of the three policies underlying trade secret protection in *Bonito Boats, Inc. v. Thunder Craft Boats, Inc.*, 489 U.S. 141, 155 (1989); see Melvin F. Jager, *Trade Secrets Law* (Thomsons Reuters 2015) § 1:5.

sion. Before turning to these, some general remarks should be made as to its conceptual contours. The Right of Privacy has been defined as "the Right of a person to be free from intrusion into matters of a personal nature"[84] or in a more succinct fashion, as the right "to be let alone".[85] In Europe, it has been codified in Article 8 of the European Convention on Human Rights[86] and is now part of the acquis communautaire since the entry into force of the Charter of Fundamental Rights of the European Union ("ChFREU") pursuant to Article 7.[87] [88] The European Court of Human Rights ("ECtHR") has interpreted that Article 8 ECHR is essentially intended to:

> ensure the development, without outside interference, of the personality of each individual in his relations with other human beings. There is therefore a zone of interaction of a person, with others, even in the public context, which may fall within the scope of private life.[89]

---

84 *Encyclopaedia Britannica*, 'Rights of privacy' <https://global.britannica.com/topic/rights-of-privacy> accessed 15 September 2018.

85 Samuel Warren and Louis Brandeis, 'The Right to Privacy' [1980] 4 Harvard LR 193, 195 (as cited in Thomas M. Cooley on Torts, *A Treatise on the Law of Torts, Or, The Wrongs which Arise Independent of Contract* (2nd edn, Callaghan 1879) 29); other definitions include the one provided by the Parliamentary Assembly of the Council of Europe "Right to live one's own life with a minimum of interference" Resolution 1165 (1998) Assembly debate on 26 June 1998 (24$^{th}$ Sitting). Doc. 8130, report of the Committee on Legal Affairs and Human Rights (rapporteur: Mr Schwimmer), Doc. 8147, opinion of the Committee on Culture and Education (rapporteur: Mr Staes) and Doc. 8146, opinion of the Social, Health and Family Affairs Committee (rapporteur: Mr Mitterrand).

86 Article 8 of the Convention for the Protection of Human Rights and Fundamental Freedoms (European Convention on Human Rights, as amended on 1 June 2010) (ECHR) reads as follows:
"1. Everyone has the right to respect for his private and family life, his home and his correspondence.
2. There shall be no interference by a public authority with the exercise of this right except such as is in accordance with the law and is necessary in a democratic society in the interests of national security, public safety or the economic wellbeing of the country, for the prevention of disorder or crime, for the protection of health or morals, or for the protection of the rights and freedoms of others".

87 Article 7 of the Charter of Fundamental Rights of the European Union [2012] OJ C326/391 (ChFREU) sets out that: "Everyone has the right to respect for his or her private and family life, home and communications".

88 Both provisions are rooted in the Universal Declaration of Human Rights (adopted 10 December 1948 UNGAs 217 A (III) (UDHR), Art 12.

89 *Von Hannover v Germany* (2005) 40 EHHR 1, para 50.

As is apparent from the above, privacy arguments appear best suited for physical persons. Corporations do not present the personality attributes a priori protected by such a right that would ultimately justify trade secrets protection.[90]

Notwithstanding this, the ECtHR in *Société Colás Est v France*,[91] a case concerning the inspection of the premises of various companies during the course of an investigation by the French Competition Authority, held that "in certain circumstances the rights guaranteed by Article 8 of the Convention may be construed as including the right to respect for a company's registered office, branches and other business premises".[92] [93] In view of this and following a dynamic interpretation of the ECHR, the scope of Article 8(1)ECHR might be extended to the protection of telephone, mail or electronic communications in the context of an inspection of premises.[94] The CJEU has followed a more extensive approach and has stated that the privacy right "cannot be taken to mean that the professional or commercial activities of either natural or legal persons are excluded.[95] In the same vein, it has concluded that "the protection of business secrets is a general principle".[96]

Consequently, from a deontological perspective, even if it could be agreed that legal persons are entitled to a right of privacy, it is still unclear whether or not trade secrets fall under the scope of its protection, as resorting to a moral right to commercial privacy for corporations is seemingly weak. As noted above, such a right can best be explained in the context of personal relationships, but it is unsatisfactory when applied to corporations and the protection of their undisclosed information.[97]

On the other hand, following a utilitarian rationale, trade secrets protection ensures that companies have a so-called "Laboratory Zone" in which

90 Robert G. Bone 1998 (n 15) 286-288; Tanya Aplin and others 2012 (n 22) para 3.31.

91 *Société Colás Est v France* (2004) 39 EHRR 17.

92 *Société Colás Est v France* (2004) 39 EHRR 17, para 388.

93 A more detailed account of this issue is provided by Tanya Aplin, 'A right of privacy for corporations?' 475-505 in Paul L.C. Torremans (ed), *Intellectual Property and Human Rights* (Kluwer Law International 2008).

94 Tanya Aplin 2008 (n 93) 14.

95 Case C–450/06 *Varec SA v Belgium* [2008] ECR I-581 para 48.

96 Case C–450/06 *Varec SA v Belgium* [2008] ECR I-581 para 48; Gianclaudio Malgieri, 'Trade Secrets v Personal Data: a possible solution for balancing rights' [2016] 6 International Data Privacy LR 1, 9.

97 Robert G. Bone 1998 (n 15) 288-289.

to develop their inventions or business strategies in confidence.[98] Trial and error is essential to any innovative process and it is most effectively carried out under conditions of secrecy. It is also crucial to preserve the novelty of an innovation until the application date.[99] A similar rationale can be applied with respect to commercial and business information; a market strategy cannot be known to competitors to succeed.[100] As noted by the Commission, "every IPR starts with a secret".[101]

As a whole, the protection of "business privacy" in its utilitarian dimension appears as a key element to encourage both innovation and competition in the market. If secrecy were not protected at all and every market participant had access to a competitor's information, incentives to innovate and compete with better products would disappear.[102]

### C) Conclusion on the doctrines underlying trade secrets protection

A survey of the main legal justifications underlying trade secrets protection reveals that deontological theories seem intrinsically vague. In effect, resorting to commercial moral standards, natural labour value principles and contractarian doctrines does not seem to provide solid legal grounds to justify some of the pillars upon which trade secrets laws are premised. Under the commercial ethics theory, reverse engineering and the limitation of post-contractual obligations do not appear legitimate. Equally, following labour value doctrines, the creation of information should confer a property right in rem on its creator, irrespective of the concealed nature of the information, which furthermore should not be subject to any exceptions and limitations. Similar considerations apply to contractarian theories:

98 This argument is discussed by Ansgar Ohly, 'Reverse Engineering: Unfair Competition or Catalyst for Innovation?' 540, 547 in Joseph Drexl and others (eds), *Patents and Technological Progress in a Globalized World* (Springer 2009).

99 Florian Schweyer, *Die rechtliche Bewertung des Reverse Engineering in Deutschland und den USA* (Mohr Siebeck 2012) 431-432.

100 Ansgar Ohly, 'Der Geheimnisschutz im deutschen Recht: heutiger Stand und Perspektiven' [2014] GRUR 1, 3.

101 Commission, 'Explanatory Memorandum, Proposal for a Directive of the European Parliament and of the Council on the protection of undisclosed know-how and business information (trade secrets) against their unlawful acquisition, use and disclosure' 2.

102 Jerome H. Reichman, 'Legal Hybrids Between the Patent and Copyright Paradigm' [1994] 94 Columbia LR 2432, 2506 noting that competition presupposes the lead time conferred by secrecy.

there is no actual evidence that the assumptions upon which they are premised would take place in the real world.

Consequently, it is submitted that utilitarian theories provide a more solid justification for the enactment of rules that regulate the protection of trade secrets and the resulting limitation on the flow of information among market participants that such protection entails. As argued above,[103] trade secrets legislation protects factual secrecy, allowing the creator of information to internalise the benefits of its (incremental) innovations, thereby preventing potential market failures in the development of information that is not eligible for protection under the general IPRs framework. Crucially, it creates incentives to encourage market experimentation and the development of business as such. According to the incentives to disclose rationale, trade secrets legal regimes also lower the transaction costs associated with the commercial exploitation of confidential information, foster cooperation between market participants and prevent the fragmentation of information within the internal sphere of a company. Most importantly, trade secrets laws prevent wasteful arms races in the adoption of protective measures and provide companies with a Laboratory Zone in which to develop their innovations without third party interference.[104]

Whereas some of the doctrines analysed above, such as the contractarian theories and incentives to innovate rationale, are common to other IPRs (patents and copyright), others serve conflicting interests. For instance, the incentives to disclose doctrine serves different objectives to the disclosure function under patent law. Such a tension inevitably leads to the question of how trade secrets interrelate with other IPRs and whether they should even be conceptualised as a species of them. This complex topic is the object of analysis in the following section (§ 3).

## *§ 3 Dissecting the legal nature of trade secrets: between IPRs and unfair competition*

The legal nature of secret information is one of the most contested aspects of the law of trade secrets. There has been a longstanding debate regarding whether they should be considered property rights or even be protected as

103 See chapter 1 § 2 B) I.

104 Contrary, Robert G. Bone 1998 (n 15) concludes that there is no normative theory capable of justifying trade secrets protection.

an IPR. This tension is a common theme in other areas of intellectual property law and stems from the different conceptions of property in civil law countries and the "Anglo-American legal system".[105] In the former, the property right is understood as a single and solid right that the owner has in respect of the material object.[106] It is regarded as the most complete and absolute right that one can enjoy in an asset.[107] By contrast, property in common law is a broader notion that comprises a number of situations where a person has "some exclusive rights, though not absolute, to use a resource".[108] As regards intellectual property, the problem lies in the extension of the property metaphor to the protection of intangible assets, because originally it was only envisaged to protect real property.[109] Therefore, some commentators suggest that intellectual property should be considered a "unique form of legal protection" that is specifically tailored to deal with the protection of public goods.[110]

This controversy is even more prominent in the field of trade secrets, as they present a hybrid legal nature within the IPRs spectrum, and share some of the features of IPRs and some of the unfair competition paradigm.[111]

---

105 Thomas Dreier, 'How much 'property' is there in intellectual property?' 116, 116-117 in Helena R. Howe and Jonathan Griffiths (eds), *Concepts of Property in Intellectual Property Law* (CUP 2013); Ralf Michaels, 'Property', *The Max Planck Encyclopaedia of European Private Law* (OUP 2012) 1371 noting that: "The term property is ambiguous. Sometimes property designates a right in an object; sometimes it designates the object itself: a person has property in an object, and the object is her property. Understood as a right, property is the most comprehensive right that one can have over an object. It encompasses the right to use and enjoy, the right to exclude and the power to dispose".

106 Thomas Dreier 2013 (n 105) highlighting that "the effects of this different understanding of the legal concept of what constitutes property in general runs like a red thread through the history of intellectual property protection in most, if not all civil law states".

107 Séverine Dusollier, 'The commons as a reverse intellectual property-from exclusivity to inclusivity' 258, 265 in Helena R. Howe and Jonathan Griffiths (eds), *Concepts of Property in Intellectual Property Law* (CUP 2013).

108 Séverine Dusollier 2013 (n 107) 265.

109 Mark. A. Lemley, 'Property, Intellectual Property, and Free Riding' [2004] 83 Texas LR 1031, 1033.

110 Mark A. Lemley 2004 (n 109) 1031-1032; see also Lionel Bently, 'Trade Secrets: 'Intellectual property' but not property?' in Helena R. Howe and Jonathan Griffiths (eds), *Concepts of Property in Intellectual Property Law* (CUP 2013).

111 Stanisław Sołtysiński, 'Are Trade Secrets Property?' [1986] IIC 331-356 distinguishes between property and subjective rights.

The following sections intend to map out the complex topic of the legal nature of trade secrets protection, following a two-fold approach. In the first place, the relationship and overlaps between trade secrets law and other IPRs (patents, copyrights, trade marks and the database right) are examined in section A. Next, section B looks into whether trade secrets themselves can be the object of an IPR. To this end, the prevailing academic and case law views on this topic are surveyed.

## A) The unsettled relationship between trade secrets and IPRs

### I. Trade secrets and patents[112]

The relationship between the patent system and trade secrecy is not settled. These two means of appropriation have often been regarded as mutually exclusive.[113] Such an approach, nevertheless, overlooks many aspects of the interplay between the two regimes. In fact, trade secrets protection supplements the patent system in a number of ways. In view of this, the following sections provide an analysis of the three possible scenarios in which trade secrets and patents may interact: (i) trade secrets prior to patenting; (ii) preferring trade secrecy to patents, and (iii) combining patent protection with trade secrets protection.[114]

---

112 Similar considerations would apply in the context of utility models that are characterised, among others, by a (i) flexibility on the level of novelty (innovations are usually required to be regionally or even locally new); (ii) a lower level of inventiveness and (iii) a shorter term of duration than patents (the period of durations in countries that do provide for utility models protection ranges from five to twenty years); see further on this issue Uma Suthersanen, 'Utility Models and Innovation in Developing Countries' (2006) ICTSD Issue Paper No. 13, 2 <http://unctad.org/en/docs/iteipc20066_en.pdf> accessed 15 September 2018 and Henning Grosse Ruse-Khan, 'The International Legal Framework for the protection of Utility Models' (2012) WIPO Regional Seminar on the Legislative, Economic and Policy Aspects of the Utility Model System, Kuala Lumpur <http://www.wipo.int/edocs/mdocs/aspac/en/wipo_ip_kul_12/wipo_ip_kul_12_ref_t2b.pdf> accessed 15 September 2018.

113 For instance Michael Risch 2011 (n 113) 168 noting that "Patent law and trade secret law cannot be co-extensive because trades secrets must be secret and patents must be publicly disclosed"; contrary, David D. Friedman, William M. Landes and Richard A. Posner, 'Some Economics of Trade Secret Law' [1991] 5 JEP 61, 64.

114 The legal analysis of this section is conducted based on the framework created by the European Patent Convention, as it governs the application and grant pro-

## 1. Trade secrets prior to patenting

Pursuant to Article 52(1) of the European Patent Convention,[115] patents shall only be granted for inventions if they are new, involve an inventive step and are susceptible to industrial applicability.[116] Frequently, before reaching the patentability stage, undertakings must conduct costly and lengthy research and development endeavours, particularly in order to come up with an invention with some degree of industrial applicability.[117] This process should be carried out in a working environment where secrecy is guaranteed for the purposes of ensuring novelty, the Laboratory Zone referred to above.[118] Conversely, the invention would fall into the public domain and would not meet the patentability standards. In practice, stakeholders also take this time to assess, from a business perspective, whether to apply for a patent or opt for informal protection (such as secrecy, lead time or complexity).[119]

Under the legal framework created by the EPC, an invention can be exploited secretly without detriment to the possibility of obtaining a patent for it later on.[120] Notwithstanding this, prior to filing an application with the patent office, the holder of the information should be careful not to disclose it. In this regard, it is important to note that the priority date is crucial for two reasons: it indicates the date at which novelty is assessed

---

cess for European patents and has shaped patent law in the 28 Member States. The three identified scenarios follow the scheme presented by Lionel Bently, 'Patents and trade secrets' 57 para 3.62 in Neil Wilkof and Shamnad Basheer (eds), *Overlapping Intellectual Property Rights* (OUP 2012).

115 Convention on the Grant of European Patents (European Patent Convention) of 5 October 1973 (as revised by the Act revising Article 63 EPC of 17 December 1991 and the Act revising the EPC of 29 November 2000) (EPC).

116 See also Article 27(1) TRIPs.

117 Lionel Bently 2012 (n 114) para 3.58; Robert P. Merges, 'Priority and Novelty Under the AIA' [2012] 27 Berkeley Technology LJ 1023, 1044.

118 See chapter 1 § 2 B) IV.

119 This is further developed by Katrin Hussinger, 'Is Silence golden? Patent versus secrecy at the firm level, Governance and the Efficiency of Economic Systems' (2005) ZEW Discussion Papers 04-78, 16 <https://ideas.repec.org/p/zbw/zewdip/2883.html> accessed 15 September 2018 noting that the strong reliance on secrecy takes places for early-state inventions that will be marketed afterwards.

120 Lionel Bently 2012 (n 114) para 3.62; Rudolf Kraßer and Christoph Ann, *Patentrecht* (6th edn, C.H. Beck 2009) § 16 IV, Rdn 2; similarly, in the U.S. with the adoption of The Leahy-Smith America Invents Act, Pub. L. No. 112-29, 125 Stat. 284 (2011) (America Invents Act of 2011 or AIA), see 35 U.S.C. § 102(a)(1).

and the date at which the invention can be used without compromising potential patents.[121]

The novelty requirement plays a central role in understanding the complementarity between secrecy and patents. The basic framework for the assessment of this patentability condition is laid down in Article 54 EPC, which as a general rule provides that an invention is new if it does not form part of the state of the art (paragraph 1). In turn, the state of the art is composed of everything that is made available to the public (paragraph 2).[122] No territorial or time limits shall apply for establishing relevant disclosures, provided that there is an actual possibility of acquiring the knowledge.[123] This can be oral, written or even refer to public prior uses that make the invention accessible. There are also no restrictions regarding the type of media in which the information is made available.[124]

Typically, the question that arises in connection with trade secrets is whether marketing a product in which a secret invention is embodied renders it automatically available and thus part of the public domain. Consistent case law from the Boards of Appeal of the European Patent Office ("EPO") indicates that the use of an invention is only regarded as novelty-destroying if it is possible for members of the public to acquire knowledge of that subject matter on the relevant priority day. This includes not only the external examination of the product, but also the obtention after further analysis of the intrinsic features (those which do not need to interact with external conditions to become apparent).[125] Against this background, it should be noted that pursuant to settled case law from the Boards of Appeal of the EPO, if it is possible to reverse engineer the secret, the invention will lack novelty for the purposes of patent law, provided that there

---

121 Lionel Bently 2012 (n 114) para 3.62.

122 See Article 54 EPC.

123 The EPC follows an absolute novelty approach. For instance, in T 355/07 (28 November 2008) the Boards of Appeal of the European Patent Office (EPO) considered that the theoretical possibility of having access to the information included in a document on a particular date renders it available to the public as of that date, regardless of whether on that date a member of the public actually inspected the file; see also Rudolf Kraßer and Christoph Ann 2009 (n 120) Kapitel 3, § 17 I a) 1; William Cornish, 'The Essential Criteria for Patentability of European Inventions: Novelty and Inventive Step' [1983] IIC 765, 765-766.

124 Joel Nägerl and Lorenz Walder-Hartmann, 'Differentiation from the state of the art' 129, 142-150 in Maximilian Haedicke and Henrik Timmann (eds), *Patent Law A Handbook on European and German Patent Law* (C.H. Beck 2014).

125 Lionel Bently and Brad Sherman, *Intellectual Property Law* (4th edn, 2014 OUP) 536.

was no confidentiality obligation restricting the use or dissemination of such knowledge and no additional inventive effort is required.[126]

Notably, secret information disclosed in confidence is not regarded as available.[127] The existence of a confidentiality obligation can derive either from an express or a tacit agreement.[128] If, on the other hand the recipient of secret information covering a patentable invention reveals it, for example breaching a duty of secrecy, such a disclosure is deemed non-prejudicial when assessing novelty.[129] In this case, the holder of the information has six months to file for a European patent.[130] If the disclosure takes place before the six months prior to the filing of the application, it will lack novelty and thus will be part of the state of the art.[131]

All in all, the legal framework created by the EPC affords some level of protection to an inventor who relies on secrecy prior to patenting. This approach is in line with the argument that "every IPR starts with a secret"[132]

---

126 G 1/92 [1993] OJ EPO 277, 279; see further Guidelines for Examination in the EPO. Part G. Chapter IV. Section 6.2.1 noting that "subject matter should be regarded as made available to the public by use or in any other way if, at the relevant date, it was possible for members of the public to gain knowledge of the subject-matter and there was no bar of confidentiality restricting the use or dissemination of such knowledge (…). This may, for example, arise if an object is unconditionally sold to a member of the public, since the buyer thereby acquires unlimited possession of any knowledge which may be obtained from the object. Even where in such cases the specific features of the object may not be ascertained from an external examination, but only by further analysis, those features are nevertheless to be considered as having been made available to the public. This is irrespective of whether or not particular reasons can be identified for analysing the composition or internal structure of the object".

127 See Article 55(1)(a) EPC.

128 Lionel Bently 2012 (n 114) para 3.68; T 830/90 [1994] OJ EPO 713 and T 681/01 (28 November 2006) para 2.8, where the Technical Board of Appeal noted that the supply of a product does not necessarily entail a tacit agreement as to confidentiality.

129 Guidelines for Examination in the EPO. Part G. Chapter V. Section 3; see also Rudolf Kraßer and Christoph Ann 2009 (n 120) Kapitel 3, § 16.A.IV. Rdn 2.

130 Guidelines for Examination in the EPO. Part G. Chapter V. Section 2.

131 Article 55(1) EPC; this point was later clarified by the EPO Enlarge Board of Appeal in G 2/99 [2001] OJ EPO 83, where it was noted that the relevant date to calculate the six months period was the actual date of filing before the EPO and not the priority date.

132 Commission, 'Explanatory Memorandum, Proposal for a Directive of the European Parliament and of the Council on the protection of undisclosed know-how and business information (trade secrets) against their unlawful acquisition, use and disclosure' 2.

and highlights the complementarity of patents and trade secrets as appropriation methods.[133] Inventors can rely on secrecy during the development phase and apply for patents to protect their inventions during the marketing phase. Notwithstanding this, the EPC also imposes temporal restrictions on unlawful disclosure in order to encourage early patenting.[134]

### 2. Preferring trade secrets over patents

#### a) Analysis of economical empirical evidence

Contrary to the general belief that patents protect a company's most valuable inventions, empirical evidence suggests that alternative mechanisms, such as secrecy and lead-time advantage, are the preferred methods of appropriating returns from innovation.[135] This is true at least in the EU,[136] the UK,[137] Switzerland[138] and the U.S.[139] Indeed, it has been reported that in the UK, only 4% of the companies engaging in innovative activities applied for a patent between 1998 and 2006.[140] This figure is only slightly higher for undertakings operating in the U.S., where only 5,5% of the

133 Anthony V. Arundel, 'The relative effectiveness of patents and secrecy for appropriation' [2001] 30 Research Policy 611-624.

134 Lionel Bently 2012 (n 114) para 3.68.

135 Bronwyn H. Hall, Christian Helmers, Mark Rogers and Vania Sena, 'The Choice between Formal and Informal Intellectual Property: A Review' [2014] 52 Journal of Economic Literature 1, 6.

136 Anthony V. Arundel 2001 (n 133) 611-624.

137 UK Innovation Survey 2007.

138 Najib Harabi, 'Appropiability of Technichal Innovations an Empirical Analysis' [1995] 24 Research Policy 981-992.

139 Over the last decades, a number of studies have addressed the preferred means of appropriation in the U.S. The most well-known ones are two: Richard C. Levin, Alvin K, Klevorick, Richard R. Nelson and Sidney G. Winter 'Appropriating the Returns from Industrial Research and Development' [1987] 18 Brookings Papers on Economic Activity 783-832; and Wesley Cohen, Richard R. Nelson, John P. Walsh, 'Protecting Their Intellectual Assets: Appropriability Conditions and Why U.S. Manufacturing Firms Patent (or Not)' (2000) National Bureau of Economic Research Working Paper 7552 <http://www.nber.org/papers/w7552> accessed 15 September 2018.

140 Bronwyn H. Hall, Christian Helmers, Mark Rogers and Vania Sena, 'The importance (or not) of patents to UK Firms' (2013) NBER Working Paper No. 19089 <http://www.nber.org/papers/w19089> accessed 15 September 2018.

manufacturing companies hold patents for their inventions.[141] With regard to these statistics, this section surveys the underlying economic factors that determine whether firms will opt to apply for patents or rely on other informal appropriation mechanisms instead.

For the purposes of the current research, Arundel's survey is reviewed as it provides the most accurate insight into the preferred methods for protecting innovations by EU firms during a certain period.[142] Arundel's study looks into the data gathered from 1990 to 1992 in the Community Innovation Survey ("CIS") of six EU Member States (Germany, Luxemburg, the Netherlands, Belgium, Denmark and Ireland), as well as Norway and analyses the responses of 2.849 R&D performing firms. His research intends to answer mainly three questions. In the first place, he examines the relative importance of secrecy and patents for European manufacturers. Next, he considers whether small firms believe that patents are of greater value than secrets as opposed to larger firms. Finally, he looks into the factors that affect the value of secrecy in contrast to patents.[143]

With regard to the relative importance of secrecy, the respondents in the CIS were asked to take into account not only trade secrets and patents as potential appropriation means to maintain and increase the competitiveness of innovations, but also three other parameters, namely (i) design registration, (ii) complexity of product design,[144] and (iii) lead-time advantage over competitors.[145] At the same time, a distinction was drawn between product and process innovations. The results are illustrated in Table 1 below:

141 Natarajan Balasubramanian and Jagadeesh Sivadasan, 'What happens when firms patent? New evidence from U.S. economic census data' [2011] 93 The Review of Economics and Statistics 126, 126-127.

142 Anthony V. Arundel 2001 (n 133) 611-624.

143 Anthony V. Arundel 2001 (n 133) 614.

144 Complexity of product design refers to a product of high intricacy that requires considerable resources to be reverse engineered; see further Pamela Samuelson and Suzanne Scotchmer 2002 (n 226) 1619.

145 The term lead-time advantage (also known as the first mover advantage) refers to "the ability of pioneering firms to earn positive economic profits (i.e. profits in excess of capital). (…) It arises from three primary sources (1) technological leadership, (2) preemption of assets, and (3) buyer switching costs" according to Marvin B. Lieberman, 'First-Mover Advantage' [1988] 9 Strategic Management J 41, 41-42.

TABLE 1. PERCENTAGE OF 2849 R&D-PERFORMING FIRMS THAT GIVE THEIR HIGHEST RATING TO EACH APPROPRIATION METHOD

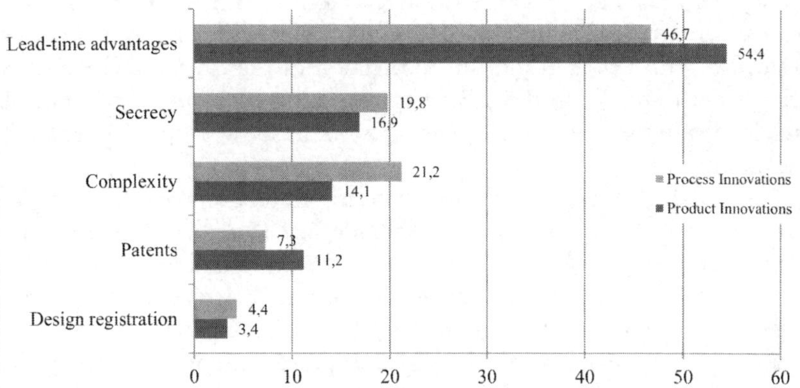


As is apparent from the above reproduced table, lead-time advantage (the first mover advantage) was deemed the preferred method of appropriation for product innovation by 54,4% of the respondents, followed by secrecy (16,95%), complexity of product design (14,1%), patents (11,2%) and design registration (3,4%). As regards process innovations, lead-time advantage also received the highest rating score (54,4%), followed by the complexity of the product (21,2%), and secrecy (19,8%).[146] Notably, in regard to process innovations, the complexity of the product was considered more effective to secure returns from innovation than secrecy. In contrast, patents were the preferred option only for 7,3% of the R&D companies.

146 The UK Innovation Survey 2007 provided similar results. The preferred methods for protecting innovations among the more than 28.000 undertakings surveyed between 2004 and 2006 were confidentiality agreements (18%), lead-time advantage (15%) and secrecy (13%). In contrast, only 8% of the sampled companies ranked patents as highly important means of protecting innovations. In the U.S., the survey evidence conducted by Weseley Cohen and others 2000 (n 139) shows that for product innovations secrecy and lead-time are perceived as the two most effective appropriation mechanisms. This means that in more than 50% of the product innovations in which undertakings resorted to lead-time and secrecy, effective protection was achieved. At the other end of the spectrum, patents were only regarded as effective means of appropriation in 34.83% of the innovations. As regards process innovations, secrecy was regarded as the most effective mechanism of appropriation (50.59%), followed by lead-time (38.43%). Patents were only effective in 23.30% of the cases in which companies resorted to them.

This is in line with the idea that process patents are likely to disclose too much information to competitors in their specification, as it is generally considered that they are easier to invent around than product patents.[147] Also, when process innovations are kept secret, they are less likely to be examined by third parties and thus protection can last beyond the twenty-year patent term.[148] On the other hand, keeping a product innovation secret is seemingly more difficult, as it can be inspected upon purchase of the product.[149]

Turning to the size of firms, in regard to product innovations, a higher percentage of small firms considered trade secrets to be more important than patents as compared to larger firms. The data gathered from the CIS survey suggests that there is a correlation between the size of the firm and the relative importance of secrecy, when compared to patents.[150] However, this correlation does not exist in regard to process innovations, where the relative value of secrecy and patents is similar across firms of all sizes. Special emphasis should be given to the responses provided by small R&D-intensive firms, as on average they regarded patents as more important than small R&D-performing firms.[151]

Other factors that come into play in the assessment of the relative value of secrecy and patents are the firm's own innovative strategies and the sector in which they are applied. As noted in the previous paragraph, R&D-intensive firms tend to attach greater value to patents. Most importantly, there are significant variations across manufacturing sectors. Patents are most valued by firms when the development of the invention is very cost-

147 Bronwyn Hall, Christian Helmers, Mark Rogers and Vania Sena 2014 (n 135) 380.

148 Wesley Cohen and others 2000 (n 139) 10.

149 Richard C. Levin and others 1987 (n 139) 795.

150 Anthony V. Arundel 2001 (n 133) 617; similar conclusions were reached by Serge Pajak, 'Do innovative firms rely on big secrets? An analysis of IP protection strategies with the CIS 4 survey' [2016] 25 Economics of Innovation and New Technology 516; Knut Blind, Jakob Edler, Rainer Frietsch and Ulrich Schmoch, 'Motives to patent: Empirical evidence from Germany'[2006] 35 Research Policy 655-672 studied the German scenario and came to the conclusion that the importance of patents increases according to the size of the firm. Larger firms tend to rely more on patents as means of appropriation than smaller ones, which prefer informal means. This is also the case in the UK according to the studies of Alan Hughes and Andrea Mina, 'The Impact of the Patent System on SMEs' (2010) Centre for Business Research, University of Cambridge Working Paper No.411 Working Papers <https://www.uspto.gov/sites/default/files/aia_implementation/ipp-2011nov08-ukipo-1.pdf> accessed 15 September 2018.

151 Anthony V. Arundel 2001 (n 133) 616-617.

ly, but its imitation is actually very cheap.[152] Thus, the pharmaceutical and chemical industries are two of the most paradigmatic examples of sectors where there is a strong reliance on patents.[153]

As a whole, the prevalence of lead-time advantage and secrecy over patents as the preferred appropriation mechanisms both for product and process innovations seems intrinsically linked to the disclosure requirement provided for in patent law.[154] Secrecy plays a central role in ensuring a technological head start, which is irretrievably hindered by patent disclosure.[155]

### b) Advantages of secrets over patents

Protecting information through the law of trade secrecy entails a number of advantages over patents for their holders. The three most salient ones are that: (i) the protection is available without burdensome administrative procedures and at a very low cost, (ii) critical information is not disclosed to competitors, and (iii) protection may extend beyond the twenty-year term. Each of these features are examined in turn.

The grant of a patent is subject to a formal (and in some instances lengthy)[156] procedure of application to national offices.[157] In addition, patent applications must be drafted in a very specific manner, which in most countries involves engaging the services of qualified patent attorneys.

---

152 Anthony V. Arundel 2001 (n 133) 618-619.

153 Richard C. Levin and others 1987 (n 139) 796; empirical evidence on the positive effects of the patent system in the pharmaceutical and chemical sector is provided by Edwin Mansfield 'Patents and Innovation: An Empirical Study' [1986] 32 Management Science 173-181.

154 Wesley Cohen and others 2000 (n 139) 14 provide empirical evidence (Figure 5), according to which the main reason not to apply for a patent is the ease to invent around by competitors; a similar point is raised in Richard C. Levin and others 1987 (n 139) 802-803.

155 See Alexandra K. Zaby, 'Losing the lead: Patents and the disclosure requirement' (2005) Tübinger Diskussionsbeitrag No. 296 <http://nbn.resolving.de/urn:nbn:de:bsz:21-opus-20528> accessed 15 September 2018.

156 For a more detailed account see Eugenio Hoss, 'Delays in Patent Examination and their Implications under the TRIPS Agreement' (Master Thesis, MIPLC 2010/11) <http://ssrn.com/abstract=2166853> accessed 15 September 2018.

157 Article 4 A PC; for a detailed account of the European and German grant proceedings see Felix Landry, 'The proceedings for grant' 338-501 in Maximilian Haedicke and Henrik Timmann (eds), *Patent Law Handbook* (2013 C.H. Beck).

Furthermore, if international protection is sought, costly translations for the selected countries are required.[158] Similarly, most patent offices demand the payment of maintenance fees yearly throughout the life of the patent.[159]

Conversely, under the law of trade secrets undisclosed information is protected as long as it is not publicly known and without the need to comply with burdensome administrative procedures.[160] As a result, information can be protected automatically and at a lower cost. However, pursuant to Article 39(2)(c) TRIPs, the holders of information must take reasonable measures to protect the secret nature of their information.[161] It is generally accepted that the cost of implementing protective measures is lower than the fixed patentability costs (these include the average price of patenting and the maintenance cost of the patent throughout its life), particularly for trade secrets of modest value, as from a rational perspective the investment made in protecting trade secrets should never be higher than their actual value.[162]

The most relevant advantage provided by the law of trade secrets as opposed to the patent system is that it affords protection to inventions without disclosing relevant information to competitors. Patent law ensures that the holder can benefit exclusively from his innovation for a certain period of time, subject to the condition that the patent is published and thus accessible to the public at large.[163] As indicated above,[164] a number of empirical studies show that the disclosure requirement is the main reason why holders of information choose informal means to protect their inventions. They fear that the description of an innovation in the patent specification may instruct competitors on how to invent around before the expiry of the

158 As provided by Article 22 PCT; this point is further elaborated in Lionel Bentley 2012 (n 114) 62.

159 See for instance the schedule of fees and expenses applicable to patents granted by the EPO <http://www.epo.org/law-practice/legal-texts/official-journal/2014/etc/se3/p1.html> accessed 15 September 2018 and the USPTO <http://www.uspto.gov/learning-and-resources/fees-and-payment/uspto-fee-schedule#Patent%20Fees> accessed 15 September 2018.

160 Roger M. Milgrim, *Milgrim on Trade Secrets* (Matthew Bender 2014) § 1.06 [2]; see James Pooley 2002 (n 66) § 3.01 [3-5]; Lionel Bently 2012 (n 114) 62.

161 This requirement is developed further in chapter 2 § 1 A) IV. 2. d).

162 Michael Risch 2007 (n 15) 43.

163 Friedrich-Karl Beier and Josef Straus, 'The Patent System and Its Informational Function – Yesterday and Today' [1977] IIC 387, 397.

164 See chapter 1 § 3 A) I. 2. a).

patent term.[165] Furthermore, innovations that do not fulfil the patentability standards because they are not regarded as new or inventive will be dedicated to the public after the publication of a patent application, even if a patent is not granted, thus forfeiting trade secrets protection. These factors explain the prevalence of trade secrets over patents as a means of appropriating returns from innovation across different industries.[166]

Thirdly, the protection of innovations through secrecy may last for as long as the inventor is able to keep the invention secret,[167] whereas with patents the term of protection is limited to twenty years from filing.[168] In theory, trade secrets may extend for as long as the secret remains unveiled. Prime examples of this are the Coca-Cola formula for the so-called "Merchandise 7x" flavouring or KFC's famous "11 herbs and spices" sauce.[169] However, this feature of trade secrets is an advantage only for those inventions that are not easy to study.[170]

The foregoing analysis has been conducted from the perspective of the trade secret holder. However, it is important to bear in mind that the patent system is based on four pillars that take into account not only the private interest of the inventor, but also the general interest of society. According to Machlup, the grant of an exclusive right on a patent is justified on the basis of four grounds that partially overlap with the justifications outlined with respect to trade secrets protection:[171] (i) the intellectual property thesis, (ii) the reward thesis, (iii) the incentive thesis and (iv) the

---

165 See Article 93(1)(a) EPC; but also 35 U.S.C. § 122 (2008) (U.S. Patent Act) regarding the confidential status of applications; William Landes and Richard Posner 2003 (n 38) 362-363; Suzanne Scotchmer 2004 (n 41) 83 noting that "Nevertheless, inventors generally prefer to avoid disclosure because it is difficult to protect all of the knowledge disclosed in a patent. Trade secrecy is especially attractive if the inventor thinks that the trade secret would never leak out and never be rediscovered independently by someone else. However, choosing trade secrecy undermines the well-thought-out objectives of the patent system".

166 Sabra Chartrand, 'Patents; Many companies will forgo patents in an effort to safeguard their trade secrets' *New York Times* (New York, 5 February 2001) C00005.

167 Michael Risch 2011 (n 113) 168.

168 See Article 38 TRIPs, Article 63 EPC and Article 33 TRIPs. However, it should be borne in mind that TRIPs only lays down minimum standards of protection and thus, the patent term may extend beyond twenty years.

169 Robbie Brown and Kim Severson, 'Recipe for Coke? One More to Add to the File' *New York Times* (New York, 19 February 2011) WK3.

170 Michael Risch 2011 (n 113) 168; William Landes and Richard Posner 2003 (n 38) 362.

171 See chapter 1 § 2.

disclosure thesis.[172] The first two are of a deontological nature and consider that individuals have a natural right in their inventions and should be rewarded for their contribution to society (following the Lockean labour law theory described in § 2 A) II of this chapter).[173] Under the incentive thesis, the exclusive patent right is granted in order to encourage technical and scientific progress.[174] As outlined above,[175] the disclosure thesis contends that the main goal of the patent system is to make publicly available information that otherwise would be concealed by its holder in order to encourage further development. Following this rationale, the patent system is pictured as a trade-off between the inventor and society.[176]

In the light of the above, it should be highlighted that although the justifications for the protection of trade secrets and patents present some common ground, they also present notable differences owing to the hybrid legal nature of trade secrets and the fact that protection is only envisaged against misappropriation. Turning first to the deontological arguments, pursuant to the labour value thesis, both the patent holder and the trade secrets holder have a natural right in their inventions and the information that they have generated.

In the same vein, contractarian theories are also applicable to justify both trade secrets protection and the general legal framework created by IPRs.[177] With respect to the latter, Merges, in his seminal book *Justifying Intellectual Property*, submits that individuals in the Original Position

172 A more detailed account on the justifications of the patent system is provided by Fritz Machlup in his seminal article 'Economic Review of the Patent System' (1958) Study No. 15 of the subcommittee on the Judiciary-United States Senate 85th Congress, 2nd session, Washington, 20-21; Rudolf Kraßer and Christoph Ann 2009 (n 120) § 3 II.

173 Friedrich-Karl Beier, 'Traditional and Socialist Concepts of Protecting Inventions' [1970] IIC 328, 330-332.

174 Similarly, William Fisher 'Theories of Intellectual Property' 168, 173 in Stephen R. Munzer (ed), *New Essays in the Legal and Political Theory of Property* (CUP 2001); Friedrich-Karl Beier 1970 (n 173) 333 noting that "The incentive thesis views the main purpose of patent protection in its function to stimulate the profit expectations of the inventor and to encourage enterprises to invest capital in research, development, and exploitation of new inventions".

175 A more comprehensive account of this principle is provided in chapter 1 § 2 B) II.

176 See Friedrich-Karl Beier 1970 (n 173) 336-338; but see Robert P. Merges and Richard R. Nelson, 'On the complete economics of patent scope' [1990] 90 Columbia LR 839, 868 arguing that the trade-off analysis is too simplistic and appropriate consideration should be paid to other factors.

177 Robert P. Merges, *Justiffying Intellectual Property Law* (HUP 2011) 112, 135-136.

would agree on granting IPRs (including patents) to creators and inventors despite the unequal distribution of resources among members of a society that this would entail. He argues that such an incentive would encourage the most creative/inventive individuals to pursue this kind of activity, which would ultimately result in a net positive distributional effect. In other words, the individuals in the worst position in society would still benefit from the products covered by IPRs. Consequently, he concludes that the unfair allocation of resources may appear justified and should be part of the essential liberties to which every individual is entitled.[178]

In contrast, the patent reward theory is not applicable to trade secrets protection, as trade secrets holders do not publish the subject matter covered by the secret, which in addition is not necessarily innovative. In fact, upon disclosure, protection ceases. Therefore, the holder of valuable secret information does not participate in the trade-off between the inventor and society and will not be entitled to obtain an absolute erga omnes right to exploit the information concerned.

With respect to the commercial ethics theory, its application to patent rights is highly questionable, based on the fact that patents are absolute property rights with erga omnes effects. This means that the patent holder is protected against the exploitation of products in which the invention is embodied by any third party.[179] Consequently, the standard of liability is a strict one, unlike the one applicable to trade secrets, where protection is afforded only in case of unlawful acquisition, use and disclosure of information. Hence, while trade secrets protection may be justified on the basis that it is necessary to enforce honest commercial practices in the marketplace among competitors, the strict patent liability standard precludes any analogous consideration in the field of patents. Indeed, in patent infringement cases, the appraisal of negligence or wilfulness on the side of the in-

---

178 Robert P. Merges, *Justifying Intellectual Property Law* (HUP 2011) 112.

179 In this regard, it should be noted that Article 28 the TRIPs Agreement sets out the following minimum standards of protection with regard to the rights conferred by a patent:
"1. A patent shall confer on its owner the following exclusive rights:
(a)where the subject matter of a patent is a product, to prevent third parties not having the owner's consent from the acts of: making, using, offering for sale, selling, or importing for these purposes that product;
(b) where the subject matter of a patent is a process, to prevent third parties not having the owner's consent from the act of using the process, and from the acts of: using, offering for sale, selling, or importing for these purposes at least the product obtained directly by that process".

fringer does not play a role during the assessment of the acts that trigger liability in direct infringement cases, with the exception of those situations where the defendant uses a process or offers to use a process.[180] In the latter case, the plaintiff must prove that the defendant knew or that it was obvious from the circumstances that use of the process without consent would result in an infringement.[181]

Following utilitarian arguments, at first glance it seems that the fact that under the law of trade secrets an invention that may be eligible for patent protection can be perpetually exploited without disclosing to the public at large its technical innovation runs counter to the last two theoretical justifications put forward with respect to the patent law systems: the incentive thesis and the disclosure thesis. There is social value in the disclosure of an invention that is undermined if the trade secret holder is able to reap the fruits indefinitely.[182] In such a case, society would not be able to build on existing knowledge and develop follow-on innovation.[183] As noted above, cumulative innovation is central to the development of technological progress.[184] In the words of Scotchmer, "intellectual property should be designed to achieve the right balance of protection for innovators, protection for consumers, and opportunity for rivals to make improvements. Protection through secrecy can obstruct these objectives".[185] However, following the conclusions previously outlined,[186] trade secrets protection does provide certain incentives to generate information (that may be both of an innovative and non-innovative nature) and allows for lower transaction costs, which despite not fulfilling the patent disclosure function, incentivise information sharing among market participants and within the internal sphere of firms. Consequently, it is submitted that the incentive

180 Lionel Bently and Brad Sherman 2014 (n 125) 610 and 624-625.

181 Lionel Bently and Brad Sherman 2014 (n 125) 619; along the same lines see § 9(2) Patentgesetz in der Fassung der Bekanntmachung vom 16. Dezember 1980 (BGBl. 1981 I S. 1), das zuletzt durch Artikel 4 des Gesetzes vom 8. Oktober 2017 (BGBl. I S. 3546) geändert worden ist (German Patent Act).

182 See Fritz Machlup 1985 (n 172) 76; Suzanne Scotchmer 2004 (n 41) 83; Surblyte Gintare, *The Refusal to Disclose Trade Secrets as an Abuse of Market Dominance – Microsoft and Beyond* (Stämpfli 2011) 92.

183 Katherine J. Strandburg, 'What does the public get? Experimental use and the patent bargain?'[2004] 57 Wisconsin LR 81, 107-118 discussing the interplay between the incentive to disclose and the incentive to innovate within the patent system and its effects on follow-on innovation.

184 See chapter 1 § 2 B) I.

185 Suzanne Scotchmer 2004 (n 41) 26.

186 See chapter 1 § 2 B) II.

thesis and the disclosure thesis under patent law and the trade secrets legal regime are not completely mutually exclusive.

As a final consideration, it should be noted that the two additional utilitarian arguments that have been discussed with respect to trade secrets protection are not extrapolatable to the patent system. With respect to the limit to the arms race argument, it should be observed that according to the strict liability rules followed in patent law, patentees do not have to invest in costly self-help measures to protect their inventions. Once the patent is granted, the patentee will be protected against any unauthorised acts of exploitation in the market of the products in which the patented invention is embodied or that have been directly obtained from a new patented process.[187] This is further reinforced by the fact that the adoption of reasonable measures under the circumstances to protect the undisclosed nature of a trade secret is not a requirement for protection under patent law.

In the same vein, the privacy rationale is not applicable to justify patent legal regimes, as knowledge diffusion is one of the principles upon with the patent system is built. In fact, pursuant to the PCT, patent applications are published at the latest eighteen months after filing[188] and according to the EPO, upon grant, the patent specification is also published in the European Patent Bulletin.[189] Notwithstanding this, it should be recalled that following the utilitarian dimension of the privacy rationale explained above,[190] it is of utmost importance that the secrecy of the invention is not lost prior to the submission of the patent application. Prospective patent applicants should be guaranteed a Laboratory Zone in which to develop their innovations without the interference of third parties.

#### c) The risks of secrecy

The protection of innovations through secrecy involves considerable risks, in contrast to patents. The most salient one is the revelation of the information. Upon disclosure, information ceases to be protected and enters the

187 Please note that some countries confer provisional protection to the applicant from the date of publication and until the date of publication of mention of its grant is published in the Patent Office Bulletin. In Europe, such a right is regulated under Articl 67 of the EPC, which confers upon the applicant the same protection provided for granted patents in the designated contracting state.

188 See Article 21 PCT and 93 EPC.

189 See Article 98 EPC.

190 See chapter 1 § 2 B) IV.

public domain. It is not possible to recoup the confidential nature once it is lost. As noted by Sir John Donaldson M.R. during the course of the so-called "Spycatcher" litigation in England:

> Confidential information is like an ice cube. Give it to the party who undertakes to keep it in his refrigerator and you still have an ice cube by the time the matter comes to trial. Either party may then succeed in obtaining possession of the cube. Give it to the party who has no refrigerator or will not agree to keep it in one, and by the time of the trial you just have a pool of water which neither party wants. It is the inherently perishable nature of confidential information which gives rise to unique problems.[191]

Against this background, it is important to outline the four main scenarios in which secrets may be revealed,[192] namely: (i) with the publication of the information by its holder; (ii) if the information is independently generated and made available; (iii) if the secret is unveiled through lawful means such as reverse engineering; and (iv) as a result of a breach of a duty of confidence.

In the first scenario, a lack of due diligence may lead the trade secret holder to disclose his own invention. Sometimes scientists publish their inventions in journals, unaware of how the novelty requirement operates within the patent system. Subsequently, in the assessment of their application by the patent office their own publication is regarded as prior art.[193] Similarly, if an inventor applies for a patent that in the end is not granted, the application will be published and the secret contained therein will fall into the public domain. As a result, the invention will be protected neither by patent law nor as a trade secret.[194]

According to the second scenario, even if an invention is successfully concealed by the trade secret holder, it is possible that a competitor will be

---

191 *Attorney General v Newspaper Publishing Plc and Others* [1989] 2 FSR 27(Ch), 48.

192 As noted by Lionel Bently 2012 (n 114) para 3.27-3.51.

193 EPO T 381/87 [1990] OJ EPO 213 dealing with an invention published before the priority date in an article submitted to a scientific journal by the three inventors.

194 This has been confirmed by case law in the UK (*Mustad v Son v Dosen and another* [1964] 1 WRL 109 (HL)); Germany (BGH GRUR 1975, 206 – *Kunststoffschaum-Bahnen*) and also in the United States (*Timely Products Corp v. Arron* 523 F 2d 288 (2d Cir. 19751975)); for a more detailed account of the underlying policy see Friedrich-Karl Beier and Josef Straus, 'The Patent System and Its Informational Function – Yesterday and Today' [1977] IIC 387, 387.

able to generate it independently. Nowadays most technological progress is built upon prior innovations and thus it is possible that two competing firms will manage to develop the same invention separately.[195] This is particularly problematic if the second inventor obtains a patent covering the secret innovation, as according to consistent case law from the EPO, a secret or inherent use does not anticipate the invention unless it is accessible to the public. Thus, the first inventor will not be able to rely on such a use to invalidate the patent.[196]

In this context, another problem that may arise is the potential infringement of the patent by the first inventor. To overcome this, most European jurisdictions have developed a so-called "prior user right", which entitles the holder of a secret invention to continue using it, despite the grant of a valid patent.[197] Such a defence was developed on the basis of fairness arguments and with the purpose of counterbalancing the effects of the first-to-file system. It is generally accepted that the trade secret holder who has invested time and work and incurred high costs to use the invention should not be deprived of the fruits of his work by a third party's patent application.[198] In Germany for instance, the exercise of the prior user right is conditioned upon the fulfilment of two requirements. In the first place, the

195 Suzanne Scotchmer, 'Standing on the Shoulders of Giants: Cumulative Research and the Patent Law' [1991] 5 JEP 29, 29 noting that "most innovators stand on the shoulders of giants, and never more so than in the current evolution of high technologies, where almost all technical progress builds on a foundation provided by earlier innovators".

196 See T 472/92 [1998] OJ EPO 161, where the Board of Appeal held that the mere delivery of materials did not render them publicly available; see also more generally G 1/92 [1993] OJ EPO 277, where the Enlarged Board of Appeal deemed that if an invention is accessible on the date of priority, it is dedicated to the public.

197 Article 122(5) EPC establishes the so-called "intervening rights", which operate in a similar manner to prior user rights. Pursuant to this provision, if a person in good faith has used or prepared to use an invention which is the object of a published EP application or a granted EP, between the time a loss of rights occurred and the time of publication of the mention of re-establishment of rights, he may continue to use it in the course of his business. Notwithstanding this, substantive issues concerning the acquisition, scope and transferability of prior user rights is subject to the national legislation of the EPC Contracting States. As regards TRIPs, it is generally accepted that prior user rights to fall within the general scope of Article 30 TRIPs. Prior user rights are regulated for instance in § 12 of the German Patent Acct and § 64 of the UK Patents Act 1977.

198 Rudolf Kraßer and Christoph Ann 2009 (n 120) § 34 II a. 2; a similar position was expressed by the German Federal Supreme Court in one of its decisions on § 12 of the German Patent Act (BGH GRUR, 2010, 47, 48 –*Füllstoff*), where the

patented invention must have actually been used (or arrangements to use it must have been made) in Germany before the priority date. Secondly, the inventor must be in possession of the invention. If these two conditions are met, the patent cannot be enforced against the trade secret holder.[199] However, as the prior user right (unlike the patent right) is not of an exclusive nature, its holder will not be able to enforce it against third parties.[200]

In the U.S., historically there was no general "prior user's right" defence, as it was only envisaged for business method patents.[201] Until the America Invents Act ("AIA") was passed, the patent system was premised on the first to invent principle, where non-disclosing uses could be invoked as the basis for invalidating a patent application.[202] Under the new framework created by the AIA, the paradigm shifted and as of March 16, 2013 it became closer to a first-to-file system.[203] In view of that, § 273 U.S. Patent Act[204] was amended in order to create a general defence allowing any per-

court noted that "The purpose of Section 12 PatG is, for reasons of fairness, to safeguard an existing previously initiated vested right of the prior user, and hence to prevent the unfair destruction of values created in a permissible and, in particular, lawful manner. His (the prior user's) efforts, time and capital in existing assets, which are utilised to exploit the invention, or in which the will to do so has been confirmed, ought not to have been invested for nothing, nor should such a vested right be stripped of value by someone else's patent application". translation by Johannes W. Bukow, 'Defences' § 9c I, Rdn 98 in Maximilian Haedicke and Henrik Timmann (eds), *Patent Law Handbook* (2013 C.H. Beck).

199 Johannes W. Bukow, 'Defences' § 9c II in Maximilian Haedicke and Henrik Timmann (eds), *Patent Law Handbook* (2013 C.H. Beck).

200 Rudolf Kraßer and Christoph Ann 2009 (n 120) § 34 II a. 3; a more detailed account of the prior user right falls outside the scope of the present research. However, see The Tegernsee Group 'Consolidated Report on the Tegernsee user consultation on substantive Patent Law Harmonization (Tegernsee V)' (2014), 75-101 <http://www.epo.org/news-issues/issues/harmonisation_de.html> accessed 15 September 2018.

201 For a general overview of the prior user rights in the U.S. see The Tegernsee Group 'Report on Prior User Right (Tegernsee III)' (2012), 8-9 <http://www.epo.org/news-issues/issues/harmonisation_de.html> accessed 15 September 2018; see further Lionel Bently 2012 (n 114) para 3.40.

202 See 35 U.S.C. §§ 102 (g) (2008), which is not applicable to patents filed after 1 March 2013, subject to the provisions of the AIA.

203 For an introduction to the rules laid down before the AIA was passed see Mark A. Lemley, 'Does "Public Use" Mean the Same Thing It Did Last year?' [2014] 93 Texas LR 1119, 1123-1125.

204 U.S Patent Act, Public Law 593, 66 Stat. 792 (1952) (codified as amended at 35 U.S.C. §§ 1 et seq) (U.S. Patent Act).

son who acting in good faith had used the invention in the U.S. in a commercial context to continue using the invention after the grant of the patent. However, the prior user can only avail himself of this defence if the relevant use occurred at least one year before the filing date or the date of public disclosure of the patentee who relies on the one-year grace period provided for in § 102(b).[205]

The two additional scenarios in which the right in a trade secret is lost, i.e. when it is lawfully acquired through reverse engineering and when it is unlawfully acquired, used or disclosed are examined in the following chapters,[206] as they are of paramount importance in striking an optimal balance between the trade secrets regime and the IPRs system and are deemed essential limitations for the construction of a solid public domain.

In sum, it can be concluded that the choice between patent protection and trade secrets when they are both mutually exclusive will depend on the interplay of a number of factors. Ultimately, from an economic perspective, the holder of information will prefer trade secrets protection if the costs of the patent system are too high compared to the value of the invention or the expected profit is lower than their value.[207] Rational inventors will choose the most profitable option. This would be the case if the patentable invention took longer to reverse engineer than the twenty-year patent term.[208] In the latter case, the objectives pursued by the patent system and the trade secrets legal regime seem incompatible, as the trade secrets owner may be able to reap the fruits of his endeavours indefinitely.

### 3. Simultaneous protection of trade secrets and patents

The academic literature has paid little attention to the complementarity relationship between patents and trade secrets, even though in practice it plays an essential role in planning the strategic protection of intangible assets and maximising returns from innovative activities.[209]

---

205 35 U.S.C. § 102(b).

206 Chapter 3 § 5 C) III provides an account of the misappropriation doctrines under the TSD and chapter 6 § 2 B) examines reverse engineering practices.

207 William Landes and Richard Posner 2003 (n 38) 359.

208 William Landes and Richard Posner 2003 (n 38) 359.

209 William Cornish, David Llewellyn and Tanya Aplin, *Intellectual Property: Patents, Copyright, Trade Marks and Allied Rights* (8th edn, Sweet&Maxwell 2013) para 8-03 noting that "In actual practice, patents are often secured for a central invention, while much that is learned in the process of bringing it into commer-

Trade secrets are not only key in early-stage inventions,[210] but also when innovations can be protected simultaneously both by trade secrets and patents. In this case, companies will often make use of both appropriation mechanisms.[211] On the one hand, processes or products that fulfil the patentability criteria will be protected under the patent law regime. On the other hand, more specific information that is not necessary for the purposes of providing an enabling disclosure in the patent application will be concealed.[212] Usually, such information refers to the precise way in which the inventor performed the claimed product or process and it is disclosed through licensing agreements.[213]

This complementarity relationship is enhanced by the fact that "trade secret law reaches into a number of corners patent law cannot".[214] The spectrum of subject matter eligible for protection is broader for trade secrets than for patents, particularly in Europe where patents covering software and business models are difficult to obtain. However, trade secrets protection may be invoked to protect business plans, customer lists and so-called "negative know-how" against use by third parties.[215] The EPO consideres that this type of information lacks inventiveness and hence falls outside the scope of protection of patent law. Yet, it is effectively protected against misappropriation by the law of trade secrets. Furthermore, in some cases inventors must wait up to three years for the patent office to decide

---

cial production is tied up as secret 'know-how' by means of confidence undertakings".

210 See chapter 1 § 3 A) I. 1.

211 Lionel Bently 2012 (n 114) para 3.78; Anthony V. Arundel 2001 (n 133) 613.

212 Elisabetta Ottoz and Franco Cugno, 'Patent-Secret Mix in Complex Product Firms' [2008] 10 American Law & Economics R 142.

213 In the U.S., such practices may appear more controversial, as pursuant to 35 U.S.C. § 112 (a) (2011) the inventor must disclose to the public the best mode he knows for performing the invention. That is, of all the embodiments covered within the scope of a claim, the most effective one has to be specified. The fact that the inventor concludes a licensing agreement that includes several recommendations as to how to practice the invention not described in the patent may suggest that he has failed to comply with the "best mode requirement". Yet, this has been simplified after the adoption of the AIA, by virtue of which, the best mode is no longer an accepted defence in an infringement suit; Robert P. Merges and John F. Duffy, *Patent Law and Policy, Cases and Materials* (6th edn, Lexis Nexis 2013) 263; Lionel Bently 2012 (n 114) para 3.78.

214 Mark A Lemley 2008 (n 15) 331.

215 David S. Almeling, 'Seven Reasons Why Trade Secrets are Increasingly Important' [2012] 27 Berkeley Technology LJ 1091, 1112.

whether to grant protection.[216] As a result and for practical reasons, in fast-moving industries like the software industry, patents are rarely applied for.[217]

Hence, simultaneous reliance on both appropriation mechanisms provides protection of additional subject matter, enhances exclusivity, provides additional remedies in the event of litigation and acts as a fall-back position if the other IPR is not enforceable.[218]

## II. Trade secrets and copyright

As argued in the previous section, upon perfunctory analysis trade secrets are usually associated with patentable subject matter. Nevertheless, overlaps may also occur with regard to copyright. To name some, technical drawings or software can be afforded protection under both regimes.[219] Notwithstanding this, relying on such a two-tiered scheme may come into conflict with one of the goals upon which the copyright system is built: promoting access to new works. Indeed, modern copyright law aims at striking an adequate balance between the public interest in education, research and access to information on the one hand, and the exclusive proprietary right granted to the author to incentivise further creation on the other.[220] Ultimately, concealing information that is eligible for copyright protection prevents its dissemination to the public at large. The tensions

---

216 On average grant procedures at the EPO take three years and three months <http://www.epo.org/service-support/faq/own-file.html#faq-274.v> accessed 15 September 2018; similarly, the USPTO grant procedure lasts around 27,4 months pursuant to the USPTO, 'Performance and Accountability Report' (2014) 128 <https://www.uspto.gov/about/stratplan/ar/USPTOFY2014PAR.pdf.> accessed September 15, 2018; this period is substantially shorter if the application takes place before offices that do not conduct a substantive examination, but rather a mere registration.

217 Mark A. Lemley 2008 (n 15) 332.

218 Elisabetta Ottoz and Franco Cugno 2008 (n 212) 156.

219 Diane L. Zimmerman, 'Trade secrets and the "philosophy" of copyright: a case of culture crash' 299, 300 in Rochelle C. Dreyfuss and Katherine J. Strandburg (eds), *The Law and Theory of Trade Secrecy: A Handbook of Contemporary Research* (Edward Elgar 2011), where the author notes that "technical drawings and specifications are eligible for copyright protection and at the same time may embody information that the author may wish to conceal".

220 See Recital Fifth of the WIPO Copyright Treaty (adopted 20 December 1996, entered into force 6 March 2002) 2186 UNTS 121 (WCT): "Recognizing the need to maintain a balance between the rights of authors and the larger public

arising from such an overlap of regimes are best explained in connection to computer programs, which are taken as an example case due to their economic significance and the fact that mass-market computer program producers rely on a dual protection strategy to secure returns from their innovations.[221]

Indeed, computer programs can be protected simultaneously under the law of trade secrets and copyright. Pursuant to Article 10(1) TRIPs both the source[222] and the object code[223] fall within the material scope of the Berne Convention[224] as a form of literary work.[225] Notwithstanding the aforementioned, in practice, software manufacturers protect the source code of a program through trade secrets and resort to copyright for the object code. The rationale for this is two-fold: users prefer the functionality of the object code of programs and, most importantly, software developers are inclined to keep the source code a trade secret, and thus hinder the access to the market of third parties seeking to compete with the new com-

---

interest, particularly education, research and access to information, as reflected in the Berne Convention"; however Recital 22 of the Council Directive (EC) 2001/29 on the harmonisation of certain aspects of copyright and related rights in the information society [2001] OJ L167/10 (Information Society Directive) highlights that "The objective of proper support of dissemination of culture must not be achieved by sacrificing strict protection of rights or by tolerating illegal forms of distribution of counterfeited or pirated goods".

221 James Pooley 2002 (n 66) § 3.02 [3] 3-23.

222 The Oxford Advanced Learner's Dictionary defines 'source code, n' as "a computer program written in text form that must be translated into another form, such as machine code, before it can run on a computer" (OALD Online, 9th edn, OUP 2015) <https://www.oxfordlearnersdictionaries.com/definition/english/source-code?q=source+code> accessed 15 September 2018.

223 The Oxford Advanced Learner's Dictionary defines 'object code, n' as "the language into which a program is translated using a compiler or an assembler" (OALD Online, 9th edn, OUP 2015) <https://www.oxfordlearnersdictionaries.com/definition/english/object-code?q=object+code> accessed 15 September 2018.

224 Berne Convention for the Protection of Literary and Artistic Works (9 September 1886) 828 UNTS. 221 (BC).

225 Several commentators have called into question the characterisation of computer programs as "literary works": Sean Gordon, 'The Very Idea! Why Copyright Law is an Inappropriate Way to Protect Computer Programs' [1998] 1 EIPR 10; Jerome H. Reichman 1994 (n 102) 2432; Pamela Samuelson and others, 'A Manifesto Concerning the Legal Protection of Computer Programs [1994] 94 Columbia LR 2308; Tanya Aplin, 'Subject Matter' 49, 51-53 in Estelle Derclaye (ed), *Research Handbook on the Future of EU Copyright Law* (Edward Elgar 2009).

puter program.[226] However, the source code can be partially reconstructed in an imperfect way through the use of decompilation programs, which allow reverse engineering of the object code and thereby reveal the source code.[227]

Under EU Copyright law, as set forth in Article 6(1) and 6(2) of the Software Directive,[228] decompilation is only deemed lawful if it is required in order to develop an interoperable program[229] and if the three following restrictive conditions are all met, namely:

(i) The acts of decompilation shall only be carried out by the licensee or another person entitled to use the copy;
(ii) The information should not have previously been available to the person who wishes to achieve interoperability;
(iii) Only the original parts of the program which are necessary in order to develop an independent generated interoperable program can be subject to decompilation processes.

Against this background, it appears that trade secrets are a crucial asset for the fast-moving software industry, where many firms decide to keep their interfaces undisclosed in an attempt to capture the market. Indeed, concealing the information through which interoperability between the different programs (so-called "interfaces")[230] is achieved allows the software developer to control the applications created for its platform and limit their

226 Pamela Samuelson and Suzanne Scotchmer, 'The law and economics of reverse Engineering' [2002] 111 Yale LJ 1575, 1608.

227 Jerome H. Reichman, 'Computer Programs as applied scientific know-how: implications of copyright'[1989] 42 Vanderbilt LR 639, 701; Pamela Samuelson and Suzanne Scotchmer 2002 (n 226) 1614, where the authors quote a technologist who notes that reverse engineering (decompilation) does not reveal the programm's inner secrets. According to the expert, these are embodied in the source code and do not appear in the object code after its conversion. Also, reverse engineering of computer programs is described as a very costly and difficult process.

228 Directive of the European Parliament and of the Council 2009/24/EC of 23 April 2009 on the legal protection of computer programs [2009] OJ L122/9 (Software Directive).

229 In this regard, it should be noted that "interoperability" is defined in Recital 10 of the Software Directive "as the ability to exchange information and mutually to use the information which has been exchanged".

230 The Oxford English Dictionary defines 'interface, n' as "A device or program enabling a user to communicate with a computer" (*OED Online*, OUP June 2013) <https://en.oxforddictionaries.com/definition/interface> accessed 15 September 2018.

availability to competitors, thus exploiting the resulting network effects.[231] This has important legal consequences, both from a copyright and competition law perspective. However, providing a more detailed account of the former exceeds the limits of the present research and the implications of applying competition law as a necessary limitation to trade secrets protection is analysed in chapter 6.[232]

Aside from the overlap tensions outlined above, it is noteworthy that trade secrets law also provides an incentive to create information where copyright is not available, in line with the market experimentation incentive purported by Duffy and Abramowicz. Indeed, copyright only protects the expression of literary and artistic works.[233] Ideas, facts and processes fall outside of its material scope of application.[234] Hence, trade secrets law seems to have been designed to protect non-creative "sweat of the brow" information, which results from economic investment or intellectual effort.[235] Unlike copyright, trade secrets law only requires that information is secret and derives its value from its undisclosed nature.[236] Thus, business plans or customer lists that are not original in their selection and arrangement are still protectable as undisclosed information. The implications derived from protecting information for the mere fact of keeping it undisclosed are developed in greater detail below.[237]

### III. Trade secrets and trade marks

In the context of trade mark law, there is virtually no possibility that the subject matter protected by trade marks and trade secrets will overlap.[238] Indeed, trade marks are valuable because they convey information to con-

231 Pamela Samuelson and Suzanne Scotchmer 2002 (n 226) 1617.

232 Legal scholars have thoroughly examined the multiple issues raised by Article 6 of Software Directive, both from an IP law and a competition law perspective. A more detailed account of this topic is provided in chapter 6 § 2 B) IV. 2).

233 See Article 2 BC.

234 Michael Risch 2011 (n 113) 152.

235 The "sweat of the brow" doctrine was first developed in the United States and purported that copyright should be a reward for the labour, time and cost invested in compiling facts. Such a theory was expressly rejected by the U.S. Supreme Court in *Feist Publ'ns, Inc. v. Rural Tel. Serv. Co.*, 499 U.S. 340 (1991).

236 Michael Risch 2011 (n 113) 175.

237 Chapter 1 § 3 B).

238 Michael Risch 2011 (n 113) 178.

sumers, whereas the value of trade secrets lies in their concealed nature.[239] However, in some cases, relying on trade secrets and trade marks at the same time as means of appropriation provides further incentives to create both types of information.[240]

This is best illustrated through the example of luxury perfume producers that market fragrances under famous fashion brands and rely simultaneously on trade mark and trade secrets protection in order to recoup the investment made in their development and maximise profits.[241] As is examined in chapter 5, perfume manufacturers try to keep the formula and composition of their perfumes undisclosed in order to avoid potential imitations of their high-end perfumes, which can nevertheless be easily unveiled through not very complex reverse engineering techniques. Consequently, in order to capture the market, they also invest substantial amounts in marketing campaigns to create an aura of exclusivity for their fine fragrances.

Against this background, the importance of trade mark protection for the perfume industry was underscored in the famous *L'Oréal v Bellure*[242] case decided by the CJEU, where the L'Oréal Group brought legal action against a manufacturer of so-called "smell-alike perfumes" in the UK (Bellure) and two of its distributors (Malaika and Starion) on the basis of an infringement of its trade mark rights. According to the fact-pattern of the decision, Bellure produced imitations (conveying similar olfactory messages) of famous fragrances including "Trésor", "Miracle", "Anais-Anais" and "Noa",[243] as well as of the bottles and packaging of "Trésor" and "Miracle". These were subsequently marketed by Malaika and Starion and their retailers through comparison lists that indicated the correspondence between the smell-alike perfumes and the famous fragrances by referring to the word mark under which they were protected. In the second instance, the Court of Appeal of England and Wales submitted a number of questions for a preliminary ruling before the CJEU regarding the protection conferred by the Trade Mark Directive ("TMD")[244] to marks having a repu-

239 See Article 39(2)(b) TRIPs.

240 Michael Risch 2011 (n 113) 178.

241 A detailed account of the relationship between perfumes, trade secrets and other IPRs is provided in chapter 5 of this dissertation.

242 Case C–487/07 *L'Oréal v Bellure* [2009] ECR I-05185.

243 A detailed overview of this case is provided in chapter 5 § 3 D) II. 2.

244 Directive (EU) 2015/2436 of the European Parliament and of the Council of 16 December 2015 to approximate the laws of the Member States relating to trade marks [2015] OJ L336/1 (Trade Mark Directive or TMD).

tation and its interrelation with the Misleading and Comparative Advertising Directive.[245]

In its ruling, the CJEU held that a third party takes unfair advantage of the reputation or distinctiveness of a mark when he intends to "ride on the coat tails of the mark with a reputation" in order to take advantage of its power of attraction, position or prestige without providing any financial compensation. Thus, the finding of trade mark infringement does not require either likelihood of confusion among the relevant consumers, or detriment to the distinctive character or repute of the mark.[246]

With respect to the possibility of the use of trade marks in comparative advertisements (such as comparison lists) by any third party, where the essential origin function of the trade mark is not affected (i.e. designation of origin of the goods and services protected), but such use is likely to play a significant role in the promotion of the goods and services of the other party, the CJEU held that such conduct would only be deemed lawful if it did not affect any of the other trade mark functions. In this context, specific reference was made to the communication, investment and advertisement functions.[247] Otherwise, the acts of comparative advertisement would amount to trade mark infringement.[248]

As regards comparative advertisement, the CJEU held that any explicit or implicit statement in a comparative advertisement that presents goods or services as imitations of marks with a reputation shall be regarded as an infringement for the purposes of Article 4(g) MCAD. In addition, such conduct would be regarded as taking unfair advantage of the reputation of the famous mark, as per Article 4(f) MCAD.[249]

The foregoing analysis demonstrates the complementarity relationship between trade marks and trade secrets, in particular when the secrets can be easily unveiled through reverse engineering practices and where it is not possible to resort to the protection of any formal IPR, other than trade marks. In this context, trade marks may provide additional incentives to create information by conferring an aura of luxury and exclusivity to products that incorporate secret information, thereby allowing their manufac-

245 Directive of the European Parliament and of the Council 2006/114/EC of 12 December 2006 concerning misleading and comparative advertising [2006] OJ L376/21 (Misleading and Comparative Advertisement Directive or MCAD).

246 As per Article Article 10(2)(c) TMD.

247 The uncertanty sorrounding the trade mark functions discussion is outlined in chapter 5 § 3 C) II. 2. below.

248 As per Article 10(3)(f) of the TMD.

249 Case C–487/07 *L'Oréal v Bellure* [2009] ECR I-05185, paras 75-79.

tures to internalise the cost of creation and development of the said products.

## IV. Trade secrets and the database right: the protection of investment as such

Although not as self-evident as in the case of patent rights, the sui generis right introduced by the European legislator to protect databases may also overlap with the subject matter protected by the law of trade secrets. After all, both legal regimes aim at protecting investments. However, whereas the sui generis regime aims at protecting the investment made in the *compilation* of data,[250] trade secrets law, following the incentives to innovate theory, is justified because it protects the investment made in the *creation* of valuable information.[251] The interplay between these two legal regimes is examined in section 1. Thereafter, the possibility of resorting to trade secrets protection in the absence of sui generis protection is analysed in section 2.

### 1. The EU two-tier legal regime for the protection of databases and its interplay with trade secrets protection

In the EU, the legal protection of databases was harmonised in the highly contested Database Directive, by virtue of which a two-tier regime of protection was established and a uniform notion of database was introduced. Pursuant to Article 1(2), a database is defined as "a collection of independent works, data or other materials arranged in a systematic or methodical way and individually accessible by electronic and other means". This definition, together with Recitals 13 and 14, reveals that the protection covers both compilations of data or other materials that are arranged, stored and accessed by means that include electronic, electromagnetic or electro-optical processes or analogous processes, as well as non-electronic databases.

250 See Recital 40 of the Database Directive: "Whereas the object of this sui generis right is to *ensure protection of any investment* in obtaining, verifying or presenting the contents of a database for the limited duration of the right; whereas such investment may consist in the deployment of financial resources and/or the expending of time, effort and energy (emphasis added). "

251 See chapter 1 § 2 B) I.

Under the harmonised system, on the one hand, copyright protection is afforded to the structure[252] of those databases that by reason of the selection and arrangement of their contents constitute the *author's own intellectual creation*.[253] In this case, the term of protection extends to seventy years after the death of the author. However, the Directive expressly clarifies that copyright protection does not cover the contents of the database concerned, i.e. the data gathered, which may be the object of independent protection by other rights, such as trade secrets or formal IRPs.[254]

On the other hand, the European legislator created a sui generis right for the maker of a database who carries out substantial investment (assessed from a qualitative and/or quantitative perspective) in the obtention, verification or presentation of its contents.[255]

The term of duration of the sui generis right is fifteen years from the date of completion of the database or the date on which it was made available.[256] Yet, in practice, such a term may be extended further if substantial changes in the contents of the database are introduced. Following the wording of Article 10(3) along with Recital 55, the mere update or verification of the content of the database will be considered as a new investment

252 The emphasis on the structure of the database is set out in Recital 15 of the Database Directive, which provides that: "Whereas the criteria used to determine whether a database should be protected by copyright should be defined to the fact that the selection or the arrangements of the contents of the database is the author's own intellectual creation; whereas such protection should cover the structure of the database".

253 The CJEU clarified in Case C–604/10 *Football Dataco Ltd and Others v Yahoo! UK Ltd and Others* (CJEU, 1 March 2012), para 38 that the originality requirement of "author's own intellectual creation is satisfied when, through the selection or arrangement of the data which it contains, its author expresses his, creative ability in an original manner by making free and creative choices (…) and thus stamps his 'personal touch;'" this is in line with previous case law of the CJEU, such as Case C–5/08 *Infopaq International v Danske Dagblades Forening* [2009] ECR I-6569, paras 47-48, where the originality standard was also defined by reference to the "author's intellectual creation".

254 See Artice 3(2) of the Database Directive: "The copyright protection of databases provided for in this Directive shall not extend to their contents and shall be without prejudice to any rights subsisting in those contents themselves".

255 Article 7(1) and (2) of the Database Directive; see further Estelle Derclaye, 'Databases sui generis right: what is a substantial investment?' [2005] IIC 2-30 providing an insighful analysis of the notion of substantial investment.

256 See Article 10 of the Database Directive.

worthy of protection for fifteen additional years.[257] In the context of the sui generis right, the EU legislator stated again that its scope of protection should not affect the rights existing in respect of its contents.[258] Indeed, sui generis protection is only applicable to "databases as collection of data".[259]

In essence, the sui generis right grants the maker of the database the exclusive right to:

(i) prevent unauthorised third parties from *extracting* and *re-utilizing* the whole or a *substantial* part of the contents of the database,[260] without prejudice to any other existing rights on its contents[261] and;

(ii) prevent unauthorised third parties from *extracting repeatedly* and *systematically* insubstantial parts of the database, implying acts that would conflict with the normal exploitation of the database.

From the above considerations, it appears that in theory (i) the content of a database may constitute the object of a trade secret (i.e. with respect both to individual data and data sets as a whole), whereas (ii) its selection and arrangement may merit protection under copyright law and/or (iii) the investment made in the obtention, verification or presentation of its contents may be the object of the sui generis right. Therefore, the three regimes of protection may overlap and protect two distinct aspects of a database: its structure (through copyright) and its contents (but only against substantial extraction and re-utilisation, in the case of the sui generis database right, and against unlawful acquisition, use and disclosure, in the case of trade secrets law).

---

257 P. Bernt Hugenholtz 'Something Completely Different: Europe's Sui Generis Database Right' 205, 215 in Susy Frankel and Daniel Gervais (eds), *The Internet and the Emerging Importance of New Forms of Intellectual Property* (Wolters Kluwer 2016); Matthias Leistner, 'The Protection of Databases' 427, 443-444 in Estelle Derclaye (ed), *Research handbook on the future of EU Copyright* (Edward Elgar 2009) noting that Article 10(3) of the Database Directive should be costrued as referring to the investment effort of the database maker which gives rise to a new sui generis right that may overlap with the pre-existing one. In this case, the author argues that the scope of protection would comprise only the parts of the new database that were the object of the new investment.

258 See Article 7(4) of the Database Directive.

259 Josef Drexl 2016 (n 426) 21.

260 As regards the interpretation of the expression "substantial investment" the CJEU still has to take a stand on the threshold of investment required for a database to merit protection under copyiright law, as noted by P. Bernt Hugenholtz 2016 (n 257) 212

261 See Article 7(4) of the Database Directive.

However, upon closer examination, the assessment of whether the information included in a database can qualify as a trade secret appears more problematic. As discussed in § 1, the cornerstone upon which trade secrets protection is built is precisely its concealed nature. Yet, the rationale underlying the creation of a two-tier regime of protection was to foster the growth and development of a strong database industry in the EU, which ultimately aims at the commercial exploitation of the databases.[262]

Consequently, if the holder of the database makes it available to a large number of market participants under no obligation of confidence, its contents may be considered generally available within a given industry, and accordingly the secrecy requirement may not be satisfied.[263] Likewise, if the database consists of elements in the public domain, even if it is li-

---

262 See Recital 11 of the Database Directive; see further Commission, 'Green Paper on Copyright and Challenge of Technology – Copyright Issues Requiring Immediate Action COM (88) 172, final' [1988] OJ C71, para 6.2.1, where it was noted that "The worldwide turnover of electronic publishing in 1985 amounted to 5 billion U.S. dollars. Of this, the United States were responsible for more than 4/5 of the total turnover, but the value of the total market produced by Germany, France and the United Kingdom represented 350 million dollars. Obstacles to the free flow of information between Member States must be removed *if the Community is to develop a competitive role in the information services market*" (emphasis added); against this background, it should be observed that the Commission concluded that the Database Directive had not managed to boost the database industry in Europe. However, this statement has been criticised by Matthias Leistner 2009 (n 257) 428 who argues that it was based on dubious data.

263 This was the case in the competition judgements rendered by the CJEU in Joined Cases C-241/91 P and C-242/91 *Radio Telefis Eireann (RTE) and Independent Television Publications (ITP) v Commission of the European Communities* [1995] ECR I-00743 (know as "*Magill*"), which concerned the refusal to license a database comprising a weekly TV guide in the territories of Ireland and Northern Ireland, where no comprehensive TV guide existed at that time. Each of the three television stations that broadcasted in these territories published their own guide covering their own programs and licensed the contents of their databases to newspapers on a free-of charge basis. The defendant, Magill TV Guide Ltd intended to publish a weekly comprehensive guide compiling the data of the three TV stations, but was sued by them on the basis of an infringement of their copyright over said compilations of data. In the first instance, the court granted an injunction preventing Magill from publishing the program listings. Subsequently, Magill lodged a complaint before the European Commission, on the basis of an abuse of market dominance by the TV station, by virtue of which the Commission ruled that there had been a breach of Article 102 of the TUE (ex Article 86 of the EEC). Upon appeal, the GCEU (then Court of First Instance) questioned whether copyright protection should be afforded to the TV pro-

censed under confidentiality obligations, the content of the database will not be regarded as secret, unless the selection and arrangement result in a discrete entity protectable as a combination secret.[264] The mere expenditure of time and money to gather known information into a searchable database does not automatically confer the database or the individual data trade secrets protection.[265] Equally, if a competitor of an electronic database maker duplicates the contents of the protected database in an unauthorised manner, for instance through so-called "screen-scraping practices",[266] and uploads the content to an Internet website for a substantial period of time, the database holder will not be able to claim trade secrets protection against the general public who accessed the website in good faith. Enforcement will only be available against the party that acquired and uploaded the information without authorisation.

Notwithstanding the aforementioned, in the three scenarios mentioned above, the original database maker could still rely on the sui generis right to file a claim against unauthorised extraction or re-utilisation of the database contents. Indeed, one of the main justifications presented by the European legislator for the creation of the sui generis database right was that the creation of databases required large investments of money and effort, but the unauthorised access and copy could be carried out at a much lower price.[267] From a copyright perspective, if the structure of the database meets the "author's own intellectual creation" originality thresh-

---

gramme listings, as they "were not in themselves secret, innovative or related to research. On the contrary, they were mere factual information in which no copyright could therefore subsist". (as reported in Case T–76/98 *Independent Television Publications Ltd v Commission* [1991] ECR II-575, para 29). However, such considerations were not taken into account in the decision rendered by the CJEU.

264 On the protection of combination secrets see chapter 4 § 4 C) II. 5.

265 Sharon K. Sandeen, 'A Contract by Another Name is Still a Contract: Examining the Effectiveness of Trade Secrets Clauses to Protect Database' [2005] 45 IDEA 119, 134.

266 The term 'screen scrapping, n' is defined in the Oxford English Dictionary as "The action of using a computer program to copy data from a website" (*OED Online*, OUP June 2013) <https://en.oxforddictionaries.com/definition/screen_scraping> accessed 15 September 2018.

267 See Recital 7 of the Database Directive. However, it should be noted that such a justification has been highly contested in the light of the findings of the Commission, in 'DG Internal Market and Services Working Paper. First evaluation of Directive 96/9/EC on the legal protection of databases,' where it was stated that "The economic impact of the "sui generis" right on database production is unproven". Indeed data from the Gale Directory of Databases, the largest exist-

old, the author shall have the exclusive right to prevent the unauthorised reproduction, translation, adaptation, arrangement and alteration of its expression, as well as any form of distribution to the public of its expression.[268]

In the legal analysis of the interplay between trade secrets protection and database protection, the mandatory limitation set out in Article 8(1) of the Database Directive plays a central role. Pursuant to this provision, the database maker cannot prevent the *lawful user*[269] of a database from *extracting* and/or *re-utilising insubstantial* parts of its contents (for any purposes). Any agreement to the contrary by the parties will be null and void, as per the wording of Article 15 of the Directive. Thus, contractual confidentiality obligations cannot override such a mandatory limitation. Consequently, if the "insubstantial" data are subsequently re-utilised and as a result disclosed to third parties, the assessment of secrecy with respect to that specific data may be compromised. Yet, the legal issue lies in determining when the extraction and reutilisation of data is to be considered "insubstantial", and therefore, whether the entire dataset can be considered readily ascertainable for the purposes of trade secrets protection, particularly as the Database Directive does not provide any interpretative guidance on how to measure the threshold of insubstantial extraction and re-utilisation.[270]

### 2. The problem of protecting created data under the sui generis database right and the possibility of resorting to contractual protection

Since its adoption, the Database Directive has garnered substantial criticism among legal commentators, as it was perceived that the introduction of such a new exclusive right would create a monopoly over the compiled

---

ing database directory at that time and which contained statistics indicating the growth of the global database industry since the 1970s showed that the production of database in the EU in 2004 had receaded to pre-Directive levels.

268 See Article 5 of the Database Directive.

269 A detailed account of the meaning of "lawful user" in the context of Article 8 and 9 of the Directive is provided by Estelle Derclaye, *The legal protection of Databases* (Edward Elgar 2008) 120-126, where the author concludes that the term "lawful user" should be interpreted as referring to the user "with a contract of lawful acquirement". However, the author concludes that the interplay between Article 7(5) and Article 8(1) renders the concept of *lawful user* superfluous, as pursuant to Article 7(5) "anyone (lawful user or not) is authorised to extract and re-utilize insubstantial parts".

270 P. Bernt Hugenholtz 2016 (n 257) 213-214.

information, thereby hampering freedom of information and competition, particularly as regards the development of secondary markets.[271] A major area of concern was so-called "sole-source databases", in which the information is created as a by-product in the course of other business activities and, consequently, it is only available from such unique sources.[272]

In 2004 the CJEU shed some light on the scope of protection of sole-source databases by rendering a series of decisions in which it clarified that the sui generis database right does not cover the investment made in the *creation* of data, but only the investment made in the *obtention* of data.[273] Thereby, the CJEU introduced the so-called "Spin-off Doctrine",[274] initially developed by Dutch courts in the interpretation of the EU sui geneis database legal regime, and ruled, among other things, that the investment made in fixtures lists for English and Scottish football did not require an investment "independent of that required for the creation of the data contained in that list".[275] Accordingly, for an investment to be eligible for protection under the sui generis right it has to "refer to the resources used to seek out existing independent materials and collect them in a database".[276] Following the CJEU's view, the reason for such a division is that the Database Directive was created to incentivise the creation of processing and storage mechanisms for pre-existing data, not the creation of data as such.[277] On a more abstract level, by introducing such a limitation, the CJEU intended to prevent the creation of an exclusive right on informa-

271 Matthias Leistner 2009 (n 257) 427.

272 Matthias Leistner 2009 (n 257) 434.

273 See Case C–444/02 *Fixtures Marketing Ltd v Organismos prognostikon agonon podosfairou AE (OPAP) 1* [2004] ECR I-10549; Case C–46/02 *Fixtures Marketing Ltd v Oy Veikkaus Ab* [2004] ECR I-10396; Case C–203/02 *The British Horseracing Board Ltd v William Hill Organization Ltd* [2004] ECR I-10415 and Case C–338/02 *Fixtures Marketing v Svenska Spel AB* [2004] ECR I-10497.

274 The application of the Dutch spin-off doctrine by the CJEU is discussed further by Mark J. Davison and P. Bernt Hugenholtz, 'Football fixtures, horse races and spin-offs: the ECJ domesticates the database right' [2005] 27 EIPR 113, 114-115.

275 Case C–46/02 *Fixtures Marketing Ltd v Oy Veikkaus Ab* [2004] ECR I-10396, para 44.

276 Case C–203/02 *The British Horseracing Board Ltd v. William Hill Organization Ltd* [2004] ECR I-10415, para 42; however Mark J. Davis and P. Bernt Hugenholtz, 'Football fixtures, horseraces and spin-offs: The ECJ domesticates the database right' [2005] 27 EIPR 113-118 note that the distinction between synthetic data and observed data is not self-evident.

277 Case C–203/02 *The British Horseracing Board Ltd v William Hill Organization Ltd* [2004] ECR I-10415, para 36.

tion that would not be available otherwise.[278] However, such a distinction has been criticised by many academics for not being as "self-evident" as the court initially argued.[279] Indeed, in the application of the Spin-off Doctrine held by the CJEU in *Football Dataco*, the Court of Appeal of England and Wales noted that such a distinction does not apply to *observed* data, such as the goals scored in the course of a football match, which according to the court should not be regarded as *created* data for the purposes of database protection.[280]

In the context of trade secrets, such a distinction inevitably leads to the question of whether, in the event that neither copyright nor sui generis protection are available for a specific database, it would still be possible to rely on trade secrets protection through contractual clauses, such as non-disclosure agreements ("NDAs"). The interplay between the Database Directive and inter partes contractual provisions was clarified by the CJEU in the context of a "screen scraping" case in 2015 (*Ryanair Ltd v PR Aviation)*.[281] According to the decision, Ryanair brought legal actions against PR Aviation, the operator of a website that allowed users to search for flights and compare prices, for an infringement of Ryanair's "rights relating to its data set"[282] and the breach of the terms and conditions applicable to its website. As a preliminary remark, it should be noted that the data displayed on PR Aviation website's was acquired from Ryanair's website upon acceptance of Ryanair's terms and conditions, which was not contested throughout the proceedings. Indeed, pursuant to the said terms and conditions, the website could only be used for private non-commercial purposes and the obtention of data through screen scraping practices was prohibited.[283]

---

278 Herbert Zech, 'Data as a Tradable Commodity' 51, 73 in Alberto De Franceschi (ed), *European Contract Law and the Digital Single Market – The Implications of the Digital Revolution* (Insertia 2016).

279 P. Bernt Hugenholtz, 'Data Property: Unwelcome Guest in the House of IP' (2017), 8 <https://www.ivir.nl/publicaties/download/Data_property_Muenster.pdf> accessed 15 September 2018.

280 *Football Dataco & Others v Stan James Plc & Others and Sportradar GmbH & Other* [2013] EWCA Civ 27 (CA).

281 Gintare Surblyte, 'Data as a Digital Resource' (2016) Max Planck Institute for Innovation and Competition Research Paper No. 16-12, 19-22 <https://dx.doi.org/10.2139/ssrn.2849303> accessed 15 September 2018; Case C–30/14 *Ryanair Ltd v PR Aviation BV* (CJEU, 15 January 2015).

282 Case C–30/14 *Ryanair Ltd v PR Aviation BV* (CJEU, 15 January 2015), para 17.

283 Case C–30/14 *Ryanair Ltd v PR Aviation BV* (CJEU, 15 January 2015), para 16: "the use of automated systems or software to extract data from this website or of

Upon appeal, the Dutch Supreme Court submitted a preliminary question to the CJEU, asking whether the use of a database that does not qualify either for copyright or sui generis protection can be contractually limited, in view of the unwaivable nature of the limitations set out in Article 6(1) and Article 8 of the Databases Directive, as per Article 15. In its legal reasoning, the CJEU concluded that any contractual agreements regulating the use of a database that does not qualify for protection under either of the two harmonised regimes (sui generis or copyright) should be admissible, as the unwaivable nature of the limitations provided for in Article 15 is only applicable to those databases that are eligible for protection under the harmonised framework created by the Database Directive.[284]

Drawing on the above, it is submitted that in practice NDAs may play a central role in the protection of databases that do not satisfy the requirements of protection of either of the two legal regimes set out in the Database Directive, provided that their diffusion within a given industry is rather limited (i.e. that the holder retains control over the use and disclosure of the information). However, such an outcome seems rather paradoxical considering the lawful user limitation laid down in Article 8(1) of the Database Directive. Whereas the maker of a database protected under the sui generis right shall always allow the extraction and re-utilisation of insubstantial parts of its database, such a possibility can be contractually excluded for those databases that do not satisfy the requirements of protection laid down under the harmonised system. Consequently, the limitations introduced by the European legislator in the scope of protection of the two-tier harmonised database regime to avoid the creation of information monopolies are not applicable with regard to those databases that present a lower threshold of originality and investment or even sole-source databases, where information is not accessible in any other possible manner. This may in fact lead to the creation of the facto information monopolies on pre-existing data.[285]

As a final note, it should be underscored that the distinction between *generated* data as opposed to *obtained* data is of utmost importance in the

www.bookryanair.com for commercial purposes "screen scraping" is prohibited unless the third party has directly concluded a written licensing agreement with Ryanair in which permits access to Ryanair's price, flight and timetable for the sole purpose of price comparison".

284 Case C–30/14 *Ryanair Ltd v PR Aviation BV* (CJEU, 15 January 2015), para 39.

285 Gintare Surblyte 2016 (n 281) 23-25 highlighting the competition law implications of contractual clauses that prohibit screen-scrapping.

wake of the Data Economy.[286] As noted by Drexl, the inclusion of sensors in smart products (for example in connected cars) that *collect* data or the performance of Big Data analysis that results in the *creation* of new data are not investments relevant to the obtention of data in the sense of Article 7(1) of the Database Directive. Therefore, these data sets do not qualify for protection under the sui generis database right.[287] In the same vein, the possibility of relying on copyright protection seems unlikely, as to benefit from such protection the selection and arrangement of the contents of the database have to reflect the author's "personal stamp" and, in the Data Economy, big data sets are usually generated automatically by machines and consequently there is no "human intellectual achievement".[288] Another hurdle in the application of the sui generis legal regime to large datasets is the lack of *extraction* of data in the course of big data analysis, where "the code comes to the data" thus precluding any actionable conduct under the Database Directive.[289]

It is precisely for the aforementioned reasons that several commentators have contended that the EU framework for the protection of databases was drafted on the basis of outdated technology and that the limitations as to its scope of protection and subject matter are not applicable to the protection of large data sets created in the context of the Data Economy.[290]

---

286 For a terminological clarification of these terms see chapter 4 § 4 F) 1.

287 Josef Drexl 2016 (n 426) 21; against this background, Andreas Wiebe, 'Protection of industrial data – a new property right for the digital economy?' [2016] GRUR Int 877, 879 argues that in order to accommodate the sui generis database regime to the Data Economy, the CJEU should abandon the Spin-off Doctrine and afford protection to the data generated by the database maker; in this regard, P. Bernt Hugenholtz 2017 (n 279) 8 supports a more nuanced approach by noting that the distinction between *created* data and *observed* data is of utmost importance in the context of protection of industrial data "as, sensor data produced by a radar system or observation satellite are likely to qualify as data 'observed', and concomitant investments may thus be taken into account when applying the database right. Conversely, computer-generated airline schedule data squarely falls under the rubric of 'created' data excluded by the European Court".

288 Herbert Zech 2016 (n 278) 70 ; a survey of the main views of selected Data Protection Authorities on the issue of Big Data is provided by Bart van der Sloot and Sascha van van Schendel, 'Ten Questions for Future Regulation of Big Data: A Comparative and Empirical Legal Study' [2016] 7 JIPITEC 110.

289 Josef Drexl 2016 (n 426) 22.

290 Josef Drexl 2016 (n 426) 22.

### V. Conclusion on the relationship between trade secrets and IPRs

As a whole, the picture that emerges from the analysis conducted in the previous section is that there are strong synergies between trade secrets and formal IPRs (particularly patents, but also copyright and the sui generis database right). Indeed, the similarities and overlaps between the two appropriation regimes are so strong that many view trade secrets as a species of IPRs.[291]

A central element in the protection of IPRs is their exclusive erga omnes nature. In this regard, it is worth noting that in the case of trade secrets, exclusivity is achieved ex ante through the adoption of de facto physical or legal measures that conceal information from third parties. However, protection is only afforded against unlawful acquisition, use and revelation of the information.

Against this background, the fact that trade secrets confer a certain degree of exclusivity has been viewed by some commentators as an indicator that trade secrets constitute a species of IPRs. The implications of adopting such an approach are elaborated in the following section from a comparative law perspective, from which a number of considerations are drawn.

## B) Trade secrets as the object of intellectual property law: considerations for Europe

Traditionally, intellectual property was considered as the best mode to incentivise creation and innovation.[292] This assumption stems from the non-exclusive and non-rival nature of intangible goods and the difficulties associated with their exploitation. As outlined above, if the creator is not able to recoup the investment made in the development of an invention or creative work, the incentives to engage in creative and innovate activities may disappear, leading to a suboptimal level of innovation in the market.[293]

Against this background, and in order to overcome the market failure inherent to the exploitation of any intangible good, exclusive rights are

291 See for instance Christoph Ann, 'Know-how- Stiefkind des Geistiges Eigentums?'[2007] GRUR 39; Mark A. Lemley 2008 (n 15) 311-353.

292 Suzanne Scotchmer 2004 (n 41) 8 "Neoclassical economics has established the traditional view that intellectual property (rights) are the best mode to incentivise creative and innovative activity".

293 Séverine Dusollier 2013 (n 107) 258-259.

granted so as to allow the inventor (or creator) to recover the exclusivity and non-rivalry over his innovations (or creations). Following the systematic division of goods into three levels (consumption, production and innovation), the creation of property rights at one level yields the development of market competition at the next level. Thus, IPRs are conceived as a necessary competitive restriction at the production level to enhance competition at the innovation level.[294] However, concerns have also been raised as to whether attaching the traditional proprietarian consequences to IPRs may be detrimental to lawful "free-riding uses" and lead to the overcompensation of creators.[295]

As regards trade secrets, the application of the exclusivity paradigm to their protection has been widely discussed. The root of the discussion revolves around the fact that exclusivity is obtained through factual secrecy and no qualitative threshold has to be met, unlike formal IPRs, where protection is conditioned upon meeting a certain degree of originality (copyright), novelty and inventiveness (patent law) or being able to distinguish the source of the goods and services (trade mark law). For the purposes of answering one of the research questions that guide the present thesis (i.e. whether trade secrets should be regarded as the object of an IPR), in the first place, the similarities and differences that emerge from conducting a comparative law analysis are reviewed (section I). Next, the implications of considering information as property are discussed (section II). Finally some insights and perspectives are presented on the basis of the foregoing analysis for the application of the TSD by national legislators and the judiciary (section III).

294 Michael Lehmann, 'The Theory of Property Rights and the Protection of Intellectual and Industrial Property' [1985] IIC 525, 537-540.

295 In this context, Mark A. Lemley 2004 (n 109) 1046-1050 identifies the following most salient costs of overcompensating creators: (i) the distortion of competition in the market which creates static efficiencies; (ii) the impairment of further creation and innovation; (iii) rent seeking behaviour is also favoured by the expectation of achieving IPRs protection; (iv) administrative costs derived from the enforcement of IPRs and (v) overinvestment in research and development.

## I. Comparative legal analysis

### 1. International intellectual property convention system

The PC does not include any explicit reference to the protection of trade secrets. It only clarifies that the repression of unfair competition is one of the objects of industrial property (Article 1(2) PC), which in turn leads to the question of whether trade secrets protection falls within the scope of unfair competition.[296] Similarly, the WIPO Treaty, in its definition of intellectual property, does not mention either trade secrets or confidential information.[297]

At the international level, undisclosed information was only first explicitly accorded protection in Article 39 TRIPs.[298] However, the agreement addresses the issue of whether trade secrets are property in a rather open-ended manner. On the one hand, TRIPs anchors the protection of trade secrets on unfair competition provisions by referring to Article 10bis PC. On the other hand, Article 1(2) TRIPs regards undisclosed information as one of the "categories of intellectual property" laid down in the agreement.[299] Such an inconsistent regulation derives from the conflicting views of the negotiating parties, which, pursuant to Article 32 VCLT, constitute "supplementary means of interpretation" of international treaties.[300] Developing countries purported that one of the defining features of IPRs is the disclosure of the information protected, whereas trade secrets, as their name implies, are defined by their confidential nature.[301] At the other end of the

296 This issue is discussed in detail in chapter 2 § 1 A) III.

297 See Article 2 (VIII) of the Convention Establishing the World Intellectual Property Organisation (signed on 14 July 1967 and amended on 28 September 1979).

298 Markus Peter and Andreas Wiebe, 'Art. 39' Rdn 3 in Jan Busche and Tobias Stoll (eds), *TRIPs* (Carl Heymanns 2013).

299 Article 1 (2) TRIPs: "For the purposes of this Agreement, the term "intellectual property" refers to all categories of intellectual property that are the subject of Sections 1 through 7 of Part II"; in this regard, it is particularly noteworthy that Section 7 of Part II deals with the protection of undisclosed information.

300 Article 32 of the Vienna Convention on the Law of Treaties (adopted 23 May 1969) 1155 UNTS 331 (VCLT).

301 The Peruvian, Indian and Brazilian delegations were particularly belligerent in this regard. The Indian position can be found in the following documents: India made clear its position in GATT Doc. MTN.GNG/NG11/14; Brazil formally objected to the protection of trade secrets as IPRs in an official communication dated 11 December.1989 (GATT Doc. MTN.GNG./NG11/W/57, para 48); simi-

spectrum, industrialised countries led by the US[302] and the Swiss[303] delegations were of the opinion that undisclosed information is to be regarded as an IPR that confers exclusive rights in order to protect the intellectual efforts necessary for its creation.[304]

A review of the academic literature on this matter sheds little light.[305] Some commentators are of the opinion that the express reference to unfair competition rules enshrined in Article 39(1) TRIPs, along with the fact that the wording of Article 1(2) TRIPs mentions "categories of intellectual property" and not just IPRs, are clear indicators that no proprietary exclusive right on trade secrets exists.[306] In this context, it is noted that the terminology used to draft Article 39 is distinctly different to that used in connection to other IPRs such as trade marks and patents. In some ways, it seems that TRIPs has deliberately avoided the use of proprietary language.[307] For instance, trade secrets holders are referred to as the persons who have the information "lawfully within their control", and not the "owners" of information. What is more, Article 39 does not confer the right to exclude the alleged infringer, but simply "the possibility of preventing information (...) from being disclosed to, acquired by, or used by others".[308] Even though at first glance this may appear trivial, such a distinction entails an important legal nuance. Pursuant to Article 39 TRIPs, it does not matter what the title in the trade secret is; what matters is that the alleged holder possesses the information, that is, that the secret informa-

---

larly, Peru expressed a similar view in its official communication (GATT Doc. MTN.GNG/NG11/W/45, para 10).

302 The U.S. position is reflected in GATT Doc. MTN.GNG/NG11/9, 6, para 11.

303 The Swiss delegation formally expressed its view on the proprietary regime for trade secrets during the course of the Uruguay Round in a number of documents, such as GATT Doc. MTN.GNG/NG11/W/38/Add.1.

304 Markus Peter and Andreas Wiebe, 'Art. 39' Rdn 4 in Jan Busche and Tobias Stoll (eds), *TRIPs* (Carl Heymanns 2007).

305 The lack of a clear-cut answer at the international level is highlighted in Michael Dorner, *Know-how Schutz im Umbruch* (Carls Heymanns 2013) 306-307.

306 Carlos Correa, *Trade Related Aspects of Intellectual Property Rights, A commentary on the TRIPs Agreement* (OUP 2007) 366-367; Tanya Aplin, 'Right to Property and Trade Secrets' 421, 429-431 in Christophe Geiger (ed), *Research Handbook on Human Rights and Intellectual Property* (Edward Elgar 2015).

307 Lionel Bently, 'Trade Secrets Intellectual Property but not property?' 60, 91 in Helena R. Howe and Jonathan Griffiths (eds), *Concepts of property in Intellectual Property Law* (CUP 2013).

308 Lionel Bently 2013 (n 307) 91.

tion is lawfully under his physical control.[309] Similarly, the fact that the negotiating parties agreed on the expression "undisclosed information" rather than the more common terms trade secret or know-how is understood as an attempt to avoid the proprietary connotation of the latter.[310]

More importantly, the fact that Article 39(1) TRIPs premises the protection of trade secrets upon an unfair competition provision, namely Article10bis PC, makes clear that trade secrets are not property in the sense that they do not create an exclusive right.[311] In this context, Wadlow argues that Article 10 PC protects a right that is in essence completely different to a property right. As argued in chapter 2 below, the scope of this provision is confined to protection against unfair conduct by a competitor. As a result, the assessment of the "fairness" of a specific behaviour should be conducted on a case-by-case basis, taking into consideration the individual circumstances of each instance.[312]

By contrast, a more literal interpretation of the TRIPs provisions that govern trade secrets protection has also been supported by legal scholars. Such an approach suggests that trade secrets are to be regarded as IPRs under the legal framework created by the TRIPs Agreement mainly for two reasons. In the first place, any interpretation that, contrary to the wording of Article 1(2), does not regard undisclosed information as IPRs is to be rejected, as the WTO Appellate Body has consistently stated that treaties should be construed so as to avoid conflicts (principle of effective interpretation).[313]

Furthermore, pursuant to Article 31(1) of the VCLT "a treaty shall be interpreted in good faith in accordance with the *ordinary meaning* to be given

---

309 Nuno Pires de Carvalho, *The TRIPs Regime of Antitrust and Undisclosed Information* (Wolters Kluwer 2007) para 39.2.38.

310 Carlos Correa 2007 (n 306) 368; see also GATT Doc. MTN.GNG/NG11/20.

311 Tanya Aplin 2015 (n 306) 429 noting that "(…) By linking the protection of trade secrets to unfair competition it seems that while trade secrets may be "industrial property" or even "intellectual property" this does not require a focus on property protection".

312 Christopher Wadlow, 'Regulatory data protection under TRIPs Article 39(3) and Article 10bis of the Paris Convention: Is there a doctor in the house?' [2008] IPQ 355, 397.

313 See WTO, *Argentina – Footwear (EC)*, WTO Appellate Body Report, WT/DS121/AB/R (14 December 1999) para 81 and footnote 72 thereto; see also WTO, *United States –Upland Cotton*, WTO Appellate Body Report, WT/DS267/AB/ (2 March 2005); a more detailed account on the interpretation of treaties by the WTO Appellate Body is provided by Isabelle Van Damme, 'Treaty Interpretation by the WTO Appellate Body' [2010] 21 EJIL 605-648.

to the terms of the treaty in their context and in view of its object and purpose".[314] Accordingly, in line with this guiding principle, if trade secrets are not regarded as an IPR, the enforcement provisions set forth in Part III of TRIPs should not be applied in connection to undisclosed information. Yet, such an interpretation would again violate the principle of effective interpretation, especially in connection to Article 41(1) TRIPS, which sets forth that the enforcement provisions (in Part III of TRIPs) should be applied to any act of infringement of IPRs that falls under the scope of TRIPs, including Article 39. Similarly, it would also clash with the special provisions on the safeguarding of confidential information embedded in Articles 42 and 43(1) TRIPs.[315]

In this regard, it is worth noting that a number of bilateral agreements have also included undisclosed information within the scope of intellectual property. For instance, the Euro-Mediterranean Agreement between the EC and Egypt in the Joint Declaration on Article 37 and Annex VI stated that:

> For the purpose of this Agreement, intellectual property includes, in particular, copyright, including copyright in computer programmes, and neighbouring rights, patents, industrial designs, geographical indications, including appellations of origin, trademarks and service marks, topographies of integrated circuits, as well as the protection against unfair competition as referred to in Article 10 bis of the Paris Convention for the Protection of Industrial Property (Stockholm Act, 1967) and *protection of undisclosed information on 'know-how'* (emphasis added).[316]

Drawing on the above, it seems that the obligation to protect undisclosed information enshrined in Article 39 TRIPs was specifically tailored so as to leave open the possibility of its protection at the national level through

314 Article 31 VCLT.

315 Marco Bronckers and Natalie McNelis, 'Is the EU Obliged to improve the Protection of Trade Secrets? An Inquiry into TRIPS, the European Convention on Human Rights and the EU Charter of Fundamental Rights' [2013] 34 EIPR 673, 677.

316 See Euro-Mediterranean Agreement establishing an Association between the European Communities and their Member States, of the one part, and the Arab Republic of Egypt, of the other part [2004] OJ L304; similar provisions can be found in Article 10. 2 (2) of the of the Free Trade Agreement between the European Union and its Member States, of the one part, and the Republic of Korea, of the other part [2010] OJ L127/6.

non-proprietary means. Bently goes even further and suggests that "TRIPs seems to have deliberately preserved the very possibility that confidential information might be intellectual property but not property".[317] This author takes the view that intellectual property is becoming a genus different from property rights, as is traditionally understood.[318] As a whole, the twofold approach of TRIPs seems to highlight the hybrid legal nature of trade secrets. The rules that govern infringing conduct are tailored according to unfair competition principles, whereas their enforcement follows the traditional remedies structure available in intellectual property law.

## 2. Common law approach

### a) England

Traditionally, English Courts have rejected the idea that information can be protected through a property right. It is generally agreed that the House of Lords settled the proprietary debate in the *Boardman v Phipps* ruling,[319] which concerned the violation of an equitable fiduciary obligation. The defendant, Mr Boardman, was the solicitor of a trust and in the course of his duties acquired information regarding the value and performance of one of the undertakings held by the trust. He later used it for his own benefit. The plaintiff, a beneficiary who came to know that Mr Boardman had used the data for his own advantage, brought an action, arguing among other things that the information was actually the property of the trust. When giving the judgement, the majority expressed their opposition to conceptualising information as property and argued that:

> in general, information is not property at all. It is normally open to all who have eyes to read the real and ears to hear. The true test is to determine in what circumstances the information has been acquired. If it has been acquired in such circumstances that it would be a breach of confidence to disclose it to another then courts of equity will restrain the receipt from communicating it to another. (…) *But in the end the real truth is that it (confidential information) is not property in any normal*

317 Lionel Bently 2013 (n 307) 91.
318 Lionel Bently 2013 (n 307) 91.
319 *Boardman v Phipps* [1967] 2 AC 46 (HL).

> *sense, but equity will restrain its transmission to another if in breach of some confidential relationship* (emphasis added).[320]

Likewise, in a more recent decision by the Court of Appeal, *Douglas v Hello!*,[321] Lord Phillips expressly rejected such a possibility, stating that "confidential or private information, which is capable of commercial exploitation but which is only protected by the law of confidence, does not fall to be treated as property that can be owned and transferred".[322] In Lord Phillips' view, if confidential information were to be regarded as property, such a right could in turn be enforced against third parties, irrespective of whether the recipient of the information was aware of its private or confidential condition. Thus, he concluded that "the right depends upon the effect on the third party's conscience of the third party's knowledge of the nature of the information and the circumstances in which it was obtained".[323]

In the same vein, the legal scholarship has repeatedly expressed its reluctance to treat confidential information as property, mostly for the same reasons put forward by in *Douglas v Hello!*, i.e. it would allow for restraining third parties and accidental acquirers, regardless of whether they should have been aware that the information was confidential.[324] Aplin, Bently, Johnson and Malynic have argued that, in most cases, confidential information is described as property merely in a metaphorical sense, simply to refer to "ownership" of confidential information or "the confider's right in contract and equity".[325] A similar view has been taken by most commentators[326] and the Law Commission Report on Breach of Confidence, where it is argued that "the nature of confidential information is such as to place it in a category of its own, distinct from that of property".[327]

---

320 *Boardman v Phipps* [1967] 2 AC 46 (HL), 127 F-128A.

321 *Douglas v Hello! Ltd and others* [2007] UKHL 21.

322 *Douglas v Hello! Ltd and others* [2007] UKHL 21, [119].

323 *Douglas v Hello! Ltd and others* [2007] UKHL 21, [126].

324 Tanya Aplin and others 2012 (n 22) para 4.108 by confidential acquired it should be understood "those who accidentally find confidential information".

325 Tanya Aplin and others 2012 (n 22) para 4.74.

326 See William Cornish, David Llewellyn and Tanya Aplin 2013 (n 209) paras 8-50-8-54; see also Roger M. Toulson and Charles M. Phipps, *Confidentiality* (3rd edn, Sweet&Maxwell 2012) paras 2-025-061.

327 Law Commission, *Law Commission Report on Breach of Confidence* (Law Com No 110, 1981) 9 notwithstanding, in *Voila ES Nottinghamshire Ltd and Nottinghamshire County Council v Dowen* [2010] EWCA Civ 1214 (CA), the Court of Ap-

Notwithstanding the aforesaid, the English Courts have recently regarded trade secrets (as opposed to the broader notion of confidential information)[328] as the object of an IPR for the purposes of the European Union's Intellectual Property Rights Enforcement Directive ("Enforcement Directive").[329] In particular, the Court of Appeal in *Vestergaard v Bestnet*[330] stressed that the proportionality of the enforcement measures principle spelt out in Article 3(2) of the concerned Directive was also applicable to a trade secrets claim. It further concluded that "it is accepted that a claim for misuse of technical trade secrets such as the present is a claim to enforce an intellectual property right".[331] Indeed, there are a number of provisions in UK statutes that regard confidential information as Intellectual Property, such as the Atomic Energy Authority Act,[332] the Building Societies Act[333] and the Corporation Tax Act 2009.[334] This doctrinal position has led some commentators to argue that confidential information falls within the scope of intellectual property, but not property as such.[335]

---

peal concluded that possession of confidential commercial information can be protected on the basis of Article 1 of the First Protocol to the European Convention of Human Rights; a more detailed legal analysis of this decisions and its consequences is provided in Tanya Aplin,'Confidential Information as property?' [2013] 24 King's LJ 172–201.

328 The conceptual distinction is clarified further in chapter 3 § 3 B) below.

329 Directive of the European Parliament and the Council 2004/48/EC of 29 April 2004 on the enforcement of intellectual property rights [2004] OJ L195/16 (Enforcement Directive).

330 *Vestergaard Frandsen A/S v Bestnet Europe Ltd* [2011] EWCA Civ 424 (CA). The case at hand concerned the misappropriation of a trade secret regarding the manufacturing of anti-mosquito nets by two departing employees.

331 *Vestergaard Frandsen A/S v Bestnet Europe Ltd* [2011] EWCA Civ 424 (CA), [56]; for a critical debate on this decision, see Tanya Aplin and others 2012 (n 22) para 17.05 noting that the expansion of the Enforcement Directive to protect trade secrets was left for Member States, particularly in the light of the Commission, 'Commission Statement on Directive 2004/48/EC' [2005] OJ L94/37.

332 See Atomic Energy Authority Act 1986, s 8.

333 The Building Societies Act 1997, s 92A(3).

334 The Corporation Tax Act 2009, s 712 (3).

335 Lionel Bently 2013 (n 307) 91.

### b) U.S.

In the United States, the property debate has been at the core of the legal discussion since the XIX century.[336] Until recently, an analysis of the most relevant legal sources provided no definitive answer.[337] Yet, this debate now seems to be settled with the adoption of the Defend Trade Secrets Act of 2016 ("DTSA").[338] Pursuant to Sec. 1 amending § 1836 on Civil proceedings:

> APPLICABILITY TO OTHER LAWS .—This section and the amendments made by this section shall not be construed to be a law pertaining to intellectual property for purposes of any other Act of Congress.

According to the above reproduced provision, it seems that trade secrets shall not be regarded as a species of IPR. Yet, upon closer examination, the expression "for the purposes of any other Act of Congress" appears to have been drafted to establish a hierarchy of norms in order to avoid any potential overlap with other IPRs regulated under Federal Law (i.e. patents and copyright), rather than to clarify the legal nature of trade secrets protection and the implications derived from it. In this regard, it has been suggested that such a categorisation intended to preserve the safe harbour of online intermediaries in the event that a user unlawfully discloses a trade secret, as per § 230 of the Communications Decency Act,[339] which is not applicable for intellectual property law infringements.[340] It is most likely that in

336 For a detailed account of the evolution of the history of the law of trade secrets in the United States as regards the property theory see Robert G. Bone 2011 (n 15) 46.

337 Charles Tait Graves, 'Trade Secrets as property: Theory and Consequences' [2007] 15 JIPL 39, 62; in the commentary to the Restatement (First) of Torts § 757 (Am. Law Inst. 1939) it was expressly noted that the proprietarian approach had been frequently advanced and rejected, as "good faith" was the prevailing underlying policy justification. Notwithstanding this, the UTSA and the Restatement (third) of Unfair Competition do not take a clear stand. Only in the Restatement (Third) of Unfair Competition it is mentioned that the term property is still frequently applied and that the legal nature debate has had a rather limited effect in practice.

338 Defend Trade Secrets Act of 2016, Pub. L. No. 114-153, 130 Stat. 376 (2016) (codified at 18 U.S.C. § 1831, et seq.) (DTSA).

339 Communications Decency Act of 1996, Pub. L. No. 104-104, 110 Stat. 133-145 (1996) (codified as amended at 47 U.S.C. § 223 (1934).

340 As per 47 U.S.C. § 230(e)(2) which provides that "Nothing in this section shall be construed to limit or expand any law pertaining to intellectual property"; this argument is submitted by Eric Goldman, 'The Defend Trade Secrets Act

the near future the wording and implications of such a provision will be the object of a comprehensive and in-depth analysis by courts and academia.

Indeed, commentators in the U.S. are divided between those who assert the property nature of trade secrets[341] and those who deny it and are in favour of affording protection to confidential information through liability rules.[342] A minority supports a middle ground approach, regarding trade secrets as comprising a bundle of rights.[343]

A review of the Supreme Court case law on this matter sheds little light on the controversy. On the one hand, in *E.I. DuPont de Nemours Powder Co. v. Masland*, which concerned the misappropriation of confidential information by a departing employee the court noted that:

> The word property, as applied to trademarks and trade secrets is an unanalysed expression of certain secondary consequences of the factor that the law makes some rudimentary requirements of good faith. Whether the plaintiffs have any valuable secret or not the defendant knows the facts, whatever they are, through a special confidence that he has accepted. *The property may be denied but the confidence cannot be*. Therefore, the starting point for the present matter is not property or

---

Isn't an "Intellectual Property " Law' [2017] 33 Santa Clara High Technology LJ 541, 542-546.

341 Roger M. Milgrim 2014 (n 160) § 2.01[2] highlights that the rights in a trade secrets are intangible intellectual property. Those rights include the right to use information, to disclose it to others (for instance the employees, licensees and other persons subjected to a confidential relationship) and seek redress in the event of unauthorised user or disclosure to third parties; a similar position is adopted by Mark A. Lemley 2008 (n 15) 311-353.

342 William Landes and Richard Posner 2003 (n 38) 355 noting that "a trade secret is not property in the same sense that real and personal property and even copyrights and patents are because it is not something that the possessor has the (more or less) exclusive right to enjoy it"; see further Pamela Samuelson, 'Information as Property: Do Ruckelshaus and Monsanto Carpenter Signal a Changing Direction in Intellectual Property Law' [1988] 38 Catholic University LR 365, 375 noting that "It is simply unnecessary to call trade secrets "property" to enforce confidences and penalize those who use improper means to obtain valuable secret"; the same author in a later article notes that "Although trade secret law is sometimes clustered for the sake of convenience under the general rubric of 'intellectual property' rights, this does not alter the essential nature of trade secrets as a form of unfair competition" Pamela Samuelson, 'Principles for Resolving Conflicts Between Trade Secrets and the First Amendment' [2007] 58 Hastings LJ 777, 807.

343 This case is reported by Michael Risch 2007 (n 15) 23-26.

> due process of law, but that the defendant stood in confidential relations with the plaintiffs, or one of them (emphasis added).[344]

As is apparent from the above reproduced paragraph, Justice Holmes suggested that trade secrets should be afforded protection on the basis of the general concepts of fair and equitable conduct, not property.[345] This statement is usually cited by those who believe that the breach of a duty of confidence is central to any misappropriation claim, the so-called "Confidential Relationship School",[346] and has been followed by courts both at the state level and in the Federal Circuit.[347]

Conversely, those who argue that the bundle of rights that the trade secret holder claims on his secrets is best labelled as property rely on another landmark decision from the U.S. Supreme Court: *Rueckelhaus v. Monsanto Co.*[348] In this ruling from 1984 the court took a different view on the property debate, which was more in line with the so-called "Property School".[349] The facts of the case are as follows. Monsanto submitted research data on a pesticide in order to obtain marketing approval from the Environmental Protection Agency ("EPA"), which was subsequently used and disclosed by the agency for the purposes of assessing a competitor's application on the basis of the Federal Insecticide and Rodenticide Act ("FIFRA"). Thereafter, Monsanto filed a lawsuit arguing that the FIFRA provisions on the use and disclosure of data submitted for obtaining marketing approval constituted a taking of property that violated the Fifth Amendment of the U.S. Constitution.[350] Upon appeal to the Supreme

344 *E.I. DuPont de Nemours Powder Co. v. Masland*, 244 U.S. 100, 102 (1917).

345 Pamela Samuelson 1988 (n 341) 374-375.

346 James Pooley 2002 (n 66) 1.02[8] 1-16, 1-17.

347 In the Federal Circuit see for example *Servo Corp. of Am. v. General Electric Co.*, 393 F.2d 551, 555 (4th Cir. 1968) where the court held that "the gravamen in a trade secrets case is a breach of confidence, rather than an infringement in a property right; hence, reliance on innocent sources of information involving no breach of duty, is an essential element of the defence that the secrets were previously disclosed" and *Northern Petrochemical Co. v. Tomlinson*, 484 F.2d 1057, 1060 (7th Cir. 1973) noting that "A trade secret, unlike a patent or copyright, has no proprietary dimension. A suit to redress the theft of the secret is one grounded in tort, with the act of theft comprising the misfeasance against which the law protects".

348 *Ruckelshaus v. Monsanto Co.*, 467 U.S. 986 (1984).

349 James Pooley 2002 (n 66) § 1.02[8] 1-18, 1-19.

350 The Fifth Amendment provides that "No person shall be (…) deprived of life, liberty, or property, without due process of law; nor shall private property be taken for public use, without just compensation".

Court, it was held that owing to the intangible nature of trade secrets, the property right conferred by them is defined by the "extent to which the owner of the trade secret protects his interest from disclosure to others".[351] In the course of its legal reasoning, the court further noted that trade secrets share many of the features of other forms of tangible property, as they can be assigned or constitute the object of a trust.[352] Consequently, the court concluded that the provisions of the FIFRA resulted in the taking of property that was not supported under the Fifth Amendment of the U.S. Constitution.[353]

The previous analysis further highlights the tension arising from the hybrid nature of trade secrets, which safeguard confidential information on the basis of liability rules akin to what in continental law is referred to as unfair competition, while also presenting some of the features of property rights. It appears that common law jurisdictions have adopted an "integrated approach", whereby the holder of secret information has a bundle of rights over such information and a number of these rights present the characteristics of property.[354] Against this background, it seems that the root of the discrepancies as to the legal nature of trade secrets derives from the "flexibility" of the property notion in common law jurisdictions and the many purposes for which it is applied.[355]

---

351 *Ruckelshaus v. Monsanto Co.*, 467 U.S. 986 (1984) 1002.

352 *Ruckelshaus v. Monsanto Co.*, 467 U.S. 986 (1984) 1002.

353 After *Ruckelshaus v. Monsanto Co.*, 467 U.S. 986 (1984) a number of decisions have followed the "Property School", such as the Supreme Court of Hawaii in the context of a marriage separation *Teller v. Teller*, 53 P.3d 240, 247-249 (Haw. 2002); against this background, Roger M. Milgrim 2014 (n 160) 61, § 2.01[1]-[2] notes that "practically all jurisdictions have recognized that a trade secret is property, or, stated more precisely, that the possessor of a trade secret has a property right in it that permits the possessor to restrict use and disclosure of it in many situations".

354 James Pooley 2002 (n 66)§ 1.02[8] 1-20, 1-21.

355 This argument is raised by William Cornish, David Llewellyn and Tanya Aplin 2013 (n 209) para 8-50 with resepect to the English conceptualisation of property, due to the fact that common law jurisdictions in general understand the term property in a more flexible manner than civil law countries; see chapter 1 § 3 B).

## 3. Civil law approach

European civil law jurisdictions do not provide a uniform answer as to the legal nature of trade secrets. This section explores the different solutions followed in two of the EU jurisdictions where this topic has been more widely discussed, namely Italy and Germany.

### a) Italy

In recent years, the proprietary debate in Italy has attracted substantial attention from European academics, particularly since the enactment of the Industrial Property Code in 2005. Pursuant to Article 1, trade secrets (or more accurately secret information) are regarded as a species of IPRs.[356] In the original version of the Code (Article 99), which was later amended, the protection of secret information was envisaged against mere acquisition, use and disclosure.[357] This gave rise to widespread criticism, as it was perceived that the new Italian regulation had created an "exclusive and absolute (erga omnes) proprietary regime".[358] Under the first version of the new Code, a trade secret holder would be entitled to prevent use or disclosure resulting from independent creation or reverse engineering, regardless of the breach of a confidentiality obligation or the unlawfulness of the behaviour. Thus, when the Code was amended in 2010, Article 99 was modified such that in order to find infringement there had to be evidence of

356 Article 1.1 of the Italian Industrial Property Code (Decreto legisltaivo 10 febbraio 2005, n. 30 1 Codice della proprietà industriale, a norma dell'articolo 15 della legge 12 dicembre 2002, n. 273, aggiornato a seguito del decreto legislativo di correzione 13 agosto 2010, n. 13) sets forth that: "For the purposes of this Code, the expression industrial property comprises trademarks and other distinctive signs, geographical indications, designations of origin, designs, inventions, utility models, topographies of semiconductors, confidential commercial information and new planet varieties" (translation by the author).

357 Giorgio Floridia and others, *Diritto Industriale Proprietà Intellettuale e concorrenza* (4th edn, Giappichelli Editore 2012) 207.

358 Gustavo Ghidini and Valeria Falce, 'Trade secrets as intellectual property rights: a disgraceful upgrading – Notes on an Italian reform' 140 in Rochelle C. Dreyfuss and Katherine J. Strandburg (eds), *The Law and Theory of Trade Secrecy: A Handbook of Contemporary Research* (Edward Elgar 2011).

abusive conduct by the alleged infringer.[359] Despite the new wording, commentators remain sceptical about the new regime enshrined in Article 99. Some contend that the new code has strengthened the protection of trade secrets, which have now become the object of an autonomous IPR, because under the newest version of Article 99 the behaviour is unfair in itself, as in most cases the parties are aware that the information belongs to a third party.[360]

Interestingly, it has been pointed out that the establishment of such enhanced protection responds to the structure of Italy's industrial landscape, which is mostly made up of SMEs. It is generally believed that firms of this type usually regard the patent system as being too costly and in most cases prefer to resort to secrecy as a means of appropriating returns from innovation.[361] Thus, Article 99 was tailored so as to meet the needs of Italy's SMEs. This, however, begs the question of whether the trade-off imposed by the patent system has been in some way bypassed.[362]

### b) Germany

The legal nature of trade secrets has also been extensively examined in Germany, particularly in connection to the relevant provisions of the German Civil Code ("BGB") applicable to their enforcement.[363] Indeed, the discussion is not only a doctrinal one. If trade secrets are considered an IPR, they should be protected pursuant to the property guarantee of the German Constitution (Article 14) and §§ 823 I, 812 I, and 687 II BGB.[364] However, only a few judicial decisions from the 1950s have actually dealt with the issue. In 1955, in the context of a bankruptcy case, the Supreme Court of

---

359 Article 99(1) of the Italian Industrial Property Code provides that: "Without prejudice to unfair competition law, the rightful holder of the information and the experiences set forth in Article 98, shall be entitled to prevent third parties not having his consent from acquiring, using and disclosing the information in an abusive manner , unless acquired independently by the third party" (translation by the author).

360 Giorgio Floridia and others, *Diritto Industriale Proprietà Intellettuale e concorrenza* (4th edn, G Giappichelli Editore 2012) 207.

361 Gustavo Ghidini and Valeria Falce 2011(n 358) 149-150.

362 Gustavo Ghidini and Valeria Falce 2011(n 358) 149-150.

363 Bürgerliches Gesetzbuch in der Fassung der Bekanntmachung vom 2. Januar 2002 (BGBl. I S. 42, 2909; 2003 I S. 738), das zuletzt durch Artikel 6 des Gesetzes vom 12. Juli 2018 (BGBl. I S. 1151) geändert worden ist.

364 Ansgar Ohly 2014 (n 100) 3.

the Republic of Germany held that the holder of a secret process had an exclusive right in it ("*Auschlussrecht*").[365] Notwithstanding this, some months later, the same court stated in another case dealing with technical undisclosed information that the holder did *not* have an *absolute exclusive* and *prohibitory right* in the information and that the applicable laws were the relevant provisions of the BGB and the Act Against Unfair Competition ("UWG").[366]

From an academic perspective, the debate remains unsettled. While some view trade secrets as an absolute IPR,[367] others reject such a categorisation.[368] In this regard, Drexl suggests that trade secrets lack one of the features common to all IPRs, i.e. their exclusive nature. As a result, they cannot be considered as one of the rights that fall under the broader umbrella of intellectual property. He convincingly argues that IPRs afford erga omnes protection to their right holders against use by any third parties in the manner set forth in the relevant statutes.[369] Trade secrets, instead, are only protected against unlawful acquisition, use and disclosure. According to Drexl, this difference is an essential one, as it renders trade secrets protection a tort law ("*Deliktsrecht*") resulting from the unlawfulness of the behaviour.[370]

In a similar vein, Beyerbach concludes that the undisclosed character of trade secrets precludes their inclusion within the IPRs spectrum. Crucially, any trade secret holder achieves protection without publicising the information, and hence does not participate in the trade-off between the holder and the general public envisaged by the intellectual property system.[371]

---

365 BGH GRUR 1955, 388, 389 – *Dücko.*

366 Gesetz gegen den unlauteren Wettbewerb in der Fassung der Bekanntmachung vom 3. März 2010 (BGBl. I S. 254), das zuletzt durch Artikel 4 des Gesetzes vom 17. Februar 2016 (BGBl. I S. 233) geändert worden ist (UWG); BGH GRUR 1955, 468, 472 – *Schwermetall-Kokillenguß.*

367 Christoph Ann, 'Know-how- Stiefkind des Geistiges Eigentums?' [2007] GRUR 39, 42 highlighting the economic dimension of know-how as an IPR.

368 Hans-Jürgen Ahrens and Mary-Rose McGuire, *Modellgesetz für Geistiges Eigentum, Normtext und Begründung* (GRUR 2012) 50; Mary-Rose Mcguire, 'Know-how:Stiefkind, Störenfried oder Sorgenkind?' [2015] GRUR 424, 426.

369 Josef Drexl, 'Die Verweigerung der Offenlegung von Unternehmensgeheimnissen als Missbrauch marktbeherrschender Stellung' 437, 449 in Reto Hilty and others (eds), *Schutz von Kreativität und Wettbewerb* (C.H. Beck 2009).

370 Josef Drexl 2009 (n 369) 449; Gintare Surblyte 2011(n 182) 59-60.

371 Hannes Beyerbach, *Die geheime Unternehmensinformation* (Mohr Siebeck 2012) 222.

Dorner is also wary of categorising trade secrets as property rights, as he believes that this amounts to an "Hypertrophy of IPRs".[372] In the case of trade secrets, this is achieved by expanding the subject matter protected, rather than creating a sui generis right.[373] He illustrates this by referring to the broad scope of paragraph 2 of § 17(2) UWG, the simultaneous protection of software through copyright and trade secrets and the protection of confidential information through procedural law.[374]

A middle ground approach is purported, among others, by Ohly, who is of the opinion that trade secrets protection appears to fall somewhere between one of the market behaviour rules set forth in the UWG and an IPR.[375] Following this viewpoint, trade secrets are regarded as an "imperfect intellectual property right" ("*unvollkommenes Immaterialgüterrecht*"), owing to the fact that they share some of the features of traditional IPRs and others of the market behaviour rules enshrined in the UWG.[376] From a dogmatic perspective, Ohly suggests that not every IPR confers upon its holder the right to enforce it without taking into account the lawfulness of the alleged infringer's conduct, as in the case of patent rights.[377] This is best illustrated by referring to trade marks and copyright. The infringement of the former is usually conditioned upon unfair behaviour such as the creation of likelihood of confusion or taking unfair advantage

---

372 Michael Dorner 2013 (n 305) 315-318; the concept of Hypertrophy of IPRs is further developed by Brigitte Zypries, 'Hypertrophie der Schutzrechte?' [2004] GRUR 977, 980.

373 William Cornish, 'The Expansion of Intellectual Property Rights' 9 in Gerhard Schricker, Thomas Dreier and Annette Kur (eds), *Geistiges Eigentum im Dienst der Innovation* (Nomos 2001).

374 Michael Dorner 2013 (n 305) 315-318.

375 Ansgar Ohly 2014 (n 100) 3.

376 Ansgar Ohly 2014 (n 100) 4; a similar view is expressed by Hans-Jürgen Ahrens and Mary-Rose McGuire 2012 (n 366) where trade secrets are conceptualised as a special protection position ("*sonstige Schutzposition*"); this argument is further developed by Mary-Rose McGuire 2015 (n 368) 424, where the author suggests that the system articulated by §§ 17-19 UWG together with § 823 II BGB does not afford absolute protection to the secret holder. Rather, it confers subjective right against unlawful acquisition, use and disclosure. Hence, the author purports that the legal nature debate results from the different ways in which the concept intellectual property is understood. For some, IPRs confer an absolute right to the holder of the intangible good, while others view it as a set of rules that regulate different types of extisting conduct ("*Lebenssachverhalten*"); see further *Harte-Bavendamm*/Henning-Bodewig, *Gesetz gegen den unlauteren Wettbewerb (UWG)*( 4th edn, C.H. Beck 2016) '§§ 17-19' Rdn 2.

377 Ansgar Ohly 2014 (n 100) 4.

of the distinctive character and reputation of the mark.[378] Similarly, copyright does not afford protection against independently created works. Hence, he concludes that IPRs constitute a bundle of rights, some of which are tighter laced than others. It is in this context that he submits that trade secrets can be regarded as an "imperfect species of IPRs". However, this dogmatic characterisation should not lead to enhancing the material limits laid down in the protection of trade secrets, particularly vis-à-vis bona fide third party acquirers, as the right in a trade secret is not a right in rem with erga omnes effects.[379] In the following section, it is argued that such a conceptualisation should be extended to the interpretation of the TSD. Indeed, this seems to be the approach adopted by the German legislature in the implementation of the TSD, as noted in the comments to § 3 of the Proposed Trade Secrets Act.[380]

### 4. European Union approach

As outlined in the previous sections, EU Member States have different views on whether trade secrets should be considered a species of IPRs or a set of unfair competition rules. Interestingly, there is not a single provision of the acquis communautaire that expressly addresses this issue and even the wording of the TSD appears unclear.

The Technology Transfer Block Exemption Regulation, in force until the end of April 2014, defined IPRs as including "industrial property rights, know-how, copyright and neighbouring rights".[381] However, in its newest version, IPRs are defined as "industrial property rights, in particu-

378 See Article 10(2)(c) TMD.

379 Ansgar Ohly 2014 (n 100) 4.

380 See § 3 of the Proposed Trade Secrets Act: "(...) es sich bei Geschäftsgeheimnissen zwar in gewisser Weise um Immaterialgüterrechte handelt, aber anders als bei Patenten, Marken und Urheberrechten keine subjektiven Ausschließlichkeits- und Ausschließungsrechte vorliegen können, weil der rechtliche Schutz allein von der Geheimhaltung der Information abhängt und nicht von anderen Voraussetzungen wie einer Eintragung oder einer besonderen Schöpfungshöhe. Um Innnovation und Wettbewerb weiterhin zu ermöglichen, werden daher Geschäftsgeheimnisse nicht völlig der Gemeinfreiheit entzogen und ihrem Inhaber mit Wirkung gegenüber jedermann zugeordnet, sondern es wird lediglich ein bestehender Zustand rechtlich abgesichert".

381 See Article 1 (1)(g) of the Commission Regulation (EC) No 772/2004 of 27 April 2004 on the application of Article 81 (3) of the Treaty to categories of technology transfer agreements [2004] OJ L123/11.

lar patents and trade marks, copyright and neighbouring rights".[382] Thus, the latter version has omitted any reference to know-how.

More recently, the EU legislator has adopted an ambiguous wording when addressing the legal nature of trade secrets in the TSD. On the one hand, it incorporates the "honest commercial practices" benchmark contained in the PC in the assessment of the types of conduct that are deemed unlawful and the exceptions and limitations thereto.[383] The non-proprietary nature of trade secrets is reinforced by the language used in Article 2(2), which refers to trade secrets holders instead of trade secrets owners.[384] In the same vein, the Impact Assessment notes that the application of the Enforcement Directive to trade secrets was declined because "trade secrets are not intellectual property rights" and that regarding them as an IPR would add confusion.[385] However, on the other hand, Recital 16 expressly mentions that the provisions of the Directive shall not create an *exclusive right* on the information they protect, but notably no reference to intellectual property is made.[386]

In the light of the above, it is submitted that the Directive does not require Member States to protect trade secrets as IPRs.[387] Instead, the legislature has opted to emphasise the unfair competition nature of the relevant

---

382 Commission Regulation (EU) No 316/2014 of 21 March on the application of Article 101 (3) of the Treaty on the Functioning of the European Union to categories of technology transfer agreements [2014] OJ L93/17 (TTBER).

383 Annette Kur, Reto Hilty and Roland Knaak, 'Comments of the Max Planck Institute for Innovation and Competition of 3 June 214 on the Proposal of the European Commission for a Directive on the Protection of Undisclosed Know-How and Business Information (Trade Secrets) Against Their Unlawful Acquisition, Use and Disclosure of 28 November 2013, COM(2013) 813 Final' [2014] IIC 45, para 11 (MPI Comments).

384 As noted by Tanya Aplin, 'A critical evaluation of the proposed Trade Secrets Directive' [2014] IPQ 257, 260-261.

385 Commission, 'Impact Assessment accompanying the document proposal for a Directive of the European Parliament and of the Council on the protection of undisclosed know-how and business information (trade secrets) against their unlawful acquisition, use and disclosure' SWD(2013) 471 final, 267-268; Tanya Aplin 2014 (n 384) 260 further refers to the fact that Recital 1 of the TSD views trade secrets protection as a compliment or alternative to IPRs.

386 Recital 16 TSD: "In the interest of innovation and to foster competition, the provisions of this Directive should not create any exclusive right to know-how or information protected as trade secrets".

387 Tanya Aplin 2014 (n 384) 260-261 is of the opinion that the wording used in the Directive is so flexible that it even allows for a certain degree of leeway in terms of whether it is mandatory to implement unfair competition provisions.

liability conduct. Yet, it does not mandate either that Member States that do protect trade secrets as IPRs amend their legislation and regulate trade secret protection only by reference to unfair competition rules.[388] This would disregard the overall functioning of the intellectual property system, where unfair competition rules regularly supplement the protection afforded by IPRs, such as trade marks or design rights.[389]

Against this background, it should be borne in mind that there is also a constitutional dimension to the property debate vis-à-vis trade secrets in the EU. Article 17(2) of the ChFREU mandates Member States to protect intellectual property under the general property clause. However, so far, the CJEU has not ruled on whether trade secrets fall within the scope of protection of this provision and the implications that such a categorisation may entail with respect to the rights conferred by national trade secrets legal regimes. In addition, according to the constitutional approach, confidential information should also be afforded protection pursuant to the general freedom to conduct a business laid down in Article 16 of the ChFREU. This provision encompasses all economic and business activities of a company, as well as the competitive position of all of the economic actors.[390]

A number of commentators have expressed scepticism regarding the possibility of considering trade secrets as a form of intellectual property rights in the context of the TSD because they understand that this would lead to higher standards of protection to the advantage of corporate actors. In particular, it is argued that this would (i) result in the application of stricter liability principles (in particular with respect to third party liability); (ii) narrow the manner in which exceptions and limitations are construed (with respect to reverse engineering and independent creation); and (iii) impose stringent enforcement remedies.[391] Furthermore, it has been suggested that the minimum harmonisation approach adopted in the Directive seems problematic, as in its implementation, Member States may adopt higher standards of protection.[392] Consequently, it is submitted that

388 This would be, for instance, the case of Italy.

389 Ansgar Ohly 2014 (n 100) 4.

390 Hannes Beyerbach, *Die geheime Unternehmensinformation* (Mohr Siebeck 2012) 305.

391 Tanya Aplin 2015 (n 306) 432 noting that "in the context of the EU, it is argued that classification as 'possessions' and 'intellectual property' within Article 17 Charter is likely to create pressure to increase the scope of protection".

392 Valeria Falce, 'Looking for (Full) Harmonization in the Innovation Union' [2015] IIC 940, 959.

the maximum standards laid down in Article 1(1) TSD, which safeguard the exceptions and lawful means of acquiring, using and disclosing secret information, are essential to ensure a proper balance between the interests of trade secrets holders and the intellectual property system.[393]

Drawing on the above, it is concluded that the emphasis in the implementation by Member States should not lie in the specific label under which trade secrets are categorised (either as unfair competition rules or imperfect intellectual property rights), but rather in their material limits. As convincingly argued by Ohly, the protection conferred to a trade secret holder should not be enhanced in the event that they are in fact regarded as an imperfect form of IPRs by the national legislators, particularly with respect to the application of the exceptions and limitations and the liability of bona fide third party acquirers. The right in a trade secret should not be viewed as an absolute erga omnes right (such as patent rights) and its enforcement should always be conditioned upon the appraisal of the fairness in the acquisition, use and disclosure of the information concerned.[394]

## II. Considering information as the object of property rights

### 1. Preliminary remarks: the problematic conceptualisation of information as such as the object of IPRs

Ultimately, the property debate in the context of trade secrets leads to the question of whether information as such should be regarded as the object of property rights and whether it should be protected within the scope of IPRs. Indeed, information and information relationships are regulated by multiple fields such as contract law, tort law, data protection, administrative law and even environment law, to name some.[395] Intellectual property is among those fields, as the grant of exclusive rights unquestionably limits the free access to and flow of information. However, a historical analysis shows that one of the goals of the intellectual property regime in the EU

393 See chapter 6 § 2.

394 Ansgar Ohly 2014 (n 100) 4.

395 Thomas Dreier, 'Regulating information: Some thoughts on a perhaps not quite so new way of looking to intellectual property' 35, 42 in Josef Drexl and others (eds), *Technology and Competition, Contributions in Honour of Hanns Ullrich* (Larcier 2009); Hannes Beyerbach, *Die geheime Unternehmensinformation* (Mohr Siebeck 2012) 5-6.

has been to promote the dissemination of information and knowledge, rather than to limit its access through the creation of property rights.[396]

To be sure, IPRs are granted for a restricted period of time, limited in scope and only for those inventions and creations that meet a certain qualitative threshold.[397] For this reason, intellectual property intends to afford the lowest level of protection necessary to encourage innovation and creation.[398] Notwithstanding this, in the information society, information as such has become a very valuable commodity, which some consider is worth protecting.[399]

However, characterising information as the object of property rights is difficult for a number of reasons. In the first place, as noted above, there is no uniform definition of information,[400] which allows for distinguishing it

---

396 In the Communication from the Commission, 'Europe 2020: a strategy for smart, sustainable and inclusive growth, Brussels,' COM(2010) 2020 final, 11-14, the Commission established three priorities within the framework of the Europe 2020 Strategy, namely, (i) smart growth, (ii) sustainable growth and (iii) inclusive growth. Particularly, the second pillar, smart growth, intends to enhance the role of knowledge and innovation as drivers for growth in the EU. According to the Commission, this calls for an improvement of the quality of education and research performance, as well as promoting the transfer of innovation and knowledge within the common market.

397 Séverine Dusollier, 'Pruning the European intellectual property tree: in search of common principles and roots' 24, 37 in Christophe Geiger (ed), *Constructing European intellectual property* (Edward Elgar 2013). The author identifies a continuum of four levels, which to some extent are present in the requirements of protection of every IPR, even though not at the same time. These are creation-novelty-adequacy-investment. The creation requirement refers to the intellectual intervention of the author. Novelty is conceptualised as an objective threshold that looks into the prior existence of the intellectual object now produced. Adequacy indicates that the object of protection serves the purpose of the IP for which it is applied. Finally, investment refers to the financial investment in the creation of the object.

398 Mark A. Lemley 2004 (n 109) 1031.

399 Pamela Samuelson 1988 (n 341) 367.

400 Thomas Dreier 2009 (n 395) 42; Thomas Hoeren, 'Zur Einführung: Informationsrecht' [2002] JuS 947, 947 notes that "Niemand weiß, was Information ist"; in a similar vein, Hannes Beyerbach, *Die geheime Unternehmensinformation* (Mohr Siebeck 2012) 5 refers to information as a "definiens indefiniblis".

from other concepts such as knowledge[401] or data.[402] Most famously, it has been stated that "information is information, not matter or energy".[403] Dreier notes that information has been defined, as a message, pattern, sensory input or even a property in physics (etc.). He further adds that none of these explanations share a common ground and in some instances they contradict each other. Furthermore, the intangible nature and inherent leakiness of information make it very difficult for the possessor to maintain a certain degree of exclusivity in its use.[404] Consequently, information presents the same non-rivalrous and non-exclusive nature, which is common to other forms of intangible assets that are afforded protection under the general umbrella of IPRs.

In the light of the above, trade secrets law seems tailored to protect certain categories of information that fall outside the traditional realm of IPRs,[405] such as incremental innovations that are considered obvious by the patent office, business models or compilations of data that are not eligible for protection under the Database Directive but are maintained undisclosed. Yet, this in turn may have a negative impact on access to information, innovation and market competition.

The following sections further explore the legal problems surrounding the categorisation of information as such as the object of an IPR and its consequences for trade secrets law. First, section 2 starts by analysing the leading case in the U.S. on this topic ; then, some additional arguments following a semiotics approach are presented in section 3; next, in section 4, the sui generis "data producer's right" proposed by the Commission is used as an example case to illustrate the problems of creating exclusive rights on information as such; finally section 5 concludes.

---

401 In the Oxford English Dictionary, 'knowledge, n' is defined as "Facts, information, and skills acquired through experience or education; the theoretical or practical understanding of a subject" (*OED Online*, OUP June 2013) <https://en.oxforddictionaries.com/definition/knowledge> accessed 15 September 2018.

402 For the purposes of the present research, 'data, n' will be tentatively defined as "Facts and statistics collected together for reference or analysis" (*OED Online*, OUP June 2013) <https://en.oxforddictionaries.com/definition/data> accessed 15 September 2018.

403 Thomas Dreier 2009 (n 395) 42 (as cited in N. Wiener, *Cybernetics, or control and communication in animal and machine* (2nd edn, MIT Press 1961) 132).

404 Pamela Samuelson 1988 (n 341) 368-369.

405 Michael Risch 2011 (n 113) 175.

## 2. The debate in the U.S.: INS v. Associated Press and its influential dissent

The proprietary debate reached the U.S. Supreme Court in the famous *INS v. Associated Press* case, where the court recognised a quasi-property right in a specific kind of information, news items.[406] In the case at hand, the parties competed in the distribution of news throughout the U.S. during the First World War. Associated Press ("AP") filed a lawsuit against International News Service ("INS"), owned by the newsprint magnate Randolph Hearst, for appropriating its news, after the defendant was barred from using the allied lines.[407] In effect, despite the ban, INS continued to report news to the west coast, leveraging the time difference. Crucially, the news was lawfully acquired from bulletin boards and early editions of the newspapers on the east coast and subsequently telegraphed to INS customers on the west coast.[408]

In the ratio decidendi, the U.S. Supreme Court first noted that no copyright protection was available on the reported news items based on two factors: firstly, most of the news was rewritten and copyright law only affords protection to expression, not ideas; and secondly, the news described daily ordinary matters and as such lacked originality and did not qualify for copyright protection.[409] Hence, upon their publication, the news items were deemed to be part of the public domain. Notwithstanding this, Justice Pitney recognised that a property interest subsisted between the parties, which was nevertheless not enforceable against the public in general.[410] Such a property right was derived from the amount of time, money

406 *INS v. Associated Press*, 248 U.S. 215 (1918).

407 The news on First World War was reported using the Allies telegraph lines. Due to the critical reports of the Allies' performance by INS, the company was denied use of the allied lines; this was reported by the New York Times in 'News Pirating Case in Supreme Court' *The New York Times* (New York, 3 May 1918) 14.

408 In addition, INS bribed AN's employees in order to receive the information before the publication of the newspapers and induced them to breach their confidentiality obligations. However, these types of conduct were not the object of the appeal before the U.S. Supreme Court.

409 *INS v. Associated Press*, 248 U.S. 215, 234 (1918).

410 *INS v. Associated Press*, 248 U.S. 215, 235 (1918): "Regarding the news, therefore, as but the material out of which both parties are seeking to make profits at the same time and in the same field, we hardly can fail to recognize that for this purpose, and as between them, it must be regarded as quasi-property, irrespective of the rights of either against the public".

and labour that AP had invested in gathering the news and the value that those without knowledge of the news were willing to pay. As a result, the court granted an injunction on the grounds that the competitor had misappropriated the plaintiff's investment in an enterprise. Next, the majority spelt out four factors that have become central to any misappropriation action in the United States.[411] In the first place, there must have been a substantial investment in the production of an article with market value. Second, the defendant must be in direct competition with the plaintiff. Furthermore, there must be some free-riding (reaping without sowing) on his investment. Fourth, the act of misappropriation must result in a substantial reduction in the incentive to yield the goods and services misappropriated.[412]

The line of reasoning explained above was contested by Justice Brandeis in his famous dissent, where he called into question the extension of property rights in news items based on two arguments. In the first place, he expressed concern about the creation of a new private right that may allow anyone who had invested labour, skill and money in something to claim a semi-property right in it, against third parties.[413] In the words of Justice Brandeis:

> The plaintiff has no absolute right to the protection of his production; he has merely the qualified right to be protected against the defendant's acts, because of the special relation in which the latter stands, or the wrongful method or means employed in acquiring the knowledge, or the manner in which it is then used.[414]

411 Matthias Leistner, 'The Legacy of International News Service v Associated Press (USA)' 33, 34 in Christopher Heath and Anselm Kamperman Sanders (eds), *Landmark Intellectual Property Cases and Their Legacy* (Kluwer Law International 2010).

412 Matthias Leistner 2010 (n 411) 34; at 39-41 the author further notes that later in time the INS test for misappropriation was substantially narrowed down by the U.S. Court of Appeal for the Second Circuit in *National Basketball Association (BA) v. Motorola Inc.* 105 F.3d 841 (2d Cir. 1997). In its legal reasoning, the court noted that a central element in the INS case was the time-sensitivity of news items. Hence, the court argued that the misappropriation action as tailored in INS was only applicable to misappropriation of hot news.

413 *INS v. Associated Press*, 248 U.S. 215, 262-263 (1918).

414 *INS v. Associated Press*, 248 U.S. 215, 251 (1918).

Next, he argued that this situation would result in a limitation of the right to use general knowledge and ideas.[415] Against this backdrop, Justice Brandeis considered that in order to reconcile the private right with the public interest, such a right may only be created by the legislature and based on articulate and clear limitations.[416]

This dissent was very influential in the following years, as it explored for the first time the implications of expanding the intellectual property regime to the mere protection of information based on the cost, time and labour devoted to garnering it.[417] Most notably, it drew special attention to one of the cornerstones of the intellectual property system, according to which abstract ideas should not be protected by law, but should remain free:[418]

> The general rule of law is, that the noblest of human productions-knowledge, truths, ascertained, conceptions, and ideas became, after voluntary communication to others, free as the air to common use.[419]

This general principle is most clearly stated in copyright law under the idea/expression dichotomy: only the expression, not the underlying idea, is protected by copyright.[420] Similarly, patent law only protects technical features. This can be inferred from the exclusion list set forth in Article 52(2) EPC and the fact that inventions must be susceptible of industrial application (Article 57 EPC). As regards trade marks, the CJEU clarified in *Dyson v Registrar of Trade Marks* that a trade mark application consisting of all of the conceivable appearances of a product in a non-specific manner cannot be regarded as a sign under the TMD. Otherwise, the holder of the trade mark would obtain a competitive advantage that may limit competition in the market.[421]

---

415 *INS v. Associated Press*, 248 U.S. 215, 240 (1918); and also at page 250 (Brandeis Dissent).

416 *INS v. Associated. Press*, 248 U.S. 215, 263 (1918).

417 Matthias Leistner 2010 (n 411) 37-38.

418 Séverine Dussollier 2012 (n 397) 35-37.

419 *INS v. Associated Press*, 248 U.S. 215, 250 (1918).

420 The idea/expression dichotomy is one of the general principles enshrined in most national copyright systems. At the international level, it has been explicitly codified in Article 9(2) of TRIPs and Article 2 of the WCT. Yet, at the EU level, it is only referred to in Article 1(2) of the Software Directive; see Mireille van Eechoud and others, *Harmonizing European Copyright Law* (Kluwer Law International 2009) 34-35.

421 In Case C–321/03 *Dyson Ltd v Registrar of Trademarks* [2007] ECR I-687 the CJEU dealt with the refusal to register as a trade mark all conceivable shapes of

### 3. Semiotics approach to the property debate

The legal analysis of *International News Service v. Associated Press*[422] underscores that information can be separated from its physical carrier,[423] in the same way that a text and the book in which it is embedded are two distinct objects.[424] Accordingly, this may lead to the distinction of three different layers when addressing information as an object: (i) the semantic level, as regards the meaning of the information; (ii) the syntactic level, as regards the signs and their interrelation; and (iii) the physical level, as regards the carrier. Against this background, semiotics doctrines have identified three types of information that correlate with the previous sequence of levels: semantic information, syntactic information and structural information.[425] Following this rationale, the story told in a book is semantic information, whereas the text of the book, understood as a sequence of letters and words devoid of any meaning, is syntactic information and the book as such is the physical carrier (real property) and, therefore, structural information.[426]

The creation of IPRs confers exclusivity over certain types of information. For instance, patent rights confer exclusivity over specific technical information, which relates to semantic information, whereas copyright and design rights provide exclusivity over syntactic information.[427] Indeed, as outlined in the previous section, pursuant to Article 9(2) TRIPs copyright protection extends only to the expression (syntactic information) of ideas, which are semantic information. Likewise, design rights are only protected against their reproduction in a physical embodiment, which is also syntactical information.[428]

The case of trade secrets is a particular one, as the object of protection is semantic information, but unlike patent rights, exclusivity is not achieved

---

a transparent collecting bin forming part of the external surface of a vacuum cleaner.

422 *INS v. Associated Press*, 248 U.S. 215 (1918).

423 Herbert Zech, 'Information as Property' [2015] 6 JIPITEC 192 para 9.

424 Herbert Zech 2015 (n 423) para 9.

425 Herbert Zech 2015 (n 423) para 14.

426 This example is presented by Josef Drexl, 'Designing Competitive Markets for Industrial Data – Between Propertisation and Access' (2016) Max Planck Institute for Innovation & Competition Research Paper No. 16-13, 12 <https://ssrn.com/abstract=2862975> accessed 15 September 2018.

427 Herbert Zech 2015 (n 423) paras 25-28.

428 Herbert Zech 2015 (n 423) para 28.

by conferring exclusive rights over the said semantic information. Instead, exclusivity is a pre-condition that derives from the factual condition of secrecy.[429] Therefore, trade secrets law merely protects factual exclusivity against the unauthorised acquisition, use and disclosure of semantic information that has commercial value due to its secret nature and has been subject to reasonable efforts under the circumstances to protect its concealed nature. Crucially, the protection conferred by trade secrets does not extend to information acquired through independent creation or reverse engineering (unless the parties have contractually agreed to the contrary). Consequently, semantic information is not protected as such, only against specific tortious conduct. Such a distinction is of the greatest importance, because conferring exclusive rights over semantic information vests the holder of the right with greater powers than creating rights over syntactic information. As a result, the reduction of the public domain is also substantially larger in the former case.[430]

In the light of the above, it is submitted that the "honest commercial practices" benchmark should remain at the centre of the appraisal of the lawfulness of the alleged infringing types of conduct in order to avoid the creation of a right in rem over semantic information. Following this line of reasoning, the limitations laid down with respect to trade secrets protection should also always be observed in their enforcement. Otherwise, trade secrets protection would have a disruptive effect within the overall IPRs legal framework.

A similar rationale speaks against the introduction of the data producer's right contemplated by the Commission in the context of the Building a European Data Economy,[431] as analysed in the following section.

---

429 Herbert Zech 2015 (n 423) para 26.

430 In this context, Herbert Zech 2015 (n 423) para 31 notes that the creation of property rights over semantic information calls for a stronger justification than establishing property rights over syntactic information. Hence, copyright becomes more problematic if the protection of works protected under copyright law extends not only to its expression, but also its content.

431 See Commission, 'Building a European Data Economy Initiative' COM(2017) 9 final.

### 4. Example case: data producer's right

In the context of the Digital Single Market initiative and mostly owing to the increasing role of data as a driver for innovation,[432] the Commission evaluated the possibility of introducing a new EU-wide novel sui generis right for the protection of so-called "machine-generated data"[433] (also referred to as "industrial data" or "non personal data")[434] with a potentially erga omnes effect.[435] This debate was spurred for the most part by the automotive industry[436] and has been particularly intense among German authors, who are divided between those that support the need to create a sui generis right that allocates ownership rights on raw data,[437] and those that argue that the existing liability regimes (such as tort law, criminal and trade secrets law) are applicable to the emerging data markets and are wary of the consequences for innovation and competition that the creation of such a new right would entail.[438]

As a result of this debate, in January 10, 2017, the Commission announced that it was considering the possibility of introducing a new sui

432 OECD, 'Data-Driven Innovation: Big Data for Growth and Well-Being' (OECD Publishing 2015) 4 <http://dx.doi.org/10.1787/9789264229358-en> accessed 15 September 2018.

433 Herbert Zech 2016 (n 278) 53 and 74 defines data as "machine-readable encoded information". However, in the context of the sui generis right, the author suggests that the subject matter of protection should be limited to "machine-readable coded information that is defined only by its representative characters (bits) irrespective of its content (data delimited on the syntactic level)".

434 See Andreas Wiebe 2016 (n 287); in the following, the term "industrial data" will be used.

435 P. Bernt Hugenholtz 2017 (n 279) 5; Commission, 'Building a European Data Economy Initiative' COM(2017) 9 final, 13 and more specifically Commission, 'Commission Staff Working Document on the free flow of data and emerging issues of the European data economy' SWD(2017) 2 final, 33-38.

436 P. Bernt Hugenholtz 2017 (n 279) 1-2.

437 Herbert Zech 2016 (n 278) 51-79; Michael Lehmann, 'European Market for Digital Goods' 111-126 in Alberto de Franceschi (ed), *European Contract Law and the Digital Single Market – the Implications of the Digital Revolution* (Intersentia 2016).

438 Josef Drexl and others, 'Position Statement of the Max Planck Institute for Innovation and Competition of 26 April 2017 on the European Commission's Public consultation on Building the European Data Economy' (2017) Max Planck Institute for Innovation & Competition Research Paper No. 17-08 <https://ssrn.com/abstract=2959924> accessed 15 September 2018.

generis right for industrial data[439] in order to foster "the tradability of non-personal or anonymised machine-generated data as an economic good".[440] The contours of the right were not precisely defined, even though in the Building a European Data Economy Communication it was noted that it related to the "right to use and authorise the use of non-personal data", which would be vested on the "data producer", which could be either the *owner* or *long-term user* (i.e. the lessee) of the device concerned.[441] This would allow for unlocking machine-generated data controlled de facto by the manufacturer of the device.[442] According to the Working Document, two possibilities were considered:

(i) the introduction of a right in rem allowing the data producer to enforce it against third parties with erga omnes effect, including the right to assign and license such a right, or

(ii) the creation of a defensive right of a tortious nature imposing liability in case of misappropriation, similar to the liability regime laid down in the TSD.

The proposal garnered substantial criticism among academics and stakeholders, as it was perceived that the creation of such a right was not well founded and was alien to the general IPRs system, particularly if the EU legislator opted to introduce an in rem right with erga omnes effects.[443]

From an economic perspective, it was argued that neither of the two utilitarian justifications most frequently invoked for IPRs were applicable in the context of industrial data, namely (i) the incentives to innovate theory, and (ii) the prospect theory. In connection to the former, it was noted that the Commission had not provided sufficient evidence regarding the need to confer exclusivity to data producers in order to provide additional incentives to generate and collect data.[444] Indeed, in the Data Economy sheer amounts of data were already being generated as by-products of most of the services provided therewith, such as platforms, or in the context of

439 Commission, 'Building a European Data Economy Initiative' COM(2017) 9 final, 12.

440 Commission, 'Commission Staff Working Document on the free flow of data and emerging issues of the European data economy' SWD(2017) 2 final, 5.

441 Commission, 'Building a European Data Economy Initiative' COM(2017) 9 final, 13.

442 Josef Drexl and others 2016 (n 438) para 9.

443 P. Bernt Hugenholtz 2017 (n 279) 5; Josef Drexl and others 2017 (n 442) paras 8-19.

444 Josef Drexl 2016 (n 426) 30-33.

the Internet of Things ("IoT").[445] In other words, there was no "public good problem" to be solved.[446] The prospect theory submits that IPRs are justified because they provide additional incentives to commercialise the subject matter of protection.[447] Yet again, the Commission failed to provide evidence of whether data producers and data holders were in fact facing difficulties in the commercialisation of their data.[448]

From a legal perspective, the introduction of a new data producer's right in the acquis communautaire also encountered criticism, mainly on the grounds that it would lead to "disruptive overlaps" with existing IPRs, generate legal uncertainty and hinder the free flow of information.[449] In particular, Hugenholtz holds that if a property right is recognised over machine-generated data, tension will arise with existing copyright rules, leading to "competing claims of ownership in the same content".[450] He illustrates this in a very convincing manner by reference to the protection afforded by copyright to cinematographic works. If a sui generis right over digital data were introduced, a picture shot with a digital camera would be protected both under copyright and under the sui generis data producer's right. Furthermore, in such a context, the owner of the camera could claim ownership of the digital images, along with the competing ownership

---

445 P. Bernt Hugenholtz 2017 (n 279) 4; for the purposes of the present analysis, the broad definition of Internet of Things ("IoT") outlined by the OECD, 'Digital Economy Outlook' (OECD Publishing 2015) 61 <http://dx.doi.org/10.1787/9789264232440-en> accessed 15 September 2018 will be followed. According to this definition, the IoT encompasses "all devices and objects whose state can be read or altered via the Internet, with or without the active involvement of individuals. This includes laptops, routers, servers, tablets and smartphones, all of which are often considered to form part of the "traditional Internet". However, as these devices are integral to operating, reading and analysing the state of IoT devices, they are included here. The IoT consists of a series of components of equal importance – machine-to-machine communication, cloud computing, big data analysis, and sensors and actuators. Their combination, however, engenders machine learning, remote control, and eventually autonomous machines and systems, which will learn to adapt and optimise themselves".

446 An overview of the public good problem is provided by Wolfgang Kerber, 'A New (Intellectual) Property Right for Non-Personal Data? An Economic Analysis' [2016] GRUR Int 989, 997.

447 The prospect theory was developed by Edmund Kitch, 'The Nature and the Function of the Patent System' [1977] 20 Journal of Law and Economics 265; Josef Drexl 2016 (n 426) 33-34.

448 Wolfgang Kerber 2016 (n 446) 998.

449 P. Bernt Hugenholtz 2017 (n 279) 10.

450 P. Bernt Hugenholtz 2017 (n 279) 10-11.

claim by the authors of the film (music composer, producer, director and scriptwriter).[451] In turn, this would affect the exceptions and limitations under copyright law and the sui generis database right, unless similar exceptions and limitations were introduced for the sui generis data producer's right.[452] For instance, the right to extract and use insubstantial parts of a database by the lawful user regulated under Article 8(1) of the Database Directive could be undermined by the operation of the data producer's right in the individual data. As a final note, Hugenholtz convincingly argues that the fact that the Commission claimed that the subject matter of protection under the new sui generis right only covers syntactic information (not semantic information) would not prevent disruptive overlaps, because in many instances the reproduction of the semantic layer (for example, a film) requires the use of the syntactic layer (such as the digital file in which the film is embedded).[453]

Similar criticism was echoed by stakeholders in the context of the Consultation on the Building a European Data Economy Initiative, where most of the respondents noted that the investment made in the collection of data was sufficiently protected "through the Database and Trade Secrets Protection Directives, requiring no additional regulation".[454] In the same document, it was noted that the majority had submitted that the crucial issue was not to vest ownership rights in raw data, but rather to promote access to the said data.[455]

As a result, in a more recent communication, "Towards a common European data space" the Commission acknowledged the respondent's view and proposed a number of principles that should inform contractual practices in order to ensure "fair and competitive markets for the IoT objects and for products and services that rely on non-personal machine-generated data created by such objects".[456] The five principles that were spelt out refer to: (i) transparency in the access and sharing of data; (ii) the shared value of industrial data; (iii) the need to respect the commercial interests of data holders and data users; (iv) the need to ensure undistorted

451 P. Bernt Hugenholtz 2017 (n 279) 10-11.

452 P. Bernt Hugenholtz 2017 (n 279) 12.

453 P. Bernt Hugenholtz 2017 (n 279) 11-12.

454 Commission, 'Synopsis Report on the Consultation on the Building a European Data Economy Initiative,' 5.

455 Commission, 'Synopsis Report on the Consultation on the Building a European Data Economy Initiative,' 5.

456 Commission, 'Towards a common European data space' COM(2018) 232 final, 9-10.

competition and (v) the need to minimise data-lock in.[457] In addition, due to the dynamic nature of the emerging data markets, further consultations with stakeholders and sectorial measures were announced.[458]

## 5. Concluding remarks on the treatment of information as property

The analysis conducted above underscores the disruptive effects that the creation of a new IPR covering information as such (raw data at the syntactic level) would have on the protection of information at the semantic level.

IPRs are granted not only as a reward for creators and innovators. One of the main objectives of the intellectual property system is to incentivise the dissemination of information and allow its use for subsequent innovation and creation and, at the same time, foster competition in the market. However, affording protection to abstract ideas and information as such runs counter to the disclosure function[459] and may also have a negative impact on market competition and follow-on innovation. If access to information is essential in order to enter a given market, monopolisation may occur if the law affords protection against such access. As a result, it is crucial that the protection of information and access to it is not regulated in a restrictive manner.[460]

Ultimately, regarding information as the object of a property right may also affect fundamental freedoms such as the freedom of expression and information laid down under Article 10 ECHR and Article 11 of the ChFREU. Even though the ECtHR has stated that the protection afforded under these provisions to commercial speech is less than for political discourse,[461] states cannot impose information restrictions, for instance, by

457 Commission, 'Towards a common European data space' COM(2018) 232 final, 9-10.

458 Commission, 'Towards a common European data space' COM(2018) 232 final, 10-11.

459 Similar criticism has been raised in connection to the sui generis right in the EU created by the Database Directive. In this regard see Estelle Derclaye, 'Intellectual Property Rights on Information and Market Power- Comparing European and American Protection of Database' [2007] IIC 275, 297.

460 Josef Drexl 2011 (n 50) 183.

461 See *Hertel v Switzerland* (1998) 28 EHHR 534.

introducing property rights over information, unless this is mandated by law and appears necessary in the context of a democratic society.[462]

In the light of the above considerations, it appears necessary to find a suitable definition of information vis-à-vis intellectual property and establish clear boundaries between protectable and non-protectable types of information.[463] Indeed, an adequate definition of information should always be contextualised and tailored according to the problem it intends to solve.[464] This is particularly relevant in order to avoid the creation of an exclusive right over semantic information, if none of the utilitarian rationales for intellectual property apply.

In this context, it seems advisable to include a general provision within the acquis communautaire where it is specifically mentioned that abstract ideas and general principles should be free for everyone to use, in order to limit the ever-extending trend of granting proprietary rights over intangible assets without sound justifications.[465] This is also consistent with one of the governing principles of unfair competition, whereby beyond the realm of exclusivity afforded by intellectual property law, any achievement that provides a competitive advantage to its users should be free for everyone to enjoy. In fact, it is a well-established principle that unfair competition is not concerned with valuable achievements, but rather looks into the appraisal of a conduct.[466] Yet again, this raises the issue of defining whether an idea is sufficiently abstract and whether a conduct is contrary to honest commercial practices.

Similar concerns would apply in the event that trade secrets were regarded as the object of an IPR *with exclusive erga omnes* effects. In such a case, the protection of subject matter explicitly excluded by other types of IPRs, such as incremental innovations that do not meet the inventive step test or databases that do not qualify for protection under the two-tier harmonised system of protection, may end up enshrined within the intellectual property system for the mere fact of being kept undisclosed.[467] With these considerations in mind, some of the implications of the interplay between intellectual property and unfair competition in the realm of trade secrets are presented in the following section, in the wake of the TSD.

---

462 P. Bernt Hugenholtz 2017 (n 279) 13-14; in this regard see *Ashby Donald and Others v France* App no 36769/08 (ECtHR, 10 January 2013).

463 Pamela Samuelson 1988 (n 341) 398.

464 Thomas Dreier 2009 (n 395) 37.

465 Also suggested by Séverine Dussollier 2012 (n 397) 35-37.

466 Annette Kur 2014 (n 27) 16.

467 See chapter 1 § 3 B) II. 1.

## III. Dissecting the proprietary debate in the light of the harmonised framework created by the TSD

The examination conducted throughout this chapter shows that there is lack of consensus concerning the legal nature of trade secrets. Drawing on the previous analysis, this section outlines some policy considerations regarding the relevance and consequences of characterising trade secrets as a species of IPRs. Even though this debate is mostly of an academic nature, it has important practical implications, particularly as regards the application of the Enforcement Directive and the relevant provisions under the Rome II Regulation.[468] The first topic is discussed in greater detail in chapter 3, where the TSD is analysed. At this point, it suffices to note that only a few EU Member States apply the Enforcement Directive in connection to trade secrets[469] and that the TDS does not clarify its relationship with the Directive already in force.

From a private international law perspective, it is noteworthy that if the protection of trade secrets is regarded as an act of unfair competition, the law applicable to such obligations should be governed by Article 6(2) (together with Article 4) of the Rome II Regulation (i.e. the law of the country where the damage occurs). If, in contrast, trade secrets are deemed to be one of the categories of IPRs, Article 8(1) should be applied (i.e. the law of the country in which protection is sought).[470] The guiding principle pursuant to the Commission's Proposal of July 2003, is that industrial espionage, breach of contract and disclosure of business secrets fall within the categories of bilateral unfair commercial practices regulated in Article 6(2) of the Rome II Regulation, which refers to Article 4 of the same Regu-

---

468 Regulation (EC) No 864/2007 of the European Parliament and of the Council of 11 July 2007 on the law applicable to non-contractual obligations (Rome II) [2007] OJ L199/40.

469 Pursuant to the Baker McKenzie, 'Study on Trade Secrets and Confidential Business Information in the Internal Market' (MARKT/2011/128/D) (2013), 26 <http://ec.europa.eu/growth/tools-databases/newsroom/cf/itemdetail.cfm?item_id=8269> accessed 15 September 2018 these countries are Italy, Portugal (to the extent the law implementing the Enforcement Directive is applicable to unfair competition), the Slovak Republic, Romania and arguably also the UK according to *Vestergaard Frandsen A/S v Bestnet Europe Ltd* [2011] EWCA Civ 424 (CA), [56].

470 Annette Kur, Reto Hilty and Roland Knaak 2014 (n 383) para 17.

lation.[471] Following the latter provision, the applicable law is that of the place where the damage occurs (*lex loci damni*) (Article 4(1)).[472] Yet, if the parties have a common residence, the law of that country shall be applicable (Article 4(2)), whereas Article 4(3) introduces a so-called "escape clause" to the previous paragraphs and deems applicable the law of the country that has manifestly the closest connection to the misappropriation of the confidential information.

From a dogmatic perspective, trade secrets present some features that are similar to those of an IPR and at the same time others that are fundamentally different and seem closer to those of unfair competition.[473] Turning first to the similarities, both trade secrets and IPRs protect non-rival and non-exclusive intangible goods. In practice, this may lead to an overlap between the two regimes of protection, as examined in previous sections.[474] For instance, as noted above, copyright and trade secrets overlap in regard to the protection of source code.[475] Also, secrecy can protect technical in-

---

471 Commission, 'Proposal for a Regulation of the European Parliament and the Council on the Law Applicable to non-contractual obligations ("ROME II")' COM (2003) 427 final, 16; the Proposal notes that even though industrial espionage, breach of contract and disclosure of business secrets may have a negative impact on a particular market, these cases should be regarded as bilateral and not as falling under the more general conflict of law norm laid down in Article 6(1).

472 Christopher Wadlow, 'Trade secrets and the Rome II Regulation on the law applicable to non-contractual obligations' 30 EIPR [2008] 309-319; Valeria Falce 2015 (n 392) 960.

473 Ansgar Ohly 2013 (n 13) 35; Matthias Leistner, 'Unfair Competition and Freedoms of Movement', *Max Planck Encyclopaedia of European Private Law* (OUP 2012) 1718 provides a very illustrative first approximation to the concept of unfair competition. He notes that: "from a European Perspective, 'unfair competition' does not exist as a clearly defined, unitary concept. However, despite all the differences in the scope and characterization, all Member States have developed instruments based on the principle of fairness to control Commercial activities. A common feature of all these mechanisms is the condition that the regulated activities or practices must be of commercial nature. Thus, unfair competition law regulates market behaviour. Beyond this common starting point, a clear-cut demarcation of unfair competition from other fields of law as well as common identification of the objectives of the law of unfair competition can hardly be achieved, given the wide variety of statutes and case law in the Member States".

474 See chapter 1 § 3 A); a detailed account of the overlap between trade secrets and IPRs is provided in Estelle Derclaye and Matthias Leistner, *Intellectual Property Overlaps* (Hart 2011) 21.

475 See chapter 1 § 3 A) II.

formation that actually meets the patentability standards, but for competitive reasons is kept undisclosed. In favour of their characterisation as IPRs, it should be noted that trade secrets can be the object of a licensing agreement and that they can also be sold and assigned.[476] In effect, trade secrets are a very valuable asset for their holders, just like any other IPR.[477] The remedies available in most jurisdictions are similar to those available in the event of IPR infringement.[478] As a final remark, it should be noted that trade secrets protection, just like any other IPR, is subject to limitations. The most widely accepted ones are reverse engineering and independent creation.[479]

Yet, there are also substantial differences. Undisclosed information need not be novel and inventive (as in patent law) or meet a certain originality threshold (as in copyright).[480] Its protection depends to a large extent on the factual assessment of whether the secrecy requirement is fulfilled. Central to the protection of trade secrets in every jurisdiction is that once information becomes generally known it falls into the public domain and thus ceases to be eligible for protection[481] and that secret information must derive independent value from its undisclosed nature, which is frequently expressed in terms of the cost of creation.[482] Crucially, trade secrets do not afford any sort of protection against the independent generation of information.[483] As a result, two competitors may possess the same secret and in both instances be worthy of protection. Information remains free. In contrast, patent law protects against independent creation or reverse engineering of the patented invention. Similarly, copyright protects against the reproduction of the same exact expression, while trade marks preclude the use of identical or similar signs for identical or similar goods and services.

In this regard, it has been suggested that trade secrets are fundamentally different to IPRs, which, by definition, have an exclusive nature. The latter

---

476 Stanisław Sołtysiński 1986 (n 111) 332 noting that this is the case at least in Switzerland and Germany.

477 *Harte-Bavendamm*/Henning-Bodewig (n 376) §§ 17–19 UWG Rdn 2.

478 A detailed account of the relationship between Enforcement Directive and the TSD is provided in chapter 3 § 5 C) II. 1.

479 Mark A. Lemley 2008 (n 15) 138 purports that conceptualizing trade secrets as IPRs draws attention to the requirements and limitations of trade secrecy law.

480 See chapter 4 § 4 E) II.

481 Ansgar Ohly 2014 (n 100) 3; Tanya Aplin and others 2012 (n 22) chapter 5 on the attributes if confidentiality; also James Pooley 2002 (n 66) § 4.04.

482 Michael Risch 2011 (n 113) 175.

483 This is developed further in chapter 6 § 2 A).

afford absolute erga omnes proprietary rights to their holders if the relevant liability conditions are fulfilled.[484] Indeed, exclusivity is one of the pillars upon which the intellectual property system is built. This is best illustrated by taking the case of patent law, where direct infringement is found irrespective of whether the defendant knew that his behaviour amounted to the violation of a patent right.[485] However, it is also true that other formal IPRs require unlawful action by the defendant as a precondition for finding liability. This is the case in trade mark law, where infringement is subject to creating likelihood confusion by the conflicting sign or taking unfair advantage of the reputation of the registered mark.[486] To be sure, secrecy encourages some degree of exclusivity, as it confers upon its holder the right to restrict others from using the information concerned until it becomes public.[487]

The characterisation of trade secrets as intellectual property ultimately begs the question of whether there is a *numerus clausus* of IPRs, meaning that they must be statutorily recognised, as in the case of property law.[488] In this regard, it is worth noting that intellectual property attempts to strike a balance between two conflicting interests: the interest of holders in protecting their intangible goods, and the interest of the general public in accessing information.[489] From a dogmatic perspective, it has been suggested that case law can ascertain the intellectual property nature of certain legal positions ("*Rechtsposition*") even if these are not statutorily defined, as in the case of trade secrets (or know-how).[490] Yet, access to information can be hindered by the recognition of such new rights. This, in turn may run counter to the general principle that propounds the freedom to imi-

---

484 Josef Drexl 2009 (n 369) 449.

485 Lionel Bently and Brad Sherman 2014 (n 125) 610; conversely, indirect infringement requires, among others, knowledge by the defendant that the supplied items are suitable and intended for the infringement. For an overview of the requirements for finding indirect patent infringement in Germany see Peter Mes, 'Indirect Patent Infringement' [1999] IIC 531, 535; Neils Holder and Josef Schmidt, 'Indirect patent infringement – latest developments in Germany' [2006] 28 EIPR 480-484.

486 Ansgar Ohly 2014 (n 100) 3.

487 See Mark A. Lemley 2008 (n 15) 122.

488 Ansgar Ohly, 'Gibt es einen Numerus clausus der Immaterialgüterrechte?' 105 in Ansgar Ohly and others (eds), *Perspektiven des Geistiges Eigentums und Wettbewerbsrechts* (C.H. Beck 2005).

489 Ansgar Ohly 2005 (n 488) 107.

490 Ansgar Ohly 2005 (n 488) 114.

tate products in the market, unless covered by an IPR.[491] To avoid such a conflict, Ohly indicates that it is essential that in those areas with legal lacunae, courts weigh the conflicting interests against each other and, only when appropriate, accord legal protection akin to that of IPRs. He is of the opinion that such a judicial practice would allow for delineating in a more precise manner the contours of permitted and forbidden acts of imitation, rather than restricting in general the possibility of copying in the market.[492]

With respect to the consequences of expanding the scope of intellectual property rights, many have propounded that in recent decades we have witnessed a hypertrophy of IPRs.[493] Most notably, at the turn of the century, Cornish warned that "the expansion of IPRs is not an automatic good".[494] Property rights confer upon their owners broad exclusivity to realise the "economic potential" of the protected good and enforce it against third parties, without the limitations posed by unfair competition and equity rules.[495] In this context, characterising trade secrets as an IPR may amount to an expansion of intellectual property law by expanding the scope of the subject matter covered by IPRs, as in the case of the protection of databases through copyright law. Such an expansion may further lead to restricting lawful uses of confidential information.[496]

On the contrary, some commentators have purported that including trade secrets within the realm of IPRs would in practice constrain, rather than expand, the scope of protection, by attaching sound limitations to the exercise of the rights conferred, such as reverse engineering, independent discovery or whistle-blowing.[497] In this regard, Bently argues that from a taxonomic perspective, "intellectual property" has become a separate category, different to property as such. Owing to its novel status, its contours are imprecise, as are the consequences that derive from attaching such a label, which are different to those derived from traditional property rights. He thus concludes that trade secrets are intellectual property, but not property.[498]

---

491 Michael Dorner 2013 (n 305) 313-314.
492 Ansgar Ohly 2005 (n 488) 121.
493 Michael Dorner 2013 (n 305) 313-318.
494 William Cornish 2001 (n 373) 21.
495 William Cornish 2001 (n 373) 16-17.
496 Michael Dorner 2013 (n 305) 313-314, 317.
497 Lionel Bently 2013 (n 307) 92; also Mark A. Lemley 2008 (n 15) 353; Charles Tait Graves 2007 (n 337) 45.
498 Lionel Bently 2013 (n 307) 89-91.

On the basis of the foregoing analysis several conclusions can be drawn. First, applying the metaphor of property to trade secrets is a complex matter, mainly due to the broad meaning and flexible interpretations that the different jurisdictions give to the concept. Finding a universal consensus on the legal nature issue appears rather implausible.[499] It is submitted that trade secrets regimes are bound to sit on the fence between unfair competition and intellectual property law. Ohly refers to the entitlement of a trade secret "as an imperfect form of intellectual property".[500] After all, the TRIPs Agreements conceptualises undisclosed information as one of the "categories of intellectual property" that fall under their scope of protection. Thus, it seems advisable and consistent with the TSD that no legal consequences derive from the characterisation of trade secrets either as the object of an IRR or as protected under unfair competition rules.[501] In the former case, trade secrets protection should not be enhanced by those Member States that adopt a property-oriented approach, particularly in the assessment of the lawfulness of the means used to acquire, use and disclose the information concerned and the liability of third party acquirers and employees. By the same token, the existing limitations to the rights conferred by a trade secret should always be observed.[502] Otherwise, the balance of interests struck by the patent system (and also the general intellectual property legal framework) will be negatively affected to the detriment of the general interest in accessing information.[503]

## § 4 *Conclusion*

The starting point in the examination of the optimal scope of secrecy is to understand the extent to which valuable information merits protection for the mere fact of being kept secret. To this end, § 2 has underscored that both deontological and utilitarian explanations justify trade secrets legal regimes. Yet, it is submitted that utilitarian rationales provide more convincing grounds, particularly with regard to the configuration of the rights conferred. As noted by the Commission, "every IPR starts with a secret".[504]

---

499 This was best illustrated during the negotiation of the TRIPs Agreement.
500 Ansgar Ohly 2013 (n 13) 35.
501 Ansgar Ohly 2013 (n 13) 35.
502 Ansgar Ohly 2014 (n 100) 4.
503 Tanya Aplin 2015 (n 306) 435-436.
504 Commission, 'Proposal for a Directive of the European Parliament and of the Council on the protection of undisclosed know-how and business information

Drawing on the statement above, § 3 has looked into the legal nature of trade secrets following a two-tier approach. On the one hand, the relationship between trade secrets and formal IPRs has been examined with regard to patents, copyright and the database right. The results of this enquiry highlight that the former supplement the patent system in a number of ways and are crucial not only in early-stage inventions (the so-called "Laboratory Zone"), but also when innovations can be protected simultaneously by informal and formal means. Yet, the assessment of the interplay between patents (but also copyright and the database right) and trade secrets appears more problematic when they are mutually exclusive. Indeed, data shows that secrecy is the preferred option to appropriate returns on innovation, together with other informal means of protection, such as lead time advantage or product configuration. Hence, throughout chapter 1, it has been argued that resorting to secrecy for the protection of patentable subject matter may have a negative effect on the disclosure function on which the patent system (and in general the intellectual property system) is built, and may lead to a wasteful duplication of efforts, hinder the competitive process in the market and ultimately affect negatively follow-on innovation. Against this background, it has been suggested that trade secrets protection should not extend to mere abstract ideas, in line with the limitations set forth in the realm of formal IPRs.

Bearing the above in mind and following the analysis of the legal nature of trade secrets, this chapter has looked into the suitability of characterising trade secrets as pure IPRs or rather as falling into the realm of unfair competition rules and the implications that such a characterisation may have on the appropriate scope of secrecy. The better view, it is submitted, is that the legal system for the protection of trade secrets has an inherently hybrid nature. The relevant liability rules appear to be drafted as unfair competition norms, whereas their enforcement resembles that of IPRs. In this vein, it is argued that no legal consequences should derive from characterising trade secrets protection as one or the other, i.e. the scope of protection should not be enhanced if trade secrets are regarded as IPRs.

On the basis of the foregoing analysis, chapter 2 first looks into the minimum standards of protection set forth in the applicable multilateral international treaties (i.e. the TRIPs Agreement and the soft law WIPO Model Provisions) and then examines the main features of the U.S. legal regime, which has had a great influence on the development of trade secrets pro-

---

(trade secrets) against their unlawful acquisition, use and disclosure' COM (2013) 813 final, 2 (Explanatory Memorandum).

tection in most EU jurisdictions and, in particular, in the configuration of the minimum standards of protection set forth by the TSD.

# Chapter 2. Trade secrets protection in the international context

## *§ 1 International legal sources for the protection of undisclosed information*

A comprehensive and insightful understanding of the secrecy-openness dichotomy requires an in-depth analysis of the minimum standards of protection set forth at the international level. The contours of the secrecy requirement within the EU should be shaped in light of the obligations and flexibilities set forth in international treaties (§ 1) and by taking into account the legal system in place in the U.S., the jurisdiction upon which such obligations were modelled (§ 2).

Indeed, the international protection of trade secrets was only explicitly included in multilateral conventions in 1994 with the adoption of the TRIPs Agreement.[505] Before then, academics had extensively discussed whether Article 10bis PC was applicable to trade secrets protection.

The following sections map out the international legal framework set forth by Article 10bis PC together with Article 39 TRIPs.[506] To that end, section A looks into the legal system for the protection of undisclosed information established in Article 39 TRIPs. In particular, this section provides a critical analysis of (i) the general framework created by TRIPs; (ii) the negotiation history of the relevant provisions dealing with trade secrets; (iii) the general obligation to protect undisclosed information established in Article 39(1) TRIPs; and (iv) the scope and requirements for protection laid down in Article 39(2). Then, section B examines the WIPO Model Provisions on unfair competition and their implications for trade secrets protection.[507]

505 Daniel Gervais, *The TRIPs Agreement* (4th edn, Sweet&Maxwell 2012) 541.

506 For a general overview of the international IPRs convention system, see Annette Kur and Thomas Dreier, *European Intellectual Property Law* (Edward Elgar 2013) 10-31.

507 The study of Article 39(3) TRIPs has been deliberately left outside the scope of the present research, because providing a comprehensive and rigorous analysis of the legal issues that it poses falls outside the limits of this study.

## A) International minimum standards of protection: The TRIPs Agreement and the protection of undisclosed information

### I. General framework

Some regard the TRIPs Agreement as the "most innovative" of the WTO agreements.[508] It was negotiated to address the deficiencies of the Convention system in force at the time.[509] In essence, it intended to overcome (i) the fragmented coverage of IPRs; (ii) the lack of effective enforcement mechanisms and dispute settlement systems and (iii) the problems posed by the limited membership.[510]

Against this background, developed countries pushed to enhance the standards of IPRs protection enshrined within the system of the General Agreement of Trade and Tariffs of 1947.[511] Initially, this was addressed during the Uruguay Round of Multilateral Trade Negotiations, which ultimately led to the adoption in 1994 of the "Agreement Establishing the World Trade Organisation", whereby the WTO was set up.[512] The TRIPs Agreement was included as ANNEX C and is therefore an integral part of the WTO Agreement adopted in Marrakech on 15 April 1994.[513]

The inclusion of TRIPs within the WTO legal framework entails a number of advantages. First, due to its "single undertaking nature", all WTO

508 Peter Van den Bossche and Werner Zdouc, *The Law and Policy of The World Trade Organization* (3rd edn, CUP 2013) 952; in the same vein Daniel Gervais 2012 (n 505) para 1.12 notes that the TRIPs Agreement "together with the 1967 Stockholm Conference that adopted the revise Berne and Paris Convention and Created the World Intellectual Property Organization (WIPO), is undoubtedly the most significant milestone in the development of intellectual property in the twentieth century".

509 The issues posed by the international conventions before TRIPs is explained in greater detail by Paul Katzenberger and Annette Kur, 'TRIPs and Intellectual Property' 10-16 in Friedrich-Karl Beier and Gerhard Schricker (eds), *IIC Studies, Studies in Industrial Property and Copyright Law, From GATT to TRIPs – The Agreement on Trade-Related Aspects of Intellectual Property Rights* (Weinheim 1996).

510 Peter Van den Bossche and Werner Zdouc, *The Law and Policy of The World Trade Organization* (3rd edn, CUP 2013) 953.

511 General Agreement on Tariffs and Trade (adopted 30 October 1947) 55 UNTS 194 (GATT Agreement); Articles XX (d), IX, XII:3(c)(iii) and XVIII:10 of the GATT Agreement made explicit reference to IPRs.

512 Marrakesh Agreement Establishing the World Trade Organization (adopted 15 April 1994) 1867 UNTS 154 (WTO Agreement).

513 For a more detailed analysis of the background that led to the adoption of the TRIPs Agreement see Annette Kur and Thomas Dreier 2013 (n 506) 21-25.

members are bound to implement into their domestic legal orders the minimum standards of protection[514] for all of the categories of IPRs set forth in TRIPs, including trade secrets or "undisclosed information".[515] Ultimately, this has resulted in a substantial "approximation of extra-territorial treatment of immaterial property"[516] across the 164 Members of the WTO.[517] Likewise, one of the most significant achievements of TRIPs is that it brings IPRs-related disputes between states under the WTO's Dispute Settlement Understanding ("DSU"), thus providing an effective international enforcement mechanism.[518] Despite its limitations and the rise of bilateralism,[519] it is undisputed that TRIPs has achieved a minimum level of harmonisation of intellectual property protection at the international level.

The following section maps out the negotiation history of Article 39 TRIPs, upon which the international legal framework for the protection of trade secrets is built.

---

514 See Article 1(1) TRIPs: "Members may, but shall not be obliged to implement in their law more extensive protection than is required by this Agreement, provided that such protection does not contravene the provisions of this Agreement".

515 Marco Bronckers, 'The Impact of TRIPs: Intellectual Property Protection in Developing Countries' [1994] 31 Common Market LR 1245, 1249 while discussing the "single package nature" of the WTO notes that "the Uruguay Round negotiations towards a single package have been criticised for weakening the resistance of developing countries to proposals like the TRIPs agreement that may be inimical to their interests", as trade concessions were conditioned upon stronger IP protection.

516 Josef Straus, 'Implications of the TRIPs Agreement in the Field of Patent Law' 160, 163 in Friedrich-Karl Beier and Gerhard Schricker (eds), *IIC Studies, Studies in Industrial Property and Copyright Law, From GATT to TRIPs – The Agreement on Trade-Related Aspects of Intellectual Property Rights* (Weinheim 1996).

517 According to the WTO's website <http://www.wto.org/english/thewto_e/whatis_e/tif_e/org6_e.htm> accessed 15 September 2018.

518 See Article 64(1) TRIPs; for a more in-depth analysis on the interplay between TRIPs and the WTO's DSU see Karen D. Lee and Silke von Lewinski, 'The Settlement of International Disputes in the field of Intellectual Property' 278-328 in Friedrich-Karl Beier and Gerhard Schricker (eds), *IIC Studies, Studies in Industrial Property and Copyright Law, From GATT to TRIPs – The Agreement on Trade-Related Aspects of Intellectual Property Rights* (Weinheim 1996); see also Daniel Gervais 2012 (n 505) paras 2.704-2.716.

519 For a discussion on this topic see Graeme B. Dinwoodie, 'The International intellectual property law system: new actors, new institutions, new sources' [2006] 10 Marquette IPLR 206, 214.

## II. Negotiation history of Article 39 TRIPs[520]

During the initial discussions of the Uruguay Round in 1986, intellectual property did not occupy a prominent position in the negotiation agenda, and it only acquired a notorious role in the last few years prior to the adoption of TRIPs.[521] As some sources note, IPRs were included in the Punta del Este Declaration[522] due to the efforts of a group of U.S. industry leaders who sought to establish an international system for the protection of IPRs that mirrored the United States' intellectual property legislation.[523]

Against this background, Sandeen distinguishes three stages in the negotiation process of Article 39 TRIPs. During the early phase (1987–1988) the U.S., the EC and the representatives of different industry groups issued several proposals addressing the potential scope of trade secrets protection.[524] Most notably, the U.S. advocated for treating trade secrets as IPRs.[525] During the "Mid-Term Phase" (1989–1990), the discussions about whether trade secrets were a form of IPRs and hence should be included under the shelter created by TRIPs and how comprehensive their regulation should be, were the prime focus of the negotiations.[526] The Indian government strongly objected to affording proprietary protection to trade secrets and insisted that protection should be premised on Article 10bis PC. It further noted that it would be preferable to regulate trade secrets protection through contract and under civil laws.[527] In 1990, fourteen other developing countries endorsed India's position and expressed their opposition to negotiating further on trade secrets, as they should not be considered as

520 For a comprehensive analysis of the negotiation of Article 39 TRIPs see UNCTAD-ICTSD, *Resource Book on TRIPS and Development* (CUP 2005) 520-526.

521 Marco Bronckers, 'The Impact of TRIPs: Intellectual Property Protection in Developing Countries' [1994] 31 Common Market LR 1245, 1245.

522 WTO/GATT Ministerial Declaration on the Uruguay Round (Declaration of 20 September 1986).

523 Sharon K. Sandeen, 'The limits of trade secret law: Article 39 of the TRIPs Agreement and the Uniform Trade Secrets Act on which it is based' 537, 539 in Rochelle C. Dreyfuss and Katherine J. Strandburg (eds), *The Law and Theory of Trade Secrecy: A Handbook of Contemporary Research* (Edward Elgar 2011).

524 This section follows the approach adopted by Sharon K. Sandeen 2011 (n 523) 542.

525 UNCTAD-ICTSD, *Resource Book on TRIPS and Development* (CUP 2005) 523.

526 Sharon K. Sandeen 2011 (n 523) 542.

527 See GATT Doc. MTN.GNG/NG11/W/37, paras 46-47.

IPRs.[528] As a result, the standards of protection of trade secrets were mostly negotiated by developed countries.[529]

During the final stage, the so-called "Drafting Phase" (1990–1991), each of the delegations of the EC,[530] the U.S.[531] and Switzerland[532] submitted a draft agreement on trade-related aspects of IPRs. These were used as the basis for "The Anell (or Chairman's) Draft".[533] The wording of the latter agreement shows that in July of 1990 divergences persisted regarding substantive standards for trade secrets protection, as a number of items appeared bracketed. First, there was a difference of opinion regarding whether actual commercial value was required or if potential value would suffice. Furthermore, the parties to the negotiation failed to agree on a single term to designate the subject matter of protection, and several terms were used interchangeably. The U.S. leaned towards the term "trade secrets"; while Switzerland suggested "proprietary information" and the EC proposed "undisclosed information", the latter of which eventually prevailed over the other proposals.[534] Finally, a non-exclusive list of acts that were deemed contrary to honest commercial practices was included in the main body of the text. There was also a lack of consensus on whether liability should extend to third parties who "had reasonable grounds to know" that the information had been acquired unlawfully.[535]

After a number of discussions, the Group of Negotiation on Goods submitted another draft agreement on IPRs (the so-called "Brussels Draft") included in the Draft Final Act Embodying the Results of the Uruguay Round of Multilateral Trade Negotiations.[536] In essence, it contained three

528 See GATT Doc. MTN.GNG/NG11/16.

529 According to Nuno Pires de Carvalho, *The TRIPS Regime of Antitrust and Undisclosed Information* (Kluwer Law International 2008) paras 39.2.26-39.2.27 the unwillingness of developing countries to participate in the discussions on trade secrets resulted in the adoption of Article 39(2) TRIPs with a wording that does not reflect the actual interests of developing countries. He refers to it as a "strategic mistake" during the negotiation process.

530 See GATT Doc. MTN.GNG/NG11/W/68.

531 See GATT Doc. MTN.GNG/NG11/W/70.

532 See GATT Doc. MTN.GNG/NG11/W/73.

533 See GATT Doc. MTN.GNG/NG11/W/76.

534 On the terminology issue, Nuno Pires de Carvalho 2008 (n 529) para 39.2.22 highlights that the EC's proposed term 'undisclosed information' was crucial to the negotiations because many parties opposed to include 'trade secrets' within the text of the agreement, as they believed that it would directly imply the recognition of proprietary or exclusive rights.

535 Sharon K. Sandeen 2011 (n 523) 550-551.

536 See GATT Doc. MTN.TNC/W/35/Rev. 1.

minor changes to the Anell Draft.[537] First, any reference to actual or potential commercial value of the protected information was deleted. Most notably, the examples of dishonest commercial practices were listed in a footnote, as proposed by the U.S. Likewise, only one of the provisions regarding government use, the one that referred to test data submitted to governments, was included in the Brussels Draft.

In the months that followed the adoption of the Brussels Draft, agricultural provisions were the main focus of the negotiations.[538] Hence, discussions concerning IPRs were pushed into the background until December 1991, when a new and simplified version of the agreement was included in the second Draft Final Act Embodying the Results of the Uruguay Round of Multilateral Trade Negotiations, generally known as the "Dunkel Draft".[539] This preliminary version was presented on a "take-it-or-leave-it basis"[540] and served as the basis for the TRIPs Agreement.

With regard to trade secrets, the outcome of the above negotiation process led to the adoption of Article 39, which governs the protection of undisclosed information in the international legal system created by TRIPs. It consists of three paragraphs and a footnote:

> Article 39
> 1. In the course of ensuring effective protection against unfair competition as provided in Article 10bis of the Paris Convention (1967), Members shall protect undisclosed information in accordance with paragraph 2 and data submitted to governments or governmental agencies in accordance with paragraph 3.
> 2. Natural and legal persons shall have the possibility of preventing information lawfully within their control from being disclosed to, acquired by, or used by others without their consent in a manner contrary to honest commercial practices (10) so long as such information:
> (a) is secret in the sense that it is not, as a body or in the precise configuration and assembly of its components, generally known among or readily accessible to persons within the circles that normally deal with the kind of information in question;
> (b) has commercial value because it is secret; and
> (c) has been subject to reasonable steps under the circumstances, by the person lawfully in control of the information, to keep it secret.

537 Sharon K. Sandeen 2011 (n 523) 551.
538 Daniel Gervais 2012 (n 505) para 1.25.
539 See GATT Doc. MTN.TNC/W/FA.
540 Daniel Gervais 2012 (n 505) paras 1.27-1.28.

3. Members, when requiring, as a condition of approving the marketing of pharmaceutical or of agricultural chemical products which utilize new chemical entities, the submission of undisclosed test or other data, the origination of which involves a considerable effort, shall protect such data against unfair commercial use. In addition, Members shall protect such data against disclosure, except where necessary to protect the public or unless steps are taken to ensure that the data are protected against unfair commercial use.
Footnote 10
For the purpose of this provision, "a manner contrary to honest commercial practices" shall mean at least practices such as breach of contract, breach of confidence and inducement to breach, and includes the acquisition of undisclosed information by third parties who knew, or were grossly negligent in failing to know, that such practices were involved in the acquisition.

As is apparent from the above, the first section links the protection of undisclosed information and test data submitted to governments to the general obligation of ensuring protection against unfair competition established in Article 10bis PC. Paragraph 2 focuses on the right of individuals and undertakings to prevent the acquisition, disclosure and use of secret information in a manner contrary to honest commercial practices. More specifically, footnote 10 provides a list of non-exclusive types of conduct that are regarded as unfair commercial practices. Paragraph 3 creates an obligation for Member States to protect undisclosed data submitted to governmental agencies in order to obtain marketing approval for pharmaceutical or agricultural chemical products. Each of these sections are analysed in turn, with the exception of Article 39(3) TRIPs. The legal and public policy implications of the obligations laid down in this provision are so far-reaching that providing a comprehensive analysis of them falls outside the scope of the present research.

## III. The architecture of the general obligation to protect undisclosed information: Article 39(1)TRIPs

### 1. Hybrid nature of the protection

Article 39(1) TRIPs serves two purposes: it declares that Member States are bound to protect undisclosed information by means of unfair competition pursuant to Article 10bis PC and it provides the general framework for the interpretation of paragraphs 2 and 3.[541]

However, it is not the only provision in TRIPs that refers to the PC. By virtue of Article 2(1) TRIPs, WTO Member States are compelled to comply with the minimum standards of protection set forth in Articles 1 through 12 and Article 19 PC.[542] Thus, the specific reference in Article 39 TRIPs to Article 10 PC reinforces the hybrid legal nature of trade secrets and anchors their protection in unfair competition rules.

To provide greater legal certainty, the following section investigates the meaning of Article 10bis PC in the context of TRIPs.

### 2. Construing Article 10bis PC in the context of undisclosed information

Following the line of argument explained above, the international protection of unfair competition is premised on Article 10bis PC, which has been the object of several revisions since it was first included in the PC.[543] The wording of the provision now in force is as follows:

Article 10*bis*

(1) The countries of the Union are bound to assure to nationals of such countries effective protection against unfair competition.
(2) Any act of competition contrary to honest practices in industrial or commercial matters constitutes an act of unfair competition.
(3) The following in particular shall be prohibited:

541 Markus Peter and Andreas Wiebe 2013 (n 304) Art. 39 Rdn 10-11.

542 Article 2(1) TRIPs: "In respect of Parts II, III and IV of this Agreement, Members shall comply with Articles 1 through 12, and Article 19, of the Paris Convention (1967)"; see further Josef Drexl, 'Nach "GATT und WIPO": Das TRIPs-Abkommen und seine Anwendung in der Europäischen Gemeinschaft' [1994] 43 GRUR Int 777, 787; Gintare Surblyte 2011 (n 182) 26.

543 For an exhaustive analysis of the legislative evolution see Stephen P. Ladas, *Patents; Trademarks, and Related Rights – National and International Protection* (HUP 1975) 1684; Christopher Wadlow, *The Law of Passing-off* (4th edn, Swett&Maxwell 2011) 65 - 93; also Marcus Höpperger and Martin Senftleben, 'Protection Against Unfair Competition at the International Level – The Paris Convention, the 1996 Model Provisions and the Current Work of the World Intellectual Property Organisation' 61, 62-63 in Retro Hilty and Frauke Henning-Bodewig (eds), *Law Against Unfair Competition* (Springer 2007).

(i) all acts of such a nature as to create confusion by any means whatever with the establishment, the goods, or the industrial or commercial activities, of a competitor;
(ii) false allegations in the course of trade of such a nature as to discredit the establishment, the goods, or the industrial or commercial activities, of a competitor;
(iii) indications or allegations the use of which in the course of trade is liable to mislead the public as to the nature, the manufacturing process, the characteristics, the suitability for their purpose, or the quantity, of the goods.

Paragraph (1) contains a "general clause" that mandates contracting parties to protect nationals of (other) Union Member States against acts of unfair competition.[544] Crucially, paragraph (2) defines what constitutes an act of unfair competition.[545] This definition is completed in paragraph (3) with a list of three specific instances that are regarded as unfair and thus prohibited at the national level.[546] The first example refers to the creation of confusion in the market, while the second alludes to acts aimed at the disparagement of a competitor. Both of them fall under the category of traditional consumer protection. On the other hand, the third instance refers to misleading practices and, as such, intends to protect the interests of both competitors and consumers.[547] Notably, no reference to trade secrets or undisclosed information is made.

Since the Hague Conference in 1925, there has been much debate about whether the general clause set forth in paragraph (1), together with the definition provided in paragraph (2) has an overarching normative effect

544 In order to comply with this requirement, Member States are not obliged to enact special legislation; see further Georg H. C. Bodenhausen, *Guide to the application of the Paris Convention* (BIRPI 1967) 143.

545 For an exhaustive analysis of the actual meaning of "act of competition contrary to honest practices" in Article 10bis PC see Frauke Henning-Bodewig and Heijo E. Ruijsenaars, *Protection against Unfair competition* (WIPO 1994) 28-134; Christopher Wadlow 2011 (n 543) 2-014 - 2-031

546 In this regard, Georg H. C Bodenhausen 1977 (n 544) 143 notes that the wording of paragraphs (ii) and (iii) of Article 10bis PC is phrased in such a manner that these provisions should be considered as "self-executing" in the jurisdictions where such possibility is envisaged.

547 Frauke Henning-Bodewig and Heijo E. Ruijsenaars 1994 (n 545) 18, noting that the last example spelt out in Article 10bis(3) was only added to the body of the Treaty in 1958 during the Revision Conference in Lisbon.

on the specific examples listed in Article 10bis(3).[548] Today, most commentators agree that protection against unfair competition extends beyond the scope of the three examples listed in Article 10bis. Bodenhausen resorts to the Washington Act[549] to conclude that these examples "constitute only a minimum".[550] Similarly, the WIPO study on the "Protection against unfair competition" takes the same view and submits that these instances are not to be construed as being exhaustive, but rather as minimum standards to be afforded by Union Member states.[551] In addition, the study provides a list with a number of "acts not expressly mentioned in Article 10bis" that are frequently regarded by courts as unfair practices and accordingly are more often regulated by statues. Crucially for the purposes of the present research, these include (i) the violation of trade secrets, but also (ii) comparative advertisement; (iii) taking undue advantage of another's achievements "free riding"; and (iv) other acts of unfair competition.[552]

In contrast, Cornish highlights that the obligation set forth in Article 10bis PC has generally been interpreted as referring to making false and misleading statements. He notes that it is not generally understood to include actions against the appropriation of ideas marketed in a competitor's product. In particular, he adds that trade secrets and the slavish imitation of products do not fall within its scope.[553]

548 The third example of Article 10bis (paragraph 3) was only included to the text at the Lisbon Conference in 1958.

549 Washington Act (adopted 2 June 1911, entered into force 1 May 1913) TRT PARIS 006.

550 Georg H. C. Bodenhausen 1977 (n 544) 145.

551 Frauke Henning-Bodewig and Heijo E. Ruijsenaars 1994 (n 545) 18.

552 Frauke Henning-Bodewig and Heijo E. Ruijsenaars 1994 (n 545) 48-68.

553 William Cornish, 'The International Relations of Intellectual Property' 52 Cambridge LJ 46, 61; Gerald Reger, *Der internationale Schutz gegen unlauteren Wettbewerb und das TRIPS-Übereinkommen* (Carl Heymanns Verlag 1999) 122; in the same vein Christopher Wadlow, 'Regulatory data protection under TRIPs Article 39(3) and Article 10bis of the Paris Convention: Is there a doctor in the house?' [2008 ] IPQ 355, 368 noting that "Art. 10*bis*, despite the superficial breadth of its language, in fact confines itself to requiring protection against a range of misrepresentation-based acts of unfair competition corresponding to those enumerated in para 3 (i)-(iii). I entirely agree, and with the corollary that doctrines of unfair competition based on supposed acts of misappropriation alone are altogether outside the scope of Art. 10*bis*, because there was never sufficient international consensus as to what was fair and what was unfair in this context".

In the light of the foregoing, it is submitted that Article 39 expands the scope of Article 10bis PC to the protection of trade secrets, which is therefore lex specialis to the latter provision.[554]

What seems more problematic is clarifying the meaning of *"any act of competition contrary to honest practices"*, which lies at the core of Article 10bis(2) PC.

The starting point should be to construe the term "competition" in each jurisdiction according to the specific parameters usually applied therein.[555] The PC is an international treaty, and as such it should be interpreted in an autonomous manner.[556] Consequently, official and private acts fall clearly outside the scope of application of Article 10bis PC.[557] Yet, the open wording of the provision leaves a certain margin of discretion to the Member States so that for instance, in some jurisdictions a direct competitive relationship between the parties is not necessarily required.[558]

Second, the Convention introduces an element of *fairness* when referring to honest practices.[559] Following the general rule of interpretation in the VCLT, treaties are to be interpreted "in good faith in accordance with the ordinary meaning to be given to the terms of the treaty in their context and in the light of its object and purpose".[560] Consequently, as is apparent from paragraph 3, the scope of Article 10bis is limited to honest practices in the context of industrial or commercial matters, which may be different to the standards applied in other areas, such as liberal professions.[561] These may also vary from country to country or may evolve with time.[562] As Ladas indicates:

---

554 Gintare Surblyte 2011 (n 182) 27; Markus Peter and Andreas Wiebe 2013 (n 304) Art. 39 Rdn 10.

555 Georg H. C. Bodenhausen 1977 (n 544) 144.

556 Frauke Henning-Bodewig, 'International Unfair Competition Law' 53, 57 in Reto Hilty and Frauke Henning-Bodewig (eds), *Law Against Unfair Competition* (Springer 2007).

557 Frauke Henning-Bodewig, 'Internationale Standards gegen unlauteren Wettbewerb' [2013] GRUR Int 1, 5.

558 Frauke Henning-Bodewig and Heijo E. Ruijsenaars 1994 (n 545) 23; Georg H. C. Bodenhausen 1977 (n 544) 144.

559 Christopher Wadlow 2011 (n 543) para 2-025.

560 See Article 31 VCLT.

561 Christopher Wadlow 2011 (n 543) para 2-025; notwithstanding this, Marcus Höpperger and Martin Senftleben 2011 (n 543) 64 critically note that the establishment of the relevant behavior pattern will strongly depend on how the circle is defined.

562 Frauke Henning-Bodewig and Heijo E. Ruijsenaars 1994 (n 545) 23.

> morality, which is the source of the law of unfair competition, is a simple notion in theory only. In fact it reflects customs and habits anchored in the spirit of a particular community. There is no clear objective standard of feelings, instincts, or attitudes toward a certain conduct. Therefore, specific prescriptions involving uniform evaluation of certain aspects are extremely difficult.[563]

Bearing this in mind, Bodenhausen highlights that when establishing the meaning of "honest practices in industrial or commercial matters" courts will also have to consider "honest practices established in international trade".[564] Thus, it is submitted that the *splendidly imprecise*[565] expression of "any act of competition contrary to honest commercial or industrial practices" can be narrowed down through objective criteria.[566]

As a whole, Article 10bis PC set a general and flexible minimum standard of protection against acts of unfair competition and defined three conducts that should always be deemed unlawful across all members of the Union. Modern unfair competition is premised on (i) the protection of competitors (the original purpose), (ii) the protection of consumers and more recently (iii) the safeguarding of competition in the interest of the public at large.[567] The open nature of Article 10bis has enabled it to adapt to evolving trends in unfair competition and encompass all of the interests referred to above under its normative framework. Most importantly, it provides the basis upon which the assessment of when the acquisition, use and disclosure of trade secrets is unlawful, as per Article 39(2) TRIPs examined in section IV.

---

563 Stephen P. Ladas 1975 (n 543) 1685.

564 Georg H. C. Bodenhausen 1977 (n 544) 144.

565 In the words of William Cornish, 'The International Relations of Intellectual Property' [1993] 52 Cambridge LJ 42, 61.

566 Frauke Henning-Bodewig, 'Internationale Standards gegen Unlauteren Wettwerb' [2013] GRUR Int 1, 7; along these lines, Jacob notes referring to the TMD in Case C-2/00 *Hölterhoff v Freiesleben* [2002] ECR I-4187 that: "The precise delimitation of 'honest practices' is of course not given in the Trade Marks Directive. By its very nature, such a concept must allow of certain flexibility. Its detailed contours may vary from time to time and according to the circumstances, and will be determined in part by various rules of law which may themselves change, as well as by changing perceptions of what is acceptable, however, there is a large and clear shared core concept of what constitute honest conduct in trade, which may be applied by the courts without great difficulty and without any excessive danger of diverging interpretations".

567 Frauke Henning-Bodewig and Heijo E. Ruijsenaars 1994 (n 545) 24-25.

## IV. Article 39(2) TRIPs

### 1. Scope of the obligation

Article 39(2) TRIPs defines the scope of the obligations outlined in section III. In essence, it compels Member States to ensure that the person lawfully in control of undisclosed information is entitled to prevent its unauthorised disclosure, acquisition or use in a manner contrary to honest commercial practices by a third party. This shows that trade secrecy law is not concerned with the subject matter of secrecy, but instead focuses on the manner in which trade secrets are acquired, used or disclosed.[568] What is actually protected is the selective disclosure of information under specific circumstances.[569] Hence, the acquisition of information based on someone's own effort, such as reverse engineering or independent discovery, should be deemed lawful.[570]

In order to comply with the obligation laid down in paragraph 2, Member States are not required to enact specific legislation dealing with trade secrets protection, in line with Article 1(1) TRIPs.[571] As long as trade secret holders have the possibility of preventing unlawful acquisition, use or disclosure, WTO Member States are not in breach of the TRIPs obligations.[572] This is particularly relevant in common law jurisdictions that have no specific legislation on the subject. In these cases, effective protection is usually achieved through the development of "a body of case law" that clarifies the means of redress available in the event of trade secret misappropriation. If such body does not exist, it may seem advisable for Member States to take legislative measures.[573]

---

568 Nuno Pires de Carvalho, *The TRIPs Regime of Patent Rights* (3rd ed, Kluwer Law International 2010) para 39.1.49.

569 Daniel Gervais 2012 (n 505) para 2.486.

570 Nuno Pires de Carvalho 2010 (n568) para 39.1.49.

571 Article 1 TRIPs: "1. Members shall give effect to the provisions of this Agreement. Members may, but shall not be obliged to, implement in their law more extensive protection than is required by this Agreement, provided that such protection does not contravene the provisions of this Agreement. Members shall be free to determine the appropriate method of implementing the provisions of this Agreement within their own legal system and practice".

572 Nuno Pires de Carvalho 2010 (n 568) para 39.94; Markus Peter and Andreas Wiebe 2013 (n 304) Art. 39 Rdn13.

573 Tanya Aplin and others 2012 (n 22) para 22-07; Nuno Pires de Carvalho 2010 (n 568) para 39.94

In addition, the wording of Article 39 specifically accords protection to both natural and legal persons. To avoid any explicit reference to "property" or "ownership" of the information, Article 39(2) resorts to the notion of "control".[574] The use of this term is closely connected with the requirement to take reasonable steps to keep the information secret, as spelt out in littera (c) of Article 39(2) TRIPs. The person who takes measures to keep the information undisclosed is regarded as the possessor of the information in question and thus, as the trade secret holder, irrespective of the nature of his legal title in the secret. Hence, if the creator of the secret data decides to share them with a second party for their mutual benefit, in the event of misappropriation both parties are regarded as holders, such as in the licensor-licensee relationship. Therefore, both may seek legal redress against a third party who obtains the information improperly.[575]

Protection is subject to the condition that the holder lawfully acquires the trade secret. If the information is obtained in an improper or illegal manner, the person in control of the information will not be able to enforce it against third parties. For instance, if an employee bound by a confidentiality agreement discloses secret information to a competitor because of bribery, the competitor is not considered to be in control of the information for the purposes of Article 39(2) TRIPs. The unlawful holder is consequently unable to prevent any third party from acquiring, using or disclosing the information.[576] Ultimately, the unlawfulness of the conduct shall be determined according to national law.[577]

The rights relating to trade secrets include the rights to (i) prevent their disclosure, (ii) acquisition and (iii) use by third parties.[578] The inclusion of *use* as a relevant conduct that may trigger liability is particularly relevant, as it does not require the trade secret holder to provide evidence that the information was acquired without consent from a specific source, which in practice is not always feasible. The mere unlawful use of secret information is deemed enforceable.[579] The exercise of these rights is subject to two cumulative conditions: (i) the actions previously listed must be carried out without the holder's consent and (ii) in a "manner contrary to honest com-

574 Tanya Aplin and others 2012 (n 22) para 22.10.

575 Tanya Aplin and others 2012 (n 22) 22.10.

576 Tanya Aplin and others 2012 (n 22) para 22.11.

577 Markus Peter and Andreas Wiebe 2007 (n 304) Art. 39 Rdn 15.

578 Daniel Gervais 2012 (n 505) para 2.486 notes that "the inclusion of 'use' is helpful as it does not require a positive identification of the source of information, which may not always be easy to determine".

579 Daniel Gervais 2012 (n 505) para 2.487.

mercial practices". Thereby, Article 39(2) introduces an element of fairness, which should be interpreted in the light of the normative framework created by the PC. In this regard, and as noted above,[580] there is no single interpretation of honest commercial practices; it is a flexible test in which all relevant interests can be weighed against each other. Such an assessment depends upon the values that govern each society at a particular moment in time.[581] Nevertheless, its open-ended nature unavoidably entails a degree of legal uncertainty.[582]

Crucially, footnote 10 attempts to shed light on the meaning of this phrase in the context of trade secret misappropriation. However, as no standard definition seems suitable, the provision provides two examples of practices that should always be deemed unlawful and that constitute the minimum standards of protection: breach of contract (or inducement to do so) and breach of confidence.[583] This reference seems problematic insofar as it does not limit the admissibility and content of confidentiality clauses.[584] In the footnote, it is further explained that acquisition by third parties who knew or were grossly negligent in failing to know that breach of contract or breach of confidence had occurred should be deemed contrary to honest commercial practices. This clarifies that any other conduct carried out by third parties such as industrial espionage, theft or bribery also fall under the scope of TRIPs. Hence, gross negligence triggers the same legal response as actual knowledge.[585]

In light of this, the main criterion to assess whether an obligation of secrecy exists is the knowledge (or the obligation to know) that the information was acquired, used and disclosed in confidence.[586] However, the final draft, unlike previous proposals, does not afford protection in the event of accidental disclosure.[587]

580 See chapter 2 § 1 A) III. 2.
581 Carlos Correa 2007 (n 306) 371.
582 Ansgar Ohly 2013 (n 13) 41.
583 Daniel Gervais 2012 (n 505) para. 2.487. These are just examples, the protection of trade secrets goes further.
584 Hanns Ullrich, 'Techchnologieschutz nach TRIPS: Prinzipien und Probleme' [1995] GRUR Int 623, 630, footnote 36.
585 Rudolf Kraßer, 'The Protection of Trade Secrets in the TRIPs Agreement' 216, 224 in Friedrich-Karl Beier and Gerhard Schricker (eds), *IIC Studies, Studies in Industrial Property and Copyright Law, From GATT to TRIPs – The Agreement on Trade-Related Aspects of Intellectual Property Rights* (Weinheim 1996).
586 Nuno Pires de Carvalho 2008 (n 529) para 39.2.46.
587 Gerald Reger 1999 (n 553) 275.

Likewise, it is also noteworthy that TRIPs does not afford protection against the lawful acquisition of third parties who are not in a contractual relationship with the holder of the information. This would be the case, for instance, if the information were acquired through reverse engineering.[588] Crucially, TRIPs provisions regulating undisclosed information do not specifically refer to the exceptions and limitations to the rights conferred by a trade secret.[589] These are thus inherent to its definition: trade secrets are only enforceable against unlawful conduct.

## 2. Requirements for protection

Article 39(2) also lays down the three requirements that information has to meet to be "protectable". Namely, it (i) has to be secret, (ii) have commercial value due to its secret nature and (iii) have been subject to reasonable steps to keep it secret under the circumstances. As a general remark, it should be noted that these were tailored following the conditions for liability described in section 1(4) Uniform Trade Secrets Act ("UTSA"), although minor amendments were introduced.[590]

Each of these elements is analysed in turn.

### a) Information

TRIPs defines trade secrets as information.[591] As explained above,[592] the expression "undisclosed information" was adopted over the more common terms "trade secret" or "proprietary information" because it seemed a neutral concept and thus avoided a link to a particular legal system or existing intellectual property standards.[593] However, TRIPs also refers to trade se-

588 Rudolf Kraßer 1996 (n 585) 223.

589 Unlike three-step test enshrined for copyright (Article 13 TRIPs), patents (Article 30 TRIPs), industrial designs (Article26(2) TRIPs) and more generally trade marks (Article 17 TRIPs); for an overview of the exceptions and limitations subject to the three-step-test see Henning Grosse Ruse-Kahn, 'The Protection of Intellectual Property in International Law' (OUP 2016) para 12.43.

590 Uniform Trade Secrets Act (Am. Law Inst. 1979) (UTSA); see chapter 2 § 2 B) I.

591 Nuno Pires de Carvalho 2008 (n 529) para 39.2.36.

592 See chapter 1 § 3 B) I. 1.

593 Daniel Gervais 2012 (n 505) para 2.486; Gerald Reger 1999 (n 553) 256.

crets as "manufacturing and business secrets" in Article 34(3) and as "confidential information" in Article 43(1).

Bearing in mind the difficulties of finding one suitable definition of the concept of "information" outlined in chapter 1,[594] such a term should be construed vis-à-vis trade secrets in the widest possible manner to include any kind of "knowledge obtained from investigation, study, or instruction",[595] but not abstract ideas. In contrast to patentable subject matter, it covers both technical and commercial information such as formulas, test data, customer lists and negative knowledge.[596] Unlike Article 1711 (2) NAFTA, TRIPs does not require WTO Member States to protect information embodied or fixated in a given instrument.[597]

Yet, to be protected, information must be related to trade, interpreted in a broad sense.[598] Such a limitation derives from the commercial value requirement mentioned in subparagraph (b) of Article 39(2) TRIPs. Therefore, private information falls outside the scope of protection of the agreement.[599] Against this background, Carvalho suggests that the key element is the possibility of "economic competition of any sort" and puts forth the example of non-profit universities who compete for subsidies.[600] Consequently, protection could extend beyond those cases where there is a direct competitive relationship between the parties.

---

594 See chapter 1 § 3 B) II. 1.

595 See The Merriam-Webster Dictionary definition of 'information, n' (*Merriam-Webster Dictionary Online*) <https://www.merriam-webster.com/dictionary/information> accessed 15 September 2018; in the same vein, Pamela Samuelson 1988 (n 341) 368 footnote 19 notes that "Information is not an easy term to define with precision. Yet, at least some tentative definition of the term is necessary to address such questions as whether information is the same as or different from data, knowledge or rumour".

596 Markus Peter and Andreas Wiebe 2013 (n 304) Art. 39 Rdn 7; but see more generally chapter 1 § 3 B) II.

597 North American Free Trade Agreement (United States-Canada-Mexico) (adopted 17 December 1992, entered into force 1 January 1994) ILM 289 (NAFTA); Article 1711 (2) NAFTA: "A Party may require that to qualify for protection a trade secret must be evidenced in documents, electronic or magnetic means, optical discs, microfilms, films or other similar instruments".

598 Nuno Pires de Carvalho 2008 (n 529) para 39.2.32; Gerald Reger 1999 (n 553) 256-257.

599 Markus Peter and Andreas Wiebe 2013 (n 304) Art. 39 Rdn 7; Gerald Reger 1999 (n 553) 256.

600 Nuno Pires de Carvalho 2008 (n 529) para 39.2.32.

### b) Secrecy: Information not generally known or readily accessible

The secrecy requirement in Article 39 is defined in subparagraph (a) as a relative standard.[601] This means that to be protected, information must not be known solely by the holder of the information (which amounts to absolute secrecy). Hence, a secret will not lose its confidential nature if it is imparted to employees or if it is disclosed in the context of a licensing agreement.[602] According to TRIPs, trade secrets remain undisclosed so long as they are not "generally known among or readily accessible to persons within circles that normally deal with the kind of information in question".[603] Some authors compare this reference to the knowledge of the person having ordinary skills in the art in patent law.[604]

The secret nature of information is lost somewhere between absolute secrecy and general knowledge. However, TRIPs does not provide an absolute test to assess whether a certain piece of information should be considered part of the public domain. The practical implementation of the criterion spelt out in subparagraph (a) is left to Member States to regulate.[605] Hitherto, no case law stemming from the WTO Dispute Settlement Bodies has interpreted the meaning of this provision.

---

601 Nuno Pires de Carvalho 2008 (n 529) para 39.2.48; for a more detailed analysis of the relative nature of secrecy see François Dessemontet, 'Protection of Trade Secrets and Confidential information' 271, 283 in Carlos Correa and Abdulqawi A. Yusuf (eds), *Intellectual Property and International Trade* (2nd edn, Wolters Kluwer 2008).

602 Nuno Pires de Carvalho 2008 (n 529) para 39.2.52; Markus Peter and Andreas Wiebe 2013 (n 304) Art. 39 Rdn 19; Gerald Reger 1999 (n 553) 261.

603 This expression is very similar to the wording used both in the Restatement (First) of Torts and in the UTSA, which state that the information must be "readily ascertained by proper means". Indeed, the definition of secrecy included in Article 39(2) of TRIPs was also largely influenced by the definition of Article 1 Sec. 7(2) of the Commission Regulation (EEC) No 556/89 of 30 November 1988 on the application of Article 85 (3) of the Treaty to certain categories of know-how licensing agreements [1989] OJ L061, where it was noted that: "The term "secret" means that the know-how package as a body or in the precise configuration and assembly of its components is not generally known or easily accessible, so that part of its value consists in the lead-time the licensee gains when it is communicated with him; it is not limited to the narrow sense that each individual component of the know-how should be totally unknown or unobtainable outside the licensor's business".

604 Daniel Gervais 2012 (n 505) para 2.486.

605 Gerald Reger 1999 (n 553) 260.

Finally, Article 39(2)(a) clarifies that information can be protected even if it is known as a whole ("body") but the precise configuration and assembly of its components remains unknown. This is to be understood as meaning that even if some of the elements of a particular secret are in the public domain, the information considered as a whole may still remain secret. That may be the case, for instance, of a customer list where some of the names and contact data embodied therein are known to competitors. The list considered as a unit could still be protected as a trade secret.[606] This is also the main argument used to justify the application of the trade secrets legal regime to test data protection or big data scenarios.

c) Commercial value

Undisclosed information only falls under the scope of protection of Article 39(2) TRIPs if it has (i) commercial value due to its (ii) secret nature.[607] This means that there must be a causal link between the secret nature of the information and its value (i.e. the information must provide a competitive advantage to its holder).[608] The commercial value must not derive solely from the secrecy of the information.[609] Nonetheless, its secret nature must have an impact on the competitive advantage it confers. If the disclosure, use or acquisition of the information does not affect its value, Article 39(2) TRIPs is not applicable.[610] However, it is possible that information maintains some value after disclosure. The relevant yardstick is the fact that the information that is kept undisclosed confers a competitive advan-

606 Gerald Reger 1999 (n 553) 262; Markus Peter and Andreas Wiebe 2013 (n 304) Art. 39 Rdn 19.

607 According to Gerald Reger 1999 (n 553) 262 this requirement is similar to the "Geheimhaltungsinteresse" under German law.

608 Markus Peter and Andreas Wiebe 2013 (n 304) Art. 39 Rdn 22; Daniel Gervais 2012 (n 505) para 2.487; Nuno Pires de Carvalho 2008 (n 529) para 39.2.58 highlights that "commercial value" means "competitive value".

609 Markus Peter and Andreas Wiebe 2013 (n 304) Art. 39 Rdn 22.

610 Nuno Pires de Carvalho 2008 (n 529) para 39.2.60; in the words of François Dessemontet 2008 (n 601) 280: "The Commercial value requirement is but a threshold, below which no protection may be granted".

tage to the trade secret holder.[611] Similarly, secret information without commercial value does not fall under the scope of this provision.[612]

At first glance, the term "commercial" may indicate that the minimum standards of protection are only applicable with respect to information that relates to "the activity of buying and selling, especially on a larger scale".[613] However, most commentators and WTO Member States have construed the term "commercial" beyond trading activities, in line with the second broadest acceptation laid down in the Oxford English Dictionary: "making or intended to make a profit".[614] Consequently, the relevant yardstick is that the unauthorised disclosure of the information hinders the competitive position of the person lawfully controlling the information.[615] Hence, it is submitted that the results of research and development activities carried out by non-profit organisations, such as universities, should fall under the subject matter protected by Article 39(2) TRIPs.

There has been a longstanding debate on whether the value of information should be actual or potential, which has also recently been discussed with regard to the TSD. During the negotiation of the TRIPs Agreement, the U.S proposed the inclusion of an explicit reference to both concepts, even though the final text is silent on this point.[616] Correa believes that information must have actual value, while Carvalho holds the opposite view.[617] The latter convincingly argues that potential value should also be protected because the only difference is that potential value is unlocked af-

611 Markus Peter and Andreas Wiebe 2013 (n 304) Art. 39 Rdn 22; Nuno Sousa e Silva, 'What exactly is a trade secret under the proposed Directive?' [2014 ] 9 JIPLP 923, 930.

612 Markus Peter and Andreas Wiebe 2013 (n 304) Art. 39 Rdn 22.

613 Definition of 'commerce, n' (*OED Online*, OUP June 2013) <https://en.oxforddictionaries.com/definition/commerce> accessed 15 September 2018.

614 According to the definition of 'commercial, adj' (*OED Online*, OUP June 2013) <https://en.oxforddictionaries.com/definition/commercial> accessed 15 September 2018.

615 NunoPires de Carvalho, *The Trips Regime of Patents and Test Data* (4th edn, Wolters Kluwer Law 2014) 535; similar views were expressed by the EU legislator in Recital 14 TSD: "Such know-how or information should be considered to have a commercial value, for example, where its unlawful acquisition, use or disclosure is likely to harm the interests of the person lawfully controlling it, in that it undermines that person's scientific and technical potential, business or financial interests-, strategic positions or ability to compete" and by the U.S. legislature in the Restatement (Third) of Unfair Competition §39 (Am. Law Inst. 1995) Reporters' Note 449.

616 See Article 13 GATT Doc. MTN.GNG./NG11/W/70.

617 Carlos Correa 2007 (n 306) 373.

ter the fulfilment of conditions that are not verified.[618] However, denying protection to information with potential value would exclude information generated in the context of research and development. In turn, this would undermine the complementary relationship between trade secrets and the patent system, as every company should have a space in which to develop its innovations without the interference of competitors or third parties.[619] In this context, it is submitted that it suffices if the trade secret confers "an advantage that is more than trivial".[620]

#### d) Reasonable steps to maintain secrecy

The only formality spelt out in TRIPs vis-à-vis the protection of undisclosed information is that "it is subject to reasonable steps under the circumstances to keep it secret".[621] Such a condition stems from the UTSA, and its suitability has been the object of a long standing debate.[622] Essentially, its inclusion in the body of the law of trade secrecy has been justified on two grounds. First, the adoption of precautionary measures reveals that the holder of the information has an interest in keeping it undisclosed. It provides notice of confidentiality in a manner similar to the notice of registration in other IPRs, such as trade marks.[623] Similarly, it has been argued that it provides evidence of the existence and value of a secret that deserves protection.[624]

As a final remark, undisclosed information does not have to be fixated to be protected under TRIPs nor does it have to be identifiable. Criticism has been raised regarding the absence of the latter criterion, as it does not

---

618 Nuno Pires de Carvalho 2008 (n 529) para 39.2.56.

619 See chapter 1 § 2 B) IV.

620 Nuno Pires de Carvalho 2008 (n 529) para 39.2.57; similarly, Tanya Aplin and others 2012 (n 22) para 22.14 argue that "The information must have some objective commercial value which is more than trivial".

621 Nuno Pires de Carvalho 2008 (n 529) para 39.2.62

622 Robert G. Bone 2011 (n 15) 46.

623 François Dessemontet 2008 (n 601) 284.

624 Mark A. Lemley, 'The surprising virtues of treating trade secrets as IP rights' 109, 136 in Rochelle C. Dreyfuss and Katherine J. Strandburg (eds), *The Law and Theory of Trade Secrecy: A Handbook of Contemporary Research* (Edward Elgar 2011); *Rockwell Graphic Systems, Inc. v. DEV Industries, Inc.*, 925 F.2d 174 (7th Cir. 1991).

seem possible to enforce the obligation of confidence, the object of which has not been clearly identified in judicial proceedings.[625]

### B) Considerations from a soft law perspective: The WIPO Model Provisions on the protection of unfair competition

In 1996, the WIPO Model Provisions on the protection of unfair competition ("WMP") were issued following the publication of an international WIPO-commissioned study on the same topic.[626] The intention was to provide standard provisions to be used in drafting or improving the unfair competition legislations of different Member States based on Article 10bis PC.[627] In fact, the notes accompanying the body of the text highlight that the WMP's objective is to implement the obligations established in Article 10bis PC.[628]

As regards the content, Article 1 establishes a general prohibition of unfair commercial practices, similar to Article 10(2)bis PC. This general clause is supplemented with five additional provisions that spell out acts or practices that should be regarded as unlawful. The WMP expressly refer to causing confusion with respect to another's enterprise or its activities (Article 2); damaging another's goodwill or reputation (Article 3); misleading the public (Article 4); discrediting another's enterprise or activities (Article 5); and unfair competition with respect to secret information (Article 6).

Before discussing Article 6 on secret information, some remarks should be made regarding the legal nature of the WMP. This instrument is not a binding international treaty for all Member States that ratify it. In fact, it has not been formally ratified by any member of the WTO.[629] Similarly, it is not to be regarded as a body of soft law principles as such,[630] even though it aims at achieving similar objectives i.e. to serve as a model for

625 Daniel Gervais 2012 (n 505) para 2.486.

626 Frauke Henning-Bodewig and Heijo E. Ruijsenaars 1994 (n 545).

627 Charles Gielen,'WIPO and Unfair Competition' [1997] 19 EIPR 78, 78; a critical view is provided by William Cornish 'Genevan Bootstraps' [1997] 19 EIPR 336-338.

628 Frauke Henning-Bodewig and Heijo E. Ruijsenaars 1994 (n 545) 6, note 1.01.

629 Marcus Höpperger and Martin Senftleben 2011 (n 543) 73.

630 For an overview of the legal nature of soft law principles see Hartmut Hillgenberg, 'A Fresh Look at Soft Law' [1999] 10 EJIL 499-515.

lawmakers and courts.[631] The WMP were adopted to guide the implementation of international obligations in the field of unfair competition.[632]

Regarding substantive law, Article 6 WMP seems to nest the protection of undisclosed information in unfair competition provisions, even more clearly than Article 39(2) TRIPs. In fact, the former has a similar structure to Article 39 TRIPs. Paragraph (1) sets forth a general obligation to protect secret information in commercial and industrial activities against disclosure, acquisition or use without the consent of the holder in a manner contrary to honest commercial practices. In contrast to TRIPs, "the person lawfully in control of the information" is referred to as the "rightful holder". Next, paragraph 2 provides a list of acts that should be deemed contrary to honest commercial practices, similar to footnote 10 of the TRIPs Agreement, but with an additional example, namely, industrial or commercial espionage. Paragraph (3) defines secret information in the same terms as Article 39(2) TRIPs, that is, information must be secret, have commercial value due to its secret nature and be subject to reasonable steps under the circumstances to keep it secret. Finally, paragraph 4 proposes a regulation of test data submitted for marketing approval.[633] One of the main differences with Article 39(3) TRIPs is that it is aimed at entrepreneurs who use information provided by authorities. Unlike TRIPs, paragraph 4 WMP it is not addressed to the authorities that should ensure the relevant protection.[634]

Looking back and from a legislative perspective, it seems that the impact of the WMP on the regulation of trade secrets protection has been rather limited, having most certainly been outshined by the minimum standards set forth in the TRIPs Agreement.

## *§ 2 Trade secrets protection in the U.S.*

As discussed in § 1, the international legal regime for the protection of trade secrets has been greatly influenced by the U.S. legal regime. A com-

---

631 Marcus Höpperger and Martin Senftleben 2011 (n 543) 73; as Frauke Henning-Bodewig, *International Handbook on Unfair Competition* (C.H. Beck 2013) 29 highlights: "It should be unambiguously pointed out that the Model Provisions are neither binding law nor soft law, but merely a model for law-making activities without any legal commitment".

632 Marcus Höpperger and Martin Senftleben 2011 (n 543) 73.

633 Similar to Article 39(3) TRIPs.

634 Charles Gielen,'WIPO and Unfair Competition' [1997] 19 EIPR 78, 81.

prehensive analysis of the law of trade secrets in most EU Member States and, in particular, the way in which the secrecy requirement has been construed is not possible without a deeper understanding of its regulation in this jurisdiction.

The protection of intangible assets through trade secrets has garnered more scholarly attention in the U.S. than in any EU Member State, both from a legal and an economic perspective.[635] Indeed, trade secret litigation in the U.S. has increased exponentially since the 1950s,[636] unlike in any EU Member States, where the evidence shows that trade secret holders are still reluctant to take up legal proceedings in the event of misappropriation out of fear of disclosing secret information during litigation.[637]

The remainder of the chapter investigates the legal system for the protection of trade secrets in the U.S., in order to examine the way in which secrecy has been construed therein. Section A starts by outlining the evolution of trade secrets protection and its underlying justifications along with the most relevant legal sources. Next, section B focuses on the definition of trade secrets and the legal requirements for their protection, and particularly, the secrecy requirement. Thereafter, section C discusses the legal regime for the protection of trade secrets created by the UTSA, together with the Restatement (First) of Torts, the Restatement (Third) of Unfair Competition and the recently adopted Defend Trade Secrets Act of 2016. Finally, some conclusions are drawn.

## A) Evolution of trade secret law in the U.S.: main legislative sources

As opposed to other IPRs, the law of trade secrecy was only developed in the U.S. in the XIX century with the rise of industrial capitalism.[638] While

---

635 For a general account of trade secret law in the United States see: Roger M. Milgrim 2014 (n 160); James Pooley 2002 (n 66); Vincent Chiappetta 1999 (n 24); Charles Tait Graves 2007 (n 337) 39; Chris Montville, 'Reforming the Law of Proprietary Information' [2007] 56 Duke LJ 1159; Christopher Rebel J. Pace, 'The Case for a Federal Trade Secrets Act' [1995] 8 Harvard Journal of Law & Technology 427, 435-442; Michael Risch 2007 (n 15).

636 David S. Almeling and others, 'A Statistical Analysis of Trade Secret Litigation in Federal Courts' [2009-2010] 45 Gonzaga LR 291, 301.

637 Baker McKenzie 2013 (n 469) 129.

638 Robert G. Bone 1998 (n 15) 251.

patent and copyright protection were premised on the U.S. Constitution[639] and regulated mostly in federal statutes, trade secrets protection was built upon common law principles and has only recently been codified into law. Until the adoption of the DTSA in May 2016, trade secrets protection in the U.S. was mostly state law.[640] It is generally agreed that only in 1868 did the Supreme Court of Massachusetts provide for the first time a complete view of trade secrets protection in *Peabody v. Norfolk.*[641]

In the development of the law of trade secrecy in the U.S., it is possible to differentiate five phases.[642] In the early days (1860 –1920) trade secrets were regarded as a form of property. During this period, the secrecy precautions requirement was developed by the courts with two purposes. On the one hand, it gave notice of confidentiality to employees and other third parties. On the other hand, the adoption of such measures was interpreted by some courts as a form of possession, necessary to assert property rights in common law.[643]

During the second phase (1920–1940), the courts relied less on the property theory, whilst unfair competition became the dominant approach to justify trade secrets protection. Accordingly, case law placed special emphasis on the unfairness of the defendant's conduct, i.e. the unlawfulness

639 Famously, U.S. Const. art. I, § 8, cl.8 empowers Congress "To promote the Progress of Science and useful Arts, by securing for limited Times to Authors and Inventors the exclusive Right to their respective Writings and Discoveries".

640 Michael Risch 2007 (n 15) 6; notwithstanding, prior to the adoption of the DTSA there were two federal sources of trade secret protection, namely (i) the criminal provisions of the Economic Espionage Act Pub. L. No. 104-294, 110 Stat. 3488 (1996) (codified as amended at 18 U.S.C.§§ 1831 et seq. (2016) (EEA)), and (ii) the prohibition to disclose trade secrets by federal employees codified in 18 U.S.C. § 1905 (2012).

641 *Peabody v. Norfolk*, 98 Mass. 452, 458 (1868): "If (a person) invents or discovers, and keeps secret, a process of manufacture, whether a proper subject for a patent or not, he has not indeed an exclusive right to it as against the public, or against those who in good faith acquire knowledge of it; but he has a property in it, which a court of chancery will protect against one who in violation of contract and breach of confidence undertakes to apply it to his own use, or to disclose it to third persons".

642 Robert G. Bone 2011 (n 15) 49-58; for a more a general account of the evolution of trade secret protection in the U.S. see Catherine Fisk, 'Working Knowledge: Trade Secrets, Restrictive Covenants in Employment, and the Rise of Intellectual Property' [2001] 52 Hastings LJ 441 and Sharon K. Sandeen, 'The Evolution of Trade Secret Law and why courts commit error when they do not follow the Uniform Trade Secrets Act' [2010] 33 Hamline LR 493.

643 Robert G. Bone 2011 (n 15) 49-50.

of the acquisition, use or disclosure, rather than the existence of ownership rights.[644] As a result of the increasing importance of unfair competition as a means to protect trade secrets, the American Law Institute included trade secrets protection in the Restatement (First) of Torts published in 1939.[645] Of its 971 sections, only two deal with the protection of trade secrets: while § 757 provides the necessary liability requirements, § 758 limits the liability of third parties that acquire undisclosed information without notice of its secret nature.[646] Notably, the Restatements are not to be regarded as a source of primary law.[647] Their main purpose is to provide an account of the common law principles developed in the U.S. as a result of judicial decisions and case law derived from the application of statutes enacted and in force.[648]

During the third period (1940–1979), the so-called "Dominance of the Unfair Competition Theory" courts relied mostly on the unlawful nature of the defendant's conduct following the stipulations of the Restatement (First) of Torts.[649] Notwithstanding this, some decisions still referred to the notion of property.[650]

The adoption of the UTSA in 1979 was a real turning point in the harmonisation of trade secrets protection in the U.S. and marked the begin-

644 Robert G. Bone 2011 (n 15) 52 -54.

645 Restatement (First) of Torts § 757 (Am. Law Inst. 1939).

646 Remarkably the Restatement (First) of Torts § 759 (Am. Law Inst. 1939) establishes liability for the acquisition of business information that does not qualify for trade secrets protection.

647 Robert Denicola, 'The Restatements, the Uniform Act and the status of American trade secret law' 18, 19 in Rochelle C. Dreyfuss and Katherine J. Strandburg (eds), *The Law and Theory of Trade Secrecy: A Handbook of Contemporary Research* (Edward Elgar 2011).

648 Restatement (First) of Torts § 757 (Am. Law Inst. 1939); for a critical analysis of the Restatements and the role of the American Law Institute see Kristen David Adams, 'Blaming the Mirror: The Restatements and the Common Law' [2007] 40 Indiana LR 205-270 and Sharon K. Sandeen 2010 (n 642) 539, who notes that "The purpose of the Restatement was (and is) not to codify the law, but rather to clarify and simplify the law by providing an easy-accessible and clear statement of what the members of the ALI thought was the majority of the states on various points of law".

649 Robert G. Bone 2011 (n 15) 55.

650 See for instance, *National Starch Products, Inc. v. Polymer Industries, Inc.*, 273 App. Div. 732, 735 (1948).

ning of the fourth phase.[651] It was approved by the National Conference of Commissioners on Uniform State Laws following a recommendation from the American Bar Association with the aim of (i) addressing the uneven development of the law among states and (ii) clarifying the remedies and the standards provided for in common law.[652] Its main purpose was to achieve uniformity and to codify the common law rules on trade secrets protection.[653] Ultimately, it sought to establish a unitary definition of the notions of trade secret and misappropriation as well as a statute of limitations.[654] It has been suggested that its publication was partially triggered by the fact that the Restatement (Second) of Torts included no provisions on trade secrets protection, unlike the first version of 1939.[655]

Regarding its legal nature, similar to the Restatements, the UTSA has "no law-making authority".[656] Its main goal is to serve as a model to be followed by states when regulating trade secrets protection.[657] It is not merely intended to "restate existing law, but to make and codify the law".[658] Thus far, the UTSA has been implemented by 47 states, the District of Columbia, Puerto Rico and the Virgin Islands. In addition, the states of New York and Massachusetts have introduced bills to implement it.[659]

In 1995, the American Law Institute issued the Restatement (Third) of Unfair Competition, which regulated, among others, deceptive marketing,

---

651 A second version of the UTSA was approved in 1985 with some amendments as regards the injunctions, damages and the effect of legislation provisions; James Pooley 2002 (n 66) § 2.03 [7] highlights that the existence of two versions and the nuances in the implementation at a state level are a hurdle in the achievement of uniformity.

652 See UTSA Preparatory Note (1979) 1; see also James Pooley 2002 (n 66)§ 2.03 [1]; Robert Denicola 2011 (n 647) 20-21.

653 James Pooley 2002 (n 66) § 2.03 [1].

654 James Pooley 2002 (n 66) § 2.03 [1] 2-13 critically suggests that as a result "one might argue that the state of trade secret law is today more conflicting and uncertain than it was in 1979".

655 See UTSA Preparatory Note (1979) 1.

656 Robert Denicola 2011 (n 647) 20-21; contrary, Sharon K. Sandeen 2010 (n 642) 540 notes that "whereas the Restatement series is secondary authority of what the law is, the UTSA is primary authority".

657 William E. Hilton, 'What sort of improper conduct constitutes misappropriation of a trade secret' [1990] 30 IDEA 287, 290.

658 Sharon K. Sandeen 2010 (n 642) 540.

659 According to the National Conference of Commissioners and Uniform State Laws <http://www.uniformlaws.org/Act.aspx?title=trade%20Secrets%20Act> accessed 15 September 2018.

trade mark law, the right of publicity and trade secrets protection.[660] The inclusion of the latter after the promulgation and success of the UTSA may appear superfluous.[661] As noted by the reporters, "the rules in this Restatement are applicable both to common law actions and actions under the Uniform Trade Secrets Act or analogous civil legislation".[662] Hence, the provisions in the Restatement (Third) have been applied to construe the provision of the UTSA and at the same time overcome the deficiencies of the Restatement (First) of Torts 1939.[663]

The extent to which the UTSA displaced the application of the common law principles embedded in case law and § 757 and § 758 of the Restatement (First) of Torts has been widely discussed. Indeed, the evidence shows that in most cases both federal and state courts apply the UTSA's principles.[664] They refer to the UTSA alone, but also to case law decided as a result of its application. Notwithstanding this, sometimes courts also cite the UTSA together with case law where the UTSA is not mentioned. Finally, some courts also refer to cases where the UTSA is not hinted at whatsoever. In this context, regarding the definition, it is noteworthy that according to a study conducted by Risch, 75,36% of the surveyed state cases refer primarily to the one provided in the UTSA, while in federal courts this percentage rises to 81,03% of the cases cited.[665]

In line with the codification process described above, in 1996 the U.S. Congress passed the Economic Espionage Act ("EEA") with the aim of enhancing criminal protection against the unlawful appropriation of information.[666] In the early 1990s, there was growing concern about the importance of intangible assets for U.S. companies and their increasing vulnera-

660 Restatement (Third) of Unfair Competition (Am. Law Inst. 1995).

661 Robert Denicola 2011 (n 656) 21.

662 See Reporters' Note of the Restatement (Third) of Unfair Competition §39 (Am. Law Inst. 1995).

663 James Pooley 2002 (n 66) § 2.04 [1] 2-32 and Robert Denicola 2011 (n 656) 22.

664 Michael Risch, 'An Empirical Look at Trade Secret Law's Shift from Common to Statutory Law' (2013) Working Paper No. 2012-2008, 11-12 <http://ssrn.com/abstract=1982209> accessed 15 September 2018; in the article the author conducts an empirical study with the purpose of assessing the influence of common law principles after the enactment of the UTSA. The cases selected for the study are the same ones as the ones used by David S. Almeling and others 2009-2010 (n 636) 291.

665 Michael Risch 2013 (n 664) 11-12.

666 Economic Espionage Act, Pub. L. No. 104-294, 110 Stat. 3488 (1996) (codified as amended at 18 U.S.C. §§ 1831 et seq. (2016)).

bility to (international) industrial espionage.[667] Crucially, the EEA set forth a federal criminal action for trade secrets misappropriation with a focus on international espionage.[668] Yet, owing to its criminal law nature, its study falls outside the scope of the present research.

As a whole, due to the prevalence of state law and the overlap of legislative sources, it was not accurate to refer to *a single* law of trade secrets in the U.S. Indeed, there were multiple laws that resulted from the courts' applications of different theories and interpretations of the scope of protection conferred by trade secrets law.[669] In view of this, and after a five-year negotiation process,[670] in 2015 the U.S. Senate Committee reported to Congress the proposal to amend the EEA, the so-called DTSA with the aim of providing federal jurisdiction for private civil actions derived from trade secret misappropriation. On April 27, 2016, Congress passed the bill, which became Public Law No. 114-153 on May 11, 2016, thereby creating a civil federal action for trade secret misappropriation. Notably, pursuant to 18 U.S.C. § 1836 (b)(1), the competence of Congress to legislate on trade secrets protection at the federal level stems from the so-called "Commerce Clause" embedded in the U.S. Constitution,[671] and not in the "Progress of Science and Useful Arts Clause", which served as the legislative basis to regulate patent and copyright protection at the federal level.[672] As a result, it is only possible to bring a civil federal claim for trade secret misappropriation when the secret in question relates to a product or service used in or intended for use in interstate or foreign commerce.[673]

The following section explores the different concepts of trade secrets and the legal requirements embodied in the Restatements, the UTSA and the DTSA.

---

667 See H.R. No 3723, 4023-4024 (1996).

668 For a general account of the EEA see Rochelle C. Dreyfuss, 'Trade Secrets: How Well Should We Be Allowed to Hide them? The Economic Espionage Act of 1996' [1998] 9 Fordham IP Media & Entertainment LJ 1-44.

669 Robert Denicola 2011 (n 656) 20-21.

670 John Cannan, 'A [Mostly] Legislative History of the Defend Trade Secrets Act of 2016' [2017-2019] 109 Law Library Journal 363, 372.

671 U.S. Const. art. I, § 8, cl. 3.

672 U.S. Const. art. I, § 8, cl.8.

673 See Sharon K. Sandeen and Christopher B. Seaman,'Toward a Federal Jurisprudence of Trade Secret Law' [2017] 32 Berkeley Technology LJ 829, 888 comparing the Commerce Clause Provision in the DTSA with the one in the Lanham Act and concluding that "the DTSA's jurisdiction appears narrower because (unlike the Lanham Act) there must be actual or intended use of the secret 'related to a product or service' in 'interstate or foreign commerce.'"

## B) Definition of a trade secret and requirements for protection in the U.S.

### I. Definitional aspects

In the U.S., there is no uniform definition of a trade secret. Instead, it is regarded that virtually any useful information[674] is eligible for protection, as opposed to the subject matter protected under copyright and patent laws.[675] The difficulty of establishing a suitable definition is because trade secret regulation was originally developed on the basis of common law and consequently resulted from a factual assessment conducted on a case by-case basis.[676] Notwithstanding this, courts most often refer to the following three definitions:

The first is embedded in comment b of § 757 of the Restatement (First) of Torts (1939) and stipulates:

> A trade secret may consist of a formula, pattern, device or compilation of information which is used in one's business, and which gives him an opportunity to obtain an advantage over competitors who do not know or use it.

This definition has been extensively quoted in case law and is still often referred to by courts despite the fact that the Restatement (Second) of Torts (1979) omits any reference to trade secrets protection.[677] It has often been regarded as the bedrock of modern trade secret law.[678] In addition to providing a definition, comment b in the Restatement (First) of Torts spells

---

674 The four definitions analysed under this section provide that trade secrets' subject matter is information. The considerations outlined in chapter 2 § 1 A) IV. 2. a) are therefore also applicable to the U.S. jurisdiction.

675 James Pooley 2002 (n 66) § 1.01; similarly, Roger M. Milgrim 2014 (n 160) § 1.01 1-4 notes that "the definition of trade secret is thus unlimited as to any particular class or kind of matter and may be contrasted with matter eligible for patent or copyright protection, which must fall into statutorily defined categories"; in this regard the Iowa Supreme Court concluded that "there is virtually no category of information that cannot, as long as the information is protected from disclosure to the public, constitute a trade secret". *U.S. West Communications, Inc. v. Office of Consumer Advocate*, 498 N.W.2d 711, 714 (Iowa 1993).

676 James Pooley 2002 (n 66) § 1.01 1-3.

677 James Pooley 2002 (n 66) § 1.01 1-3; this definition is applied in old decisions, but also in more recent judgements; see for instance *Vacco Indus., Inc. v. Van Den Berg*, 5 Cal. App. 4th 34, 49-50 (Cal. Ct. App. 1992).

678 James Pooley 2002 (n 66) § 2.02[1] 2.

out a list of non-exclusive factors to be considered in establishing the existence of a trade secret. The relevant text reads as follows:[679]

> An exact definition of a trade secret is not possible. Some factors to be considered in determining whether given information is one's secret are:
> (1) the extent to which information is known outside the of his business;
> (2) the extent to which it is known by and other involved in his business ;
> (3) the extent of measures taken by him to guard the secrecy of the information;
> (4) the value of the information to him and his competitors;
> (5) the amount of effort or money expended by him in developing the information;
> (6) the ease or difficulty with which the information could be properly acquired or duplicated.

The second definition that is most commonly quoted by courts was included in § 1(4) UTSA and, unlike the previous definition, enumerates three specific and binding requirements:

> Information, including a formula, pattern, compilation, program, device, method, technique, or process, that:
> (i) derives independent economic value, actual or potential, from not being generally known to, and not being readily ascertainable by proper means by, other persons who can obtain economic value from its disclosure or use, and
> (ii) is subject to efforts that are reasonable under the circumstances to maintain its secrecy.

The third definition is in the Restatement (Third) of Unfair Competition § 39 (1995):

> A trade secret is any information that can be used in the operation of a business or other enterprises and that is sufficiently valuable and secret to afford actual or potential economic advantage over others.

679 Restatement (First) of Torts § 757 Comment b (Am. Law Inst. 1939).

Table 2 shows a comparison of the Restatement First factors and the UTSA requirements for the protection of trade secrets:[680]

| TABLE 2: THE RESTATEMENT FIRST FACTORS AND THE UTSA | |
|---|---|
| **Restatement First Factors** | **UTSA Requirements** |
| 1. The extent to which the information is known outside the claimant's business | Not generally known (UTSA § 1(4)(i)) |
| 2. The extent to which it is known by employees and others involved in the business. | Not generally known and subject to reasonable efforts to maintain secrecy (UTSA § 1 (4)(ii)) |
| 3. The extent of measures taken by the claimant to guard the secrecy of the information. | Subject to reasonable efforts to maintain secrecy (UTSA § 1 (4)(ii)) |
| 4. The value of the information to the business and its competitors | Derives independent economic value from not being generally known or readily ascertainable (UTSA § 1(4)(i)) |
| 5. The amount of effort and or money expended by the business in developing the information. | |
| 6. The ease or difficulty with which the information could be properly acquired or duplicated by others. | Readily ascertainable by proper means (UTSA § 1(4)(i)) |

As is apparent from Table 2, the most important difference between the Restatement (First) of Torts and the UTSA is that the latter does not require the trade secret holder to invest money or effort in the creation of the information. This is in line with the Supreme Court's viewpoint in the *Feist* decision, where the "sweat of the brow doctrine" was explicitly rejected in the context of copyright.[681] Accordingly, pursuant to the UTSA, information created with little effort can be protected under trade secrets law

680 Table 2 is a reproduction of the one included in Sharon K. Sandeen 2010 (n 642) 522.

681 See *Feist Publ'ns, Inc. v. Rural Tel. Serv. Co.* 499 U.S. 340, 349-350 (1999): "It may seem unfair that much of the fruit of the compiler's labor may be used by others without compensation. (…) As applied to a factual compilation, assuming the

in the same manner as information that is developed over the course of a long time and with substantial investment.[682]

Likewise, as opposed to the definition of a trade secret set forth in comment b § 757 of the Restatement (First) of Torts, the UTSA deleted any reference to the use of the trade secret by its holder. Initially, such a requirement was introduced following the same rationale that governs the "use in commerce" requirement in trade mark law, and it was drafted with the purpose of avoiding the information's owner preventing its use in commerce in the event that he did not use it.[683] However, in the UTSA, a different approach was adopted, as it was deemed that undisclosed information that is not used commercially may still have independent commercial value.[684] This would be true in the case of a market leader who develops a trade secret manufacturing process and, with time, develops a better one. Even if the first one is no longer applied by the company, he may still want to keep it undisclosed to avoid its use by competitors.[685] In addition, the UTSA stated most clearly that there must be causality between the secret nature of the information and its commercial value and that the holder should adopt measures to protect it. Hence, the adoption of measures was codified as a requirement for protection under the UTSA, not just as a factor signalling the existence of valuable information worth protecting. Similarly, the comments on the UTSA further clarified that protection is also to be afforded to negative knowledge; that is, information resulting from experiments that do not work and hence cannot be used in practice, but which may nevertheless be of great value for competitors, as it would allow them to avoid costly and lengthy experiments.[686]

---

absence of original written expression, only the compiler's selection and arrangement may be protected; the raw facts may be copied at will. This result is neither unfair nor unfortunate. It is the means by which copyright advances the progress of science and art".

682 Sharon K. Sandeen 2010 (n 642) 522, 523.

683 Michael Risch 2007 (n 15) 48.

684 Restatement (First) of Torts § 757 Comment b (Am. Law Inst. 1939): "The definition of 'trade secret' contains a reasonable departure from the Restatement of Torts (First) definition which required that a trade secret be "continuously used in one's business". The broader definition in the proposed Act extends protection to a plaintiff who has not yet had an opportunity or acquired the means to put a trade secret to use".

685 Michael Risch 2007 (n 15) 48.

686 See UTSA Comments to § 1: "The definition includes information that has commercial value from a negative viewpoint, for example the results of lengthy and

The UTSA also overcame some definitional issues posed by the Reporter's comment to the Restatement (First) of Torts. According to comment b, business information about singular events was regarded as ephemeral and hence did not fall under the scope of trade secrets protection. This referred to the salary of employees, the date for launching a product or the amount of a secret bid for a contract, to name some.[687] Such a limitation does not appear in the UTSA and seems better suited for protecting information resulting from research activities.[688]

In the light of these considerations, it is important to note that the definition of a trade secret is inconsistently applied in case law. This leads to striking consequences particularly in the field of departing employees with respect to the information that they are allowed to use after the termination of their employment.[689] Under similar circumstances, courts will allow some employees to use certain information, while they will prevent others from using it based on the cause of action invoked, the state where the case is litigated or the judge that hears the case.[690] For instance, the same NDA regulating the use of a trade secret after the termination of an employment relationship may be considered enforceable by some courts even if the alleged trade secret is part of the public domain, whereas others

---

expensive research which proves that a certain process will not work could be of great value to a competitor".

687 Restatement (First) of Torts § 757 Comment b (Am. Law Inst. 1939): "It differs from other secret information in a business (see § 759) in that it is not simply information as to single and ephemeral events in the conduct of the business, as, for example, the amount or other terms of a secret bid for a contract or the salary of certain employees, or the security investments made or contemplated, or the date fixed for the announcement of a new policy or for bringing out a new model or the like".

688 James Pooley 2002 (n 66) § 4.05[1] 4-45, 4-46.

689 Charles Tait Graves, 'Trade Secrecy and Common Law Confidentiality: The Problem of Multiple Regimes' 77, 79-80 in Rochelle C. Dreyfuss and Katherine J. Strandburg (eds), *The Law and Theory of Trade Secrecy: A Handbook of Contemporary Research* (Edward Elgar 2011).

690 Charles Tait Graves 2011 (n 689) 79-80.

consider that the object of protection has ceased to exist,[691] thereby forfeiting trade secrets protection.[692]

Having the above in mind, the Federal legislator in the recently adopted DTSA seemingly leans towards a definition of trade secret that is practically identical to the one laid down in the EEA, with some minor variations:

> (3) the term "trade secret" means all forms and types of financial, business, scientific, technical, economic, or engineering information, including patterns, plans, compilations, program devices, formulas, designs, prototypes, methods, techniques, processes, procedures, programs, or codes, whether tangible or intangible, and whether or how stored, compiled, or memorialized physically, electronically, graphically, photographically, or in writing if—
>
> > (A) the owner thereof has taken reasonable measures to keep such information secret; and
> >
> > (B) the information derives independent economic value, actual or potential, from not being generally known to, and not being readily ascertainable through proper means by, another person who can obtain economic value from the disclosure or use of the information;[693]

The main difference between the definition enshrined in the UTSA and the one above is that the latter defines the type of information eligible for protection (i.e. financial, business, scientific, technical, economic or engineering information) and provides additional examples of the subject matter covered. It refers to tangible and intangible "plans, designs, prototypes, procedures and programs or codes". In addition, it clarifies that the information may be stored or compiled, not only in a physical support, but also electronically, photographically, graphically or in writing. Information need not be fixated at all to merit protection. A side-by-side comparison of

---

691 According to Charles Tait Graves 2011 (n 689) 89 footnote 23 citing *Allen v. Creative Serv., Inc.*, 1992 WL 813643 2 (R.I. 1992) (unpublished), where the court noted that "while every business interest is not worthy of protection through a restrictive covenant, a business interest worthy of such protection need not rise to the level of a trade secret".

692 According to Charles Tait Graves 2011 (n 689) 89 footnote 23 citing *International Settlement Design, Inc. v. Hickez*, 1995 WL 864463, 5 (Penn. Ct., 1995), (unpublished) where the court noted that "since we have already concluded that the information here does not rise to the level of a 'trade secret' as defined in the Pennsilvania law, it cannot be contractually protected".

693 18 U.S.C. § 1839 (3).

both definitions reveals that the DTSA spells out categories of protectable information instead of resorting to the broader term of "information" like the UTSA does, which may limit the subject matter of actions brought under the former. This will ultimately depend on the interpretation carried out by federal courts.[694] As a final note, the DTSA clarifies that private information falls outside the scope of federal criminal and civil actions.

Despite the divergence in how the notion of a trade secret is construed, three common requirements for protection appear in the UTSA and the DTSA and are most frequently invoked by courts.[695] These coincide with those set out in Article 39(2) TRIPs and refer to fact that the information (i) is not generally known or readily ascertainable, (ii) has economic value due to its secrecy and (iii) is subject to reasonable measures to keep it secret. Each of these is analysed in turn.

## II. Requirements for protection

### 1. Secrecy: information not generally known or readily ascertainable

The secrecy requirement is essential in the legal framework for the protection of confidential information.[696] Indeed, "by definition, a trade secret is something which has not been placed in the public domain".[697] The U.S. Supreme Court has repeatedly indicated that state laws dealing with unfair competition cannot afford protection to information that is publicly known. In one of its seminal decisions on trade secrets, *Kewanee Oil Co. v. Bicron Corp.*, the court noted, "that which is in the public domain cannot be removed therefrom by action of the State".[698] Ultimately, this reflects one of the key underlying policies of the intellectual property system, ac-

---

694 Sharon K. Sandeen and Christopher B. Seaman 2017 (n 673) 888-905.

695 Sharon K. Sandeen and Christopher B. Seaman 2017 (n 673) 906.

696 Mark A. Lemley 2008 (n 15) 342.

697 *Sinclair v. Aquarius Electronics, Inc.*, 116 Cal.Rptr. 654, 661 (Cal. Ct. App. 1974).

698 See *Kewanee Oil Co. v. Bicron Corp.*, 416 U.S. 470, 481 (1974); similarly in *Bonito Boats, Inc. v. Thunder Craft Boats, Inc.*, 489 U.S. 141, 156-157 (1989) the U.S. Supreme Court clarified that "A State law that substantially interferes with the enjoyment of an unpatented utilitarian or design conception which has been freely disclosed by its author to the public at large impermissibly contravenes the ultimate goal of public disclosure and use which is the centrepiece of federal patent policy".

cording to which there is a public interest and social benefit in sharing ideas.[699]

The UTSA and DTSA, similar to Article 39(2) TRIPs, use two expressions to define the notion of secrecy. They stipulate that the information object of the trade secret should be neither "generally known" nor "readily ascertainable" by people who could obtain economic advantage from its disclosure. This is to be understood as meaning that information must be unknown to the public at large, but also to those who could obtain economic advantage from the disclosure of the information.[700] Consequently, even if the trade secret is only well-known within a given industry, but not the general public, it loses its confidential nature.[701]

The UTSA and the DTSA, in the same way as the Restatement (First) of Torts and the Restatement (Third) of Unfair Competition, adopt a relative secrecy approach, which is essential for the economic exploitation of the information concerned.[702] As underscored in *Metallurgical Industries Inc. v. Fourtek. Inc.*:

---

699 Charles Tait Graves and Alexander Macgillivray, 'Combination Trade Secrets and the Logic of Intellectual Property' [2004] Santa Clara High Technology LJ 261, 268-269.

700 According to UTSA Comment to § 1(4): "The language 'not being generally known to and not being readily ascertainable by proper means by other persons' does not require that information be generally known to the public for trade secret rights to be lost. If the principal person/persons who can obtain economic benefit from information is/are aware of it, there is no trade secret".

701 The Supreme Court has clearly enshrined this principle in two of the most important decisions in trade secrets law. In *Ruckelshaus v. Monsanto Co.*, 467 U.S. 986, 1002 (1984) it noted that "information that is public knowledge or that is generally known in an industry cannot be a trade secret". Similarly, in *Kewanee Oil Co. v. Bicron Corp.*, 416 U.S. 470, 475 (1974) it was argued that "the subject of a trade secret must be secret, and must not be of public knowledge or of a general knowledge in the trade or business"; see further Sharon K. Sandeen 2010 (n 642) 523.

702 The first two factors of the Restatement (First) of Torts § 757 comment b (Am. Law Inst. 1939) refer to the extent to which the information is known outside the plaintiff's business and the extent to which it is known by employees and others involved in the business; similarly, the Restatement (Third) of Unfair Competition §39 (Am. Law Inst. 1995) comment b notes that "to qualify as a trade secret, the information must be secret. The secrecy, however, need not be absolute(...) Information known by persons in addition to the trade secret owner can retain its status as a trade secret if it remains secret from other to whom it has potential economic value".

> A holder may divulge his information to a limited extent without destroying its status as a trade secret. To hold otherwise would greatly limit the holder's ability to profit from his secret. If disclosure to others is made to further the holder's economic interests, it should, in appropriate circumstances, be considered a limited disclosure that does not destroy secrecy.[703]

Indeed, one of the soundest theories underlying trade secrets protection, the so-called "incentives to disclose theory", holds that trade secrets legislation lowers transaction costs associated with the commercial exploitation of confidential information (such as licensing agreements) and therefore enhances cooperation between market participants and facilitates organisation within a company.[704]

With respect to the interplay between the secrecy requirement and the disclosure function in the patent system, case law has considered that the issuance of a patent discloses the trade secrets described in the specification. This is crucial to ensure the appropriate balance between both legal regimes.[705] Regarding patent applications, pursuant to 35 U.S.C § 122 of the U.S. Patent Act,[706] the information contained therein remains confidential during the examination process and only enters the public domain after the publication of the application (18 months after the filing if international protection is sought) or upon issuance of the patent.[707] In con-

703 *Metallurgical Industries v. Fourtek Inc.*, 790 F.2d 1195, 1200 (5th Cir. 1986).

704 Chapter 1 § 2 B) II.

705 For instance, *On-Line Technologies, Inc. v. Bodenseewerk Perkin-Elmer GmbH,* 386 F.3d 1133, 1141 (Fed. Cir. 2004) it was noted that: "after a patent has been issued, the information contained within it is ordinarily regarded as public and not subject to protection as a trade secret"; similarly the Texas Supreme Court in *Hyde Corporation v. Huffines*, 314 S.W.2d 763, 773 (1958) concluded that "upon the granting of a patent upon any of the claims contained in the application, the file is no longer held in confidence by the Patent office but the contents thereof become public property (…) Consequently, the secrets disclosed by the application and its amendments are available to the world".

706 35 U.S.C. § 122. Confidential status of applications: "Application for patents shall be kept in confidence by the Patent and Trademark Office and no information concerning the same given without authority of the applicant or owner unless necessary to carry out the provisions of any Act of Congress or in such special circumstances as may be determined by the Commissioner".

707 Restatement (Third) of Unfair Competition §39 (Am. Law Inst. 1995) comment f: "Information disclosed in a patent or contained in published materials reasonably accessible to competitors does not qualify for protection".

trast, the abandonment or rejection of the application prior to publication does not result in the disclosure of the information contained therein.[708]

The second prong of the secrecy requirement set forth by the UTSA and DTSA is that information is not "readily ascertainable by proper means". The comment in § 1 UTSA explains that information that is available in trade journals, reference books or published materials is deemed as being "readily ascertainable".[709] Similarly, it is noted that when a trade secret is apparent through observation of the product in which it is embodied, it loses its secret nature. Consequently, marketing a product does not necessarily reveal all related trade secrets.[710] First, information about its process of development and manufacture may remain undisclosed unless it can be inferred from the examination of the product. Second, the item's design or other secrets may not be evident. In such cases, the trade secret lasts for as long as it takes to reverse engineer the product.[711]As noted in *Hamer Holding Group, Inc. v. Elmore*:

> The key to secrecy is the ease with which information can be developed through other proper means: if the information can be readily duplicated without involving considerable time, effort or expense, then it is not secret.[712]

Notwithstanding this, in practice, defining when the acquisition of information is readily ascertainable and when it is subject to a process of reverse engineering is complex, but nonetheless relevant. Information that can on-

708 35 U.S.C § 122.

709 UTSA Comment § 1: "Information is readily ascertainable if it is available in trade journals, reference books, or published materials. Often, the nature of the product lends itself to being readily copied as soon as it is available on the market. On the other hand, if reverse engineering is lengthy and expensive, a person who discovers the trade secret through reverse engineering can have a trade secret in the information obtained from reverse engineering".

710 James Pooley 2002 (n 66) § 4.04[3]4-34; Restatement (Third) of Unfair Competition §39 (Am. Law Inst. 1995) comment f: "Public sale of product does not preclude continued protection against the improper acquisition or use of information that is difficult, costly or time-consuming to extract through reverse engineering; " along the same lines see *American Can Co. v. Mansukhani*, 728 F.2d 818, 819 -820 (7th Cir. 1982) stating that the fact that someone else might have discovered the secret by fair means such as reverse engineering does not protect the unlawful acquirer.

711 This is particularly relevant in industries with short product life cycles such as the computer software industry.

712 See *Hamer Holding Group, Inc. v. Elmore*, 560 N.E.2d 907, 918 (Ill. App. Ct. 1990).

ly be obtained through reverse engineering is protectable as a trade secret prior to the reverse engineering process. By contrast, readily ascertainable information is not accorded protection at all, as it is regarded that it does not fulfil the secrecy requirement. A more detailed study of specific scenarios under which secret information is disclosed and its effect on the protectability of said information is provided in chapter 4.

## 2. Independent economic value

Similar to Article 39(2) TRIPs, the UTSA and DTSA demand that information derives independent economic value resulting from its secret nature.[713] This phrase codifies the "competitive advantage" factor set forth in comment b of § 757 of the Restatement (First) of Torts (1939).[714] In essence, it means that the secret nature of the information must confer upon the trade secret holder an advantage over its competitors, irrespective of the inherent value of the good or service in which it is embodied.[715] In the words of the Supreme Court in *Ruckelshaus v. Monsanto*, "the value of a trade secret lies in the competitive advantage it gives to its owner over competitors".[716] Thus, the asserted trade secret must not be valuable only in the abstract.[717] However, such an advantage need not be considerable, just "more than trivial".[718] This requirement is crucial, as it allows to draw the line between protectable and non-protectable information. Most information concerning professional matters is deemed confidential. Yet, only information that confers a competitive advantage to its holder is deemed a trade secret.[719] This has been construed in the widest sense, in line with

---

713 See UTSA § 1(4)(i): "derives independent economic value, actual or potential, from not being generally known to, and not being readily ascertainable (…)".

714 Similarly, comment e of the Restatement (Third) of Unfair Competition §39 (Am. Law Inst. 1995) stresses that "a trade secret must be of sufficient value in the operation of a business or another enterprise to provide an actual or potential economic advantage over others who do not possess the information".

715 *Abba Rubber Co. v. Seaquist,* 286 Cal.Rptr. 2d 518, 526 (Cal. Ct. App. 1991).

716 *Ruckelshaus v. Monsanto Co.*, 467 U.S. 986, footnote 15 (1984).

717 Sharon K. Sandeen 2010 (n 642) 524.

718 Restatement (Third) of Unfair Competition §39 (Am. Law Inst. 1995) comment e.

719 Roger M. Milgrim 2014 (n 160) § 1 understands that "not every commercial secret can be regarded as a trade secret. In business most matters are considered confidential; however only secrets affording a demonstrable competitive advantage may be properly considered trade secrets".

comment b of the Restatement (Third) of Unfair Competition, which provides that: "Although rights in trade secrets are normally asserted by businesses and other commercial enterprises, nonprofit entities such as charitable, educational, governmental, fraternal, and religious organizations can also claim trade secret protection for economically valuable information such as lists of prospective members or donors".

Notably, the Church of Scientology relied on this requirement to enforce trade secret rights over the Church's funder works that had been disseminated through the Internet.[720] In *Religious Tech. Ctrl. v Netcom On-Line Com,* the District Court for the Northern District of California noted that religious materials can be the object of a trade secret, because there is "no category of information (that) is excluded from protection as a trade secret because of its inherent qualities".[721] In addition, it was further noted that the Church's spiritual training materials were eligible for trade secret protection because they had a "significant impact on the donations received by the Church", and therefore had commercial value.[722]

Crucially, the UTSA, the DTSA and the Restatement (Third) of Unfair Competition indicate that value may be actual or potential. This approach departs substantially from the "continuous use" requirement laid down in the Restatement (First) of Torts, and according to some commentators, it was introduced to ensure the protection of research and development efforts.[723]

Some of the criteria that have been suggested to assess whether information is valuable and therefore worth copying are: (i) whether a competitor or another third party is trying to obtain the information; (ii) the identification of the information as having commercial value by competitors and consumers;[724] (iii) the actual use of the information; and (iv) the measures taken by the holder to prevent misappropriation.[725]

---

720 *Religious Technology Center v. Netcom On-Line Com.*, 923 F. Supp 1231(N.D. Cal. 1995).

721 *Religious Technology Center v Netcom On-Line Com.*, 923 F. Supp 1231, 1251 (N.D. Cal. 1995).

722 *Religious Technology Center v Netcom On-Line Com.*, 923 F. Supp 1231, 1253 (N.D. Cal. 1995).

723 James Pooley 2002 (n 66) § 2.03[2] 2-14, 2-15.

724 Daniel Gervais 2012 (n 505) para 2.488.

725 Nuno Pires de Carvalho 2008 (n 529) para 39.2.57; in the U.S., case law refers tot he following factors based on Restatement (First) of Torts § 757 (Am. Law Inst. 1939): "(1) the extent to which the information is known outside of the plaintiff's business; (2) the extent to which the information is known by employees and others involved in the plaintiff's business; (3) the extent of measures

The quantification of commercial value is most complex in the field of undisclosed information, and it usually appears in connection with the assessment of damages in the event of trade secret misappropriation.[726] It has been generally accepted that it should be calculated on the basis of the holder's lost profits, the reasonable royalties that should have been paid in the context of a licensing agreement or the account of the defendant's profits.[727]

By way of illustration, consider a hypothetical market for goods lifts consisting of 10 sellers and 10.000 businesses that may use this equipment within their premises. In this hypothetical market, it is uncertain which of these companies use goods lifts and which rely on other transportation means such as escalators. Seller A has a list of 1.500 businesses to which he has sold goods lifts in the past. If the content of A's customer list is unknown to the other nine competitors, it will be regarded as a trade secret, as its disclosure would allow the other market participants to target individual consumers. In the event that the other nine competitors are aware that each of the businesses enumerated in A's list are goods lift consumers, the list has no independent economic value. Under those circumstances, the identities are already known to A's competitors and cannot be protected under the law of trade secrecy, as they do not provide a competitive advantage.

The burden of proving that the information confers a competitive advantage by virtue of its secret nature lies with the trade secret holder. He can provide direct evidence by showing advantageous use in his own business.[728] Yet, in practice, most holders rely on circumstantial evidence, such as investments in research and development,[729] security measures adopted to protect the secrecy of the information[730] and that others may be willing

taken by the plaintiff to guard the secrecy of the information; (4) the value of the information to the plaintiff's business and to its competitors; (5) the amount of time, effort and money expended by the plaintiff in developing the information; and (6) the ease or difficulty with which the information could be properly acquired or duplicated by others", according to *Learning Curve Toys Incorporated v. Playwood Toys Incorporated,* 342 F. 3d 714, para 38 (7th Cir. 2003).

726 Nuno Pires de Carvalho 2008 (n 529) para 39.2.59.

727 Nuno Pires de Carvalho 2008 (n 529) para 39.2.59.

728 Restatement (Third) of Unfair Competition §39 (Am. Law Inst. 1995) comment e.

729 *Gates Rubber Co. v. Bando Chemical Industries, Ltd et al.*, 9 F.3d 823, 848 (10th Cir. 1991).

730 *Rockwell Graphic Systems, Inc. v. DEV Industries, Inc.*, 925 F.2d 174, 179 (7th Cir. 1991).

to pay to access the information.[731] From a legal perspective, it has been suggested that the economic value due to the secrecy requirement differentiates trade secrets protection from common law. In a breach of contract or tort law claim, it is not necessary to show either economic value or secrecy.[732]

As a final remark, research shows that the value requirement is rarely invoked before U.S. federal courts during the litigation of trade secrets. In the few instances where it has been, the existence of value has been assumed or its threshold has been interpreted to be low.[733]

### 3. Reasonable measures to maintain secrecy

The third and last requirement set forth in § 1(4) UTSA (and the DTSA)[734] specifies that information must be subject to "efforts that are reasonable under the circumstances to maintain its secrecy". This is consistent with the relevant case law, which provides that this requisite be fulfilled separately from the secrecy requirement,[735] but departs from the multifactor test approach enshrined in the Restatement (First) of Torts and the Restatement (Third) of Unfair Competition. In the latter, precautionary measures were regarded as mere evidence of secrecy, value and improper appropriation.[736] It has been argued that its inclusion in the UTSA as a separate condition derives from the negotiation history of the act and the removal of the originally envisaged requirement that secret information had to be in a tangible form. The adoption of protective measures was aimed at defining the scope of trade secrets, similar to the copyright fixation requirement.[737]

---

731 *Tan-Line Studios Inc. v. Bradley*, 1 U.S.P.Q.2d 2032, 2038 (E.D. Pa. 1986).

732 Michael Risch 2007 (n 15) 38.

733 David S. Almeling and others 2009-2010 (n 636) 319.

734 18 U.S.C. § 1839(3) (B).

735 Robert G. Bone 2011 (n 15) 57.

736 Restatement (Third) of Unfair Competition §39 (Am. Law Inst. 1995) comment g: "Whether viewed as an independent requirement or as an element to be considered with other factors relevant to the existence of a trade secret, the owner's precautions should be evaluated in light of the other available evidence relating to the value and secrecy of the information. Thus, if the value and secrecy of the information are clear, evidence of specific precautions taken by the trade secret owner may be unnecessary".

737 Robert G. Bone 2011 (n 15) 57 footnote 45 citing an informal conversation with Sharon K. Sandeen; see also Sharon K. Sandeen 2010 (n 642) 526-527.

Subsequently, and due to the influence of the U.S. delegation during the negotiations of the TRIPs Agreement, the reasonable measures requisite was included as a requirement for protection in Article 39(2)(c) TRIPs and is now a minimum standard for the protection of trade secrets in all WTO Member States.[738] However, such an inclusion has not been without criticism.

### a) Assessment of the "reasonableness" of the measures adopted

The UTSA and the DTSA do not require the holder of the information to take all possible measures, nor do they demand any level of efficacy. Essentially, they require the trade secret owner to adopt "reasonable measures under the circumstances". From an economic perspective, trade secret holders should aim at achieving a balance between the measures taken and their viability.[739] In the words of Posner, "The question is whether the additional benefit in security would have exceeded (the) cost (of protection)".[740] Indeed, the adoption of all possible measures would lead to an over-investment in the protection of information, which may adversely affect innovation, create inefficiencies and ultimately hinder the "spirit of inventiveness".[741]

---

738 See chapter 2 § 1 A) IV.2. d).

739 Victoria A. Cundiff, 'Reasonable Measures to Protect Trade Secrets in a Digital Environment' [2009] 49 IDEA 359, 363.

740 *Rockwell Graphic Systems, Inc. v. DEV Industries, Inc.*, 925 F.2d 174, 180 (7th Cir. 1991); similarly, Richard Posner, 'Trade Secret Misappropriation: A Cost-Benefit Response to the Fourth Amendment Analogy' [1992] 106 Harvard LR 461, 473-478 arguing that instead of comparing the "reasonable measures under the circumstances" yardstick with the "reasonable expectation of privacy" benchmark set forth in the Fourth Amendment, courts should apply a cost-benefit analysis to assess whether the owner has taken reasonable precautions: "Courts should require to firms to invest in precautionary measures until the marginal cost of those measures equals the marginal expected economic loss in the event of misappropriation, that is, the value of the to the trade secret to the owner multiplied by the decrease of the risk that the trade secret will be discovered by a competitor brought about by taking additional precautions".

741 Victoria A. Cundiff 2009 (n 739) 363; William Landes and Richard Posner 2003 (n 38) 369; Douglas Gary Lichtman 2004 (n 80) 32; see also *E.I. du Pont deNemours & Company v Christopher et al.*, 431 F.2d 1012, 1016 (5th Cir. 1970): "Our tolerance of the espionage game must cease when the protections required to prevent another's spying cost so much that the spirit of inventiveness is damped".

This is best illustrated in the *DuPont v. Cristopher*[742] case decided by the Court of Appeals of the Fifth Circuit in 1970. DuPont was in the process of building a plant for the production of methanol through an unpatented process that gave DuPont a competitive advantage over other producers. One of its competitors hired the defendant to take aerial photographs while the facilities were under construction and before the roof was built. As a result, parts of the secret process were exposed from a bird's eye view, and the court had to decide whether aerial photography under these circumstances is an improper means of obtaining a trade secret. The court ruled that taking secret information without the permission of its right holder, if reasonable precautions to preserve secrecy are adopted, is improper. In particular, the court noted that it would be too burdensome to ask DuPont to cover the manufacturing facility while it was under construction:

> We should not require a person or a corporation to take unreasonable precautions to prevent another from doing that which he ought not to do in the first place. Reasonable precautions against predatory eyes we may require, but an impenetrable fortress is an unreasonable requirement, and we are not disposed to burden industrial inventors with such a duty in order to protect the fruits of their efforts.[743]

In the light of the above, the reasonableness of the measures should be assessed against the specific circumstances of each case and considering the nature of the threat to disclosure, the value of the trade secret and the cost of the potential security mechanisms.[744] In fact, "what may be reasonable measures in one context may not necessarily be so in another".[745]

The UTSA and DTSA are silent on the nature of the measures to be adopted by trade secrets holders.[746] Notwithstanding this, legal commenta-

---

742 *E.I. du Pont deNemours & Company v. Christopher et al.*, 431 F.2d 1012, 1017 (5th Cir. 1970).

743 *E.I. du Pont deNemours & Company v. Christopher et al.* 431 F.2d 1012, 1017 (5th Cir. 1970).

744 James Pooley 2002 (n 66) § 4.04. [2] 2-27.

745 See also *Matter of Innovative Construction Systems, Inc.*, 793 F.2d 875, 884 (7th Cir. 1986).

746 Restatement (Third) of Unfair Competition §39 (Am. Law Inst. 1995) comment g: "Precautions to maintain secrecy may take many forms, including physical security designed to prevent unauthorized access, procedures intended to limit disclosure based upon the "need to know", and measures that emphasize to recipients the confidential nature of the information such as nondisclosure agreements, signs, and restrictive legends".

tors have drawn a distinction between "standard" and "non-standard" measures.[747] The former include physical methods (e.g. building fences); technical methods (e.g. protecting information through passwords or encryption); legal methods (e.g. NDAs) and enforcement/detection methods (e.g security cameras), as well as IT measures. The latter refer to measures adopted when the holder does not rely on standard measures. They usually consist of fragmenting information, and a prime example is the assembly of products containing secret information in different locations.[748]

The evidence suggests that during litigation, the most relevant measures courts take into account to support a finding that reasonable efforts have been adopted are agreements with employees and third parties and, to a lesser extent, establishing restrictions to access information within an undertaking.[749] Agreements with employees can consist of non-competition covenants, non-solicitation, employment contracts, confidentiality agreements and invention assignment agreements. For third parties, such as suppliers, trade secret holders most frequently resort to NDAs.[750]

### b) Criticism

Three reasons are most frequently invoked by case law and academia in the U.S. to explain the imposition of such a requirement: (i) to give notice of confidentiality to third parties, (ii) to provide evidence of the value of the trade secret and (iii) to prevent misappropriation through the adoption of self-help measures.[751]

However, in recent years, it has been widely discussed whether the reasonable measures requirement is entirely in line with the above outlined modern justifications for trade secrets protection. Bone, in his seminal article "Trade secrecy, innovation and the requirements of secrecy precautions",[752] casts doubt upon the adverse impact that such a requirement may have on access to information.[753] The author submits that two of the arguments generally put forward to justify demanding such measures in all

747 Michael Risch 2007 (n 15) 43.
748 Michael Risch 2007 (n 15) 43.
749 David S. Almeling and others 2009-2010 (n 636) 322-323.
750 David S. Almeling and others 2009-2010 (n 636) 322.
751 Victoria A. Cundiff 2009 (n 739) 363; *Rockwell Graphic Systems, Inc. v. DEV Industries, Inc,*. 925 F.2d 174, 179 (7th Cir. 1991); Michael Risch 2007 (n 15) 45-47.
752 Robert G. Bone 2011 (n 15) 46-76.
753 Robert G. Bone 2011 (n 15) 46.

cases are in fact superfluous: (i) notice of confidentiality can be provided without resorting to specific measures and (ii) it is possible to provide evidence of the actual existence and value of a trade secret without showing that particular precautions were adopted.[754]

Against this background, the author reviews the general policies supporting the protection of trade secrets and their intersection with the "reasonable steps requirement".[755] From an economic perspective, the first justification argues that trade secrets protection should be encouraged to promote incentives to create. However, demanding reasonable steps to protect the secrecy of information ultimately increases the cost of innovation and the enforcement of trade secrets.[756] The second economic reason presented is that providing effective legal protection in the event of trade secret misappropriation avoids (over) investing in costly self-help measures. However, by requiring firms to adopt reasonable protective measures, the law gives normative value to investment in precautionary measures, as their adoption becomes a requirement of protection that defines the subject matter covered, which may easily lead to over-investment. As a third justification, trade secrets laws encourage licensing and the commercial exploitation of information. In this context, Bone argues that these activities would be encouraged by the law of trade secrets, even if the holders of secret information were not required to adopt reasonable measures under the circumstances to protect the information.

From a deontological perspective, it has been suggested that trade secrets protection should be understood in terms of a firm's right to privacy.[757] However, Bone dismisses this argument in the context of the reasonable steps requirement, essentially due to the fact that privacy does not always call for specific measures and is not appropriate in the context of trade secrets protection.[758] Notwithstanding this, the author concludes that it could be possible to justify such a requirement based on a potential reduc-

754 Robert G. Bone 2011 (n 15) 46.
755 As outlined in chapter 1 § 2.
756 Robert G. Bone 2011 (n 15) 58-62.
757 Robert G. Bone 2011 (n 15) 66.
758 Robert G. Bone 2011 (n 15) 66; in this regard, it is submitted that *Bone* does not contemplate the utilitarian dimension of privacy in trade secrets protection, as outlined in chapter 1 § 2 B) IV.

tion of enforcement costs[759] and signalling benefits.[760] However, he is of the opinion that further research is required to demand the application of the "reasonable steps requirement" in all cases.[761]

It is noteworthy that Lemley comes to the same conclusion. He essentially holds that the main advantage of the law of trade secrets is that it limits the investment in the event that no such legislation existed. Consequently, conferring normative value to the establishment of a minimum level of investment should not be regarded as an end in itself.[762]

Risch conversely argues that demanding some efforts to maintain secrecy ensures that the adopted measures are efficient from an economic perspective. If no protection against trade secret misappropriation is afforded, the holders of valuable, confidential information would still adopt precautionary measures to avoid losing it. Similarly, if the holders of undisclosed information could adopt less than reasonable precautions, they would tend to under-protect information. Hence, requiring reasonable measures serves the purpose of finding an equilibrium in investments to protect secret information[763]

In the light of the above, it is submitted that it is not possible to establish a clearly defined standard that provides the number and types of mea-

---

759 Robert G. Bone 2011 (n 15) 67-75 argues that a potential explanation for the "reasonable measures requirement" is that it prevents process costs, i.e. the adoption of very costly self-help measures, which may be higher than litigation costs, as well as the error costs that arise in the context of "frivolous" trade secrets lawsuits, particularly against former employees.

760 In this context, Robert G. Bone 2011 (n 15) 72-74 notes that the adoption of reasonable measures under the circumstances may be justified because it provides information to competitors about the value of the secret concerned and the behaviour of the holder. By reducing such information asymmetries it allows to invest in the obtention of the most valuable trade secrets and avoids "the waste that results from obtaining the trade secrets unlawfully only to be sued and enjoined from using it".

761 Robert G. Bone 2011 (n 15) 76.

762 Mark A. Lemley, 'The surprising virtues of treating trade secrets as IP rights' 109, 136 in Rochelle C. Dreyfuss and Katherine J. Strandburg (eds), *The Law and Theory of Trade Secrecy: A Handbook of Contemporary Research* (Edward Elgar 2011); similarly, Jonathan R. Chally 2004 (n 44) 1293-1295 arguing that the "reasonable measures requirement" should only be taken into consideration by courts when an innovator may have revealed the information voluntarily. Furthermore, it is suggested that not demanding trade secret holders to adopt reasonable efforts is the most efficient approach, as it guarantees that the holder and potential competitors do not undertake unnecessary activities.

763 Michael Risch 2007 (n 15) 45.

sures necessary to define "reasonable", this will have to be assessed according to the specific circumstances of each case.[764] Furthermore, despite Risch's arguments, it seems unlikely that, in the event that no trade secrets protection is afforded, holders of valuable confidential information would under-invest in protective measures. Applying the prisoner's dilemma line of reasoning, if the parties are uncertain about the efforts and investments competitors make in finding their valuable information, they will most likely adopt the highest possible means to protect the competitive advantage the trade secret confers. Ultimately, the maximum threshold of investment is determined by the value of the advantage conferred by the subject matter of the trade secret.

### C) The legal regime for the protection of trade secrets under the UTSA, the DTSA and the Restatements of the law

Trade secrets protection cannot only be achieved through the regime of confidentiality created by the Restatements of the Law, the UTSA and more recently the DTSA. Other regimes play a crucial role in achieving such protection, including non-competition covenants, confidentiality agreements and tort law. The overlap between the multiple regimes has crucial doctrinal and practical implications, but its analysis falls outside the scope of the present research.[765] This study focuses on the interpretation of misappropriation as regulated in the UTSA and the Restatements as well as the case law that applies them. Finally, some remarks on the new features introduced by the DTSA are made.

The Restatement (First) of Torts in § 757[766] prevents the unauthorised *use* or *disclosure* of a trade secret.[767] Some years later, the UTSA extended the misappropriation conduct to the *acquisition* of another's trade secret by improper means and condemned both actual and threatened behaviours.[768] In § 1(2) UTSA (which has been almost identically reproduced

---

764 David S. Almeling and others 2009-2010 (n 636) 321.

765 For an in-depth study of the four regimes of protection and their practical implications see Charles Tait Graves 2011 (n 689) 77-108.

766 See Restatement (First) of Torts § 757 (Am. Law Inst. 1939).

767 Similarly, the U.S. Supreme Court in *Kewanee Oil Co. v. Bicron Corp.*, 416 U.S. 470, 475-476 (1974) indicated that the protection accorded to a trade secret was against the disclosure or use of information as a result of a breach of a confidentiality duty or the acquisition of knowledge through improper means.

768 See § 2(a) UTSA.

in the DTSA)[769] misappropriation may consist of six specific types of conduct. The first one, as described in § 1(2)(i) refers to acquisition knowing (or with reason to know) that the trade secret was obtained through improper means. Next, § 1(2)(ii)(A) alludes to the use or disclosure of secret information without consent by a person who had used improper means to acquire it. The third conduct in § 1(2)(ii)(B) (I) extends liability to those used or disclosed another's trade secret with knowledge (or who should had known under the circumstances) that it had been acquired through improper means.

The behaviours subsequently described refer to acts of misappropriation resulting from a breach of a duty of confidence. Section 1(2)(ii)(B)(II) prevents the use or disclosure of a trade secret when the information was acquired under a duty to maintain its secrecy or limit its use. The fifth category imposes liability on the use or disclosure of secret information by a third party when such information was obtained knowing or with reason to know that the acquirer was under a duty of confidence with the trade secret holder. Specifically, it encompasses the disclosure of former employees in the context of their new employment relationship.[770] Finally, § 1(2)(ii)(C) governs liability in the event of accidental or mistaken acquisition.

As discussed in chapter 1, one of the main features of trade secrets in contrast to other IPRs is that they only confer protection against improper taking or "misappropriation".[771] This does not prevent mere copying; anyone is free to inspect a publicly available product or reverse engineer it.[772] Hence, the use of "improper means" lies at the very foundation of the law of trade secrecy: the maintenance of commercial morality.[773] Comment f in § 757 of the Restatement (First) of Torts convincingly notes that providing a list with numerus clausus of such means is not feasible. The UTSA attempts to shed light on the matter by giving an open-ended list of exam-

769 18 U.S.C. § 1839(5).

770 James Pooley 2002 (n 66) § 2.03.

771 Misappropriation is the term used in the UTSA; similarly, the Supreme Court in *Kewanee Oil Co. v. Bicron Corp.*, 416 U.S. 470, 475-476 (1974) stated that "the protection accorded to a trade secret holder is against the disclosure or unauthorized use of the trade secret by those to whom the secret has been confided under express or implied restrictions of nondisclosure and none-use. The law also protects the holder of a trade secret against disclosure or use when the knowledge is gained, not by the owner's volition, but by some 'improper means.'"

772 Robert G. Bone 1998 (n 15) 250.

773 Restatement (First) of Torts § 757 (Am. Law Inst. 1939) comment f noting that improper means "In general (…) are means which fall below the generally accepted standards of commercial morality and reasonable conduct".

ples, including "theft, bribery, misrepresentation, breach or inducement of a breach of a duty to maintain secrecy, or espionage through electronic or other means".[774] However, the means used to acquire a trade secret can be regarded as "improper" even if they are not independently wrongful.[775] Ultimately, the assessment of whether the means can be deemed "improper" should be based on a flexible case-by-case analysis considering a number of factors and leaving considerable room for judicial discretion.[776] As noted by the 5th Circuit in *DuPont v. Cristopher*:

> Improper will always be a word of many nuances, determined by time, place and circumstances. We therefore need not proclaim a catalogue of commercial improprieties. Clearly, however, one of its commandments does say that 'thou shall not appropriate a trade secret through deviousness under circumstances in which countervailing defences are not reasonably available.[777]

Crucially, in the Commentary in § 1 UTSA notes that "proper means" encompass, among others, (i) discovery by independent invention;[778] (ii) discovery by reverse engineering;[779] (iii) discovery as a result of licensing a product by the trade secret owner; (iv) observation of the item in public use or display; and (v) review of published literature.[780] In a similar vein, the DTSA sets forth that "reverse engineering" and "independent derivation" constitute lawful means of acquiring a trade secret.[781]

---

774 See UTSA § 1 (1) and 18 U.S.C. § 1839 (6) (A) ; in the same vein, Restatement (Third) of Unfair Competition § 43 (Am. Law Inst. 1995) comment c refers among others to the following types of conduct: entering a competitor's offices without permission; spying a competitor's telephone conversations; inducing a trade secret holder to disclose secret information through using deceptive means as regards representation; see 18 U.S.C. § 1839 (6) (A).

775 Restatement (Third) of Unfair Competition § 43 (Am. Law Inst. 1995) comment c.

776 For a detailed analysis of the way in which courts in the U.S. have construed "improper means" William E. Hilton, 'What sort of improper conduct constitutes misappropriation of a trade secret' [1990] 30 IDEA 287.

777 *E.I. du Pont deNemours & Company v. Christopher et al.*, 447 431 F.2d 1012, 1017 (5th Cir. 1970).

778 *Kewanee Oil Co. v. Bicron Corp.*, 416 U.S. 470, 476 (1974); also Roger M. Milgrim 2014 (n 160) § 7.02.

779 *Kewanee Oil Co. v. Bicron Corp.*, 416 U.S. 470, 476 (1974); also Roger M. Milgrim 2014 (n 160) § 7.02.

780 Commentary to § 1(1) UTSA.

781 18 U.S.C. § 1839 (6) (B).

With regard to enforcement, if the plaintiff prevails, state courts usually award monetary damages, as well as injunctive relief.[782] Against this background, the adoption of the DTSA has introduced greater legal certainty, as it sets forth a comprehensive array of remedies in the event of trade secret misappropriation. These include (i) the grant of an injunction against threatened or actual misappropriation;[783] (ii) the award of damages for the actual loss caused by the misappropriation of the trade secret; as well as of any damages derived from any unjust enrichment caused by the infringing conduct[784] and (iii) the award of exemplary damages (up to twice the amount of regular damages) if the trade secrets is misappropriated with wilfulness and malice.[785] When a claim is made in bad faith, the prevailing party may apply for attorney's fees.[786]

Remarkably, as a novel feature, the DTSA allows the holder of a trade secret to apply (ex parte) for an order providing the civil seizure of property to prevent further dissemination of the secret information.[787] Yet, such an order is only granted under exceptional circumstances if an immediate and irreparable injury is likely to occur if such seizure is not ordered.[788]

Likewise, the DTSA provides that the *owner* of a trade secret has legal standing to bring legal proceedings.[789] This aspect was not regulated in the UTSA and ultimately bears the question of whether licensees have legal standing to sue.[790] As a final remark, the DTSA expressly provides that its provisions should not be interpreted as pre-empting or displacing any remedies of civil and criminal nature on the misappropriation of trade secrets set forth by federal, state and common law.[791] However, Sandeen and Seaman have warned of the difficulties that federal courts will encounter in interpreting the DTSA and applying the pre-existing body of state case law to fill the gaps of the DTSA.[792]

782 For a general overview of the remedies available, see James Pooley 2002 (n 66) Chapter 7 and Roger M. Milgrim 2014 (n 160) chapter 3.

783 18 U.S.C. § 1836 (b) (3) (A).

784 18 U.S.C. § 1836 (b) (3) (B) (i).

785 18 U.S.C. § 1836 (b) (3) (C).

786 18 U.S.C. § 1836 (b) (3) (D).

787 18 U.S.C. § 1836 (b) (2) (A) (i).

788 18 U.S.C. § 1836 (b) (2) (A) (ii).

789 18 U.S.C. § 1836 (b) (1); see further Victoria A. Cundiff and others, 'The Global Harmonisation of Trade Secret Law: The Convergence of Protection for Trade Secrets in the US and EU' [2016] 38 EIPR 738, 741.

790 See further Victoria A. Cundiff and others 2016 (n 789) 741.

791 18 U.S.C.§ 1838.

792 Sharon K. Sandeen and Christopher B. Seaman 2017 (n 673) 912.

## *§ 3 Conclusion*

Chapter 2 has reviewed the minimum standards of protection set forth at the international level regarding trade secrets (i.e. Article 39 TRIPs and Article 10bis PC), which all WTO Member States are bound to implement in their domestic legal regimes. These mostly coincide with those laid down in the most relevant sources of law in the U.S. (the UTSA and the DTSA), which shows the prevalence of the U.S. delegation during the negotiation process of Article 39 TRIPs.

To merit protection, information must (i) be secret; (ii) derive independent commercial value from its concealed nature, and (iii) the holder must adopt reasonable measures under the circumstances to keep it undisclosed. These three cumulative requirements are closely interconnected and ultimately reveal that the law of trade secrets is concerned with the protection of investments made in the creation of valuable information, but only against specific behaviours that do not comply with the accepted market practices. Information is protected by the mere fact of being kept undisclosed and providing its holder with a competitive advantage. No additional qualitative threshold beyond secrecy has to be met. As a result, if the information is disclosed, the competitive advantage disappears. In this context, this chapter has argued that the "commercial value" requirement laid down in Article 39(2)(b) TRIPs shall be interpreted in a broad sense so as to include any potential act of competition between the parties, as well as both actual or potential value in line with Article 1(4) UTSA. In the same vein, the expression "readily ascertainable" should be considered synonymous to "readily accessible", which under Article 1(4) UTSA must be carried out "through or by proper means".

As such, only when the acquisition, use or disclosure is carried out in a manner contrary to honest commercial practices is the holder of the information able to seek legal redress.

With the above in mind, the following chapter looks into the scattered regulation of trade secrets protection across several EU Member States, which led to the alignment of national legal regimes in this field of law. In particular, the methodology of comparative law is applied to study the legal regimes for the protection of trade secrets in England and Germany before the implementation of the TSD and the emerging harmonised legal framework according to the provisions of the TSD.

# Chapter 3. Fragmented protection of trade secrets across the EU leading to a harmonised system: study of the English and German models and the emerging common framework

## *§ 1 Scattered protection across the internal market before the implementation of the Trade Secrets Directive: Different models*

Until the adoption of the TSD, the legal framework for the protection of trade secrets had not been harmonised in the EU. However, all Member States offered some level of redress, in line with the minimum standards set forth in Article 39 of the TRIPs Agreement. The regimes, nevertheless, differed substantially and the level of protection was very limited in some jurisdictions.[793] Such a fragmented legislative landscape was described by some as a "patchwork"[794] and to some extent resulted from the overlap of regimes that are applicable to safeguarding secret information within national jurisdictions. Beyond specific rules dealing with trade secrets, contractual agreements between the parties play a central role in their enforce-

793 Hogan Lovells, 'Study on Trade Secrets and Parasitic Copying (Look-alikes) – Report on Trade Secrets' (MARKT/2010/20/D) (2012) para 290 <ec.europa.eu/internal.../docs/trade-secrets/120113_study_en.pdf> accessed 15 September 2018; see also Recital 6 TSD: "Notwithstanding the TRIPS Agreement, there are important differences in the Member States' legislation as regards the protection of trade secrets against their unlawful acquisition, use or disclosure by other persons. For example, not all Member States have adopted national definitions of a trade secret or the unlawful acquisition, use or disclosure of a trade secret, therefore knowledge on the scope of protection is not readily accessible and that scope differs across the Member States. Furthermore, there is no consistency as regards the civil law remedies available in the event of unlawful acquisition, use or disclosure of trade secrets, as cease and desist orders are not always available in all Member States against third parties who are not competitors of the legitimate trade secret holder. Divergences also exist across the Member States with respect to the treatment of a third party who has acquired the trade secret in good faith but subsequently learns, at the time of use, that the acquisition derived from a previous unlawful acquisition by another party".

794 Hogan Lovells 2012 (n 793) para 5.

ment, along with labour law provisions. Furthermore, most Member States set forth criminal penalties in the case of industrial espionage.[795]

Despite the myriad of legal sources that regulated trade secrets protection in national jurisdictions before the adoption of the TSD, Ohly identified six pre-eminent models across the Single Market.[796] In the first place, he referred to Sweden, the only Member State where a specific statute for the protection of trade secrets had been passed before the adoption of the TSD. The Swedish Act on the Protection of Trade Secrets (1990:409) was enacted in 1990, prior to the approval of the TRIPs Agreement, mainly as a result of the absence of a general unfair competition act and the increasing legal challenges posed by industrial espionage and employee mobility.[797] Next, he mentioned the so-called "IP model", which is best exemplified by the Italian legal system. As noted above,[798] the Italian Industrial Property Code of 2005 included trade secrets within the spectrum of rights traditionally protected under Intellectual Property Law. Indeed, Italy was the first jurisdiction to adopt such a strong property approach. Thirdly, France followed a so-called "hybrid model", whereby manufacturing trade secrets ("*secrets de fabrique*") were included within the Intellectual Property Code.[799] However, trade secrets in the broadest sense ("*secret d'affaires*") were afforded protection only on the basis of general tort law, unfair competition and criminal sanctions.[800] Certain jurisdictions like Spain or Switzerland built their trade secret regimes on civil provisions enshrined within their unfair competition acts.[801] This was the case with Article 6 of

795 By way of illustration, see Articles 278-80 of the Spanish Criminal Code (Ley Orgánica 10/1995, de 23 de noviembre, del Código Penal).

796 Ansgar Ohly 2013 (n 13) 27-28; however, some jurisdictions do not follow any of the above identified models. This is, for instance, the case of Malta, where trade secrets are only protected contractually. In the Netherlands, a general principle of tort law, unlawful act, is applied to misappropriation cases; see further Hogan Lovells 2012 (n 793) paras 159-170.

797 Marianne Levin, 'Trade Secret Protection and the Computation of Damages under Swedish Law' 735, 737 in Thomas Dreier, Horst-Peter Götting, Maximilian Haedicke, Michael Lehmann (eds), *Perspektiven des Geistigen Eigentums und des Wettbewerbsrechts* (C.H. Beck 2005).

798 See chapter 1 § 3 B) I. 3, a).

799 See Article L621-1 Code de la propriété intellectuelle (version consolidée au 25 avril 2016) (French Intellectual Property Code).

800 Jérôme Passa, 'La protection des secrets d'affaires en droit français' 47 in Jacques de Werra (ed), *La protection des secrets d'affaires* (Schulthess 2013).

801 Ansgar Ohly 2013 (n 13) 27-28.

the Swiss Unfair Competition Act[802] and Article 13 of the Spanish Act against Unfair Competition.[803] Notwithstanding this, in these legal systems accessory criminal liability was also foreseen in the event of industrial espionage. In the fifth model, the one followed in countries like Austria, Poland and Germany, protection was built upon criminal provisions that were part of the respective unfair competition acts.[804] Finally, common law jurisdictions such as England and the Republic of Ireland had not enacted any provisions to deal with trade secrets, not even from a criminal law perspective. Effective protection was achieved through the breach of confidence action, which covers confidential information in general i.e. private information, government secrets, and artistic and literary information.[805]

In the light of such a scattered legal framework, the last two models are studied, taking as example cases the German (§ 2) and English jurisdictions (§ 3). By application of the methodology of comparative law, the following sections analyse the legal mechanisms in place in these two national systems, which furthermore belong to two different legal traditions (civil and common law, respectively), in order to achieve effective protection of valuable secret information. Furthermore, both legal regimes were highly influential during the negotiation and configuration of the harmonised system and therefore constitute the point of departure to critically analyse the emerging common framework introduced by the TSD (§ 5). From a methodological perspective, it should be noted that the research for this thesis was completed before the implementation of the TSD in both jurisdictions, and consequently, no reference to resulting harmonised framework in these jurisdictions is made.

## *§ 2 Trade secrets protection in Germany before the implementation of the TSD*

The present section delves into the protection of trade secrets in Germany prior to the implementation of the TSD. The German jurisdiction is a civil law jurisdiction with a long tradition of protecting confidential informa-

802 Bundesgesetz gegen den unlauteren Wettbewerb (UWG) vom 19. Dezember 1986 (Stand am 1. Juli 2016).

803 Ley 3/1991, de 10 de enero, de Competencia Desleal (Spanish Unfair Competition Act).

804 Ansgar Ohly 2013 (n 13) 27-28.

805 See more generally Tanya Aplin and others 2012 (n 22).

tion, which has led to a rich body of case law. Section A briefly examines the development of trade secrecy law since its inception in the late XIX century. Next, section B looks into three of the main fields of law that regulated trade secrets disclosure. In this context, special emphasis is given to the intersection between unfair competition law and criminal law.

## A) Development of the law of trade secrets

The protection of trade secrets in Germany until the mid-XIX century consisted mostly of scattered pieces of legislation that set forth criminal liability with respect to the misappropriation of trade secrets in specific sectors that were considered of particular relevance for the states economies.[806] Indeed, legislatures concentrated mostly on criminal protection due to the particular vulnerability of secret information and the fact that it was deemed that the persons liable for misappropriation did not have the financial resources to pay for the damages arising from their conduct.[807]

The seed of the system was built upon the German Unfair Competition Act, dated 27 Mai 1899,,[808] which was mostly concerned with the protection of the duty of confidence that the employee owed to the employer, as per § 9 paragraph 1 UWG 1896.[809] In addition, liability was also extended to third parties that had obtained secret information as a result of any of the breaches described in paragraph 1 or in breach of any other law or in a manner contrary to honest commercial practices (and to the detriment of competitors in all instances).[810] Some years later, in 1909, following the influence of embroidery and lace manufacturers, the German legislature de-

806 As noted by Florian Schweyer 2012 (n 99) 390.

807 *Harte-Bavendamm*/Henning-Bodewig (n 376) §§ 17-19 UWG Rdn 6.

808 Gesetz zur Bekämpfung des unlauteren Wettbewerbs 1986 ("UWG 1986").

809 According to Florian Schweyer 2012 (n 99) 390; § 9 paragraph 1 UWG 1886 provided the following: "Mit Geldstrafe bis zu dreitausend Mark oder mit Gefängniß bis zu einem Jahre wird bestraft, wer als Angestellter, Arbeiter oder Lehrling eines Geschäftsbetriebes Geschäfts- oder Betriebsgeheimnisse, die ihn vermöge des Dienstverhältnisses anvertraut oder sonst zugänglich geworden sind, während der Geltungsdauer des Dienstverhältnisses unbefugt an Andere zu Zwecken des Wettbewerbes oder in der Absicht, dem Inhaber des Geschäftsbetriebes Schaden zuzufügen, mittheilt".

810 According to Florian Schweyer 2012 (n 99) 390, § 9 paragraph 2 UWG 1896 provided the following: "Gleiche Strafe trifft denjenigen, welcher Geschäfts- oder Betriebsgeheimnisse, deren Kenntniß er durch eine der im Absatz 1 bezeichneten Mittheilungen oder durch eine gegen das Gesetz oder die guten Sitten

cided to regulate in a separate provision protection against the so-called "piracy of models" ("*Vorlagenfreibeuterei*"), which now corresponds to § 18 UWG.

The following section provides an overview of three of the main legal regimes under which the protection of trade secrets is regulated in Germany. To this end, first, the constitutional dimension of trade secrets protection is briefly examined (§ I). Next, the dissertation looks into the unfair competition provisions that deal with trade secrets and their intersection with criminal law (§ II). Finally, some remarks regarding the applicability of general civil law provisions are made (§ III).

## B) Legal regime for the protection of trade secrets

### I. Constitutional Law

As outlined in chapter 1, from a civil law perspective, in Germany, it is unclear to what extent trade secrets fall under the category of IPRs or property rights. However, such a discussion has a constitutional dimension. In effect, if trade secrets are regarded as a species of property or a "legal interest" that merits protection,[811] the so-called "property guarantee" ("*Eigentumsgarantie*") provided for in § 14(1) of the German Constitution[812] and all of the implications derived from it should apply to their protection,[813] in particular, §§ 823 I, 812 I, and § 687 II of the BGB.

Against this backdrop, tension arises between "the property guarantee" and the "occupational freedom right" set forth in § 12(1) of the German

---

verstoßende eigene Handlung erlangt hat, zu Zwecken des Wettbewerbes unbefugt verwerthet oder an Andere mittheilt".

811 Stanisław Sołtysiński 1986 (n111) 351; in the same vein, Axel Beater, *Unlauterer Wettbewerb* (2nd edn, C.H. Beck 2011) § 9 Rdn 24 noting that: "Eigentum ist weit auszulegen und erfasst nicht allein Sacheigentum im Sinne des bürgerlichen Rechts, sondern sämtliche vermögenswerten privaten Rechte, die dem Einzelnen ähnlich wie das Sacheigentum zur privaten Nutzung und Verfügung zugeordnet sind. Solche vermögenswerten Rechtspositionen können z.B. Geschäftsgeheimnisse im Sinne der §§ 17 ff UWG. "

812 Grundgesetz für die Bundesrepublik Deutschland in der im Bundesgesetzblatt Teil III, Gliederungsnummer 1001, veröffentlichten bereinigten Fassung, das zuletzt durch Artikel 1 des Gesetzes vom 13. Juli 2017 (BGBl. I S. 2347) geändert worden ist.

813 *Ohly*/Sosnitza, *Gesetz gegen den unlauteren Wettbewerb* (7th edn, C.H. Beck 2016) §§ 17-19 Rdn 8.

Constitution, particularly in the context of departing employees and the information that they should be free to use in a new position.[814] This issue garnered a lot of attention during the negotiation of the TSD, and is mostly decided on a case-by-case basis, taking into consideration all of the relevant interests of each specific situation. A more detailed account of this topic and the principles applied by German courts in the ponderation of both rights is provided in chapter 6.[815]

## II. Unfair competition law and its intersection with criminal law

The main provisions that govern the legal regime for the protection of trade secrets in the German jurisdiction are enshrined in §§ 17 through 19 UWG. In essence, the primary objective of this statute is to regulate market practices in order to protect competitors, consumers, other market participants and, ultimately, the general public.[816] To this end, § 3 UWG (as amended in 2015) sets forth a general broad clause (§ 3(1) UWG) prohibiting unfair commercial practices (i) among companies in business-to-business relations; (ii) from non-business entities (such as non-governmental organisations); and (iii) with respect to consumers in business-to-consumer relations.[817] In addition § 3(2) UWG establishes a second general clause specifically for the protection of consumers, in the sense harmonised under Article 5(2) of the Unfair Commercial Practices Directive.[818] Both gen-

814 Ansgar Ohly 2014 (n 100) 10.

815 Chapter 6 § 1 A) II. 1. a) cc).

816 See § I UWG: "This Act shall serve the purpose of protecting competitors, consumers and other market participants against unfair commercial practices. At the same time, it shall protect the interests of the public in undistorted competition; " Ansgar Ohly, 'Unfair Competition', *Max Planck Encyclopaedia of European Private Law* (OUP 2012) 1172; Frauke Henning-Bodewig, 'A New Act Against Unfair Competition IIC [2005] 421, 423 stating that: "Originally, the UWG only served the interest of "honest competitors", and thus, to use modern terminology, a "B2B" regulation" and concluding that with time public interest and consumer protection were also recognised as "being of equal importance".

817 Ohly/*Sosnitza* (n 813) § 3 Rdn 6-7.

818 Ohly/*Sosnitza* (n 813) § 3 Rdn 69; Directive 2005/29/EC of the European Parliament and of the Council of 11 May 2005 concerning unfair business-to-consumer commercial practices in the internal market and amending Council Directive 84/450/EEC, Directives 97/7/EC, 98/27/EC and 2002/65/EC of the European Parliament and of the Council and Regulation (EC) No 2006/2004 of the European Parliament and of the Council [2005] OJ L149/22 (Unfair Commercial Practices Directive).

eral clauses are drafted in a flexible manner so as to allow a broad construction of the "unfair commercial practices" notion, which inevitably entails a certain degree of legal uncertainty.[819] To some extent, this uncertainty is narrowed down by the inclusion of a number of examples of unfair commercial practices with regard to competitors in § 4 UWG and with respect to consumers in § 4a UWG (aggressive commercial practices), § 5 UWG (misleading commercial practices) and § 5a UWG (misleading by omission).[820]

For the purposes of this research, §§ 17 and 18 UWG set out criminal liability in the event of unauthorised communication, acquisition, securing or exploitation of trade secrets, which furthermore trigger civil liability as acts of unfair competition. Drawing on these provisions, § 19 UWG provides that abetting to commit the offences therein established shall also be penalised.[821] This regulation is rather uncommon in view of the systems implemented in other European jurisdictions, where criminal law sanctions and unfair competition remedies are regulated in separate statutes.[822] However, in Germany, the criminal law regime was considered the most appropriate system to protect trade secrets mainly for two reasons, namely: (i) the special vulnerability of trade secrets ("*die besondere Verletzlichkeit*"), and (ii) the difficulty of obtaining appropriate and effective remedies in law.[823] The approach adopted by the German legislature when regulating trade secrets protection demands conditional intent to trigger not only criminal liability, but also civil liability, which is a much higher standard than the one introduced by the TSD (and differs from the applicable gross negligence standard in the U.S. and footnote 10 TRIPs). Accordingly, the two-fold nature of the provisions regulating trade secrets protection in the UWG is likely to be reviewed with the implementation of the TSD.[824]

---

819 Ansgar Ohly 2014 (n 98) 541.

820 Ansgar Ohly 2014 (n 98) 541.

821 Natalie Ackermann-Blome and Joanna Rindell, 'Should trade secrets be protected by private and/or criminal law? A comparison between Finnish and German laws' [2018] 13 JIPLP 78, 78.

822 Hogan Lovells 2012 (n 793) 251, according to which only Austria, Poland and Romania have adopted a similar approach.

823 Henning Harte-Bavendamm, '§ 77 Schutz von Geschäfts- und Betriebsgeheimnissen (§§ 17-19 UWG)' in Michale Loschelderr and Willi Erdmann (eds), *Wettbewerbsrecht* (4th edn, C.H. Beck 2010) § 77 Rdn 3.

824 Mary-Rose McGuire, 'Der Schutz von Know-how im System des Immaterialgüterrechts' [2016] GRUR 1000, 1002; Natalie Ackermann-Blome and Joanna Rindell (n 821) 86; the proposed Trade Secrets Act deletes §§ 17-19 UWG and

Throughout the next sections, the main provisions that regulate trade secrets protection under the two-fold unfair competition and criminal law regime are studied.

### 1. § 17 UWG Trade secrets disclosure

As already stated, the core regulation of trade secrets protection in Germany is built upon § 17 UWG, which provides the following:

(1) Whoever as the employee of a business communicates, without authorisation, a trade or industrial secret with which he was entrusted, or to which he had access, during the course of the employment relationship to another person for the purposes of competition, for personal gain, for the benefit of a third party, or with the intent of causing damage to the owner of the business shall be liable to imprisonment not exceeding three years or to a fine.

(2) Whoever for the purposes of competition, for personal gain, for the benefit of a third party, or with the intent of causing damage to the owner of the business, acquires or secures, without authorisation,
   1. a trade or industrial secret
   a) by using technical means;
   b) by creating an embodied communication of the secret; or
   c) by removing an item in which the secret is embodied;
   or
   2. without authorisation, uses or communicates to anyone a trade secret which he acquired through one of the communications referred to in subsection (1), or through an act of his own or of a third party pursuant to number 1, or which he has otherwise acquired or secured without authorization shall incur the same liability.[825]

In essence, § 17 identifies three types of conduct as criminal offences, *i.e.* (i) the unauthorised disclosure of trade secrets by an employee; (ii) the unauthorised procurement (acquisition) or securing of trade secrets by any third party; and (iii) the unauthorised exploitation or communication of the information obtained. Each of these is analysed in turn.

---

adopts a gross negligence standard with respect to civil liability. However, it still contains criminal provisions.

825 English Translation extracted from <http://www.gesetze-im-internet.de/englisch_uwg/englisch_uwg.html#p0139> accessed 15 September 2018.

### a) Unauthorised trade secret disclosure in the course of employment

Section 17(1) UWG proscribes the unauthorised disclosure of trade secrets in the course of employment. The essential feature of the behaviour described in this provision is that it can exclusively be carried out by a person in an employment relationship with the company.[826]

The term employed person ("*beschäftigte Person*") refers not only to employees ("*Angestellter*"), but also to workers ("*Arbeiter*") and apprentices ("*Lehrlinge*").[827] In fact, the courts have construed this expression in a wide sense, so as to include not only business executives and members of the board,[828] but also unskilled workers, such as trainees, cleaning staff and messengers.[829] The driving factor is that the infringer learnt about the secret information as a result of his relationship with the company.[830] His qualification, the salary that he receives or the type of tasks that he performs are irrelevant for the purposes of this provision.[831] Thus, partners and shareholders are deemed to fall outside the scope of § 17(1) UWG if they do not have a direct relationship with the undertaking.[832] Crucially, there must be causality between the obtention of the trade secret and the employment relationship. In this context, the decisive factor is whether the information could have been acquired outside of the employment relationship.[833]

The object of protection of § 17(1) UWG is a commercial or industrial secret that was entrusted to the employee, or that became known to him by reason of his employment relationship.[834] In particular, a secret is deemed to have been entrusted ("*anvertraut*") when it is conveyed to the employee under an explicit obligation of confidentiality or when such an

---

826 *Ohly*/Sosnitza (n 813) § 17 Rdn 13.
827 *Ohly*/Sosnitza (n 813) § 17 Rdn 13.
828 *Ohly*/Sosnitza (n 813) § 17 Rdn 13; Richard Schlötter, *Der Schutz von Betriebs- und Geschäftsgeheimnissen und die Abwerbung von Arbeitnehmern* (Carl Heymanns Verlag 1997) 144-145.
829 Henning Harte-Bavendamm 2010 (n 823) § 77 Rdn 18.
830 *Ohly*/Sosnitza (n 813) § 17 Rdn 13.
831 Rudolf Kraßer, 'Der Schutz des Know-how nach deutschem Recht' [1970] GRUR 587, 591; Henning Harte-Bavendamm (n 823) § 77 Rdn 18.
832 *Ohly*/Sosnitza (n 813) § 17 Rdn 13.
833 Richard Schlötter 1997 (n 828) 145-146; Gintare Surblyte 2011 (n 182) 57.
834 Michael Knospe, 'Germany' 62 in Melvine F. Jager (ed), *Trade secrets throught the world* (2012 Thomsom West) 15:12.

obligation can be inferred from the specific circumstances of the case.[835] Similarly, access ("*zugänglich geworden ist*") to undisclosed information during the performance of work activity also gives rise to confidentiality obligations.[836] Furthermore, the employee is bound not to disclose the information developed by him in the course of his employment relationship.[837] This is particularly relevant with regard to inventions, as follows from the Act on Employee Inventions ("*Arbeitnehmererfindungsgesetz*").[838] Specifically, § 24 of this statute sets forth a general presumption, whereby the ownership of the invention is vested on the undertaking instead of the employee, irrespective of whether the former had actual knowledge of its existence.[839]

As regards the scope of the liable conduct, it includes the *unauthorised communication* of the trade secret to anyone when carried out for at least one of the following purposes ("*Absicht*"): (i) for competitive purposes; (ii) for personal gain, (iii) for the benefit of a third party, or (iv) with the intention of causing damage to the enterprise or its owner.[840]

Case law has interpreted that the act of communication ("*Mitteilung*") covers any disclosure that makes trade secrets available to any third parties.[841] However, § 17(1) UWG does not require the recipient to have acquired active knowledge of the information, as the mere possibility of accessing it is regarded as sufficient.[842] As such, the disclosure can be carried out either orally or in a written form.[843] Likewise, pursuant to § 13 of the

---

835 *Köhler*/Bornkamm/Feddersen, *Gesetz gegen den unlauteren Wettbewerb* (36 edn, C. H. Beck 2018) § 17 Rdn 51.

836 *Ohly*/Sosnitza (n 813) § 17 Rdn 14; Henning Harte-Bavendamm 2010 (n 823) § 77 Rdn 19.

837 Henning Harte-Bavendamm 2010 (n 823) § 77 Rdn 19.
*Ohly*/Sosnitza (n 813) § 17 Rdn 14.

838 Gesetz über Arbeitnehmererfindungen in der im Bundesgesetzblatt Teil III, Gliederungsnummer 422-1,
veröffentlichten bereinigten Fassung, das zuletzt durch Artikel 7 des Gesetzes vom 31. Juli 2009 (BGBl. I S. 2521)
geändert worden ist (Act on Employee Inventions).

839 Michael Knospe (n 834) 15:17; BGH GRUR 1977, 539, 540–*Prozessrechner;* see further § 24 of the Act on Employee Inventions.

840 Michael Knospe (n 834) 15:17; *Harte-Bavendamm*/Henning-Bodewig (n 376) § 17 Rdn 14-17.

841 *Ohly*/Sosnitza (n 813) § 17 Rdn 15; *Köhler*/Bornkamm/Feddersen (n 835) § 17 Rdn 19; Harte-Bavendamm (n 823) § 77 Rdn § 21.

842 *Köhler*/Bornkamm/Feddersen (n 835) § 17 Rdn 28.

843 *Ohly*/Sosnitza (n 813) § 17 Rdn 15; *Köhler*/Bornkamm/Feddersen (n 835) § 17 Rdn 19; Henning Harte-Bavendamm 2010 (n 823) § 77 Rdn 21.

German Criminal Code,[844] an omission that leads to the disclosure of a trade secret may also be penalised under § 17(1) UWG, but only if the offender is in a guarantor position.[845] In that regard, it is worth noting that the recipient of the information can be anyone that it is not acquainted with the secret, such as competitors or colleagues of the infringer.

The act of communication carried out by the employee must be unauthorised ("*unbefugt*"), that is, contrary to an obligation of confidentiality.[846] Notwithstanding this, courts have ruled that such a disclosure might not trigger criminal liability when a ground of justification exists.[847]

Likewise, in its criminal law dimension, § 17(1) UWG requires that the secret is intentionally disclosed and that the infringer has actual knowledge of the secret nature of the information. Although negligent activity does not qualify for a relevant disclosure pursuant to § 17(1) UWG,[848] it has been generally accepted that conditional intent ("*Bedingter Vorsatz*") suffices with regard to all of the objective elements of the actus reus.[849] In the same vein, a mere attempt is also subject to criminal liability pursuant to § 17(3) UWG.[850]

In order to trigger liability, the act of communication must have been completed during the term of the infringer's employment. Accordingly, the disclosure of secret information after termination of the employment relationship can only give rise to an action for a breach of contractual obligations or an offence under paragraph 2 of § 17(2) UWG.[851] The rationale behind this provision is to promote labour mobility and this is examined in greater detail in chapter 6.[852]

---

844 Strafgesetzbuch in der Fassung der Bekanntmachung vom 13. November 1998 (BGBl. I S. 3322), das zuletzt durch Artikel 1 des Gesetzes vom 30. Oktober 2017 (BGBl. I S. 3618) geändert worden ist (StGB or German Criminal Code).

845 *Ohly*/Sosnitza (n 813) § 17 Rdn 15.

846 *Köhler*/Bornkamm/Feddersen (n 835) § 17 Rdn 21.

847 Typical examples of justification grounds include Einwillung (§ 138 StGB), Aussagepflicht (§ 38I Nr 6); Rechfertigender Notstand (§ 34 StGB); Notwehr (§ 32 StGB) and Selbdthilfe (§ 229 BGB); as noted by *Köhler*/Bornkamm/Feddersen (n 835) § 17 Rdn 21-21a,

848 Michael Knospe (n 834) 15:52.

849 Gerhard Janssen and Gabriele Maluga, '§ 17 Verrat von Geschäfts- und Betriebsgeheimnissen' in Wolfgang Joecks and Klaus Miebach (eds), *Münchener Kommentar zum StGB* (1st edn, C.H. Beck 2010); *Harte-Bavendamm*/Henning-Bodewig (n 376) § 17 Rdn 13.

850 Axel Beater (n 811) § 22 Rdn 1885.

851 *Ohly*/Sosnitza (n 813) § 17 Rn 15-16; *Köhler*/Bornkamm/Feddersen (n 835) § 17 Rdn 22.

852 Axel Beater (n 811) § 22 Rdn 1885.

In sum, it appears that the scope of § 17(1) UWG is limited to the protection of trade secret holders from the unauthorised disclosure of confidential information by their employees during the course of their labour relationship. However, the UWG in subsequent provisions expands the scope of protection afforded to trade secrets. In particular, the following section examines the legal framework set forth with regard to so-called "industrial espionage".

b) Industrial espionage

The German trade secrets legal regime draws on the roots of the special vulnerability of confidential information against acts of industrial espionage.[853] Under the current legislation, this unlawful behaviour is captured in paragraph 1 of § 17(2) UWG. Pursuant to this provision, the unauthorised procurement ("*sich verschaffen*") or securement ("*sichern*") of a trade secret triggers criminal liability if it is carried out through (i) the use of technical devices or means; (ii) the physical reproduction of the secret information; or (iii) the misappropriation of the object in which the confidential information is incorporated.

One of the distinguishing features of paragraph 1 of § 17(2) UWG is that the unlawful conduct described therein can be carried out by any person (not only employees, unlike § 17(1) UWG).[854]

However, the actus reus is limited to the unauthorised procurement and securement of trade secrets. The former consists of the acquisition of secret information. Hence, if the trade secret is embodied in a given object, its procurement requires obtaining possession of the said item (e.g. a CD containing confidential information).[855] By contrast, if the trade secret is not embodied in any object, its procurement arises from the mere acquisition of the information that constitutes the trade secret. For instance, this would be the case if the infringer memorised the chemical formula used to manufacture a pharmaceutical product. An act of securement takes place when the infringer incorporates secret information in a permanent form; among others, through recording or scanning the data.[856] Yet, often establishing the exact boundaries between these concepts appears rather implau-

853 *Harte-Bavendamm*/Henning-Bodewig (n 376) §§ 17-19 Rdn 6.
854 *Harte-Bavendamm*/Henning-Bodewig (n 376) § 17 Rdn 43.
855 *Ohly*/Sosnitza (n 813) § 17 Rdn 17; Richard Schlötter 1997 (n 828) 156-157.
856 *Ohly*/Sosnitza (n 813) § 17 Rdn 18.

sible, as some acts encompass both types of conduct simultaneously.[857] By way of illustration, this would be the case if the infringer acquired a CD with secret data (procurement), made a copy of the confidential information on his personal desktop and sent it through his private e-mail account to a third party (securement).[858]

The conduct referred to above must be carried out by at least one of the improper means described in paragraph 1 of § 17(2) UWG. If the trade secret is acquired in any other way, the conduct falls outside the scope of this provision.[859] As such, it is regarded that paragraph 1 of § 17(2) UWG identifies and penalises three types of behaviours that constitute a particularly dangerous form of espionage, irrespective of whether the acquired confidential information is subsequently used or disclosed.[860]

The first of the improper means described in paragraph 1 of § 17(2) refers to the procurement or securement of information through "technical means". Case law has construed these terms in a wide sense, so as to include all devices that can be used for such purposes;[861] for example, photographic and recording cameras, as well as the use of computers or other devices to decompile and analyse secret information.[862]

Secondly, the "physical reproduction of the secret information" also constitutes one of the unlawful means of acquiring a trade secret pursuant to paragraph 1 § 17(2) UWG. This provision refers to the reproduction of the trade secret and typically occurs when the infringer makes a photocopy or builds a replica of a machine.[863]

Finally, paragraph 1 of § 17(2) UWG prevents the "misappropriation of an object or device incorporating the secret". This provision refers to the unauthorised acquisition of the item in which the trade secret is embodied, and it includes all actions that allow the infringer to possess the object and use it or allow its use by a given third party.[864] Among others, courts

857 *Ohly*/Sosnitza (n 813) § 17 Rdn 18.
858 *Ohly*/Sosnitza (n 813) § 17 Rdn 18.
859 *Ohly*/Sosnitza (n 813) § 17 Rdn 19.
860 *Harte-Bavendamm*/Henning-Bodewig (n 376) § 17 Rdn 43; Thomas Hören und Reiner Münkner, 'Die neue EU-Richtlinie zum Schutz von Betriebsgeheimnissen und die Haftung Dritter' [2018] CCZ 85, 85.
861 *Harte-Bavendamm*/Henning-Bodewig (n 376) § 17 Rdn 44.
862 *Harte-Bavendamm*/Henning-Bodewig (n 376) § 17 Rdn 44.
863 *Ohly*/Sosnitza (n 813) § 17 Rdn 19.
864 *Ohly*/Sosnitza (n 813) § 17 Rdn 19; *Harte-Bavendamm*/Henning-Bodewig (n 376) § 17 Rdn 44.

have held that the misappropriation of photographs and storage devices may fall within the scope of paragraph 1 of § 17(2) UWG.[865]

As a final note, it should be stressed that in its criminal law dimension, paragraph 1 of § 17(2) UWG requires that the offender acts at least with intent ("*Vorsatz*") or conditional intent ("*Bedingter Vorsatz*").[866] The infringer must know or at least have reason to know that he had acquired or secured a trade secret under at least one of the improper means described in paragraph 1 of § 17(2) UWG and with one of the following purposes: (i) for competitive purposes; (ii) for personal gain, (iii) for the benefit of a third party, or (iv) with the intention of causing damage to the enterprise or its owner.[867] The following section, in which the general prohibition set out in paragraph 2 of § 17(2) UWG is examined, analyses in more detail the implications of demanding intent on the side of the infringer.

c) General prohibition

Finally, paragraph 2 of § 17(2) UWG sets forth a broader prohibition, whereby (i) the use or communication of a secret obtained through an unlawful disclosure from an employee pursuant to § 17(1) UWG or (ii) the unauthorised procurement or securement of confidential information by any of the means set out in paragraph 1 of § 17(2) UWG or by any other means shall trigger criminal liability. Notably, such a broad prohibition renders unlawful any unauthorised acquisition of a trade secret, if it is carried out by either an employee or a third party.[868] In this regard, it should be noted that the use of the same terminology as in the previous types of conduct but in a completely different context has been vehemently criticised.[869] This provision is particularly relevant with regard to the behaviour of former employees, as it captures the exploitation of secrets obtained by employees in an unlawful way while they were still in an employment relationship with the trade secret holder.[870]

---

865 *Ohly*/Sosnitza (n 813) § 17 Rdn 19; *Harte-Bavendamm*/Henning-Bodewig (n 376) § 17 Rdn 44.

866 Natalie Ackermann-Blome and Joanna Rindell (n 821) 82; *Ohly*/Sosnitza (n 813) § 17 Rdn 24 refers to dolus eventualis.

867 *Harte-Bavendamm*/Henning-Bodewig (n 376) § 17 Rdn 25.

868 *Harte-Bavendamm*/Henning-Bedewig (n 376) 17 Rdn 47.

869 Thomas Hören und Reiner Münkner 2018(a) (n 860) 85.

870 *Ohly*/Sosnitza (n 813) § 17 Rdn 20; *Harte-Bavendamm*/Henning-Bodewig (n 376) § 17 Rdn 44.

Crucially, due to its criminal law nature, paragraph 2 of § 17(2) UWG, just like the other relevant types of conduct analysed under § 17 UWG, restricts the liability of former employees and third parties to cases where they acted with intent ("*Vorsatz*"). Yet, positive knowledge that the information has been acquired through the means set out in § 17(1) UWG and paragraph 1 of § 17(2) UWG is not required. It is generally accepted that conditional intent suffices ("*Bedingter Vorsatz*").[871] Accordingly, if the infringer is aware that the information may have been obtained in an unlawful manner pursuant to the previous relevant types of conduct and willingly closes his eyes to it, liability will also arise with respect to indirect acquisition.[872] Crucially, the intent comprises all of the objective elements of the offence. Hence, if the infringer mistakenly believes that he is under an obligation to disclose a trade secret, no liability will arise.[873] In addition, the employee or any other third party must have disclosed the trade secret for at least one of the following purposes ("*Absicht*"): (i) for competitive purposes; (ii) for personal gain, (iii) for the benefit of a third party, or (iv) with the intention of causing damage to the enterprise or its owner.[874]

In view of this, it appears that the standard of liability set out in the UWG with respect to third parties is higher than under the TRIPs Agreement (under footnote 10 of Article 39(2)), and Article 4(4) TSD, by virtue of which gross negligence suffices.[875] Hence, the level of protection of trade secret holders against third party misappropriation is much lower than in other EU jurisdictions, such as England (or even the U.S.).

## 2. § 18 UWG Use of models

In the UWG of 1909 the German legislature decided to regulate in a separate provision protection against the so-called "piracy of models" ("*Vorlagenfreibeuterei*"). This amendment was introduced as a result of complaints raised by embroidery and lace manufacturers, who argued that their trade

---

871 Thomas Hören und Reiner Münkner 2018(a) (n 860) 85.

872 Mary-Rose McGuire, Björn Joachim, Jens Künzel and Nils Weber,'Protection of Trade Secrets through IPR and Unfair Competition Law' (2010) AIPPI Report Question Q215, 10 <http://aippi.org/wp-content/uploads/committees/215/GR215germany_en.pdf> accessed 15 September 2018.

873 *Ohly*/Sosnitza (n 813) § 17 Rdn 20; Thomas Hören und Reiner Münkner 2018(a) (n 860) 85.

874 *Harte-Bavendamm*/Henning-Bodewig (n 376) § 17 Rdn 14-17.

875 Rudolf Rudolf Kraßer 1996 (n 585) 224.

secrets were being revealed through the unlawful use of their templates and models.[876] In its current wording, § 18 UWG provides the following:

> § 18 UWG Use of models
> (1) Whoever, acting without authorisation, uses or communicates to another person models or instructions of a technical nature, particularly drawings, prototypes, patterns, segments or formulas, entrusted to him for the purposes of competition or for personal gain shall be liable to imprisonment not exceeding two years or to a fine.
> (2) An attempt shall incur criminal liability.
> (3) The offence shall be prosecuted upon application only, unless the criminal prosecution authority considers that it is necessary to take *ex officio* action on account of the particular public interest in the criminal prosecution.
> (4) Section 5, number 7, of the Criminal Code shall apply *mutatis mutandis*.[877]

Nowadays, this provision aims at protecting technical knowledge that is supplied by the trade secret holder in the context of know-how agreements or during the negotiation of other kinds of contracts.[878] However, its scope of application is limited to two specific kinds of industrial secrets, i.e. models ("*Vorlagen*") and technical instructions ("*Vorschriften technischer Art*"). The former refer to means that are used as prototypes for the production of new items or the delivery of new services, subject to fixation.[879] The latter include the commands and teachings that must be followed in the implementation of technical processes.[880] Segments and formulas, as well as computer programs are often cited by academia and case law as paradigmatic examples of instructions of a technical nature in the sense of § 18 (UWG).[881]

---

876 *Ohly*/Sosnitza (n 813) § 18 Rn 2.

877 Translation obtained from the German Ministry of Justice website <http://www.gesetze-im-internet.de/englisch_uwg/englisch_uwg.html#UWGengl_000P17> accessed 15 September 2018.

878 *Harte-Bavendamm*/Henning-Bodewig (n 376) § 18 Rdn 55.

879 *Köhler*/Bornkamm/Feddersen (n 835) § 18 Rdn 9 stating that: "Vorlagen sind Mitteln, die als Grundlage oder Vorbild für die Herstellung von neuen Sachen oder Dienstungen dinen sollen"; Köhler further notes that the Models ("*Vorlagen*") can be fixated either in a particular embodiment (an exemplary) or in an abstract depiction (such as a description or representation).

880 *Köhler*/Bornkamm/Feddersen (n 835) § 18 Rdn 10.

881 *Ohly*/Sosnitza (n 813) § 18 Rdn 5.

The actus reus consists of the unauthorised communication of models and technical instructions that were entrusted to the infringer in the course of trade for the purposes of hindering competition or for a personal gain.[882]

Case law has again construed the term entrusted ("*anvertraut*") in a wide sense. It includes all the models and technical instructions that the trade secret holder conveyed to another undertaking under an obligation of confidentiality (express or implied from the specific circumstances of the case).[883] However, it is essential that the trade secret was communicated to the confidant with the sole purpose of it being used in the interest of the holder.[884]

Finally, it is necessary that the secret information is conveyed in the course of trade ("*im geschäftlichen Verkehr*") in order to be protected pursuant to § 18 UWG. The limited scope of application of this provision has been criticised by a number of commentators, who regard that it is out of date in the digital world and, consequently, it will most likely be deleted with the implementation of the TSD in Germany.

## III. Civil law

The current wording of the UWG sets forth criminal sanctions in the event that §§ 17 and 18 are infringed, but makes no reference to the civil protection afforded in such circumstances.[885] Notwithstanding this, it is generally accepted by courts and academia that trade secret holders are entitled, among other remedies, to claim damages, exercise the right of information and apply for injunctive relief.[886] In that regard, it is worth noting that since § 19 UWG was amended in 2004,[887] no general consensus exists on a

882 Axel Beater (n 811) § 22 Rdn 1887.

883 *Ohly*/Sosnitza (n 813) § 18 Rdn 6; *Köhler*/Bornkamm/Feddersen (n 835) § 18 Rdn 11.

884 *Ohly*/Sosnitza (n 813) § 18 Rdn 6.

885 *Köhler*/Bornkamm/Feddersen (n 835) § 17 Rdn 51.

886 *Harte-Bavendamm*/Henning-Bodewig (n 376) § 17 Rdn 58.

887 Before the 2004 UWG amendment, § 19 UWG set forth the right to claim damages in the event of infringement of §§ 17 and 18 UWG. Accordingly, § 19 provided that: "Violations of the provisions of Sections 17 and 18 also result in liability for damages caused thereby. Where there are several parties, they are jointly and severally liable" (translation from Michael Knospe (n 834) para § 15:32). Notwithstanding this, such a provision was deemed superfluous and was consequently deleted from the Act in the UWG reform of 2004; see in this regard

civil legal basis that triggers their applicability. As regards the available means of redress, Ohly makes a clear-cut distinction between criminal accessory claims ("*Strafrechtsakzessorische Ansprüche*") and civil autonomous claims ("*Zivilrechtsautonome Ansprüche*").[888] The former only arise if the objective elements of the offence ("*objektiver Tatbestand*") and the mens rea or subjective elements of the offence ("*subjektiver Tatbestand*") described in §§ 17 and 18 UWG are carried out by the infringer. The latter, on the other hand, can be claimed irrespective of any finding of criminal liability.[889] In the following section, for the purposes of clarity, the different legal mechanisms available to enforce trade secrets protection in the civil jurisdiction are outlined in accordance with Ohly's classification, with the aim of providing a better and clearer understanding of the legal issues surrounding the enforcement of trade secrets in Germany.

### 1. Criminal accessory claims

Despite the lack of statutory provisions dealing with the enforcement of trade secrets, as stated above, case law provides that any violation of §§ 17 and 18 UWG may trigger claims both for damages and injunctive relief. Hence, in order to award damages, courts resort to the general clause of 823 II BGB, which provides that a duty of compensation arises if a breach of statute intended to protect another person is found.[890] Likewise, injunctive relief is usually granted in accordance with Article 1004 BGB, pursuant to which the possibility of obtaining an injunction if an interference with a property right occurs is established.[891]

---

*Ohly*/Sosnitza (n 813) § 17 Rdn 35; *Köhler*/Bornkamm/Feddersen (n 1299) § 17 Rdn 52.

888 For a more detailed analysis see Ansgar Ohly 2014 (n 13) 7-11.

889 Ansgar Ohly 2014 (n 13) 12.

890 § 823BGB Liability in damages: "(1) A person who, intentionally or negligently, unlawfully injures the life, body, health, freedom, property or another right of another person is liable to make compensation to the other party for the damage arising from this.(2) The same duty is held by a person who commits a breach of a statute that is intended to protect another person. If, according to the contents of the statute, it may also be breached without fault, then liability to compensation only exists in the case of fault" (translation obtained from the German Ministry of Justice website <http://www.gesetze-im-internet.de/englisch_bgb/englisch_bgb.html#> accessed 15 Sepember 2018).

891 § 1004 BGB – Claim for removal and injunction: "(1) If the ownership is interfered with by means other than removal or retention of possession, the owner

Against this background, an infringement of a trade secret pursuant to § 17 and § 18 UWG is regarded as a breach of § 3a UWG, by virtue of which "the breach of a statutory provision that is also intended to regulate market behaviour in the interest of market participants if the infringement affect the interests of consumers, other entrants or competitor shall be deemed unfair". In the light of the above, a violation of §§ 17 or 18 UWG is deemed to contravene the general prohibition of unfair commercial practices set forth in § 3 I UWG through the application of § 3a UWG.[892] Based on § 3 I UWG, the trade secret holder is entitled to claim the remedies set forth in chapter 2 of the UWG, namely elimination and injunctive relief (§ 8 UWG);[893] compensation for damages (§ 9 UWG); and confiscation of profits (§ 10 UWG). Nonetheless, such a possibility has been highly contested by some commentators on the basis that the behaviours described in §§ 17 and 18 UWG cannot be understood as a provision regulating market behaviour. In particular, it has been argued that IPRs do not fall under such a category, as indeed they are meant to protect individual rights.[894]

---

may require the disturber to remove the interference. If further interferences are to be feared, the owner may seek a prohibitory injunction" (translation obtained from the German Ministry of Justice website <http://www.gesetze-im-internet.de/englisch_bgb/englisch_bgb.html#> accessed 15 Sepember 2018).

892 *Ohly*/Sosnitza (n 813) § 17 UWG Rdn 44; Franz Hofmann, '"Equity" im deutschen Lauterkeitsrecht? Der "Unterlassungsanspruch" nach der Geschäftsgeheimnis-RL' [2018] WRP 1, 3 para 10.

893 BGH GRUR 1964, 31 – *Petromax II.*

894 Against this background, Wolfgang Schaffert, '4 Nr 11' Rdn 68 in Peter W. Heermann and others (eds), *Münchener Kommentar zum Lauterkeitsrecht* (1st edn, C.H. Beck 2006) argues that exclusive rights and particularly §§ 17-18 UWG do not intended to regulate competition in the market through the establishment of the equal barriers and the creation of equal opportunities among competitors. Contrariwise, he concludes that such provisions do not establish any market behaviour rules ("*Marketverhaltungsregeln*") in the interest of consumers and thus, fall outside the scope of § 3a UWG. As such, the infringement of the above- mentioned provisions cannot be regarded as anticompetitive if it systematically leads to a competitive advantage; the opposite view is held by Ohly 2014 (n 13) 12, who notes that the behaviours described in the UWG provisions that regulate trade secret protection, i.e. §§ 17-18 UWG do not take place before any market activity, as in this scenario the relevant market consists of information and not the products. Hence, he concludes that the tension between market behaviour rules and individual rights is only apparent, as he affirms that IPRs protect individual rights and at the same time establish market behaviour rules. In particular, it is stressed that IPRs determine the behaviours that are allowed in the market.

## 2. Civil autonomous claims

Civil autonomous claims arise irrespective of the finding of criminal liability pursuant to § 17 and § 18 UWG. Their applicability has proven extremely relevant in practice, as the UWG provisions that expressly regulate trade secrets protection only sanction wilful infringement.[895]

The most relevant civil autonomous claims refer to contractual obligations, and are applicable to the breach of know-how agreements and the use and disclosure of trade secrets by departing employees. In such a context, performance or damages can be claimed on the basis of § 280 I BGB.[896] The applicability of this provision only requires negligence ("*Leichte Fahrlässigkeit*").[897] In addition, fault is presumed in those cases where the breach of a duty is established, as per the second phrase of § 280 I BGB.[898]

Likewise, § 4(3)(c) UWG precludes the offering of goods or services that are replicas of goods or services of a competitor if he dishonestly obtained the knowledge or documents needed for the replicas. This provision may be applied in the event that the replicas embody a trade secret obtained unlawfully.[899] More generally, if not all of the liability conditions set out in §§ 17-18 UWG are fulfilled, courts may still regard that the conduct of a competitor falls under the general obstruction of competition clause set out in § 4(4) UWG, which in turn contravenes the general prohibition of unfair commercial practices set forth in § 3 I UWG and the remedies established in connection with it.[900]

As a final note, it should be pointed out that if trade secrets are regarded as the object of a property right, they shall be protected pursuant to § 823 I (damages in the event of unlawful, wilful or negligent injury of another's property), § 812 I (duty of restitution), and § 687 II (false agency without

895 *Ohly*/Sosnitza (n 813) § 17 Rdn 36.

896 § 280 (1) BGB sets out that: "If the obligor breaches a duty arising from the obligation, the obligee may demand damages for the damage caused thereby. This does not apply if the obligor is not responsible for the breach of duty"; (translation obtained from the German Ministry of Justice website <http://www.gesetze-im-internet.de/englisch_bgb/englisch_bgb.html#p0841> accessed 15 September 2018).

897 *Ohly*/Sosnitza (n 813) § 17 Rdn 43.

898 *Ohly*/Sosnitza (n 813) § 17 Rdn 43.

899 Ansgar Ohly 2014 (n 13) 12.

900 *Köhler*/Bornkamm/Feddersen (n 1299) § 17 Rdn 52.

specific authorisation) BGB.[901] However, this remains highly contested, as no consensus on the legal nature of trade secrets in Germany exists.[902]

### *§ 3 Trade Secrets Protection in England before the implementation of the TSD – The law of confidentiality*

The analysis of the law of confidentiality should start by noting that in the UK three different jurisdictions coexist, namely (i) England and Wales; (ii) Northern Ireland; and (iii) Scotland. The first two are common law jurisdictions, while the law in Scotland has a hybrid nature, as it draws both from common law and Roman law origins.[903] As regards trade secrets, the England and Wales jurisdiction has the most developed body of case law and will be used as the case of study in this dissertation. In fact, judicial review regards that the law of confidentiality in Northern Ireland and Scotland is very similar to the law in England and Wales, even though the Scottish system is viewed as being less developed.[904]

In England, trade secrets protection is mostly achieved through contractual provisions and the breach of confidence action, which protects confidential information in general.[905] Notably, trade secrets are protected through the same action that covers other kinds of confidential information, such as artistic and literary information, government secrets[906] and private information,[907] without distinction by subject.[908]

Unlike most civil law countries and the U.S., in England no specific provisions dealing with the protection of trade secrets have been enacted into law.[909] Remarkably, the English legal regime does not contain criminal law provisions penalising industrial espionage,[910] the most common form

---

901 Ansgar Ohly 2014 (n 100) 3.
902 See chapter 1 § 3 B) 3. b).
903 Hogan Lovells 2012 (n 793) paras 240-241.
904 Hogan Lovells 2012 (n 793) paras 241.
905 Tanya Aplin and others 2012 (n 22) para 1.01.
906 *Attorney General v Guardian Newspapers Ltd (No 2)* [1990] 1 AC 109 (HL).
907 *Campbell v MGN Ltd* [2004] 2 AC 457 (HL).
908 William Cornish, David Llewellyn and Tanya Aplin 2013 (n 209) para 8-07.
909 In the Law Commission 1981 (n 327) 101 it was argued in favour of establishing a statutory action for breach of confidence in the interests of clarity and legal certainty.
910 The Law Commission published a Discussion Paper (Law Commission, *Legislating the Criminal Code: Misuese of Trade Secrets* (Law Com No 150, 1997)) arguing in favour of the establishment of a criminal liability regime for the deliberate

of trade secrets protection found in other jurisdictions. Consequently, criminal liability for the misappropriation of trade secrets is covered by other offences, such as conspiracy to defraud or theft (but only with regard to a physical object in which a trade secret is embodied).[911] It is a well-established principle that "there is no confidence as to the disclosure of inequity".[912]

The breach of confidence action has considerable breadth, as it "enables any person who has an interest in information that is confidential to prevent others who have received, or acquired the information with notice of its confidential quality from using or disclosing the information".[913]

Case law has set forth that information must present three elements in order to be protected.[914] First, it must entail the quality of confidence. Second, it must have been disclosed in circumstances implying an obligation of confidence. Third, an unauthorised use of the information detrimental to the owner of the information must have taken place.[915]

The following sections delve into the protection of trade secrets in England and Wales under the legal framework created by the breach of confidence action, with the aim of providing a better understanding of the notion of confidentiality. To this end, first section A introduces a number of preliminary remarks regarding the withdrawal of the UK from the EU and its effects on the trade secrets legal regime. Thereafter, section B examines the development of the action since the mid-XIX century, while section C analyses the four causes of action that have traditionally been invoked in cases of breach of confidence and the applicable liability requirements.

---

misuse of trade secrets, but this proposal was never passed; see further Carl Steele and Anthony Trenton, 'Trade secrets: the need for criminal liability' [1998] 20 EIPR 188-192.

911 William Cornish, David Llewellyn and Tanya Aplin 2013 (n 209) para 8-55; Lionel Bently and Brad Sherman 2014 (n 125) 1197; Allison Coleman, *The Legal Protection of Trade Secrets* (Sweet&Maxwell 1992) Chapter 7; pursuant to the Theft Act 1968, s 1 "theft", is the "dishonest appropriation *of property* belonging to another with the intention of permanently deriving the other of it". In turn, s 4 establishes that property also refers to "intangible property". However, a substantial number of cases have stated that information does not fall under the category of "intangible property".

912 Law Commission Report 1997 (n 910) 59, citing *Garstide v Outram* [1857] 26 LJ Ch 113.

913 Tanya Aplin and others 2012 (n 22) para 1.01.

914 The three elements that constitute the breach of confidence action were first established in *Coco v. A.N.Clark (Engineers) Ltd* [1969] RPC 41 (Ch), 46.

915 *Coco v A.N.Clark (Engineers) Ltd* [1969] RPC 41 (Ch), 48.

## A) A note on Brexit

On June 23, 2016, 51,9% of the electorate in the UK voted in favour of leaving the EU, following a referendum called for by the European Union Referendum Act of 2015.[916] The results of the referendum were confirmed by the Parliament of the UK in both of its Houses, leading to the adoption of the European Union Notification of Withdrawal Bill.[917] Consequently, on March 29, 2017 the UK Government notified the European Council about its decision to abandon the EU (popularly referred to as “Brexit”), in accordance with the procedure set out in Article 50(2) TUE.[918] At this stage, the European Council and the UK are still in the process of negotiating the terms of the Withdrawal Agreement, which will establish the specific date after which the EU Treaties and secondary legislation of the EU will no longer be applicable in the UK and will also govern the relationship between the parties after that date. In the absence of such an agreement and pursuant to Article 50(3) TEU, the EU legal system will cease to apply two years after the withdrawal notification date (29 March 2019).

Despite the imminent withdrawal of the UK from the EU, the United Kingdom Intellectual Property Office (“UKIPO”) has launched a consultation, which includes a proposal to implement the Directive.[919] Irrespective of the outcome of the consultation, the UK played a fundamental role during the negotiation of the TSD, mostly due to the sophisticated and diverse body of case law developed by English courts that allowed stakeholders to achieve an effective level of protection against trade secrets misappropriation. Therefore, the study of the English model in the context of the TSD remains relevant for the purposes of the present research, even after the withdrawal of the UK from the EU.

---

916 European Union Referendum Act 2015 (c. 36)

917 European Union Notification of Withrawal Bill 2017.

918 According to the UK notification under Article 50 TEU dated 29 March 2017 <http://data.consilium.europa.eu/doc/document/XT-20001-2017-INIT/en/pdf> accessed 15 September 2018.

919 According to Will Smith and Robert Williams, ‘Brexit and the Trade Secrets Directive - the Clock is Ticking (16 October 2017) <https://www.twobirds.com/en/news/articles/2017/uk/brexit-and-the-trade-secrets-directive-the-clock-is-ticking> accessed 15 September 2018.

## B) Development of the law of confidentiality

The origin of the breach of confidence action has often been described as "obscure". Until the early XIX century, the protection of confidentiality was articulated through an array of legal doctrines established in contract law, employment law, criminal law, copyright law and patent law, as well as in the law of inheritance.[920] The basis for the existing breach of confidence action was not settled until the mid-XIX century through two landmark cases: *Prince Albert v Strange*[921] and *Morison v Moat*.[922] These decisions set out the core principles upon which the current breach of confidence action is built, as outlined below.

In the first ruling, the plaintiff obtained an injunction preventing the publication of a catalogue of etchings made by Prince Albert and Queen Victoria for their amusement and private use. The defendant was an employee of the printer in Windsor where the etchings were printed. He decided to make additional copies and compile them in a catalogue, without authorisation from Prince Albert and Queen Victoria. In its ruling, the court stated that the plaintiff had a property right in the etchings and was therefore entitled to exclude the defendant "against the invasion of such right". Notwithstanding this, the most significant contribution of the decision was the finding that a duty of confidence might exist separately from a contractual obligation.[923]

In *Morison v Moat*,[924] the plaintiffs were granted an injunction to prevent the use of a secret recipe to manufacture a cure-all medicine called "Morison's Universal Medicine". The inventor, the plaintiff's father (James Morison), had entered into a partnership with the defendant's father, Thomas Moat, to exploit the invention, under the condition that he did not disclose it. Shortly before his death, Thomas Moat revealed the secret to his son, Horatio Moat, who started producing and marketing the medicine on his own account. As a result, the plaintiffs sought an injunction to restrain such marketing activities. The High Court of Chancery granted the injunction and held that Thomas Moat must have revealed the secret recipe to his son in breach of the contract (and confidence) or he

920 Tanya Aplin and others 2012 (n 22) para 2.02.

921 *Prince Albert v Strange* [1849] 2 De G & Sm 652.

922 *Morison v Moat* [1851] 9 Hare 241.

923 In *Prince Albert v Strange* [1849] 2 De G & Sm 652; ER 293; 1 Mac & G 25, 44 the Court stated that: "a breach of trust, confidence or contract would of itself entitle the plaintiff to an injunction".

924 *Morison v Moat* [1851] 9 Hare 241.

must had acquired it "surreptitiously". Notably, *Morison v. Moat* is regarded as the first authority where "the liability for third-party recipients of trade secrets" was established.[925]

In the mid-XX century, the English courts established a broader equitable jurisdiction, on the basis of good faith rather than property and contract.[926] In *Saltman Engineering v Campbell Engineering* the court stated that "the obligation to respect confidence is not limited to cases where the parties are in contractual relationship".[927] Instead, the court found an implied duty of confidentiality, whereby an obligation of confidence may stem from a relationship where information is imparted under certain circumstances and without a contract.[928]

Despite the recent developments, many aspects of the breach of confidence action remain open, such as the jurisdictional basis and the liability of innocent acquirers. Likewise, the rise of new technologies, such as Artificial Intelligence and Big Data, poses additional challenges that courts will have to address in the near future. The following section analyses the legal regime for the protection of confidential information under the breach of confidence action in England.

## C) Legal regime for the protection of confidential information under the breach of confidence action

### I. Jurisdictional basis for the action

The legal nature and scope of the breach of confidence action has been the object of debate by scholars and case law, and hitherto no consensus exists on this matter.[929]

On the one hand, it has been argued that there is no single concept that clarifies or comprises all of the causes of action for what has traditionally

925 Tanya Aplin and others 2012 (n 22) para 2.90.

926 William Cornish, David Llewellyn and Tanya Aplin 2013 (n 209) para 8-07.

927 *Saltman Engineering v Campell Engineering* [1948] 65 RPC 203 (CA), 211.

928 Tanya Aplin and others 2012 (n 22) para 2.90; Roger M. Toulson and Charles M. Phipps 2012 (n 326) paras 1-046 - 1-050; Law Commission 1981 (n 327) para 3.11.

929 Law Commission 1981 (n 327); Gareth Jones, 'Restitution of Benefits Obtained in Breach of Another's Confidence' [1970] 86 LQR 463.

been called breach of confidence.[930] On the other hand, more recently, it has been suggested that the said action is of a sui generis nature and, as such, does not fall strictly under one conventional category.[931] The latter view became increasingly popular during the negotiation of the TSD in the light of the new obligations set forth by its implementation.[932]

Courts have mostly relied on four different causes of action, (predominantly contract, equity and to a lesser extent tort and property) to decide on an alleged breach of confidence case.[933] In the light of the above, the following sub-sections intend to provide an overview of the doctrinal grounds of the action.

### 1. Contract

Courts have extensively invoked contractual obligations in order to protect confidential information, on the basis of both express and implied terms of a contract.[934]

The main issues raised by the enforcement of express terms relate to post-employment obligations that prevent employees from using their acquired skills and knowledge.[935] As such, these contractual provisions have often been deemed unenforceable as an "unreasonable restraint of trade".[936] In contrast, courts have stated that it is possible to infer an obligation of confidence from a contract, even though the contract is silent on

930 Roger M. Toulson and Charles M. Phipps, *Confidentiality* (2nd edn, Sweet&Maxwell 2006) 2 noting that "No single concept satisfactorily explains or encompasses all species of the action for what has traditionally been called breach of confidence".

931 Tanya Aplin and others 2012 (n 22) para 4.09

932 Lionel Bently and Brad Sherman 2014 (n 125) 1139.

933 Tanya Aplin and others 2012 (n 22) para 4.09; Allison Coleman 1992 (n 911) 37 arguing that contract is the main jurisdictional base for actions.

934 John Hull, 'The licensing of trade secrets and know-how'155, 167 in Jacques de Werra (ed), *Research Handbook in Intellectual Property Licensing* (Edward Elgar 2013) argues that the modern course of action is grounded on an equitable duty of good faith; Tanya Aplin and others 2012 (n 22) para 4.13; Allison Coleman 1992 (n 911) 38.

935 Kate Brearley and Selwyn Bloch, *Employment covenants and confidential information* (Butterworths1993) 70.

936 Allison Coleman 1992 (n 911) 41-44.

that point, if the said obligation is necessary to comply with the object of the contract.[937]

Notwithstanding this, contract law is also subject to limitations and has proven insufficient in answering questions regarding third party liability in breach of contract i.e. situations where there is a disclosure from the confidant who received the information under a duty of confidence to a third party.[938] In these cases, the protection of confidential information should be sought through equity or tort law, as contract law does not provide a legal basis to enjoin the use of the trade secret by the third party outside of the contractual relationship .[939]

## 2. Equity

Originally, the equitable jurisdiction[940] provided supplementary remedies in situations in which authorities or statutory law might not fully address the issue concerned or provided inequitable solutions.[941] In the mid-IVX century, the Court of Chancery was established as a new and distinct court in England,[942] with the aim of creating a body of law based on "principles of justice"[943] that afforded remedies not granted by the increasingly rigid system developed in common law courts.[944] Within this legal framework, the breach of confidence action sought to protect an "equitable right in the confidentiality of information".[945]

Nowadays, the equitable jurisdiction essentially plays two roles vis-à-vis the breach of confidence action. First, it supports the legal jurisdiction exercised by courts on the basis of contractual confidence obligations. In the

937 Tanya Aplin and others 2012 (n 22) para 4.18.

938 Tanya Aplin and others 2012 (n 22) para 4.36.

939 Tanya Aplin and others 2012 (n 22) para 4.36.

940 The Black's Law Dictionary defines 'equity,n' as "The system of law or body of principles originating in the English Court of Chancery and superseding the common and statute law (together called "law" in the narrower sense) when the two conflict" *Black's Law Dictionary* (9th edn, West Publishing 2009).

941 'equity, n', *Black's Law Dictionary* (9th edn, West Publishing 2009).

942 *Encyclopaedia Britannica*, 'Equity' <https://www.britannica.com/topic/equity> accessed 15 September 2017.

943 'equity, n', *Black's Law Dictionary* (9th edn, West Publishing 2010).

944 *Encyclopaedia Britannica*, 'Equity' <https://www.britannica.com/topic/equity> accessed 15 September 2017.

945 Andrew Burrows and David Feldman, *Oxford Principles of English Law* (2nd edn, OUP 2009) 1311.

event that courts find a breach in the contractual obligation of confidence, an injunction may be granted only on the basis of equitable conduct. Second, equity provides an additional jurisdiction to prevent breach of confidence irrespective of the existence of any legal rights, substantially expanding courts' jurisdiction on this subject.[946]

In particular, the independent equitable jurisdiction allows courts to restrain the breach of confidence in three situations where the law provides no remedy.[947] First, equity can serve to restrain parties to a confidential disclosure that are not in a contractual relationship. This may occur, for example, if one of the parties to a negotiation that ultimately broke off seeks to benefit from the disclosed information. Second, equity provides the basis for court intervention where a third party receives confidential information from a confidant in breach of his obligation of confidence. Typically, this might be the case where the recipient of the information knows that the said information was acquired in breach of an equitable or contractual obligation. Third, the equitable jurisdiction also allows for restraining third parties that have acquired information without being bound by a confidential relationship. This covers both the surreptitious acquisition of information and acquisition with knowledge of its confidential nature by any third party.[948]

Against this backdrop, it is noteworthy that from the same fact pattern both contractual and equitable obligations may arise and eventually even overlap.[949] In this scenario, courts have either applied both jurisdictions or proceeded on the equitable basis alone, at their own discretion.[950] In fact, the Supreme Court of England, in one of its latest decisions on trade secrets protection, *Vestergaard v Bestnet*,[951] relied on equity as the applicable cause of action.

### 3. Property

The possibility of restraining unauthorised uses of confidential information has frequently been justified on the basis of a property right.[952] How-

946 Tanya Aplin and others 2012 (n 22) para 4.38.
947 Tanya Aplin and others 2012 (n 22) paras 4.43-4.46.
948 Tanya Aplin and others 2012 (n 22) para 4.46.
949 Allison Coleman 1992 (n 911) 46-47.
950 Tanya Aplin and others 2012 (n 22) para 4.48.
951 *Vestergaard Frandsen A/S v Bestnet Europe Ltd* [2013] UKSC 31.
952 Allison Coleman 1992 (n 911) 48.

ever, this argument has been, and still is, the object of a vehement debate both by case law and the legal scholarship, and is by no means settled, as discussed in chapter 1.[953]

## 4. Tort[954]

In the past, tort law was frequently invoked by courts to take action for the protection of confidential information. Nowadays such a jurisdictional basis seems confined to the protection of personal privacy, pursuant to Article 8 ECHR.[955]

Indeed, as noted above,[956] one of the most remarkable features of the English breach of confidence action is that it protects a wide range of interests, and among them, the protection of personal information has given rise to a rich body of case law.[957] This is particularly relevant because under English law there is no specific legislation that explicitly recognises the right to privacy.[958]

Notwithstanding this, for years courts repeatedly rejected the creation of a general tort of privacy, as it was deemed that this fell under the scope of the competences of the Parliament.[959] Accordingly, several bills aiming at

953 A more detailed account of this topic is provided in chapter 1 § 3 B) I. 2. a).

954 'Tort,n', *Black´s Law Dictionary* (9th edn, West Publishing 2009) "A tort is a legal wrong committed upon the person or property independent of contract. It may be either (1) a direct invasion of some legal right of the individual; (2) the infraction of some public duty by which special damage accrues to the individual; or (3) a violation of some private obligation by which like damage accrues to the individual".

955 Roger M. Toulson and Charles M. Phipps 2012 (n 326) 2-017: "It is therefore right that the courts have now come to recognise explicitly that there are separate (sometimes overlapping) causes of action in contract of equity for breach of confidence and in tort for infringement of privacy".

956 See chapter 3 § 3 B).

957 Ansgar Ohly and Agnès Lucas-Schloetter, *Privacy, Property and Personality* (CUP 2005) 85.

958 Tanya Aplin, 'The future of the breach of confidence action and the protection of privacy' [2007] Oxford University Commonwealth J 137, 137 refers to the "piecemeal protection of privacy by different areas of the law".

959 See Lord Hoffman in *Campbell v MGN Limited* [2004] 2 AC 457 (HL), [14] and *Wainwright v Home Office* [2003] 3 WLR 1137 (HL); contrary, Tanya Aplin 2007 (n 958) 137 argues in favour of the establishment of a limited tort of privacy, namely misuse of private information; also Lord Nicholls in *Campbell v MGN Limited* [2004] 2 AC 457 (HL), [43].

the creation of a statutory right of privacy were debated during the second half of the XX century, even though none of them was successfully passed.[960] Instead, the effective protection of privacy was achieved through the application of existing causes of action, such as breach of confidence.[961]

The major turning point in the protection of privacy and its intersection with the breach of confidence action was the enactment of the Human Rights Act in 1998 ("HRA"), which implemented the European Convention of Human Rights.[962] Most notably, Lord Nicholls, in his minority opinion in *Campbell v MGN Ltd,*[963] argued in favour of the inclusion of the misuse of private information within the scope of the breach of confidence action as a liability tort on the basis of the new developments in the privacy right introduced by the HRA. This opinion was followed in some subsequent decisions, such as *McKennith v Ash*.[964]

By contrast, several commentators have argued in favour of establishing a separate tort for the misuse of private information, instead of including it within the already broad scope of the breach of confidence action.[965] This was also the view purported in the Law Commission Report and it remains the object of an intense debate.[966] Yet, providing a more detailed account on the law of privacy in England falls outside the scope of this study.

---

960 A number of Bills intending to provide a statutory regulation of privacy were proposed first by Lord Mancroft in 1961, Alexander Lyon in 1967, Brian Walden in 1969, William Cash in 1987 and John Browne in 1989; among the many Reports that studied the subject of privacy, two are particularly relevant: Gerald Dworkin, 'The Younger Committee Report on Privacy' [1973] 36 Modern LR 399-406 and the Law Commission 1981 (n 909).

961 Tanya Aplin 2007 (n 958) 137; Ansgar Ohly and Agnès Lucas-Schloetter 2005 (n 957) 75-77 state that there are four objections that have impeded the definition of a general right of privacy, namely: (i) the difficulty of providing a definition; (ii) whether privacy is a sufficiently distinctive and coherent value to form the basis of a corresponding coherent substantive legal right; (iii) the inherent difficulty of striking a balance between personal privacy and wider public interest values in freedom of expression; and (iv) a general right to privacy does not seem to fit well.

962 Ansgar Ohly and Agnès Lucas-Schloetter 2005 (n 957) 86 note that, "In a more recent phase of development, breach of confidence has been given a new breadth and strength in the wake of the Human Rights Act 1998 in a series of cases involving press intrusions and the disclosure of private facts"

963 *Campbell v MGN Ltd* [2004] 2 AC 457 (HL), [14].

964 *McKennitt v Ash* [2006] EWCA Civ 1714 (CA), [8].

965 Tanya Aplin and others 2012 (n 22) paras 4.114-1.117.

966 Law Commission 1981 (n 327) para 6.2; Allison Coleman 1992 (n 911) 47.

After examining the potential causes of action invoked for the protection of confidential information, it is possible to conclude that, to some degree, they overlap with the ones resorted to by German legislation and courts. Indeed, trade secrets in both jurisdictions are enforced mostly on the basis of contractual (express or implied) obligations, but also tort law. Similarly, in both jurisdictions, the debate as to the legal nature of trade secrets remains inconclusive and consequently there is uncertainty surrounding their enforcement. Yet, in Germany no correlation with the equitable jurisdiction cause of action exists.

In the light of the above analysis, the following section examines the relevant liability requirements in the form of a four-step-test, which aims to interrogate the confidential (or secret) nature of the information.

## II. Liability requirements

The conditions necessary to find liability under the breach of confidence action were first established in the landmark case *Coco v A.N.Clark (Engineers) Ltd*[967] and have been repeatedly followed by subsequent case law. The relevant facts of the case and the legal reasoning are scrutinised in the following paragraphs.

In 1965, the plaintiff, Marco Paolo Coco, designed a new motorcycle, which was known among the parties as the "Coco moped". In April 1967, he entered into negotiations with the defendant, A.N. Clark (Engineers) Limited, with the aim of establishing a partnership to manufacture the vehicle. After some time and the disclosure of very precise information relating to the design of the motorbike the negotiations ultimately broke off. Shortly afterwards, the defendant learnt that A.N. Clark (Engineers) Ltd had started to produce their own motorcycle, the so-called "Scamp moped", which incorporated an engine based on the plaintiff's design. As a result, the plaintiff brought a motion for interlocutory relief on the basis of an alleged breach of confidence.

In its ruling, Megarry J set forth the requirements that trigger liability under this action:

> First, the information itself, in the words of Lord Greene, M.R. in the Saltman case (...), must "have the necessary quality of confidence about it". Secondly, that information must have been imparted in circum-

967 *Coco v A.N.Clark (Engineers) Ltd* [1969] RPC 41 (Ch).

> stances importing an obligation of confidence. Thirdly, there must be an unauthorised use of that information to the detriment of the party communicating it.[968]

The three cumulative relevant requirements described above have been followed by most of the subsequent authorities in finding a breach of confidence. They are: (i) the quality of confidence of the information; (ii) the verification of specific circumstances importing an obligation of confidence; and (iii) the existence of an unauthorised use detrimental to the party source of the communication.

In its legal reasoning, the court started by analysing the second of these requirements and concluded that the information had been conveyed in circumstances importing an implied obligation of confidence. In doing so, Megarry J developed a test according to which:

> If the circumstances are such that any *reasonable man* standing in the shoes of the recipient of the information would have realised that upon reasonable grounds the information was being given to him in confidence, then this should suffice to impose him the equitable obligation of confidence (emphasis added).[969]

Notwithstanding this, the analysis of the first requirement led the court to conclude that Mr Coco had not provided strong evidence that the information was of a confidential nature, as all of the engine components were available on the market separately. As the three conditions were deemed cumulative, the court dismissed the motion subject to the payment of 5s 0d per engine produced.

On the basis of the previous requirements, the English courts have developed a four-step test in order to assess whether information shall be protected under the breach of confidence action. The four steps are as follows:[970]

(i) Is the subject matter of the information eligible for protection under the breach of confidence action?
(ii) Does the information possess the necessary quality of confidence?
(iii) Has the information been imparted in circumstances importing an obligation of confidence?

968 *Coco v A.N.Clark (Engineers) Ltd* [1969] RPC 41 (Ch), 47.
969 *Coco v A.N.Clark (Engineers) Ltd* [1969] RPC 41 (Ch), 48.
970 As noted by John Hull in a personal communication with the author.

(iv) Has the information been disclosed in an unauthorised manner detrimental to the confider?

The following sections analyse the last three liability requirements. First, some remarks as to the quality of confidence are laid down. Section 2 then looks into the content of the obligation of confidence, while section 3 studies the types of conduct that fall within the "unauthorised use" requirement. The first step of the test, which enquires about the subject matter eligible for protection under the breach of confidence action, is examined in chapter 4.[971]

### 1. The quality of confidence

The quality of confidence of information is a requirement for protection under each of the jurisdictional causes of action examined under section I.[972] Yet, in the case of private information it seems that case law has emphasised that there should be a "reasonable expectation of privacy", which may trigger protection under Article 8 HRA.[973]

The general principle is that for information to qualify as confidential it must not be generally accessible and, consequently, must not form part of the public domain. In such an assessment, courts usually interrogate whether skill and labour are required to access or obtain the information concerned. Thus, in the realm of trade secrets, the term "confidential" appears to be a synonym of the term "secret", which follows from the fact that the breach of confidence action was developed to protect the undisclosed nature of information.[974] It is for this reason that case law does not

971 See chapter 4 § 2 B) II.

972 Tanya Aplin and others 2012 (n 22) para 5.02; Roger M. Toulson and Charles M. Phipps 2012 (n 326) 3-078.

973 Human Rights Act 1998; Tanya Aplin and others 2012 (n 22) para 5.02; *Campbell v MGN Ltd* [2004] 2 AC 457 (HL), 465-466.

974 Roger M. Toulson and Charles M. Phipps 2012 (n 326) 3-112; in the words of Bingham L.J. in *Attorney General v Guardian Newspapers Ltd (No 2)* [1988] 2 WLR 805 (CA): "Forty-four years ago there can have been few, if any, national secrets more confidential than the date of the planned invasion of France. Any crown servant who divulged such information to an unauthorised recipient would plainly have been in flagrant breach of his duty. But it would be absurd to hold such a servant bound to treat the date of the invasion as confidential on or after (say) 9 June 1944 when the date had become known to the world. A pursuit might say that the Allies, as confiders and owners of the information, had by their own act destroyed its confidentiality and so disabled themselves

require formalities with respect to the mode of expression of the information: the object of protection is the underlying ideas and thoughts (semantic information) and not their expression, unlike copyright.[975] Consequently, the general principle is that information need not be expressed in a tangible form to merit protection.[976] The attributes of confidence and the specific circumstances under which the confidential nature of information is lost are examined further in chapter 4.

### 2. The obligation of confidence

As mentioned above,[977] in order to find liability under the breach of confidence action, "information must have been imparted in circumstances importing an obligation of confidence".[978] This obligation may arise in a variety of contexts, as a result of a contract (express or implied) or in equity. Below, the four main situations that give rise to such an obligation are examined, namely (a) disclosure by confider to confidant; (b) accidental acquisition; (c) surreptitious acquisition; and (d) third party liability.[979]

#### a) Disclosure by confider to confidant

In the most common case of liability for breach of confidence a person provides information to another on the condition that he will not disclose it.[980] Such an equitable obligation of confidence arises when there is a direct relationship between the parties; among others, as a result of a contract, due to the existence of a fiduciary relationship between the parties or depending on the manner in which the information is conveyed.[981] This

---

from enforcing the duty, but the common sense view is that the date, being public knowledge, could no longer be regarded as the subject of confidence".

975 Tanya Aplin and others 2012 (n 22) para 5.10.

976 For instance, in *Terrapin Ltd v Builders' Supply Co (Hayes) Ltd* [1962] RPC 375 (Ch), 389 Roxburgh J noted that no distinction should be made with respect to the form in which information is expressed, whether orally or in writing.

977 See chapter 3 § 4 B) II. 2.

978 *Coco v A.N.Clark (Engineers) Ltd* [1969] RPC 41 (Ch), 47.

979 Private information may also give rise to an obligation of confidence; yet, its study falls outside the scope of the present research.

980 William Cornish, David Llewellyn and Tanya Aplin 2013 (n 209) para 8.20.

981 Lionel Bently and Brad Sherman 2014 (n 125) 1160-1161.

latter case appears particularly controversial, as identifying in a precise manner all of the circumstances that give rise to an obligation of confidentiality seems problematic.[982] Furthermore, numerous cases point to different tests to determine whether such an obligation arises.[983]

When assessing the existence of a confidentiality obligation on the recipient, most authorities resort to the so-called "reasonable man" test outlined by Megarry J in *Coco v Clark*,[984] whereby an obligation of confidence exists if a "reasonable man" would deem that the information was communicated in a confidential manner. To a large extent, this is an objective factual assessment based on the knowledge of the recipient.[985] Consequently, if information is conveyed, and it is expressly stated that it is secret, it is going to be difficult to argue that a reasonable man would regard it otherwise. However, this has proven more challenging if confidentiality is to be inferred from the circumstances of the case, where a number of elements such as the commonly held views, usages and trade practices of the industry are taken into account by the court deciding on the matter.[986]

Against this background, it is submitted, in line with recent scholarly work, that the preferred test should be the so-called "notice of confidentiality" test, which to a large extent is built on the "reasonable man" yardstick

---

982 Lionel Bently and Brad Sherman 2014 (n 125) 1161; Roger M. Toulson and Charles M. Phipps 2012 (n 326) para 3-008 noting that it would be "almost impossible to compile a list of all the relationships likely to give rise to duties of confidentiality. They include agents, trustees, partners, directors, employees; professional people; holders of public and private offices; people in close personal relationships; and many others"; similarly, Law Commission 1981 (n 327) para 4.2: "to compile an exhaustive list of such relationships would not be practicable and even if it were, the list would be of limited value because the extent of the obligation of confidence varies according to the exact nature of the relationship".

983 As reviewed in Tanya Aplin and others 2012 (n 22) para 7.02-7.52.

984 Among others, this test is referred to in *De Maudsley v Palumbo* [1996] FSR 447 (Ch); *Mars UK Ltd v Teknowledge Ltd* [2000] FSR 138 (Pat); likewise, Roger M. Toulson and Charles M. Phipps 2012 (n 326) 3-008 highlight that "the common thread is that a reasonable person would understand them as involving an obligation of confidentiality".

985 Lionel Bently and Brad Sherman 2014 (n 125) 1161 highlight that "it is a subjective but assessed in the light of the knowledge of the recipient"; William Cornish, David Llewellyn and Tanya Aplin 2013 (n 209) para 8-20 consider that this test implicitly refers to a "somewhat diffuse notion of good faith", as the obligation of confidence may be breached by unintentional behaviours.

986 Lionel Bently and Brad Sherman 2014 (n 125) 1161.

referred to above.[987] The former considers whether "the circumstances in which the information was acquired or received indicate (objective) knowledge or notice of confidentiality of the information".[988] To conduct this assessment, a number of factors are weighed against each other, namely, (i) the nature of the information; (ii) the measures adopted to preserve confidentiality; (iii) the manner of in which the information was acquired or disclosed; (iv) the perception of the parties, that is, whether they regard the information as being confidential; and (v) whether the information was disclosed for a limited purpose.[989]

Similar to the "reasonable man" yardstick, the notice of confidentiality test demands that the alleged confider has an objective knowledge that the information in question is being disclosed in a confidential manner. However, under the second test, such an assessment may be influenced by the subjective intention or tacit views of the parties.[990] Hence, the subjective element is introduced not with regard to the confidential (secret) nature of

---

987 Tanya Aplin and others 2012 (n 22) para 7.36.

988 Tanya Aplin and others 2012 (n 22) para 7.37

989 Tanya Aplin and others 2012 (n 22) para 7.36; on this point, the Second edition of Gurry on Breach of confidence departs from the first edition, where it was deemed that the limited purpose test should be the prevailing criterion to assess confidentiality, as per para 7.02: "an obligation will exist whenever confidential information is imparted by a confider for a limited purpose. In these circumstances the confidant will be bound by a duty not to use the information or any purpose other than that for which it was disclosed"; similarly, Roger M. Toulson and Charles M. Phipps 2012 (n 326) 3-012 argue that "where information of a personal or confidential nature is obtained or received in the exercise of a legal power or to furtherance of a legal duty, the recipient will in general owe a duty to the person from whom it was obtained or to whom it relates not to use it for unrelated purposes".

990 Tanya Aplin and others 2012 (n 22) paras 7.38-7.39; *De Maudsley v Palumbo* [1996] FSR 447 (Ch), 457, where Judge Knox favoured an objective test informed by the appraisal of subjective views: "The test in my view is objective-the question is where the circumstances such as to import a duty of confidence and, if so, the obligation is not to be avoided simply by not addressing the problem. On the other hand, I accept that a factor, and it may be an important factor, is whether the parties did in fact regard themselves as under an obligation to preserve confidence, just as is a proven trade or industry usage in that regard but I do not accept that the test is exclusively subjective as to the parties' intentions"; by contrast, Jacob J in *Carflow Products (UK) Ltd v Linwood Securities* [1996] FSR 424 (Ch), 428 favoured a subjective test. He argued that under the breach of confidence action, unlike in contract law, the subjective views of the parties had to be taken into consideration, because equity "looks at the conscience of the individual.

the information, but rather with respect to the appraisal of whether an obligation to keep it secret arises.

b) Accidental acquisition

The accidental acquisition of secret information takes place when no direct relationship between the parties exists. It covers situations where one of the parties obtains certain information that is regarded as confidential by the other, as a result, directly or indirectly, of an accident, negligence or a mistake on the part of the party who knew that the information was of a confidential nature.[991] This would be the case, for example, if a member of the public fortuitously found a confidential document on the street that had been lost by the holder of the information.[992] The information is acquired without surreptitious means, merely as a result of carelessness. Nonetheless, despite the fact that no relationship between the parties exists, a duty of confidence may arise.[993]

The leading opinions among legal scholars restrict such a possibility to situations where the acquirer knows that the information is confidential or "is deliberately blind to the likelihood of it being confidential".[994] The underlying rationale is to protect confidential information as such based on

991 Tanya Aplin and others 2012 (n 22) para 7.46.

992 Lionel Bently and Brad Sherman 2014 (n 125) 1163.

993 Lionel Bently and Brad Sherman 2014 (n 125) 1163.

994 Roger M. Toulson and Charles M. Phipps 2012 (n 326) para 3-07.6 This statement is based on a passage from Lord Goff in *Attorney General v Guardian Newspapers Ltd (No 2)* [1990] 1 AC 109 (HL), 281-282: "A duty of confidence arises when confidential information comes to the knowledge of a person (the confidant) in circumstances where he has notice, or is held to have agreed, that the information is confidential, with the effect that it would be just in all circumstances that he should be precluded from disclosing the information to others. I have used the word "notice" advisedly, in order to avoid the (here unnecessary) question of the extent to which actual knowledge is necessary; though I of course understand knowledge to include circumstances where the confidant has deliberately closed his eyes to the obvious (...) I have expressed the circumstances in which the duty arises in broad terms (...) to include certain situations beloved of law teachers –where an obviously confidential document is wafted by an electric fan out of the window into a crowded street into a crowded street, or when an obviously confidential document, such as a private diary, is dropped in a public place, and it is then picked by a passer-by".

the knowledge that the information was confidential, instead of a pre-existing confidential obligation.[995]

c) Surreptitious acquisition

The surreptitious acquisition of information refers to the obtention of information through "reprehensible means".[996] It encompasses a broad array of activities, such as theft of confidential documents or products to name a few, and may arise in a variety of contexts.[997] The main difficulty in applying the breach of confidence action stems from the lack of a relationship between the parties involved.[998] In fact, The Law Commission Report on Breach of Confidence from 1981 concluded that it was questionable whether an obligation of confidence might arise based only on the use of reprehensible means in the acquisition of information.[999]

Notwithstanding this, subsequently commentators and a number of cases argued in favour of establishing liability on the basis that the acquirer knew that the information was confidential and such knowledge derived from the means through which it was obtained.[1000]

One of the most relevant cases in this regard was *Shelley Films v Rex Featured Limited*,[1001] which concerned the publication of photographs taken during the shooting of a film based on the famous novel Frankenstein by Mary Shelley. The disputed photographs depicted one of the actors in character and were taken inside the studio premises without authorisation

995 Tanya Aplin and others (n 22) para 7.51.
996 Law Commission 1981 (n 327) para 4.7.
997 Tanya Aplin and others (n 22) para 7.53 provide a non-exhaustive list of types of conduct that can be considered to be "surreptitious acquisition". In particular, they mention the following examples: "secret photographic filming, or otherwise recording activities of a person or business, hacking into an encrypted computer to access documents or email correspondence; tapping a telephone or intercepting mail into the post".
998 Tanya Aplin and others 2012 (n 22) para 7.54.
999 Law Commission 1981 (n 327) para 4.10; Roger M. Toulson and Charles M. Phipps 2012 (n 326) 3-031 argue that this statement is largely based on the finding of Megarry VC in *Malone v Commissioner of Police of the Metropolis* (No 2) [1979] 2 All ER 620 (Ch), where it was argued that the accidental acquisition of information (in the case at hand by overhearing a conversation or tapping a phone conversation) did not give rise to an obligation of confidence.
1000 Tanya Aplin and others 2012 (n 22) para 7.55.
1001 *Shelley Films Limited v Rex Features Limited* [1994] EMLR 134 (Ch).

and despite the existence of signs that prohibited the taking of pictures. The plaintiff, the company that produced the film, sought an injunction on the basis of copyright infringement and breach of confidence and argued that the dissemination of the photographs would run counter to the film's marketing strategy. In the legal grounds of the decision, Martin Mann QC ruled that it was impossible under the specific circumstances of the case that the photographer was not aware that the information was of a confidential nature and that he was not allowed to convey it to others.[1002] It further noted that the producing company had an "obvious and stated commercial interest in protecting its substantial investment by, minimally, being able to provide an undisrupted production environment and to control the timing and manner of the release of information about the film (…)".[1003] Hence, the existence of a commercial interest also appears to be one of the elements that courts weigh up when assessing breach of confidence.[1004]

### d) Third party liability

The liability of third parties is still, to date, one of the most controversial topics in the field of trade secrecy law. It refers to situations where information is imparted during the course of a confidential relationship and is later disclosed in breach of confidence to a third party by the confidant. Thus, it differs from the accidental or surreptitious acquisition of information in that negligence, mistake or reprehensible means are not involved (just unauthorised disclosure) and there is an obligation of confidence between the holder of the information and the party that reveals it.[1005] The main legal question that arises is whether the recipient outside of the initial confidential relationship is bound by an obligation of confidence.[1006] Against this background, a distinction must be drawn between two main

1002 *Shelley Films Limited v Rex Features Limited* [1994] EMLR 134 (Ch), 148.

1003 *Shelley Films Limited v Rex Features Limited* [1994] EMLR 134 (Ch),148.

1004 Chris D.L. Hunt, 'Rethinking Surreptitious Takings in the Law of Confidence' [2011] IPQ 66 where it is argued that obligations of confidence should not extend to surreptitious takers owing to the absence of a pre-existing relationship. The author argues that imposing liability under breach of confidence would distort the main policies underpinning the action, i.e. relationship preservation and remedying unconscionable conduct.

1005 Tanya Aplin and others 2012 (n 22) para 7.103.

1006 Lionel Bently and Brad Sherman 2014 (n 125) 1028.

situations: (i) the acquisition of information that occurs with knowledge of the breach, and (ii) acquisition by an indirect recipient who is not aware of the confidential nature of the information.

In the first scenario, the case law provides that a third party who receives confidential information knowing that it is confidential will come under an obligation not to disclose it at the time that he receives it.[1007] The extent of knowledge required to come under such a duty is linked to the failure of the third party to "observe the standard which would be observed by an honest person placed under those circumstances",[1008] in line with footnote 10 of the TRIPs Agreement.[1009] Similarly to the accessory liability for breach of trust or fiduciary obligation, dishonesty has been cited by some commentators and in some authorities as a prerequisite to finding third party recipients liable for breach of confidence. In this regard, Toulson and Phipps concluded that:

> The important thing is that for a third party to be held liable in equity for a breach of confidence, more is required than merely careless, naive or stupid behaviour; there must be awareness of the fact that the information was confidential or willingness to turn a proverbial blind eye.[1010]

This passage was later interpreted by Buxton LJ in *Thomas v Peace*[1011] as meaning that dishonesty could be inferred both from the fact that the recipient had actual knowledge of the wrongness and the mere fact that he closed his eyes to it. Bearing this in mind, Aplin, Bently, Johnson and Malynic hold a different view in the second edition of *Gurry on Breach of Confidence*.[1012] In essence, they suggest that dishonest behaviour on the part of the third party should not be considered as a requisite to finding liability. Rather it should be interpreted as a factor pointing towards the existence of actual knowledge. In support of this view, reference is made to *Prince*

---

1007 *Schering Chemicals Ltd v Falkman Ltd* [1982] QB 1(CA), 27 (Shaw LJ); *Attorney General v Guardian Newspapers Ltd (No 2)* [1990] 1 AC 109 (HL), 260 where Lord Keith stated that: "it is a general rule of law that a third party who comes into possession of confidential obligation which he knows to be such, may come under a duty not to pass it to anyone else".

1008 *Royal Brunei Airlines Sdn. Bhd v Philip Tan Kok Ming* [1995] 2 AC 378 (PC), 390.

1009 Roger M. Toulson and Charles M. Phipps 2012 (n 326) 3-069 and Lionel Bently and Brad Sherman 2014 (n 125) 1028-1029.

1010 Roger M. Toulson and Charles M. Phipps 2012 (n 326) para 3-071.

1011 *Susan Thomas v Elizabeth Pearce and Another* [2000] FSR 718, 721.

1012 Tanya Aplin and others 2012 (n 22) paras 7.110-7.111

*Albert v Strange* and the legal position of one of the defendants, Mr Judge. He acquired a number of copies of etchings made by the Queen and Prince Albert for their private use from one of the employees (Mr Middelton) of the printer at Windsor where the impressions had been printed off and intended to make a public exhibition with them. Mr Middelton had in turn taken copies of them in a surreptitious manner.[1013] As regards the liability of Mr Judge, the court ruled that he had obtained the etchings knowing that Mr Middelton must have acquired them with "faithlessness, fraud and treachery".[1014] Hence, the Court of Chancery granted an injunction on the basis of an equitable jurisdiction, restraining him from exhibiting the etchings and publishing the catalogue.

In the second scenario, the recipient acquires information without being aware of its confidential nature. This would be the case, for instance, if an employer conveyed a trade secret to one of his employees and the latter revealed it to his subsequent employer without him knowing that the information was in fact one of his competitor's secrets.[1015] In such cases, the general principle is that if a person receives information innocently, he is liable as of the date on which he was given notice that the information was obtained as a result of a breach of confidence.[1016]

Both approaches seem to be in line with the solution presented by the EU legislature in Article 4(4) of the TSD, by virtue of which, the liability of third parties is established if at the time of the acquisition, use or disclo-

1013 *Prince Albert v. Strange* [1849] 2 De G & Sm 652, 714.

1014 *Prince Albert v. Strange* [1849] 2 De G & Sm 652, 714.

1015 A similar case was decided in *English & American Insurance Co Ltd. v Herbert Smith 2* [1988] FSR 232 (Ch), where the papers of the council acting for the plaintiff in an action pending in the Commercial Court were sent by mistake to the solicitors of the other party. Upon reception of the documents the solicitors did not read the content, but informed their clients, who instructed them to look through the documents. As a result, an action for breach of confidence was brought against the solicitors of the defendant in order to restrain the use of information obtained from those papers. The Judge granted the injunction, arguing that as a general rule, the equitable jurisdiction may provide relief against the world and that only bona fide purchasers for value without notice were excluded from liability. He further noted that in the case at hand, there had been a deliberate decision to acquire the confidential information, which was taken with knowledge that the papers were of a confidential nature. Hence, he concluded that the defendants had no right to use the information contained in the privileged document, as it belonged to the plaintiff.

1016 John Hull, *Commercial Secrecy* (1st edn, Sweet&Maxwell 1998) para 4.185; see *Malone v Commissioner of Police of the Metropolis (No 2)* [1979] 2 All ER 620 (Ch).

sure they knew (or should have known under the circumstances) that the information had been obtained unlawfully. Hence, knowledge (or reason to know) are at the centre of the assessment of the liability of third parties, both in the English jurisdiction and the TSD, following a gross negligence liability standard.

As a final note, it is worth highlighting that the position of bona fide purchasers for value remains controversial, as it has been argued that innocent third parties that in good faith "incurred detriment by paying for the information or perhaps incurring expense of money or effort in consequence of obtaining it (for example in further research and development)" may be exempted from liability.[1017] This approach stems from one of the passages in *Morison v. Moat,* where Turner V.C. noted that the purchaser for value in good faith may be in a different position from other innocent third parties:

> It might indeed be different if the Defendant was a purchaser for value of the secret without notice of any obligation affecting it; and the Defendant's case was attempted to be put upon this ground...but I do not think that this view of the case can avail him ... So far as the secret is concerned he is a mere volunteer deriving under a breach of trust or of contract.[1018]

In the light of the above, some commentators have debated the existence of a bona fide defence for value that covers innocent third party recipients in good faith.[1019] The implications of adopting this general defence are better explained with an example. Let us take the case of a businessman (X) who pays for confidential information from another (Y) without knowing that the information was obtained by Y breaching the confidence of another person (P). If the above referred to defence is generally accepted, P will not be able to obtain either an injunction or damages against X, even after giving him notice of confidentiality.[1020]

As a result of the foregoing analysis, the preferred approach is a flexible one, where all of the circumstances of the case are balanced against each other taking into account the divergent interests of the parties.[1021] The

---

1017 Tanya Aplin and others 2012 (n 22) para 7.129.

1018 *Morison v Moat* [1851] 9 Hare 241, 263-264.

1019 For a more in-depth analysis of this issue see Tanya Aplin and others 2012 (n 22) para 7.121.

1020 A similar example was first presented by Gareth Jones, 'Restitution of Benefits Obtained in breach of another's Confidence' [1970] 86 LQR 463, 48.

1021 Tanya Aplin and others 2012 (n 22) paras 7.136-7.143.

bona fide acquisition of information should not afford an absolute right to continue using the information.[1022] Rather, it should be one of the factors taken into consideration by courts when deciding whether to grant the relief. Among these, a key factor should be whether the acquirer of the information changed his position on the information before learning about its confidential nature.[1023] That would be the case, for instance, if the acquirer of the information had invested in new machinery or hired new employees based on the disclosure of confidential information. Under such circumstances, providing economic compensation for using the confidential information appears to be more appropriate than granting an injunction.[1024] The EU legislature has included a similar approach in Article 13 TSD, by virtue of which national courts may allow a third party to continue using a trade secret after receiving notice of its infringing nature provided that adequate compensation is paid (damages in lieu of injunctions).[1025]

### 3. Unauthorised use

Pursuant to *Coco v AN Clark*, the third requirement to find breach of confidence requires that the information is communicated without authorisation and to the detriment of the party conveying it.[1026] Thus, in the first place it is necessary to establish the scope of the obligation of confidence in order to determine whether it has been breached by use, disclosure or some other act.[1027] If the obligation stems from an express term in a contract, the scope is determined by means of interpreting the relevant provisions. By contrast, if the duty of confidentiality arises implicitly or in equity, the assessment will be a factual one. It will ultimately depend upon the specific circumstances surrounding each particular case.[1028] Accordingly,

---

1022 Roger M. Toulson and Charles M. Phipps 2012 (n 326) paras 3-063- 3-064 are also reluctant to accept a general bona fide defence for value, as the transfer of property rights does not apply to the position of third party acquirers.

1023 For a more detailed analysis see Tanya Aplin and others (n 22) 7.140

1024 Tanya Aplin and others 2012 (n 22) para 7.140.

1025 See further chapter 3 § 5 C) IV. 4. b).

1026 *Coco v A.N.Clark (Engineers) Ltd* [1969] RPC 41 (Ch).

1027 Lionel Bently and Brad Sherman 2014 (n 125) 1172-1173 highlight that under English law the use and disclosure of information may be restricted, but not the acquisition. Accordingly, they argue that British law might be in breach of TRIPS, which refers to the disclosure, acquisition and use of information.

1028 Lionel Bently and Brad Sherman 2014 (n 125) 1161.

the scope of the obligation is to be determined by what "a reasonable person standing in the shoes of the defendant would understand is not permitted".[1029]

In order to find liability under the breach of confidence action it is crucial to show "derivation", that is, that the information in question has been "directly or indirectly" acquired from the confider.[1030] Hence, when information has been generated independently or obtained from other sources no liability arises.[1031] In practical terms, this means that during litigation the plaintiff should provide evidence that the defendant acquired the information from him. A clear example would be the case of an employee who uses one of his former employer's secrets. In this case, the employer should prove that the employee acquired the information from him.

Furthermore, the defendant's state of mind at the time that he receives or uses the information should not be taken into consideration for the purposes of determining whether an obligation has been breached (the fourth prong).[1032] It is irrelevant for the breach whether the defendant acted in good faith or not, or had actual knowledge of the secret nature of the information.[1033]

As stated above, Megarry J in *Coco v AN Clark* raised the question of whether the misuse of confidential information must be detrimental to the confider in order to trigger liability under the breach of confidence action; i.e. whether damage is an essential element of the action. To date the answer to this question remains unclear, as the case law has provided divergent solutions.[1034]

---

1029 Tanya Aplin and others 2012 (n 22) para 10.50.

1030 *Saltman Engineering v Campell Engineering* [1948] 65 RPC 203 (CA), 213 (Lord Green MR).

1031 Tanya Aplin and others 2012 (n 22) para 15.03; Lionel Bently and Brad Sherman 2014 (n 125) 1176.

1032 William Cornish, David Llewellyn and Tanya Aplin 2013 (n 209) para 8-38 .

1033 Lionel Bently and Brad Sherman 2014 (n 125) 1177.

1034 William Cornish, David Llewellyn and Tanya Aplin 2013 (n 209) para 8-39; in *Douglas v Hello! Ltd and others* [2007] UKHL 21, [111]-[115] and in *Attorney General v Guardian (No 2)* [1990] 1 AC 109 (HL), 270 (Lord Griffith), it is submitted that it is necessary to show detriment to find liability under a breach of confidence action, whereas in the same decision at 256 Lord Keith states, "So I would think it a sufficient detriment to the confider that the information given in confidence is to be disclosed to persons whom he would prefer not to know of it, even though the disclosure would not be harmful to him in any positive way".

Cornish argues that the finding of liability by the mere breaking of confidence is problematic. In particular, he observes that the breach of confidence action imposes limitations on the freedom to use information. Thus, as a matter of public interest, such a restriction requires "sufficient reason".[1035] He further supports the detrimental use requirement by noting that in most economic torts proof of damage is an essential part of an actionable tort.[1036]

By contrast, Aplin, Bently, Johnson and Malynic suggest that the detriment requirement is already encompassed by the nature of the information and the scope of the obligation. Where an obligation exists, it is indeed likely that an infringement will cause a detriment. However, in certain scenarios where that might not be the case, such as technical secrets and private information, it is argued that the detriment is conceived as a loss of the potential licence fee.[1037]

Indeed, a review of the relevant case law shows that damage is a condition to find liability only with regard to government secrets, not private information[1038] or commercial secrets.[1039]

## III. The "springboard doctrine"

One of the most notable features of the English legal system in the field of confidential information is the development of the so-called "springboard doctrine". Basically, this doctrine seeks to prevent a situation where a person who breaches an obligation benefits from such conduct.[1040] Accordingly, courts may grant injunctive relief in order to prevent the recipient of confidential information obtaining an "unfair start" over their competitors.[1041] It mainly aims at fulfilling two policy objectives, i.e. fostering the

1035 William Cornish, David Llewellyn and Tanya Aplin 2013 (n 209) para 8-39.
1036 William Cornish, David Llewellyn and Tanya Aplin 2013 (n 209) para 8-39.
1037 Tanya Aplin and others 2012 (n 22) para 15.43.
1038 *McKennitt v Ash* [2006] EWCA Civ 1714 (CA).
1039 Lionel Bently and Brad Sherman 2014 (n 125) 1177.
1040 Lionel Bently and Brad Sherman 2014 (n 125) 1151; Roger M. Toulson and Charles M. Phipps 2012 (n 326) 4-025 noting that, "The object of the springboard doctrine is merely to ensure that the recipient of confidential information does not obtain an unfair start by misuse of information received in confidence".
1041 Lionel Bently and Brad Sherman 2014 (n 125) 1151; Roger M. Toulson and Charles M. Phipps 2012 (n 326) 4-025.

duty of confidentiality by reducing the potential benefits of using the information disclosed and encouraging "fair relationships" among competitors.[1042] It was first formulated in *Terrapin Ltd v Builders' Supply Co (Hayes) Ltd* by Roxburh J, who noted that:

> As I understand it, the essence of this branch of the law, whatever the origin may be, is that as a person who has obtained information in confidence is not allowed to use it as a springboard for activities detrimental to the person who made the confidential communication, and springboard it remains even when all the features have been published or can be ascertained by an actual inspector or member of the public.[1043]

Notwithstanding this, some of its features are highly controversial. It has been argued that this doctrine goes against the general principle according to which once information enters the public domain it cannot be protected under the breach of confidence action.[1044] This issue was addressed by the Law Commission Report on Breach of Confidence. In essence, it was stated that information should not be regarded as effectively in the public domain until it would be "reasonably possible for an interested member of the public in fact to use the information even though some of the information was already available to the public".[1045] In this regard, subsequent decisions have required that protection is only afforded with regard to the unfair advantage that the defendant would obtain if no injunction were granted. Accordingly the scope of such an injunction should not extend beyond the duration of the unfair advantage.[1046] Furthermore, in some cases, courts have required the defendants to pay for the information.[1047]

---

1042 Lionel Bently and Brad Sherman 2014 (n 125) 1151.

1043 *Terrapin Ltd v Builders' Supply Co (Hayes) Ltd* [1962] RPC 375 (Ch), 391; the decision was rendered in 1959 but only reported in 1967.

1044 Roger M. Toulson and Charles M. Phipps 2012 (n 326) 4-025.

1045 Law Commission 1981 (n 327) para 4.31.

1046 Roger M. Toulson and Charles M. Phipps 2012 (n 326) 4-025; in *Sun Valley Foods Ltd v Vincent* [2000] FSR 825 (Ch), 834-837 it was ruled that the grant of an injunction was subject to the persistence of the unfair advantage on the date of the order.

1047 John Hull 1998 (1016) para 3.43.

## § 4 Concluding remarks on the comparative law analysis

The comparative analysis conducted above underscores that despite the existence of common ground on certain aspects of the protection of trade secrets, there are also substantial differences in their regulation in Germany and England. These range from the lack of clarity as to the cause of action that parties may invoke in England to the two-fold nature of trade secrets protection envisaged in the German UWG. As regards enforcement, there is also uncertainty surrounding the remedies available in Germany and the applicability of the Enforcement Directive in England.[1048] Most notably, in both jurisdictions other unsettled issues include the information that departing employees are free to take to their new positions and the assessment of the liability of third parties. Crucially, there is also uncertainty surrounding the circumstances under which reverse engineering should be deemed lawful.

Similarly, showing that a detriment to the holder of information has taken place is not necessary in England (per se), whereas in Germany the UWG lays down that the acquisition, use and disclosure of trade secrets must be carried out "for the purposes of competition, for personal gain, for the benefit of a third party, or with the intent of causing damage to the owner of the business, " which ultimately leads to a different conceptualisation of when misappropriation has taken place.

Notably, the standard of liability of third parties seems higher in Germany under the scheme set out in the UWG, where at the minimum conditional intent is required as a result of the criminal law nature of the provision. By contrast, the standard of liability in England is much more flexible and is built upon knowledge and "the observance of the standard which would be observed by a honest man".[1049]

In the light of the substantial divergences and their impact on the construction of the Single Market, the EU legislature decided to take legal action to harmonise this area of law. On April 14, 2016 the European Parliament passed the TSD, which provides for minimum standards of protection against the unlawful acquisition, use and disclosure of confidential business information. The main features of the Directive and its legal implications for the assessment of the optimal scope of secrecy constitute the object of study of the remainder of this chapter.

---

1048 This aspect will become irrelevant after the withdrawal of the UK from the EU.

1049 Roger M. Toulson and Charles M. Phipps 2012 (n 326) para 3-070.

## *§ 5 The emerging common framework: a critical study of the Trade Secrets Directive*

### A) Background of the Directive

In November 2013, after months of hermetic negotiations, the Commission issued the much-anticipated Proposal for a Directive on the protection of trade secrets.[1050] This legislative initiative falls within the framework of the Comprehensive intellectual property strategy adopted in May 2011, aimed at the suppression of the remaining barriers within the Internal Market and the achievement of a "true Single Market" for IPRs by 2020.[1051] Strengthening the existing legal regime for the protection of IPRs was identified by the Commission as one of the linchpins of an Innovation Union and an essential factor in order to ensure a growing labour market and the continued competitiveness of the whole EU economy.[1052]

In the 2011 IPRs Strategy, the Commission took the view that the existing disparities in the national regimes led to a fragmented protection of trade secrets within the Internal Market, as examined throughout chapter 3.[1053] In particular, it was noted that the substantial inconsistencies on the national level regarding the nature and scope of trade secrets, as well as the available means of redress and remedies resulted in different levels of protection across the EU. Furthermore, it echoed the increasing vulnerability of trade secrets in relation to unlawful disclosure, acquisition and use.

---

1050 Commission, 'Proposal for a Directive of the European Parliament and of the Council on the protection of undisclosed know-how and business information (trade secrets) against their unlawful acquisition, use and disclosure' COM (2013) 813 final (Commission Proposal).

1051 Commission, 'Communication from the Commission to the European Parliament, the Council, the European and economic and social committee and the committee of the regions. A Single Market for Intellectual Property Rights. Boosting creativity and innovation to provide economic growth, high quality jobs and first class products and services in Europe' COM (2011) 287 final, 3 <http://eur-lex.europa.eu/legal-content/EN/TXT/HTML/?uri=CELEX:52011DC0287&from=EN> accessed 15 September 2018 (Commission, A Single Market for Intellectual Property Rights).

1052 IPRs are regarded by the Commission as a crucial driver for innovation and creativity. As such, it is believed that enhancing the protection of IPRs within the internal market will foster the EU's economic growth, cultural diversity and international competitiveness; for a more detailed account of the EU's 2011 IPRs Strategy, see Commission, A Single Market for Intellectual Property Rights (n 1051).

1053 Commission, A Single Market for Intellectual Property Rights (n 1051) 6.

Notwithstanding this, it was concluded that further evidence was required before taking an EU approach in this area.

In the light of the above, in March 2011 a study on the legal framework for the protection of trade secrets and parasitic copying in the (at that time) 27 Member States was commissioned to Hogan Lovells International LLP. The primary objective of the study was to conduct a comparative law analysis in order to clarify the legal regime and practices in all of the jurisdictions of the EU. The final report was published in January 2012 and in essence it confirmed what the Commission had hesitantly pointed out in the 2011 strategy: "the law in relation to trade secrets in the EU is a collage".[1054] The outcome of the study showed that there were substantial differences among the 27 Member States with regard to core issues, such as the actual definition of the information that could be protected as a trade secret; the legal basis for protection, i.e. unfair competition, tort law and criminal law; the status of trade secrets as IPRs; the applicability of the Enforcement Directive; and the remedies and means of redress available.[1055]

In June 2012, the Commission held a conference in Brussels entitled "*Trade Secrets: Supporting Innovation, Protecting Know-how*" with the aim of facilitating a dialogue with stakeholders. During the conference, the differences among the (at that time) 27 jurisdictions and the economic importance of trade secrets protection in ensuring competitiveness and innovation were analysed and some of the potential policy options were examined.[1056]

Following the conference with representatives from the industry, a statistical on-the field survey was conducted by Baker McKenzie LLP on behalf of the Commission in order to assess the actual relevance of trade secrets and confidential business information as drivers for innovation, competitiveness and economic growth in the EU. By the end of the consultation period, more than 537 undertakings had participated in the survey, which was included as part of a more extensive study dealing with the economic structure of trade secrets protection in the European Union.[1057] From an economic perspective, the Baker McKenzie empirical study revealed that trade secrets constituted an essential element for performance, growth and competitiveness for the vast majority of the companies that re-

1054 Hogan Lovells 2012 (n 793) para 290.

1055 Hogan Lovells 2012 (n 793) paras 288-304.

1056 For further information see <http://ec.europa.eu/growth/tools-databases/newsroom/cf/itemdetail.cfm?item_id=8270> accessed 15 September 2018.

1057 Baker McKenzie 2013 (n 469) 12.

sponded to the survey (74% of them attached medium or high importance to trade secrets). In the same vein, over a third of them expressed concerns regarding the loss of confidential information.[1058] In this context, current and former employees, together with competitors and suppliers were identified as the main sources of risk. The study further indicated that trade secrets misappropriation (whether actual or merely an attempt) results in a "loss of sales (56%), costs for internal investigation (44%), increased expenditure for the protection (35%), cost for negotiating settlements (34%), and costs for prosecuting and litigating (31%)".[1059]

Notably, most of the participants supported a potential EU action in order to establish common rules regarding the protection of trade secrets. In particular, participants showed a preference for harmonisation in four areas, which guided the legislative process led by the Commission. The issues of concern highlighted by the participants were: (i) the clarification of the information that can be protected as a trade secret (55%); (ii) the prohibition of acts of misappropriation and the definition of such types of conduct (45%); (iii) the establishment of common rules vis-à-vis criminal sanctions (35, 5%) and (iv) ensuring confidentiality during litigation.

At the same time, from December 2012 until March 2013 the Commission carried out an open consultation focussed on the perception and use of trade secrets, which attracted the participation of 386 respondents. Among the contributors were not only private undertakings and business organisations, but also citizens and professionals. The outcome of the consultation showed that most citizens (75%) deemed that trade secrets protection was not a key element for R&D and that the existing legal framework was already too stringent, whereas the vast majority of the responding companies regarded trade secrets as an essential element for R&D and their competitiveness.[1060]

After conducting the aforementioned studies and consultations, the Commission concluded that there was a case for harmonisation. Thus, the ordinary legislative procedure was initiated,[1061] and on November 2012 the "Proposal for a Directive of the European Parliament and of the Council

1058 Baker McKenzie 2013 (n 469) 122-123.

1059 Baker McKenzie 2013 (n 469) 129.

1060 Commission, 'Explanatory Memorandum of the Proposal for a Directive of the European Parliament and of the Council on the protection of undisclosed know-how and business information (trade secrets) against their unlawful acquisition, use and disclosure' 6.

1061 The ordinary legislative procedure within the EU is regulated in Articles 289 (1) and 294 of the TFEU, and as its name indicates, it is the most common pro-

on the protection of undisclosed know-how and business information (trade secrets) against their unlawful acquisition, use and disclosure"[1062] was published. Along with it, an Impact Assessment was issued by the Commission, in which it was essentially restated that the existing scattered legal protection was detrimental to the competitiveness of the internal market[1063] and five potential policy options were analysed.[1064]

In line with the ordinary legislative procedure, on May 14, 2014 the Council of the European Union presented its General Approach to the proposed Directive.[1065] After months of negotiations, the European Parliament and Council adopted the final Draft of the TSD on June 8, 2016.

The following sections examine the new legal framework created by the TSD. To this end, section B explores the legal basis and ground for harmonising trade secrets protection within the EU legal framework. Next, a legal analysis of the new obligations set out in the Directive and their implications for the assessment of secrecy is conducted in section C below.

---

cedure followed to enact EU legislation. Prior to the entry into force of the Lisbon Treaty in December 2009, most of the legislative initiatives were started by the Commission upon the request of the Council or the European Council. However, the legislative process is now governed by the co-decision procedure, which essentially consists of the adoption, both by the European Parliament and by the Council of the regulations, directives or decisions, of a proposal presented by the Commission. A more detailed account of the legislative procedures in the EU falls outside the scope of the present research. Nonetheless, the following authors provide an insightful analysis of this topic: Paul Craig and Gráinne de Búrca, *EU Law, Text, Cases, and Materials* (5th edition OUP 2011) 121-133; Jörn Axel Kämmerer, 'European Commission', *The Max Planck Encyclopaedia of European Private Law* (OUP 2012) 563-565 and Walter Frenz, *Handbuch Europa-Recht*, vol 6 (1st edn, Springer 2011) 501-528.

1062 Commission, 'Proposal for a Directive of the European Parliament and of the Council on the protection of undisclosed know-how and business information (trade secrets) against their unlawful acquisition, use and disclosure' COM (2013) 813 final.

1063 Impact Assessment (n 385) 18-21.

1064 Impact Assessment (n 385) 43-45.

1065 Council, 'General Approach on the Proposal for a Directive of the European Parliament and of the Council on the protection of undisclosed know-how and business information (trade secrets) against their unlawful acquisition, use and disclosure' 2013/0402 (COD) (Council's Proposal) <http://register.consilium.europa.eu/doc/srv?l=EN&f=ST%209870%202014%20INIT> accessed 15 September 2018.

## B) Legal basis and grounds for harmonising trade secrets protection

As mentioned in the first chapter of this dissertation, finding a sound justification to harmonise trade secrets protection within the EU is both necessary and desirable to ensure the good functioning of the internal market. For some, the aspirational rhetoric of the TSD resembles that of the Database Directive, which has not fulfilled the economic improvements it was supposed to bring about.[1066] The remainder of this section surveys the main objectives of the TSD and analyses the legal basis upon which the legislative initiative is based.

The Directive aims to provide a sufficient and comparable level of redress across all Member States against the misappropriation of trade secrets, even though it only provides for minimum standards of protection.[1067] One of the main goals of the EU is to ensure the creation of a Single Market without frontiers in which the four freedoms, "free movement of goods, persons, services and capital", are accomplished.[1068] To achieve the creation of the internal market, over time the CJEU has developed a consistent body of case law preventing the adoption of trade rules by Member States that may directly (or indirectly) hinder trade within the EU.[1069]

---

1066 This argument is raised by Tanya Aplin 2014 (n 384) 259; a comprehensive evaluation of the economic impact of the Database Directive is provided in Commission, 'First evaluation of Directive 96/9/EC on the legal protection of databases' (2005) DG Internal Market and Services Working Paper 24, where it is noted that the sui generis right "economic impact on database production is unproven".

1067 See Recital 10 TSD.

1068 See Article 26(2) TFEU; in this regard, it is noteworthy that the Treaty does not establish a single right of economic free movement. Instead, a bundle of rights and prohibitions is set forth, in order to limit unjustified restrictions on the freedom of movement and establishment, which would ultimately affect trade between Member States; see further Richard Gordon, *EC Law in judicial review* (1st edn, OUP 2007) para 16.01.

1069 Case 8/74 *Procureur du Roi v Dassonville* [1974] ECR I-837, 852: " All trading rules enacted by Member States which are capable of hindering, directly or indirectly, actually or potentially, intra-Community trade are to be considered as measures having an effect equivalent to quantitative restrictions". The scope of this rule was subsequently limited by the CJEU in Joined Cases C-267/91 and C-268/91 *Keck and Mithurard* [1993] ECR I-6097, para 16, where the Court noted that: "contrary to what has previously been decided, the application to products from other Member States of national provisions restricting or prohibiting certain selling arrangements is not such as to hinder directly or indi-

As regards trade secrets, the disparities among the different national legal regimes resulted in different subject matter being protected and different interpretations of when an unlawful acquisition, use and disclosure of confidential information had occurred.[1070] The available means of enforcement also varied from one Member State to another.[1071] Consequently, it was regarded that this might hamper the free movement of employees (persons), services and goods.

Ohly provided an example of the latter case, which he warned was rather extreme. He explained that it might not be possible to import a product in which a trade secret is embodied into other EU markets, if protection is afforded in the destination market and not the original one.[1072] He further added that from an EU law perspective, this would run counter to the principle of free movement of goods, which can only be limited in two instances: (i) to protect intellectual property (Article 36 TFEU);[1073] and (ii) to protect fair competition following the doctrine set forth by the CJEU in *Cassis de Dijon*.[1074] Similarly, the different national rules on non-

---

rectly, actually or potentially, trade between Member States within the meaning of the Dassonville judgement (Case 8/74 *Procureur du Roi v Dassonville* [1974] ECR I-837*): "so long as those provisions apply to all relevant traders operating within the national territory and so long as they affect in the same manner, in law and in fact, the marketing of domestic products and of those from other Member States*" (emphasis added).

1070 Hogan Lovells 2012 (n 793) para 304.

1071 Ansgar Ohly 2013 (n 13) 39.

1072 Ansgar Ohly 2013 (n 13) 39.

1073 Article 36 TFEU provides the following: "The provisions of Articles 34 and 35 shall not preclude prohibitions or restrictions on imports, exports or goods in transit justified on grounds of public morality, public policy or public security; the protection of health and life of humans, animals or plants; the protection of national treasures possessing artistic, historic or archaeological value; or the *protection of industrial and commercial property. Such prohibitions or restrictions shall not, however, constitute a means of arbitrary discrimination or a disguised restriction on trade between Member States* (emphasis added)";Gintare Surblyte 2011 (n 182) 47 further notes that trade secrets are not covered by Article 36 TFEU.

1074 Case 120/78 *Rewe-Zentrale AG v Bundesmonopolverwaltung für Branntwein (Cassis de Dijon)* [1979] ECR I-649, para 8: "Obstacles to movement within the Community resulting from disparities between national laws relating to the marketing of the products in question must be accepted in so far as those provisions may be recognized as being necessary in order to satisfy *mandatory requirements* relating in particular to the effectiveness *of fiscal supervision*, the protection of *public health, the fairness of commercial transactions* and the *defence of the consumer*" (emphasis added).

disclosure obligations after the termination of a contractual relationship might negatively affect the mobility of employees from one country to another. In the light of the foregoing, he convincingly concluded that the uneven legislative framework constituted an obstacle to trade and that harmonisation seemed the most appropriate mechanism to overcome it.[1075]

Aplin held a different view, which was largely based on the results of the Baker McKenzie Industry Survey referred to above. In the first place, she looked into the figures on the risk of exposure and the attempts at misappropriation suffered by the respondents in the last ten years. As regards the first, 38% of the enterprises were of the opinion that the risk had increased, whereas 20,5% reported at least one misappropriation attempt in the last decade. Out of those, only 5,2% had suffered more than five attempts. She considered that those numbers were not particularly alarming and cast doubt upon whether a harmonised system of protection would yield more investment in innovation. According to the survey, 29% of the respondents adopted different measures if they operated in several jurisdictions. In her view, this indicated that there would not be substantial savings in the means adopted by firms in protecting secrecy, which in turn would not result in a higher investment in R&D. The same rationale was applied in connection to collaborative research, as only 24% of the respondent companies were of the opinion that more collaborative opportunities would derive from the alignment of national legislation. However, it is here submitted that the fact that two out of ten market participants had suffered a misappropriation attempt in the last ten years and that three out of ten of the surveyed companies adopted different protection measures if they operated in more than one market seems persuasive enough to justify the alignment of national laws in the field of trade secrets.[1076]

With the above analysis in mind, the Preamble of the TSD clarifies that the competence to harmonise trade secrets protection across the EU stems from Article 114 TFEU, which sets forth the power of the Parliament and the Council to legislate on measures necessary to ensure the proper functioning of the Single Market. This aspect is further developed in several recitals, where it is explicitly stated that the existing scattered legal framework has a negative impact on the creation of a Single Market without internal barriers to trade.[1077]

1075 Ansgar Ohly 2013 (n 13) 39.

1076 Tanya Aplin 2014 (n 384) 260; the empirical survey commented results can be found in Baker McKenzie 2013 (n 1057) 126 and the following.

1077 See Recitals (4) and (8) TSD.

Notwithstanding this, legal scholars have warned of the excessive reliance of EU legislative powers on this provision to approximate national regimes, and the little attention that is often paid to whether the national divergences actually have a negative effect on intra-community trade.[1078] The CJEU in its *Tobacco Advertising* decision emphasised that Article 114 TFEU should serve as the legal basis only when the divergences among Member States are likely to hinder the Fundamental Freedoms and thus affect the good functioning of the Single Market.[1079] In this context, the role of the Impact Assessment as a means to examine the advisability of taking a legislative action at the EU level is becoming increasingly relevant, as it compels the EU legislature to take into consideration the advantages and disadvantages of each of the policy options analysed.[1080]

As noted above, the Commission prepared an Impact Assessment in which five potential policy options to address the fragmentation of the Single Market vis-à-vis trade secrets were examined. The first one was to maintain the existing status quo, i.e., keeping the scattered legal protection. The second alternative presented compelled Member States to raise awareness and provide information about the existing means of redress in the case of misappropriation of trade secrets. Option 3 considered the harmonisation of national civil law vis-à-vis the unlawful acts of misappropriation (but excluded remedies and the preservation of confidentiality of trade secrets during legal proceedings). Option 4, by contrast, called upon Member States to harmonise their legal regimes with regard to the available civil law remedies and to implement measures to ensure secrecy during litiga-

1078 Paul Craig and Gráinne de Búrca, *EU Law, Text, Cases and Materials* (5th edn, OUP 2011) 92-93; this point is further developed by Stephen Weatherhill, 'Competence Creep and Competence Control' [2004] 23 Yearbook European L 1.

1079 Case C–376/98 *Germany v European Parliament and the Council* [2000] ECR I–8419, para 84 where the Court noted that "(…) A measure adopted on the basis of Article 100a of the Treaty (now Article 114 TFEU) must genuinely have as its object the improvement of the conditions for the establishment and functioning of the internal market. If a mere finding of disparities between national rules and of the abstract risk of obstacles to the exercise of fundamental freedoms or of distortions of competition liable to result therefrom were sufficient to justify the choice of Article 100a as a legal basis, judicial review of compliance with the proper legal basis might be rendered nugatory. The Court would then be prevented from discharging the function entrusted to it by Article 164 of the EC Treaty (now Article 220 EC) of ensuring that the law is observed in the interpretation and application of the Treaty".

1080 Paul Craig and Gráinne de Búrca, *EU Law, Text, Cases and Materials* (5th edn, OUP 2011) 93.

tion. Finally, harmonising both civil law and criminal law remedies was also considered.[1081]

In the end, the preferred policy option was to align the laws of the Member States with regard to national civil law remedies against the misappropriation of trade secrets, that is, to implement option 4. This was deemed the most advantageous of the available alternatives, as it would allow the owners to seek protection vis-à-vis infringing parties and stop imports from third countries. According to the Impact Assessment, the harmonisation of rules that ensure the preservation of confidentiality during legal proceedings should boost litigation. All in all, legal certainty should be improved and, accordingly, cooperation between undertakings should also be facilitated. This should ultimately strengthen the incentives to innovate.[1082]

Consequently, the Impact Assessment concluded that the adoption of the TSD was justified on the basis of two grounds.[1083] Firstly, the ineffective protection of trade secrets discouraged innovation activities (including those that take place at a cross-border scale) due to, on the one hand, the low expected value of innovation relying on trade secrets and the higher costs of protecting it, and on the other, the "higher business risk when sharing trade secrets". This hindered innovation and creativity and diminished investment (Recital 4), which in turn lowered the incentive to engage in cross-border innovative activities (Recital 8). Secondly, it was suggested that the different scope of protection and means of redress available across the 28 Member States caused trade secrets holders to risk losing their competitive advantage and thus reduced their competitiveness. As a result, the Commission determined that there was a case for harmonisation.

## C) Legal analysis of the TSD

The body of the TSD is divided into a Preamble and four chapters, from which the first three correspond to the three main areas of trade secrets law that are harmonised. The following sections critically analyse the main provisions of the Directive. In the first place, some general remarks regarding the principles that inform it are outlined (section I). Next, the subject matter and scope of application of the Directive are examined (section II).

1081 Impact Assessment (n 385) 57-58.
1082 Impact Assessment (n 385) 64-65.
1083 Impact Assessment (n 385) 40-41.

Section III then looks into the types of conduct that are considered lawful, as well as those that are considered infringing and the exceptions thereto. Finally, the main obligations in connection to the enforcement of trade secrets are analysed in section IV.

## I. General remarks

A detailed analysis of the Directive reveals that the EU legislature has adopted a flexible approach in the regulation of trade secrets protection. This is apparent from the number of open-ended clauses that refer to the general standard of honest commercial practices (in line with Article 10bis(2) PC) enshrined in most of the provisions that regulate the scope of protection, the list of lawful means of acquisition, use and disclosure of trade secrets spelt out in Article 3 and the list of exceptions in Article 5.[1084] Flexibility is central in order to achieve a well-balanced Directive that allows for weighing up all of the relevant interests in each individual case.[1085] Nonetheless, this legislative technique may interfere with the harmonisation objective pursued by the TSD, as the meaning of "honest commercial practices" may be construed differently in each of the 28 Member States.[1086] In fact, this standard is mostly applied as part of the acquis communautaire in the field of trade marks and was excluded from the scope of the Unfair Commercial Practices Directive.[1087] Ultimately, divergences in this field should be solved by the CJEU as part of the EU secondary law interpretation.[1088]

The TSD provides for minimum harmonisation and explicitly mentions that Member States can establish stronger protection than that foreseen in the Directive.[1089] Nonetheless, certain restrictions have also been included

---

1084 This argument is raised in Annette Kur, Reto Hilty and Roland Knaak 2014 (n 383) para 10; Mary-Rose McGuire 2016 (n 824) 1006, particularly when compared with the German system as per §§ 17-19 UWG, which followed an "Alles-oder-Nichts-Prinzip" .

1085 Annette Kur, Reto Hilty and Roland Knaak 2014 (n 383) para 6.

1086 Tanya Aplin 2014 (n 384) 260; a more detailed account of the meaning of the expression "honest commercial practices" is provided in chapter 2 § 1 A) III. 2).

1087 Annette Kur, Reto Hilty and Roland Knaak 2014 (n 383) para 10.

1088 Tanya Aplin 2014 (n 384) 265; see further Article 267 of the TFEU. In the words of Martin Höpner, 'Der Europäische Gerichtshof als Motor der Integration' [2011] 21 Berlin J Soziol 203, 204: "The ECJ (now CJEU) has become the engine of European Integration".

1089 As per Recital 10 TSD.

in order to ensure compliance with specific obligations.[1090] Some of the most relevant ones provide that Member States shall not adopt higher standards as regards the definition of lawful acquisition, use and disclosure of trade secrets (Article 3) or interfere with the exceptions laid down in Article 5 of the Directive. In this context, it has been suggested that the maximum harmonisation approach adopted by the TSD precludes Member States from including additional exceptions and lawful means of acquiring a trade secret.[1091] With respect to the enforcement of secrets, national legal regimes should put in place the procedures, measures and remedies necessary to ensure the availability of civil redress against the misappropriation of trade secrets (Article 6(1)) and ensure that these are governed by the principles of fairness, equity and proportionality (Articles 6(2)) and 7(1)). In the interest of legal certainty, national legislatures are compelled to set forth a statute of limitations, which shall not exceed 6 years (Article 8). In line with the objective of protecting secrecy during litigation, Member States shall ensure that the parties, witnesses or any other persons that have access to a trade secret during the course of a misappropriation proceedings are not allowed to use it or disclose it after the legal proceedings have ended (Article 9(1)), provided that it has not become generally known or a final judicial decision has held that it does not meet the statutory requirements of protection. Likewise, as an alternative to precautionary measures, it shall always be possible to continue using an allegedly infringing secret upon the lodging of specific guarantees by the defendant to compensate for any eventual damage (Article 10(2)). However, this does not include the disclosure of the information. In addition, the possibility of granting an injunction and the conditions to which it is subject are regulated as a maximum standard of protection (Article 13).

To be sure, the minimum harmonisation approach conflicts with the ultimate goal of the Directive, i.e. to eliminate barriers within the internal

---

1090 Article 1(1) paragraph 2 TSD: "Member States may, in compliance with the provisions of the TFEU, provide for more far-reaching protection against the unlawful acquisition, use or disclosure of trade secrets than that required in this Directive, provided that compliance with Articles 3, 5, 6, Article 7(1), Article 8, the second subparagraph of Article 9(1), Articles 9(3) and (4), Articles 10(2), Article 11, 13 and Article 15(3) is ensured.

1091 Christian Alexander, 'Gegenstand, Inhalt und Umfang des Schutzes von Geschäftsgeheimnissen nach der Richtlinie (EU) 2016/943 1034' [2017] WRP 1034, para 19.

market.[1092] Allowing Member States to provide for stronger protection may also raise concerns as to the relationship between trade secrets and IPRs.[1093] From a policy perspective, strengthening the legal regime of trade secrets protection benefits the trade secret holder, but may also have a negative impact on cumulative innovative and creative activities, as there is social value derived from the sharing of information.[1094] However, the fact that reverse engineering and independent discovery are regarded as lawful means of acquiring secret information and at the same time maximum standards of protection prevents the creation of an exclusive right and ensures an equilibrium with the IPRs system (and particularly patent law), in accordance with the wording of Recital 16.

Another remarkable feature of the Directive is that many central aspects of trade secrets protection are left unregulated. The three most salient ones are: (i) non-disclosure and non-competition agreements after the termination of an employment relationship; (ii) the ownership of trade secrets in cooperation agreements; and (iii) the establishment of claims for information and preserving evidence.[1095] As regards the first of these, The Comments of the Max Planck Institute for Innovation and Competition ("the MPI Comments") highlight that despite the practical relevance of this topic, it does not appear likely that the Directive can provide a univocal answer that foresees all of the potential situations of conflict without interfering with national labour and contract law.[1096] The latter points will be dis-

1092 IFRA, 'Comments on the Proposal for a Directive on the Protection of Undisclosed Know-How and Business Information (Trade Secrets)' (2014) 2 <http://www.ifraorg.org/en-us/library/tag/21005/s0> accessed 15 September 2018; see further Valeria Falce 2015 (n 392) 958, arguing that full harmonisation would allow for ensuring uniform transposition among all 28 EU jurisdictions and creating a "level playing field so as to incentivize and facilitate know-how and the exchange of sensitive information agreements, as well as any form of cooperation among enterprises, inventors and trade secret owners operating in Europe"; similar Mary-Rose McGuire 2016 (n 824) 1005; however, industry representatives have welcomed such an approach, as they believe that the existing differences among Member States are an insurmountable obstacle and Member States should be able to establish stronger protection. In this regard see IP Federation, 'The EU Trade Secrets Directive' (2014) Policy Paper PP04/15, 1 <https://www.ipfederation.com/news/ip-federation-comments-on-the-compromise-text-for-the-eu-trade-secrets-directive/> 15 September 2018.

1093 Valeria Falce 2015 (n 392) 948.

1094 See chapter 1 § 2 B) II. on the incentives to disclose theory in the context of trade secrets.

1095 Annette Kur, Reto Hilty and Roland Knaak 2014 (n 383) paras 8-9.

1096 Annette Kur, Reto Hilty and Roland Knaak 2014 (n 383) paras 8-9.

cussed in connection with the concept of trade secret holder[1097] and the enforcement measures.[1098]

As a final observation, it should be highlighted that the TSD represents a step forward in the harmonisation of the law of unfair competition in the EU.[1099] In line with this, Recital 17 expressly mentions that because of reverse engineering activities, innovators and creators are exposed to parasitic competition and slavish imitation practices "that free ride on their reputation and innovation efforts".[1100] Hence, the Directive calls on the Commission to investigate whether there is a need to take EU-wide action in this area, although it notes that it is not the purpose of the TSD to harmonise unfair competition in general. The wording used in this recital raises concerns insofar as it does not seem to take into account that fairness and legal protection against parasitic copying and slavish imitation are viewed differently across EU jurisdictions[1101] and that the general principle in competitive economies is that of freedom of imitation, which may be limited only by the operation of IPRs.[1102] Ultimately, such a statement indicates that in the near future these areas will guide the Commission's legislative action.

---

1097 See chapter 3 § 5 C) II. 2.

1098 See chapter 3 § 5 C) IV.

1099 Valeria Falce 2015 (n 392) 957.

1100 Recital 17 TSD: "In some industry sectors, where creators and innovators cannot benefit from exclusive rights and where innovation has traditionally relied upon trade secrets, products can nowadays be easily reverse-engineered once in the market. In those cases, those creators and innovators may be victims of practices such as parasitic copying or slavish imitations that free ride on their reputation and innovation efforts. Some national laws dealing with unfair competition address those practices. While this Directive does not aim to reform or harmonize unfair competition law in general, it would be appropriate that the Commission carefully examine the need for Union action in that area".

1101 Hogan Lovells, 'Study on Trade Secrets and Parasitic Copying (Look-alikes) – Report on Parasitic Copying' (MARKT/2010/20/D) paras 106-109 (2012) <https ://www.google.com/url?sa=t&rct=j&q=&esrc=s&source=web&cd=1&cad=rja&uact=8&ved=2ahUKEwiy8tzludndAhWDaFAKHfYHC3UQFjAAegQICRAC&url=http%3A%2F%2Fec.europa.eu%2Finternal_market%2Fiprenforcement%2Fdocs%2Fparasitic%2F201201-study_en.pdf&usg=AOvVaw2Ws2o9bYEnYOj5RM9bFb8y> accessed 15 September; more generally Frauke Henning-Bodewig and others, *International Handbook on Unfair Competition* (C.H. Beck 2013) para 73.

1102 Ansgar Ohly, 'The Freedom of Imitation and Its Limits – A European Perspective' [2010] IIC 506, 520-524.

## II. Scope of application and subject matter covered

### 1. Scope of application

Article 2 lays down the positive scope of application of the Directive, by defining the concepts of "trade secret",[1103] "trade secret holder", "infringer" and "infringing goods". Conversely, Article 1(2) sets forth the negative scope of application and expressly notes that the rules laid down in the Directive shall not affect the exercise of the fundamental rights of freedom of expression and information, as laid down in the ChFREU. In addition, the national and EU law provisions that mandate the disclosure of trade secrets for reasons of public interest shall remain unaffected. In a similar vein and in the interest of employee mobility, Article 1(3) clarifies that no restrictions on the mobility of employees can be grounded on the provisions of the TSD.[1104]

Recital 39 further delimits the material scope vis-à-vis other areas of law and expressly provides that the provisions set forth in the Directive shall not interfere with "the application of other relevant law in other areas including intellectual property rights and the law of contract". These clarifications are of paramount importance to ensure legal certainty, in particular with regard to employment relations.[1105]

In addition, Recital 35 provides that the rights and obligations embedded within the Data Protection Directive[1106] shall remain unaffected.[1107] In this regard, it should be noted that since the adoption of the TSD, the Data Protection Directive has been repealed by the General Data Protection Regulation ("GDPR"),[1108] which contains no express clarification as to its relationship with the TSD. However, since Recital 35 TSD expressly pro-

---

1103 A detailed account of the concept of trade secret laid down in the TSD is provided in chapter 4 § 3.

1104 See chapter 6 § 1 A).

1105 Annette Kur, Reto Hilty and Roland Knaak 2014 (n 383) paras 14 and 15.

1106 Directive of the European Parliament and of the Council 95/46/EC of 24 October 1995 on the protection of individuals with regard to the processing of personal data and on the free movement of such data [1995] OJ L281/0031 (Data Protection Directive).

1107 Annette Kur, Reto Hilty and Roland Knaak 2014 (n 383) paras 14-15.

1108 Regulation (EU) 2016/679 of the European Parliament and of the Council of of 27 April 2016 on the protection of natural persons with regard to the processing of personal data and on the free movement of such data, and repealing Directive 95/46/EC (General Data Protection Regulation) [2016] OJ L119/01 (GDPR).

vides that the rights of the data subject to access, obtain the rectification, erasure or blocking of the data should not be affected by the TSD and as those same rights are included in the GDPR, it seems that the general principle embedded in Recital 35 TSD should also govern the relationship with the GDPR.[1109] Yet, uncertainty remains as to the relationship between the TSD and the new rights envisaged in the GDPR, such as data portability.[1110] Furthermore, Recital 63 GDPR notes that the right of access to personal data by the data subject "should not adversely affect the rights or freedoms of others, including *trade secrets* or intellectual property and in particular the copyright protecting the software. However, the result of those considerations should not be a refusal to provide all information to the data subject". Therefore, it seems that the observance of the rights laid down in the TSD is not absolute and, depending on the specific circumstances of the case, the data subject may have the right to access his personal information, even if it constitutes a trade secret or part of it. Similar concerns were presented in the Opinion of the European Data Protection Supervisor, where it was expressly recommended that an adjudication process be created including national protection authorities, in the event that tension arose between the data subject rights and the trade secret holder rights.[1111]

The relationship between the Enforcement Directive and the TSD is also problematic. Recital 39 TSD provides that in the event that the two overlap, the application of the latter should be favoured as lex specialis.[1112] This statement begs the question of whether the Enforcement Directive is to be

1109 Surblyte Gintare, 'Data Mobility in the Digital Economy' (2016) Max Planck Institute for Innovation & Competition Research Paper No. 16-03, 15 <https://papers.ssrn.com/sol3/papers.cfm?abstract_id=2752989> accessed 15 September 2018.

1110 Ibid.

1111 See European Data Protection Supervisor, 'Opinion of the European Data Protection Supervisor on the proposal for a directive of the European Parliament and of the Council on the protection of undisclosed know-how and business information (trade secrets) against their unlawful acquisition, use and disclosure' (2014), para 22 <https://edps.europa.eu/data-protection/our-work/publications/opinions/protection-undisclosed-know-how-and-business_en> accessed 27 September 2018.

1112 Recital 39 TSD provides that: "This Directive should not affect the application of any other relevant law in other areas, including intellectual property rights and the law of contract. However, where the scope of application of Directive 2004/48/EC of the European Parliament and of the Council and the scope of this Directive overlap, this Directive takes precedence as lex specialis".

applied to trade secrets in those areas that are not regulated in the latter Directive, namely with regard to the obligation to provide and preserve evidence,[1113] information duties,[1114] and the liability of intermediaries.[1115] Indeed, in 2005 the Commission issued a statement on the rights that were deemed to fall under the scope of protection of the Enforcement Directive and no reference to trade secrets or unfair competition was made.[1116] Notwithstanding this, according to Recital 13 of the Enforcement Directive, Member States are free to extend its scope of application to unfair competition. Against this background, a few jurisdictions have extended the obligations enshrined in the Enforcement Directive to the protection of undisclosed information.[1117] In this respect, it should be noted that during the initial stage of the TSD negotiations, the Commission considered whether the application of the Enforcement Directive to trade secrets would be an adequate solution to achieve effective protection across the Single Market. This option was dismissed based on the argument that trade secrets were not an IPR.[1118] In view of the remaining uncertainty, it is argued that the relationship between the Enforcement Directive and the Trade Secrets Directive will most likely have to be clarified by the submission of a preliminary question to the CJEU.

Another potentially conflicting aspect that has already been outlined above is the applicable law from a private international law perspective, which is explicitly excluded from the scope of the Directive pursuant to Recital 37.[1119] The law applicable to IPR infringement disputes is governed by Article 8, para 1 of the Rome II Regulation (the law of the place in

---

1113 Articles 6 and 7 Enforecement Directive.

1114 Article 8 Enforcement Directive.

1115 Article 11(3) of the Enforcement Directive.

1116 Commission, 'Commission Statement concerning Article 2 of Directive 2004/48/EC of the European Parliament and of the Council on the enforcement of intellectual property rights' [2005] OJ L94/37: "The Commission considers that at least the following intellectual property rights are covered by the scope of the Directive: copyright, rights related to copyright, sui generis right of a database maker, rights of the creator of the topographies of a semiconductor product, trademark rights, design rights, patent rights, including rights derived from supplementary protection certificates, geographical indications, utility model rights, plant variety rights, trade names, in so far as these are protected as exclusive property rights in the national law concerned".

1117 Italy, Portugal, Slovak Republic, Rumania and arguably the UK, as noted in Baker McKenzie 2013 (n 1057) 26.

1118 Impact Assessment (n 385) 267-268.

1119 See chapter 1 § 3 B) III; see further Recital 37 TSD: "This Directive does not aim to establish harmonised rules for judicial cooperation, jurisdiction, the

which the damage occurs). By contrast, if trade secrets misappropriation is regarded as an act against unfair competition, Articles 6 and 4 of the Rome II Regulation should be applied (the law of the place in which protection is sought). For the sake of legal certainty, it would have been advisable for the TSD to clarify the applicable law in the case of infringement, even though it clearly seems to lean towards an unfair competition approach.[1120]

As a final remark, it is worth noting that the Directive is limited to civil redress, despite the fact that the comparative law study carried out by Hogan Lovells shows that there are substantial disparities as regards the configuration of criminal penalties and the sanctions imposed in the event of trade secrets infringement.[1121] In the Impact Assessment, the Commission took the view that the alignment of criminal law provisions in the field of trade secrets was not appropriate owing to the lack of harmonisation of criminal law at the EU level, the potential deterrence effect it may shield in regard to employment mobility, and the proportionality principle that governs criminal law.[1122]

## 2. Definition of trade secret holder and infringer

The concept of "trade secret holder" is defined in Article 2(2) as a natural or legal person who is *lawfully in control of the information*, in line with Ar-

recognition and enforcement of judgements on civil and commercial matters, or deal with applicable law. Other Union instruments which govern such matters in general terms, should, in principle, remain equally applicable to the field covered by this Directive"; and as noted by Thomas Hören and Reiner Münker, 'Die EU-RL für den Schutz von Geschäftsgeheimnissen und ihre Umsetzug' [2018] WRP 150, 151 para 4.

1120 This is developed in Annette Kur, Reto Hilty and Roland Knaak 2014 (n 383) para 17.

1121 Hogan Lovells 2012 (n 793) paras 254-256.

1122 Impact Assessment (n 385) 64-65; Björn H. Kalbfus, 'Die EU-Geschäftsgeheimnis-Richtlinie - Welcher Umsetzungsbedarf besteht in Deutschland?' [2016] GRUR 1009, 1009; the consultations for the Directive started while the Anti-Counterfeiting Trade Agreement (ACTA) was still being negotiated and was eventually rejected by the European Parliament on June 2012. In this post-ACTA scenario, the Commission considered that any attempt to harmonise criminal sanctions would face strong opposition from the Parliament and the citizens of the EU in general.

ticle 39(2) TRIPs.[1123] Article 4(1) further adds that the trade secret holder is the person entitled to apply for the measures, procedures and remedies set forth in chapter III of the Directive.

Against this background, it might be noted that the Directive does not refer to the owner, but instead resorts to the notion of *control*.[1124] Hence, the decisive factor is not who has created the information, but rather who exercises control over it.[1125] Yet, the TSD does not provide any rules regarding the assessment of the control over the information and the establishment of the ownership of trade secrets; this is left unregulated.[1126] Accordingly, it is up to the Member States to set forth the rules that determine who is the rightful holder and who has a standing to sue. This is particularly relevant in the context of collaborative agreements and with regard to the possibility that exclusive and non-exclusive licensees bring legal action against alleged infringers,[1127] in contrast to the DTSA, which refers to "owners".[1128] The wording used by the Directive also leaves open whether those who obtain a trade secret after reverse engineering a marketed product or employees who gain knowledge of secret information during the course of their employment with consent should also be regarded as trade secret holders.[1129] It has been suggested that the Directive should not aim at providing such a detailed and precise regulation, but instead it should be agreed upon contractually between the parties or determined by the application of the relevant law.[1130] Indeed, the ownership of trade secrets is largely dependent on the regulation of employee creations and in-

1123 Article 39(2) TRIPs provides that: "*Natural and legal persons* shall have the possibility of preventing information lawfully within their control from being disclosed to, acquired by, or used by others without their consent in a manner contrary to honest commercial practices (10) so long as such information (...)" (emphasis added).

1124 On this specific issue, the TSD differs from the DTSA, pursuant to which only owners have legal standing.

1125 Thomas Hören and Reiner Münker 2018(b) (n1119) para 9.

1126 Thomas Hören and Reiner Münker 2018(b) (n1119) para 9.

1127 Tanya Aplin 2015 (n 306) 435.

1128 Further Victoria A. Cundiff and others 2016 (n 789) 740 note that: "Plaintiffs may argue that this definition confers standing to more than just the owner or exclusive licensee of the trade secret, such as non-exclusive licensee who controls the trade secret, which potentially broadens the application of the Directive as compared with the DTSA".

1129 Tanya Aplin 2014 (n 384) 264; Christian Alexander 2017 (n 1091) para 69 convincingly argues that those that create the trade secret independently should also be regarded as trade secret holders.

1130 Annette Kur, Reto Hilty and Roland Knaak 2014 (n 383) para 9.

ventions, which in most Member States consist of a piecemeal regulation in the employment and labour statutes.[1131] Consequently, aligning the regulations of Member States with regard to such a complex topic might have exceeded the scope of harmonisation in the context of trade secrets. However, the absence of a uniform approach may lead to a divergent solution among Member States' courts and may potentially interfere with the harmonisation goals pursued by the Directive.[1132]

At the other end of the spectrum, the term infringer is defined as "any natural and legal person who has unlawfully acquired, used or disclosed trade secrets". This provision is one of the milestones of the Directive, as it provides common ground across the EU on the potential liability of legal persons for trade secrets misappropriation.

### 3. Infringing goods

The term infringing goods is used to refer to "goods the design (in French "*conception*"), characteristics, functioning, production process or marketing of which significantly benefit from trade secrets unlawfully acquired, used or disclosed". This definition poses a number of interpretative questions, particularly in connection with the causal relationship between trade secrets and the infringing goods.

Firstly, in accordance with Recital 26 TSD, it appears that the term "infringing goods" refers both to products and the provision of services. However, while it is true that establishing causality between the design and manufacturing process of a product and a trade secret may be rather straightforward, this appears more problematic in other instances, such as in the provision of services based on the unlawful acquisition, use or disclosure of a trade secret or the marketing strategy followed to commercialise certain products. In particular, it has been suggested that according to the literal wording of Article 2(4) TSD, if a company unlawfully acquires a competitor's customer list to position his products in the marketplace better, the product as such may be considered as infringing, even though its characteristics bear no connection with the misappropriated

1131 For an overview of the provisions that govern the ownership of employee inventions in Germany see Kurt Bartenbach and Franz-Eugen Volz, *Arbeitnehmererfindungen* (6 edn, Carl Heynemanns Verlag 2014).

1132 Tanya Aplin 2014 (n 384) 265.

list.[1133] In this respect, the MPI Comments convincingly conclude that it is beyond the scope of the Directive to regard as infringing products that are commercialised under a marketing campaign that was conceived on the basis of an unlawfully acquired customer list.[1134]

In this context, it is worth noting that initially the Draft Proposed by the Commission in 2013 referred to goods, the *quality* of which significantly benefitted from the misappropriated trade secret. The inclusion of this term was vehemently criticised, as it was noted that ascertaining the relationship between the quality of a product and a trade secret is extremely difficult. It was argued that the term "characteristics" was more suitable, as it encompassed a broader spectrum of features other than just its quality. In the final version of Article 2(4), the expression "quality" was replaced by "characteristics".[1135] However, surprisingly Recital 28 still refers to the quality of the product resulting from the misappropriation of trade secrets in the context of the seizure of products and the prohibition of importation, which may lead to an over-extensive application of this provision.

Indeed, requiring that the "infringing goods" "significantly benefit" from the allegedly infringed trade secret seems a very open-ended standard that puts little emphasis on the causal link between the production of the goods and the actual use of a trade secret.[1136] This benchmark is manifestly different to the test usually applied in other fields of intellectual property.[1137] For instance, in patent law, in order to find an infringement it is required that the products are "directly" obtained from the patented pro-

1133 Thomas Hören und Reiner Münker 2018(a) (n 860) 86.

1134 Annette Kur, Reto Hilty and Roland Knaak 2014 (n 383) para 23; GRUR, 'Opinion on the proposal for a Directive on the protection of undisclosed know-how and business information (trade secrets) against their unlawful acquisition, use and disclosure, COM (2013) 813 final', para 1.b) <http://www.grur.org/uploads/tx_gstatement/2014-03-19_GRUR_Stellungnahme_zum_Know-how-Schutz_EN.pdf> accessed 15 September 2018 .

1135 Annette Kur, Reto Hilty and Roland Knaak 2014 (n 383) para 23.

1136 GRUR, 'Opinion on the proposal for a Directive on the protection of undisclosed know-how and business information (trade secrets) against their unlawful acquisition, use and disclosure, COM (2013) 813 final', 5 <http://www.grur.org/uploads/tx_gstatement/2014-03-19_GRUR_Stellungnahme_zum_Know-how-Schutz_EN.pdf> accessed 15 September 2018; also Thomas Hören und Reiner Münker 2018(a) (n 860) 86; Björn H. Kalbfus 2016 (n 1122) 1014.

1137 Tanya Tanya Aplin 2014 (n 384) 267-269.

cess[1138] or that a third party knows that the means supplied to him are intended to infringe a patented invention.[1139]

Against this background, some have suggested that if at least half of the total expenditure required for the development, production or distribution of a product can be attributed to the trade secret, it should be regarded as "infringing".[1140] However, such an absolute test seems too rigid, because with complex products that incorporate multiple inventions (for example, smart phones), if only one of them is misappropriated, it is likely that it represents less than 50% of the total expenditure in view of the other inventions incorporated in the product. However, the product as such should be considered as infringing. Consequently, it is submitted that courts should follow a more nuanced approach, whereby the percentage of expenditure in the development, production and marketing is just one of the factors to be taken into consideration, alongside the importance of the information for the commercial success of the product or service rendered or the potential harm to the lawful holder, to name some. In this regard English courts resort to a degree test in order to consider whether a given product infringes a trade secret, which seems particularly pertinent:[1141]

> It is not every derived product, process or business which should be treated as camouflaged embodiment of the confidential information and not all on-going exploitation of such products, processes or business should be treated as continued use of the information, it must be a matter of degree whether the extent and importance of the use of the confidential information in such a continued exploitation of the derived material should be viewed as continued use of the information.[1142]

In the light of the previous arguments, it appears that courts will have to emphasise the need to establish a causal link between the trade secret and the allegedly infringing good, which will ultimately be a matter of degree. Otherwise, the potential to regard goods as infringing may be too far-

---

1138 See Article 64(2) EPC: "If the subject matter of the European patent is a process, the protection conferred by the patent shall extend to the products directly obtained by such process"; see further Article 25 Agreement on a Unified Patent Court.

1139 Agreement on a Unified Patent Court [2013] OJ C175/1 (Agreement on a Unified Patent Court), Article 26 (1).

1140 Christian Alexander 2017 (n 1091) para 107.

1141 Tanya Aplin 2014 (n 384) 268.

1142 *Ocular Sciences Ltd v Aspect Vision Care Ltd* [1997] RPC 289, [404].

reaching, much broader than the concepts traditionally applied in intellectual property law and expand to items that bear no factual connection with the confidential information in question. Ultimately, this may impose undue limitations on the ability of other market participants to commercialise competing products.[1143]

## III. Scope of protection: the assessment of misappropriation and lawful conducts

Chapter III of the Directive sets forth the circumstances under which the acts of acquisition, use and disclosure of trade secrets are deemed lawful (Article 3) or unlawful (Article 4), and the exceptions thereto (Article 5). The following sections delve into the study of the scope of protection of the TSD following the systematic structure of this chapter. Hence, it starts by examining the cases of lawful acquisition, use and disclosure (section 1); next, it looks into the regulation of the types of infringing conduct (section 2) and finally it studies the exceptions to the latter (section 3).

### 1. Lawful acquisition, use and disclosure

Article 3 spells out a number of types of conduct that should be considered lawful, thereby enhancing legal certainty for market participants[1144] and maintaining the equilibrium with the intellectual property law system. From a systematic perspective, the types of conduct regulated under Article 3 seem to exclude ex ante liability for misappropriation, while the exceptions set out under Article 5 require the competent judicial authorities to carry out a balancing test, taking into account the specific circumstances of the case.[1145]

Firstly, in accordance with most Member States' practice, the Directive clarifies that independent discovery or creation shall be considered lawful means of acquiring undisclosed information (Article 3(1)(a) TSD). This topic is discussed further in chapter 6[1146] as one of the limitations to secrecy. For now, it suffices to note that regarding independent discovery as a

1143 Christian Alexander 2017 (n 1091) para 107.
1144 Christian Alexander 2017 (n 1091) para 74.
1145 Thomas Hören and Reiner Münker 2018(b) (n 1119) para 19.
1146 Chapter 6 § 2 A).

lawful way to acquire confidential information is consistent with the fact that trade secrets are not deemed the object of an exclusive right (Recital 16) and at the same time maintains the balance with the intellectual property system.[1147]

One of the milestones of the Directive is the introduction of a general clause that allows for reverse engineering lawfully acquired products. Article 3(1)(b) defines this as the "Observation, study, disassembly or test of a product or object that has been made available to the public or that is lawfully in the possession of the acquirer of the information who is free from any legally valid duty to limit the acquisition of the trade secret".

The establishment of common ground rules on reverse engineering represents a major step forward in the light of the divergent interpretations adopted by the EU Member States[1148] and their economic impact on the Internal Market.[1149] Indeed, with the introduction of the general reverse engineering exception, the EU has taken a similar approach to the governing principle in the U.S., where it has been accepted for many years and is deemed a necessary counterbalance to the patent system. In effect, the U.S. Courts and the DTSA regard reverse engineering as a valid and powerful defence against misappropriation actions.[1150] The implications of such an approach for the interpretation of secrecy are further discussed in chapter 6.[1151]

In addition, Article 3(1)(c) deems lawful the acquisition of information that constitutes a trade secrets if it is acquired by employees (or employees'

1147 James Pooley 2002 (n 66) § 5.01[1] 5-3.

1148 In Germany, for instance, reverse engineering was not allowed as such. Following the German Federal Supreme Court Decision RGZ 1935 149, 329, 335–*Stiefeleisenpresse*, courts should assess whether the information is obtained through great difficulty and cost, that is, whether it is secret. If that is the case, the obtention of information through reverse engineering will be deemed unlawful.

1149 Baker McKenzie 2013 (n 1057) 125.

1150 Against this background, it is important to note that the UTSA does not expressly refer to independent creation or reverse engineering as exceptions to the rights in a trade secret; Roger M. Milgrim 2014 (n 160) § 1.05(2), 1.07(01) argues that courts have regarded both of them as an inherent corollary to the secrecy requirement. Consequently, a number of States have incorporated these exceptions into the wording of their Trade Secrets Acts. This is the case of § 3426.1(a) of the California Civil Code.

1151 Chapter 6 § 2 B).

representatives) during the exercise of their right to information and consultation, as regulated under EU or national statues.[1152]

In line with the flexibility principle that informs the Directive, Article 3(1)(d)[1153] resorts to a broad unfair competition clause and provides that the acquisition of a trade secret should be regarded as lawful so long as it is in accordance with honest commercial practices. Ultimately, the appraisal of whether secret information has been lawfully acquired will depend upon the interpretation of the *broader* and *splendidly imprecise* expression of what is regarded as "honest commercial practices".[1154] As noted above, such a flexible approach may contribute to enhancing the legal fragmentation among Member States, but at the same time may allow for better adaptation to the evolving technological means and the different legal traditions. Some have in fact drawn parallels between this provision and the fair use limitations that govern trade mark and copyright limitations in the U.S. legal system.[1155]

Finally, Article 3(2) provides that the acquisition, but also the use and disclosure mandated or permitted pursuant to EU or national provisions should be deemed lawful.[1156]

## 2. Types of infringing conduct

In line with the minimum standards set out in Article 39(2) TRIPs, the EU legislator stipulated that the unlawful acquisition, use and disclosure of trade secrets constitute infringing types of conduct. Due to their broad scope, these rules appear to be related more to unfair competition than to intellectual property law provisions, which seems to indicate that the Directive leans towards an unfair competition approach, even though this is not expressly mentioned in the text.[1157] Remarkably, the Directive does not define any of the infringing types of conduct. Instead, the EU legisla-

1152 Christian Alexander 2017 (n 1091) para 74.

1153 Ultimately, the unlawful acquisition, use and disclosure of secret information is premised on acts contrary to honest commercial practices, as per Art 4(2)(b) TSD.

1154 For a detailed account of the interpretation of the "honest commercial practices" see chapter 2 § 1 A) III. 2.

1155 Thomas Hören and Reiner Münker 2018(b) (n 1119) para 23.

1156 This is discussed further in chapter 4 § 4 C) 2. c).

1157 Contrary, Mathias Lejeune 'Die neue EU Richtlinie zum Schutz von Know-How und Geschäftsgeheimnissen' [2016] CR 330, 331.

ture preferred to spell out a list of examples and included a final open-ended clause that refers to the general standard of "general commercial practices" enshrined in Article 10bis PC with regard to unlawful acquisition. Consequently, some commentators have argued that Article 4 sets forth a "blacklist" of types of conduct that, when carried out by the infringer, are *objectively* deemed unlawful (strict liability).[1158] However, this statement is not completely accurate, particularly because the liability of third parties and importers requires at least gross negligence.

In the light of the above consideration, the following four sections look into the types of conduct that are deemed illicit by the Directive, namely the unlawful acquisition of secret information (section a); the unlawful use and disclosure of trade secrets (section b); the liability of third parties (section c); and the import and export of infringing goods (section d).

### a) Unlawful acquisition

Pursuant to Article 4(2), the acquisition of a trade secret will only be regarded as unlawful if it is carried out without the consent of the trade secret holder.[1159] Next, the Directive provides a number of examples of actions that are to be considered unlawful acquisition of undisclosed information. These are the "unauthorised access to, appropriation of, or copy of any documents, objects, materials, substances or electronic files, lawfully under the control of the trade secret holder, containing the trade secret or from which the trade secret can be deduced".[1160] Thereupon, section (b) clarifies that any other conduct contrary to honest commercial practices may also be deemed an unlawful acquisition under the circumstances. Thereby, it expands the scope of Article 4(2) beyond the acts previously listed. Ultimately, the inclusion of such a flexible clause is in line with Article 10bis of the PC and Article 39(2) TRIPs and underscores the unfair competition nature of the protection afforded by Directive.[1161] It also provides sufficient leeway to adapt to future technological developments that

1158 Mary-Rose McGuire 2016 (n 824) 1007-1006; Clemens Koós, 'Die europäische Geschäftsgeheimnis-Richtlinie – ein gelungener Wurf? Schutz von Know-How und Geschäftsinformationen – Änderungen im deutschen Wettbewerbsrecht' [2016] MMR 224, 225.

1159 Björn H. Kalbfus 2016 (n 1122)1013.

1160 Article 4(2)(a) TSD.

1161 Thomas Hören and Reiner Münker 2018(b) (n 1119) 152.

may create new means of misappropriating information that could not have been foreseen at the time that the TSD was drafted.

At this point, it is worth noting that in the first draft presented by the Commission, "intentionality" or "gross negligence" were prerequisites to regard an acquisition as unlawful. Yet, such an approach was criticised because these standards of fault should only be taken into consideration in the establishment of sanctions, not vis-à-vis the infringing conduct as such.[1162] In addition, it was suggested that section (b), which has an overarching effect, is an unfair competition law provision, where fault is not a requirement to find liability.[1163] In this context, it is not required that the acquisition of a trade secret is detrimental to the trade secret holder or that it is carried out "for the purposes of competition", "for personal gain", "for the benefit of a third party", or "with the intent of causing damage to the owner of the business or trade secret holder", as required by several national jurisdictions before the adoption of the Directive, such as Spain (Article 13(3) of the Spanish Unfair Competition Act) and Germany (as per § 17 UWG).

In the Commission's draft, additional examples of types of infringing conduct were also included, namely theft, bribery and deception. However, these are criminal law concepts that require, at least, an implicit intent on the part of the infringer to be actionable. Gross negligence is insufficient to find criminal liability in these cases.[1164] More importantly, these offences have not been harmonised across the 28 EU Member States. Therefore, inconsistencies in their interpretation may have arisen, thus hampering the ultimate harmonisation objective.[1165] In view of this, in the final version "intentionality" and "gross negligence" were omitted as preconditions to find an infringement under Article 4(2).[1166] Similarly, theft, bribery and deception were deleted from this provision, in line with the exclusion of harmonisation in the field of criminal sanctions. However, this has given rise to some criticism from commentators, who understand

---

1162 Annette Kur, Reto Hilty and Roland Knaak 2014 (n 383) para 27 noting that "as a matter of principle, fault on the part of the infringer should only play a role when determining the sanctions. As such, a claim for damages usually requires fault, while it is not taken into consideration in a claim for injunctive relief"; Mary-Rose McGuire 2016 (n 824) 1007; Mathias Lejeune 2016 (n 1157) 334.

1163 Annette Kur, Reto Hilty and Roland Knaak 2014 (n 383) para 27.

1164 Annette Kur, Reto Hilty and Roland Knaak 2014 (n 383) para 27.

1165 Tanya Aplin 2014 (n 384) 265.

1166 Thomas Hören and Reiner Münker 2018(b) (n 1119) 153.

that the mere fact that any of the types of conduct spelt out in Article 4(2) TSD are objectively carried out allows for the application of the sanctions set out in chapter III of the TSD is at odds with many national legal regimes (namely Germany) and equates trade secretes protection with IPRs protection.[1167]

b) Unlawful use and disclosure

Article 4(3) regulates the unlawful "use" and "disclosure" of trade secrets. The term "use" refers to the commercial exploitation of the secret in any manner, whereas the term "disclosure" captures the act of making available information to unauthorised third parties or the general public.[1168]

Just as in the case of unlawful acquisition, this provision also requires lack of consent. In addition, the infringer (a) must have acquired the trade secret unlawfully, as per article 4(2); or (b) must be in breach of a confidentiality agreement or a duty to maintain secrecy; or (c) must be in breach of a contractual or any other duty to limit the use of the trade secret.[1169]

Following the legal reasoning applied above in connection with unlawful acquisition, intentionality and gross negligence were deleted from the final draft as preconditions for finding liability in the case of unlawful use and disclosure.[1170] This has not been without criticism, as many have suggested that the objective nature of the liability set forth in paragraphs 2 and 3 of Article 4 affords intellectual property-like protection to trade secret holders, because if the types of conduct that they refer to are objectively carried out, they will trigger the same consequences as formal IPRs infringement.[1171] However, such an approach disregards the fact that Article 3 and 5 seem to provide sufficient safeguards against erga omnes enforcement of trade secrets irrespective of the manner in which the information is acquired. Consequently, the EU legislature rightfully stipulated that fault should only play a role in connection to acquisition by third parties, as discussed in the following section.[1172]

---

1167 Thomas Hören and Reiner Münker 2018(b) (n 1119) 153.
1168 Christian Alexander 2017 (n 1091) para 74.
1169 Mathias Lejeune 2016 (n) 333-334.
1170 Tanya Aplin 2014 (n 384) 265.
1171 Thomas Hören and Reiner Münker 2018(b) (n 1119) para 15.
1172 Annette Kur, Reto Hilty and Roland Knaak 2014 (n 383) para 31.

### c) Third party liability

The term "third party liability" refers to those situations where information is obtained from someone who is under an obligation of confidence or someone who has acquired it unlawfully, and it is subsequently used or disclosed by the third party, who has not breached any duty of confidence as such, or employed improper means to obtain it. This issue is addressed in Article 4(4) of the Directive, which to a large extent mirrors the wording of § 1(2)(ii)(B) UTSA.[1173] In essence, it expands the scope of the unlawful use or disclosure of a trade secret to any third parties who knew or should have known under the circumstances that the information was acquired by a person who acquired it, used it or disclosed it unlawfully.[1174] The secret may have been obtained directly or indirectly from another person.

The wording of Article 4(4) refers to "knowledge" and the fact that the trade secret holder "should have known under the circumstances" that the information was unlawfully acquired. This seems to introduce an element of fault in the appraisal of liability by imposing a duty of care on the side of the acquirer, in line with footnote 10 of the TRIPs Agreement, where gross negligence (not strict liability) is the applicable liability standard in the case of third party acquisition.[1175] The rationale behind this provision is to prevent third parties hiding behind a so-called "veil of wilful ignorance".[1176] However, this has also given rise to criticism from some commentators, who believe that the fact that the mere "knowledge" and "gross negligence" in the use of a trade secret illicitly obtained suffices to trigger the sanctions set out in chapter III of the Directive leads an overprotection of the trade secret holder.[1177] Such an approach seems to be in line with the prevailing case law in England, but broadens the liability of third par-

1173 § 1(2)(ii)(B) UTSA provides that, "Misappropriation includes acquisition by one who knows "or has reason to know" that the secret was acquired by improper means, or who gets it from such a person and thereafter uses or discloses it"; in a similar vein, see Restatement (Third) of Unfair Competition § 40 (Am. Law Inst. 1995) comment d.

1174 Article 4(4) TSD.

1175 Mathias Lejeune 2016 (n 1157) 334; footnote 10 of the TRIPs Agreement, provides as an example of practices contrary to honest commercial practices in the context of undisclosed information "the acquisition of undisclosed information by third parties who knew, or were grossly negligent in failing to know, that such practices were involved in the acquisition".

1176 James Pooley 2002 (n 66) § 6.04[1] 6-31.

1177 Thomas Hören and Reiner Münker 2018(b) (n 1119)153.

ties in Germany, which is limited to conditional intent ("*Vorsatz*" or "*Bedingter Vorsatz*").[1178]

This complex scenario is best illustrated with an example. Let us take for instance the case of a supplier of raw materials (Raw S.L.) that provides exclusively all the necessary materials and compounds to a French cosmetic firm (Beauty Care) for the production of a very effective antiaging cream (Stop fine lines), which competitors have since unsuccessfully tried to reverse engineer and which is the company's most valuable trade secret. As the sole supplier, the members of the Board of Raw S.L. and its chemists (Mr. Smith) have had access to the formula of Stop fine lines under strict confidentiality obligations. After some years, the parties cannot reach an economic agreement and the supply contract is terminated. A few weeks after the termination of the agreement, Raw S.L. approaches a competing cosmetic company in Germany (SKIN Harmony) claiming that it has developed a cream that is just as effective as Stop fine lines (the so-called "Magic Cream") and offers to provide the formula to SKIN Harmony under the condition that Raw S.L. becomes the sole provider of SKIN Harmony. Once the new product reaches the market, SKIN Harmony realises, upon receiving a cease and desist letter from Beauty Care, that the new competing product in fact uses the secret formula of their best-selling cream Stop fine lines, with a few minor variations regarding the perfume used. Under this factual scenario and following the new Directive rules, Raw S.L. could be held liable for trade secrets infringement pursuant to Article 4(3) (unlawful disclosure) and SKIN Harmony under Article 4(4) from the date on which the cease and desist letter was sent.[1179]

Against this background, Article 13(3) TSD along with Recital 29 provides further guidance regarding the potential liability of a legal or natural person who gained knowledge of a trade secret in good faith but after some time became aware that the information had been acquired from the original holder in an unlawful manner. In such a case, where appropriate, instead of granting injunctions or corrective measures that would disproportionately affect the third party, national courts shall award a pecuniary compensation (i.e. damages in lieu of injunction), in line with the bona

1178 Björn Kalbfus 2016 (1305) 1014.

1179 To avoid such situations in the context of departing employees, in the U.S. it is a common practice that employers demand that their new employees sign written statements declaring that their new position will not require them to breach any duty of confidence; see further James Pooley 2002 (n 66) § 6.04[1] 6-31.

fide defence for value discussed in the context of England.[1180] This should not exceed the amount of a reasonable royalty for the period of time for which the use of a trade secret could have been prevented, as analysed below.[1181]

Finally, the liability of third parties in the digital age raises the question of whether intermediary service providers (such as Reddit or Facebook) may be considered liable under Article 4(4) TSD for the mere hosting of information that was unlawfully acquired, used or disclosed by a third party that uses the services provided by these intermediaries to disseminate the trade secret. In particular, liability may arise if upon being notified by the trade secret holder about the infringing nature of the information, the intermediary service provider does not proceed to take it down. In such a context, it may be considered that the intermediary is carrying out a disclosure that triggers liability under Article 4(4) TSD and which falls outside of the scope of the hosting safe harbour established in Article 14(1) of the Directive on electronic commerce.[1182] Pursuant to paragraph (a) of this this provision, "actual knowledge" of the infringing conduct triggers liability for the service provider. Considering this uncertainty and the fact that the TSD does not allude to the responsibility of intermediaries, unlike Article 11 of the Enforcement Directive, it seems that the CJEU will ultimately have to provide guidance regarding the potential liability of intermediary service providers for the disclosure of trade secrets that they host, the relationship between the TSD and Article 11(3) of the Enforcement Directive and the applicability of the safe harbour established in Article 14(1) of the Directive on electronic commerce.

#### d) Import and export

Article 4(5) of the Directive sets out additional circumstances that constitute an unlawful use of a trade secret. This paragraph aims to preserve the good functioning of the internal market against (i) the exportation of infringing goods manufactured within the EU into another Member State,

1180 Chapter 3 § 3 C) II. 2. d).

1181 Chapter 3 § 5 C) IV. 4. b).

1182 Directive 2000/31/EC of the European Parliament and of the Council of 8 June 2000 on certain legal aspects of information society services, in particular electronic commerce, in the Internal Market [2000] OJ L178 (Directive on Electronic Commerce).

and (ii) the importation of goods manufactured outside the Single Market. The wording of the provision is as follows:

> The production, offering or placing on the market of infringing goods, or the importation, export or storage of infringing goods for those purposes, shall also be considered an unlawful use of a trade secret where the person carrying out such activities knew, or ought, under the circumstances, to have known that the trade secret was used unlawfully within the meaning of paragraph 3.

In the Explanatory Memorandum, the Commission noted that in recent years confidential information has become increasingly vulnerable due to a number of factors, including globalisation, outsourcing, longer supply chains and the increased use of ICT. This, in turn, can lead to a situation where goods manufactured outside of the EU by an infringer have to compete in the internal market with those produced by the trade secret holder.[1183] Accordingly, Recital 28 highlights the importance of banning the importation or storage of these goods with the aim of putting them into the market. Such a prohibition has crystallised in Article 4(5), reproduced above, and appears to echo the spirit of the ACTA, which was finally rejected by the European Parliament in July 2012 after a long and controversial negotiation process.[1184]

The starting point of this analysis should be to note that Article 4(5) TSD proscribes the use of infringing goods and not the trade secret as such.[1185] It suffices that the traders know or have reason to know that the products derived from the trade secrets of a third party are being unlawfully produced, offered or placed in the market, or exported, imported or stored for any of these purposes.[1186] In such a context, the liability of importers and exporters extends to every member of the distribution chain who had "knowledge" or should have known under the circumstances that the trade secret was used unlawfully. Consequently, the applicable stan-

---

1183 Commission, 'Explanatory Memorandum of the Proposal for a Directive of the European Parliament and of the Council on the protection of undisclosed know-how and business information (trade secrets) against their unlawful acquisition, use and disclosure' 3.

1184 In essence, the Agreement aimed at strengthening the effective enforcement of IPRs at an international level vis-à-vis "the proliferation of counterfeit and pirated goods".

1185 Thomas Hören und Reiner Münker 2018(a) (n 860) 86.

1186 Thomas Hören und Reiner Münker 2018(a) (n 860) 86.

dard of liability is the same one as with respect to third parties, as set out in Article 4(4) TSD.[1187]

To be sure, the rules spelt out in Article 4(5) affect not only the export of products from third countries, but also intra-Community trade, which may lead to restraint of the free movement of goods under Article 34 TFEU.[1188] Such a limitation could nonetheless be justified as a mandatory requirement to protect fair competition following the *Cassis de Dijon* Doctrine and its subsequent development by the CJEU.[1189] Yet, forbidding the production, offering or placing in the market of infringing goods already ensures the protection of trade secrets across the 28 Member States. Hence, as argued in the MPI Comments, such a restriction appears unnecessary and should only be taken into consideration as regards export and import activities vis-à-vis third countries.[1190] The MPI Comments also convincingly note that the Directive should have expressly clarified that any importing and exporting conduct that is carried out for personal use is not to be regarded as infringing, based on the fact that the personal use of goods that embody a trade secret is not regarded as unlawful either.[1191]

Finally, it should be stressed that trade secrets do not fall under the scope of the Customs Regulation[1192] and that the Directive does not refer to the establishment of any border control measures, which may facilitate the entrance of infringing goods into the Single Market. This, on the other hand, is consistent with the fact that trade secrets are not regarded as an exclusive right and thus should not fall under the scope of protection of a Regulation that deals with the enforcement of IPRs by customs authorities.

---

1187 Thomas Hören and Reiner Münker 2018(b) (n 1119) para 18.

1188 Annette Kur, Reto Hilty and Roland Knaak 2014 (n 383) para 34.

1189 See chapter 3 § 5 B).

1190 Annette Kur, Reto Hilty and Roland Knaak 2014 (n 383) para 34, stressing that "the European legislature should not enact provisions thar are specifically aimed at hindering the cross-border movement of goods within the internal market".

1191 Annette Kur, Reto Hilty and Roland Knaak 2014 (n 383) para 34.

1192 Council Regulation 608/2013 of 12 June 2013 concerning customs enforcement of intellectual property rights and repealing Council Regulation (EC) No 1383/2003 [2013] OJ L181/1 (Customs Regulation), Article 2 defines "intellectual property" as meaning trade marks; designs; copyright and related rights; geographical indications; patents; supplementary protection certificates for medicinal products and plant protection products; community and national plant varieties right; topography of semiconductor products; and utility model and trade names.

## 3. Exceptions

Article 5 spells out a list of four exceptions to the rights conferred by Article 4, which attempt to reconcile the interests of trade secret holders in keeping their information undisclosed and the concerns of third parties in accessing and using such information.[1193] Unlike the types of conduct set out in Article 3 TSD, the exceptions are conceptualised as specific limitations to the rights conferred by a trade secret that should be assessed on a case-by-case basis by courts, weighing the specific competing interests at stake in order to proceed to the enforcement of the rights, where appropriate.[1194] These exceptions have been phrased in an open-ended manner to safeguard (a) the right to freedom of expression and information; (b) whistle-blowing; (c) the disclosure of secrets by workers to their representatives in the course of their representation task; and; (d) the protection of a legitimate interest recognised by Union or national law. Each of these will be analysed in turn.

One of the main concerns raised during the negotiation of the Directive was that the fundamental right to freedom of expression and information (recognised in Article 11 ChFREU)[1195] was not hindered by the establishment of common ground rules on the protection of trade secrets,[1196] especially in connection with investigative journalism.[1197] To this end, Article 5(a) provides for a general exception that permits the acquisition, use and disclosure of a trade secret, if it is necessary in order to exercise the abovementioned freedoms. This is in line with the case law of the ECtHR that provides that the principle of freedom of information and expression has to be weighed against the interest of maintaining information in confidence considering the specific circumstances of the case, as per Article 10(2) ECHR.[1198] Ultimately, the inclusion of such an exception seems redundant, in view of the fact that Article 1(2)(a) TSD already sets forth that

---

1193 Annette Kur, Reto Hilty and Roland Knaak 2014 (n 383) para 38.

1194 Christian Alexander 2017 (n 1091) 1014.

1195 The right to Freedom of expression and information is expressly recognised in Article 11 of the ChFREU.

1196 This point is raised by the Commission, 'Public Consultation On The Protection Against Misappropriation Of Trade Secrets And Confidential Business Information, Summary Of Responses,' 11 <http://ec.europa.eu/growth/industry/intellectual-property/trade-secrets/index_en.htm> accessed 15 September 2018; in the same vein see Mathias Lejeune 2016 (n 1157) 334.

1197 Björn H. Kalbfus 2016 (n 1122)1015.

1198 Christian Alexander 2017 (n 1091) para 114.

the Directive shall not affect the exercise of the right to freedom of expression and information, including respect for pluralism and the media.

Notably, paragraph (b) introduces common ground rules on the liability of so-called "whistle-blowers". The Oxford Dictionary defines them as persons who inform "on a person or organisation regarded as engaging in unlawful or immoral activity".[1199] Accordingly, the acquisition, use or disclosure of secret information does not trigger the application of the measures, procedures and remedies set out in the Directive, when they are performed:

> For revealing a misconduct, wrongdoing or illegal activity, provided that the respondent acted for the purpose of protecting the general public interest.

This is typically the case for an employee who reveals criminal or dangerous conduct by his employer. Prime examples include the sale of tax evaders' data to the competent national authorities or the disclosure of environmental damage caused by a company.[1200] The establishment of such a defence was one of the most contested aspects during the negotiation process and was redrafted on several occasions.[1201] It is one of the features that has garnered more attention from media and civil organisations in the wake of the WikiLeaks and Panama Papers cases. However, there are still a number of civil organisations and political parties that claim that the protection for whistle-blowers is too weak and that the most recent political developments call for the enactment of a new and more comprehensive Directive on their protection.[1202]

The whistle-blower exception is only applicable if the person revealing the information acts with the aim of "protecting the general public interest".[1203] Pursuant to Recital 21 TSD, the public interest would include

---

1199 'whistle-blower, n' (*OED Online*, OUP June 2013) <https://en.oxforddictionaries.com/definition/whistle-blower> accessed 15 September 2018.

1200 Ansgar Ohly 2013 (n 13) 43.

1201 Victoria A. Cundiff and others 2016 (n 789) 744 noting that no similar provision has been included in the DTSA.

1202 The European Corporate Observatory, 'A New Right To Secrecy For Companies, And A Dangerous EU Legislative Proposal Which Must Be Rejected' (30 March 2016) <https://corporateeurope.org/power-lobbies/2016/03/trade-secrets-protection> accessed 15 September 2018.

1203 Jean Lapousterle, Christophe Geiger, Norbert Olszak and Luc Desaunettes, 'What protection for trade secrets in the European Union?' (2015) Centre for International Intellectual Property Studies (CEIPI) Research Paper No. 2015-02, 8 <https://ssrn.com/abstract=2970461> accessed 15 September 2018.

among others, disclosures for the benefit of public safety, consumer protection, public health and environmental protection.[1204] However, legal uncertainty may arise as regards the interpretation of the wording of paragraph (b), in particular in connection to the differentiation between "misconduct, wrongdoing or illegal activity" and their relationship with the public interest.[1205] These terms are undoubtedly broad and the constellation of acts they may cover ranges from the mere misuse of a company's resources to the disclosure of a hygiene scandal.[1206]

Furthermore, the wording of the provision does not clarify when the acquisition, use and disclosure of a trade secret is to be regarded as *necessary* and thus unenforceable.[1207] Rather than providing a universal standard, it seems that the assessment of necessity should be appraised on a case-by-case basis, in such a manner that it is possible to take into consideration the individual circumstances and all of the relevant interests at stake. Hence, the protection of whistle-blowers will have to be assessed in accordance with the extensive case law of the ECtHR on the subject.[1208] In addition, pursuant to Recital 20, if one of the requirements for the application of Article 5(b) is missing, judicial authorities may not enforce trade secrets protection when the whistle-blower believed in good faith that his conduct complied with the requirements set out in this provision.[1209] In this regard, it should further be borne in mind that the Directive does not aim to harmonise criminal law.[1210] Consequently, the revelation of a secret, when justified on the basis of a prevailing public interest, may not trigger civil sanctions, but may still be subject to criminal law liability under the relevant national provisions.[1211]

---

1204 Christian Alexander 2017 (n 1091) para 116.

1205 IP Federation, 'The EU Trade Secrets Directive' (2014) Policy Paper PP04/15, 3 <https://www.ipfederation.com/news/ip-federation-comments-on-the-compromise-text-for-the-eu-trade-secrets-directive/> 15 September 2018; Thomas Hören and Reiner Münker 2018(b) (n 1119) para 25.

1206 Tanya Aplin 2014 (n 384) 272.

1207 Tanya Aplin 2014 (n 384) 272.

1208 Jean Lapousterle, Christophe Geiger, Norbert Olszak and Luc Desaunettes, 'What protection for trade secrets in the European Union?' (2015) Centre for International Intellectual Property Studies (CEIPI) Research Paper No. 2015-02, 8 <https://ssrn.com/abstract=2970461> accessed 15 September 2018.

1209 Christian Alexander 2017 (n 1091) para 117.

1210 Impact Assessment (n 385) 57-58.

1211 Against this background, Mathias Lejeune 2016 (n 1157) 334 notes that in Germany the right of an employee to disclose the circumstances and conduct of an employer is not an absolute one. According to case law from the German Con-

The inclusion of paragraph (c) regarding the disclosure of secrets by workers to their representatives ensures that the rules laid down in the Directive are not used to circumvent the safeguards provided for in national labour legislations. However, the application of this exception is confined to situations where the disclosure (i) is carried out in the course of legitimate exercise by the employee representatives of their functions, (ii) and is necessary in order to perform such functions.[1212]

Finally, paragraph (d) sets forth that when the acquisition, use and disclosure are carried out with a view to protecting a legitimate interest, liability does not arise. This is an open balancing clause, which allows for weighing in the interests of trade secret holders and third parties,[1213] when none of the previously analysed exceptions are applicable.[1214] Crucially, this provision provides that the "legitimate interest" must be "recognised by Union or national law". This allows for taking into consideration some of the objectives promoted by the EU in the assessment of lawfulness. Of particular relevance in the context of trade secrets are innovation (Article 173 TFEU) and competition (Article 101-103, 116 and 117 TFEU).[1215] Yet, the scope of this exception is so broad and flexible that it may allow courts to consider any relevant interest that may inform the action of the EU powers in the years to come.

## IV. Enforcement

As noted above, the initial intention of the Commission was to expand the scope of application of the Enforcement Directive to undisclosed information. However, this possibility was declined, based among other reasons, on the argument that trade secrets are not IPRs.[1216] Consequently, chapter III of the TSD, which also constitutes its central part, extensively regulates enforcement, mirroring the former Directive, even though some relevant

---

stitutional Court, the interest in the disclosure of information has to be balanced against the right of the company to keep the information undisclosed. However, Lejeune anticipates that the implementation of this provision into German Law will not be very problematic.

1212 Christian Alexander 2017 (n 1091) para 119.

1213 Annette Kur, Reto Hilty and Roland Knaak 2014 (n 383) para 38.

1214 Christian Alexander 2017 (n 1091) para 120.

1215 Tanya Aplin 2014 (n 384) 271-272.

1216 The relationship between the Enforcement Directive and the TSD is analysed in chapter 3 § 5 C) II. 1. above.

omissions and specific provisions on procedural aspects have been included in order to address the particularities raised by trade secrets protection. The remainder of this chapter analyses the main features of the enforcement of trade secrets as laid down in the TSD. To this end, section 1 examines the general principles that should guide the enforcement of trade secrets. Next, some legal considerations as to the limitation period set forth in Article 8 are presented in section 2. Section 3 then looks into the specific measures that Member States may adopt to preserve confidentiality during litigation. Finally, the remedies against trade secrets infringement are analysed in section 4.

## 1. General provisions

Article 6 of the Directive lays down a general obligation for Member States to implement the measures, procedures and remedies necessary to ensure the availability of civil redress against trade secrets misappropriation. These should not only be fair and equitable, but also effective and dissuasive.[1217] Likewise, they should be applied by national courts in a manner that is not too complicated and costly or involves unreasonable delays.[1218]

Most notably, Article 7 TSD places special emphasis on the principle of proportionality and the prevention of abusive litigation. This echoes the concerns expressed by the respondents in the economic survey carried out by Baker McKenzie, in which 23,6% of the participants considered that harmonisation in the field of trade secrets would spur abusive litigation and consequently raise market barriers for competitors.[1219] On this point, the TSD follows the structure implemented in the Enforcement Directive, where compensation in the case of abuse of litigation is left to Member States to regulate. Yet, a lack of harmonisation on such a salient aspect may lead to a structural imbalance, whereby trade secrets holders could seek redress if their rights were infringed, but those who face unfounded claims could not seek compensation across the several EU jurisdictions.[1220]

---

1217 Article 6 (2)(a) TSD and Article 6(2)(c) TSD.

1218 Article 6 (2)(b) TSD is very similar to Article 3(1) Enforcement Directive.

1219 Baker McKenzie 2013 (n 1057) 131.

1220 This argument is raised in Annette Kur, Reto Hilty and Roland Knaak 2014 (n 383) para 41; the MPI Comments also highlight that the sanctions envisaged in the case of abusive litigation should be just as efficient and have the same deterring effect as those applicable in the event of infringement; see further Mathias Lejeune 2016 (n 1157) 335.

To offset this potential imbalance, Article 7(2) provides that judicial authorities may, if requested by the defendant, award damages, impose sanctions or order the dissemination of the judicial decision when the claim is deemed manifestly unfounded and the plaintiff is found to have initiated the proceedings in bad faith, in accordance with national law. Pursuant to Recital 22, such conduct may have as its ultimate purpose, for example, delaying or limiting the defendant's access to the market or harassing or intimidating him.[1221] As a whole, the wording of the provision poses several interpretative questions, which will be discussed in the following paragraphs.[1222]

First, it is worth noting that the Directive does not provide guidance as to how courts are to assess whether a claim is ill-founded and if defendants can bring an action or file a counterclaim.[1223] Furthermore, the provision refers to sanctions in a generic manner, and does not specify the particular measures that should be adopted beyond the publication of the decision and the possibility of claiming damages.[1224] Following wording of the Directive, the measures that judicial authorities may adopt are left to the Member States. This runs counter to the harmonisation goals pursued by the Directive, as sanctions may vary substantially from country to country.

Finally, some authors take the view that the defendant should be able to claim full compensation for the cost that he incurred as a result of the abusive litigation. This is particularly relevant in those jurisdictions where the amount of the attorney's fees that the prevailing party can recoup is statutorily limited in order to ensure equality of arms between the parties.[1225]

## 2. Limitation period

With a view to enhancing legal certainty, Article 8 TSD mandates Member States to lay down a limitation period to take legal action. In essence, such a limitation aims at imposing a duty of care and the obligation to monitor the use of trade secrets on right holders.[1226]

---

1221 See Recital 22 TSD.

1222 Mathias Lejeune 2016 (n 1157) 335 notes that such a possibility is not provided for under German law, but its inclusion in the TSD as a minimum standard is to be welcomed.

1223 Annette Kur, Reto Hilty and Roland Knaak 2014 (n 383) para 42.

1224 Annette Kur, Reto Hilty and Roland Knaak 2014 (n 383) para 43.

1225 Annette Kur, Reto Hilty and Roland Knaak 2014 (n 383) para 44.

1226 See Recital 23 TSD.

Pursuant to Article 8, it is up to the Member States to determine when the limitation period begins, its duration and the circumstances that may be invoked to interrupt or suspend it. The only restraint is that it shall not exceed six years.[1227] Even though the latter approach appears weak from a harmonisation perspective, it might also be overambitious to interfere to such a large degree with Member States' procedural law.[1228] In this context, it has been suggested that information is afforded protection as a trade secret for as long as the requirements set out in Article 2(1) TSD are complied with, similarly to the protection afforded in Germany under § 4 (3) UWG regarding the offering of goods and services that are replicas of the ones offered by competitors.[1229]

### 3. Preservation of confidentiality during litigation

Drawing upon the results of the empirical study conducted by Baker McKenzie,[1230] the Directive has introduced specific measures to preserve secrecy during litigation. Before its adoption, only a limited number of jurisdictions had put in place effective means to protect confidentiality. This is crucial to ensure that the object of the proceedings, undisclosed information, is not lost during litigation.[1231] In the absence of such measures, information would become publicly known by the mere fact of bringing legal proceedings and the enforcement of trade secrets would be substantially hindered. In the light of this and in accordance with the right to a fair trial recognised in Article 47 ChFREU, the Directive sets forth two general obligations.

---

1227 Thomas Hören and Reiner Münker 2018(b) (n 1119) para 33.

1228 Tanya Aplin 2014 (n 384) 275.

1229 Christian Alexander 2017 (n 1091) para 72.

1230 Baker McKenzie 2013 (n 1057) 131 noting that lack of trust in the judicial system and fear of losing the trade secret were identified as two of the reasons that dissuaded trade secret holders from seeking legal redress after misappropriation.

1231 Hogan Lovells 2012 (n 793) para 301, considers that: "The courts need to have means to protect secret information during proceedings. This can be achieved with confidential schedules to pleadings and restricting the disclosure of information during trial and in the judgement itself. At the moment there is inconsistency between Member States on the use of "in camera" hearings (hearings excluding the public) and the protection of information contained in court documents".

Firstly, Article 9(1) provides that Member States are bound to ensure that the parties and any other persons who intervene in the legal proceedings do not disclose or use information of a confidential nature that they have acquired during the course of litigation, even after the legal proceedings have ended, provided that the information has not lost its secret nature over time or that there is a final court decision that stipulates that the object of the proceedings no longer meets the requirements of protection.[1232]

The general obligation set forth in Article 9(1) is conditioned upon the submission of an application by the interested party with the competent judicial authorities where the alleged trade secret is clearly identified. Yet, in the implementation of the TSD, Member States may also allow judicial authorities to act on their own motion.

Thereafter, Article 9(2) spells out a list of three specific measures that national courts may adopt ex parte or on their own initiative (if allowed by national law) with the purpose of maintaining secrecy during litigation. These include: (a) restricting access to documents where the trade secret is disclosed, and (b) restricting access to the hearings and their transcripts. In order to avoid the leakage of information to competing parties, the circle of people that have access to evidence or hearings should be limited to those for whom this is strictly necessary. However, in order to comply with the transparency demands set out in Article 47 ChFREU, the Directive provides that such a circle should always include at least the legal representatives of the parties and one natural person from each of the parties, as well as any other legal representatives in accordance with national law, who are also under an obligation of confidence.[1233] Finally, paragraph (c) of the provision sets out that any passages of the ruling where trade secrets are disclosed may be deleted or redacted from the published decision.

In deciding whether to adopt the measures referred to above, courts should weigh up the interests of the parties to the proceedings, but also any potential harm to third parties (as per Article 9(3) TSD).

1232 Mary-Rose McGuire 2016 (n 824) 1007-1008, highlighting the similarities with the German "in camera hearings"; in this regard, Mathias Lejeune 2016 (n 1157) 335-336 notes that until the implementation of the TSD the application of the said proceedings to trade secrets cases was subject to a balance of interests test of the competing interests of the parties.

1233 As per Recital 25 TSD; consequently Björn H. Kalbfus 2016 (n 1122)1015-1016 notes that the TSD does not call for the introduction of a true "in camera hearing" in the German sense, because at least one representative and legal person from each party should be allowed.

## 4. Remedies available in case of infringement

The remedies laid down in the TSD are very similar to those enshrined in the Enforcement Directive. They are of a civil nature and encompass provisional and precautionary measures (Article 10), injunctions and corrective measures (Article 12), damages (Article 14) and the publication of judicial decisions (Article 15). Yet, there are some salient differences. The TSD does not harmonise the measures for providing and preserving evidence[1234] or the right to information, which are left to Member States to regulate.[1235] The following sections start by providing an analysis of the remedies set forth in the TSD and conclude by looking into the policy reasons that may justify the exclusion of some of the remedies embedded in the Enforcement Directive.

### a) Provisional and precautionary measures

It usually takes some time from the moment a trade secret holder realises that their rights are being infringed to the final judicial decision on the merits, just as with any other IPR.[1236] To avoid the right holder's interests being hindered during this time, the Directive lays down in Article 10(1) a number of provisional and precautionary measures that national competent judicial authorities should adopt at the request of the trade secret holder against the alleged infringer. These include: (a) a temporary cessation of, or prohibition on the use or disclosure of the infringed trade secret; (b) a prohibition on the manufacture, offering and placing on the market of the infringing products, as well as their import and export or storage for the same purpose. Finally, paragraph (c) provides for the seizure and delivery of the suspected infringing goods with the purpose of precluding their entrance in the internal market.

In line with the Enforcement Directive,[1237] the TSD sets out in Article 10(2) the possibility that the allegedly infringing conduct might continue (use, but not disclosure), provided that appropriate guarantees are lodged.[1238] Such an approach poses a number of issues as regards trade se-

---

1234 See Article 7 Enforcement Directive.
1235 See Article 8 Enforcement Directive.
1236 Lionel Bently and Brad Sherman 2014 (n 125) 1100.
1237 See Article 9( 1)(a) Enforcement Directive.
1238 Mathias Lejeune 2016 (n 1157) 336.

crets, particularly as the object of protection, undisclosed information, would be put at risk.[1239] One of the principles upon which the law of trade secrets is built is that once the secret becomes generally known it no longer merits protection. Hence, if its subsequent use is allowed, secrecy might be lost. In this context, it is noteworthy that the Directive does not mention whether acquisition may be permitted upon the lodging of the appropriate guarantees. Following the above rationale, in the interest of secrecy, it should be deemed as falling outside the scope of Article 10(2) TSD. Consequently, it is submitted that the wording of Article 10(2) interferes with one of the main goals pursued by the TSD, ensuring that secrecy is preserved during litigation.

In a similar vein, Article 11(2) spells out a number of criteria that should be duly examined by the competent judicial authority when granting the measures envisaged in Article 10(1). Accordingly, courts should take into consideration the value of the secret, the steps adopted to protect it, the conduct of the defendant, the impact of an unlawful use or disclosure, as well as the effect of the adoption of interim measures on the parties. This provision has no corresponding rule in the Enforcement Directive and it also raises a number of interpretative questions. According to its wording, the assessment of proportionality should be carried out based on the specific circumstances of each case, and deems the criteria listed as an open-ended enumeration of examples.[1240] Yet, surprisingly, among those, no reference is made to the urgency of the measures. From a procedural law perspective, the grant of interim measures is justified by the negative consequences that waiting for a final decision on the main proceedings may entail. Thus, the urgency of the measures is of paramount importance in the appraisal of the pertinence of their adoption.[1241] In this vein, it is worth noting that pursuant to Article 11(4) TSD, the grant of precautionary measures is in any case conditioned upon the establishment of the appropriate securities by the applicant.[1242]

Remarkably, the Directive foresees the revocation of any interim measures adopted in accordance with Article 10 if proceedings are not instituted within a reasonable period, as set forth by the competent judicial authorities, or, in the absence of such a determination, after 20 working days

1239 Annette Kur, Reto Hilty and Roland Knaak 2014 (n 383) para 50.
1240 See Article 11(2) TSD.
1241 Annette Kur, Reto Hilty and Roland Knaak 2014 (n 383) para 52.
1242 Mathias Lejeune 2016 (n 1157) 337.

(or 31 calendar days, whichever is longest).[1243] Similarly, if the requirements for protection, as per Article 2(1) TSD, are no longer fulfilled for reasons independent of the conduct of the defendant, the application of interim measures should also be revoked. This would typically be the case for a trade secret that becomes publicly known and thus loses one of its essential qualities, its secret nature.

b) Injunctions and corrective measures

A trade secret is infringed when its acquisition, use or disclosure is regarded as unlawful, pursuant to the wording of Article 4 (in conjunction with Article 3 and Article 5). In such a case, the holder is entitled to ask the court to adopt an array of measures against the infringer (Article 12(1)). These include: (a) the cessation of, or prohibition on the use and disclosure of the trade secret; (b) the prohibition on producing, offering and placing on the market goods in which the trade secret is embodied, or their import, export and storage to this end; (c) the adoption of corrective measures in connection to the infringing goods; and (d) the destruction of all or part of any document, object, material, substance or electronic file containing or embodying the trade secret, as well as their delivery to the applicant. The corrective measures available are stipulated in 12(2) and encompass (a) the recall of the infringing goods from the market; (b) the modification of the infringing goods with the purpose of eliminating their infringing features; and, (c) the destruction of the infringing goods, as well as any documents (both physical and electronic) or other items where the trade secret is disclosed.

The wording of Article 12(1)(b) has been regarded as redundant and superfluous by some, as the types of conduct therein described are already regarded as infringing by Article 4(5) TDS and thus fall under the scope of Artice 12(1)(a).[1244] While such criticism is well-founded, it is true that such clarification, albeit redundant, may avoiding differences in the implementation among Member States. Similarly, bearing in mind that the main purpose of the Directive is to restore the market position of the trade secret holder by conferring upon him a lead time advantage, the content of paragraph 2 of Article 13(1) appears particularly relevant.[1245] This provision

1243 As per Article 11(3)(a) TSD.

1244 Annette Kur, Reto Hilty and Roland Knaak 2014 (n 383) para 54.

1245 Mary-Rose McGuire 2016 (n 824) 1007.

stipulates that the duration of injunctions can be limited, but courts should always ensure that they are sufficient to eliminate commercial advantage gained by the misappropriation, in line with the springboard doctrine discussed in connection with the English breach of confidence action.[1246]

Considering the interim measures regulation and with a view to limiting the liability of bona fide third parties, Article 13(3) foresees the possibility of establishing alternative financial compensation instead of granting injunctions or corrective measures (i.e. damages in lieu of injunctions). The continuous use of the trade secret or the marketing and distribution of the goods in which it is embodied is only possible if (i) the information was acquired in good faith, as a sort of bona fide defence, (ii) the execution of the injunctions or corrective measures in question would be very harmful to the acquirer, and (iii) the monetary compensation seems reasonable.[1247] In addition, Article 13 provides that when damages are awarded instead of an injunction, the said compensation shall not exceed the royalties that the parties would have agreed if the misappropriated trade secret had been licensed.[1248] Ultimately, this provision equates the position of the third party infringing user with that of the lawful user.[1249] In addition, it shows a clear parallel with Article 12 of the Enforcement Directive, even though its scope of application is more limited (it is only applicable to bona fide acquirers) and its implementation into national legislation is mandatory as a maximum standard of protection, and not optional, as in the case of the Enforcement Directive.[1250] As a final note, Recital 29 provides that the award of damages in lieu of injunction shall not be permitted when it results in an infringement of any other provision (such as labour law or criminal law) and it may harm consumers. In view of this, it is submitted here that a central factor in assessing whether granting an injunction is disproportionate should be whether the acquirer of the information changed his position on the information before learning about its confidential nature, for instance, by buying new machines or hiring new

1246 See chapter 3 § 3 C) III.

1247 See Article 13(3) TSD; however, establishing the amount of the said licences may in practice prove quite difficult.

1248 As discussed in chapter 3 § 3 C) II. 2.d) in connection to the liability of third parties.

1249 Clemens Koós 2015 (n1158) 227; Franz Hofmann, '"Equity" im deutschen Lauterkeitsrecht? Der "Unterlassungsanspruch" nach der Geschäftsgeheimnis-RL' [2018] WRP1, para 27.

1250 See Article 1(1) TSD.

employees to develop, produce or commercialise a new product on the basis of such information.[1251] Also, due consideration should be paid to the likelihood that by allowing the use of the trade secret it becomes generally known or easily accessible.

### c) Damages

The TSD foresees the award of damages in the event of infringement, the most common remedy in the enforcement of IPRs.[1252] Just as in the intellectual property scenario, compensation through damages intends to restore the holder of secret information to the position in which he would have been prior to the unlawful acquisition, use and disclosure.[1253] The assessment of damages follows a similar scheme to that laid down in the Enforcement Directive,[1254] which represents considerable progress in view of the divergent approaches followed by national regimes before the adoption of the TSD and the legal uncertainty that it entailed. Accordingly, three calculation methods are foreseen.[1255] In the first place, the plaintiff can claim the lost profits resulting from the infringement of his trade secret. Alternatively, the compensation can be calculated on the basis of the unfair profits made by the defendant following the misappropriation of the trade secret. In this context, the Directive also mentions that the trade secret holder can claim moral damages derived from the infringement. The third option is the computation of damages as a lump sum, using as a benchmark the reasonable royalties that the trade secret holder would have received in the case of licensing. In all of those cases, the award of damages is conditioned upon the finding of at least gross negligence on the side of the infringer, "who knew or ought to have known" that the acquisition, use or disclosure of the information was illicit.[1256] Nonetheless, it should be noted that in the light of the CJEU decision in *Jørn Hansson v Jungpflanzen*, it has been contested whether damages under Article 13(1)(a)

1251 For a more detailed analysis see Tanya Aplin and others (n 22) para 7.140

1252 Lionel Bently and Brad Sherman 2014 (n 125) 1117.

1253 See Recital 30 TSD.

1254 For an overview of the assessment of damages in the Enforcement Directive see Annette Kur, 'The Enforcement Directive - Rough Start, Happy Landing?' [2004] IIC 821, 827-830.

1255 Thomas Hören and Reiner Münker 2018(b) (n 1119) para 33.

1256 Mary-Rose McGuire 2016 (n 824) 1007; Franz Hofmann 2018 (n 1249) para 14.

of the Enforcement Directive (and by extension under Article 14(2) TSD) may be calculated on the basis of the infringer's profits.[1257]

With respect to the regulation of damages, two features stand out. In the first place, there might be a great asymmetry between the infringer's profits and the lost profits on the side of the right holder. In effect, the unlawful acquisition, use and disclosure may render the information generally known. In this context and linked to the lack of an exclusive nature of trade secrets as opposed to other IPRs, the trade secret holder would lose the object of protection. By contrast, the profits gained by the infringer may be rather limited if compared to the economic consequences that losing the trade secret entails. Secondly, it is unclear in which context moral (or immaterial) damages should arise, which is an aspect that has been particularly controversial in the implementation of the Enforcement Directive.[1258] If one accepts the privacy justification, moral damages could derive from the violation of a privacy right.[1259]

Against this background, paragraph 2 of Article 14(1) TSD provides that in the implementation of the Directive, Member States may restrict the liability for damages of employees towards their employers in the case of unlawful acquisition, use or disclosure of a trade secret if they have acted without intent. At first glance, the wording of this provision seems obscure, as it is not clear whether it should also apply to former employees. Following a systematic and teleological interpretation, and bearing in mind that fostering employee mobility is one of the principles that informs the Directive, it is submitted that the non-intentional disclosure of departing employees should fall under the scope of such a limitation.

#### d) Publication of the judicial decision

In line with Article 15 of the Enforcement Directive, if the plaintiff prevails, he may request that the court publishes the judicial decision at the expense of the infringer. In such a case, all of the necessary measures to

1257 Case C–481/14 *Jørn Hansson v Jungpflanzen Grünewald GmbH* [2016] (CJEU, 9 June 2016) para 42; Franz Hofmann 2018 (n 1249) para 14.

1258 GRUR, 'Opinion on the proposal for a Directive on the protection of undisclosed know-how and business information (trade secrets) against their unlawful acquisition, use and disclosure, COM (2013) 813 final' (2014), para 5.b) <http://www.grur.org/uploads/tx_gstatement/2014-03-19_GRUR_Stellungnahme_zum_Know-how-Schutz_EN.pdf> accessed 15 September 2018.

1259 See chapter 1 § 2 B) IV.

preserve the secret nature of the information should be adopted in accordance with the rules laid down in Article 9 TSD.

In the assessment of the suitability of the publication and proportionality of such a measure, a number of factors should be taken into consideration. These include, among others, the potential harm to the reputation of the infringer, the value of the secret and the likelihood of further use or disclosure. During the final phase of the negotiation process, some amendments were introduced with a view to enhancing the privacy of the infringer and preventing his personal identification, which have crystallised in paragraph 2 of Article 15(3) of the Directive.[1260]

e) Claims for information and preserving evidence

One of the central differences between the Enforcement and the TSD is that the latter does not establish any obligations concerning claims for preserving evidence[1261] and for obtaining orders as to the origin or distribution networks of the infringing goods.[1262] These are left to Member States to regulate, and, as a result, their availability will ultimately depend on national law provisions. Consequently, the practices among member states may vary from one country to another, putting at risk the harmonisation goals. Yet, it is true that claims for information and preserving evidence may be unduly used to acquire confidential business data. In view of this, it is submitted that a uniform EU framework on the protection of trade secrets should also have included rules on these issues and ensured that the necessary safeguards were adopted to avoid abuses on the side of the plaintiff.[1263]

Moreover, this approach is consistent with the fact that placing infringing goods on the market, and their import or export is regarded as an unlawful use of a trade secret, pursuant to Article 4(5) of the Directive. As a result, the wording of the provisions regulating claims for information should be adapted to ensure that the plaintiff is able to learn not only the

1260 Article 15(3) para 2 TSD: "The competent judicial authorities shall also take into account whether the information on the infringer would be such as to allow a naural or legal person to be identified and, if so, whether publication of that information would be justified, in particular in the light of the possible harm that such measures may cause to the privacy and reputation of the infringer".

1261 See Articles 6 and 7 Enforcement Directive.

1262 See Article 8 Enforcement Directive.

1263 Annette Kur, Reto Hilty and Roland Knaak 2014 (n 383) para 56.

channels of distribution, the quantity and the prices of infringing goods, but also the identities of the subsequent acquirers.[1264] This seems crucial to prevent subsequent infringements and assess the extent to which the confidential information has been made available.

## § 6 Conclusion

Drawing from the foregoing legal analysis, it is submitted that despite some criticism, the alignment of national Member States' laws on the protection of trade secrets is justified as a measure that is necessary to ensure the good functioning of a Single Market without barriers, in which the fundamental freedoms are accomplished (particularly the free movement of goods and workers).

Indeed, the comparative law examination conducted above has underscored that the legal regimes for the protection of trade secrets across the Single Market prior to the implementation of the TSD were completely scattered and, consequently, the level of protection varied substantially from one member state to another. For instance, the liability threshold for third parties was much higher in Germany than in England. In the former jurisdiction, conditional intent was required on the side of the infringer and at least one of the following purposes in the performance of the relevant conduct: a competitive purpose, a personal gain, to benefit a third party or to hinder the position of the trade secret holder. In contrast, in England liability arose merely if the standard of care followed by a honest person placed under the same circustances was not observed.

In the light of the above, it is submitted that the Directive manages to strike a balance between the interest of trade secrets holders in keeping their information concealed and the interest of third parties in accessing such information. This is mostly achieved through the establishment of a number of flexible and open-ended clauses in the provisions that govern the appraisal of the lawfulness of the allegedly infringing conduct, which mostly resort to the general standard of honest commercial practices embedded in Article 10bis PC and the inclusion of common ground regarding the standard of liability of third parties, which requires at least gross negligence on the side of the infringer. Likewise, the consideration of independent discovery and reverse engineering as lawful forms of obtaining a trade secret is also crucial to maintain the aforementioned equilibrium.

1264 Annette Kur, Reto Hilty and Roland Knaak 2014 (n 383) para 57.

They are essential to ensure the complementarity between the patent system and the trade secrets regime. In this context, the EU legislature has further laid down an array of exceptions to the rights conferred by a trade secret that safeguard the fundamental freedoms of expression and information and most notably deem as lawful whistle-blowing conduct. The applicability of such exceptions will ultimately depend on the balance of interests conducted by the competent national authorities, considering the individual circumstances of the case.

Such a flexible approach presents both advantages and disadvantages. On the one hand, it allows for considering all of the relevant interests in each individual case and adapting to future technological developments, a key aspect in the protection of trade secrets. Yet, on the other, it may also lead to divergent interpretations of the same provision among Member States, thus hindering the ultimate harmonisation objective. As a whole, it seems that establishing minimum standards with regard to the civil protection of trade secrets (as well as maximum standards with respect to central aspects such as the exceptions, as well as lawful and unlawful conduct) will enhance legal certainty across the Single Market.[1265]

Remarkably, it is submitted that the Directive does not provide a univocal answer as to the legal nature of trade secrets. Only Recital 16 refers to this matter and spells out that the provisions of the Directive should not create an exclusive right. However, such a statement does not clarify whether the misappropriation of confidential information is to be protected as an infringement of an IPR, a property right or just as an act of competition contrary to honest commercial practices under unfair competition rules. The Directive seems to adopt an unfair competition approach in the provisions that regulate the unlawful acquisition, use and disclosure of trade secrets, as they keep referring to the standard of honest commercial practices. On the other hand, the list of remedies spelt out in chapter III mostly corresponds to those envisaged for the infringement of an IPR. Wisely, the EU legislature has not attached specific legal consequences to the categorisation of information as the former or the latter. However, as noted above,[1266] this has implications outside the scope of the Directive vis-à-vis the applicable law in the case of infringement and the relationship

1265 A different view is purported by Tanya Aplin 2014 (n 384) 279, where the author notes that, "only a modest amount of harmonisation is likely to ensue from implementation of this Directive".

1266 Chapter 1 § 3 III.

with the Enforcement Directive. In this context, clarification will ultimately have to be sought by reference to the CJEU.

From a policy perspective, the Commission and the Council expect that the implementation of the Directive will yield enhanced competitiveness and cross-border innovation, which ultimately should lead to remarkable employment growth. Yet, only time will tell whether these ambitious objectives will be met or, to phrase it better, if any causal link between the harmonisation of trade secrets law in the EU and an improvement in the economic results within the Single Market can be established. Without doubt, the comprehensive regulation of the measures, procedures and remedies that trade secret holders may claim in the enforcement of their rights creates a level-playing fied for stakeholders across the EU.

As a final note, it is also noteworthy that the Directive sheds little light on the interpretation of the secrecy requirement, as the definition provided in Article 2 simply reproduces the wording of Article 39(2) TRIPs. In addition, by virtue of Article 1(3)(b) and Recital 14, the skills and knowledge acquired by employees during the normal course of their employment are excluded from the scope of protection in the interest of employee mobility. Again, the legislature provides little guidance regarding how to delineate the contours of such information.

In view of the increasing vulnerability of information in the digital age, the following chapter is devoted to the study of the notion of secrecy and, more specifically, to the analysis of the circumstances under which information enters the public domain. Having regard to the harmonisation goals pursued by the TSD, it proposes a number of case-specific guiding principles to ensure a homogeneous interpretation of this notion across the different EU Member States.

# Chapter 4. Mapping the notion of secrecy

## *§ 1 Secrecy in the digital age*

### A) Increasing vulnerability of confidential information

The advent of new technologies in the globalised world has allowed individuals and companies to generate and share information at a much faster pace than ever before. The flow of information is unprecedented to the point that some suggest that we now live in a "data centred economy".[1267] In effect, the ever-growing amount of data available, mostly through the Internet, may be deployed to unlock new sources of economic development, foster scientific progress and scrutinise governments' actions.[1268] Despite the numerous advantages, the increase in information is creating a host of new problems. Indeed, it is becoming more and more difficult to ensure data security and personal privacy.[1269]

Legislators all around the globe are trying to adapt to the changes brought about by the widespread and constant information exchange. A prime example of this is the comprehensive reform of the Data Protection framework undertaken by the EU Commission with the adoption of the GDPR and the publication of the Final Report on the e-commerce sector inquiry led by the Commission.[1270] In the same vein, in 2012, the U.S. Federal Government announced the Big Data Research and Development Initiative, which aimed at facilitating the gathering, organisation and access to big sets of digital data.[1271] The adoption of the DTSA in the U.S. and the

---

1267 'Data, data everywhere' *The Economist* (London, 25 February 2010) <http://www.economist.com/node/15557443> accessed 15 September 2018; see further Gintare Surblyte, '6th GRUR Int / JIPLP Joint Seminar: Internet search engines in the focus of EU competition law – a closer look at the broader picture' [2015] GRUR 127, 130.

1268 'Data, data everywhere' *The Economist* (London, 25 February 2010) <http://www.economist.com/node/15557443> accessed 15 September.

1269 Ibid.

1270 Commission, 'Final report on the E-commerce Sector Inquiry' COM(2017) 229 final <http://ec.europa.eu/competition/antitrust/sector_inquiry_final_report_en.pdf> accessed 15 September 2018.

1271 'Obama Administration unveils "Big Data" Initiative: Announces $ 200 million in new R&D investments' (29 March 2012) <https://www.whitehouse.gov

TSD in the EU is set against this backdrop. The convergence of protection on both sides of the Atlantic was prompted, among other reasons, by the increasing vulnerability and strategic importance of confidential information.[1272] In effect, the Impact Assessment prepared by the Commission during the TSD legislative process identified five main factors underpinning the increasing difficulties in concealing trade secrets, which partially correspond to those mentioned by the perfume industry representatives.[1273] They are: (i) labour mobility, (ii) globalisation, (iii) longer supply chains, (iv) the information-intensive economy that we live in, and (v) the shortening of production cycles and the rise of fast-moving industries.[1274]

Without doubt, it is now easier to store large amounts of business sensitive information in a single spreadsheet document or on a computer hard drive, which can also be downloaded within seconds on to a USB thumb-drive or uploaded to the cloud and reach a broader audience much faster.[1275] Even though this clearly facilitates the effective management of information within firms, it also increases the risk of leakage of valuable information. By way of illustration, in 2006 the Texas District Court had to decide on a preliminary injunction preventing a former employee who had downloaded the equivalent of 1,5 million raw pages on to several USB thumb-drives before leaving his job and had subsequently copied the downloaded files on to his personal computer and the system of his new employer from working for any competitor.[1276] The use of servers also poses new risks for trade secret holders, as the vast amounts of data that were previously stored in physical cabinets or document warehouses are now available to hundreds of employees in a company through the mere clicking a mouse.[1277] Similar concerns apply to the general use of laptop computers, which allow employees to take valuable information outside the premises of their companies or to remotely access it from anywhere in

---

/sites/default/files/microsites/ostp/big_data_press_release.pdf> accessed 15 September 2018.

1272 Victoria A. Cundiff and others 2016 (n 789) 738.

1273 See chapter 5 § 4 B).

1274 Impact Assessment (n 385) 15-16.

1275 Elizabeth A. Rowe, 'Contributory Negligence, Technology, and Trade Secrets' [2009] 17 George Mason LR 1, 14.

1276 In *Anadarko Petroleum Corp. v. Davis*, 2006 WL 3837518 (S.D. Tex. Dec. 28, 2006) the court denied the preliminary injunction, but the parties entered into an Agreed Order, whereby the competitor unterook to return all proprietary information and to refrain from using such information.

1277 Elizabeth A. Rowe 2009 (n 1275) 14.

the world through virtual private networks ("VPN").[1278] This has facilitated both the physical misappropriation of information (for instance, through the theft of the laptop), as well as unauthorised access to data stored on a server or computer by hackers.[1279]

Furthermore, the advent of digital technologies has made the dissemination of valuable secret information easier; now it can be done with the "mere push of a button".[1280] Notably, this has been facilitated by the widespread use of email communications within companies that allow employees to send sensitive information from their corporate account to their personal accounts, or even to competitors, as well as instant messaging services, such as Skype and Google Hangouts. Similarly, posting confidential information on the Internet has become an increasing threat for companies, which risk losing their valuable trade secrets if an employee inadvertently or maliciously posts them on an Internet website and, as a result, the information becomes generally known.[1281]

In view of the above, it is undeniable that in the digital age it has become much harder to conceal information from competitors and the public at large. This, in turn, calls into question how secrecy should be construed vis-à-vis its frontiers with the public domain and, ultimately, enquires about the optimal scope of protection. The following section underscores the main difficulties in this regard.

## B) Constructing the public domain

Defining the boundaries of the public and private spheres is of utmost importance in every legal system. In the realm of intellectual property, this is particularly challenging, as constructing and defining the contours of private rights and the intangible objects to which they refer is seemingly more complex than with regard to tangible property.[1282]

In the context of confidentiality, "the public domain" is an expression that has been used for decades to designate information that cannot be the

1278 Elizabeth A. Rowe 2009 (n 1275) 14.
1279 Elizabeth A. Rowe 2009 (n 1275) 14.
1280 Elizabeth A. Rowe 2009 (n 1275) 16.
1281 Elizabeth A. Rowe 2009 (n 1275) 16.
1282 Nari Lee, 'Public domain at the interface of trade mark and unfair competition law: The case of referential use of trade marks' 309, 309 in Nari Lee, Ansgar Ohly, Annette Kur, Guido Westkamp (eds), *Intellectual Property, Unfair Competition and Publicity* (Edward Elgar 2014).

object of trade secrets protection.[1283] More generally, it has also been deployed to refer to "material that is unprotected by Intellectual Property Rights".[1284] Indeed, the construction of the public domain has been studied extensively in connection to copyright and patents. However, in the field of trade secrets it has attracted less scholarly discussion. This mostly results from the casuistic nature of trade secrets protection, as well as from the fact that there is no universally accepted definition of the public domain. Its boundaries change from jurisdiction to jurisdiction and evolve with time.[1285] Thus, an innovation that was initially kept secret by an undertaking may be discovered by competitors through reverse engineering or independent creation and enter the realm of the public domain after some time. Similarly, it has been suggested that the abstract definition of the public domain does not necessarily correspond to the actual information that a departing employee may use in his new employment.[1286]

Despite these inherent difficulties, mapping the public domain has normative significance, as it allows for identifying the relevant values underpinning its components.[1287] To be sure, a solid public domain is necessary to foster creativity and innovation.[1288] More specifically, according to Samuelson, it allows for creating new knowledge, and encourages competition through imitation, as well as follow-on innovation. Thus, a robust public domain is essential to promote access to information in the academic, scientific and cultural spheres.[1289] In the field of trade secrets this is even more problematic, as the subject matter protected may never enter

1283 Charles Tait Graves 2007 (n 337) 39, footnote 145; see for instance in the US: *Kewanee Oil Co. v. Bicron Corp.*, 416 U.S. 470, 484 (1974) stating that "by definition a trade secret has not been placed in the public domain"; similarly *Storage Tech. Corp. v. Custom Hardware Eng'g & Consulting Inc.*, 421 F.3d 1307, 1319 (Fed Circ. 2005) "Information that is in the public domain cannot be appropriated by a party as its proprietary trade secret"; *VD, Inc. v. Raytheon Co.*, 769 F.2d 842 (1st Cir. 1985): "Once a trade secret enters the public domain, the possessor's exclusive rights to the secret are lost".

1284 James Boyle, 'Foreword: The Opposite of Property?' [2003] 66 Law and Contemporary Problems 1, 30.

1285 Pamela Samuelson, 'Challenges in Mapping the Public Domain' 7, 13 in P. Bernt Hugenholtz and Lucie Guibault (eds), *The Public Domain of Information* (Kluwer International Law 2006).

1286 Charles Tait Graves 2007 (n 337) 87-88.

1287 Pamela Samuelson 2006 (n 1285) 13.

1288 Nari Lee 2014 (n 1282) 311.

1289 Pamela Samuelson 2006 (n 1285) 13; for a more detailed overview of the discussion surrounding the public domain see Lawrence Lessig, *Free Culture* (The Penguin Press 2004).

the public domain. Unlike formal IPRs, trade secrets are not subject to any time limitation.[1290] Thus, the pool of information available to individuals and companies is diminished as the protection of trade secrets increases.[1291]

In the light of the above, determining whether a specific piece of information has lost its secret nature and accordingly entered the public domain is crucial to assess whether it can be used by third parties other than the original holder or the recipient of the information bound by a confidentiality obligation, or whether such an obligation remains enforceable. This is essential, for instance, in the case of departing employees who may intend to use information that they have acquired during the course of their employment relationship or for licensees that wish to cease paying their licensing fees. At the same time, as explained in chapter 1, the protection of a company's secret valuable information appears necessary and justified from a utilitarian perspective (and to a certain extent, also from a deontological one).[1292] Thus, in view of the increasing challenges in concealing digital information, it is of utmost importance to find the appropriate balance between the secret sphere and the public domain. The following sections are devoted to analysing the principles that govern such an appraisal: namely, whether something is generally known or readily accessible.

To this end, first the different concepts and requirements of trade secrets protection followed in Germany and England before the implementation of the TSD are examined (§ 2). From this comparative analysis, some interpretative principles regarding the definition of trade secrets laid down in Article 2 TSD and the subject matter protected are proposed (§ 3). Next, the dissertation goes on to examine the essential features of the notion of secrecy in greater depth, namely the degree of secrecy required (§ 4 A), the concept of readily ascertainability (§ 4 B), and the effects of the disclosure (§ 4 C) through the lenses of English, German and U.S. case law. In the light of this comparative analysis, some conclusions as to the interpretation of the relevant circles doctrine are drawn (§ 4 D). Thereafter, in § 4 E, the secrecy standard is compared to other IPRs, such as novelty in patent law and originality in copyright law, with a view to finding an equilibrium between the different legal regimes. Next, the possibility of resorting to trade secrets protection for Big Data sets is analysed under § 4F (Excursus).

---

1290 William van Caenegem 2014 (n 7) 13-14.

1291 William van Caenegem 2014 (n 7) 14.

1292 See chapter 1 § 2.

The ultimate goal of this investigation is to underscore the principles that courts across EU jurisdictions should follow in order to determine, in a consistent manner, whether information is part of the public domain or remains secret pursuant to Article 2(1)(a) TSD. Notwithstanding the aforementioned, such an analysis is largely factually driven. For that reason, it is only possible to outline general guiding principles.

## § 2 *Different concepts and requirements for protection of trade secrets before the implementation of the TSD*

### A) Concept and requirements for the protection of trade secrets in Germany

#### I. Distinction between Geschäftsgeheimnis and Betriebsgeheimnissen

In Germany, unlike other jurisdictions, no statutory definition of trade secrets exists. Instead, the following working definition has been developed by the courts:

> A trade secret is information which relates to a particular business, is known only to a narrow limited number of persons, so is secret, and under the express or identifiable (as a rule, commercial) owner's will, which is based on a legitimate interest, is intended to be kept secret.[1293]

Article 17 UWG distinguishes between two categories of trade secrets, namely commercial secrets ("*Geschäftsgeheimnisse*") and industrial secrets ("*Betriebsgeheimnisse*"). The former refers to the business-related information of an undertaking,[1294] such as customers' and suppliers' data, or contractual and cost estimation documents,[1295] while the latter encompasses technical information.[1296] Among others, courts have ruled that industrial

---

1293 Translation by Gintare Surblyte 2011 (n 182) 49; BGH MMR 2006, 815, 816 – *Kundendatenprogramm*; BGH GRUR 2003, 356, 358 – *Präzisionsmessgeräte.*
1294 Gintare Surblyte 2011 (n 182) 49.
1295 *Ohly*/Sosnitza (n 813) § 17 Rdn 5.
1296 *Harte-Bavendamm*/Henning-Bodewig (n 376) § 17 Rdn 1.

secrets are manufacture and assembly processes,[1297] formulas[1298] or computer programs.[1299]

At first glance, the division of trade secrets into two categories might appear merely formal, as no definition of any of these concepts is provided, either in § 17 UWG or throughout the Act. Notwithstanding this, during the *travaux préparatoires* of the UWG (1896) it was extensively debated whether commercial information should be covered by the legal regime for the protection of trade secrets.[1300] Accordingly, an explicit distinction was included for the purposes of clarity, which unequivocally stated that commercial information fell within the scope of § 9 UWG 1896 (now § 17 UWG). However, in practice, no substantial legal consequences arise from such a distinction[1301] other than the exclusive application of § 18(1) UWG to industrial secrets ("*Betriebsgeheimnisse*").[1302] Thus, the terms "business secret" ("*Unternehmensgeheimnis*") and "economic secrets" ("*Wirtschaftsgeheimnis*") are often used as generic terms ("*Oberbegriff*").[1303]

## II. Requirements for the protection of trade secrets

As stated in the previous section, the definition of trade secrets that has been followed by case law requires that (i) information, (ii) must be connected to a particular business, (iii) must not be public, but only known by a limited circle of people, (iv) must be kept secret by the express will of the trade secret holder, and (v) the desire to keep the information secret must be based on an economic interest.[1304]

---

1297 BGH GRUR 1963, 367 – *Industrieböden.*

1298 BGH GRUR 1980, 750 – *Pankreaplex.*

1299 BGH GRUR 1977, 539 – *Prozessrechner*; *Köhler*/Bornkamm/Feddersen (n 835) § 17 Rdn 12a.

1300 Björn H. Kalbfus, *Know-how Schutz in Deutschland zwischen Strafrecht und Zivilrecht-welcher Reformbedarf besteht?* (1st edn, Carl Heymanns Verlag 2011) 70.

1301 Lutz Lehmer, *UWG: Kommentar zum Wettbewerbsrecht* (Luchterhand 2007) 555; *Ohly*/Sosnitza (n 813) § 17 Rdn 5, Axel Beater (n 811) § 22 Rdn 686; *Köhler*/Bornkamm/Feddersen (n 835) § 17 Rdn 4a.

1302 Lutz Lehmer 2010 (n 1301) 555.

1303 *Ohly*/Sosnitza (n 813) 17 Rdn 5; Gintare Surblyte 2011 (n 182) 49; Björn H. Kalbfus 2011 (n 1300) 70; *Harte- Harte-Bavendamm*/Henning-Bodewig (n 376) § 17 Rdn 1; hereinafer, the generic term "trade secret" will be used.

1304 BGH GRUR 2009, 603, Rdn 13 – *Versicherungsvertreter*; Hirsch/Ann/*Brammsen*, *Münchener Kommentar zum Lauterkeitsrecht* (2nd edn, C.H. Beck 2014) § 17 Rdn 8; Florian Schweyer 2012 (n 99) 458.

The following sections analyse the requirements for the protection of information as a trade secret in the German jurisdiction.

## 1. Information

The working definition adopted by the German courts refers to facts ("*Tatsachen*"). The use of this term has been criticised for not being sufficiently precise, because the law of trade secrets protects information about facts ("*Tatsachen*") and not the facts themselves.[1305]

## 2. Information connected to a business — Geschäftsbezogenheit

In Germany, information can only be protected as a trade secret if it can be ascribed to a particular business,[1306] i.e. the information must be "used in relation to the business"[1307] or owned and controlled by the said business.[1308] No other requirements regarding the content or the object of the secret information have to be met.[1309]

Consequently, private secrets[1310] and information that stems from universities and research institutions do not fall within the scope of §§ 17 and 18 UWG.[1311] This contrasts with the broad scope of the English breach of confidence action and the broad interpretation of commercial value followed by courts in the U.S. The rationale behind such a limitation derives from the very foundations of unfair competition.[1312] The legal regime for the protection of trade secrets was established with the intention of safeguarding the "exercise without disruption of the business activity"[1313] of

1305 See Stephan Hillenbrand, *Der Begriff des Betriebs- und Geschäftsgeheimnisses* (Herbert Utz Verlag 2017) 28 and Björn H. Kalbfus 2016 (n 1122)1010 with further references.

1306 See Florian Schweyer 2012 (n 99) 458; Gintare Surblyte 2011 (n 182) 50.

1307 Rudolf Kraßer 1970 (n 831) 589; Michael Knospe (n 834) § 15:5; Gintare Surblyte 2011 (n 182) 49.

1308 Florian Schweyer 2012 (n 99) 458; Michael Knospe (n 834) 15:5.

1309 Axel Beater (n 811) Rdn 1878.

1310 *Ohly*/Sosnitza (n 813) § 17 Rdn 6.

1311 Florian Schweyer 2012 (n 99) 458 noting that in other jurisdictions, like the United States, they are actually considered trade secrets.

1312 *Harte-Bavendamm*/Henning-Bodewig (n 376) § 17 Rdn 2.

1313 *Harte-Bavendamm*/Henning-Bodewig (n 376) § 17 Rdn 2.

the trade secret holder in order to preserve the market position that he had obtained through his secret knowledge and experience.[1314]

From the outset it was controversially discussed, as happened in most jurisdictions, whether the information protected under the trade secrets legal regime should meet the patentability requirements set forth in the German Patent Act.[1315] In 1907, one of the first decisions rendered by the Supreme Court of the German Reich regarding trade secret protection, the *Pomril*[1316] judgement, ruled out such a possibility, stating that: "It is not relevant whether the (...) process was new in the sense of §§ 1,2 of the Patent Act (...)".[1317] Later on in the same decision, it was further noted that a known process could be the object of a trade secret only if by keeping the information secret the trade secret holder could achieve a certain competitive advantage.[1318] The principles set out by the *Pomril* decision have been incorporated by subsequent case law.[1319]

Likewise, courts have repeatedly stated that it is irrelevant whether the information is secret as such, or whether only its relationship with the business is kept secret. This issue was first clarified by the Supreme Court of the German Reich in the *Stiefeleisenpresse* decision.[1320] In the legal reasoning of this landmark case, the court noted that a known process could be the object of a trade secret, as long as its use by the business was not disclosed. It further added that the relationship with the company lasted for as long as the trade secret holder had a legitimate economic interest in keeping the relationship between the process and the undertaking confidential. Hence, the relationship with the company is not lost by the mere fact of selling the product in which the trade secret is embodied.[1321]

---

1314 *Harte-Bavendamm*/Henning-Bodewig (n 376) § 17 Rdn 2.

1315 See § 3 German Patent Act.

1316 RGZ 1907 65, 333, 335 – *Pomril.*

1317 RGZ 1907 65, 333, 335 – *Pomril* (...)"kommt es nicht darauf an, ob das Promil Verfahren in dem Sinne neu war, in dem eine Erfindung nach §§ 1, 2 des Patentsgesetz neu sein muß, wenn die patentfähig sein soll". This point of view has been reiterated in subsequent case law, for example: RGZ 1935 149, 329, 335– *Stiefeleisenpresse;* BGH GRUR 1995, 424, 426 – *Möbelpaste.*

1318 RGZ 1907 65, 333, 335 – *Pomril*; RGZ 1935 149, 329, 334 – *Stiefeleisenpresse,* BGH GRUR 1995, 424 – *Möbelpaste.*

1319 Florian Schweyer 2012 (n 99) 459.

1320 RGZ 1935 149, 329, 335 – *Stiefeleisenpresse.*

1321 *Ohly*/Sosnitza (n 813) § 17 Rdn 6.

In this context, it has been stated that the *information connected to business* requirement correlates with the condition that "information is lawfully within the control" of its holder, spelt out in Article 39(2) TRIPs.[1322]

### 3. Secrecy — Nichtoffenkundigkeit

By definition, the subject matter of trade secrets protection must not be in the public domain.[1323] Pursuant to the prevailing view in case law, information will be regarded as secret as long as it is neither generally known nor easily accessible.[1324] The threshold for assessing these requirements is the so-called "circle of experts" ("*Fachkreise*") but also the competitors, whose actions are ultimately the object of the UWG regulation.[1325]

Information will only be regarded as secret if it is "only known by a limited circle of people".[1326] Consequently, in Germany, the relevant yardstick has become whether the trade secret owner maintains control over the number and type of persons who know or who have access to the information.[1327] Thus, courts do not resort to a precise numerical value in order to evaluate if the "number of persons who have knowledge of the information is sufficiently limited".[1328] Instead, a case-by-case analysis is con-

---

1322 *Ohly*/Sosnitza (n 813) § 17 Rdn 6.

1323 Michael Knospe (n 834) 15:8.

1324 Florian Schweyer 2012 (n 99) 459, Michael Knospe (n 834) 15:8; *Ohly*/Sosnitza (n 813) § 17 Rdn 7; *Harte-Bavendamm*/Henning-Bodewig (n 376) § 17 Rdn 3.

1325 Florian Schweyer 2012 (n 99) 461; Thomas Reimann,'Einige Überlegungen zur Offenkundigkeit im Rahmen von §§ 17 ff. UWG und von § 3 PatG' [1998] GRUR 298, 299; BGH GRUR 2012, 1048 Rdn 21 – *Movicol (Zulassungsantrag)*: "Das BerGer. hat zutreffend angenommen, dass es nicht zu einer den Geheimnischarakter ausschließenden allgemeinen Bekanntheit führt, wenn die Zulassungsunterlagen einem begrenzten – wenn auch unter Umständen größeren – Personenkreis zugänglich waren, etwa den auf Grund des Arbeitsvertrags zur Verschwiegenheit verpflichteten Betriebsangehörigen oder auch bestimmten Kunden und Lieferanten. Nichts anderes gilt, soweit die Unterlagen den mit der Vorbereitung und Prüfung des Zulassungsantrags dienstlich befassten Personen bekannt geworden sind"; this topic is further elaborated in chapter 4 § 4 D) III.

1326 *Ohly*/Sosnitza (n 813) § 17 Rdn 8.

1327 *Ohly*/Sosnitza (n 813) § 17 Rdn 8; Rudolf Kraßer, 'Grundlagen des zivilrechtlichen Schutz von Geschäfts- und Betriebsgeheimnissen sowie von Knowhow' [1977] GRUR 177, 178.

1328 Michael Knospe (n 834) 15:4.

ducted,[1329] where the decisive factor is the likelihood of a disclosure to any third parties, in particular competitors, not bound by a confidentiality obligation.[1330] Hence, courts have deemed that the trade secret holder is in control of the secret, not only among his employees, who are bound by their labour contracts, but also with regard to licensees and contract manufacturers, so long as they are expressly bound by a confidentiality obligation.[1331]

As stated above, information will be deemed public and thus not protectable under trade secrets law, not only if it is generally known, but also if it may be easily accessed ("*leichte Zugänglichkeit*").[1332] This requirement comprises both actual access and the possibility of accessing the information concerned.[1333] In patent law, a disclosure that is theoretically accessible by any third party is considered novelty destroying pursuant to § 2 of the German Patent Act,[1334] whereas under the trade secrets regime, the accessibility requirement has been construed in a much narrower and "specific" sense.[1335] Information that can only be obtained in an extremely difficult manner is considered to meet such a condition and consequently can be protected as a trade secret.[1336] This highlights one of the defining features of trade secrets vis-á-vis other IPRs: in order to be protected information must fulfil neither the technical novelty criterion as applied in patent law, nor the originality requirement necessary to grant copyright law.[1337]

In the light of the above, a new standard for the assessment of secrecy was developed by case law, according to which "information which in its specific manifestation can only be obtained through great difficulty and cost ("*große Schwierigkeit und Opfer*") is considered to be secret".[1338] In contrast, information that can be learned by the interested parties without such difficulty is deemed to be dedicated to the public and thus part of the public domain. The development of this standard was considered neces-

---

1329 *Ohly*/Sosnitza (n 813) § 17 Rdn 8.
1330 *Harte-Bavendamm*/Henning-Bodewig (n 376) § 17 Rdn 4; Rudolf Kraßer 1977 (n 1327) 177.
1331 Rudolf Kraßer 1977 (n 1327) 179.
1332 Florian Schweyer 2012 (n 99) 461.
1333 Rudolf Kraßer 1977 (n 1327) 179; Florian Schweyer 2012 (n 99) 462.
1334 See § 2 German Patent Act.
1335 Henning Harte-Bavendamm 2010 (n 823) § 77 Rdn 11.
1336 Rudolf Kraßer 1977 (n 1327) 179; Thomas Reimann 1998 (1325) 298, 299.
1337 Hirsch/Ann/*Brammsen* (n 1304) § 17 Rdn 13; BGH GRUR 1995, 424, 426 – *Möbelpaste.*
1338 Rudolf Kraßer 1977 (n 1327) 179.

sary in order to protect competitors who acquired a secret independently and through a high investment of effort and costs.[1339] Thus, information does not necessarily lose its secret nature if third parties achieve similar results independently.[1340]

## 4. Will to keep the information secret — Geheimhaltunsgswille

The fourth requirement applied by courts sets forth that information must remain undisclosed as a result of the will of the trade secret holder.[1341] The rationale behind this subjective requisite[1342] is to differentiate mere unknown information from information that is intentionally kept secret.[1343] The will to observe confidentiality must stem from the holder and it can be agreed upon orally or in a written form,[1344] even though it will often be inferred from the circumstances of the case.[1345] Courts have construed the intent requirement in a broad sense, encompassing both the "potential" and the actual intent.[1346] In addition, it has been suggested that if such intent is unclear, employees should presume that "all knowledge and processes, whose existence is unknown outside the inner sphere of the particular business and that play a role in its competitive position",[1347] are kept undisclosed as a result of the express will of the trade secret holder.[1348] Thus, the burden of proof lies with the employee, who will have to provide evidence that the employer did not intend to keep the information undisclosed.[1349] Likewise, actual knowledge of the secret information by the employer is not required, so long as if he had in fact been acquainted

---

1339 Rudolf Kraßer 1977 (n 1327) 179; Henning Harte-Bavendamm 2010 (n 823) § 77 Rdn 10.

1340 Henning Harte-Bavendamm 2010 (n 823) § 77 Rdn 10.

1341 BGH GRUR 1964, 31 – *Petromax II.*

1342 Gintare Surblyte 2011 (n 182) 51.

1343 *Ohly*/Sosnitza (n 813) § 17 Rdn 11; Henning Harte-Bavendamm 2010 (n 823) § 77 Rdn 12.

1344 Henning Harte-Bavendamm 2010 (n 823) § 77 Rdn 12.

1345 Henning Harte-Bavendamm 2010 (n 823) § 77 Rdn 12.

1346 Axel Beater (n 811) § 22 Rdn 1880.

1347 Henning Harte-Bavendamm 2010 (n 823) § 77 Rdn 12; BGH GRUR 2006, 1044 Rdn 19 – *Kundendatenprogramm.*

1348 Henning Harte-Bavendamm 2010 (n 823) § 77 Rdn 12.

1349 Henning Harte-Bavendamm 2010 (n 823) § 77 Rdn 12; Florian Schweyer 2012 (n 99) 468, Michael Knospe (n 834) 15:4.

with it he would have intended to keep it secret.[1350] This general presumption refers to the situation where information was developed by employees but still had to be communicated to employers, and it was introduced for practical purposes, because there is always a period of time between the actual invention and the act of communication.

This requirement has been strongly criticised by several commentators, who believe that the way in which it is tailored nowadays renders it a superfluous condition for protection.[1351] Some argue that establishing such a fiction appears redundant and should be abandoned.[1352] Hence, the only relevant yardstick should be whether the trade secret holder had disclosed the information and consequently it had become generally known.[1353]

### 5. Interest in keeping the information secret — Geheimhaltungsinteresse

The will to keep information secret ("*Geheimhaltungswille*") is closely connected with the last requirement set forth by case law for protecting trade secrets, namely the interest in keeping the information undisclosed ("*Geheimhaltungsinteresse*").[1354] Nowadays, it is generally accepted by case law and academia that the trade secret holder must have a justifiable economic interest in keeping the information secret, as the mere intention is deemed an inadequate subjective parameter for assessing trade secrets protection.[1355] Such an objective condition was essentially introduced with the aim of ensuring that the owner could not arbitrarily establish the information covered by the trade secret, irrespective of whether an objective un-

1350 Florian Schweyer 2012 (n 99) 468; BGH GRUR 1977, 539 – *Prozessrechner.*

1351 In that sense, Henning Harte-Bavendamm 2010 (n 823) § Rdn 12 states that "Die Erkannbarkeit dieses Willens mag für die Strafbarkeit wegen Geheimnisverrat von Bedeutung sein, jedoch nicht für den Begriff des Geheimnisses und nicht unbedingt für zivilrechtliches Vorgehen".

1352 *Ohly*/Sosnitza (n 813) § 17 Rdn 11.

1353 *Ohly*/Sosnitza (n 813) § 17 Rdn 11.

1354 Rudolf Kraßer 1970 (n 831) 590.

1355 In this sense, BGH GRUR 1955, 424, 425– *Möbelwachspaste*: "Der Begriff des Betriebsgeheimnisses außer dem Willen zur Geheimhaltung ein berechtigtes wirtschaftliches Interesse des Betriebsinhabers an der Geheimhaltung voraussetze"; *Ohly*/Sosnitza (n 813) § 17 Rn 12; *Köhler*/Bornkamm/Feddersen (n 835) § 17 Rdn 9; Henning Harte-Bavendamm 2010 (n 823) § 77 noting that "Außer dem Willen zur Geheimhaltung ist ein berechtigtes wirtschaftliches Interesse des Betriebsinhabers an der Geheimhaltung erforderlich".

derlying justification existed.[1356] In that regard, it should be noted that §§ 17 and 18 of the UWG are criminal law provisions and accordingly set forth criminal penalties in the event of infringement.[1357]

The ground for the assessment of the so-called "justifiable interest" is based on the competitive advantage gained by keeping the specific information secret, in line with Article 39(2)(b) TRIPs. Hence, case law has introduced a general presumption, whereby a legitimate economic interest will be assumed if the disclosure of the information hinders the rightholder's position in the market, or conversely, it leads to an improvement in the competitor's position.[1358] However, this does not mean that the trade secret must have economic value as such.[1359] Likewise, as already stated with regard to the secrecy requirement, it is not necessary that the object of protection is undisclosed information from a company, such as a secret method of manufacture. It suffices that its relationship with the business is kept secret. For instance, based on the previous example, the method for manufacture could be generally known, but if its use by a given company remains secret this relationship could constitute the object of trade secrets protection.[1360]

As a final consideration, it should be pointed out that it is irrelevant whether the protected secret deals with immoral or unlawful information.[1361] Notwithstanding this, a disclosure might be justified on the basis of third parties' best interests and, arguably, an obligation to do so may arise in the event of an emergency situation pursuant to § 34 of the Criminal Code.[1362]

---

1356 Henning Harte-Bavendamm 2010 (n 823) 13; *Ohly*/Sosnitza (n 813) § 17 Rdn 12.

1357 Gintare Surblyte 2011 (n 182) 47.

1358 *Köhler*/Bornkamm/Feddersen (n 835) § 17 Rdn 9.

1359 *Köhler*/Bornkamm/Feddersen (n 835) § 17 Rdn 9.

1360 *Köhler*/Bornkamm/Feddersen (n 835) § 17 Rdn 9.

1361 Henning Harte-Bavendamm 2010 (n 823) § 77 Rn 13; *Köhler*/Bornkamm/Feddersen (n 835) § 17 Rdn 9; Stephan Hillenbrand, *Der Begriff des Betriebs- und Geschäftsgeheimnisses* (Herbert Utz Verlag 2017) 75.

1362 Henning Harte-Bavendamm 2010 (n 823) § 77 Rdn 13; *Köhler*/Bornkamm/Feddersen (n 835) § 17 Rdn 9.

## B) The notion of confidentiality in England

### I. Concepts of confidential information and trade secret in England

The inclusion of trade secrets within the general legal framework created by the breach of confidence action has led to the establishment of a very complex system, where the boundaries between privacy and secrecy have progressively faded, causing the concepts to merge. In numerous rulings, English courts have sought to provide a uniform interpretation of essential concepts, such as confidential information, trade secrets and know-how.[1363] The following paragraphs attempt to shed light on the complex and at times confusing terminology used in case law when applying the breach of confidence action.

*Confidential information* is most adequately defined as the general term used to refer to information that is protected under the breach of confidence action.[1364] As mentioned previously, its scope covers all types of information without restrictions on the subject matter of protection,[1365] irrespective of the format in which it is presented.[1366]

As regards *trade secrets*, no statutory definition of this term has been enacted into law in England.[1367] A detailed study of the authorities on the subject reveals that the English courts have mostly avoided precisely delineating the semantic contours of this concept.[1368] As such, trade secrets refer to one of the several categories of information that are protected under the

1363 The difficulties of establishing a uniform interpretation of confidential information were already outlined by Lord Megarry in *Thomas Marshall (Exports) Limited v Guinle* [1979] FSR 208 (Ch), 209 where he held that "it is far from easy to state in general terms what is confidential information or trade secret".

1364 John Hull, 'Trade Secret Licensing: the art of the possible' [2009] 14 JIPLP 203, 205.

1365 Tanya Aplin and others 2012 (n 22) para 6.02 state that confidential information can be generally classified in four kinds, i.e. trade secrets, artistic and literary information, government secrets and personal information. However, it is further noted that "the boundaries separating these categories are not always easy to draw and there is a certain amount of overlapping".

1366 Lionel Bently and Brad Sherman 2014 (n 125) 1144.

1367 Notwithstanding, the Freedom of Information Act 2000, s 43(1) refers to trade secrets.

1368 John Hull 2013 (n 934) 158.

breach of confidence action,[1369] although some commentators argue that the courts have applied this phrase such that is has a two-fold meaning.[1370]

The first and more restrictive approach limits the scope of trade secrets to post-employment restraints on former employees, based both on express and implied duties of confidentiality.[1371] This was the case in *Helmet Integrated Systems Ltd v Tunnard*, where Moses J noted that former employees should be free to use and apply for their own benefit the skill and knowledge acquired and developed during the course of an employment relationship, even if it entails competing with the former employer. However, he added that they should not benefit from information regarded as a trade secret.[1372]

Conversely, the prevailing and broader approach uses the term trade secrets as a "synonym for commercial and industrial confidential information",[1373] similarly to Article 2(1) TSD. Indeed, Megarry J in *Thomas Marshall (Exports) Limited v Guinle* stated that trade secrets are information concerning industrial and trade settings that meets the following four requirements:

(i) First, the disclosure of the information would be detrimental to its holder or to the benefit of a competitor or any other third party;
(ii) Second, the owner should believe that the information concerned is secret;
(iii) Third, the holder's belief under the two previous requirements "must be reasonable";
(iv) Fourth, information must be assessed according to the "usage and practices of the particular industry or trade concerned".[1374]

Against this background, the traditional distinction between technical secrets and business secrets is also applicable. In particular, *know-how* is con-

1369 John Hull 2013 (n 934) 161.

1370 Tanya Aplin and others 2012 (n 22) para 6.06.

1371 See among others *Faccenda Chicken Ltd v Fowler* [1987] Ch 117 (CA), 136 where *Neil LJ* highlighted that: "The implied term which imposes an obligation on the employee as to his conduct after the termination of the employment is more restricted in scope than that which imposes a general duty of good faith. It is clear that the obligation not to use or disclose information may cover secret processes of manufacture such as chemical formulae (…), or designs or special methods of construction (…), and other information which is of sufficiently degree of confidentiality as to amount to a trade secret".

1372 *Helmet Integrated Systems Ltd v Tunnard* [2007] FSR 385 (CA), 445-446.

1373 Tanya Aplin and others 2012 (n 22) para 6.06.

1374 *Thomas Marshall (Exports) Limited v Guinle* [1979] FSR 208 (Ch), 229.

sidered to encompass two kinds of technical information.[1375] On the one hand, it is used to refer to non-patented practical information that has been developed through experience and testing and that is secret, substantial and identified.[1376] On the other hand, know-how has been used to designate the set of skills and knowledge that employees acquire during the course of their employment. This was the view supported, among others, by Sir Thomas Bingham M.R. in *Lancashire Fire Ltd v Lyons*, where it was held that:

> The normal presumption is that information which the employee has obtained in the ordinary course of his employment, without specific steps such as memorising particular documents, is information which he is free to take away and use in alternative employment.[1377]

With the above clarification in mind, the following section delves into two of the four conditions that are necessary to find liability under the breach of confidence action mentioned above: (i) the subject matter capable of protection, and (ii) the confidential nature of the information.[1378]

## II. Subject matter capable of protection

One of the most notable features of the English legal system is the fact that the breach of confidence action places no restrictions on the type of information protected and the format in which it is conveyed.[1379] Accordingly, the action has been invoked to protect both oral and written information,[1380] as well as drawings,[1381] photographs[1382] and products.[1383] Notwithstanding this, courts have developed four limitations as to the information that falls under its scope of protection. Consequently, trivial information, information that is vague, immoral information and false infor-

1375 Tanya Aplin and others 2012 (n 22) para 6.10; John Hull 2009 (n 1364) 206.
1376 Similar to Article 1(i) TTBER.
1377 *Lancashire Fires Limited v S.A. Lyons & Company Limited and Others* [1996] FSR 629 (CA), 656.
1378 See chapter 3 § 3 C) II.
1379 Lionel Bently and Brad Sherman 2014 (n 125) 1144.
1380 *Fraser v Thames Television Ltd* [1984] QB 44 (QB).
1381 *Morison v Moat* [1851] 9 Hare 241.
1382 *Douglas v Hello! Ltd and others* [2007] UKHL 21.
1383 *Vestergaard Frandsen A/S v Bestnet Europe Ltd* [2013] UKSC 31; *Helmet Integrated Systems Ltd v Tunnard* [2007] FSR 16 (CA).

mation are not eligible for protection.[1384] Each of these exceptions will be analysed in turn.

1. Commercial value: protection of trivial information?

As a first general limitation, case law has provided that trivial information may not be subject to a confidential obligation. Famously, Megarry J in *Coco v A.N.Clark (Engineers) Ltd* stated that "equity ought not to be invoked merely to protect *trivial tittle-tattle*, however confidential".[1385] Yet, the decision provided no further guidance on how to assess such a requirement. The Oxford dictionary defines *tittle-tattle* as referring to "casual conversation about other people, typically involving details that are not confirmed as true; gossip".[1386] In line with this definition, in *Attorney General v Guardian Newspapers Ltd* Lord Goff stressed "the duty of confidence applies neither to useless information, nor to trivia".[1387] However, in *Stephens v Avery*[1388] the notion that information concerning an extramarital affair between two people published in a tabloid was not eligible for protection under the breach of confidence action was rejected. In this case, the plaintiff, Mrs Stephens, conveyed in confidence certain information of a private nature to one of the defendants, Mrs Avery. In particular, the information related to a lesbian relationship between the plaintiff and Mrs Telling, who because of the affair was murdered by her husband. Subsequently, Mrs Avery communicated the information about the lesbian relationship to one of the most prominent tabloids in the UK, "The Mail on Sunday", in which an article revealing details of the relationship was published in July 1984. As a result, Mrs Stephens brought an action for a breach of confidence. Upon Appeal, Sir Nicolas noted that the exclusion of "trivial tittle-tattle" information in *Coco v A.N.Clark (Engineers) Ltd* was exclusively concerned with information that was of industrial value and expressed scepti-

1384 Lionel Bently and Brad Sherman 2014 (n 125) 1144.

1385 *Coco v A.N.Clark (Engineers) Ltd* [1969] RPC 41 (Ch), 48; later Judge Dean in *Moorgate Tobacco Co, Ltd v Philip Morris Ltd* (No 2) [1984] 156 CLR 414, 438.

1386 'tittle-tattle, n' (*OED Online*, OUP June 2013) <https://en.oxforddictionaries.com/definition/tittle-tattle> accessed 15 September 2018.

1387 Lord Goff in *Attorney General v Guardian Newspapers Ltd (No. 2)* [1990] 1 AC 109 (HL), 282.

1388 *Stephens v Avery* [1988] FSR 510 (Ch).

cism about considering the sexual conduct of an individual as trivial tittle-tattle information.[1389]

Accordingly, courts have been wary of regarding information as trivial, partially due to the uncertainty and difficulty related to the consideration of what constitutes trivial information,[1390] which in practice has led to a reduction in the applicability of this limitation.[1391]

Notwithstanding this, in the field of trade secrets, some decisions have demanded information to be commercially valuable or at least attractive, in line with Article 2(1)(b) TSD.[1392] Yet, a survey of the cases involving trade secrets protection reveals that most of them do not expressly refer to the value of the information, as it is often deemed that companies would not bring legal action if the information concerned did not have a certain "value".[1393]

More recently, the notion of "objective value" was used as one of the factors that signalled whether the information possessed the necessary quality of confidence.[1394] In addition, in the landmark decision from the House of Lords *Douglas v Hello and other Ltd* the fact that the parties entered into an agreement covering the protection of information was considered crucial in assessing the confidential nature of the pictures of the wedding that had been misappropriated.[1395] In view of this, it appears that "commercial value" as such is not a normative requirement under the breach of confidence

1389 *Stephens v Avery* [1988] FSR 510 (Ch), 515.

1390 Lionel Bently and Brad Sherman 2014 (n 125) 1000.

1391 Lionel Bently and Brad Sherman 2014 (n 125) 1001.

1392 For instance, in *Thomas Marshall (Exports) Limited v Guinle* [1979] FSR 208 (Ch), 229 it was stated that one of the requirements to find liability was that the disclosure of the information should cause a prejudice to the owner or an advantage to competitors or third parties; see further Lionel Bently and Brad Sherman 2014 (n 125) 1000; Gintare Surblyte 2011 (n 182) 78.

1393 Tanya Aplin and others 2012 (n 22) para 5.51; however, in *Nichrothermc Electrical Co Ltd v Percy* [1956] RPC 272 (Ch) the plaintiffs brought legal action for the misappropriation of a machine that presented no commercial value.

1394 *HEFCE v Information Commissioner and the Guardian News and Media Ltd* (EA/2009/0036, 10 January 2010) [48].

1395 See *Douglas v Hello! Ltd and others* [2007] UKHL 21 [325] (Lord Brown): "Having paid £1m for an exclusive right it seems to me that OK! ought to be in a position to protect that right and to look to the law for redress were a third party intentionally to destroy it. Like Lord Hoffmann, I would uphold OK!'s claim, as Lindsay J did at first instance, on the ground of breach of confidence"; however Lord Walker [299] held the opposite view, by noting that "the confidentiality of any information must depend on its nature, not on its market value".

action in England, but it is a strong indicator of the existence of information that is worth protecting.[1396]

## 2. Information that is vague

In addition to being non-trivial, the general principle is that confidential information should be specific i.e. clear and identifiable.[1397] Vague or general information is excluded from the scope of the breach of confidence action.[1398] In effect, as noted in *Terrapin Ltd v Builders' Supply Co (Hayes) Ltd.* by Roxburh J, confidential information must be "something that can be traced to a particular source and not something which has become so completely merged in the mind of the person informed that it is impossible to say from what precise quarter he derived the information which led to the knowledge which he is found to possess".[1399]

Identifying the information for which protection is sought is crucial not only to establish the duration of an injunction and the amount of damages due, but also to elucidate whether an actual breach has occurred.[1400] It also appears of paramount importance in the context of the licensing agreements in order to delineate the scope of the contracts.[1401]

Such a limitation has often been invoked by courts as a ground to deny granting an injunction preventing the use of a "generalized body of information".[1402] Consequently, injunctions should be drafted in a very specific manner so as to allow defendants to know with certainty which conducts are permitted and which are forbidden. This is particularly relevant, for instance, in injunctions relating to post employment restraints as regards trade secrets.[1403] In the event of litigation, the trade secrets that former employees are not allowed to use after the termination of their employment relationship should be clearly identifiable in any potential injunction. It is

1396 Nevertheless, Roger M. Toulson and Charles M. Phipps 2012 (n 326) 3-081 suggest that "There must be some value to the party claiming confidentiality (not necessarily commercial) in the information being treated as confidential".

1397 Roger M. Toulson and Charles M. Phipps 2012 (n 326) para 3-086.

1398 Lionel Bently and Brad Sherman 2014 (n 125) 1001-1003.

1399 *Terrapin Ltd v Builders' Supply Co (Hayes) Ltd* [1962] RPC 375 (Ch), 391; a detaied account of this case is provided in chapter 6 § 2 B) III. 3).

1400 Tanya Aplin and others (n 22) para 5.74.

1401 John Hull 2009 (n 1364) 208.

1402 Tanya Aplin and others (n 22) para 5.74.

1403 Roger M. Toulson and Charles M. Phipps 2012 (n 326) para 3-088.

essential to distinguish them from general skills and knowledge, which every employee should be free to use.[1404] The importance of identifying the information that constitutes the trade secret in order to find liability under the breach of confidence action was restated by the Supreme Court in *Vestergaard v Bestnet,* a case concerning an alleged breach by a former employee.[1405]

The above should not be understood to mean that simple ideas cannot be protected, even though the more novel or original ideas are, the more likely they are to merit protection.[1406] As opposed to copyright law, the breach of confidence action affords protection to ideas without the need to show their specific expression.[1407] By way of illustration, the ideas for a new TV programme[1408] and an innovative concept of a dance club were deemed confidential.[1409] Yet again, the courts have struggled to draw a line with regard to when an idea is sufficiently detailed. Notably, this requirement has been construed as meaning that the concept or idea must be "sufficiently developed to be capable of being realized".[1410] This is analysed further in the assessment of the secrecy requirement vis-à-vis IPRs normative standards.[1411]

1404 *Faccenda Chicken Ltd v Fowler* [1987] Ch 117 (CA), 122-123.

1405 *Vestergaard Frandsen A/S v Bestnet Europe Ltd* [2013] UKSC 31, [22]: "It would seem surprising if Mrs Sig could be liable for breaching Vestergaard's rights of confidence through the misuse of its trade secrets, given that she did not know (i) the identity of those secrets, and (ii) that they were being, or had been, used, let alone misused. The absence of such knowledge would appear to preclude liability, at least without the existence of special facts".

1406 See Tanya Aplin and others 2012 (n 22) para 5.55.

1407 William Cornish, David Llewellyn and Tanya Aplin 2013 (n 209) para 8-10 note that "an idea for something to be elaborated may attract legal protection as confidential information where there is nothing that generates copyright".

1408 *Fraser v Thames Television Ltd* [1984] QB 44 (QB).

1409 *De Maudsley v Palumbo* [1996] FSR 447 (Ch).

1410 Lionel Bently and Brad Sherman 2014 (n 125) 1145-1146 noting that this is criterion was first developed in the Supreme Court of Victoria in *Tablot v General Television Corp* [1981] RPC 1.

1411 Chapter 4 § 4 E) II 2).

### 3. Immoral and false information

In England the general principle is that immoral information is not eligible for protection under the breach of confidence action.[1412] However, as no generally accepted code of morality exists, courts have shown reluctance to apply this limitation. For instance, in *Stephens v Avery*, while the court ruled that in abstract a duty of confidence would not be enforceable against "matters which have a grossly immoral tendency", it concluded that no common view existed on the immoral nature of sexual relationships between consenting adults.[1413]

Another unsettled issue is whether false information (i.e. inaccurate information) can be protected under the breach of confidence action, particularly due to its intersection with the defamation cause of action.[1414] A review of leading academic works on confidentiality seems to support that inaccuracies should not affect the confidential nature of the information, provided that such an action is not intended to cover a defamation claim,[1415] as noted by the Court of Appeal in *McKennitt v Ash*.[1416] This case concerned the publication of a book on the life of the plaintiff, a Canadian folk singer. In the book, private information about the singer was disclosed by the author, a former friend and business partner. As regards the falsity of the allegations, the court concluded that, "the truth or falsity of the information is an irrelevant inquiry in deciding whether the information is entitled to be protected".[1417] However, some commentators have noted that these arguments seem less persuasive with regard to non-private or non-personal matters, such as government information.[1418] Indeed, in *Financial Times Ltd & Ors v Interbrew SA* the leakage of five documents that contained false information about the acquisition of a brewery in South Africa was not deemed enforceable under the breach of confidence action, because in the words of Sedley J, "there can be no confidentiality in false information".[1419] In sum, it appears that case law under the breach of con-

1412 William Cornish, David Llewellyn and Tanya Aplin 2013 (n 209) paras 8-10.
1413 *Stephens v Avery* [1988] FSR 510 (Ch).
1414 Roger M. Toulson and Charles M. Phipps 2012 (n 326) para 3-093.
1415 Tanya Aplin and others (n 22) para 5.67; Roger M. Toulson and Charles M. Phipps 2012 (n 326) para 3-093; *McKennitt v Ash* [2006] EWCA Civ 1714 (CA).
1416 *McKennitt v Ash* [2006] EWCA Civ 1714 (CA), [86].
1417 *McKennitt v Ash* [2006] EWCA Civ 1714 (CA), [86].
1418 Tanya Aplin and others (n 22) para 5.62 and para 5.72.
1419 *Financial Times Ltd. & Ors v Interbrew SA* [2002] EWCA Civ 274 (CA), [27]-[28].

fidence action provides no clear answer as to the protection of false information.

### III. Confidential nature of the information

Crucially, in order to bring an action under an alleged breach of confidence, it must always be proved that the disclosed information is of a confidential nature i.e. "it possesses the necessary quality of confidence". Despite the widespread use of this term, few English cases seem to provide a satisfactory definition.[1420]

In assessing this requirement, courts tend to follow a pragmatic approach, where the analysis of confidentiality is considered against the specific background of every particular case.[1421]

The following sections examine the general test developed by English courts, along with the main attributes of confidentiality.

#### 1. The general test of inaccessibility

The tests developed to assess confidentiality are mostly of an objective nature, as they do not take into account the views of the parties.[1422] Indeed the "status of the information is a question of fact, not intention".[1423] Notwithstanding this, Toulson and Phipps have propounded that an implicit principle is that courts should only recognise confidentiality in those cases where it appears *reasonable* to do so.[1424] This is argued on the basis that a number of cases have resorted to the "reasonable man yardstick" when assessing the confidential nature of the information (and not just whether an obligation of confidence arises),[1425] and the fact that secrecy is

1420 John Hull 1998 (1016) para 3.03.
1421 Tanya Aplin and others 2012 (n 22) 149.
1422 Allison Coleman 1992 (n 911) 8; this was also noted in *Lancashire Fires Limited v S.A. Lyons & Company Limited and Others* [1996] FSR 629 (CA), 656: "the subjective view of the owner cannot be decisive. There must be something which is not objectively a trade secret, but something which was known, or ought to have been known, by both parties to be so".
1423 Lionel Bently and Brad Sherman 2014 (n 125) 1148.
1424 Roger M. Toulson and Charles M. Phipps 2012 (n 326) para 3-082.
1425 *Thomas Marshall (Exports) Limited v Guinle* [1979] FSR 208 (Ch), 229 and chapter 3 § 3 C) II. 2. a).

often defined by its limits, in which "reasonableness" is often invoked.[1426] Yet, this view is not supported because it introduces an element of subjectivity, ("the owner's belief -which must be reasonable- that the information is confidential") that should only be taken into account in the assessment of whether an obligation on the recipient arises, not as regards the status of the information.[1427]

In effect, most decisions follow the objective test of confidentiality first developed in *Saltman Engineering v Campbell Engineering*, where confidentiality was defined by the limitations imposed by the public domain:

> The information, to be confidential, must, I apprehend, apart from contract, have the necessary quality of confidence about it, namely it must not be something which is public property and public knowledge. On the other hand, it is perfectly possible to have a confidential document, be it a formula, a plan, a sketch, or something of that kind, which is the result of work by the maker upon materials which may be available for the use of anybody; but what makes it confidential is the fact that the maker of the document has used his brain and thus produced a result which can only be produced by somebody who goes through the same process.[1428]

As is apparent from the above passage, for information to qualify as confidential it should meet two requirements. The first is rather broad and demands that information is not "public property" or "public knowledge", i.e. part of the "public domain".[1429] Secondly, Lord Griffin suggested a test, according to which information would only be deemed confidential if it could only be acquired through the reproduction of the mental process that led to the creation of the resulting information.

In the light of the above, courts have applied the general principle of "inaccessibility" with the aim of assessing whether certain information falls into the public domain.[1430] This judgement is based on a confidentiality test developed by subsequent authorities, according to which information

---

1426 Roger M. Toulson and Charles M. Phipps 2012 (n 326) 3-082 and footnote 142 for an account of the cases in which "reasonableness" is invoked.

1427 John Hull 1998 (1016) para 3.09.

1428 *Saltman Engineering v Campell Engineering* [1948] 65 RPC 203 (CA), 215.

1429 Law Commission 1981 (n 327) 27 noting that "in referring to this requirement the courts have used a variety of expressions, but it has become increasingly common to say that the information for which protection is sought by the action of breach of confidence must not be in the public domain".

1430 Tanya Aplin and others 2012 (n 22) paras 5.14 -5.39.

will only be deemed confidential if "special intellectual skill and labour" are essential in order to reproduce it.[1431] That is understood to mean that the alleged infringer would have to go through the same burdensome mental process as the confider.[1432] This criterion is applied to information considered in its entirety, irrespective of its components.[1433]

Against this background, it is noteworthy that generally known information can also be deemed confidential, so long as intellectual skill and labour are required in order to compile it.[1434] This rationale has been applied to decide on cases concerning the confidential nature of customer lists, where the data on individual customers were also available in other trade databases. However, the lists in their entirety were regarded as confidential, as competitors had to undergo the same intellectual labour as the creators of the lists.[1435]

Drawing on the foregoing, it appears that courts in England have adopted a "relative secrecy" approach, as opposed to patent law, where the standard for assessing the novelty of an invention is an absolute one. Information can be conveyed to a limited number of people without losing its confidential nature.[1436] The issue lies in determining the extent of publication permitted. The general principle is that once information is generally accessible and widespread it cannot be regarded as confidential.[1437] Similarly,

---

1431 Tanya Aplin and others 2012 (n 22) para 5.15; *Ocular Sciences Ltd v Aspect Vision Care Ltd* [1997] RPC 289 (Ch), 375.

1432 Tanya Aplin and others 2012 (n 22) 5.16.

1433 *Coco v A.N.Clark (Engineers) Ltd* [1969] RPC 41 (Ch), 47.

1434 Tanya Aplin and others 2012 (n 22) para 5.17.

1435 *International Scientific Communications Inc v Pattinson and Others* [1979] FSR 429 (Ch), 434.

1436 Lionel Bently and Brad Sherman 2014 (n 125) 1148 ; *Franchi v Franchi* [1967] RPC 149 (Ch), 152: "Clearly a claim that the disclosure of some information would be a breach of confidence is not to be defeated simply by providing that there are other people in the world who know the facts in question besides the man as to whom it is said that his disclosure would be a breach of confidence and those to whom he had disclosed them. It must be a question of degree depending on the particular case, but if relative secrecy remains, the plaintiff can still succeed".

1437 See *Attorney General v Guardian Newspapers Ltd (No 2)* [1990] 1 AC 109 (HL), 282 where Lord Goff stated that: "In particular, once it has entered what is usually called the public domain (which means no more than that the information in question is so generally accessible that, in all the circumstances it cannot be regarded as confidential) then, as a general rule, the principle of confidentiality can have no application to it".

the fact that information can be obtained from reverse engineering should not deprive the information of its secret nature.[1438]

In this context, it should be indicated that "the status of information may change over time" and that information that is in the public domain may become secret if the public forgets the information or the relevant public changes.[1439]

In the light of the above, it is clear that establishing whether information is confidential is a question of fact that should be assessed on a case-by-case basis.[1440] Against this background, Hull refers to an Australian case in which a multi-factor test to assist in determining whether a specific piece of information presented the "necessary quality of confidence" was developed. The factors taken into consideration were:

(i) The extent to which the information was known outside the plaintiff s business;
(ii) The extent to which the information was known to employees and others inside the plaintiff's business;
(iii) The extent to which the plaintiff had taken measures to safeguard the information;
(iv) The value of the information to the plaintiff' competitors;
(v) The amount of effort expended by the plaintiff in developing the information; and
(vi) The ease or difficulty with which the information could properly be acquired.[1441]

While these factors are to be weighed against each other, the assessment of secrecy is ultimately factually driven. No normative value can be attached to either of them. In particular, the adoption of measures (factor 3), the value of the information (factor 4) and the cost of development (factor 5) signal the existence of information worth protecting, which may nevertheless be generally known.

In sum, it appears that the English notion of confidentiality is very similar to the concept of "*Nichtoffenkundigkeit*" followed under German law. In both jurisdictions, the crucial test to assess secrecy consists of looking into whether the information can only be obtained through great difficulty and

---

Paul Lavery,'Secrecy, Springboards and the Public Domain' [1998] 20 EIPR 93, 95.

1438 John Hull 1998 (1016) para 3.18.

1439 Lionel Bently and Brad Sherman 2014 (n 125) 1153.

1440 John Hull 1998 (1016) para 3.06.

1441 John Hull 1998 (1016) para 3.07 citing the Austalian case *Section Pty v DelawoodPty Ltd* [1991] 21 IPR 136.

cost (*"große Schwierigkeit und Opfer"* in Germany), which is just another way of referring to the "intellectual skill and labour" yardstick propounded in the English jurisdiction under the test of inaccessibility. However, a cardinal distinction between the two jurisdictions is that English cases seem to emphasise the need to prove that intellectual skill (not just labour) is necessary to obtain the information. In addition, English case law does not refer to the fact that information loses its secret nature when it is known among the "circle of experts" that usually deal with the information in question.[1442] The reason behind this distinction can be traced back to the fact that the scope of the breach of confidence action is not confined to the protection of trade secrets, but also covers artistic and literary information, private information and government information. However, a review of the case law concerning trade secrets reveals that decisions referring to trade secrets define the public domain by reference to a narrow field, industry or profession, similar to the "relevant circle yardstick" followed under German law.[1443]

## 2. Form of the information

In England courts have also been confronted with the issue of deciding whether the disclosure of information in a specific form leads to its disclosure in another form. This particular topic was discussed by the House of Lords in the famous *Douglas v Hello!* case, which concerned the unauthorised publication of pictures of the wedding of the actors Michael Douglas and Katherine Zeta-Jones by Hello! magazine.[1444] The pictures published by Hello! were taken without permission by an undercover photographer who had then sold them to the defendant. As a result, both the couple and OK! Magazine brought legal action against Hello! under the breach of confidence action. Crucially, some months before the event, the couple had reached an exclusive licensing agreement with OK! Magazine, granting this publication the exclusive right to publish pictures of the event in exchange for consideration. The salient issue in this case was to decide whether protection under the breach of confidence could extend to pho-

1442 Paul Lavery,'Secrecy, Springboards and the Public Domain' [1998] 20 EIPR 93, 93 suggests that this has been required in some cases in Ireland and Australia to find a breach of confidence.

1443 John Hull 1998 (1016) para 3.16.

1444 *Douglas v Hello! Ltd and others* [2007] UKHL 21.

tographs that were already in the public domain, as the pictures had been published by national newspapers some hours before OK! Magazine came out. In rendering the decision, Lord Hoffman concluded that the object of confidentiality was "any picture of the wedding", as this was the only possible way of protecting the interests of OK!.[1445]

### 3. No need to adopt reasonable measures

One remarkable difference between the English breach of confidence regime prior to the implementation of the TSD and the legal system laid down in Article 39(2) TRIPs (but also in the U.S. under the UTSA and the DTSA)[1446] is that protection is not subject to the adoption of reasonable steps by the trade secret holder to safeguard the secret nature of the information. While the adoption of such measures is assessed in a positive manner by the English courts, legal commentators seem to agree on the fact that it is not a precondition for meriting protection.[1447] Notwithstanding this, in *Thomas Marshall (Exports) Limited v Guinle* the adoption of reasonable measures was considered as one of the four requirements for the protection of trade secrets.[1448]

## *§ 3 The concept of trade secret in the Directive: considerations in the light of the comparative analysis*

### A) Preliminary remarks

The subject matter covered by the TSD is set out in Article 1(1), which "lays down rules on the protection against the unlawful acquisition, disclosure and use of trade secrets". Thereupon, Article 2(1) provides a definition of trade secrets, which is identical to the one set forth in Article 39(2) TRIPs. In order to be protected, trade secrets must (a) be information that

1445 *Douglas v Hello! Ltd and others* [2007] UKHL 21 [123]; similar considerations were applied in *Creations Records Ltd v News Group Newspaper Ltd* [1997] EWHC Ch 370 (Ch), [29] which concerned the publication by tabloids in the UK of pictures of the shooting of the cover of a rock band's forthcoming album.

1446 See § 1(4) UTSA and supra chapter 4.

1447 Lionel Bently 2012 (n 114) para 3.18.

1448 *Thomas Marshall (Exports) Limited v Guinle* [1979] FSR 208 (Ch), 229.

is not generally known or readily accessible; (b) must have commercial value due to their secret nature; and (c) must be subject to reasonable steps under the circumstances to preserve secrecy. In this regard, it is worth noting that the 28 Member States of the EU are also part of the WTO and, as such, they were bound to implement the TRIPs minimum standards of protection for IPRs in their national regimes by 1 January 1996.[1449] [1450] Thus, the inclusion in the Directive of the same definition as the one provided in the TRIPs Agreement for "undisclosed information", as a minimum standard of protection, appears to be a restatement of such an obligation and provides flexibility to Member States in its implementation.[1451]

To be sure, the object of protection of Article 2(1) TSD is information, which coincides with the subject matter protected under the breach of confidence action in England and §§ 17-19 of the German UWG.[1452] Accordingly, information is deemed secret "if it is not, as a body or in the precise configuration and assembly of its components, generally known among or readily accessible to persons within the circles that normally deal with the kind of information in question". However, upon closer examination, some uncertainty arises in connection with the meaning of some of

1449 TRIPs transitional provisions are essentially regulated in Article 65 of the Agreement. The general rule is set forth in paragraph 1, which established an automatic transitional period of one year for all WTO Members (until 1 January 1996). However, paragraphs (2) and (3) granted a four-year transitional period (until 1 January 2000) for developing countries and countries that were in the process of transformation from a centrally planned economy into a free market economy. The computing of the time referred to in Article 65 is a definite term based on the date of entry into force of the WTO Agreement. Hence, countries acceding after 1995 could not benefit from any additional transitional periods and were requested to amend their legislation before their accession, unless they qualified to benefit from the transitional periods of paragraphs (2) and (3), but only until January 1, 2000.

1450 Likewise, the European Union, as a supranational entity, became a party to the TRIPs Agreement by virtue of the Council, 'Council Decision 94/800/EC of 22 December 1994 concerning the conclusion on behalf of the European Community as regards matters within its competence, of the agreements reached in the Uruguay Round multilateral negotiations (1986-1994)' [1994] OJ L336; this is also clarified in Recital 5 TSD.

1451 In Baker McKenzie 2013 (n 1057) 5 it is noted that despite the existence of a common denominator (based on the criteria of Article 39(2) TRIPs) the definitions adopted in the different jurisdictions present divergences and in addition require particular constitutive elements.

1452 But see chapter 4 § 2 A) II. 1.

the terms used by the EU legislature and the subject matter of protection, as analysed in the following sections.

## B) Terminology

The terminology used in the Directive to refer to the term trade secret and the types of information that fall under its scope are not consistently applied. Recital 14 highlights the importance of establishing a common definition without limiting the subject matter protected against misappropriation, which should cover the protection of "know-how, business information and technological information" if two conditions are fulfilled, namely, (i) there is a legitimate interest in maintaining the confidentiality of the information, and (ii) there is also a legitimate expectation in the preservation of such confidentiality. The distinction between business and technological information mirrors the practice in most Member States before the implementation of the Directive, where case law and even some statutes differentiated between industrial secrets and commercial secrets, and presents no interpretative questions.[1453]

However, the reference to know-how is confusing. It is used in the title of the Directive and in the first sentence of Recital 1 as a full synonym of trade secret, whereas Recitals 2 and 14 instead refer to it as one of the categories of undisclosed information. This is particularly problematic, as know-how is autonomously defined in Article 1(i) TTBER in a manner that seems to partially overlap with what is usually understood by "technical trade secrets" or "technological information", as mentioned in Recital 14. The use of such confusing terminology reflects the current practice in many national jurisdictions, like Germany, where know-how is regarded as an economic term rather than a legal one.[1454] Hence, for the sake of legal certainty, it would have been best if the Directive had abandoned the use of "know-how" or clarified its relationship with Article 1(i) of the TTBER.[1455]

English courts under the breach of confidence action have also used the term "know-how" to designate the set of skills and knowledge that em-

1453 As discussed in chapter 4 with regard to Germany and England.

1454 Hannes Beyerbach, *Die geheime Unternehmensinformation* (Mohr Siebeck 2012) 103; *Ohly*/Sosnitza (n 813) § 17 Rdn 11.

1455 Tanya Aplin 2014 (n 384) 264.

ployees acquire during the course of their employment.[1456] However, such an acceptation is not supported by the TSD, which provides in Recital 14 that "the definition of trade secret excludes trivial information and the *experience and skills* gained by employees in the normal course of their employment" (emphasis added).[1457] The establishment of common ground on the information that departing employees are free to use after the termination of their employment contract represents considerable progress, as Member States' practice differed substantially on this particular aspect. Notwithstanding this, the Directive provides little guidance on how to assess the boundaries between information that is actually part of a trade secret and information that constitutes "experience and skills" that employees are free to use. The TSD resorts to a vague clause that provides great flexibility to national competent courts to conduct a balancing exercise, taking into account all of the circumstances of the specific case. Some have criticised that such a broad clause will lead to an abuse of litigation,[1458] although the Directive already provides a comprehensive array of safeguards against such practices in Articles 6 to 9.

From a legislative technique perspective, the exclusion of "experience and skills gained by employees in the normal course of their employment" from the subject matter protected by trade secrets law is more problematic. This approach creates a two-tier definition of trade secret and seems unsystematically placed within the Directive. Indeed, such an assessment should be carried out in the context of the relevant liability conducts[1459] and in particular, within the balancing exercised imposed by Article 5 TSD and not at the definition level. We will return to the provisions of the TSD that regulate post-employment obligations in chapter 6, where a number of criteria to differentiate between protected trade secrets and the skill and knowledge that employees are free to use are suggested.[1460]

1456 See chapter 4 § 2 B) I.

1457 See further Article 1(3)(b) TSD.

1458 IP Federation, 'The EU Trade Secrets Directive' (2014) Policy Paper PP04/15, 3-4 <https://www.ipfederation.com/news/ip-federation-comments-on-the-compromise-text-for-the-eu-trade-secrets-directive/> 15 September 2018.

1459 Tanya Aplin 2014 (n 384).

1460 This issue is discussed in greater detail in chapter 6 § 1 A) and has recently been the object of a comprehensive study by Magdalena Kolasa, *Trade Secrets and Employee Mobility* (CUP 2018).

## C) Commercial value

The second limb of the definition provides that information must have commercial value "because it is secret". In this regard, it is worth noting that before the implementation of the Directive, such a requirement was not foreseen either under the English breach of confidence action, or under German law. However, as indicated above, English cases dealing with trade secrets have viewed commercial value as a strong indicator that the information is worth protecting.[1461] In the same vein, the German "*Geheimhaltungsinteresse*" requirement has been interpreted as meaning that the trade secret holder has a commercial interest in keeping the information secret. Yet, in the latter jurisdiction such a requirement has also been invoked to protect secret information that does not confer commercial value, but the disclosure of which would be detrimental to a company (for instance, information that would harm the reputation of the company, or information about collusive practices that would result in antitrust sanctions).[1462] In addition, in Germany, a causality link between the concealed nature of the information and its value is not required.[1463]

Another question that was intensely discussed during the negotiation of the Directive was whether potential value suffices or actual value is required. The UTSA expressly mentions both, while TRIPs is silent on this point. Recital 14 TSD sheds light on this issue by stating that the value can be either actual or potential. As discussed previously,[1464] this is particularly relevant in the context of ensuring that R&D companies will have a Laboratory Zone in which to develop their ideas and innovations. The same recital provides further guidance on how to interpret the commercial value benchmark:

> Furthermore, such know-how or information should have a commercial value, whether actual or potential. Such know-how or information should be considered to have a commercial value, for example, where its unlawful acquisition, use or disclosure is likely to harm the interests of the person lawfully controlling it, in that it undermines that person's scientific and technical potential, business or financial interests, strategic positions or ability to compete. (…)[1465]

---

1461 Chapter 4 § 2 B) II. 1.
1462 Björn H. Kalbfus 2016 (n 1122)1011.
1463 Thomas Hören and Reiner Münker 2018(b) (n 1119) 151
1464 Chapter 1 § 2 B) IV.
1465 Recital 14 TSD.

As is apparent from the above, and in line with the principles that inform the Directive, commercial value is to be interpreted in a broad and flexible manner. It refers not only to the loss of competitive advantage, but also more generally to any harm to the scientific and technical capacity and the economic interest of the trade secret holder and his position in the market that may result from the disclosure of information. Consequently, it is submitted that protection shall also be afforded to organisations that act with no profit motive, such as universities and research institutions. This was particularly not the case under German law, where information had to be ascribed to a particular business (“*Geschäftsbezogenheit*”).

Similarly, illicit activities, such as collusive practices or information that may hamper the reputation of a company, which were protected in Germany under the *Geheimhaltungsinteresse* prong, seem to be excluded from the scope of protection of the Directive by virtue of the whistle-blower exception laid down in Article 5(b) TSD, provided that the trade secret holder intended to protect “the public interest”. Accordingly, it is submitted that national legislatures and judicial authorities should interpret that the notion of “trade secret” does not include information that the trade secret holder wishes to keep secret, but that does not affect his competitive position.

As a final note, Recital 14 also expressly excludes trivial information from the subject matter that can be protected as a trade secret. The adjective trivial is deemed to refer to things “of little value or importance”[1466] and resembles the exclusion of “trivial tittle-tattle” information under the breach of confidence action. However, drawing from the English experience, its application seems of limited relevance, as courts have struggled to draw a line between valuable and trivial information, and this will become increasingly difficult in the Digital Economy, where individual data may become valuable as a result of its inclusion in Big Data sets.[1467]

In sum, an analysis of the relevant provisions of the TSD that frame the commercial value requirement reveals that:

(i) There must be a causal link between the value of the information and its concealed nature;

(ii) The relevant factor is that the disclosure of the information hampers the ability to compete of the trade secret holder, which should be interpreted in a wide sense;

1466 ‘trivial, adj’ (*OED Online*, OUP June 2013) <https://en.oxforddictionaries.com/definition/trivial> accessed 15 September 2018.

1467 As discussed in the Excursus in chapter 4 § 4 F) II.

(iii) Consequently, information developed by entities that do not have a profit making intention (such as universities or basic research centres) may also fall under the scope of protection of the Directive;
(iv) Illicit activities and information that may hamper the reputation of a company are not included within the scope of protection of the TSD, because they do not affect the competitive position of the trade secret holder.

### D) Private and personal information

As regards the subject matter of protection, the Directive does not clarify whether secret private information that at the same time has commercial value is part of the subject matter that falls under the notion of a trade secret. This would typically be the case for celebrities who commercialise certain aspects of their private lives, such as in the *Douglas v Hello!* decision examined above.[1468] This factual scenario is covered by the breach of confidence action, but would not be protected in Germany as a trade secret because information would not meet the *Geschäftsbezogenheit* (information ascribed to a business) requirement. More generally, while it is true that in such cases the holders of secret information may have a *business* interest in commercialising unknown aspects of their lives,[1469] it is doubtful whether the EU has the competence to harmonise privacy law in such a broad manner.[1470]

More problematic is the relationship between the TSD and the GDPR. Recital 2 TSD expressly mentions "information on customers and suppliers" as one of the types of business information protected under the law of trade secrets. In turn, such information may fall under the category of personal data defined in Article 4(1) GDPR, which includes "information relating to an identified or identifiable natural person". In this regard, Recital 35 TSD clarifies that the TSD should not affect the rights and obligations laid down in the Data Protection Directive (which has been replaced by the GDPR). Hence, while it is doubtful that commercialising unknown information about someone's private life may qualify as a trade secret, it is clear that personal information may be protected as one according to Recital 35. For instance, the names and contact details included in a

1468 *Douglas v Hello! Ltd and others* [2007] UKHL 21.
1469 Tanya Aplin 2014 (n 384) 263.
1470 Ansgar Ohly 2013 (n 13) 40.

customer list, may be protected as a trade secret provided that they (i) are not generally known or readily accessible, (ii) present commercial value and (iii) are subject to reasonable measures under the circumstances to maintain them secret. In such a case, the trade secret holder shall nevertheless comply with the obligations set out in the GDPR. However, as outlined above, a systematic review of the relevant provisions of the GDPR and the TSD reveals that tension may arise between the interests of the trade secret holder in keeping information under his control undisclosed and the right of the data subject in accessing his personal data.[1471] Likewise, the distinction between private information which a priori seems excluded from the scope of the TSD and personal information which may be eligible for trade secret protection is not always a straightforward one, as for instance, the CJEU has regarded that information about professional activities or income falls within the scope of private information.[1472]

In the light of the above, it is submitted that further clarification in the TSD regarding its interplay with privacy law and personal data law would have been welcome.[1473] In this respect, it is concluded that the commercialisation of private information should not fall under the scope of trade secrets protection as harmonised by the Directive, because it does not affect the possibility of competition of any sort between the parties. As regards potential conflicts between the data subject and the trade secret holder, it is argued that as a matter of principle the access rights of data holders should prevail and, only where a clear, identifiable and substantial prejudice to the trade secret holder exists, a limitation on access rights is justified. However, in practice such a scenario seems unlikely, as personal data mostly become valuable trade secrets after their inclusion in larger data sets. Consequently, the disclosure of individual data to the data subject would theoretically not affect the value of the data because this does not imply a disclosure to competitors and, in any event, the relative value of individual data is rather low.

---

1471 Chapter 3 § 5 C) II. 1.

1472 As analysed by Juliane Kokott and Christoph Sobotta, 'The distinction between privacy and data protection in the jurisprudence of the CJEU and the ECtHR' [2013] 3 IDPL 222-228; CJEU, Joined Cases C–92/09 and C–93/09 *Volker und Markus Schecke and Eifert* [2010] ECR I-11063, para 59.

1473 Tanya Aplin 2014 (n 384) 263.

## E) Adoption of reasonable steps

The TSD sets out that in order to qualify for protection, the trade secret holder must adopt "reasonable steps under the circumstances (...) to keep it secret", in line with the UTSA, the DTSA and the TRIPs Agreement. Consequently, the adoption of measures has become a necessary requirement for protection.[1474] Yet, the comparative analysis conducted above[1475] reveals that such a condition has not been demanded by courts either in England or in Germany. Notwithstanding this, in the former jurisdiction it has been positively assessed as a strong indicator that the information is of a confidential nature. Similarly, in Germany, case law notes that the trade secret holder must have the will to keep it secret ("*Geheimhaltungwillen*"). The threshold of this subjective requirement has been interpreted as rather low, as courts mostly understand that an explicit manifestation is not necessary, and it suffices that the will to keep the information secret can be inferred from "the nature of the secret information".[1476]

Under the harmonised legal framework, by virtue of Article 2(1)(c) of the TSD, the adoption of measures (or steps) by the trade secret holder has become a necessary condition to enforce valuable secret information against any act of misappropriation.

However, this has not been without criticism. As outlined in the context of the U.S. jurisdiction, a number of commentators have warned of the consequences of including the third prong within the definition of trade secrets and the difficulties in assessing the "reasonableness" of the steps adopted".[1477] In this respect, it has been noted that if national courts apply such a requirement in a very strict manner, an overinvestment in physical measures spurring an arms race among competitors may take place.[1478] After all, trade secrets protection is afforded to information because of its undisclosed nature and, therefore, it is assumed that the holders of information adopt ex ante appropriate steps to preserve it. The MPI Comments echoed these concerns and highlighted that the term "step" should be interpreted as covering both physical and legal measures, such as express legal agreements. However, this cannot be construed as demanding that explicit confidentiality agreements are concluded individually with each per-

1474 Thomas Hören and Reiner Münker 2018(b) (n1119) 151-152.
1475 Chapter 4 § 2 A) and B).
1476 Björn H. Kalbfus 2016 (n 1122)1011 with further references.
1477 Chapter 2 § 2 B) II. 3. b).
1478 Chapter 2 § 2 B) II. 3.

son that comes under an obligation of confidence.[1479] In particular, courts should consider whether an implicit obligation exists by virtue of the relationship between the parties (for instance, employer-employee).

One aspect that is often overlooked is that including such a requirement as a normative condition for protection demands not only that the original trade secret holder, but also any potential third parties to whom the information is conveyed under an obligation of confidence (such as R&D partners or licensees), take proactive steps to safeguard the secrecy of the information in a continuous manner. Crucially, the adoption of such measures in the digital world usually involves contracting very costly IT surveillance services, which have to be updated on a regular basis to keep track of the more recent state of the art developments.[1480]

In the light of the above, it is submitted that to avoid wasteful overinvestment in protective measures:

(i) It cannot be expected that the holder of information and the third parties to whom it is conveyed (such as licensors or R&D partners) adopt all possible measures. Indeed, in the enforcement, courts should be mindful that the obligation concerns the means, not the outcome;

(ii) The reasonableness of the steps adopted to protect secrecy will depend on the specific circumstances of each individual case, but courts will have to take into consideration the nature of the threat of disclosure, the value of the trade secret and the cost of the potential security mechanisms. Consequently, the more valuable the information for which protection is sought is, the more sophisticated and costly the measures adopted should be;

(iii) The adoption of measures includes both physical and legal measures. In the absence of an express agreement, courts should take into consideration whether an implied duty of confidence existed by virtue of the relationship between the parties (for instance, between the employee and the employer).

### F) A requirement of identification of the information concerned?

As a final note, it should be stressed that the EU legislature has not included within the definition or elsewhere in the TSD the requirement that in order to be protected information must be distinguishable from other

1479 Annette Kur, Reto Hilty and Roland Knaak 2014 (n 383) paras 19-20.
1480 Thomas Hören and Reiner Münker 2018(b) (n1119) para 15.

available information.[1481] Indeed, such a condition is expressly mentioned in the definition of know-how provided in Article 1(i)(iii) TTBER, where it is indicated that know-how for the purposes of licensing agreements must be "(iii) identified, that is to say, described in a sufficiently comprehensive manner so as to make it possible to verify that it fulfils the criteria of secrecy and substantiality". At first glance, such a condition may seem obvious, but in practice it has given rise to substantial litigation in England and the U.S.[1482] Upon closer examination, the identification of the information for which protection is sought is relevant to determine the substantive cause of action and the scope of the claim, and also in the context of licensing agreements. More importantly, it is essential to avoid abusive litigation.[1483] Consequently, it is submitted that in the enforcement of trade secrets, national courts should always demand that the plaintiff identify in a clear and precise manner the information concerned, even if it is not positively codified into law.

## *§ 4 Deconstructing secrecy*

### A) Evaluating the degree of secrecy required

The comparative law analysis conducted in the previous sections,[1484] together with the examination of the main principles that govern the protection of trade secrets under the U.S. and TRIPs legal framework (chapter 2) reveal that the standard of secrecy in all of the jurisdictions studied is a relative one. In effect, absolute (or perfect) secrecy would only occur if the holder of information did not share it with any third party. Such an approach goes against the interests of the holder in exploiting his commercial and technical secrets. The law of trade secrets developed in parallel with industrial expansion, and as such, responds to the modern needs of manufacturing processes, among which collaborative work and partnerships play a central role.[1485] Consequently, it is generally accepted that the revelation of confidential secrets to employees and other parties bound by

1481 Tanya Aplin and others 2012 (n 22) para 5.73.
1482 Charles Tait Graves and Brian D. Range, 'Identification of Trade Secret Claims in Litigation: Solutions for a Ubiquitous Dispute' [2006] 5 New JTechnology IP 68, 72.
1483 Tanya Aplin and others 2012 (n 22) para 5.75.
1484 Chapter 4 § 2.
1485 James Pooley 2002 (n 66) § 4.04[2] 25-26.

confidentiality agreements will not deprive them of their secret nature.[1486] To name some, this includes licensees, contractors, members of a joint venture and R&D partners.[1487] Otherwise, the holder's ability to profit economically from his secret would be substantially hindered. Thus, it appears that the rule of thumb is that secret information can be disclosed to those for whom knowing the information is essential and who are aware of its confidential nature.[1488]

At this point, it should be recalled[1489] that the relative secrecy yardstick has also been incorporated into patent law. Pursuant to Article 55(1)(a)EPC, information disclosed in confidence is not regarded as available on the relevant date for the purposes of assessing novelty.[1490] Furthermore, if the secrecy obligation is breached, a six-month limitation period to file for a patent is granted, after which the disclosure will be novelty destroying.[1491]

The upshot of the relative secrecy approach is that several competitors can develop the same information independently, without it theoretically becoming generally known. Yet, with time, the number of market participants within a given industry that are able to come up with that information may increase, thus eroding the trade secret and the commercial advantage that it provides, which may eventually become generally known and enter the public domain.[1492]

---

1486 James Pooley 2002 (n 66) § 4.04[2] 4-26; see further *In re Matter of Innovative Construction Systems, Inc.*, 793 F.2d 875, 883 (7th Cir. 1986) where it is argued that the proprietor of the information should not necessarily be the only one who knows the secret. Its knowledge by employees who were informed or should have known from the circumstances that the information in question was confidential does not render it publicly known; see also *A.L. Labs., Inc. v. Philips Roxane, Inc.*, 803 F.2d 378, 381 (8th Cir. 1986) noting that "the fact that information or data is developed in cooperation with other companies or joint ventures, or through a consultant or other party assisting in its development, does not mean that such information or data is not a trade secret. It may still be a confidential trade secret, provided that, in fact, it is known only to the ventures or consultants and is not generally known in the industry"; see also *Kewanee Oil Co.v. Bicron Corp.*, 416 U.S. 470, 475 (1974).

1487 Björn H. Kalbfus 2011 (n 1300) 70.

1488 James Pooley 2002 (n 66)§ 4.04[2] 26; *Köhler*/Bornkamm/Feddersen (n 835) § 17 Rdn 7a; Ingo Westerman, *Handbuch Know-how-Schutz* (C.H. Beck 2007) Kapitel 1, para 33.

1489 See chapter 1 § 3 A) I. 1.

1490 Lionel Bently 2012 (n 114) para 3.64.

1491 See G 3/98 [2001] OJ EPO 62.

1492 Roger M. Milgrim 2014 (n 160) § 1.07[2].

## B) The doctrine of ready ascertainability and the principle of inaccessibility

### I. Absence of a normative standard

One of the consequences of adopting a relative standard for secrecy is that information loses its secret nature somewhere between absolute secrecy and general knowledge, in line with Article 2(1)(a) TSD and 39(2)(a) TRIPs, which distinguishes between information "generally known or readily accessible". In turn, such a standard draws from the definition enshrined in the UTSA, where secret information is defined as "not being generally known (…) and not being readily ascertainable through proper means". The TSD and TRIPs refer to the term "accessibility", instead of "ascertainability", which underscores the factual nature that governs the appraisal of the secret nature of information.[1493] In addition, neither the Directive nor the TRIPs Agreement mention that the possibility of accessing information has to be carried out "by proper means". However, this is implied by the definition of unlawful acquisition provided for in Article 4(2)(b) TSD, which outlaws any unauthorised acquisition that is contrary to "honest commercial practices".

The secrecy-public domain scale is a broad one. At one end, "impenetrable secrets", namely those that cannot be devised even after a process of reverse engineering, remain concealed and confer great competitive advantage on their holders. At the other, information that is generally known draws the boundaries of the public domain.

However, in between, information that can only be obtained after a process of reverse engineering may signal the existence of an interest worthy of protection.[1494] The difficulty lies in defining when such information is accessible (or ascertainable)[1495] with so little or no effort so that it no

1493 The term 'accesible, adj' is defined in the Oxford English Dictionary as "able to be easily obtained or used" and "easily understood or appreciated", (*OED Online*, OUP June 2013) <https://en.oxforddictionaries.com/definition/accessible> accessed 15 September 2018; while 'ascertainble, adj' is defined by reference to ascertain as "find (something) out for certain; make sure of" <https://en.oxforddictionaries.com/definition/ascertain> (*OED Online*, OUP June 2013) accessed 15 September 2018 .

1494 James Pooley 2002 (n 66) § 4.04 4-41.

1495 Ascertainibility is the concept used in the UTSA, whereas Article 39(2)(a) TRIPs refers to accessibility; Nuno Pires de Carvalho 2008 (n 529) para 39.109 considers both terms to be synonyms.

longer merits protection. This is known as the "ready accessibility area" and refers to the obtention of information as such, not just the physical support in which it is embodied.[1496] However, establishing whether information is readily accessible is a complex matter and neither TRIPs nor the TSD provide guidance regarding such an assessment.[1497] Pooley attempts to shed further light on this question through a graph that depicts the accessibility (ascertainability) spectrum:[1498]

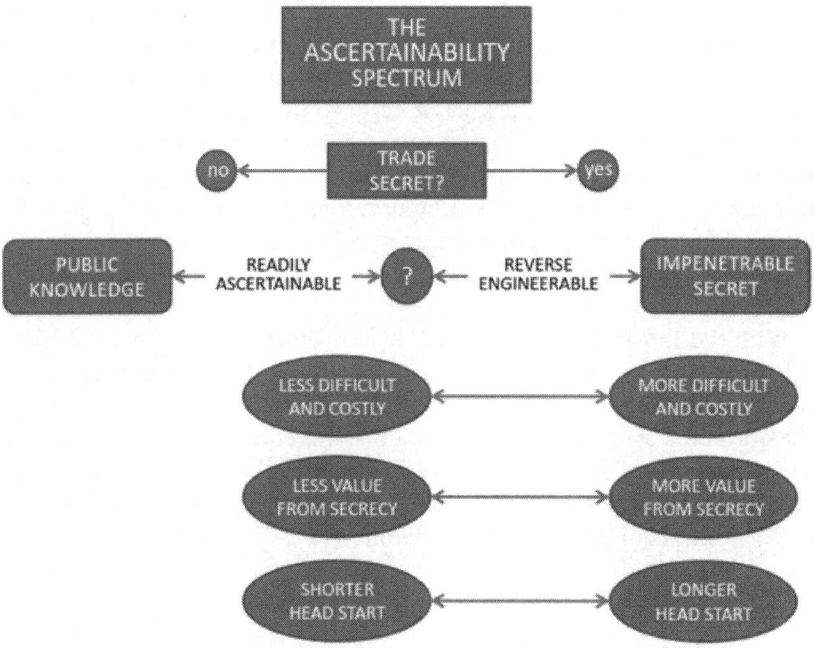


1496 Daniel Gervais 2012 (n 505) para 2.486.

1497 Gintare Surblyte, 'Enhancing TRIPS: Trade Secrets and Reverse Engineering' 725, 738 in Hanns Ullrich and others (eds), *TRIPS plus 20 – From Trade Rules to Market Principles* (Springer 2016) noting that according to the UTSA "information is readily ascertainable if it is available in trade journals, reference books, or published materials. Often, the nature of a product lends itself to being readily copied as soon as it is available on the market"; see further chapter 2 § 2 B) II. 1.

1498 Reproduced from James Pooley 2002 (n 66)§ 4.04[4] 4-42.

From the above, it can be appreciated that information that is publicly known or readily accessible does not merit protection.[1499] Thus, as the difficulty, time, labour and investment in accessing information increases, it becomes eligible for trade secrets protection. These factors signal that reverse engineering is a precondition to access information. From such a turning point onwards, the increasing difficulty further reveals that the information's economic value derived from its secrecy is higher and, in turn, the lead time advantage it confers on its holder is also longer.[1500] Such an appraisal is not merely of a theoretical nature; it is crucial to establish the duration of the injunctions in the event of misappropriation and the amount of damages. Yet again, defining the boundaries of when information is readily accessible and when it needs to undergo a process of reverse engineering is not a simple one. Nevertheless, in practice such a distinction is central. On the one hand, information that can only be obtained through reverse engineering will be protectable as a trade secret prior to undertaking such a process, whereas readily ascertainable information is part of the pool of information that any individual or company is free to use.[1501]

With the above structure in mind, it seems that the assessment of when information is readily accessible takes into account the investment (cost, time, effort, skill and labour) devoted to that end. In effect, in Germany, the prevailing standard is that of the time and effort invested in accessing the information ("*großen Zeit- oder Kostenaufwand*").[1502] In England, some cases state that information should only be regarded as confidential if it can only be acquired through the reproduction of the mental process that

1499 *Attorney General v Guardian Newspapers Ltd (No 2)* [1990] 1 AC 109 (HL), 282 stressing "the first limiting principle (which is rather an expression of the scope of the duty) is… that the principle of confidentiality only applies to information to the extent that it is confidential. In particular, once it has entered what is usually called the public domain (which means no more than that the information in question is so generally accessible that, in all circumstances, it cannot be regarded as confidential) hen, as a general rule, the principle of confidentiality can have no application to it".

1500 James Pooley 2002 (n 66)§ 4.04[4]4-42.

1501 James Pooley 2002 (n 66)§ 4.04[4]4-42.

1502 BGH GRUR, 2012, 1048 Rdn 21– *Movicol (Zulassungsantrag)*; *Ohly*/Sosnitza (n 813) § 17 Rdn 9; Henning Harte-Bavendamm, 'Wettbewerbsrechtliche Aspekte des Reverse Engineering von Computerprogrammen' [1990] GRUR 657, 660: "Nicht geheim ist, was von jedem Interessenten ohne größere Schwierigkeiten und Opfer in Erfahrung gebracht werden kann".

led to the creation of the resulting information,[1503] that is, if the information is the "product of the skill of the human brain".[1504]

Thus, when information can be acquired by third parties with an interest without incurring great labour, skill or cost, it is regarded as readily accessible and is automatically part of the public domain. Conversely, secrecy is preserved if interested third parties cannot acquire the information without such an investment.[1505] The test suggested by English authorities appears particularly pertinent: if information can only be obtained through the investment of intellectual skill it should be regarded as secret. Such a benchmark would in turn indicate that the obtention of information is subject to a process of reverse engineering through trial and error and consequently it merits protection. However, ultimately, such an appraisal is a matter of fact and degree, as it is not possible to find a normative standard that is applicable in all cases and allows to quantify secrecy.[1506]

Indeed, this reasoning has been questioned for its rather circular nature: information is deprived of its concealed nature when it is so generally accessible that it cannot be deemed secret neither in its parts nor in its entirety. However, its significance lies in the flexible nature of the assessment. In each individual case, courts have to consider whether the level of accessibility is such that in all conceivable circumstances a party bound by an alleged duty of confidentiality could not be required to fulfil such an obligation.[1507]

## II. Criticism

The inclusion of the "ready ascertainability" benchmark within the definition of secrecy has been questioned by several commentators. In particular Risch suggests that such a factor should have been included as a defence available in the event that the competitor had actually "readily ascertained

1503 *Saltman Engineering v Campell Engineering* [1948] 65 RPC 203 (CA), 215.

1504 *Ocular Sciences Ltd v Aspect Vision Care Ltd* [1997] RPC 289 (Ch), 375.

1505 BGH GRUR 1963, 367, 370 – *Industrieböden*; Rudolf Kraßer 1977 (n 1327) 179; see also conclusion of the Law Commission 1981 (n 327) 137 "Information should not be treated as being in the public domain where it is only accessible to the public after a significant contribution of labour, skill or money has been made".

1506 Lionel Bently and Brad Sherman 2014 (n 125) 530.

1507 Roger M. Toulson and Charles M. Phipps 2012 (n 326) para 3-109-3-111.

the information through independent means".[1508] He argues that the alleged misappropriator should always provide evidence that he in fact obtained the information from a different source, in line with the California Trade Secrets Law, where the "ready ascertainability" of the information is not included within the definition of a trade secret.[1509] Risch illustrates this by giving the example of a former employee who misappropriates a customer list and discloses it to his new employer (a competing firm).[1510] In this context, one could argue that the information is readily accessible on the Internet or telephone books and consequently it should not merit protection. According to Californian law, to avoid liability, the competing firm would always have to provide evidence that it conducted the search independently and gathered the relevant data without using the list compiled by the former employee. Risch understands that such an approach reduces the incentives of the owner to overprotect information and also redirects the incentives to research where it is cheaper to do so. At the same time, he suggests that it diminishes litigation costs and the associated uncertainty.[1511]

Similar arguments are raised by Unikel, who understands that the "not readily ascertainable by proper means" benchmark allows companies to deploy "improper short cuts" to obtain valuable information and avoid paying the cost of such labour, based on the mere fact that it was theoretically possible to obtain such knowledge through proper means.[1512]

Even though at first glance such propositions may seem sound, upon closer examination it seems unreasonable to demand that the defendant provide evidence that he in fact obtained the information independently. Such a reversal of the burden of proof seems unjustified and would allow for privatising information that is in fact already part of the public domain. Most importantly, it would spur abusive litigation. In addition, this is not supported by the TSD, which according to Article 11(1) TSD requires *the applicant* to prove in any case that: (i) the trade secret exists (i.e. the information complies with the requirements of protection); (ii) the applicant is the trade secret holder; and (iii) the trade secret has been ac-

1508 Michael Risch 2007 (n 15) 54.

1509 California Civil Code § 3426.1(d).

1510 This is largely based on the facts in *Abba Rubber Co. v. Seaquist*, 286 Cal.Rptr. 2d 518 (Cal. Ct. App. 1991).

1511 Michael Risch 2007 (n 15) 55.

1512 Robert Unikel, 'Bridging the "Trade Secret" Gap: Protecting "Confidential Information" Not Rising to the Level of Trade Secrets' [1998] 29 Loyola University Chicago LJ 841, 876.

quired unlawfully, is being unlawfully used or disclosed, or its unlawful acquisition, use or disclosure is imminent.[1513]

On a more general scale, the approach supported by Risch and Unikel assumes that the distinction between information generally known and easily accessible (or readily ascertainable) is a straightforward one. However, in practice it often appears to be a grey area. Indeed, even within the example proposed by Risch, it is possible to distinguish between different scenarios. On the one hand, if the disputed list concerns only the identification of all potential customers who appear in industry publications or catalogues, the content of the list should fall under the category of "readily accessible" information. In this case, it appears too burdensome to require the defendant to prove the independent generation of the information. By contrast, if the list includes references to the profitability or revenue generation gathered by the former employer over the course of his business with the investment of substantial labour and intellectual skill, the content of the list should be considered as not generally accessible (i.e. secret).[1514]

Against this background, Rowe[1515] draws a parallel with patent law and highlights that the "readily ascertainable" requirement includes "knowable but not yet generally known information" and therefore resembles the "in a printed publication" standard of patent law. According to the U.S. Supreme Court in *In re Leo M. Hall*, prior art includes "information that is sufficiently accessible, at least to the public interested in the art, so that such a one by examining the reference could make the claimed invention without further research or experimentation".[1516]

The above goes to show that it is not possible to extract a normative standard that allows for delineating with precision in all circumstances when information is readily accessible and when it maintains its secret nature. Such an assessment is to be conducted on a case-by-case basis. However, it is submitted that the deciding factor should be whether the investment of intellectual skill to gather or access the information concerned is necessary to gain actual knowledge of the "knowable information", that is, if the misappropriator has to use his rationality to gain knowledge of the information concerned, through a process of trial and error. Yet, such in-

1513 This is established as a maximum standard of protection, according to Article 1(1) TSD.

1514 James Pooley, 'The Uniform Trade Secrets Act: California Civil Code 3426' [1985] 1 Santa Clara High Technology LJ 193, 198 footnote 20.

1515 Elizabeth A. Rowe, 'Saving Trade Secret Disclosures on the Internet Through Sequential Preservation' [2007] 42 Wake Forest LR 1.

1516 *In re Leo M. Hall* 781 F.2d 897, 899 (Fed. Cir. 1986).

formation need not be novel, inventive or original.[1517] This should be viewed as an indicator that the information is secret and needs to be reverse engineered. For instance, in the case of perfumes, only a skilled chemist would be able to reconstruct the formula drawing from the analysis carried out by a gas-chromatograph spectrum after a process of trial and error to achieve the most similar results.

In practice, courts frequently rely on circumstantial evidence to assess whether information is readily apparent. This includes: (i) the steps adopted by the trade secret holder to protect the information, (ii) the difficulty for competitors to generate the same information, and (iii) the willingness of third parties to enter into licensing agreements to use the information.[1518]

In sum, the underlying reason behind the relative secrecy prong is that undisclosed information may confer upon its holder a competitive advantage and if a competitor wants to acquire it he must invest substantial time, effort and skill to do so.[1519] This is consistent with the incentives to innovate rationale: ultimately, the law of trade secrets protects investment in the creation of valuable information.[1520]

### C) Fencing secrecy by its negative dimension

Drawing on the previous analysis, it can be concluded that not every disclosure renders a trade secret generally known or readily accessible and thus unprotectable. In fact, the level of publication required to destroy secrecy depends on a number of factors. The most important of these are the kind of information concerned, the relevant part of the public who is interested in learning the information, the place, form and extent of publication and the amount of time during which the information is accessible.[1521] Indeed, due to the absence of a normative standard, it appears that secrecy is better conceptualised by reference to its negative dimension in order to establish its boundaries with the public domain. With this in

---

1517 This is developed further in Chapter 4 § 4 E), where the secrecy standard is compared to other IRPs normative standards

1518 *Rockwell Graphic Systems, Inc. v. DEV Industries, Inc.*, 925 F.2d 174, 179 (7th Cir. 1991).

1519 Rudolf Kraßer 1977 (n 1327) 179.

1520 As argued in chapter 1 § 2 B) I.

1521 Paul Lavery, 'Secrecy, springboards and the public domain' [1998] 20 EIPR 93, 95; Lionel Bently and Brad Sherman 2014 (n 125) 1148.

mind, the following section looks first into the "Third Party Doctrine" of trade secrets law in an attempt to conceptualise the different types of disclosures, drawing from Sandeen's proposal,[1522] while section II examines the effect of specific disclosures with the purpose of identifying the guiding principles that should govern the assessment of whether information still retains its secret nature.[1523] In particular, section II intends to address the challenges raised by digital disclosures.

## I. The "Third Party Doctrine" of trade secrets law and its limitations: conceptualising the different types disclosures

As outlined above,[1524] the relative secrecy requirement implies that it is possible that several persons can have access to the same information without it losing its secret nature. However, the trade secret holder must be careful when sharing such information, particularly outside the sphere of his business. According to the so-called "third-party doctrine", as conceptualised in the U.S., the mere imparting of a trade secret by its holder does not give rise to a duty of confidentiality. "It must be found in some other source of law".[1525] Indeed, pursuant to the prevailing case law in the U.S., a duty of confidentiality usually arises as a result of one of the following four situations: "(1) an express agreement; (2) an agreement implied-in-fact; (3) an agreement implied-at-law (a "quasi-contract"); or (4) a duty imposed by law either as specified in a statute (attorney-client privilege) or based upon commercial law principles".[1526] Similar considerations apply in England under the breach of confidence action, which requires that the information is "imparted in circumstances giving rise to an obligation of confidence".[1527] Likewise, in Germany, the UWG only affords protection against the unlawful acquisition, use and disclosure of information that is

1522 Sharon K. Sandeen, 'Lost in the Cloud: Information Flows and the Implications of Cloud Computing for Trade Secrets Protection' [2014] 19 Virginia JL & Technology 2.

1523 This section follows the structure implemented by James Pooley 2002 (n 66) § 4.04[2] 26 with some minor variations regarding Internet disclosures, cloud computing and the use of known information for an unkown use.

1524 See chapter 4 § 4 A).

1525 Sharon K. Sandeen 2014 (1522) 50.

1526 Sharon K. Sandeen 2014 (1522) 50.

1527 For a detailed overview of the circumstances under which an obligation of confidence arises, see chapter 3 § 3 C) II. 2.

kept secret as a result of the will of the owner.[1528] Consequently, Sandeen suggests that the salient issue in conceptualising secrecy is to identify whether sharing information with third parties that are under no confidentiality obligation automatically deprives it of its secret nature.[1529] This is particularly relevant in the digital age, as information is becoming increasingly vulnerable.

Against this background the author notes that the term "disclosure" is used in the law of trade secrets with a two-fold meaning: (i) as one of the conducts under which liability arises, together with acquisition and use,[1530] and (ii) as one of the acts that precludes trade secrets protection (secrecy-destroying acts), which can be carried out by the holder of the information, a misappropriator or any third party.[1531] In this context, she notes that the disclosure test is not just a de facto test; it has legal implications and therefore it is possible to conceptualise six types of secrecy-destroying disclosures, which are defined in narrow or broader terms based on the actors and circumstances involved.

- Type I disclosure encompasses the dissemination of information by a misappropriator. In such a context, Sandeen holds that courts should apply a narrow definition of disclosure in order to allow the trade secret owner to seek redress and prevent further dissemination of the information. The author further notes that courts in the U.S. are reluctant to consider the dissemination of information to a limited number of third parties that results from a misappropriation act as forfeiting trade secrets protection, so long as the information does not become generally known.[1532]
- Type II disclosures relate to accidental disclosures. According to the author, a narrow application of the term disclosure is supported by U.S. courts and the UTSA, by virtue of which the liability of third parties is established provided that they had knowledge of the accidental nature of the disclosure.[1533]
- Type III disclosures examine whether the information was "generally known" at the time that the misappropriation took place. This category

1528 Chapter 4 § 2 A) II. 4.
1529 Sharon K. Sandeen 2014 (1522) 50.
1530 See Article 4(3) TSD.
1531 Sharon K. Sandeen 2014 (1522) 65.
1532 Sharon K. Sandeen 2014 (1522) 65.
1533 Sharon K. Sandeen 2014 (1522) 66.

is conceptually broader than Type I and Type II, because there is no legal basis to restrict the use of what is "generally known".[1534]

- Type IV disclosures refer to "readily ascertainable" information that is excluded from the scope of protection of trade secrets and, just like Type III disclosures, these are conceptually broader than Type I and Type II.
- Type V disclosures encompasses information acquired by third parties through lawful means, such as reverse engineering and independent creations. In order to prevent overlaps with the patent system, Sandeen suggests that these types of disclosures are conceptually broader than the types of disclosures under sections I and II above.[1535]
- Type VI disclosures encompass "owner initiated disclosures" and accordingly should be conceptualised in the broadest sense, because in such a case the trade secret holder did not take the necessary steps to protect the information.[1536]

The analytical framework proposed by Sandeen provides an insightful scrutiny of the different categories of disclosures. However, it does not attach any legal consequences to the conceptualisation of disclosures as "broad", "broader", and "broadest", and, as a result, it does not create a normative standard that allows for delineating in a precise manner the contours of secrecy and the public domain. Indeed, the author expressly acknowledges that such an analytical model provides no insight into how to define disclosures with respect to trade secrets stored in the cloud.[1537] After all, as has already been argued, such an analysis is largely factually driven.

In the light of the shortcomings of the methodology proposed by Sandeen, this dissertation takes a case-oriented approach and examines specific types of disclosures and how case law in different jurisdictions has assessed their effects. Such an analysis ultimately intends to extract the guiding principles that may assist courts in determining whether a specific piece of information is part of the public domain in view of the harmonisation goals pursued by the TSD.

---

1534 Sharon K. Sandeen 2014 (1522) 67.
1535 Sharon K. Sandeen 2014 (1522) 67.
Sharon K. Sandeen 2014 (1522) 69-70.
1536 Sharon K. Sandeen 2014 (1522) 70.
1537 Sharon K. Sandeen 2014 (1522) 78-79.

## II. Effects of the disclosure

### 1. Disclosure in a patent application or specification

#### a) England as an example case

Pursuant to Article 93 EPC, European Patent applications should be published at the latest eighteen months after the date of filing or before that day at the request of the applicant. Upon publication, the trade secrets described therein lose their confidential nature. This has been confirmed by both the Federal Supreme Court in Germany[1538] and the House of Lords in England,[1539] and it is also a well-established principle under U.S. Law.[1540] Notwithstanding this, it is also a general principle that secrets related to an invention that are not disclosed in the application shall remain secret.

The controversies that may arise in this context are best illustrated in the English case *Mustad&Son v Dosen and another*.[1541] There, the plaintiffs sought to restrain the defendant, one of their former employees, from communicating confidential information regarding the process of manufacturing a machine for the production of fishhooks. Shortly after the initiation of the proceedings, the plaintiffs filed for a patent application, which in essence covered the confidential information. Upon appeal, the House of Lords ruled that regardless of the validity of the patent, "the secret, as a secret had ceased to exist"[1542] as the patent specification had been published and therefore the plaintiffs were not entitled to obtain any injunction restraining the defendants from using what was "common knowledge". Remarkably, the court also accepted that in abstract it could be possible to protect ancillary secrets that had not been disclosed in the specification, even though in the present case the plaintiff had failed to provide evidence of the existence of such information.[1543]

Another highly contested issue is whether the publication of a foreign patent application or specification may affect the secret nature of information that was independently developed by the trade secret holder. In

1538 BGH GRUR 1975, 206, 208 – *Kunststoffschaum-Bahnen*.
1539 *Mustad v Son v Dosen and another* [1964] 1 WRL 109 (HL), 111.
1540 *Conmar Products Corp. v. Universal Slide Fastener Co.*, 172 F.2d 150, 155–156 (2d Cir.1949).
1541 *Mustad v Son v Dosen and another* [1964] 1 WRL 109 (HL), 111.
1542 *Mustad v Son v Dosen and another* [1964] 1 WRL 109 (HL), 111.
1543 *Mustad v Son v Dosen and another* [1964] 1 WRL 109 (HL), 111.

*Franchi v Franchi,*[1544] the High Court of Justice of England and Wales concluded that the publication of a patent specification in Belgium also rendered the information in the public domain in England, as patent attorneys regularly reviewed foreign publications.[1545] Conversely, in Germany the Federal Supreme Court reached a different conclusion in 1962 in the *Kieselsäure* decision, in which the validity of a licensing agreement was confirmed, despite the fact that the licensed secret process was the object of a U.S. patent published sometime after the agreement was concluded.[1546]

### b) Guiding principles

In the light of the above, it is submitted that:

(i) The secrets enshrined in a patent specification are disclosed upon publication, but ancillary secrets that can only be devised with substantial intellectual skill retain their secret nature.

(ii) The withdrawal of an application prior to the eighteen months that precede the publication prevents the invention from entering the public domain. In such a case, secrecy is preserved.[1547]

(iii) Unlike the novelty prong in patent law, secrecy is not an absolute standard. However, published foreign patent applications and specifications will most likely be deemed secrecy destroying.[1548] Indeed, nowadays most patent offices have public databases available online, which allow any third party to access the published applications and specifications at no cost. In addition, these can be easily translated by automatic translation tools, allowing the recipient to get a very accurate insight into their content. During the last decade, the accessibility of obscure sources through the Internet has been widely discussed. Due to its practical importance, this topic is examined in greater detail in section 4 below.

---

1544 *Franchi v Franchi* [1967] RPC 149 (Ch).

1545 *Franchi v Franchi* [1967] RPC 149 (Ch).

1546 BGH GRUR 1962, 207, 211 – *Kieselsäure.*

1547 Pursuant to article 87(4) EPC; see furthermore Guidelines for Examination in the EPO. Part E. Chapter VIII. Section 8.1.

1548 *Ohly*/Sosnitza (n 813) § 17 Rdn 9.

## 2. Disclosure to the state and its authorities

In the XXI century, the smooth functioning of democratic states requires private companies and individuals to disclose vast amounts of data in the interests of transparency, safety and environmental protection. Both in the acquis communautaire and the national legal regimes a myriad of statutes have been enacted compelling undertakings to reveal a substantial amount of information (including trade secrets) to public authorities. This is regarded as an essential part of the democratic process.[1549] However, in the context of trade secrets, this leads to the question of whether such information is legally protected against subsequent unauthorised use or disclosure. Indeed, representatives of the perfume industry identified the disclosure of secret information to the state and its agencies as one of the main factors underlying the increasing leakage of trade secrets. This was also one of the main concerns raised by stakeholders during the negotiation of the TSD.[1550] To illustrate the legal issues that arise as a result of such disclosures, the English jurisdiction is taken as an example case of the conflicting interests that public authorities need to balance (section a). Next, the relevant provisions within the acquis communautaire (section b) and their intersection with the TSD are studied (section c). Finally, a number of guiding principles are formulated (section d). From the outset, it should be noted that this is a particularly complex topic that touches upon numerous fields of law, such as public law and data protection law. Consequently, this study is confined to the study of the effects of public bodies' disclosures from the angle of trade secrets protection.

### a) England as an example case

In England, commentators and case law seem to agree on the fact that an obligation of confidence may arise with regard to information disclosed by individuals or companies to state agencies when it is conveyed on a voluntary basis (for example in connection to public procurement);[1551] or a compulsory basis (such as in the course of a competition or a police investiga-

1549 Tanya Aplin and others 2012 (n 22) para 13.164.
1550 See chapter 5 § 4 B) II.
1551 John Hull 1998 (1016) paras 4.105-4.109

tion),[1552] and also in order to meet certain statutory conditions.[1553] The latter case usually involves the disclosure of sensitive information to a state authority to support the application to obtain permission to carry something out, such as the marketing of a cosmetic product or a new drug.[1554] The scope of the obligation of confidence in the latter scenario was discussed in *Re Smith Kline French Laboratories Ltd*[1555] where the plaintiff, a pharmaceutical company, disclosed secret information to the Department of Health in order to obtain marketing authorisation for one of its drugs in the UK. After some time, it came to the attention of the plaintiff that the Department of Health intended to use the data submitted in order to assess the applications of its competitors. Consequently, the plaintiff brought legal action based on a breach of confidence. After a number of appeals, the House of Lords ruled that the Department of Health could make use of the information in the public interest to perform its tasks.[1556] However, the court added that disclosures to third parties would result in a breach of confidence.[1557]

The above goes to show that if no express obligation of confidence between the disclosing party and the recipient authority exists, its scope should be inferred from the circumstances of the case. In particular, in *Re Smith Kline French Laboratories Ltd*[1558] the House of Lords argued that special attention should be paid to the role and purposes of the recipient authority.[1559] Hence, it was concluded that the Department of Health was entitled to use the data to perform any of "its functions" as per the relevant legislation.[1560]

In addition, confidentiality obligations have also often been tempered by the public interest defence, mostly with regard to safety and health, which may override any inter partes obligations of confidence.[1561] More

1552 This was the case in *Marcel v Commission of Police of the Metropolis* [1992] Ch 225 (CA).
1553 Tanya Aplin and others 2012 (n 22) para 13.164.
1554 John Hull 1998 (1016) paras 4.105- 4.109.
1555 *Re Smith Kline & French Laboratories Ltd* [1990] 1 AC 64 (HL).
1556 *Re Smith Kline & French Laboratories Ltd* [1990] 1 AC 64 (HL), 98E.
1557 *Re Smith Kline & French Laboratories Ltd* [1990] 1 AC 64 (HL), 98E.
1558 *Re Smith Kline & French Laboratories Ltd* [1990] 1 AC 64 (HL).
1559 Tanya Aplin and others 2012 (n 22) para 13.30.
1560 *Re Smith Kline & French Laboratories Ltd* [1990] 1 AC 64 (HL), 82.
1561 Tanya Aplin and others 2012 (n 22) para 13.37.

generally, no breach of confidence exists if the disclosure of information is mandated (or envisaged) in a statute or by a court order.[1562]

As a corollary of the public interest defence and in order to ensure transparency within democratic societies, states and their agencies are frequently under an obligation to disclose information under their control to third parties. This often conflicts with the confidentiality obligations imposed by law or agreed upon contractually between the receiving authority and the party that submits the information.[1563] Such a tension arises mostly with regard to the access rights of the data subject with respect to his personal data (according to the applicable data protection legislation) and the right of citizens to access information under the control of the state. Providing an analysis of the former case exceeds the scope of the present research. Consequently, the remainder of this section looks into the effects on trade secrets protection in the latter case, and particularly under the legal framework created by the Freedom of Information Act.[1564]

The Freedom of Information Act came into force on 1 January 2005 and, in essence, it introduced for the first time a statutory right to access information held by public authorities.[1565] The right covers all information, irrespective of its format and when it was submitted or created.[1566] As a result, public authorities are compelled to publish the information that they hold if requested to do by any third party (individuals or legal entities). Failure to comply with such a request within twenty days from the day of receipt[1567] may be appealed in the first instance before the Information Commissioner[1568] and in the second instance before the Information Tribunal.[1569]

However, the Act provides for a number of exemptions to the disclosure of information in order to ensure the protection of other potential conflicting interests. These exemptions are regulated in Part II of the Act and can be grouped into four main areas: (i) information that is already available to the third party; (ii) information on matters of public importance

1562 John Hull 1998 (1016) paras 4.109 - 4.101.

1563 Tanya Aplin and others 2012 (n 22) para 13.103.

1564 Freedom of Information Act 2000 (FOIA).

1565 Karen McCullagh, 'A tangled web of access to information: reflections on R (on the application of Evans) and another v Her Majesty's Attorney General' [2015] 21 European J of Current Legal Issues.

1566 Ibid.

1567 FOIA 2000, s 10.

1568 FOIA 2000, s 18.

1569 FOIA 2000, s 57.

(such a state defence or economic welfare); (iii) information that may prejudice private interests (as would be the case of trade secrets); and (iv) information prohibited by statute.[1570] The third category is of particular relevance for the purposes of the present research as it includes breach of confidence (s 41) and trade secrets and commercial prejudice (s 43).

The exemption set out in s 41 FOIA provides that public authorities shall not publish the information requested if this would result in a breach of confidence. More specifically, the literal wording of the provision precludes the disclosure of information if:

(a) it was obtained by the public authority from any other person (including another public authority), and
(b) the disclosure of the information to the public (otherwise than under this Act) by the public authority holding it would constitute a breach of confidence actionable by that or any other person.[1571]

The breach of confidence exemption is absolute in nature, which means that if it is applicable, the competent authorities shall not take into account other public interests.[1572] Notwithstanding this, courts have interpreted the requirement of "obtention" as not including information disclosed in the context of contractual relationships, such as in the case of public procurement.[1573] Consequently, the disclosure of sensitive data in contracts that involve public authorities shall be subsumed under the exemption set out in s 43 FOIA (commercial interest).[1574]

The commercial interest exemption provides a qualified exception regarding the publication of two categories of information: (i) trade secrets and (ii) information, the disclosure of which would "prejudice the commercial interests of any person (including the public authority holding it)".[1575] Pursuant to the Information Tribunal the term treade secret includes "something technical, unique and achieved with a degree of diffi-

1570 Tanya Aplin and others 2012 (n 22) para 13.115.

1571 FOIA 2000, s 41.

1572 Tanya Aplin and others 2012 (n 22) para 13.130.

1573 John Macdonald and Ross Crail, *John Macdonald on the Law of Freedom of Information* (3rd edn, OUP 2016) para 5.94.

1574 Notwithstanding this, John Macdonald and Ross Crail, *John Macdonald on the Law of Freedom of Information* (3rd edn, OUP 2016) para 5.408 note that presumably the majority of the information that would hinder commercial interests will also be regarded as confidential information and therefore, be subject to the exemption established in s 41 FOIA 2000, which is absolute in nature.

1575 FOIA 2010, s 43; John Macdonald and Ross Crail, *John Macdonald on the Law of Freedom of Information* (3rd edn, OUP 2016) para 5.398

culty and investment".[1576] It refers to the "highest level of secrecy".[1577] By contrast, the second category refers to disclosures that would create a commercial prejudice of any sort, including an increase in the price of a service provided to a public authority or the commercial reputation of a company.[1578] In cases where the nature of the specific piece of information is not clear, the Information Tribunal has subsumed it under the commercial interest category as "commercially sensitive" information.[1579]

However, due to the qualified nature of the exemption under s 43 FOIA, even if the requested information falls into one of the two categories referred to in the provision, the public authorities have to consider whether "the public interest in maintaining the exemption outweighs the public interest in disclosing the information", as per section 2(2)(b) FOIA. In particular, the value of the secret and the likelihood that the publication of the information will cause commercial prejudice are weighed against the public interest in transparency.[1580] In *DWP v IC*,[1581] a case concerning the disclosure of a financial model of a Government IT service provider, the Information Tribunal held that such information constituted a trade secret and that "if the information is a trade secret there is a strong public interest in protecting such a secret" because disclosure will not only negatively affect the holder's business, but will also provide competitors with an unfair commercial advantage.[1582]

In the light of the foregoing, it appears that according to the FOIA, in the case of trade secrets and other commercial information, public authorities are always requested to balance the conflicting interests before publishing the information requested.[1583] In particular, in the case of trade secrets, courts seem to recognise a strong public interest in their protection. However, such a principle is not uniformly acknowledged or applied across the

1576 *Department of Health v Information Commissioner* (EA/2008/0018, 18 November 2018) [52].
1577 *Department of Health v Information Commissioner* (EA/2008/0018, 18 November 2018) [53].
1578 Tanya Aplin and others 2012 (n 22) para 13.132.
1579 *Department of Health v Information Commissioner*, (EA/2008/0018, 18 November 2018) [54].
1580 Tanya Aplin and others 2012 (n 22) para 13.137.
1581 *DWP v IC* (EA/2010/0073, 20 September 2010).
1582 *DWP v IC* (EA/2010/0073, 20 September 2010) [84].
1583 John Macdonald and Ross Crail, *John Macdonald on the Law of Freedom of Information* (3rd edn, OUP 2016) para 16.13.

myriad of statutes that regulate the disclosure of information held by public authorities to third parties.[1584]

b) Confidentiality in the acquis communautaire and the right of access to documents

The principle of confidentiality has been incorporated into the acquis communautaire by virtue of Article 339 TFEU, which provides that:

> The members of the institutions of the Union, the members of committees, and the officials and other servants of the Union shall be required, even after their duties have ceased, not to disclose information of the kind covered by the obligation of *professional secrecy*, in particular information about *undertakings*, their *business relations* or their *cost components* (emphasis added).

It is also embedded in the ChFREU, which enshrines the principles of respect for private life (Article 7 ChFREU) and protection of personal data (Article 8 ChFREU).

In turn, such a principle has been included in a number of legal provisions of secondary EU law. For instance, in the context of competition investigations, Article 28(2) of Regulation 1/2003[1585] notes that the national and EU Competition authorities and their employees shall not disclose information "covered by the obligation of professional secrecy".

However, the observance of confidentiality is not absolute, but is subject to numerous statutory limitations that mostly follow an unsystematic approach.[1586] Just as in the UK, in the EU the general principle of confidentiality has been tempered by the right of access to documents that it is also part of the acquis communautaire, pursuant to Article 42 ChFREU and Article 15(3) TFEU. A particularly notable manifestation of this principle is Regulation 1049/2001 regarding public access to European Parliament, Council and Commission documents,[1587] which was adopted in order to

1584 Tanya Aplin and others 2012 (n 22) para 13.137.

1585 Council Regulation (EC) No 1/2003 of 16 December 2002 on the implementation of the rules on competition laid down in Articles 81 and 82 of the Treaty [2003] OJ L1/1.

1586 Tanya Aplin and others 2012 (n 22) para 13.1150.

1587 Regulation of the European Parliament and of the Council (EC) 1049/2001 of 30 May 2001 regarding public access to European Parliament, Council and Commission documents [2001] OJ L145/43 (Regulation 1049/2001).

lay down the legal framework that governs the right to access documents disclosed to the Commission, the European Parliament and the Council of the EU and to safeguard transparency during the decision-making processes of these institutions, in line with the objectives pursued by the FOIA in England.[1588]

In particular, Article 4 of Regulation 1049/2001 provides that the exercise of the right of access is subject to a number of exceptions. Specifically, pursuant to paragraph 1 of Article 4(2) of Regulation 1049/2001, access can be rejected if it would weaken the protection of "commercial interests of a natural or legal person, including intellectual property". The extent to which the reference to intellectual property encompasses trade secrets is uncertain, as examined above.[1589] However, it is undisputed that trade secrets fall under the scope of protected "commercial interests".[1590] This was the approach adopted by the CJEU in the *European Commission v Agrofert Holding a.s* case,[1591] where the court upheld a decision by the Commission in which access to a number of documents disclosed by the notifying parties during the course of a merger control process was denied to a third party ("Agrofert") that had requested it. In its legal reasoning, the Commission invoked paragraph 1 of Article 4(2) of Regulation 1049/2001 to deny access because the information requested was "commercially sensitive information relating to the commercial strategies of the notifying parties, their sales volumes, their market shares or customer relations", but no reference to trade secrets was made.[1592] Upon appeal, the CJEU held that the interpretation of paragraphs 1 and 3 of Article 4(2) established a general presumption "that the disclosure of the documents concerned undermines, in principle, the protection of the commercial interests of the undertakings involved in the merger and also the protection of the purpose of investigations relating to the control proceedings".[1593]

---

1588 Case C–404-10 P *Lagardère SCA v Éditions Odile Jacob SAS* (CJEU, 29 June 2012) para 109; John Macdonald and Ross Crail, *Macdonald on the Law of Freedom of Information* (3rd edn, OUP 2016) para 11.14.

1589 See chapter 1 § 3 B) I. 4.

1590 Tanya Aplin and others 2012 (n 22) para 13.171.

1591 Case C–477/10 P *European Commission v Agrofert Holding a.s.* (CJEU, 28 June 2012).

1592 Case C–477/10 P *European Commission v Agrofert Holding a.s.* (CJEU, 28 June 2012) para 10.

1593 Case C–477/10 P *European Commission v Agrofert Holding a.s.* (CJEU, 28 June 2012) para 64.

However, in a more recent decision concerning the disclosure of the clinical study report in the Marketing Authorisation application dossier for a medicinal product (Translanta) by the European Medicines Agency, the GCEU noted that clinical study reports do not enjoy a general presumption of confidentiality based on the implicit ground that they are "as a matter of principle and in their entirety, clearly covered by the exception relating to the protection of commercial interests of (market authorisation applicants)".[1594] The GCEU therefore held that in the assessment of whether the exception set out in the first indent of Article 4(2) of Regulation 1049/2001 may prevent the disclosure of information, the European Medicines Agency must conduct "a concrete, individual examination of each document in the application file for (Marketing Authorisation)".[1595] Indeed, the existence of such a general presumption was also denied by the GCEU with regard to a report on chemical safety submitted to the European Chemical Agency, which was requested by a competitor, also on the basis of Regulation 1049/2001.[1596]

### c) Protection of competing interests in the TSD

The competing interest between the protection of valuable commercial information held by a company and the general interest in transparency and access to documents outlined in the previous sections is also apparent in a number of provisions of the TSD. On the one hand, Article 1(2)(b) stipulates that the TSD should not affect those provisions of national and EU Law that mandate the disclosure of information (including trade secrets) to the general public or to public, administrative or judicial authorities. In this regard, Recital 11 specifically indicates that the provisions of the TSD should not affect the application of EU and national rules that demand the

1594 Case T–718/15 *PTC Therapeutics International Ltd v EMEA* (GCEU, 5 February 2018) para 53.

1595 Case T–718/15 *PTC Therapeutics International Ltd v EMEA* (GCEU, 5 February 2018) para 53.

1596 Case T–189/14 *Deza v ECHA* (GCEU, 13 January 2017) para 40: "No general presumption can therefore be inferred from the provisions of Regulation No 1907/2006. It cannot therefore be accepted that, in the context of an authorisation procedure provided for by Regulation No 1907/2006, the documents communicated to the ECHA are to be regarded as being, in their entirety, clearly covered by the exception relating to the protection of the commercial interests of applicants for authorisation".

disclosure of trade secrets to public authorities and that allow or require any subsequent disclosure and, in particular, the access to document rights set out in Regulation 1049/2001. Similarly, Article 1(2)(c) sets forth that the rules laid down in the TSD should not interfere with other national or Union law provisions that mandate or allow the disclosure of any information about businesses to public institutions, bodies and authorities in accordance with national or EU law.[1597] More generally, Article 3(2) stipulates that when the acquisition, use or disclosure of a trade secret is laid down either in national or union law provisions, it should be deemed lawful. In contrast, Recital 18 indicates that this should not be to the detriment of the obligation of confidentiality imposed on the acquirer or recipient of the information, either by national or by EU law. Most notably, this recital specifies that the Directive does not exonerate public authorities from obligations of confidence with regard to information submitted by the trade secret holder and mentions, as an example, the information acquired by contracting authorities in the course of public procurement procedures.[1598]

#### d) Guiding principles

In the light of the foregoing analysis, identifying the effect of disclosures compelled by public authorities is not straightforward, as an array of interests and legal provisions of constitutional, public and private law come into play. Notwithstanding this, the following interpretive principles are submitted:

(i) The "commercial interests (...) including intellectual property" exemption established in Article 4(2) of Regulation 1049/2001 should be deemed to include trade secrets, pursuant to the definition stipulated in Article 2(1) TSD, which is now part of the acquis communautaire.

(ii) In line with the principles that inform the practice of the CJEU with regard to the first indent of Article 4(2) of Regulation 1049/2001, the disclosure of trade secrets submitted to public authorities that is mandated or allowed by national or EU legislation and that may be subject to limitations on the basis of a commercial interest or an intellectual property right of the holder, as set out in the relevant statute, should be assessed on a case-by-case basis, in accordance with the specific cir-

1597 See Recital 11 TSD.
1598 See Recital 18 TSD.

cumstances of the case. In particular, if the disclosure of the information could cause irreparable harm to the holder, public authorities should consider whether providing partial disclosures or redacted versions could also serve public transparency purposes and protect the business interest of the parties. In such a context, it is submitted that the trade secrets holders should always be notified of the request for information by the third party or its publication and be given an opportunity to present the pertinent arguments.

(iii) If the relevant statutes set out an obligation of confidence on a national or EU authority or public body that is not observed, the said authority or public body shall be deemed liable for unauthorised use or disclosure of a trade secret. If no such obligation is stipulated, the acquisition, use and disclosure of the trade secret mandated or allowed by EU law should be considered lawful, in accordance with Article 3(2) TSD.

In sum, due to the overlap of provisions and legal interests that come into play, it is likely that further guidance from the CJEU will be sought, in line with the series of decisions rendered by the CJEU with respect to the first indent of Article 4(2) of Regulation 1049/2001.

### 3. Marketing of a product in which the trade secret is embodied

In the course of misappropriation proceedings, defendants frequently counter-claim that no such misappropriation existed, because the information lacked the necessary quality of confidence. Most frequently, they argue that by placing a product on the open market in which the trade secret was embodied, the plaintiff made it generally available, thereby preventing trade secrets protection. This section intends to map out the general principles that govern such an appraisal following the methodology of comparative law. The general proposition in the U.S. and Germany[1599] is that marketing a product, as such, does not necessarily reveal all of the trade secrets associated with it. In England, commentators and case law have not provided a uniform solution, but the prevailing view is that a certain amount of disclosure is permitted.[1600] Each of these jurisdictions is analysed in turn.

1599 Rudolf Kraßer 1970 (n 831) 590; RGZ 1935 149, 329, 330 – *Stiefeleisenpresse*.

1600 The English case law is stricter than the German and U.S. jurisprudence on this topic; as examined in chapter 6 § 2 B) below dealing with reverse engineering; for an analysis of the English approach see Tanya Aplin, 'Reverse Engi-

### a) U.S.

In the U.S., two of the main legislative sources for trade secrets protection, namely the UTSA and the Restatement (Third) of Unfair Competition, note that the marketing of a product in which a trade secret is embodied does not automatically deprive the information of its concealed nature, as long as substantial investment, time and effort are necessary to obtain it[1601] and the recipient is under no obligation of confidence.[1602] This signals that the information is subject to a process of reverse engineering and therefore it is not generally known or readily ascertainable.

Such a proposition has been restated in numerous decisions. For instance, as early as 1951, the Supreme Court of Texas held that the idea of a "metallic fishing rod that would collapse into once piece and thus serve as a walking stick"[1603] was based on "obvious" mechanical principles and could be easily imitated by "any reasonably experienced machinist that might see one for the first time or purchase it on the open market". Consequently, the Supreme Court of Texas ruled that the exhibition of the device to the public by "advertisement or sale" prevented trade secrets protection.[1604] Similarly, in 1964, the Court of Civil Appeals of Texas in El Paso held that an advertisement plan consisting of bonus cards with money amounts printed around the periphery of the card, which had been prepared by an advertising agency for the sole purpose of promoting sales in the grocery store, could not be considered a trade secret. In this respect, the court noted that the idea of punch cards was not new, as in fact similar cards were being used at the time of the alleged misappropriation in other

---

neering and Commercial Secrets' [2013] 66 Current Legal Problems 341, 347-348; *Franchi v Franchi* [1967] RPC 149 (Ch), 152.

1601 See UTSA Comment § 1: "Often, the nature of a product lends itself to being readily copied as soon as it is available on the market. On the other hand, if reverse engineering is lengthy and expensive, a person who discovers the trade secret through reverse engineering can have a trade secret in the information obtained from reverse engineering"; Restatement (Third) of Unfair Competition §39 (Am. Law Inst. 1995) comment f, Reporter's Note: "Public sale of a product does not preclude continued protection against the improper acquisition or use of information that it is difficult, costly, or time-consuming to extract through reverse engineering"; James Pooley 2002 (n 66) § 4.04 [3]4-34, 4-35.

1602 Gale R. Peterson, 'Trade Secrets in an Information Age' [1995] 32 Houston LR 385, 450.

1603 *Wissman v. Boucher*, 240 S.W.2d 278, 278 (Tex. 1951).

1604 *Wissman v. Boucher*, 240 S.W.2d 278, 278 (Tex. 1951).

cities or states. Hence, the court concluded that the cards themselves were "self-explanatory on the face".[1605]

By contrast, U.S. courts held that the formula of a jet ink acquired by an employee during the course of his employment relationship was secret, despite the fact that the jet ink had been marketed for some time before the alleged misappropriation took place. According to the deciding court, the specific composition of the jet ink was not known to others in the industry and steps had been taken to preserve its confidential nature (through employment agreements). In addition, the value and the time and effort spent in developing the jet ink formula was undisputed and, consequently, it was noted that "duplication was not so simple as to deprive (the jet ink) of trade secret status".[1606] Nevertheless, it was further suggested that "a few sophisticated competitors may have had the resources to analyse and reproduce the series 400 inks by fair means" but this did not protect the defendant, who was found liable for trade secret misappropriation.[1607] Similar principles were restated in another case decided by the Appellate Court of Illinois, where loss of secrecy was linked to the possibility of duplicating the marketed products without "time consuming and expensive analysis of products in the public domain".[1608] In *Q-CO Industries, INC. v. Hoffman*, the New York Southern District Court ruled that computer programs were eligible for trade secrets protection.[1609] In particular, the court noted that the source code of the alleged misappropriated software was not accessible to the public, because the version commercially sold was copy protected, thereby preventing users from accessing it.[1610] In this regard, the court noted that, "secrecy will not be destroyed by the wide distribution of computer programs if they are distributed in object form only".[1611] Similarly, in *Epic Syst. Corp. v. Tata Consultancy Servs*, a jury regarded that the plaintiff's medical record software and related documents constituted a trade secret,

1605 *Furr's Inc. v. United Speciality Advertising Co.*, 338 S.W.2d 762, 764 (Tex. App. 1960).

1606 *American Can Co. v. Mansukhami*, 728 F.2d 818, 819-820 (7th Cir. 1982).

1607 *American Can Co. v. Mansukhami*, 728 F.2d 818, 820 (7th Cir. 1982).

1608 *Colony Corp.of America v. Crown Glass Corp*, 430 N.E.2d 225, 227 (Ill. App. Ct.1981).

1609 *Q-CO Industries, INC. v. Hoffman*, 625 F.Supp. 608 (S.D.N.Y. 1985).

1610 *Q-CO Industries, INC. v. Hoffman*, 625 F.Supp. 608, 617-618 (S.D.N.Y. 1985).

1611 *Q-CO Industries, INC. v. Hoffman*, 625 F.Supp. 608, 618 (S.D.N.Y. 1985).

even though they were accessible to more than three hundred thousand users upon introducing the user credentials.[1612]

Importantly, a number of decisions in the U.S. have explored the concealed nature of trade secrets embedded in mass-distributed software, where concluding individual licensing agreements with users is not viable.[1613] For instance, In *Data Gene Corp. v. Digital Computer Controls Inc.* the plaintiff manufactured a new personal computer (Nova 1200), which was sold along with the engineer's drawings to allow the purchaser to do his own maintenance and repairs. The defendant, a hardware company, purchased a computer from the plaintiff (Data) and duplicated it with the aid of the diagrams provided along with the Nova 1200 minicomputer. While the parties agreed that the defendant was free to reverse engineer the lawfully purchased Nova 1200 computer, controversy arose with respect to the use of the drawings, as Data's standard contract form contained a confidentiality clause regarding the use of drawings, which was limited to maintenance, as opposed to manufacture. Such a possibility was expressly forbidden without the plaintiff's consent in writing.[1614] In view of the measures implemented by the plaintiff and the fact that the drawings had been distributed under an obligation of confidence, the Court of Chancery of Delaware ruled that the drawings retained their secret nature and the plaintiff prevailed in his claim. In this context, it was deemed that confidentiality had subsisted, although the defendant noted that at the time of the misappropriation, the drawings were available to almost six thousand users.[1615] In another case, *Data General Corp. v. Grumman Systems* the court concluded that the alleged misappropriated software remained secret because the licensing agreement included confidentiality and return upon non-use clauses.[1616] Yet, this has not been without criticism, particularly due to the potential pre-emptive effect that the Copyright Act may

---

1612 *Epic Systems Corporation v. Tata Consultancy Services Limited et al*, No. 3:2014cv00748 - Document 243 (W.D. Wis. 2015).

1613 Gale R. Peterson 1995 (n 1602) 449; see Michael Risch, 'Hidden in Plain Sight' [2016] 31 Berkeley Technology LJ 1635, 1649-1651 noting that in numerous decisions courts in the U.S. have ruled that software delivered to vendors or shown publicly had not been legally disclosed for the purposes of assessing secrecy.

1614 *Data Gene Corp. v. Digital Computer Controls Inc.*, 297 A.2d 437, 439 (Del. 1972).

1615 Miles R. Gilburne and Ronald L. Johnston, 'Trade Secret Protection for Software Generally and in the Mass Market' [1981] 3 Computer LJ 211, 230.

1616 *Data General Corp. v. Grumman Systems Support Corp.*, 36 F.3d 1147, 1167-1170 (1st Cir. 1994).

have over contractual obligations of confidentiality regarding computer programs, and especially with respect to shrink-wrap licenses.[1617] These are presented in many forms, but usually include a prohibition on reverse engineering the licensed software and become effective when the user breaks the seal or packaging in which the physical program is sold.[1618]

In sum, it appears that courts in the U.S. mostly understand that placing a product on the open market does not necessary render all of the trade secrets generally known or readily apparent, unless they can be devised upon inspecting the product with little effort.

b) England

In England, a review of the decisions that deal with the issue of whether the mere marketing of a product deprives the trade secrets embodied therein of their confidential nature also seems to indicate that a certain amount of circulation is permitted.[1619]

Such a principle appears in *Ackroyds (London) Ltd. v Islington Plastics Ltd.*[1620] In this case the defendants, plastic moulds manufacturers, entered into a contract with the plaintiff for the manufacturing of plastic swizzle sticks in the form of a Neptune's trident, based on a pattern designed by the plaintiff. Subsequently, they went on to manufacture the same tool for one of the plaintiff's main competitors. When the plaintiff found out, he decided to bring legal action against the defendant for an alleged breach of contract, as well as a breach of confidence. In the legal reasoning, with respect to the issue of confidentiality, Harver J noted that:

> (…) the mere publication of an article by manufacturing it and placing it upon the market, whether by means of work done on it or calculation or measurement which would enable information to be gained, is not necessarily sufficient to make such information available to the public. The question in each case is: Is such information available to

1617 Gale R. Peterson 1995 (n 1602) 449-450; the validity of shrink-wrap licenses has been highly contested. In this regard, see Mark A. Lemley, 'Intellectual Property and the Shrinkwrap Licenses' [1995] 68 Southern California LR 1239.

1618 Mark A. Lemley 1995 (n 1617) 1241.

1619 John Hull 1998 (n 1016) para 3.36; Tanya Aplin 2013 (n 1600) 347-348.

1620 *Ackroyds (London) Ltd v Islington Plastics Ltd* [1962] RPC 97 (Ch).

> the public? It is not, in my view *if work would have to be done upon it to make it available* (emphasis added).[1621]

As is apparent from the above, the critical factor was whether intellectual work was necessary to devise the secret information embodied in the marketed product, which ultimately led to the affirmation of the confidential nature of the pattern designed by the plaintiff. Similar principles were restated in *Alfa Laval v Wincanton,* which concerned the confidential nature of design drawings for a cheese block former machine.[1622] In the 1970s the defendant invented a cheese block former machine and some years later he assigned all of the intellectual property rights over the said machine to the plaintiff, including patents, copyright and trade secrets. However, by virtue of an agreement entered into by the plaintiff and the defendant in 1987, the defendant ceased to be involved in the design of the machines and became a mere manufacturer. At the same time, he undertook strict confidentiality obligations. A year later, the agreement was terminated and, subsequently, the defendant announced his intention to design and manufacture his own machine. Consequently, the plaintiff applied for a preliminary injunction on the basis of an alleged copyright infringement, misuse of confidential information and breach of contract. As regards the misuse of confidential information claim, Morrit J noted that confidentiality only persisted regarding the inner lining of the machine, which needed to be dismantled. However, he concluded that the external pipes could not be considered confidential, as they were "plain for everyone to see" upon marketing the product.[1623]

More recently, Arnold J had to decide whether the design of a half-size wind tunnel model of a Formula 1 racing car designed for one of the teams (Force India) was of a confidential nature, despite the fact that photographs of the vehicles had been published and certain parts had been sold by a Formula 1 memorabilia company. In deciding on the confidential status of information, he noted that:

> In cases concerning design drawings (…) much will depend on the level of generality of the information asserted to be confidential. If the claimant contends that information relating to the shape and configu-

---

1621 *Ackroyds (London) Ltd v Islington Plastics Ltd* [1962] RPC 97 (Ch), 104.

1622 *Alfa Laval Cheese Systems Ltd and Another v Wincanton Engineering Ltd* [1990] FSR 583 (Ch).

1623 *Alfa Laval Cheese Systems Ltd and Another v Wincanton Engineering Ltd* [1990] FSR 583 (Ch), 591.

> ration of the article depicted in the drawings is confidential, but the shape and configuration of the article can readily be ascertained from inspection of examples of the article which have been sold or are otherwise publicly accessible, then the claim will fail. If, on the other hand, the claimant contends that detailed dimensions, tolerances and manufacturing information recorded in the drawings are confidential, that information cannot readily be ascertained from inspection, *but only by a process of reverse engineering and the defendant has used the drawings as a short cut rather than taking the time and effort to reverse engineer,* then the claim will succeed (emphasis added).[1624]

In this context, the deciding judge held that the basic shapes of some of the parts of the Formula One cars were part of the public domain because they were ascertainable from pictures, but specified that the precise dimensions of specific parts remained concealed. Consequently, he concluded that the defendant's employees had indeed copied confidential material belonging to Force India, which the latter had supplied to the defendant for the provision of the agreed services.[1625] This finding was subsequently upheld by the Court of Appeal of England and Wales.[1626]

In the light of the above, it seems that English courts understand that the information embodied in a market product loses its secret nature if it can be obtained without the need to undergo a process of reverse engineering, that is, if no intellectual skill is necessary to devise the secret information.[1627] We will return to reverse engineering in chapter 6 as one of the main limitations of the rights conferred to the trade secret holder.[1628]

### c) Germany

In Germany, the prevailing view is that the marketing of a product does not necessarily reveal all of the trade secrets embedded therein. This was stated, for instance, by the Bavarian Higher Regional Court, in a dispute

1624 *Force India Formula One Team Ltd v 1 Malaysia Racing Team SDN BHD* [2012] EWHC 616 (Pat) [221].

1625 *Force India Formula One Team Ltd v 1 Malaysia Racing Team SDN BHD* [2012] EWHC 616 (Pat) [280],[282],[290].

1626 *Force India Formula One Team Ltd v 1 Malaysia Racing Team SDN BHD* [2013] EWCA civ 780 (CA).

1627 Tanya Aplin 2013 (n 1600) 349.

1628 Chapter 6 § 2 B) III. 3.

concerning the unlawful acquisition of a computer program incorporated into a slot machine used for gambling purposes.[1629] According to the fact-pattern of the decision, the defendant, one of the users of the slot machines, managed to decompile the computer program after using the machine several times.[1630] In this context, the court ruled that even though the slot machines had been placed on the market[1631] and that the information could be obtained after investing 70 hours of work and 5.000 German Franks (2.500€), the information remained concealed.[1632] The High Court in Bavaria concluded that it was only accessible with great difficulty and cost, which was identified as the benchmark that signals the existence of a secret worth protecting. Then, the court went on to examine whether the act of reverse engineering should be considered lawful. Consequently, under German law, information remains secret if it can only be obtained with the investment of substantial skill and labour. In particular, secrecy has been construed in a very broad sense vis-à-vis reverse engineering, as examined in chapter 6.[1633]

#### d) Guiding principles

The comparative analysis conducted above reveals that in the three jurisdictions studied a certain level of circulation is permitted; secrecy is not necessarily lost by placing a product on the market. However, it is crucial to differentiate between two types of information: (i) information about the *development* and *production* of the product concerned, and (ii) information about its *actual configuration*.[1634]

The first category refers, for example, to the secret drawings containing the precise dimensions of specific moulds used to manufacture specific

1629 BayObLG GRUR 1991, 694 – *Geldspielautomat.*

1630 BayObLG GRUR 1991, 694, 697 – *Geldspielautomat.*

1631 BayObLG GRUR 1991, 694, 695 – *Geldspielautomat* noting that "Der Geheimnischarakter der Bauart einer Maschine, oder, wie hier, der Gestaltung des Computerprogramms eines Spielautomaten, wird auch nicht dadurch aufgehoben, daß die Geräte vom Hersteller veräußert werden" and that "Kenntnis, die sich der Täter nur durch Einsatz von 70 Beobachtungsstunden und 5 000, - DM Spielgeld verschaffen kann, wird nicht 'ohne größere Schwierigkeiten und Opfer' erlangt".

1632 BayObLG GRUR 1991, 694, 697 – *Geldspielautomat.*

1633 See Chapter 6 § 2 B) III. 3).

1634 James Pooley 2002 (n 66) § 4.04 34-35.

parts of a marketed product.[1635] In this case, the information remains secret so long as the analysis of the marketed product does not disclose the dimensions of the moulds. In the second category, the information about the internal configuration of the good (internal secrets) and its functionality may not be apparent upon examination, which confers its holder a lead time advantage when compared to the rest of competitors. It remains secret and therefore protectable until it is reverse engineered.[1636] Prime examples of the latter would be a chemical formula to produce rubber goods or encrypted information embedded within a vending machine.

A similar approach has also crystallised in consistent case law from the Boards of Appeal of the EPO with regard to the assessment of novelty. As outlined in chapter 1, while examining the interplay between trade secrets and patent rights, placing a product on the open market for which patent protection is later sought is only novelty destroying if it is possible for members of the public to acquire knowledge of that subject matter on the relevant priority day. This includes the external examination of the product, as well as the obtention of the invention after further analysis of the intrinsic features (those that do not need to interact with external conditions to become apparent).[1637]

The availability of an invention embodied in a marketed product was discussed by the Enlarged Board of Appeal of the EPO in the landmark decision G-1/92. In this case, it was considered whether the chemical composition of a product is part of the state of the art when the product in which it is embodied is marketed and can be analysed and reproduced by a skilled person.[1638] In delivering its decision, the Board started by noting that one of the main goals of any technical teaching is to allow any person with ordinary skills in the art to "use" or "produce" the product concerned. To that end, he would have to use "the general technical knowledge to gather all information enabling him to prepare the said product". In such a case, if the skilled person could find out the composition or the internal structure of the product and was able to reproduce it, it should be deemed that both the product and its composition or internal structure are

1635 *Ackroyds (London) Ltd. v Islington Plastics Ltd* RPC 97.

1636 James Pooley 2002 (n 66) § 4.04 34-35.

1637 See Guidelines of Examination in the EPO. Part G. Chapter IV. Section 7.2.; on the interpretation of the availability to the public of an invention by use followed by the Enlarged Board of Appeal of the EPO, G 1/92 [1993] OJ EPO 278.

1638 G 1/92 [1993] OJ EPO 278.

part of the state of the art.[1639] Based on the above premise, the Enlarged Board of Appeal concluded that the relevant yardstick is whether the information is accessible in a "direct" and "unambiguous" manner, not whether there is a reason to "look for it".[1640] Thus, under patent law marketing, a product in which an invention is embodied does not implicitly reveal anything beyond its composition or internal structure. Indeed, extrinsic characteristics, which are solely disclosed when the product is "exposed to interaction with specifically chosen outside conditions" are not automatically revealed.[1641]

From an economic standpoint, in fast moving industries, with short product life cycles, holders of information do not usually seek patent protection, as the patent term outweighs the expected obsolescence of the secret innovation. In such a context, the lead time conferred by secrecy prior to the reverse engineering of a product is the preferred option to appropriate returns from innovation.[1642]

In sum, it can be concluded that marketing a product does not, as such, disclose any of the inventions and the trade secrets that it embodies, unless they become apparent upon its inspection and analysis. However, at this point a crucial distinction must be made. Under patent law, the mere possibility of accessing the information renders it available for the purposes of assessing its novel character, even if the information is subject to a process of reverse engineering. By contrast, in the case of trade secrets, such an assessment depends on whether third parties (i.e. the relevant circles) have *in fact* examined the marketed product and devised the secret or if the information is accessible (or apparent) with so little labour and intellectual skill that it does not appear reasonable to enforce an obligation of confidence on the acquirer of the product. Consequently, information that is acquired after a process of reverse engineering by a competitor remains eligible for trade secrets protection for as long as it does not become generally known within the industry. As a final note, it is noteworthy that under both legal regimes, the extrinsic characteristics of the product are not immediately disclosed and consequently they are eligible for both patent and trade secrets protection.

---

1639 G 1/92 [1993] OJ EPO 278.

1640 G 1/92 [1993] OJ EPO 278, 279; Guidelines for Examination in the EPO Part G. Chapter IV. Section 7.2.1.

1641 G 1/92 [1993] OJ EPO 278, 280.

1642 James Pooley 2002 (n 66) § 4.04 34-35.

### 4. Disclosures on the Internet

To be sure, the Internet has increased the pace with which, and the audience to which, specific information can be disclosed. The publication of trade secrets on the Internet constitutes a prime example of the increasing challenges that stakeholders face in keeping their secrets undisclosed. In such a context, the main issue is whether posting a piece of information on the Internet renders it automatically generally known or readily accessible. This topic has garnered substantial attention in recent years, particularly with the advent of new technologies. The following sections examine the most relevant decisions on this subject in the U.S. (section a), England (section b) and Germany (section c). Finally, some guiding principles that should aid national courts in assessing whether information has entered the public domain are formulated (section d).

#### a) U.S.

In the U.S., there is no consistent case law on the effects of internet disclosures.[1643] So far, the most relevant cases dealing with trade secret disclosure on the Internet are (i) *Religious Technology Center v. Lerma;*[1644] (ii) *DVD Copy Control Ass'n v. Bunner*[1645] and (iii) *United States v. Genovese.*[1646]

The first case, *Religious Technology Center v. Lerma* concerned a case of misappropriation of trade secrets from the Church of Scientology. The defendant (Mr Lerma), a former member of the Church, posted online information about the Church that he had acquired from a court record. Such information was regarded as a trade secret by the Church, who obtained a temporary restraining order against the defendant.[1647] Notwithstanding

1643 This issue has been explored by several academic articles, the most notable being: Elizabeth A. Rowe 2007 (n 1515) explaining that usually when a trade secret is posted on the internet, the trade secret holder loses its rights on the information and cannot prevent third parties from using it; see further Elizabeth A. Rowe, 'Introducing a Takedown for Trade Secrets on the Internet' [2007] Wisconsin LR 1041arguing that Congress should enact specific takedown legislation vis-à-vis trade secrets; also Victoria A. Cundiff 2009 (n 739) 359 reviewing the measures that the owners of secret information should adopt in order to protect them in the digital environment.

1644 *Religious Technology Center v. Lerma* 908 F.Supp. 1362 (E.D. Va. 1995).

1645 *DVD Copy Control Association Inc. v. Andrew Bunner* 75 P.3d 1 (Cal. 2003).

1646 *United States v. Genovese* 409 F.Supp.2d 253 (S.D.N.Y. 2005).

1647 *Religious Technology Center v. Lerma* 908 F.Supp. 1362, 1364 (E.D. Va. 1995).

this, prior to the issuance of the restraining order, Mr. Lerma had also sent a copy of the posted documents to an investigative reporter working for the Washington Post, Richard Leibi. The reporter ended up publishing an article in the Washington Post based on those materials. As a result, the Church of Scientology brought legal action seeking injunctive relief and damages on the grounds of copyright infringement and trade secret misappropriation against The Washington Post. The first claim on copyright was dismissed by the District Court of Virginia. As regards the trade secret claim, the court noted that the publication of a trade secret online renders it part of the public domain and thus it can no longer be afforded protection.[1648]

Similar arguments were raised by the District Court of California in a subsequent case that also concerned an alleged trade secrets misappropriation brought again by the Curch of Scientology against a former member that posted the Church's writings on an Internet USENET group.[1649] Against this fact pattern the court held that the disputed information was generally known and consequently, it did not merit protection.[1650] Notwithstanding this finding, after several months the Church filed another motion but this time providing consumer surveys.[1651] In its legal reasoning, the District Court changed its previous position and noted that the assessment of secrecy "requires a review of the circumstances surrounding the posting and consideration of the interests of the trade secret owner, the policies favoring competition and the interests, including first amendment rights, (…) of innocent third parties who acquire information of the Internet".[1652] Consequently, the preliminary injunction was issued because under such a test, it was questionable whether the information was public

1648 *Religious Technology Center v. Lerma* 908 F.Supp. 1362, 1368 (E.D. Va. 1995).

1649 *Religious Technology Center v. Netcom On-Line Commc'n Servs., Inc.*, 923 F.Supp. 1231 (N.D. Cal. 1995) (Netcom I); according to footnote 5 of this decision "Usenet news, which is one of the most popular features of the Internet, allows users of systems "subscribing" to the groups to participate by reading and "posting" messages on a particular topic, such as intellectual property rights ("misc. int-property") or table tennis ("rec.sport.table-tennis")".

1650 *Religious Technology Center v. Netcom On-Line Commc'n Servs., Inc.*, 923 F.Supp. 1231, 1256-1257 (N.D. Cal. 1995) (Netcom I).

1651 *Religious Tech. Ctr. v. Netcom On-Line Commc'n Servs., Inc.*, 1997 WL 34605244 (N.D. Cal Jan. 6, 1997) (Netcom II).

1652 *Religious Tech. Ctr. v. Netcom On-Line Commc'n Servs., Inc.*, 1997 WL 34605244 page 12. (N.D. Cal. Jan. 6, 1997) (Netcom II).

knowledge considering the difficulty in identifying potential competitors.[1653]

The second case, *DVD Copy Control Ass'n v. Bunner,*[1654] concerned the publication of a program on the Internet allowing for the decryption of information stored on DVDs (the so-called "DeSCC" program). The content scrambling system ("CSS") prevented the copying of the content of DVDs and was licensed by the DVD Copy Control Association (a trade association of businesses in the movie industry) to DVD player manufacturers under the condition that they did not reverse engineer the program. Pursuant to the plaintiff, the defendant (Mr Bunner) found the DeSCC program, which allowed for decrypting the CSS secret information, on the Internet, knowing that it had been obtained through reverse engineering in breach of the terms of the licensing agreement, and posted a link to it on his website, invoking the freedom of speech principle enshrined in the first amendment of the U.S. Constitution. On appeal, the Supreme Court of California ruled firstly that if a trade secret existed, the grant of an injunction would not contravene the first amendment and secondly, it added that the plaintiff had failed to provide evidence that the information was still secret at the time that the defendant republished it on his website. It nevertheless noted, that in theory it was possible that the secret nature of the information was not lost, as it had been posted on an "obscure site on the Internet" and detected quickly.[1655] Notwithstanding this, on remand the California Court of Appeal for the Sixth District concluded that the CSS technology was no longer secret and, consequently, held that the grant of a preliminary injunction would negatively affect the freedom of speech principle more than necessary. As a result, the decision to grant the preliminary injunction was reversed.[1656]

---

1653 Ibid.

1654 *DVD Copy Control Association Inc. v. Andrew Bunner* 75 P.3d 1 (Cal. 2003).

1655 *DVD Copy Control Association Inc. v. Andrew Bunner* 4 Cal. Rptr. 3d 69, 101 (Cal. 2003) noting that that "information posted on an obscure Internet site and detected quickly should not lose trade secret status. This position is consistent with case law holding that minor disclosures of a trade secret followed by a brief delay in withdrawing it from the public domain do not cause the trade secret to be lost".

1656 *DVD Copy Control Association Inc. v. Andrew Bunner,* 10 Cal. Rptr. 3d 185 (Cal. Ct. App. 2004); for a critical overview of first amendment defences in trade secret disclosure cases on the Internet see Pamela Samuelson, 'Principles for Resolving Conflicts Between Trade Secrets and the First Amendment' [2007] 58 Hastings LJ 777, 800-805.

The third case, *United States v. Genovese*, dealt with the publication of parts of Microsoft's source code for two of its operating systems (Windows NT 4.0 and Windows 2000) on the Internet. Following an investigation, the FBI determined that Mr Genovese was offering the source code for sale on his website for 20 USD and, therefore, he was charged for the unlawful downloading and selling of trade secrets in violation of the EEA.[1657] Mr Genovese challenged the indictment, among other reasons, on the basis that firstly, it contravened the first amendment of the U.S. Constitution, which enshrines the freedom of expression principle, and secondly, Microsoft had not adopted reasonable measures to protect it; as the defendant had obtained it from a third party.[1658] In the legal reasoning, the court indicated that the first amendment was indeed applicable to "source code and other types of trade secrets". However, the court concluded that this provision does not afford protection to third parties that intend to economically benefit from another's trade secret by "their unauthorised copying, duplicating, downloading and uploading".[1659] With respect to the reasonable measures claims, it was indicated that Mr Genovese knew that the source code had been unlawfully acquired through the circumvention of technical protection measures and therefore he "could understand" that offering to sell the source code was prohibited by law.

In the light of the foregoing analysis, it is suggested that despite the fact that ultimately secrecy is a question of fact and has to be assessed based on the circumstances of each case,[1660] courts in the U.S. have not adopted a uniform approach to the challenges posed by the Internet in connection with the secrecy requirement[1661] and the potential negative impact of injunctions on freedom of speech.[1662]

### b) England

The effects of the disclosure on the Internet of secret information were the object of a decision in 2009 by the High Court of England and Wales in

1657 *United States v Genovese* 409 F.Supp.2d 253, 255 (S.D.N.Y. 2005).
1658 *United States v Genovese* 409 F.Supp.2d 253, 254 (S.D.N.Y. 2005).
1659 *United States v Genovese* 409 F.Supp.2d 253, 256 (S.D.N.Y. 2005).
1660 Roger M. Milgrim 2014 (n 160) § 1.03-1.268.
1661 Melvin F. Jager, *Trade Secrets Law* (Thompsons Reuters 2015) § 3:39.
1662 A number of principles to resolve these types of conflicts are proposed by Pamela Samuelson, 'Principles for Resolving Conflicts Between Trade Secrets and the First Amendment' [2007] 58 Hastings LJ 777, 833-845.

*Barclays Bank Plc v Guardian News and Media Ltd.*[1663] The case concerned the leakage of nine confidential documents containing information about several transactions carried out by Barclays Bank and their tax treatment. Importantly, the court noted that it was not a case of whistle-blowing because there was no tax evasion involved, only tax avoidance, which is lawful from a legal perspective and essentially consists of optimising tax payments. According to the facts reported in the decision, one of Barclay's employees had shared the secret documents with several members of Parliament and the Guardian News. Subsequently, the newspaper published them on its website in the context of a series of articles on the topic of banking practices and financial institutions. The documents were posted only for four hours before a preliminary injunction was issued compelling Guardian News to take them down. In deciding whether they still retained the necessary confidential nature for a continuation of injunctive relief, Blake J held that in principle information that is generally available on the Internet loses its confidential nature. Notwithstanding this, under this specific fact-pattern he concluded that "very limited dissemination and only partial dissemination perhaps in some remote or expert site that is not generally available to the public without a great deal of effort, may not result in such a loss of confidentiality".[1664] The deciding factor was thus that the documents were available online for a very limited period of time, and as a result retained their confidential nature.

### c) Germany

At first glance, German case law and academia seem to indicate that the disclosure of information on the Internet deprives it of its secret nature.[1665] Indeed, in a case concerning the misappropriation of the Clinical Expert Report of a pharmaceutical product (Movicol) by a former employee who went on to work for a competitor, the Federal Supreme Court ruled that information in the Clinical Expert Report may be deprived of its secret nature if at the time of the disclosure the information was available on the Internet in German or in international specialised publications.[1666]

---

1663 *Barclays Bank Plc v Guardian News and Media Ltd* [2009] EWHC 591 (QB).
1664 *Barclays Bank Plc v Guardian News and Media Ltd* [2009] EWHC 591 (QB) 22.
1665 *Ohly*/Sosnitza (n 813) § 17 Rdn 9.
1666 BGH GRUR 2012, 1048 Rdn 24 –*Movicol* (Zuassungsantrag).

By contrast, in 2016 the Higher Regional Court of Kalsruhe ruled that the code to unlock SIM cards constituted a protectable trade secret under German law, even though the codes were available on the Internet through special unlocking software, which was made available without authorisation by the defendant upon payment of a fee. In such a context, the court concluded that the technical protection measures implemented by the plaintiff, as well as the difficulty and cost involved in obtaining the codes preserved the undisclosed nature of the information and hence it was protectable as a trade secret.[1667]

d) Guiding principles

As is apparent from the comparative analysis conducted in the previous sections, the general principle is that once information is posted on the Internet, it becomes generally known. However, in certain cases, courts in the three jurisdictions studied have ruled that the secret nature of information subsisted, despite the fact that it had been made available online.

In this context, Rowe suggests a "sequential preservation model", whereby in exceptional circumstances the publication of a trade secret on the Internet should not be deemed secrecy-destroying. According to the author, the three parameters to be weighed in are: (i) the time that the secret was available on the Internet, together with the time it took the holder to take legal action; (ii) the extent of the disclosure; and (iii) the recipient's reason to know that the information was a trade secret.[1668]

The starting point of the analytical framework proposed by Rowe should be whether at the time of the unauthorised online disclosure, the information complied with the statutory requirements of protection, i.e., whether (i) it was secret, (ii) had commercial value as a result of its secret nature, and (iii) was subject to reasonable steps under the circumstances to maintain its secret status.[1669] Clearly, if the information did not meet ex ante any of these requirements, the disclosure should not be deemed unlawful, as the object of protection had ceased to exist.

Next, the first factor proposed by Rowe takes into consideration the amount of time that the information was available online and the measures that the trade secret holder adopted upon finding out about the dis-

1667 OLG Karlsruhe MMR 2016, 562.
1668 Elizabeth A. Rowe 2007 (n 1515) 30-38.
1669 Elizabeth A. Rowe 2007 (n 1515) 33-34.

closure.[1670] According to the author, the risks associated with the dissemination of information on the Internet impose a duty of monitoring on trade secrets holders and, in correlation, a duty to take action as soon as a disclosure is identified.[1671] Such measures include launching legal actions, applying for a preliminary injunction, sending a cease and desist letter or requesting the owner of the website to take down the secret information.[1672] Reacting promptly is crucial to ensure that the object of protection is not lost. This is also in line with Recital 26 TSD, where it is noted that it "is essential to provide for fast, effective and accessible provisional measures for the immediate termination of the unlawful acquisition, use or disclosure of a trade secret", in view of the devastating effects that such conduct may have on the trade secret holder as a result of the loss of secrecy. In this context, Rowe convincingly concludes that it is unlikely that information that has been available online for more than forty-eight hours can be considered to retain its secret nature, even though this will ultimately depend on the specific circumstances of the case.[1673] Indeed, in *Barclays Bank Plc v Guardian News and Media Ltd* injunctive relief was granted on the basis that the information had only been available for four hours.[1674]

The second factor evaluates the extent of the disclosure in order to assess whether the information has become "generally known or knowable".[1675] It primarily looks into the specific characteristics of the website and the extent of the actual dissemination. In effect, disclosures on obscure websites are more likely to be non-secrecy destroying than disclosures on high-traffic websites. In addition, courts should also take into consideration whether the access was limited, for instance, restricted to members with an account. This is crucial to assess whether the relevant circles may have had access to the information concerned and as a result, may have acquired active knowledge of said information. Furthermore, due account should be paid to the amount of information published. Partial disclosures only affect the nature of the specific information disclosed.[1676]

---

1670 Elizabeth A. Rowe 2007 (n 1515) 32.
1671 Elizabeth A. Rowe 2007 (n 1515) 32-33; similar views are expressed by the EU legislator in Recital 23 TSD with respect to the limitation period.
1672 Elizabeth A. Rowe 2007 (n 1515) 33
1673 Elizabeth A. Rowe 2007 (n 1515) 33.
1674 *Barclays Bank Plc v Guardian News and Media Ltd* [2009] EWHC 591 (QB) [32].
1675 Elizabeth A. Rowe 2007 (n 1515) 33.
1676 Lionel Bently and Brad Sherman 2014 (n 125) 1148.

The third factor is the most controversial one, as it enquires into the defendant's "state of mind".[1677] According to Rowe, if the information is posted on the Internet by a misappropriator or a third party that had reason to know that the information had been misappropriated, liability should arise.[1678] A similar approach has been adopted by the EU legislator in the TSD. According to Article 4(3) TSD, the disclosure of a trade secret acquired unlawfully or in breach of a secrecy obligation or any other duty not to disclose the information triggers liability. Consequently, if the information is posted on a website, for instance, by a party in breach of an obligation of confidence, the said party will be deemed liable for the unauthorised disclosure of a trade secret. Furthermore, pursuant to Article 4(4) TSD, if the party that disseminates the information online knew or should have known under the circumstances that the information was obtained from an illicit source, such disclosure should be considered illicit and consequently trigger liability. Notwithstanding this, it seems unsound to enjoin bona fide third parties that acquire information by merely checking a website from using or disclosing the said information without knowledge or reason to know the unauthorised origin of the information. In such a context, if as a result of its wide dissemination the trade secret holder loses control over the subsequent use and disclosure of the information and it enters the public domain, the secret as such ceases to exist.[1679]

Likewise, in her analytical framework, Rowe purports that infringers should not be able to counterclaim that upon publication the obligation ceases to exists. Infringers should be liable because at the time of the disclosure the information complied with the statutory requirements for protection.[1680] This view is in line with Article 13(1) paragraph 2 TSD, which provides that when an injunction is ordered with a time limit, its "duration shall be sufficient to eliminate any commercial or economic advantage that the infringer could have derived from the unlawful acquisition, use or disclosure of the trade secret". Similarly, the TSD provides that preliminary and precautionary measures, as well as injunctions and corrective measures shall be revoked if the information no longer meets the requirements of protection "for reasons that cannot be attributed to the respon-

---

1677 Elizabeth A. Rowe 2007 (n 1515) 34.

1678 Elizabeth A. Rowe 2007 (n 1515) 36-37.

1679 Elizabeth A. Rowe 2007 (n 1515) 36.

1680 Elizabeth A. Rowe 2007 (n 1515) 35-37; Roger M. Milgrim 2014 (n 160) § 17.03 15

dent".[1681] Consequently, the fact that the information has become generally known does not exonerate of liability the infringer who publishes the information on the Internet with knowledge (or being gross negligent) of the illicit source of the information. Yet, trade secrets are not enforceable against third parties that have acquired them lawfully.

In this context, Rowe suggests that failure to act promptly upon being notified of the infringing nature of the online publication (step 1 of the sequential model) should also trigger liability.[1682] This also seems to be the prevailing legal view under the harmonised EU legal framework, where liability for bona fide third parties arises upon notification of the confidential nature of the information.[1683] This in turn raises questions regarding the potential liability of intermediaries, such as online platforms, that are used as the means to disclose the information and that do not take it down upon being notified by the trade secret holder of its infringing nature. Ultimately, the intersection between the hosting safe harbour established in Article 14(1) of the Directive on electronic commerce and the TSD will have to be subject to judicial interpretation by the CJEU.[1684]

In the light of the above, the better view, it is submitted, is that the assessment of whether information that is published on an Internet webpage loses its secret nature should be conducted on a case-by-case basis, taking into consideration the likelihood that members of the relevant public have in fact accessed the information. Crucial factors include the length of time during which the information was posted online and the measures adopted upon discovery of the publication.[1685] Courts should also take into consideration the website traffic and the extent of the disclosure (whether it is partial or total) in order to assess whether it has become generally known among the relevant circles.[1686] However, these factors should be viewed as mere guidelines with no normative value. Indeed, affording normative val-

1681 Recital 27 TSD.

1682 Elizabeth A. Rowe 2007 (n 1515) 36.

1683 See Article 4(4) TSD and 13(3) TSD and Recital 29.

1684 As analysed in chapter 3 § 5 C) III. 2. c).

1685 Similar views are expressed by Roger M. Milgrim 2014 (n 160) § 17.03 15 who notes that "publication on the Internet does not necessarily terminate trade secrets status; inasmuch as trade secret statues is an intense question of fact (…) the factual question must be answered as to whether as a matter of fact the matter is readily available or ascertainable".

1686 Pamela Samuelson, 'Reverse Engineering Under Siege' [2002] 45 Commmunications of the Association Computing Machinery 15, text acomanying footnote 7.

ue to such a test would disregard the essentially factual nature of secrecy. On the contrary, considering every single publication on the Internet as secrecy destroying would amount to an absolute test of secrecy, ignoring the principle of inaccessibility that is supported in all of the jurisdictions studied and disregarding whether the trade secret holder has control over the subsequent use and disclosure of the information concerned. As regards the third factor propounded by Rowe, it should be noted that the liability of third parties is in fact regulated under Article 4(4) TSD following a gross negligence standard, in line with footnote 10 of Article 39 TRIPs. Therefore, it seems unreasonable to enforce generally known information against third parties that consult a webpage without knowledge or reason to know the illicit source of the information. To hold otherwise would upset the balance between formal IPRs and non-formal information.

## 5. Limited content: combination secrets

Frequently, trade secrets consist of a number of elements, some of which (if not all) are part of the public domain. However, this does not necessarily preclude the application of trade secrets liability rules in the case of misappropriation. Courts in the US,[1687] England[1688] and Germany[1689] have acknowledged the existence of so-called "combination secrets", which have been defined as "a multi-element claim that, when valid, ties non-secret items of information together in a unique manner to form a trade secret".[1690] This concept presents clear parallelisms with the definition of a database provided in Article 1(2) of the Database Directive, which refers to them as the "collection of independent works, data or other materials arranged in a systematic or methodical way and individually accessible by electronic or other means". Hence, combination secrets can constitute the object of a database protected both under copyright and the sui generis right, provided that the requirements of protection under both regimes are met. However, the database sui generis legal regime also foresees that the lawful user shall be entitled to extract "insubstantial parts" of its contents,

1687 *Merck v. Smithkline Beecham Pharm Co.*, No. C.A. 15443-NC (Del. Ch 1999).

1688 *Under Water Welders & Repairers Ltd v Street and Longthorne* [1968] RPC 498 (QB), 506-507.

1689 BGH GRUR 1966, 576 – *Zimcofot.*

1690 Charles Tait Graves and Brian D. Range, 'Identification of Trade Secret Claims in Litigation: Solutions for a Ubiquitous Dispute' [2006] 5 New J of Technology IP 68, 77.

which may compromise the secret nature of the information and consequently, its elegibility for protection as a trade secret.[1691]

The protection of combination secrets is in line with Article 39(2)(a) TRIPs, which stipulates that information is secret if it "is not, as a *body or in the precise configuration and assembly of its components*, generally known among or readily accessible". Thus, following the wording of TRIPs, which has also been incorporated into Article 2(1)(a) TSD, the assembly of individually known components can also constitute the object of a trade secret.[1692]

In the following sections, several cases concerning combination secrets in the U.S. (section a), England (section b) and Germany (section c) are examined. Next, drawing from such an analysis, a number of interpretative principles regarding the protectability of combination secrets are formulated, with the purpose of finding an equilibrium with the public domain boundaries in the interests of competition, innovation and employee mobility (section d).

---

1691 Chapter 1 § 3 A) IV. 1.

1692 Gerald Reger 1999 (n 553) 362; surprisingly, the definition set out in § 2(1) of the proposed German Trade Secrets Act ("Entwurf eines Gesetzes zur Umsetzung der Richtlinie (EU) 2016/680 im Strafverfahren sowie zur Anpassung datenschutzrechtlicher Bestimmungen an die Verordnung (EU) 2016/679)") is more restrictive than the one followed by Article 2(1)(a) TSD. The German legislator has stipulated that information is secret when it is "neither as a body nor in the precise configuration and assembly of its components, generally known among or readily accessible to persons within the circles that normally deal with the kind of information in question". According to the German definition, to merit protection, information must not be generally known as a body and in its individual components simultaneously. Consequently, both requirements are cumulative under German law, and not alternative, as laid down in the TSD and TRIPs. As a result of such a narrow definition, the possibility of protecting combination secrets in Germany may be excluded in the future, because to be secret information needs to be unknown as a whole and in its individual elements, irrespective of whether the aggregation of individual components, such as data, results in a new and unknown entity; see further Luc Desaunettes, Reto M. Hilty, Roland Knaak, Annette Kur, 'Stellungnahme zum Referentenentwurf eines Gesetzes zur Umsetzung der Richtlinie (EU) 2016/943 zum Schutz von Geschäftsgeheimnissen vor rechtswidrigem Erwerb sowie rechtswidriger Nutzung und Offenlegung vom 17. April 2018' (2018), para 7 and 8 <https://www.ip.mpg.de/fileadmin/ipmpg/content/stellungnahmen/Stellungnahme_zum_Referentenentwurf_eines_Gesetzes_zur_Umsetzung_der_Richtlinie__EU__2016_943.pdf> accessed 15 September 2018.

a) U.S.

The origin of the protection of combination secrets in the U.S. can be traced back to the end of the XIX century. It emerged as a result of the intersection between labour law and trade secrets protection, after several courts refused to grant injunctions against former employees on the basis that the information for which protection was sought was in fact part of the public domain.[1693] In turn, plaintiffs usually counter-claimed that the combination of known elements deserved protection because of the new results and utility produced by the specific combination of such elements.[1694] Since the end of the XIX century, the concept of combination secrets has been incorporated into the four main sources of trade secrets law in the U.S and has given rise to a rich body of case law: the Restatement (First) of Torts;[1695] the Uniform Trade Secrets Act;[1696] the Restatement (Third) of Unfair Competition[1697] and more recently the DTSA of 2016.[1698] Most frequently, when deciding on the protection of combination secrets, courts have been confronted with the issue of deciding whether the alleged combination is common among industry members and consequently should be deemed "generally known" or instead deviates sufficiently from such practices to merit protection as a discrete entity.[1699]

1693 See Charles Tait Graves and Alexander Macgillivray 2004 (n 699) 267 with further references.

1694 *Eastman Co. v. Reichenbach*, 20 N.Y.S. 110 (1892).

1695 See Restatement (First) of Torts § 757 (Am. Law Inst. 1939) comment g, where it is noted that trade secrets may consist of a "compilation". Notably, the comment does not provide further guidance regarding the circumstances under which said "compilations" may be protected.

1696 UTSA § 1(4) defining trade secret as a "formula, pattern, *compilation*, program, device, method, technique or process" (emphasis added).

1697 Restatement (Third) of Unfair Competition §39 (Am. Law Inst. 1995) comment f: "It is the secrecy of the claimed trade secret as a whole that is determinative. The fact that some or all of the components of the trade secret are well-known does not preclude protection for a secret combination, *compilation*, or integration of the individual elements"(emphasis added).

1698 18 U.S.C. § 1839 (3) defining the term trade secrets as: "all forms and types of financial, business, scientific, technical, economic, or engineering information, including patterns, plans, *compilations*, program devices, formulas, designs, prototypes, methods, techniques, processes, procedures, programs, or codes, whether tangible or intangible, and whether or how stored, *compiled*, or memorialized physically, electronically, graphically, photographically, or in writing (…)" 1(emphasis added).

1699 Charles Tait Graves and Alexander Macgillivray 2004 (n 699) 271-272.

For instance, in 2002 the Supreme Court of Arkansas ruled in favour of Wal-Mart Inc. in a case that involved the alleged misappropriation of a trade secret by the U.S. multinational retail corporation.[1700] In 1992 the legal representative of the plaintiff ("The P.O. Market Inc.") approached a manager of a Wal-Mart store regarding an idea to execute bulk credit transactions, which essentially consisted of transferring the risk of non-payment of wholesale orders to the plaintiff, an intermediate company that would place the orders to Wal-Mart Inc. on behalf of the customers.[1701] In 1992, a number of meetings between the representatives of The P.O. Market Inc. and Wal-Mart Inc. took place under strict confidentiality but eventually the negotiations broke off.[1702] In 1993 the Wall Street Journal published an article in which it described a new purchasing programme set up by Wal-Mart Inc., by virtue of which bulk purchasers were allowed to buy goods on credit.[1703] Thereafter, The P.O. Market Inc. brought legal action against Wal-Mart Inc. for trade secrets misappropriation. The plaintiffs prevailed in the first instance, but upon appeal, the Supreme Court of Arkansas held that the alleged trade secret was not a unique concept, as it was merely "a variation of other economic models" already in the public domain. In its legal reasoning the Court noted that "any person reasonably well vested in the economics of wholesaling and credit purchasing could have put together the (...) concept".[1704]

A similar reasoning was applied by the Court of Appeals of the Federal Circuit in *Julie Research Laboratories, Inc. v Select Photographic Engineering Inc.*,[1705] where it was ruled that the retouching imaging system developed by the plaintiff consisted of a combination of twelve system design choices. These were "either obvious, widely known, easy for others to discover legitimately or disclosed in the sales literature of the plaintiff or other manufacturers".[1706] Consequently, trade secrets protection was denied.

1700 *Wal-Mart Stores, Inc. v. The P.O. Market Inc.*, 66 S.W.3d 620 (Ark. 2002).

1701 *Wal-Mart Stores, Inc. v. The P.O. Market Inc.*, 66 S.W.3d 620, 622 (Ark. 2002).

1702 *Wal-Mart Stores, Inc. v. The P.O. Market Inc.*, 66 S.W.3d 620, 623-624 (Ark. 2002).

1703 *Wal-Mart Stores, Inc. v. The P.O. Market Inc.*, 66 S.W.3d 620, 626 (Ark. 2002).

1704 *Wal-Mart Stores, Inc. v. The P.O. Market Inc.*, 66 S.W.3d 620, 634 (Ark. 2002).

1705 *Julie Research Laboratories, Inc. v. Select Photographic Engineering Inc.*, 998 F.2d 65 (2d Circ. 1993).

1706 *Julie Research Laboratories, Inc. v. Select Photographic Engineering Inc.*, 998 F.2d 65, 67 (2d Circ. 1993).

By contrast, in *Merck v. Smithkline Beecham Pharm Co,*[1707] the Court of Chancery of Delaware ruled that the commercial process for the production of a varicella vaccine developed by the Japanese pharmaceutical company, Biken, and subsequently licensed to Merck, constituted a trade secret, despite the fact that certain aspects of the laboratory process for the production of the varicella vaccine could be found in a publication from the 1970s.[1708] Against this background, the court clearly distinguished between the laboratory process described in the said publication and the commercial production process misappropriated by the defendant, because the former did not solve some of the practical problems that the manufacturers encountered in the production phase.[1709]

Likewise, in *Penalty Kick Management, Ltd. v. Coca-Cola Co.*[1710] the protection of combination secrets was affirmed. The facts of the case are as follows: in 1995 the Chief Executive of Penalty Kick Management ("the Plaintiff") developed a "beverage label marketing and production process known as Magic Windows".[1711] It essentially consisted of inserting a message on the inside of the label of the bottle that had to be read through a coloured filter once the container was emptied.[1712] In the same year, two executives of the Plaintiff met with the representatives of The Coca-Cola Co., Atlanta, GA ("the Defendant") in order to show them the marketing and production process for the new label developed by their company. During the course of the meeting, the representatives of the Plaintiff mentioned that they had filed a patent application for the Magic Windows and that everything discussed in the meeting was to be kept confidential. Sometime later, in 1996, the parties executed an NDA and started negotiating the content of the licensing agreement. However, before it was executed, the defendant examined some of the published patent applications and concluded that the Magic Window concept was in fact in the public do-

---

1707 *Merck v. Smithkline Beecham Pharm Co.*, No. C.A. 15443-NC (Del. Ch 1999).

1708 *Merck v. Smithkline Beecham Pharm Co.*, No. C.A. 15443-NC (Del. Ch 1999).

1709 *Merck v. Smithkline Beecham Pharm Co.*, No. C.A. 15443-NC 18 (Del. Ch 1999); this decision was subsequently upheld by the Supreme Court of Delaware in *Smithkline Beecham Pharmaceuticals Co. v. Merck & Co., Inc.*, 766 A.2d 442 (Del. 2000).

1710 *Penalty Kick Management, Ltd. v. Coca-Cola Co*, 318 F. 3d 1284 (11th Cir. 2003).

1711 *Penalty Kick Management, Ltd. v. Coca-Cola Co*, 318 F. 3d 1284, 1286-1287 (11th Cir. 2003).

1712 *Penalty Kick Management, Ltd. v. Coca-Cola Co*, 318 F. 3d 1284, 1286-1287 (11th Cir. 2003).

main.[1713] Hence, the defendant asked one of its label printer contractors to develop a bottle with a label, which was very similar to the Magic Windows.[1714] When the Plaintiff found out, he brought legal action against the defendant for trade secrets misappropriation and breach of the NDA. In turn, the defendant counter-claimed that the information revealed on the Magic Windows was not a trade secret and that the terms of the NDA had not been infringed. In its legal reasoning, the District Court for the Northern District of Georgia started by noting that, "the fact that some or all the elements of the trade secret are well-known does not preclude protection for trade secrets combination, compilation, or integration of the individual elements".[1715] According to the Court, a "unique combination of that information" may be eligible for protection, provided that it "adds value to the information".[1716] In view of this, the Court held that the Magic Windows constituted a trade secret because many aspects were unique if compared to the existing prior art. However, the court ruled that the Plaintiff had failed to prove that the label used by the Defendant "substantially derived" from the Plaintiff's label and came to the conclusion that the information used by the Defendant had been independently generated by him.[1717]

In sum, it appears that courts in the U.S. seem inclined to afford protection to combination secrets when the unique compilation of known information provides a solution to an unsolved problem or, more generally, when it confers additional value to the information viewed as a whole. By contrast, the mere combination of known elements should not merit protection if no intellectual skill is necessary to put it together. To hold otherwise would entail the privatisation of information already in the public domain.

1713 *Penalty Kick Management, Ltd. v. Coca-Cola Co,* 318 F. 3d 1284, 1288 (11th Cir. 2003).

1714 *Penalty Kick Management, Ltd. v. Coca-Cola Co,* 318 F. 3d 1284, 1288 (11th Cir. 2003).

1715 *Penalty Kick Management, Ltd. v. Coca-Cola Co,* 318 F. 3d 1284, 1291 (11th Cir. 2003).

1716 *Penalty Kick Management, Ltd. v. Coca-Cola Co,* 318 F. 3d 1284, 1291 (11th Cir. 2003).

1717 *Penalty Kick Management, Ltd. v. Coca-Cola Co,* 318 F. 3d 1284, 1295-1298 (11th Cir. 2003).

### b) England

The possibility of protecting combination secrets has been established in a number of landmark decisions of the English jurisdiction, such as *Coco v AN Clark Engineers Ltd,*[1718] in which Megarry J noted that, "something that has been constructed from materials in the public domain must possess the necessary quality of confidentiality".[1719] This statement clarifies that the test of inaccessibility is to be applied with respect to the information "considered as a discrete entity, independent of its component parts".[1720]

This principle was most famously acknowledged by Hawkings J in *Robb v Green*,[1721] a case concerning the unauthorised copying of the order book of the plaintiff by one of his former employees during the course of the employment relationship. The employee subsequently set up a competing business and used the copies of the book to target orders to the customers. With respect to the existence of a breach of confidence, the defendant argued that the information in the order book was publicly available in other sources.[1722] In this regard, it was held that:

> The names of all the customers are collected together in the order-book in a manner not to be found in any other book or paper to which the defendant had access. To him, therefore, the possession of a copy of the order-book would be peculiarly valuable. He would be saved the expense and delay of searches, such as would be necessary to enable him to compile such a list for himself (...) By making a copy of the order-book defendant was able to canvass at once each of his master's customers without trouble or expense.[1723]

As is apparent from the above, combination secrets will only be deemed secret if a certain degree of skill and labour is necessary to bring them together.[1724]

Such a principle was subsequently restated by Laddie J in *Ocular Sciences Ltd v Aspect Vision Care Ltd,*[1725] a case that broadly speaking involved two actions. The first concerned an alleged breach of confidence, a breach of

1718 *Coco v AN Clark Engineers Ltd* [1969] RPC 41 (Ch).
1719 *Coco v AN Clark Engineers Ltd* [1969] RPC 41 (Ch), 47.
1720 Tanya Aplin and others 2012 (n 22) para 5.16.
1721 *Robb v Green* [1895] 2 QB 1 (QB).
1722 *Robb v Green* [1895] 2 QB 1 (QB), 18-19.
1723 *Robb v Green* [1895] 2 QB 1 (QB), 18-19.
1724 John Hull 1998 (1016) para 3.28.
1725 *Ocular Sciences Ltd v Aspect Vision Care Ltd* [1997] RPC 289 (Pat).

contract and a breach of fiduciary duty, as well as a design and copyright infringement claim brought by two companies that designed, manufactured and sold contact lenses against their former employees. The second dealt with a patent infringement claim. Of particular interest for the purposes of the current analysis is that in deciding whether a booklet with all of the specifications of the lenses manufactured by the plaintiff was confidential, Laddie J questioned whether the "mere mechanical collection of data which is in public domain" could be deemed confidential. He further noted that to be treated as confidential, "there must be some product of the human brain".[1726] Such a distinction is a crucial one, as it indicates that effort, time and labour are not sufficient to confer the necessary quality of confidence upon information that is in the public domain.[1727] Thus, it appears that some intellectual skill is essential to regard the compilation of information as protectable.[1728] However, in this context, intellectual skill is to be differentiated from other IPRs normative standards such as novelty or inventive step. It is understood to refer to the trial and error process that gives rise to a unique combination of publicly available items.[1729]

### c) Germany

German commentators and case law have developed a so-called "mosaic approach" to conceptualise the protection of combination secrets, by virtue of which a combination of known elements may only constitute a trade secret if it is not known as such and derives additional value from becoming a new entity.[1730] In this scenario, it is regarded that the object of protection is the unknown combination of already known elements,[1731] which is justified on the basis that the compilation of information in a systematic manner can be very costly and time consuming. Indeed, it is the effort put into collecting and systematising the data that merits protection.[1732]

1726 *Ocular Sciences Ltd v Aspect Vision Care Ltd* [1997] RPC 289 (Ch), 375.
1727 Tanya Aplin and others 2012 (n 22) para 5.16.
1728 Tanya Aplin and others 2012 (n 22) para 5.20.
1729 John Hull 1998 (1016) para 3.28 and para 3.35.
1730 Björn H. Kalbfus 2011 (n 1300) para 138; Peter Finger, 'Die Offenkundigkeit des mitgeteilten Fachwissens bei Know-how-Verträgen' [1970] GRUR 3, 7; BGH GRUR 1966, 576 – *Zimcofot.*
1731 Charles Tait Graves and Alexander Macgillivray 2004 (n 699) 270.
1732 Björn H. Kalbfus 2011 (n 1300) para 138.

This principle was clearly stated by the Federal Supreme Court in a decision in 2006 (*Kundendatenprogramm*),[1733] which concerned the misappropriation of a client list by one of the former employees of the plaintiff who went on to work for one of its competitors (both PBC panels' manufacturers). As regards the secret nature of the information, the Federal Supreme Court held that:

> as long as a customer list does not consist merely of the list of addresses that can be easily found in public sources, it can be protected as a trade secret despite a low price for which such customer list was obtained. (...) Trade secrets do not necessarily feature as such property value (...). It derives from the nature of the customer lists that their value lies rather in the fact that they are not accessible to the competitors.[1734]

Consequently, the list, as a discrete entity, should be deemed secret if the names and additional data are gathered and assembled in a manner that would not otherwise be available to competitors.

In line with this argument, in Germany, case law and commentators have asserted that under certain circumstances the use of known information for an unknown end may merit trade secrets protection. This mostly takes place when an undertaking secretly uses a known process to achieve a result that is not known to its competitors,[1735] in a similar manner to the second medical indication exception under patent law set out in Article 54(5) EPC.[1736] However, to merit protection, it is crucial that the competitors are not aware of the use of the trade secret for that specific purpose.[1737] The object of protection is not that the company is using such a process, but rather that it can be applied to achieve an unknown result.[1738]

This was famously held by the Federal Supreme Court in a decision dated 15 March 1955 concerning a secret process to manufacture wax paste for furniture. Since 1931, the plaintiff had been producing wax paste for furniture according to a process that he had developed and kept undis-

---

1733 BGH GRUR 2006, 1044 – *Kundendatenprogramm.*

1734 BGH GRUR2006, 1044, Rdn 19 – *Kundendatenprogramm* translation by Gintare Surblyte 2016 (n 281) 12.

1735 Björn H. Kalbfus 2011 (n 1300) para 137.

1736 Article 54(5) EPC.

1737 Rudolf Kraßer 1970 (n 831) 590.

1738 Björn Joachim, Mary-Rose McGuire, Jens Künzel and Nils Weber, 'Der Schutz von Geschäftsgeheimnissen durch Rechte des Geistigen Eigentums und durch das Recht des unlauteren Wettbewerbs' [2010] GRUR Int 829, 829.

closed.[1739] In 1946 he hired one of the defendants to whom he revealed the secret manufacturing process. Subsequently, in 1948 the defendant terminated his employment relationship and started working for another company that manufactured and distributed chemical products. In February 1949, the plaintiff brought legal action based on § 17 UWG against the former employee and the new employer seeking to enjoin the further production of wax paste for furniture according to the process that he had developed.[1740] In May 1949 the parties reached a licensing agreement by virtue of which the plaintiff was entitled to receive a percentage of the turnover of the sales of the wax paste (between 5% and 6%). However, sometime later, the competitor introduced modifications to the formula and stopped paying the agreed fees to the plaintiff, which in turn led to further legal actions. Against this fact-pattern, the defendant provided evidence that the process was well-known and, consequently, the object of the licensing agreement had ceased to exist. In this context, the Federal Supreme Court ruled that a secret process could be known and still qualify for protection, provided that the use of the secret by the company to achieve a specific result was kept undisclosed.[1741] Ultimately, the appeal was dismissed because the variations introduced by the defendants were regarded as minor and, therefore, the validity of the licensing agreement was affirmed. The Federal Supreme Court later restated this argument in subsequent decisions, such as in *Kieselsäure*.[1742]

While German case law and commentators seem eager to support this principle,[1743] it is submitted here that courts should be cautious in its application, which should be limited to exceptional circumstances where the use of a known-process for an unknown use is not inferable from the state of the art and where companies have achieved a great competitive advantage because of its application. Indeed, in *Möbelpaste,* the process to manufacture the furniture wax paste was not objectively new, but was new for the competitor, who had no technical background. In such a context, it should be borne in mind that with time trade secrets erode as competitors independently generate the secret information, which in turn with time may enter the public domain. Hence, the use of a known process for an unknown result shall only be deemed secret to the extent that substantial

1739 BGH GRUR 1955, 424 – *Möbelpaste.*
1740 BGH GRUR 1955, 424, 424 – *Möbelpaste.*
1741 BGH GRUR 1955, 424, 425 – *Möbelpaste*
1742 BGH GRUR 1963, 207, 2011 – *Kieselsäure.*
1743 Björn H. Kalbfus 2011 (n 1300) para 137.

intellectual investment (a process of trial and error) by a circle of experts is necessary to link the process with the unknown result.

In the following section, a number of principles regarding the protection of combination secrets are suggested in order to avoid the privatisation of information that is in fact part of the public domain.

### d) Guiding principles

The protection of combination secrets and its implications for competition, innovation and employee mobility have been largely understudied by legal academia, yet the risks posed by such a tendency should not be overlooked.[1744] If courts affirm the protection of trade secrets that are already in the public domain by issuing injunctions against former employees or by enforcing non-competition agreements, the economic and social benefits associated with information dissemination and re-use may potentially be hindered.[1745] Furthermore, some commentators in England and the U.S. have expressed concerns about the fact that combination secrets claims may be used by plaintiffs in abusive litigation to avoid defining the specific subject matter covered by the secret information.[1746] Indeed, the comparative analysis conducted in the previous sections underscores that courts do not always evaluate the broader consequences for the public domain of confirming or denying such protection. In addition, a loose interpretation of such a principle is not in line with the TSD and the TTBER. The former notes that the injunctions and corrective measures adopted by virtue of Article 12 shall be revoked if the information no longer meets the requirements for protection (of which secrecy is one).[1747] In the same vein, the Guidelines on the application of the TTBER note that, "in the case of know-how the block exemption applies as long as the licensed know-how remains secret, except where the know-how becomes publicly known as a result of action by the licensee, in which case the exemption applies for the

---

1744 Charles Tait Graves and Alexander Macgillivray 2004 (n 699) 274.

1745 Charles Tait Graves and Alexander Macgillivray 2004 (n 699) 274.

1746 Charles Tait Graves and Brian D. Range, 'Identification of Trade Secret Claims in Litigation: Solutions for a Ubiquitous Dispute' [2006] 5 New JTechnology and IP 68, 77 -78; Roger M. Toulson and Charles M. Phipps 2012 (n 326) paras 3-086 -3-088.

1747 Article 13(2) TSD.

duration of the agreement".[1748] The general rule should be that once the secret nature of the information is lost, protection should also cease. Consequently, it is submitted that courts should be cautious when affording protection to combination secrets.

Drawing from Graves' scheme,[1749] this section proposes a number of interpretative principles that courts in the EU should take into consideration in the assessment of whether the combination of known elements (or known elements tied together with some unknown elements) merits protection as a discrete entity under Article 2(1) TSD. These principles intend to provide an analytical framework to avoid conferring exclusivity over information that is in fact already part of the public domain.

The first principle to be taken into consideration is whether "there is a functional interrelationship between the elements in the claimed combination secret".[1750] Graves suggests that courts should examine on a case-by-case basis whether the elements that constitute the trade secret are functionally interrelated in a machine, process or formula.[1751] This essentially means that the different elements have to be integrated following a "unified process that interoperates to form a unit", where all of the steps are necessary to achieve the end result.[1752] This first principle is crucial to ensure that the combination secret constitutes a discrete entity by requiring that it results from the application of a unified process. For instance, in chemical formulas, such as perfume compositions, the ingredients are frequently individually known, yet it is the interaction of the individual components that leads to a unique odour. Similarly, the value of a customer list lies in the systematic and methodical arrangement of its contents collected over time.[1753] Thus, the application of this principle would avoid rulings like *Tan-Line Sun Studios, Inc. v. Bradely*,[1754] where the methodology of the plaintiff, a tanning studio franchise, was considered protectable as a combination secret, even though it included methods of employee re-

1748 Commission, 'Guidelines on the application of Article 101 of the Treaty on the Functioning of the European Union to technology transfer agreements' [2014] OJ C89/3, para 67.

1749 Charles Tait Graves and Alexander Macgillivray 2004 (n 699) 274.

1750 Charles Tait Graves and Alexander Macgillivray 2004 (n 699) 276.

1751 Charles Tait Graves and Alexander Macgillivray 2004 (n 699) 277.

1752 Charles Tait Graves and Alexander Macgillivray 2004 (n 699) 277 citing among other U.S. cases *Saforo & Assoc., Inc. v. Porocel Corp.*, 991 S.W.2d 117, 121 (Ark.1999), where combination secrets where described as a "unified process".

1753 As noted by the BGH GRUR 2006, 1044 – *Kundendatenprogramm.*

1754 *Tan-Line Studios Inc. v. Bradley*, 1 U.S.P.Q.2d 2032 (E.D. Pa. 1986).

cruitment and training, studio layout and cash control, as well as marketing strategies, all of which were known to its competitors.[1755] In sum, it is submitted that the application of this principle would prevent the granting of protection to individual elements in the public domain that are used simultaneously by the plaintiff, i.e. the privatising of generally known information.

The second principle indicates that the combination secret as a discrete entity should have more value than the individual elements considered in isolation.[1756] This principle appears both in English case law (*Robb v Green*)[1757] and German decisions (*Kundendatenprogramm*).[1758] It essentially submits that the secret combination of known elements must be more valuable than its individual components. In addition, the value of the combination secret should be assessed against the other available alternatives, in line with the third principle proposed.[1759]

The third principle suggested by Graves enquires into whether the combination was *obvious*.[1760] At first glance, such a statement seems to contravene the general notion that trade secrets need not be novel, inventive or original. Indeed, as examined below, novelty or inventiveness in the sense of patent law are not required, nor is copyright originality.[1761] Consequently, it is submitted that the better wording, following the prevailing case law in England, is that known information should only merit protection if the combination results from the investment of "*intellectual skill*", i.e. it is a product of the mind of the trade secret holder. Indeed, information that can be automatically obtained (i.e. without the investment of intellectual skill) will rarely be regarded as secret, as it will mostly be considered "readily accessible".

Whether the plaintiffYet again, the problem lies in defining the necessary investment of "intellectual skill" from a qualitative and quantitative perspective. It is proposed here that such a standard is assessed against the existing alternatives used by the relevant circles. From a quantitative perspective, if in view of the existing alternatives the combination of known elements could be carried out automatically without further intellectual contribution from the holder that claims ownership (i.e. without undergo-

1755 *Tan-Line Studios Inc. v. Bradley*, 1 U.S.P.Q.2d 2032, para 7 (E.D. Pa. 1986).
1756 Charles Tait Graves and Alexander Macgillivray 2004 (n 699) 279-281.
1757 *Robb v Green* [1895] 2 QB 1 (QB), 17-18.
1758 BGH GRUR 2006, 1044 – *Kundendatenprogramm.*
1759 Charles Tait Graves and Alexander Macgillivray 2004 (n 699) 281.
1760 Charles Tait Graves and Alexander Macgillivray 2004 (n 699) 281.
1761 See chapter 4 § 4 E).

ing a process of trial and error), such a combination should not be eligible for protection. Linked with that, from a qualitative perspective, if the said combination does not confer any competitive advantage over the existing combinations used by other market participants, such a combination should not be deemed eligible for protection either, as the value it confers is minimal. Put simply, the combination of a specific "step of a process, part of a machine or design choice", for which a limited number of generally known or easily accessible alternatives exist with another set of known finite alternatives should be deemed to be generally known in the assessment of whether a combination trade secret exists.[1762]

The fourth principle propounds that courts should consider whether the defendant generated some of the elements of the combination independently. Graves considers this to be of utmost importance in the context of combination secrets mainly for three reasons: (i) if part of the information is already in the public domain, it is likely that the alleged misappropriator independently obtained the secret elements from public sources; (ii) if the information is common in trade with minor variations of the same basic elements, affirming protection may ultimately prevent competition among market participants; and (iii) if the defendant generated the information in an independent manner, the defendant may even file abusive litigation claims.[1763] Consequently, courts should always take into consideration whether the defendant has obtained the elements from which the combination is made from independent sources. This rationale was followed, for instance, by the District Court for the Northern District of Georgia in *Penalty Kick Management, Ltd. v. Coca-Cola Co*,[1764] where the defendant provided evidence that he had acquired the information from third party contractors. More complex appears the assessment of liability where some of the individual elements have been misappropriated, while others have been independently generated by the defendant. In this scenario, it is submitted that misappropriation should only arise with respect to the individual elements, provided that they meet the requirements for protection.[1765]

An additional principle is proposed here to avoid abusive litigation claims whereby, for the sake of legal certainty, the plaintiff must always be required to identify in a precise manner the information covered by the

---

1762 Charles Tait Graves and Alexander Macgillivray 2004 (n 699) 283.

1763 Charles Tait Graves and Alexander Macgillivray 2004 (n 699) 287.

1764 *Penalty Kick Management, Ltd. v. Coca-Cola Co*, 318 F. 3d 1284 (11th Cir. 2003); the facts of the case are summarised in chapter 4 § 4 C) II. 5. a).

1765 Charles Tait Graves and Alexander Macgillivray 2004 (n 699) 289.

trade secret, even though this is not explicitly mentioned in the TSD.[1766] Injunctions should not be granted unless the alleged infringer is informed of the information that he is free to use and that which is protected. Consequently, the individual elements that constitute the discrete entity that have been misappropriated should be clearly identifiable in the claims of the plaintiff.

As a final note, Graves holds that in order to find liability for trade secrets misappropriation, the plaintiff must prove that the defendant intended to acquire, use or disclose the combination as a whole.[1767] Under the legal framework created by the TSD, intent (or gross negligence) is only required in order to assess the liability of third parties. Consequently, such an interpretation is only supported in the present analysis with regard to acquisition by third parties.

## 6. Disclosures in the Cloud

### a) General considerations and outline of the problem

Cloud computing has been defined as "a model for enabling convenient, on-demand network access to a shared pool of configurable computing resources (…) that can be rapidly provisioned and released with minimal effort or service provider interaction".[1768] In a more succinct fashion, the Commission has described it as "the storing, processing and use of data on remotely located computers accessed over the Internet", which "makes computing power available everywhere and to anyone".[1769] The widespread use of cloud computing services has brought about numerous advantages from an information management perspective. Two of the most salient ones are that the hardware is owned by the cloud computing service provider and that the computing capabilities can be accessed by the

1766 Unlike Article 1 (1)(i)(iii) TTBER.

1767 Charles Tait Graves and Alexander Macgillivray 2004 (n 699) 287.

1768 Peter Mell and Timothy Grance, 'The NIST Definition of Cloud Computing' (2011) The National Institute of Standards and Technology Special Publication 800-145, 2 <https://www.nist.gov/publications/nist-definition-cloud-computing> accessed 15 September 2018.

1769 Commission, 'Unleashing the Potential of Cloud Computing in Europe' COM(2012) 529 final.

user over the network at any time,[1770] which essentially has allowed companies and individuals to store large amounts of data in the cloud and at the same time reduce the expenses incurred in acquiring and maintaining costly computer systems.[1771]

The legal implications of cloud computing in the context of data protection and copyright law have been the object of in-depth analysis by both academia and legislators.[1772] However, its repercussions for the law of trade secrets have garnered substantially less academic attention, even though they are closely interconnected with the increasing security issues raised by cloud computing practices. In particular, two notable issues arise in connection with the eligibility of information stored in the cloud to be a trade secret, namely: (i) whether trade secrets lose their secret status upon being uploaded to computer servers owned by cloud service providers, and (ii) whether the contractual exemption of liability by cloud services providers in the case of misappropriation negates trade secrets protection on the basis that the trade secret holder had not adopted reasonable measures under the circumstances to protect them.[1773]

A survey of the standard terms and conditions that govern the service agreements between cloud service providers and their users reveals that while many service providers are willing to ensure the adoption of certain security measures, they frequently expressly disclaim liability for the confidentiality and security of the information stored in their services.[1774] In a similar vein, in a study published in 2012 on the negotiation of cloud con-

1770 Peter Mell and Timothy Grance, 'The NIST Definition of Cloud Computing' (2011) The National Institute of Standards and Technology Special Publication 800-145, 3 <https://www.nist.gov/publications/nist-definition-cloud-computing> accessed 15 September 2018.

1771 Sharon K. Sandeen 2014 (1522) 7-8.

1772 On the issues raised by data protection in the cloud see Kuan Hon and Christopher Millard, 'What is Regulated as Personal Data in Cloud Enviroments' 165-189 in Christopher Millard (ed), *Cloud Computing Law* (OUP 2013) and more generally the European Cloud Initiative <https://ec.europa.eu/digital-single-market/en/policies/cloud-computing> accessed 18 March 2018; on the issues raised by copyright in the cloud see Lothar Determann, 'What Happens in the Cloud: Software as a Service and Copyrights' [2015] 29 Berkeley Tech LJ 1095, 1121-1126.

1773 Georgios Psaroudakis, 'Trade Secrets in the Cloud' [2016] 38 EIPR 344, 346-347.

1774 Sharon K. Sandeen 2014 (1522) 32-38; Simon Bradshaw and others, 'Contracts for Clouds: Comparison and Analysis of the Terms and Conditions of Cloud Computing Services' (2010) Queen Mary School of Law Legal Studies Research Paper No. 63/2010, 21-22 <http://dx.doi.org/10.2139/ssrn.1662374>

tracts, the authors concluded that during the negotiation process, requesting full indemnification for breach of confidence could be a "show stopper" and, at most, cloud service providers agreed to a capped liability.[1775] The rationale underlying such a limitation is to restrict liability for any security breaches that may result in trade secrets misappropriation and compromise data integrity, in view of the sheer volume of information managed by data service providers.[1776]

Furthermore, keeping information confidential has become increasingly difficult in the cloud environment, as the relevant data flows from the holder to a third party (the cloud service provider).[1777] In the context of data protection laws, the European legislator has imposed higher obligations on the controller or processor, who need to adopt the necessary organisational and security measures to mitigate such risks, taking into account the state of the art, the costs of implementation and the nature, scope, context and purposes of the processing.[1778] In particular, the GDPR specifically refers to measures such as the encryption of personal data and the ability to ensure the confidentiality of processing services and systems.[1779] In line with this, it has been argued that if the information is encrypted before being uploaded to the cloud, there is no disclosure that affects the secret nature of the information and holders can still rely on trade secrets protection.[1780] However, while it is true that unauthorised access can be minimised or even avoided by using encryption methods before storing the in-

---

accessed 15 September 2018 noting that "The majority of providers surveyed expressly include terms in their T&C making it clear that ultimate responsibility for preserving the confidentiality and integrity of the customer's data lies with the customer. A number (for example, Amazon, GoGrid, Microsoft) assert that they will make "best efforts" to preserve such data, but nonetheless include such a disclaimer. A number of providers go so far as to recommend that the customer encrypt data stored in the provider's Cloud (for example, GoGrid, Microsoft) or specifically place responsibility on the customer to make separate backup arrangements".

1775 Kuan Hon, Christopher Millard and Ian Walden, 'Negotiating Cloud Contracts: Looking at clouds from both sides now' [2012] 16 Stanford Technology LR 79, 104-105.

1776 Sharon K. Sandeen 2014 (1522) 37.

1777 W Kuan Hon and Christopher Millard, 'Control, Security, and Risk in the Cloud' 18, 19-23 in Christopher Millard (ed), *Cloud Computing Law* (OUP 2013).

1778 According to Article 32 GDPR.

1779 Article 32(1)(a) and (b) GDPR.

1780 Georgios Psaroudakis, 'Trade Secrets in the Cloud' [2016] 38 EIPR 344, 346.

formation in the cloud, these practices do not completely exclude risks, because encryption methods can be "broken" or "cracked".[1781]

b) Guiding principles

Against this background, Sandeen argues that in the digital age careful attention should be paid to the way in which information flows and consequently she proposes a multifactor test in order to assess whether the storage of trade secrets in the cloud constitutes a disclosure that would prevent the application of the trade secrets liability regime, borrowing from privacy theories.[1782]

The first factor, the so-called "Public Policy Principle", distinguishes between disclosures that preclude the application of trade secrets rules from "mere transfers". Based on the definition provided by Black's Law Dictionary,[1783] the author suggests that while a disclosure consists of the transmission of knowledge, a "mere transfer" does not.[1784] Ultimately, she argues that such a distinction is in line with the principle that selling a product does not necessarily reveal all of the secrets therein enshrined.[1785] The second factor proposes to take into consideration the purpose of the transfer and more specifically the use of the cloud service by the uploading party. In particular, due account should be paid to whether the information stored in the cloud is shared within the company (inter enterprise) or with third parties that are under no duty of confidence.[1786] In the former case, it is less likely that the information will become generally known within the relevant circles, as employees are bound by a general duty of confidence. However, disclosure to third parties, such as contractors, clients or even cloud computing servers appears more problematic. The deciding factor should be whether the purpose of the transfer is to impart knowledge or to

1781 W Kuan Hon and Christopher Millard, 'Control, Security, and Risk in the Cloud' 18, 19 in Christopher Millard (ed), *Cloud Computing Law* (OUP 2013).

1782 Sharon K. Sandeen 2014 (1522) 81-84.

1783 According to Black's Law Dictionary, the term 'disclosure, v' refers to the "act or process of making known something that was previously unkown; a revelation of facts"; while the term "transfer, v" is defined as "to convey or remove from one place or one person to another; to pass or hand over from one to another" *Black's Law Dictionary* (9th edn, West Publishing 2009)

1784 Sharon K. Sandeen 2014 (1522) 88.

1785 Sharon K. Sandeen 2014 (1522) 88.

1786 Sharon K. Sandeen 2014 (1522) 89-90.

merely pass information from one server to another.[1787] The disclosure of secret information will negate trade secrets protection if the receiving party acquired actual knowledge of the information concerned under no duty of confidence. Hence, the trade secret holder will not be able to enforce secrecy or prevent further dissemination of the information, if he cannot prove that an implied duty of confidence existed.

The third factor suggests reviewing the representations of the cloud service provider to assess whether a relevant disclosure (and not a mere transfer) has occurred and, in particular, to evaluate whether employees or other third parties connected to the cloud server provider may have accessed the information.[1788] A similar rationale is followed under the fourth factor, which enquires into the "expectations of the uploading party". This is essentially understood to mean that trade secrets protection will only be available if the trade secret holder reasonably expected the cloud server provider to maintain secrecy regarding the information uploaded.[1789] This in turn is closely connected with the fifth requirement, which looks into the functionality of the cloud storage service and whether the processing of the information is automated or requires human intervention (for example, by employees of the cloud service provider). In the latter case, there may be a disclosure of information that may render unenforceable trade secrets liability rules. This is also linked to the sixth requirement proposed by Sandeen, which looks into the ability of cloud service providers to access and use stored data.[1790] The seventh and final principle propounds that due account should be paid to whether "the cloud storage service provider has not actually accessed, seen or used the stored information".[1791]

In the light of the above multifactor test, Sandeen proposes a four-step analytical framework to evaluate whether trade secrets protection is available to information stored in the cloud. Accordingly, the first step consists of assessing whether information is transmitted beyond servers owned by the trade secret holder.[1792] The second step enquires into the nature of the flow of information and whether there was an actual disclosure or just a "mere transfer", pursuant to the proposed multifactor-test outlined

1787 Sharon K. Sandeen 2014 (1522) 89-90.
1788 Sharon K. Sandeen 2014 (1522) 89-90.
1789 Sharon K. Sandeen 2014 (1522) 92-93.
1790 Sharon K. Sandeen 2014 (1522) 96.
1791 Sharon K. Sandeen 2014 (1522) 97-98.
1792 Sharon K. Sandeen 2014 (1522) 99-100.

above.[1793] The third step analyses whether a duty of confidentiality (implied or express) exists between the cloud service provider and the trade secret holder.[1794] Finally, the fourth factor examines the measures adopted by the trade secret holder in order to preserve its trade secrets.[1795]

As a whole, it is submitted that the distinction proposed by Sandeen regarding "mere transfers" and "disclosure" seems to provide a convincing starting point to assess whether the information stored in the cloud is eligible for trade secrets protection. Only an actual transfer of knowledge between a trade secret holder and a cloud service provider or any other third party may constitute a relevant disclosure that prevents the application of trade secrets liability rules, unlike passive transmissions. Similarly, it appears of utmost importance to look into the purpose of the transfer and the functionalities of the cloud service in order to examine the nature of the disclosure, how the information is stored and who has access to it. Indeed, most cloud service providers do not have an interest in, and do not gain knowledge of, the information stored in their servers. They merely store it in a passive manner. Consequently, it is submitted here that even in the absence of express confidentiality obligations agreed upon contractually, if a cloud service provider merely stores the information passively without accessing it, the information maintains its secret nature and any unauthorised acquisition by a third party will trigger liability. This is furthermore indicated in Recital 39 GDPR, which provides that personal data should be processed in a manner that ensures appropriate security and confidentiality of the personal data.

In this context, it is argued that the analytical framework suggested by Sandeen places too much relevance on the adoption of reasonable measures under the circumstances requirement and the representations of the cloud service providers. As outlined above, in most EU jurisdictions, such a requirement is either non-existent (England) or the threshold is extremely low (Germany).[1796] As has been suggested, interpreting such a requirement in a very demanding manner would lead to an overinvestment in protective measures and spur an arms race among competitors.[1797] Hence, the fact that a cloud service provider undertakes to adopt security measures to preserve confidentiality (which is furthermore mandated by the GDPR

1793 Sharon K. Sandeen 2014 (1522) 100-101.
1794 Sharon K. Sandeen 2014 (1522) 101.
1795 Sharon K. Sandeen 2014 (1522) 102.
1796 See chapter 4 § 3 E).
1797 See chapter 4 § 3 E).

with respect to personal data) but disclaims liability for any breach should not automatically preclude trade secrets protection based on the fact that the trade secrets holder failed to adopt reasonable measures under the circumstances.[1798] However, in the unlikely event that no security measures are adopted by the cloud service provider, it is submitted here that the encryption of the information before its storage in the cloud by the trade secret holder should suffice to maintain the undisclosed nature of the information. In both scenarios, unauthorised access to the stored data (as well as any subsequent use or disclosure) by a third party that uses unlawful means to acquire the information, such as hacking the account of the user, will trigger liability under the trade secrets legal regime.

In any event, in the interest of legal certainty, it seems highly advisable that users obtain an express agreement from the cloud service provider, by virtue of which the latter undertakes to treat the information stored in its server in a confidential manner and not to disclose it to any third parties beyond its employees and on a "need-to-know" basis, even if liability in the event misappropriation is excluded. In such a contract, the trade secret holder should demand that the cloud server provider adopt reasonable security measures, in line with the requirements established in the GDPR for personal data.

In sum, the disclosure of information to the cloud service provider should not be regarded as automatically secrecy-destroying. The better view is that only the disclosure of information that involves the transfer of knowledge between parties that are not bound by a confidentiality obligation should be relevant. Furthermore, disclaimers of liability in the case of unauthorised access shall not prevent the application of trade secrets protection against third parties that access the information unlawfully.

### D) The doctrine of relevant circles

The corollary of the relative secrecy approach is that a certain number of people can access and acquire actual knowledge of the information covered by a trade secret. Yet again, the difficulty lies in establishing when the number of recipients is such that the information becomes generally known. Resorting to a numerical value in abstract (quantitative approach)

---

1798 Amazon Web Service User Agreement, para 3.1 <https://d1.awsstatic.com/legal/awsamendedCAterms/AWS%20Amended%20CA%20Terms_es.pdf> accessed 15 September 2018.

does not seem the most adequate solution, as the assessment of secrecy is largely factually driven. Article 39(2) TRIPs and Article 2(1)(a) TSD do not provide further guidance in this regard, as they only mention that information should not be known among, or be readily accessible to, "*persons within the circles that normally deal with the kind of information in question*". This statement seems to indicate that protection ceases if information is not known by the general public, but is known among members of a specific industry.[1799] Such a requirement seems to evocate the "person having ordinary skills in the art" standard applied in patent law. For secrecy to be lost the recipient of the information must "have access to normal sources of specialised information",[1800] which in turn seems to imply that he must be able to understand the content of the disclosure (in the transfer of knowledge sense). Indeed, not every member of the general public can comprehend the content of technical disclosures. By way of illustration, the publication of a complex biotechnological invention will only be understood by those with the necessary technical knowledge.

In view of the interpretative difficulties raised by the so-called "doctrine of relevant circles", the following sections explore how courts and commentators in three different jurisdictions (U.S., England and Germany) have interpreted such a condition in order to extract the applicable guiding principles (section IV).

## I. U.S.

In the U.S, the commentary to the UTSA notes that secrecy is lost when the information is generally known or readily accessible by "principal persons(s) who can obtain economic benefit from information".[1801] The

1799 François Dessemontet 2008 (n 601) 283.

1800 Daniel Gervais 2012 (n 505) para 2.486; conversely, Thomas Reimann 1998 (1323) 298, 299.

1801 See UTSA Comment to § 1 according to which: "The language 'not being generally known to and not being readily ascertainable by proper means by other persons' does not require that information be generally known to the public for trade secret rights to be lost. If the principal person / persons who can obtain economic benefit from information is / are aware of it, there is no trade secret"; see further the Restatement (Third) of Unfair Competition §39 (Am. Law Inst. 1995) comment f noting that "limited non-confidential disclosure will not necessarily terminate protection if the recipients of the disclosure maintain the secrecy of the information".

Supreme Court has further noted that relative secrecy should be assessed against the knowledge of "industry members".[1802] A review of the relevant case law suggests that courts have taken mostly two approaches when assessing from a qualitative and quantitative perspective the extent of the disclosure that renders a trade secret unprotectable. According to the first interpretation, when the majority of persons within an industry are aware of the information, protection ceases.[1803] Pursuant to the second interpretation, protection lasts until all of the members of an industry are aware of the information and consequently any competitive advantage derived from the information being kept secret disappears.[1804] In this context, due to the progressive erosion of secrecy, Unikel refers to trade secrets as "disappearing rights"[1805] and proposes an analytical framework that distinguishes between three categories of information:

- The first one, "Category 1" encompasses information that is known to substantially all persons in a particular field or industry;
- The second type, "Category 2" refers to information that is known to a majority but unknown to a minority;
- The third type, "Category 3" refers to information that is known to a minority but unknown to a majority.[1806]

Evidently, information in Category 1 falls outside the scope of trade secrets protection because it provides no competitive advantage to its holder.[1807] Conversely, information in Category 3 confers a notable competitive edge and, accordingly, is regarded as eligible for protection. The assessment of the level of protection that corresponds to Category 2 seems more problematic because its absolute competitive value is lower than in Category 3, but it may still possess relative value.[1808] In this context, Unikel suggests that only Category 3 information should be protected and that the term "minority" should be construed as meaning "less than half of persons who

1802 The Supreme Court has clearly enshrined this principle in two of its main decisions on trade secrecy law. In *Ruckelshaus v. Monsanto Co.*, 467 U.S. 986, 1002 (1984) it noted that "Information that is public knowledge or that is generally known in an industry cannot be a trade secret".

1803 See in this regard *TGC Corp. v. HTM Sports, B.V.*, 896 F. Supp. 751, 759-760 (E.D. Tenn. 1995).

1804 *Wilson. v. Barton & Ludwig Inc.*, 296 S.E.2d 74, 75 (Ga. Ct. App. 1982).

1805 Robert Unikel 1998 (n 1512) footnote 142.

1806 Robert Unikel 1998 (n 1512) 844.

1807 Robert Unikel 1998 (n 1512) 850.

1808 Robert Unikel 1998 (n 1512) 854.

could obtain economic or competitive value from its use".[1809] Even though such a proposition appears to provide great legal certainty for the trade secret holder and the alleged misappropriators, in certain industries the competitive advantage conferred by a trade secret known among, for instance, 40% of the market participants may be rather low, particularly if alternative inventions exist. Additionally, 55% of the market participants in a given industry may have obtained a secret in confidence as a result of a licensing agreement. Under Unikel's approach, one could argue that the licensing agreement should be regarded as null and void because the object of the contract has ceased to exist, even though the trade secret holder retains control over the undisclosed nature of the information.

## II. England

On the other side of the Atlantic, several English decisions have suggested that a piece of information enters the public domain when the information can be accessed "by those who have an interest in knowing it".[1810] This was for instance the deciding factor in *Franchi v Franchi,*[1811] where the High Court of Justice of England and Wales regarded a patent specification published in Belgium as generally known because patent attorneys regularly checked foreign specifications. In a similar vein, the Law Commission noted that "much information which is technically available to the public is not generally known and may in fact be known only to a handful of people".[1812] In this context, several cases allude to the fact that the accessibility of information will ultimately depend upon the skill and knowledge of the person that obtains it.[1813] For instance, Jacob J in *Cray Valley Ltd v Deltech Europe Ltd*, a case concerning the misuse of confidential information regarding formulations of resins and their manufacturing instructions, noted that "the recipes in issue here, although not published to the world in full, are to those skilled in the art of resin manufacture and

1809 Robert Unikel 1998 (n 1512) 875.

1810 Lionel Bently and Brad Sherman 2014 (n 125) 1149.

1811 *Franchi v Franchi* [1967] RPC 149 (Ch).

1812 Law Commission, *Working Paper on Breach of Confidence* (Law Com No 58 1974) 102 (as cited in Roger M. Toulson and Charles M. Phipps 2012 (n 326) para 3-116).

1813 A Roger M. Toulson and Charles M. Phipps 2012 (n 326) 3-116 with further references.

design, very ordinary".[1814] This statement seems to indicate that in England, at least in the case of technical information, the relevant factor in assessing secrecy is whether the information is accessible to people in a specific field. Such a statement highlights that the deciding factor that renders information unprotectable is the acquisition of actual knowledge beyond mere factual access to the information.

## III. Germany

Pursuant to the definition followed by German case law, for information to be considered secret it must be "known only to a narrow limited number of persons".[1815] Against this background, German commentators have identified four potential normative standards that allow for delineating when information enters the public domain in a more precise manner. Such principles will guide the present discussion.[1816]

In the first place, to maintain secrecy, information should only be shared with a limited circle of confiders ("*Begrenztheit des Mitwisserkreises*"). Accordingly, trade secrets should only be imparted to a restricted number of persons.[1817] However, such a standard is seemingly vague and open-ended because no hint as to the precise number of persons or the relationship among them can be inferred from it.[1818] Thus, in an attempt to provide more precision, some commentators have argued that the most appropriate yardstick should be that the trade secret holder has *control* over the relevant circles that know and have access to the information concerned ("*Kontrollierbarkeit des Mitwisserkreise*").[1819] Such an approach provides greater legal certainty, as it simplifies the proof hurdle. Indeed, confidentiality obligations that stem from labour contract or specific contractual NDAs are generally regarded as having sufficient probative value.[1820] Notwithstanding this, in the event of independent discovery by another competitor, the holder who first developed the secret may lose control de-

1814 *Cray Valley Ltd v Deltech Europe Ltd* [2003] EWHC 728 (Ch) [55].

1815 Translation by Gintare Surblyte 2011 (n 182) 49; BGH MMR 2006, 815, 816 – *Kundendatenprogramm*.

1816 Björn H. Kalbfus 2011 (n 1300) 85.

1817 BGH GRUR 1964, 31, 32 – *Petromax II*; BGH GRUG 1955, 424, 425 – *Möbelpaste*; *Köhler*/Bornkamm/Feddersen (n 835) § 17 Rdn 7a.

1818 Björn H. Kalbfus 2011 (n 1300) 86.

1819 See Rudolf Kraßer 1977 (n 1327) 179; *Ohly*/Sosnitza (n 813) § 17 Rdn 8.

1820 *Ohly*/Sosnitza (n 813) § 17 Rdn 8.

pending on the use that the latter makes of the information and the subsequent acquisition of the secret by lawful means.[1821]

The third interpretation regards that the doctrine of relevant circles in fact refers to the ignorance of the trade secret holder's competitors ("*Unkenntnis seitens der Wettbewerber*").[1822] On the one hand, it is clear that when all of the competitors in a market are aware of the information covered by a specific trade secret such information can no longer qualify as undisclosed.[1823] On the other, it is also true that if two competitors in a big market have developed the same trade secret independently, it retains the necessary quality of confidence. In such a scenario, with time, when more competitors are able to create it independently, the secret will erode and will end up entering the public domain. Furthermore, the economic value (understood in terms of a competitive advantage) will also decrease over time.[1824] Yet, it seems too strict (or unrealistic) to consider that secrecy is not lost until the last competitor is aware of it.[1825] For instance, in a market made up of fifty participants, if more than half of them are aware of the information it seems unlikely that courts will still regard it as secret. Another hurdle posed by this standard is that it overlooks the fact that often competitors cooperate in the context of research and development projects or strategic alliances, in which they share secret commercial and technical information. If information could not retain its secret nature, cooperation among enterprises would be hindered, thus negatively affecting innovation.[1826]

---

1821 As identified by Björn H. Kalbfus 2011 (n 1300) 86.

1822 Thomas Reimann 1998 (1323) 300 where the author notes that in Germany the protection of trade secrets is regulated by the UWG, which ultimately protects fair competition among market participants.

1823 François Dessemontet 2008 (n 601) 284.

1824 Rudolf Kraßer 1970 (n 831) 588; Gintare Surblyte, 'Enhancing TRIPS: Trade Secrets and Reverse Engineering' 725, 737 in Hanns Ullrich and others (eds), *TRIPS plus 20 – From Trade Rules to Market Principles* (Springer 2016).

1825 On the contrary, Nuno Pires de Carvalho 2008 (n 529) para 39.2.54 notes that "Secrecy, under subparagraph (a), remains until the last competitor (or the last person within the circle that normally deals with that information) obtains the desired information. If there are ten firms competing in a certain market, and nine of them know (secretly) about a process whereas the tenth does not know it, nor has it access to the information, that information is a trade secret as far as the tenth company is concerned. The important aspect is that information be not readily available to that tenth company (for example, as a result of its having been published in a scientific magazine, of which the company is not aware".

1826 Björn H. Kalbfus 2011 (n 1300) 88.

Finally, the fourth propounded principle is that information remains secret as long as the holder and the recipients of the information have a common interest in keeping it undisclosed.[1827] Such an assessment is not factually driven, and furthermore it introduces a subjective element in the interpretation of secrecy. In addition, it does not apply in cases of utmost practical relevance, such as in the relationship between an employer and an employee, particularly after the termination of the employment relationship.[1828]

## IV. Guiding principles

In sum, it seems that ultimately the most appropriate principle is the one that focuses on the assessment of the control of information disclosed by the trade secret holder, together with the possibility that the circles that actually have access to the said information are able to acquire active knowledge of it because it relates to their field of expertise.

Indeed, information will retain its secret nature provided that the trade secret holder retains control over the use and subsequent disclosure of the information concerned within the relevant circles, for instance through contractual NDAs. This ensures that the company will maintain its competitive advantage derived from the secrecy of the information for as long as it takes competitors to reverse engineer the product. It is also in line with Article 2(2) TSD, which defines the trade secret holder as the "natural or legal person *lawfully* controlling a trade secret".

With respect to the acquisition of knowledge, it should be noted that the disclosure of complex technical secrets, such as a chemical formula, should not be regarded as secrecy-destroying, unless the recipients of the information are capable of understanding the content of the secret and acquire active knowledge of it. Consequently, if the said formula is disclosed to lawyers with no chemical background in the course of a compliance process, it should not be regarded as publicly known for the purposes of assessing secrecy, unless it is further disseminated to parties that can comprehend it. In a similar vein, the assessment of secrecy should always be considered against the knowledge in the relevant industry in order to prevent the privatisation of information already in the public domain. Ultimately, such a rationale corresponds to the principle outlined with regard

1827 Björn H. Kalbfus 2011 (n 1300) 87.
1828 Björn H. Kalbfus 2011 (n 1300) 87.

to cloud disclosures, by virtue of which the disclosure of encrypted information does not render the information generally known.[1829]

### E) Secrecy as opposed to IPRs normative standards

Chapter 1 highlighted that one of the essential differences between trade secrets and formal IPRs is that to merit protection information must meet a certain qualitative threshold. In the case of patents, the information they protect must be novel and inventive. Similarly, works protected under copyright rules must be original. By contrast, in the case of trade secrets, information is protected merely by being kept undisclosed. The general principle is that no qualitative restriction beyond secrecy is required. Notwithstanding this, in a number of decisions courts in England and the U.S. have used a language that points to the introduction of limitations regarding the type of information protected, which is sometimes required to be "novel" or "original". The following sections examine the actual meaning and effects of such limitations with regard to the novelty requirement in patent law (section I) and originality in copyright law (section II). Finally, section III concludes.

#### I. Novelty

The concept of disclosure is central for the appraisal of secrecy in the context of trade secrets and novelty in the realm of patent law.[1830] The following sections underscore the differences and similarities between the two requirements in the light of the normative framework created by the EPC (section 1) and proceed to study the most relevant cases that demand novelty in the U.S. (section 2) and in England (section 3).

##### 1. Novelty under the EPC

As stated above,[1831] Article 54 EPC sets forth that for an invention to be novel it must not form part of the state of the art. The EPC is governed by

---

1829 Chapter 4 § 4 C) II. 6. b).
1830 Thomas Reimann 1998 (1323) 298.
1831 See chapter 1 § 3 A) I. 1.

the principle of "objective novelty", which is also referred to as "absolute novelty".[1832] Accordingly, patent applications are to be examined against all of the information available on the priority date, which may have been published all over the world.[1833] Furthermore, and to avoid double patenting, Article 54(3) EPC creates a legal fiction whereby patent applications filed before the relevant priority date, but published on or after that date, form part of the state of the art. Thus, under the legal framework set forth in Article 54 EPC, obscure sources are considered novelty-destroying.[1834] Furthermore, the EPO follows a strict novelty approach, by virtue of which a document is only considered novelty-destroying if all of the elements of a claim are disclosed in the document "combined within the same context".[1835]

Drawing on the foregoing analysis, the secrecy requirement has often been equated with novelty in patent law, mostly owing to the fact that trade secrets require that their object of protection is not generally known.[1836] Just as patents should not be granted over inventions already in the public domain, trade secrets should not be afforded protection if their subject matter is public.[1837] To hold otherwise would amount to a privatisation of public information.

Notwithstanding this, there seems to be a consensus regarding the fact that unlike the novelty standard in patent law, the secrecy requisite is not an absolute one.[1838] As a result, the assessment of these two requirements of protection should be different under the two different legal regimes in place. With regard to patents, as already discussed, a number of decisions from the Enlarged Board of Appeals of the EPO have established that it is not required that a person may in fact examine the prior art document or have reason to do so.[1839] By contrast, in the case of trade secrets the publication of "prior art information" is not necessarily immediately secrecy-de-

---

1832 Also in UK Patents Act 1977 (s 2) and German Patent Act (§ 1(1)).

1833 No geographical limits apply.

1834 Lionel Bently and Brad Sherman 2014 (n 125) 534.

1835 Alexander Harguth and Steven Carlsson, *Patents in Germany and Europe* (2nd edn, Wolters Kluwer 2017) 74; EPO T 0931/92 (10 August 1993).

1836 François Dessemontet 2008 (n 601) 282; Gerald Reger 1999 (n 553) 261 holds a different view and argues that the "not generally known or readily accessible" requirement is to be construed as a factual requirement with no normative value.

1837 François Dessemontet 2008 (n 601) 282.

1838 *Harte-Bavendamm*/Henning-Bodewig (n 376) § 17 Rdn 4.

1839 Chapter 1 § 3 I; Lionel Bently and Brad Sherman 2014 (n 125) 532; G 1/92 [1993] OJ EPO 277, 279 noting that "it is the fact that direct and unambiguous

stroying.[1840] Such an appraisal should be carried out on a case-by-case basis, as it does not suffice that the information is merely theoretically accessible. It is a matter of degree; it depends on the likelihood that a third party will access the theoretically generally available sources.[1841] Against this background, it has been submitted that the "not readily accessible or generally known" requirement refers to the specific possibility of third parties acquiring the information such that it is regarded as known or "knowable".[1842] Such a test is of a factual nature and unlike the novelty requirement in patent law has no normative value.[1843] Ultimately, the assessment of secrecy will depend on the possibility that the trade secret holder can exercise control over the use and subsequent disclosure of the information for which protection is sought.

The absolute nature of the novelty standard under patent law has not been without criticism, particularly in the light of the vast amount of data available through the Internet and the fact that the relevant yardstick is not actual disclosure but potential accessibility by any member of the public. In view of this, the EPO Technical Board of Appeal, in a decision concerning Internet disclosures, held that for the purpose of assessing novelty, a specific document should be accessible in a direct and unambiguous manner by known means and methods.[1844] In such a context, the proposed test is that the document (i) can be found by looking up the main keywords related to the content on a search engine, and (ii) is accessible at a URL for a period of time long enough for a person under no confidentiality obligation to access it.[1845] These requirements present some clear parallels with the sequential preservation model discussed above with regard to Internet disclosure and its effects on secrecy.[1846] Yet, while in the context of patent

---

access to some particular information is possible, which makes the latter available, whether or not there is any reason for looking for it".

1840 Rudolf Kraßer 1970 (n 831) 590.

1841 François Dessemontet 2008 (n 601) 282; similarly, Ansgar Ohly 2014 (n 100) 4: "Im Gegensatz zum Neuheitsbegriff des Patentrechts entfällt der Geheimnischarakter nicht schon automatisch dann, wenn die Information aus allgemeinzugänglichen Quellen verfügbar ist, denn es geht nicht um abstrakte Zugänglichkeit, sondern um leichte Zugänglichkeit im konkreten Fall".

1842 Elizabeth A. Rowe and Sharon K. Sandeen, *Trade Secrecy and International Transactions* (Edward Elgar 2015) para 3.18.

1843 Gerald Reger 1999 (n 553) 261.

1844 EPO T 1553/06 (12 March 2012).

1845 EPO T 1553/06 (12 March 2012); see further Guidelines for Examination in the EPO, Part G, Chapter IV. Section 7.5.

1846 See chapter 4 § 4 C) II. 4. d).

law the relevant issue is merely that the information is available for a period sufficiently long to allow for potential access by any member of the public, in the context of trade secrets due account should be paid to the extent of the actual disclosure and, in particular, the specific traffic of the website. In addition, the recipient's reason to know that the information was a trade secret also plays a role in the assessment of secrecy vis-à-vis the infringer, whereas such subjective considerations are not relevant in the assessment of the novelty standard.

In the light of the above, the following sections analyse the facts and legal reasoning followed by the most relevant decisions in the U.S. and England that have required that information should be novel, in order to shed light on the actual contours of secrecy and its intersection with the novelty requirement.

## 2. U.S. cases that demand novelty

### a) Analysis of the relevant case law

The U.S. Supreme Court, in its landmark decision regarding the potential pre-emption of trade secrets state law by federal patent law, *Kewanee Oil Co. v. Bicron Corp*, held that "novelty in the patent law sense, is not required for a trade secret.(…) However some novelty will be required if merely because that which does not possess novelty is usually known; secrecy, in the context of trade secrets, thus implies at least minimal novelty".[1847]

The aforementioned statement has been greatly influential and cited by a number of subsequent decisions, such as the 1980 decision of the District Court in Pennsylvania, *Anaconda Company v. Metric Tool & Die Company*.[1848] This case concerned the alleged misappropriation of the secret design of a machine used to manufacture telephone cord armour that protected public telephones from wear and tear by a former employee of the plaintiff.[1849] In the assessment of whether the machine in fact constituted a

1847 *Kewanee Oil Co. v. Bicron Corp., Kewanee Oil Co. v. Bicron Corp.*, 416 U.S. 470, 474 (1974).

1848 *Anaconda Company v. Metric Tool & Die Company*, 485 F. Supp. 410 (E.D. Pa. 1980).

1849 *Anaconda Company v. Metric Tool & Die Company*, 485 F. Supp. 410, 413 (E.D. Pa. 1980).

trade secret the court noted that "novelty is only required of a trade secret to the extent necessary to show that the alleged secret is not a matter of public knowledge.(…) A trade secret may be no more than a slight mechanical advance over common knowledge and practice in the art".[1850] Consequently, the court affirmed the existence of a trade secret because the precise configuration and assembly of the components made the machine "unique".[1851]

Following an analogous rationale, the United States Courts of Appeals of the Sixth Circuit ruled in *Richter v. Webstab, Inc*[1852] that an idea to include notebook covers and binders that matched trendy clothing was not protectable because it did not present sufficient "novelty".[1853] More specifically, it was argued that the idea of "using a particular design on a particular item is abstract" and consequently if the "design is not novel no legal protection is available".[1854] In addition, the court went on to note that:

> The law does not favour the protection of *abstract ideas as the property of the originator*. An idea should be *free for all to use* at least until someone is able to translate such an idea into a sufficiently useful form that it may be patented or copyrighted. Thus, competition in the use of ideas is a social good, hastening the process of innovation (emphasis added).[1855]

Thus, it was concluded that denying legal protection to abstract ideas disclosed in confidence would not have a negative impact on the flow of ideas among companies, because businesses had an interest in commercially exploiting a product, not the underlying concept.[1856]

Similar considerations were applied in a decision affecting the audiovisual industry with regard to the protection of an idea for a television series. In *Murray v. National Broadcasting Company*[1857] the Court of Appeals

---

1850 *Anaconda Company v. Metric Tool & Die Company*, 485 F. Supp. 410, 422 (E.D. Pa. 1980).

1851 *Anaconda Company v. Metric Tool & Die Company*, 485 F. Supp. 410, 422 (E.D. Pa. 1980); similar considerations apply in *Nickelson v. General Motors Corporation*, 361 F.2d 196, 199 (7th Cir. 1966), where the court noted that "trivial advances or differences in formulas or process operations are not protectable as a trade secret".

1852 *Richter v. Westab, Inc.*, 529 F.2d 896 (6th Cir. 1976).

1853 *Richter v. Westab, Inc.*, 529 F.2d 896, 901 (6th Cir.1976).

1854 *Richter v. Westab, Inc.*, 529 F.2d 896, 901 (6th Cir. 1976).

1855 *Richter v. Webstab, Inc.*, 529 F.2.d 896, 901 (6th Cir.1976).

1856 *Richter v. Westab, Inc.*, 529 F.2d 896, 901 (6th Cir. 1976).

1857 *Murray v. National Broadcasting Co., Inc.*, 844 F.2.d 988 (2d Cir. 1988).

of the Second Circuit ruled that an idea to create a sitcom that portrayed a black family in non-stereotypical roles (The Bill Cosby Show) could not be protected as a trade secret because it lacked "novelty".[1858] In this regard, the court argued that television networks had already cast black actors and that the idea for such a show had been suggested by Bill Cosby himself before the plaintiff, a former employee of the defendant (a television network), had submitted it for consideration to the executives of the network.[1859] In addition, it was noted that the plaintiff "had confused an idea with its execution"[1860] and that "when an idea consists in essence of nothing more than a variation on a basic theme (…) novelty cannot be found to exist".[1861] Against this background, it was concluded that to be protected, ideas must reflect a "genuine novelty and invention".[1862] Otherwise, they should be regarded as being in the public domain and free for everyone to use.

In view of the above, it appears that courts in the U.S. have demanded a certain threshold of novelty in trade secrets litigation mostly in two scenarios. First, it has been required in cases concerning manufacturing industries where the alleged trade secret was just a minor and often self-evident variation of existing technical solutions. Secondly, courts also seem to rely on novelty to prevent the monopolisation of abstract ideas by alleged trade secret holders.[1863] This is closely connected with the so-called "law of ideas", which is examined in the following section.

### b) The "law of ideas"

The analysis of the novelty requirement under U.S. trade secrets law would not be complete without referring to the emergence of a field of law dur-

1858 *Murray v. National Broadcasting Co., Inc.*, 844 F.2.d 988, 991 (2d Cir. 1988).
1859 *Murray v. National Broadcasting Co., Inc.*, 844 F.2.d 988, 991 (2d Cir. 1988).
1860 *Murray v. National Broadcasting Co., Inc.*, 844 F.2.d 988, 992 (2d Cir. 1988).
1861 *Murray v. National Broadcasting Co., Inc.*, 844 F.2.d 988, 993 (2d Cir. 1988).
1862 *Murray v. National Broadcasting Co., Inc.*, 844 F.2.d 988, 993 (2d Cir. 1988).
1863 James Pooley 2002 (n 66) § 4.03[1]; along the same lines the Restatement (Third) of Unfair Competition § 39 comment f concludes that "although trade secrets cases sometimes announce a "novelty" requirement, the requirement is synonymous with the concepts of secrecy and value described in this Section and the correlative exclusion of self-evident variants of the known art".

ing the second half of the XX century known as the "law of ideas".[1864] In essence, such a body of case law was developed under common law principles to address situations where the originator of an idea conveyed it to a third party, who eventually went on to exploit it without authorisation from the originator and without providing adequate compensation.[1865] In such cases, courts resorted mostly to five legal theories (the contours of which are sketchy) to provide legal redress to the originator and allow him to recover the value of his idea. The five causes of action most frequently invoked were: (i) express and (ii) implied contracts, whereby the defendant explicitly or implicitly undertook to pay a certain amount as consideration for the disclosure of the idea; (iii) property theories over the idea that prevented its unauthorised use; (iv) quasi-contract and unjust enrichment doctrines based on fairness arguments, and (v) breach of confidence, which to a large extent overlapped with trade secrets protection. These five doctrines have been the object of vehement criticism by legal commentators, mostly due to the potential disruptive effects that the "law of ideas" may have regarding the balance struck by intellectual property law and the public domain and the negative impact on innovation and creativity.[1866] Indeed, the increasing relevance of the "law of ideas" during the second half of the XX century is most adequately explained by the prevalence of the Restatement (First) of Torts, which required that a trade secret was "used in one's business".[1867] To be more precise, the comments to the Restatement noted that "a trade secret is a process or device for continuous use in the operation of the business".[1868] Consequently, courts regarded that ideas submitted for consideration to prospective business partners did not qualify for trade secrets protection, because the disclosure of the idea would not provide a continuous competitive advantage and the commercial exploitation of the products in which they were embodied rendered them generally known.[1869]

Notwithstanding the aforementioned, for the purposes of the present analysis, it is worth noting that a common threat to the five underlying

---

1864 James Pooley 2002 (n 66) § 4.03[1]; Margreth Barrett, 'The "Law of Ideas" Reconsidered' [1989] 71 J Patent & Trademark Office Society 691, 692.

1865 Margareth Barret 1989 (n 1864) 692.

1866 Melville B. Nimmer, 'The Law of Ideas' [1954] 27 Southern California LR 119, 120-140; Margareth Barret 1989 (n 1864) 757; Robert Denicola, 'The New Law of Ideas' [2014] 28 Harvard Journal of Law & Technology 195, 220-225.

1867 Restatement (First) of Torts § 757 (Am. Law Inst. 1939) comment b.

1868 Restatement (First) of Torts § 757 (Am. Law Inst. 1939) comment b.

1869 Robert Denicola 2014 (n 1866) 198-199.

theories of the "law of ideas" was that to merit protection courts required information to be *novel* and *concrete*.[1870] The *novelty* requirement was mostly interpreted with a two-fold meaning. Ideas should: (i) be either original to the plaintiff or (ii) be innovative in character (i.e. not part of the public domain), or (iii) fulfil a combination of both requirements.[1871] The first interpretation of the novelty requirement was fiercely criticised, because it allowed for privatising information that was in fact in the public domain but unknown to a minority, the alleged originator.[1872] As regards *concreteness*, case law did not provide a uniform interpretation of its conceptual contours.[1873] A number of judges understood that the idea should be presented in a tangible form or in writing, whereas some stressed that only the tangible form in which the idea was expressed would merit protection.[1874] Others held that *concreteness* should be understood as meaning that the idea should be fully developed.[1875] The latter view seems better suited to finding an equilibrium between the public domain and the interests of idea originators in recovering the cost of development of such ideas. In fact, similar considerations have been followed by English courts under the breach of confidence action.[1876]

As a final note, the enactment of the UTSA in the 1980s and more recently the DTSA, which do not require "continuous use of the secret", have allowed for overcoming the definitional problems raised by the Restatement (First) of Torts. Consequently, courts have progressively abandoned the five legal theories that dominated the "law of ideas" and subsumed such controversies under the law of trade secrets.[1877] In turn, the *novelty* and *concreteness* requirements have gradually been replaced by the

---

1870 Melville B. Nimmer 1954 (n 1866) 140.

1871 Margareth Barret 1989 (n 1864) 711.

1872 Margareth Barret 1989 (n 1864) 711.

1873 For a review of the first decisions on this topic see Melville B. Nimmer 1954 (n 1866) 140-144; Lionel S. Sobel, 'The Law of Ideas, Revisited' [1994] 1 UCLA Entertainment LR 9, 21-32.

1874 Margareth Barret 1989 (n 1864) 712-713 with further references.

1875 For instance, in *Smith v. Recrion Corporation*, 541 P.2d 663, 665 (Nev. 1975) the Supeme Court of Nevada noted that: "Concreteness pertains to the developmental stage of the idea, i.e., the idea must be sufficiently developed as to constitute a protectable interest. An ida in order to meet the test of concreteness must be ready for immediate use without any additional embellishment. The purpose of the test is to insure that the idea merits protection: That is tangibe and would not exist but for the independent efforts of its author".

1876 As examined in chapter 4 § 4 E) II. 2.

1877 Robert Denicola 2014 (n 1866) 236.

three traditional requirements under the law of trade secrets, whereby in order to merit protection, an idea must be secret, present commercial value due to its undisclosed nature, and be subject to reasonable steps under the circumstances to maintain its secret nature.[1878]

3. English cases that demand novelty under the breach of confidence action

In England, "novelty" has frequently been used to assess the protectability of secrets comprised of elements solely in the public domain (combination secrets), but also in manufacturing industries.[1879] As regards the first category, in the famous English case *Coco v Clark*,[1880] Megarry J indicated that the quality of confidence stemmed from a process of the human brain that conferred novelty, originality or even ingenuity:

> Something that has been construed solely of the materials in the public domain may possess the necessary quality of confidentiality: for something *new and confidential* may have been brought into being by the *application of the skill and ingenuity of the human brain*. *Novelty* depends on the thing itself, and not upon the quality of its constituent parts. Indeed, often, the more striking the novelty, the more commonplace its components... *whether it is described as originality or novelty or ingenuity or otherwise, I think there must be some product of the human brain which suffices to confer a confidential nature upon the information* (emphasis added).[1881]

In the same vein, in *Couthard v Disco Mix Club Ltd.*[1882] the plaintiff, a DJ, brought legal action for breach of confidence against his former DJ partners. He claimed, among other arguments, that the defendants were using a technique that he had developed for creating a beat-mix sound file that he had disclosed in confidence in the course of a partnership agreement. While delivering its judgement, the Court held that the techniques were "pretty obvious" and therefore not protectable.[1883]

---

1878 Robert Denicola 2014 (n 1866) 236.
1879 Lionel Bently and Brad Sherman 2014 (n 125) 1156.
1880 This case is analysed in chapter 3 § 3 C) II.
1881 *Coco v A.N.Clark (Engineers) Ltd* [1969] RPC 41, 47.
1882 *Coulthard v Disco Mix Club Ltd* [2000] 1 WLR 707 (Ch).
1883 *Coulthard v Disco Mix Club Ltd* [2000] 1 WLR 707 (Ch), 726.

## II. Originality

In England, as well as in the U.S., some courts have ruled that for information to be protected under the breach of confidence action it should be deemed "original".[1884]

As is examined in chapter 5[1885] in the context of perfumes, originality is also one of the criteria for protection under copyright law. So far, the originality benchmark has not been harmonised as such, either across the EU, or at the international level.[1886] However, in three of the EU Copyright Directives, originality has been defined as the "author's own intellectual creation".[1887] Such a standard was also adopted by the CJEU in the *Infopaq* decision when interpreting the notion of work under the Information Society Directive,[1888] and has been subsequently restated in a number of rulings.[1889] This interpretation and expansion has been the object of well-

1884 *Coco v A.N.Clark (Engineers) Ltd* [1969] RPC (Ch).

1885 See chapter 5 § 3 A).

1886 Elizabeth F. Judge and Daniel Gervais, 'Of Silos and Constellations: Comparing notions of Originality in Copyright Law' [2009] 27 Cardozo Arts and Entertainment LJ 375, 377 distinguish between four families of standards in copyright law: (i) the EU's "author own intellectual creation"; (ii) the US "minimal degree of creativity"; (iii) the Canadian "non-mechanical and non-trivial exercise of skill and knowledge" and (iv) the UK's "skill and labor".

1887 Database Directive (Article 3(1)), Software Directive (Article 1(3)); Directive 2006/116/EC of the European Parliament and of the Council of 12 December 2006 on the term of protection of copyright and certain related rights (codified version) [2006] OJ L372/12 (Term of Protection Directive), (Article 6).

1888 In Case C–5/08 *Infopaq International v Danske Dagblades Forening* [2009] ECR I-6569, paras 37-39 the CJEU ruled that: "copyright within the meaning of Article 2(a) of Directive 2001/29 is liable to apply only in relation to a subject matter which is original in the sense that it is its *author's own intellectual creation*. (...) The various parts of a work thus enjoy protection under Article 2(a) of Directive 2001/29, provided that they contain elements which are the *expression of the intellectual creation of the author of the work*" (emphasis added).

1889 See Case C–5/08 *Infopaq International v Danske Dagblades Forening* [2009] ECR I-6569 para 37 and subsequent decisions from the CJEU: Case C–393/09 *Bezpečnostní softwarová asociace v Ministerstvo kultury* [2010] ECR I-13971, para 45; Joined Cases C-403/08 and C-429/08 *Football Association Premier League and Others* [2011] ECR I-9083, para 97; Case C–145/10 *Eva-Maria Painer v Standard VerlagsGmbH and Others* [2011] ECR I-12533, para 87 and Case C–604/10 *Football Dataco Ltd and others v Yahoo! UK Ltd and others* (CJEU, 1 March 2012) paras 37-47; a more detailed analysis of the harmonisation of the notion of originality through the case law of the CJEU falls outside the scope of the present research; however a more comprehensive account is provided by Gernot Schulze, 'Schleichende Harmonisierung des urheberrechtlichen Werkbe-

founded criticism by legal academia, both from an intellectual property and a constitutional perspective, particularly in the UK, where the threshold of originality was comparatively lower than in continental Europe.[1890] In effect, traditionally, the English concept of originality was intended to protect works resulting from the "labour, skill or judgement" invested in creating them.[1891] In contrast, the concept of an author's own intellectual creation sets a higher bar, as following the traditional French test a work must be an expression of the author's personality.[1892]

In the context of trade secrets, the originality requirement, like the novelty prong, has been discussed in particular with regard to the entertainment and manufacturing industries, where an idea with potential to be exploited is imparted to a third party, who ends up developing and exploiting it in a commercial manner.[1893] The following sections look into how courts in the U.S. and England have construed such a requirement.

### 1. U.S.

In the U.S., a number of cases have noted that the information protected by a trade secret should present a certain degree of "originality". By way of illustration, in *Cataphote Corporation v. Hudson,*[1894] the Court of Appeals of the Fifth Circuit deemed that the techniques and processes to manufacture glass beads used by a former employee of the plaintiff that went on to create a competing firm were not protectable as a trade secret because in order to be protected, information "must possess at least that modicum of originality which will separate it from everyday knowledge".[1895] Following the same legal reasoning as the U.S. cases examined above with respect to

---

griffs? - Anmerkung zu EuGH "Infopaq/DDF"' [2009] GRUR 1019 and Silke von Lewinski, 'Introduction: The Notion of Work under EU Law' [2014] GRUR Int 1098.

1890 Eleonora Rosati, 'Originality in a work, or a work of originality: the effects of the Infopaq decision' [2011] 33 EIPR 746-755.

1891 *Ladbroke v William Hill* [1964] 1 WLR 273, 278.

1892 Elizabeth F. Judge and Daniel Gervais 2009 (n 1886) 386 note that two interpretations of the expression of an "author's own intellectual creation" are possible: (i) as a form of expressing the personhood of the author and (ii) as noting the absence of copying by the author.

1893 James Pooley 2002 (n 66) § 4.03[3] 4-21- 4-22.

1894 *Cataphote Corporation v. Hudson*, 444 F.2F 1313 (5th Cir. 1971).

1895 *Cataphote Corporation v. Hudson*, 444 F.2F 1313, 1315 (5th Cir. 1971).

the novelty requirement,[1896] the court concluded that an idea or process that is common, well known or readily ascertainable "lacks all novelty, uniqueness and originality, it necessarily lacks the element of privacy necessary to make it legally cognizable as a trade secret".[1897]

## 2. England

In England, one of the leading cases on the originality requirement within the breach of confidence action is *De Maudsley v Palumbo.*[1898] In short, the facts of the case are as follows: the plaintiff (Mr Maudsley) came up with the idea of opening a night club in London with the particularity that it could be legally open all night long and have sound equipment of the highest quality. He disclosed this idea to the defendant, Mr Palumbo, during the course of a party. A year later, the defendant opened a club, the world famous Ministry of Sound, with those same features. As a result, Mr Maudsley brought an action against Mr Palumbo for breach of confidence. In delivering the judgement, the court dismissed the action, establishing that for a literary, creative or entertainment industry idea to achieve the status of confidential information it: "(1) must contain some significant element of originality, (2) be clearly identifiable (as an idea of the confider), (3) be of potential commercial attractiveness, and (4) be sufficiently well developed to be capable of actual realisation".[1899] As regards the latter requirement, the court went on to argue that "before the status of confidential information can be achieved by a concept or idea it is necessary to have gone far from identifying a desirable goal. A *considerable degree of particularity in a definite product* needs to be shown to be the result of a mental process in question" (emphasis added).[1900]

The protectability of an idea for a new television series was also litigated before English courts, but with a different outcome than in the U.S. case *Murray v. National Broadcasting Company*[1901] examined above.[1902] In *Fraser v Thames Television Ltd*[1903] the possibility of relying on the breach of confi-

1896 See chapter 4 § 4 E) I. 2. a).
1897 *Cataphote Corporation v. Hudson*, 444 F.2F 1313, 1315 -1316 (5th Cir. 1971).
1898 *De Maudsley v Palumbo* [1996] FSR 447 (Ch).
1899 *De Maudsley v Palumbo* [1996] FSR 447 (Ch), 448.
1900 *De Maudsley v Palumbo* [1996] FSR 447 (Ch), 465.
1901 *Murray v. National Broadcasting Co., Inc.*, 844 F.2.d 988 (2d Cir. 1988).
1902 Chapter 4 § 4 E) I. 2. a).
1903 *Fraser v Thames Television Ltd* [1984] QB 44 (QB).

dence action to protect an idea for a television series about the actual experiences of three females members of a rock group was evaluated. The idea for such a series was first developed by the manager of a pre-existing three rock-girl group ("Rock Bottom"), who submitted it for consideration to a screenwriter, a television company ("Thames") and a producer (the "defendants"). During the initial negotiations, it was agreed that the three members of the band would act as the main characters of the series and that the information had been disclosed in confidence. However, the negotiations ultimately broke off and after some months, Thames, along with the other two defendants, produced a series based largely on the idea submitted by the plaintiffs, who sought damages for an alleged breach of confidence.[1904]

In its legal reasoning the court started by noting that ideas communicated orally were eligible for protection under the breach of confidence action, provided that the other requirements were met.[1905] In this regard, it further stated that to merit protection ideas must present an element of "originality", which may consist of a significant "twist or slant" on a well-known concept.[1906] Indeed, such a requirement correlates with the novelty requirement demanded in industrial settings.[1907] Against this background, it was ruled that to be protected ideas must be imparted in confidence and their content must be "(i) *clearly identifiable*, (ii) *original*, (iii) of *potential commercial attractiveness* and (iv) *capable of being realised in actuality*".[1908]

The fourth requirement has garnered substantial attention and was examined by the High Court of England in 2005 in a decision concerning the alleged misappropriation of design ideas for a cone-shaped device with a triple spiral to treat water (*Sales v Stromberg*[1909]). The court held that the idea of a triple spiral design was not protectable because it was not capable of being "put into practice in a practical way".[1910]

### III. Conclusion – protection of abstract ideas

As is apparent from the comparative analysis conducted in the previous sections, courts have applied the requirements of novelty and originality to

1904 *Fraser v Thames Television Ltd* [1984] QB 44 (QB).
1905 *Fraser v Thames Television Ltd* [1984] QB 44 (QB), 65.
1906 *Fraser v Thames Television Ltd* [1984] QB 44 (QB), 65.
1907 *Fraser v Thames Television Ltd* [1984] QB 44 (QB), 65.
1908 *Fraser v Thames Television Ltd* [1984] QB 4, 66.
1909 *Sales v Stromberg* [2006] FSR 7 (Ch).
1910 *Sales v Stromberg* [2006] FSR 7 (Ch), 111.

avoid the privatising of information already in the public domain based on trade secrets misappropriation claims. Indeed, a review of the relevant case law in the U.S. and England reveals that when courts require information to be novel or original they are ultimately enquiring into whether the information is secret or easily accessible, either because the information is in fact well-known among industry members (or even the general public) or because it is an evident variation of an existing technical solution. Consequently, it is submitted here that the novelty and originality enquiries do not constitute separate requirements of protection, but are in in fact subsumed within the general secrecy assessment. Therefore, in view of the harmonisation goals pursued by the TSD, it is advisable that courts across the EU refrain from using such terminology and confine their assessment to whether the information is in fact generally known or easily accessible.

In the same vein, the analysis of the case law examined above has underscored that courts on both sides of the Atlantic Ocean have struggled to draw a line between ideas in the public domain and those that should be afforded protection under the trade secrets regime in the U.S. and under the breach of confidence action in England. Indeed, in the U.S. this has given rise to a separate body of case law known as the "law of ideas" based on a number of legal doctrines; the contours of this remain sketchy and it has been criticised for its highly disruptive effects within the intellectual property legal system.[1911] As argued in chapter 1, abstract ideas do not merit protection either from the intellectual property regime perspective or from an unfair competition standpoint,[1912] and the same principle should be applied to the trade secrets legal regime. However, establishing when the level of abstraction is such that it precludes the privatisation of information runs as a common threat among all intellectual property doctrines.[1913]

In the light of the above, the better view it is submitted, is that courts should assess whether a specific idea imparted to a third party qualifies for protection as a trade secret by reference to the general three-step test enshrined in Article 2(1) TSD:

(i) The first step requires that information is not generally known or easily accessible. Abstract ideas will usually be devoid of such a concealed nature as no effort, skill or labour will be necessary to develop them. In the same vein, obvious variations of information in the public do-

1911 Melville B. Nimmer 1954 (n 1866) 140-144.
1912 See chapter 1 § 3 B) I.
1913 See chapter 1 § 3 B) II.

main should be considered as easily accessible and therefore not protectable either. Only more elaborate ideas developed after the investment of substantial labour, effort and intellectual skill will merit protection.

(ii) According to the second prong of the definition, ideas should only merit protection if they have commercial value (actual or potential) due to their undisclosed nature. In the context of ideas submitted for consideration to a third party, such a requirement should be understood as demanding that ideas present potential commercial attractiveness ("some kind of commercial twist").

(iii) The third limb of the definition requires that information is subject to reasonable steps under the circumstances to maintain its secret nature. This thesis has argued in favour of interpreting this requirement as a rather low threshold. In particular, as regards the protection of ideas, it will suffice that the parties execute an NDA, or that such a duty can be implied from the relationship between the parties (for example, between employer and employee).

(iv) As a final note, and in line with the arguments submitted in the present chapter,[1914] it is of utmost importance that the idea for which protection is sought is identified in a precise manner. Even though this may seem evident, it is essential to achieve an optimal equilibrium between the private sphere of a company and the public domain. In addition, it should further be required that such ideas are capable of being realised (put into practice), in other words, capable of being developed into a "finished product", in line with the English case law examined.[1915]

In sum, it appears that the more detailed and elaborate an idea is, the more likely it is to be afforded protection by courts. By way of illustration, the disclosure of a general idea for a television series that portrays a black family in a non-stereotypical manner (such as in the *Murray v. National Broadcasting Company* case)[1916] is unlikely to qualify for protection, because it falls short of the secrecy requirement. In turn, its inherent abstract nature will also substantially deprive the idea of commercial attractiveness, as commercial twists usually arise with regard to more developed concepts.

1914 See chapter 4 § 3 F).

1915 John Hull 1998 (1016) paras 3.64-3.65.
*De Maudsley v Palumbo* [1996] FSR 447 (Ch), 469; more recently, *Sales v Stromberg* [2006] FSR 7 (Ch).

1916 *Murray v. National Broadcasting Co., Inc.*, 844 F.2.d 988 (2d Cir. 1988).

However, if the idea were to be developed further and presented to a TV network or a producing company in the format of a TV Bible[1917] that subsequently went on to produce it following the guidelines outlined in the Bible without authorisation from the originator (and without paying appropriate consideration), courts would be more likely to grant relief. Indeed, similar considerations were followed by the Queen's Bench Division of the High Court of England and Wales in *Fraser v Thames Television Lt.*[1918] After all, from a practical perspective, if the information is recorded in a physical support, plaintiffs will be able to define the object of protection in a much more precise manner and thereby provide more convincing evidence of the alleged misappropriation.

More generally and from a policy perspective, it seems unsound to impose qualitative restrictions on the type of information protected under the trade secrets legal regime, since these are already embedded in the IPRs system and may conflict with the balance struck by the latter. As examined throughout this dissertation, trade secrets, unlike IPRs, do not confer erga omnes rights on their holders. They only afford protection against misappropriation and may not be enforced against third parties outside of the confidential relationship if the information is acquired by lawful means.

### F) Excursus: Trade secrets and Big Data — the way forward?

The emergence of the Data Economy has brought along a drastic shift in the use of data paradigm, as data have now become a key asset for innovation and economic growth.[1919] The inherent technical complexity of the phenomena that have arisen in this new context has given rise to numerous questions regarding the legal framework applicable to the newest data markets. Consequently, as outlined above,[1920] the Commission is contemplating several potential regulatory options in the context of the "Building

---

1917 A document used by producers and screenwriters in which the characters, the settings and the plot are explained in detail.

1918 *Fraser v Thames Television Ltd* [1984] QB 44.

1919 Josef Drexl 2016 (n 426) 9; OECD, 'Data-Driven Innovation: Big Data for Growth and Well-Being' (OECD Publishing 2015) 11-15 <http://dx.doi.org/10.1787/9789264229358-en> accessed 15 September 2018.

1920 See chapter 1 § 3 B) II. 4.

a European Data Economy Initiative".[1921] The Synopsis Report of the Consultation launched by the Commission indicated that stakeholders mostly regard that the TSD and the Database Directive already provide the most adequate framework for the protection of Big Data.[1922] Notwithstanding this, from a theoretical perspective, the application of the trade secrets legal regime to Big Data sets raises many interpretative questions.[1923] Before turning to them, it is necessary to provide some clarification regarding the functioning of the Data Economy and the concepts that are most frequently used in connection with it (section I). This is essential in order to provide a better understanding of the intersection between Big Data and the law of trade secrets, which is analysed under section II.

### I. The Data Economy and the associated phenomena

The Commission has defined the Data Economy as "an ecosystem of different types of market players -such as manufacturers, researchers and infrastructure providers- collaborating to ensure that data is accessible and usable".[1924] In such a dynamic ecosystem, new business models that are fundamentally different to the business models that dominated the web 2.0 landscape (search engines and social networks) have emerged. In the web 2.0 environment, search engines and social networks used the personal data of their users to provide them with personalised advertisements, thereby financing the provision of their services.[1925] By contrast, nowadays data

---

1921 Commission, 'Building a European Data Economy Initiative' COM(2017) 9 final.

1922 Commission, 'Synopsis Report on the Consultation on the Building a European Data Economy Initiative.' (2018) 5 <https://ec.europa.eu/digital-single-market/en/news/synopsis-report-public-consultation-building-european-data-economy> accessed 15 September 2018.

1923 The application of the sui generis database right to protect Big Data sets also appears problematic, as outlined in chapter 1 § 3 A) IV. 2. However, providing an in depth-study of this topic falls outside the scope of the present research.

1924 Commission, 'Building a European Data Economy Initiative' COM(2017) 9 final, 2.

1925 Josef Drexl 2016 (n 426) 8-9 describes the three stages of development of the Internet: "At this first stage of development the Internet emerged as an information and selling platform (web 1.0). At the second stage, new business models developed that provided consumers with other kinds of services, yet still related to information, without charging them a price. These services, such as search engines or social platforms that connect people with people (web 2.0), have become an *infrastructural resource* that can be used to create products and services for an unlimited number of purposes and in a non-rivalrous manner[1926] and, consequently, they are viewed as a valuable driver for innovation.[1927] Indeed, in the Data Economy, data analytics have turned out to be increasingly important as value creation mechanisms, mainly for two reasons: (i) on the one hand, they allow for gaining knowledge and control over the analysed objects, for example, environmental phenomena; and (ii) on the other hand, they automate decision-making processes with the use of autonomous machines, as illustrated by autonomous vehicles.[1928]

In this new ecosystem, new technologies have arisen allowing for the connectivity of machines and systems. These phenomena have been grouped together under the more general concept of the IoT, which essentially consists of "adding sensors and Internet capability to everyday physical objects",[1929] such as cars, lamp posts and refrigerators, to name some. The combination of those elements and the performance of data analysis ultimately lead to machine learning and remote control and allow for the development of autonomous machines and systems. Consequently, in recent years, the development of smart products and services has increased exponentially.[1930]

---

were often exclusively financed by advertising. Whereas at the first stage, information was largely limited to information as an object of the service, at the second stage personal data became a most important input for new kinds of business models that were information related. The advertising value of a service or platform increases with its attractiveness for private users who, in turn, provide its operator with personal data as the key input for such business models"; see further Amir Gandomi and Murtaza Haider, 'Beyond the hype: Big data concepts, methods, and analytics' [2015] 35 International J of Information Management 137, 142.

1926 OECD, 'Data-Driven Innovation: Big Data for Growth and Well-Being' (OECD Publishing 2015) 4 <http://dx.doi.org/10.1787/9789264229358-en> accessed 15 September 2018.

1927 Wolfgang Kerber 2016 (n 446) 989.

1928 OECD, 'Data-Driven Innovation: Big Data for Growth and Well-Being' (OECD Publishing 2015) 4 <http://dx.doi.org/10.1787/9789264229358-en> accessed 15 September 2018.

1929 The Economist, 'Where the smart is' (San Francisco, 11 June 2016) <https://www.economist.com/news/business/21700380-connected-homes-will-take-longer-materialise-expected-where-smart> accessed 15 September 2018.

1930 Bart van der Sloot and Sascha van Schendel, 'Ten Questions for Future Regulation of Big Data: A comparative and Empirical Legal Study' [2016] 7 JIPITEC 110 paras 16-17.

This new complex scenario is best explained through a real example case, such as the networked car.[1931] In June 2017 Volkswagen released a press statement announcing that as of 2019 some of its models would incorporate the "pWLAN" standard, which enables direct communication between vehicles, as well as transport infrastructure and international markets.[1932] The implementation of such a technology will allow for sharing real-time information gathered by the numerous sensors included in the cars on the state of the traffic, accidents and even environmental conditions within a radius of 500 metres, without the need to rely on a mobile network. It further aims at providing greater safety and traffic efficiency, helping users to avoid risky situations. The statement concludes by noting that the effectiveness of the pWLAN technology will improve with use, thereby highlighting the network effects of data sharing in the Data Economy. As a result, the note issued by Volkswagen also emphasises that the company is working together with other car manufacturers, industry partners, as well as public authorities in order to spread the inclusion of the pWLAN technology in serial production.[1933]

The big streams of data collected by tracking the activities of consumers that browse the web or by sensors incorporated into physical interconnected objects, such as in the case of the networked car outlined above, are subsequently included in larger datasets for their management and analysis.[1934] These datasets are generally referred to as "Big Data", alluding to one of the defining features of the collections of data in the Digital Economy: their sheer magnitude.[1935] However, conceptualising the Big Data phenomenon solely by reference to this parameter appears over-simplistic. Indeed, the most frequently cited definition refers to a confluence of factors, the so-called "three V's":

1931 This is the example propposed by Andreas Wiebe 2016 (n 287) 878.

1932 Volkswagen, 'With the aim of increasing safety in road traffic, Volkswagen will enable vehicles to communicate with each other as from 2019' (28 June 2017) <https://www.volkswagen-media-services.com/en/detailpage/-/detail/With-the-aim-of-increasing-safety-in-road-traffic-Volkswagen-will-enable-vehicles-to-communicate-with-each-other-as-from-2019/view/5234247/7a5bbec13158edd433c6630f5ac445da> accessed 15 September 2018.

1933 Ibid.

1934 Amir Gandomi and Murtaza Haider 2015 (n 1925) 139-140.

1935 OECD, 'Data-Driven Innovation: Big Data for Growth and Well-Being' (OECD Publishing 2015) 11 <http://dx.doi.org/10.1787/9789264229358-en> accessed 15 September 2018.

i. *Volume* alludes to the dimension of the datasets, which are measured in terabytes and petabytes.[1936]
ii. *Variety* refers to the heterogeneity of the data sources, which may be structured, but most frequently are not.[1937] Data may be obtained from a myriad of sources ranging from social media or web blogs to financial communications and sensors incorporated into physical objects.[1938] The term variety also refers to the possibility of establishing a correlation between the different data sources.[1939]
iii. *Velocity* highlights the rate at which data are generated, accessed and processed.[1940] The predictive power of data analytics is higher than ever before, allowing companies to use it in a much more precise way.[1941]

In addition to the three above-mentioned variables, it has been suggested that there are further features that are usually deployed in the common framework for characterising Big Data, namely:

iv. *Value*, which underscores that Big Data presents "low value density". That is, individual data bits as such may have little value, yet upon analysis of large amounts of collected data it is possible to obtain substantial value.[1942]

---

1936 Mike Loukides, 'What is Data Science?' (2010) <https://www.oreilly.com/ideas/what-is-data-science> accessed 15 September 2018; Amir Gandomi and Murtaza Haider 2015 (n 1930) 138.

1937 Amir Gandomi and Murtaza Haider 2015 (n 1925) 138.

1938 These are just some of the examples outlined in OECD, 'Data-Driven Innovation: Big Data for Growth and Well-Being' (OECD Publishing 2015), 14 <http://dx.doi.org/10.1787/9789264229358-en> accessed 15 September 2018.

1939 Federal Trade Commission, 'Big Data: A Tool for Inclusion or Exclusion, Understanding the issues' (2016) FTC Report, 1 <https://www.ftc.gov/reports/big-data-tool-inclusion-or-exclusion-understanding-issues-ftc-report> accessed 15 September 2018.

1940 Amir Gandomi and Murtaza Heider 2015 (n 1925) 138.

1941 Federal Trade Commission, 'Big Data: A Tool for Inclusion or Exclusion, Understanding the issues' (2016) FTC Report, 2 <https://www.ftc.gov/reports/big-data-tool-inclusion-or-exclusion-understanding-issues-ftc-report> accessed 15 September 2018.

1942 Richard Winter, 'Big Data: Business Opportunities, Requirements and Oracle's Approach' (2011) Executive Report, 2 <http://www.oracle.com/us/corporate/analystreports/infrastructure/winter-big-data-1438533.pdf.> accessed 15 September 2018.

v. *Veracity*, which refers to the unprecise and uncertain nature of the data collected, for example, when it comes to measuring customers' sentiments.[1943]

vi. *Variability and complexity*, which emphasises that data fluctuation is a common phenomenon and that individual data are obtained from multiple sources.[1944]

Notwithstanding the aforementioned, defining Big Data solely by reference to the confluence of factors spelt out above has been criticised for not signalling the different ends for which data can be used, as well as for the fact that the full potential of data is only unlocked after the large streams of individual data bits are processed and analysed.[1945] The importance of data analytics as value creation mechanisms was stressed by the Federal Trade Commission ("FTC") in a report in which the legal issues surrounding the emergence of the Big Data phenomena in the U.S. were discussed.[1946] According to the FTC, the life cycle of Big Data is divided into the following four stages: (i) collection, (ii) compilation and consolidation, (iii) data mining and analytics,[1947] and (iv) use.[1948] In the first stage of the

---

1943 Amir Gandomi and Murtaza Heider 2015 (n 1925) 138.

1944 Amir Gandomi and Murtaza Heider 2015 (n 1925) 137.

1945 OECD, 'Data-Driven Innovation: Big Data for Growth and Well-Being' (OECD Publishing 2015) 30 <http://dx.doi.org/10.1787/9789264229358-en> accessed 15 September 2018; Amir Gandomi and Murtaza Heider 2015 (n 1925) 139-140 note that "Big data are worthless in a vacuum. Its potential value is unlocked only when leveraged to drive decision making. To enable such evidence-based decision making, organizations need efficient processes to turn high volume of fast-moving data into meaningful insights".

1946 Federal Trade Commission, 'Big Data: A Tool for Inclusion or Exclusion, Understanding the issues' (2016) FTC Report, 3-4 <https://www.ftc.gov/reports/big-data-tool-inclusion-or-exclusion-understanding-issues-ftc-report> accessed 15 September 2018.

1947 A detailed account of the current trends and perspectives of data analytics see Karthik Kambatla, Giorgos Kollias, Vipin Kumar and Ananth Grama, 'Trends in big data analytics' [2014] 74 J of Parallel and Distributed Computing 2561-2573.

1948 Federal Trade Commission, 'Big Data: A Tool for Inclusion or Exclusion, Understanding the issues' (2016) FTC Report 3-4; in a similar vein see Herbert Zech, 'Data as Tradeable Commodity – Implications for Contract Law' 2 in Josef Drexl (ed), *Proceedings of the 18th EIPIN Congress: The New Data Economy between Data Ownership, Privacy and Safeguarding Competition* (Edward Elgar) (forthcoming) notes that the Data Economy is divided into four sequential stages: (i) production of data; (ii) collection of data; (iii) analysis of data and (iv) possible innovations resulting from the analysis <https://ssrn.com/abstract=3063153> accessed 15 September 2018.

value chain, data are gathered from a variety of sources, such as tracking cookies or interconnected sensors incorporated into physical devices (IoT). Next, the raw data are systematised by entities such as online ad networks, social media companies, online platforms or data aggregation entities.[1949] Crucially, during the third stage, the data are analysed in order to unveil common patterns or other characteristics across the compiled datasets. In recent years, the emergence of predictive data analytics techniques has allowed firms to anticipate new or future observations i.e. to create new data on the basis of pre-existing data sets.[1950] In effect, in the value chain of Big Data, data-based innovations can only take place after the collection of data.[1951] In the latter stage, the insights obtained from the previous phases are used in the context of process optimisation.

The complex flow of data and the multiple stakeholders that take part in the value networks[1952] that operate in the Data Economy have given rise to a high level of legal uncertainty regarding the ownership and access to data conditions.[1953] For instance, following the networked car example mentioned above, several stakeholders may have an interest in the information collected by the sensors and mobile applications incorporated in smart vehicles, including the car owner and the user, as well as navigation service providers, who may be able to improve the quality of their services through real-time analysis of the gathered data.[1954] Similarly, insurance companies may find such information useful to provide individualised

---

1949 Federal Trade Commission, 'Big Data: A Tool for Inclusion or Exclusion, Understanding the issues' (2016) FTC Report, 3-4 <https://www.ftc.gov/reports/big-data-tool-inclusion-or-exclusion-understanding-issues-ftc-report> accessed 15 September 2018.

1950 As noted by Galit Shmueli, 'To Explain or to Predict?' [2010] 25 Statistical Science 289, 291.

1951 Herbert Zech 2016 (n 278) 58.

1952 In this context, Josef Drexl 2016 (n 426) 16-17 underscores that in the "traditional economy" the value creation paradigm is of a vertical nature, where "manufacturers purchase input for the production of goods in upstream markets and then sell them through distribution chains – often including wholesales and distributors- to consumers. At each level of the production and distribution chain, some economic value is added". By contrast, in the Data Economy, value enlarges through value networks.

1953 As suggested by Andreas Wiebe 2016 (n 287) 878.

1954 See Wolfgang Kerber 2016 (n 446) 995; more generally the OECD, 'Data-Driven Innovation: Big Data for Growth and Well-Being' (OECD Publishing 2015) 14 <http://dx.doi.org/10.1787/9789264229358-en> accessed 15 September 2018 identified the following six key types of players: "(i) Internet service providers providing the backbone of the data ecosystem, (ii) IT infrastructure providers

prices to their customers based on the analysis of real-time risk and their behaviour while driving.[1955] Governmental authorities could also benefit from access to such data, as they would be able to gain an insight into the state of the traffic, or use it in managing toll systems or in crime prevention.[1956] Finally, Internet Service Providers ("ISPs") may also be interested in such data, which may allow them to provide targeted advertisements. Notably, as stressed by Drexl, a distinctive characteristic of the Data Economy is the "increasing role of Internet Intermediaries" on the basis of a twofold rationale: (i) ISPs are aware of the consumer preferences and control data interfaces, and consequently (ii) they are at a competitive advantage in the penetration of the smart products markets.[1957]

---

offering data management tools and critical computing resources including, but not limited to, data storage servers, database management software, and cloud computing resources, (iii) data analytic providers who supply software solution for data analysis including data visualisation, (iv) data providers, mainly the consumers (...), (v) governments through their open data initiatives (...), firms such as in particular data brokers and data market places (...), and increasingly owners of interconnected machines and systems (...), and last but not least (vi) data-driven entrepreneurs, who build their innovation on top of the resources provided in the data ecosystem in areas such as retail, finance, advertisement, science (...) and health (...) to name a few".

1955 'Huge volumes of data make real time insurance a possibility – Pay per risk' *The Economist* (21 September 2017) <https://www.economist.com/finance-and-economics/2017/09/21/huge-volumes-of-data-make-real-time-insurance-a-possibility> accessed 15 September 2018: "Conventional insurance works by pooling individual risks and then setting a price for that group- new drivers under 30, say. But the process can be much refined if the objects and people being insured can report to the insurer automatically, and if there is a wealth of data on the external environment. As an ever-growing number of sensors- in phones or watches, drones or cars – gathers ever-greater volumes of data, more and more activities can be assessed for real-time risk (though in the absence of pooling, some risks may become prohibitely expensive to insure)".

1956 Andreas Wiebe 2016 (n 287) 879.

1957 From a competition law perspective, Josef Drexl 2016 (n 426) 17-18 further indicates that "whereas the digital transformation of the industry decreases existing entry barriers and may even force industrial incumbents out of the market, control over data enables firms originating in the Internet sector, such as Google, to enter into and gain considerable market power in a large variety of different markets for the production and operation of smart products. Recognition of data ownership may therefore have the unwanted effect of strengthening the market power of these firms even more, while, from a competitive perspective, it would be wiser to promote access to data that is needed by other market players to operate in such markets".

In the context of the myriad of potential stakeholders that may have an interest in accessing the data created in the Data Economy environment, the most salient legal issue that arises is whether any of the applicable existing legal regimes may afford protection to industrial data or instead whether exclusivity should be granted over the said data at the collection level by the introduction of a sui generis right (prior to any innovations).[1958] As noted above,[1959] this prompted the Commission to launch a consultation in order to assess, among other options, the possibility of introducing a "data producers' right" over industrial data, as there seems to be consensus regarding the fact that industrial data, as such, are not protected by any exclusive intellectual property right.[1960] However, existing regimes such as contract law, criminal law, tort law or trade secrets may already provide a robust legal framework for industrial data governance.[1961] Providing an in-depth analysis of such a complex topic falls outside the scope of this dissertation. Thus, this thesis is confined to the study of the possibility of relying on the trade secrets legal regime for the protection of industrial data (section 2).

## II. Assessing the possibility of relying on trade secrets protection for industrial data

As noted in chapter 1, the TRIPs Agreement defines trade secrets as undisclosed information.[1962] Following the theory of semiotics, trade secrets protect information at the semantic level, i.e. information with a specific

1958 Herbert Zech 2016 (n 278) 58.

1959 Chapter 1 § 3 B) II. 5.

1960 Commission, 'Commission Staff Working Document on the free flow of data and emerging issues of the European data economy' SWD(2017) 2 final, 19 concluded that "Machine-generated and industrial data do not benefit from protection by other intellectual property rights as they are deemed not to be the result of an intellectual effort. Results of data integration, analytics, etc. can be protected, on the other hand, as a result of a protection given to the intellectual effort made into the design of the data integration process or the analytics algorithm (software)"; an overview of the academic debate is provided by Andreas Wiebe 2016 (n 287) 880; Josef Drexl and others 2017 (n 442) paras 9-17; Josef Drexl 2016 (n 426) 19-26, Michael Dorner, 'Big Data und "Dateneigentum"' [2014] CR 617, 622; Josef Drexl and others 2017 (n 442) paras 9-17.

1961 See Wolfgang Kerber 2016 (n 446) 998.

1962 See chapter 2 § 1 A) IV.

meaning.[1963] Hence, at first glance, industrial data and the algorithms used to create them seem to fall within the scope of protection of trade secrets, both according to the minimum standards set out in the TRIPs Agreement and the harmonised legal regime introduced by virtue of the TSD. However, upon closer examination, the technical specificities of Big Data and the survey of the requirements of protection that trigger liability under the TSD call for a more nuanced approach, which is analysed under section (1). Indeed, several legal scholars have criticised the TSD, stating that it was out of date even before its implementation deadline, because the European legislator overlooked its potential applicability in the Data Economy.[1964] Next, additional issues in the application of the TSD to the protection of Big Data are outlined (section 2), from which conclusions are drawn (section 3).

### 1. Reconciling the legal requirements of protection of trade secrets law with Big Data

According to the TRIPs Agreement and the TSD,[1965] information can be protected so long as: (i) it is "secret" in the sense that it is not "generally known among or readily accessible to persons within the circles that normally deal with the information in question"; (ii) it has commercial value due to its secret nature; and (iii) it has been subject to reasonable steps under the circumstances to maintain its concealed nature. The applicability of these three requirements to the large streams of data that are gathered and analysed in the context of Big Data requires specific consideration.

As regards the first requirement, it should be noted that one of the defining features of the Data Economy is the ubiquity of data collection, which allows different physical objects equipped with sensors connected to the IoT to gather the same data. Consequently, it has been argued that if the individual data can be simultaneously collected by different sensors and machines, the secrecy requirement will not be satisfied.[1966] The networked car example illustrates this in the most clear manner: if several vehicles collect the same information on the state of transit and transfer it to

---

1963 Herbert Zech 2015 (n 423) para 8.

1964 This is noted by Andreas Wiebe 2016 (n 287) 880; similarly Josef Drexl 2016 (n 426) 22.

1965 See Article 39(2) TRIPs, Article 2(1) TSD.

1966 Josef Drexl 2016 (n 426) 23.

different car manufacturers, the individual data will be deemed generally available, thus forfeiting trade secrets protection.

However, it cannot be affirmed from the outset that Big Data sets should be automatically regarded as publicly known. On both sides of the Atlantic, namely, the U.S., Germany and England, courts have construed the secrecy requirement as comprising the assembly of elements in the public domain when it results in a separate secret entity, a so-called "combination secret".[1967] This is the rationale that is usually followed with regard to the protection of customer lists, which are mostly made up of information that is publicly available, but are nonetheless deemed eligible for protection in most jurisdictions, provided that the lists as a discrete entity are not available to competitors.[1968]

Against this background, the analytical framework proposed above in the context of combination secrets appears of utmost relevance in assessing the protection of Big Data sets under the harmonised framework created by the TSD.[1969]

Pursuant to the first factor, the gathering of individual data that can be simultaneously collected by competitors will still be eligible for protection if there is a functional interrelationship between the elements in the claimed combination secret. In the context of Big Data, such a requirement is easily met, as the individual data are integrated into larger sets following a unified process.

The second factor purports that the combined elements should have more value than the individual elements considered in isolation. The application of this factor allows for overcoming the definitional problems raised by the commercial value requirement, as it has been suggested that individual data on ephemeral events as such may not fulfil this condition. In effect, in the Data Economy, the full potential of data is only unlocked after a data analytics process. In this context, the wording of Recital 14 of the TSD appears to be particularly relevant.[1970] On the one hand, it expressly clarifies that the value of data can be both "actual" and "potential",

---

1967 Chapter 4 § 4 C) II. 5.

1968 Gintare Surblyte 2016 (n 281) 11-12.

1969 Chapter 4 § 4 C) II. 5. d)

1970 See Recital 14 of the TSD: "(...) Furthermore, such know- how or information should have a commercial value, whether *actual* or *potential*. Such know-how or information should be considered to have a commercial value, for example, where its unlawful acquisition, use or disclosure is likely to harm the interests of the person lawfully controlling it, in that it undermines that person's scientific and technical potential, business or financial interests, strategic positions

which seems to indicate that individual data may be eligible for protection if, from their inclusion in larger data sets and subsequent analysis, it is possible to obtain insights that reveal common patterns or any other valuable information. On the other hand, it further indicates that "trivial information" shall not qualify for protection under the law of trade secrets. This apparent tension can be solved most effectively through the application of the methodology of statutory legal interpretation. From a semantic perspective, *trivial* is an adjective that is used to refer to items of "little value or importance".[1971] However, following a systematic interpretation of the provisions of the TSD, the exclusion of trivial information should not extend to individual data that are included in larger datasets for their subsequent analysis. Indeed, such individual data should be considered to have, at least, potential value and therefore be eligible for protection under the definition of trade secrets provided in Article 2(1) of the TSD.[1972] Their value lies in their incorporation in big data sets. Yet, in practice, establishing such a causality relationship may prove very complex for the trade secret holder.[1973]

The third factor enquires into whether the combination resulted from the investment of "intellectual skill", assessed against the existing alternatives used by the members of the relevant circles. At first glance, this principle may not appear applicable to Big Data sets, as they are mostly gathered automatically. However, it is submitted that this prong should be construed as referring to the intellectual investment in the development of the collection, processing and analysing mechanisms (mostly algorithms and code) developed by the trade secret holder. If these are known or easily accessible among the industry members (for instance, if several metasearch engines use the same sources of data and the same pre-existing scrapping program, which is furthermore well-known within an industry), the Big Data sets should not qualify for trade secrets protection, as they will not confer any competitive advantage over the existing alternatives.

Additionally, it is submitted that in the enforcement of trade secrets protection against the misappropriation of Big Data sets, courts should take into consideration whether the competitor generated the data indepen-

---

or ability to compete. The definition of trade secret excludes *trivial* information (...)"(emphasis added).

1971 'trivial, adj' (*OED Online*, OUP June 2013) <https://en.oxforddictionaries.com/definition/trivial> accessed 15 September 2018.

1972 Andreas Wiebe 2016 (n 287) 880 suggests that there may no longer be trivial information.

1973 Josef Drexl 2016 (n 426) 23.

dently or acquired it through reverse engineering (factor 4), and should demand that the plaintiff identify precisely the information concerned (factor 5). However, the latter appears rather complex in view of the sheer volume of Big Data sets and the pace at which they develop. Big Data sets are dynamic in nature.

From a practical point of view, it should be noted that technological measures that prevent the unauthorised access of third parties to the content of Big Data sets may allow data holders to achieve *de facto* exclusivity over them. In this scenario, the trade secrets legal regime may provide effective quasi exclusive protection to the trade secret holder, particularly because the protection of factual exclusivity resembles the protection of possession under civil law traditions.[1974]

As a final note, it is worth highlighting that uncertainty remains as to how courts will interpret and apply the third prong of the trade secrets definition in the context of Big Data: the adoption of reasonable measures under the circumstances to protect the secret nature of the information.[1975] However, a survey of the most relevant case law in the U.S., England and Germany indicates that the threshold is rather low. In most cases, the adoption of legal measures (such as NDAs) and physical measures (such as the fragmentation of the information, building fences or encryption of the information) is deemed sufficient.[1976] After all, one of the primary justifications of trade secrets law is to avoid wasteful arms races in the adoption of measures to protect valuable undisclosed information. In this context, following the rationale outlined with regard to Cloud Disclosures, disclaimers of liability in the case of unauthorised access shall not prevent the application of trade secrets protection against third parties that access information unlawfully.[1977] In the same vein, the mere fact that Big Data sets are stored in the Cloud does not entail a disclosure of such information to the Cloud Service Provider, as long as there is no active transfer of knowledge between the parties.[1978]

1974 Herbert Zech 2016 n (278) 63-64; Michael Dorner 2013 (n 305) 111.
1975 Josef Drexl 2016 (n 426) 23.
1976 Chapter 4 § 3 E).
1977 Chapter 4 § 4 C) II. 6. b).
1978 Chapter 4 § 4 C) II. 6. b).

### 2. Additional problems: identifying the trade secret holder and the risk of infringement

As mentioned already, in the Data Economy, the traditional concept of value chains has been replaced by the value network one, and as a result the number of stakeholders involved in the production and analysis of data (of both a personal and industrial nature) has increased exponentially.[1979] Consequently, allocating the right over secret information is particularly complex. According to Article 2(2) of the TSD, the "trade secret holder" is defined as the individual or legal entity that has "lawful control" over the secret information. Yet, in the context of Big Data, there may be numerous stakeholders who are in control of secret information in a "lawful manner".[1980] Following the networked car example, (i) the company manufacturing the physical object in which sensors are included, (ii) the producers of the sensors, (iii) the owners of the car,[1981] or (iv) any of the licensees of the information can be regarded as trade secret holders under the definition provided in Article 2(2) TSD. This goes to show that in the Data Economy, the contours of the organisation and control between companies are progressively fading.[1982]

As a corollary to the foregoing, another salient issue that arises is the difficulty in the enforcement of trade secrets, as the entities engaging in the data analytics processes may infringe the alleged trade secrets if permission is not obtained from all of the stakeholders that are considered to be lawful holders of the information concerned under Article 2(2) TSD, by virtue of an assignment or a licensing agreement. Notwithstanding the aforementioned, following the rationale put forward above in the context of Big Data analysis,[1983] individual data will rarely qualify for protection. Only those persons or legal entities lawfully in control of large data sets, the specific arrangement of which remains unknown to other market participants in the form of combination secrets, will be entitled to claim trade secrets protection. Consequently, when a legal entity intends to carry out a data analytics process, it will only have to clear the rights with the holders of the data sets that contain the aggregated data, provided that compliance with

1979 Chapter 4 § 4 F) I.
1980 Herbert Zech 2016 (n 278) 64.
1981 Andreas Wiebe 2016 (n 287) 883 noting that there may no longer be trivial information.
1982 Andreas Wiebe 2016 (n 287) 883.
1983 Chapter 4 § 4 F) II.1).

data protection laws is ensured. Consequently, the number of stakeholders from which an assignment or license will have to be acquired is substantially reduced.[1984]

### 3. Conclusion on the applicability of the trade secrets liability regime to Big Data

Legal academia is divided on the potential applicability of the TSD to the protection of Big Data sets. On the one hand, Zech considers that the lack of transparency that governs the protection of IT matters calls for careful application of the TSD.[1985] In the same vein, Wiebe highlights that with time, it will become increasingly difficult to protect data as trade secrets, and consequently, the application of the TSD will be of little practical relevance.[1986]

Notwithstanding the aforementioned, the better view it is submitted, is the one purported by Dorner and Drexl. The former suggests that the trade secrets legal regime is applicable to Big Data analysis, as the protection of individual data is alien to IPRs and data input and output can in fact meet the requirements of protection laid down in the UWG, which regulates the protection of trade secrets in Germany.[1987] Similarly, Drexl is of the opinion that the tortious nature of the protection laid down in the TSD, centred upon the lawfulness of the means used to acquire, use and disclose secret information provides the most adequate legal framework to balance the interests of stakeholders in protecting their industrial data and the interests of third parties in accessing such data. Yet, he also mentions that "clarification of the scope of trade secret protection regarding data" would be welcome.[1988]

In this context, it is submitted that courts should follow the analytical framework suggested in the context of combination secrets to assess the eligibility of Big Data sets under the legal framework created by the TSD. This would ensure a balanced solution when delineating a company's private sphere vis-à-vis the public domain. In addition, it is also line with the

---

1984 This approach does not take into account the potential data protection issues that may arise.
1985 Herbert Zech 2016 (n 278) 64.
1986 Andreas Wiebe 2016 (n 287) 883.
1987 Michael Dorner 2014 (n 1960) 623.
1988 Josef Drexl 2016 (n 426) 66.

view expressed by most of the data holders that took part in the consultation launched by the Commission with regard to the "Building a European Economy Initiative", where it was noted that the Database Directive and the TSD provided sufficient protection to the investments carried out in data collection.[1989]

## *§ 5 Conclusion*

A comparison of the definitions of a trade secret followed under the German and English jurisdictions before the implementation of the TSD reveals that despite substantial differences, both legal systems afford effective protection to valuable undisclosed information, as conceptualised under Article 2(1) TSD and in line with the minimum obligations established in Article 39(2) TRIPs. Notwithstanding this, in order to ensure uniformity across the 28 EU Member States, it is submitted that national courts should emphasise the need to establish causality between the value of information and its undisclosed nature. The concept of commercial value should be understood to refer to the ability to compete of the trade secret holder, which should be construed as including not only businesses, but also universities and research institutions. In addition, this thesis supports that the adoption of reasonable measures under the circumstances, which is not, as such, included as a normative standard in either of the studied jurisdictions, should be interpreted in a flexible manner in order to avoid wasteful arms races and promote the flow of information among market participants.

As regards the secrecy requirement, a review of the case law from the U.S., England and Germany has demonstrated that is not possible to extract a normative standard that is applicable in all circumstances to delineate the contours of protectable information and information that is in fact in the public domain. Ultimately, the assessment will depend on a number of factors such as whether substantial labour and intellectual skill are necessary to devise the secret and whether the trade secret holder retains control over the subsequent use and disclosure of said information. Consequently, it is submitted that the relative nature of secrecy is best as-

1989 Commission, 'Synopsis Report on the Consultation on the Building a European Data Economy Initiative.' (2018) 5 <https://ec.europa.eu/digital-single-market/en/news/synopsis-report-public-consultation-building-european-data-economy> accessed 15 September 2018.

sessed by reference to its boundaries with the public domain on a case-by-case basis. This is of utmost importance in order to determine the effect of disclosures in the digital age, which may be potentially automatically secrecy destroying. In this context, it is submitted that Internet disclosures and disclosures in the Cloud should be examined following the two analylitcal frameworks proposed, which place special emphasis on the actual access and the acquisition of active knowledge by the relevant circles. This thesis has also argued in favour of the protection of Big Data sets through trade secrets liability rules and in particular, through the application of the analytical framework proposed for combination secrets. By applying such a model, it is ensured that information in the public domain is not privatised therefore ensuring the equilibrium between the interests of the holders of secret information and the general interest in constructing a solid public domain.

In the light of the economic goals that the EU legislature ultimately intended to achieve with the adoption of the TSD, the following chapter focuses on the study of the strategic importance of trade secrets for certain industries and their increasing vulnerability through the application of the methodology of qualitative empirical research. To this end, the perfume industry is used as a study case to analyse the interplay between IPRs and trade secrets and the role that the latter play in appropriating returns from innovation in this manufacturing sector.

# Chapter 5. Study case: the strategic importance of secrecy in the perfume industry

## *§ 1 Preliminary remarks on the methodology applied*

Having examined the theoretical rationales underlying trade secrets protection, their legal nature and the liability conditions that inform the scope of the secrecy requirement from a comparative law perspective, this chapter addresses the increasing vulnerability and strategic importance of trade secrets in the context of the perfume industry. This manufacturing sector is used as an example case of the challenges holders face in keeping their confidential (technical and commercial) information undisclosed and of the importance of trade secrets for the competitiveness of certain sectors. To illustrate this, a three-fold approach is followed.

First, some background information about the perfume industry is provided in § 2. Next, § 3 looks into the levels of protection afforded to perfumery products by (A) copyright; (B) patents; (C) trade marks and (D) unfair competition. Other IPRs, such as utility models and design rights are not examined, due to the limited scope of the research on this topic, even though in practice perfume manufacturers may resort to them.[1990] The interplay between perfumery goods and IPRs is structured by analysing first the object and requirements of protection and then evaluating the advantages and drawbacks provided by each of the IPRs studied.

Finally, and drawing on the fact that no IPR protects perfumes as such, § 4 surveys (A) the importance of trade secrets for the fragrance industry and (B) the increasing challenges in keeping them undisclosed. This is mostly illustrated by reference to qualitative empirical research based on two semi-structured interviews conducted with the IP legal counsel of a multinational company and the maître parfumaire, Rosendo Mateu.[1991] At this point, it is worth noting that owing to the sensitive nature of the information, a substantial number of scent manufacturers declined to give interviews and the only producer that agreed did so under strict confidential-

---

1990 For a detailed overview please see Stefan Fröhlich, *Düfte als geistiges Eigentum* (Mohr Siebeck 2008) 113-121 and 170-174.

1991 Barbara DiCicco-Bloom and Benjamin F. Crabtree, 'The qualitative research interview' [2006] 40 Medical Education J 314, 316.

ity conditions; therefore, the identity of the firm can under no circumstances be revealed. The protocol of the questionnaire is attached in Annex 1 and the firm is referred to as "Perfume Company 1".

## *§ 2 The perfume industry*

The development of a new perfume involves both creative talent and technical ability. During its composition, the maître perfumaire has to combine hundreds of basic raw materials, which may be of natural or synthetic origin, to create a unique and evocative fragrance.[1992] Yet, in order to commercialise the mixture as a final product, additional ingredients such as stabilisers, colorants or antioxidants must be added. Perfumes are complex chemical solutions that require their creators to have advanced knowledge of organic chemistry to ensure their quality and security for human use.[1993] It has been estimated that the fragrance industry devotes up to 18% of its annual turnover to R&D.[1994] Beyond their technical nature, perfumes are increasingly recognised as having an artistic dimension.[1995]

Creating a new perfume is an extremely complex process and may take years before the fragrance enters the market. Even then, advertising strategies play a central role in its success.[1996] Indeed, for some the appeal of a given perfume lies largely in its luxurious character rather than the actual composition of the formula.[1997] For this reason, they are frequently commercialised through selective distribution networks, particularly those

1992 Pierre Laszlo and Sylvie Rivière, *Perfume, Arte y Ciencia* (Omega 2001) 14-23.

1993 According to IFRA, the fragrance industry devotes up to 18% of its year annual revenue to Research and Development <http://www.ifraorg.org/> accessed 15 September 2018.

1994 IFRA, 'Valuable yet vulnerable: Trade Secrets in the fragrance industry' (2013) IFRA Position Paper, 6 <www.ifraorg.org/view_document.aspx?docId=23107> accessed 15 September 2018.

1995 Agnieszka A. Machnicka, 'The Perfume Industry and Intellectual Property Law in the Jurisprudence of the Court of Justice of the European Union and National Courts' [2012] IIC 123, 124; Jean-François Blayn and others, *Questions de Parfumerie* (Corpman Editions 1988) 27-29.

1996 Pierre Laszlo and Sylvie Rivière 2001 (n 1992) 92-105.

1997 Annette Kur, Lionel Bently and Ansgar Ohly, 'Sweet Smells and a Sour Taste – The ECJ's L'Oréal decision' (2010) Max Planck Institute for Intellectual Property, Competition & Tax Law Research Paper Series No. 09-12 2, Paper No. 10/01, 2 <https://papers.ssrn.com/sol3/papers.cfm?abstract_id=1492032> accessed 15 September 2018.

aimed at the higher-end segment of the market. However, this has not prevented the proliferation of counterfeit perfumes and imitations sold through grey market channels.[1998] Similarly, in recent years, the number of companies producing and placing on the market so-called "smell-alike" perfumes has steadily increased. In this case, perfumes are marketed under another trade mark, but at the point of sale, the consumer is informed of its equivalence to other well-known perfumes.[1999]

From an industry perspective, it is important to bear in mind that perfumes marketed under the trade mark of a luxury fashion brand are rarely created in-house.[2000] Instead, they are usually developed by flavour, fragrance and active cosmetic ingredient manufacturers following the directions (briefing) of luxury brand holdings.[2001] Scent producers are mostly unknown to the public, even though they are multinational companies worth millions of Euros, and in some cases, they are even traded publicly. The biggest market players include Givaudan in Switzerland; Takasago Int, Corp. in Japan; International Flavors & Fragrances Inc. in the U.S.; and Symrise AG in Germany. The spectrum of products that they manufacture ranges from fine fragrances (20%) to household products and detergents (50%) and personal care products (30%).[2002] During the last decade, these companies have actively lobbied to enhance the protection of scents through IPRs.

Indeed, this topic has garnered much attention in recent years, particularly after a series of decisions by the CJEU dealing with perfumes and trade mark law. Perfumes as such are not the object of any IPR. Yet, some of their intangible features may fall within the scope of specific IPRs. The following sections delve into the relationship between perfumes and

---

1998 Annette Kur, Lionel Bently and Ansgar Ohly, 'Sweet Smells and a Sour Taste – The ECJ's L'Oréal decision' (2010) Max Planck Institute for Intellectual Property, Competition & Tax Law Research Paper Series No. 09-12 2, Paper No. 10/01, 2 <https://papers.ssrn.com/sol3/papers.cfm?abstract_id=1492032> accessed 15 September 2018.

1999 This topic is discussed in detail in chapter 5 § 3 D) below.

2000 Only a few luxury maisons like Chanel, Hermès and Guerlain have their own in-house perfumists.

2001 Interview with Perfumist Rosendo Mateu (see Annex 2);

2002 Interview with Perfumist Rosendo Mateu (see Annex 2); also Antoon Quaedvlieg,'Copyright and Perfume: Nose, Intellect and Industry' (2011) 6, 7 (English translation by Margaret Platt-Homme) <http://www.klosmorel.com/en/our-people/antoon-quaedvlieg/publications/copyright-and-perfume-nose-intellect-and-industry/> accessed 15 September 2018.

IPRs (§ 3), prior to analysing the strategic importance of trade secrets for the perfume industry and the difficulties in concealing information (§ 4).

### *§ 3 The protection of perfumes through IPRs*

#### A) Copyright

In 2006, the Supreme Courts of both the Netherlands and France ruled on the protection of perfumes under copyright law and remarkably they came to conflicting decisions. The former concluded in *Kecofa v. Lancôme*[2003] that the definition of what constitutes a work laid down in Article 10 of the Dutch Copyright Act is not exhaustive and thus does not preclude the protection of scents. Yet, three days earlier the French Supreme Court held that perfumes could not be the object of copyright protection owing to their industrial nature.[2004] This shows that the eligibility of perfumes as artistic works is by no means settled among EU Member States. The following sections explore such a possibility by examining whether perfumes can be regarded as the object of copyright protection (section I) and whether they fulfil the requirements set out in international conventions and most national regimes (section II). Finally, some conclusions as to the advantages and drawbacks of resorting to such means of protection are analysed in section III.

#### I. Object of protection

Traditionally, the perfume industry has sought to protect three distinct aspects of a perfume through author's rights: its formula, the aromatic impression it conveys and its composition.[2005] According to Article 2(1) BC, copyright affords protection to literary and artistic works, "irrespective of the form or mode in which they are expressed". Consequently, if copyright protection is afforded to a perfume's formula, such protection will be limited to the perception of the "set of chemical symbols showing the elements

---

2003 *Kecofa B.V. v. Lancôme parfumes et beauté. Et cie* S.N.C, No. C04/327 Hoge Raad (16 June 2006).

2004 Nejla *Bsiri-Babur v. Haarmann &Reimer et al*, Cass. Civ. 1st ch., 13 June 2006, *Propr. Intell.* 2006, 442-443.

2005 Stefan Fröhlich, *Düfte als Geistiges Eigentum* (Mohr Siebeck 2008) 21.

present in a compound and their relative proportions".[2006] From a practical standpoint, this appears to be of little relevance, because there seems to be consensus among chemists on the fact that a specific aromatic message can be achieved through the implementation of different formulas. These are, after all, only one of the possible descriptions of a fragrance, whilst chemical compositions act as their support.[2007] Thus, commentators who are in favour of affording copyright protection to perfumes suggest that the object of protection should be their aromatic message (i.e. the aromatic impression a perfume conveys).[2008]

## II. Requirements for protection

Thus far, copyright law has not been fully harmonised in the EU. The legislations of Member States have only been aligned in specific areas, such as software and database protection.[2009] As a result, the requirements for protection beyond the harmonised subject matter and the obligations provided for in international treaties are left for Member States to regulate. The following sections survey three of the more common requirements of protection set forth by national copyright laws and their applicability to the

---

2006 'formula,n' (*OED Online*, OUP June 2013) <https://en.oxforddictionaries.com/definition/formula> accessed 15 September 2018.

2007 J-Ch Galloux, 'Profumo di diritto – Le principe de la protection des fragrances par le droit d'auteur, note sous TGI Paris, 26 mai 2004' [2004] 36 Recueil Dalloz 2641, 2642.

2008 See further J-Ch Galloux, 'Profumo di diritto – Le principe de la protection des fragrances par le droit d'auteur, note sous TGI Paris, 26 mai 2004' [2004] 36 D 2641, 2642; see further Sergio Balañá Vicente, 'La perfumería toma posiciones en torno al derecho de autor "¿...fumus boni iuris?"' [2005] 19 Pe.i. 37, 48-49; a number of French decisions also support this view, particularly *L'Oréal v. Bellure, TGI Paris, 3rd ch., 26 May 2004, D. 2004*; 2641-2645 conversely, the Dutch Court of Appeal's in Hertogenbosch, *Lancôme Parfums et Beauté et Cie S.N.C., v. Kecofab B.V.*, C0200726/MA (8 June 2004) para 4.11.2 noted that the perfume's composition should be the object of protection, because the aromatic message can only be sensorily perceived in a subjective manner. The composition is sufficiently concrete and stable to be considered as a work for the purposes of copyright law. This decision was later upheld by the Dutch Supreme Court in *Kecofa B.V. v. Lancôme parfumes et beauté. Et cie* S.N.C, No. C04/327HR (16 June 2006).

2009 A detailed account of the Directives that harmonise copyright law is provided in Thomas Dreier and P. Bernt Hugenholtz, *Concise European copyright law* (2nd ed, Kluwer Law International 2016).

fragrance industry. To merit copyright protection, perfumes should be deemed literary and artistic works (section 1), be original (section 2) and be capable of being perceived through the senses (section 3).

## 1. Literary and artistic work

As noted above, Article 2(1) BC mandates Member States to protect "artistic and literary works" and provides a non-exclusive list of examples, in which no reference to perfumes is made.[2010] The recognition of fragrances as a form of artistic creation has been at the centre of the discussion in both legal academia and case law, particularly in France, the cradle of the perfume industry. The main argument against acknowledging their artistic nature is that they are created through the implementation of a set of skills and knowledge in an industrial context. Indeed, in 1975 the Paris Court of Appeals rejected the notion that fragrances could be protected under copyright law due to the industrial nature of their production.[2011] Yet, in later years, a number of decisions from lower courts followed a different line of argument. Most notably, in *Thierry Mugler Parfums v. GLB Molinard* (1999),[2012] *Beauté Prestige International v. Bellure* (2004)[2013] and *L'Oréal v. Bellure* (2004),[2014] the French courts concluded that the process of creating a fragrance goes beyond mere "*savoir-faire*"; fragrances were deemed an "*ouvre de l'esprit*" created through intellectual research with the aim of achieving an aesthetic composition.[2015] In a similar vein, commentators

---

2010 Claire Guillemin, *Law & Odeur* (Nomos 2016) 152; WIPO, *Guide to the Berne Convention for the Protection of Literary and Artistic Works* ( WIPO Publications 1978) para 2.7.

2011 *Rochas v. de Laire*, CA Paris, 4th ch., 3 July 1975, *Gaz. Pal.*21-22 January 1976, pp. 43-45(as cited by Stefan Fröhlich, *Düfte als Geistiges Eigentum* (Mohr Siebeck 2008) 21).

2012 *Thierry Mugler Parfums v. SA GLB Molinard* , T.com. Paris, 15th ch., 24 Septembre 1999, *LPA* 3 March 2000, pp 13-16.

2013 *Beauté Prestige International v. Bellure and Euro Media*, CA Paris, 17 September 2004, *Propr. Intell.* 2005, pp. 47-49 (as cited by Estelle Derclaye, 'One on the nose for Bellure: French appellate court confirms that perfumes are copyright protected' [2006] 1 JIPLP 377-379).

2014 *L'Oréal v. Bellure, TGI Paris, 3rd ch., 26 May 2004, D 2004*; 2641-2645.

2015 *Beauté Prestige International v. Bellure and Euro Media*, CA Paris, 17 September 2004, *Propr. Intell.* 2005, pp. 47-49 (as cited by Estelle Derclaye, 'One on the nose for Bellure: French appellate court confirms that perfumes are copyright protected' [2006] JIPLP 377-379).

have argued that the distinction between artistic creations (concerning the aesthetic effect achieved) and industrial creations (constrained by technical and commercial limitations) contravenes the principle of "unity of the art" and results in an artificial classification. After all, the chemical composition of a perfume is always guided by its aesthetic purpose.[2016] These arguments did not seem persuasive enough for the French Supreme Court, which settled the debate in a decision from 2006 where it was ruled that, "the fragrance of a perfume, which results from the simple implementation of a skill may not benefit from the protection of copyright".[2017]

In line with the French Supreme Court, the European Copyright Society ("ECS"), in its opinion on the pending *Levola Hengelo v Smilde Foods BV*,[2018] case which concerns a request for a preliminary ruling submitted by a Dutch court to the CJEU on the possibility of protecting taste under the Information Society Directive, has identified two additional problems with conceptualising the taste of a food product as such (as well as smells) as an "artistic work". In the first place, the ECS convincingly submits that smells are "raw materials" that, just as abstract ideas, are excluded from the scope of Article 2(1) BC.[2019] Second, the ECS further argues that the BC only covers creations that can be "accessed or perceived" by the senses of "sight and hearing" in contrast to the senses of "taste, smell and touch".[2020] At the time that the BC was negotiated, smells and tastes in connection to food or perfumery goods were already valuable, but were nonetheless not included as examples of artistic and literary works in the BC. Consequently, their inclusion as subject matter protected under the BC could only be achievable by amending the convention with the approval of all parties.[2021]

2016 André Bassard, 'La composition d'une formule de parfum est-elle une (oeuvre de l'esprito au sens de la loi du 11 mars 1957?' [1979] 118 RIPIA 461, 463.

2017 *Nejla Babur v. Haarmann &Reimer et al*, Cass. 1st Civ., 13 June 2006, *Propr. Intell. 2006*, 442-443 (translation by Brad Spitz, <http://kluwercopyrightblog.com/2014/02/17/france-no-copyright-protection-for-perfume/> accessed 25 January 2018).

2018 Case C–310/17 *Levola v Hengelo Smilde Foods BV* submitted for a preliminary ruling on 29 May 2019.

2019 European Copyright Society, 'Opinion on the pending reference before the CJEU in Case 310/17 (copyright protection of tastes)' (19 February 2018) para 17 <https://europeancopyrightsocietydotorg.files.wordpress.com/2018/03/ecs-opinion-on-protection-for-tastes-final1.pdf> accessed 15 September 2018.

2020 Ibid paras 17-19.

2021 Ibid para 18.

## 2. Originality: author's own intellectual creation

Neither the BC nor TRIPs provide a uniform definition of "originality".[2022] However, all jurisdictions demand that works, in order to be eligible for copyright protection, achieve a minimum originality threshold.[2023] In this respect, common law (copyright) and civil law systems ("*droit d'auteur*") have traditionally followed different understandings of this notion. In the UK, case law requires "independent creation" and "skill and labour" to find copyright protection.[2024] In the U.S., until the famous Supreme Court decision *Feist*, courts followed a similar approach under the "sweat of the brow" doctrine.[2025] However, in *Feist* the Supreme Court expressly rejected such a principle[2026] and introduced the "creative choices" benchmark at the centre of the assessment of originality.[2027] By contrast, in civil law countries under the author's right system, the threshold was much higher, as it was required that works bore the personal stamp of the author as a

---

2022 Daniel Gervais, 'The compatibility of the skill and labour standard with the Berne Convention and the TRIPs Agreement' [2004] 26 EIPR 75, 77: the author notes that the term "originality" is used throughout the BC with three different meanings: (i) first, it is used to refer to a work created by an author (Article 14ter (1)); (ii) it also applied to designate a work which will be reproduced or adapted (Arts. 2(3), 8, 11(2), 11*ter*(2), 14(2), Art.IV of the Appendix and (iii) lastly, it refers to an intellectual creation that falls under the scope of protection of the Convention.

2023 In Europe, see for instance, Article 10(1) of the Spanish Intellectual Property Act (Real Decreto Legislativo 1/1996, de 12 de abril, por el que se aprueba el texto refundido de la Ley de Propiedad Intelectual, regularizando, aclarando y armonizando las disposiciones legales vigentes sobre la materia) ; § 2 (1) of the German Copyright Act (Urheberrechtsgesetz vom 9. September 1965 (BGBl. I S. 1273), das zuletzt durch Artikel 1 des Gesetzes vom 1. September 2017 (BGBl. I S. 3346) geändert worden ist.); in the U.S. see Copyright Act, Public Law 94-553, 90 Stat. 2541 (1976) (codified as amended at 17 U.S.C. § 102 (a).) (U.S. Copyright Act).

2024 *University of London Press v University Tutorial Press* [1916] 2 Ch 601 (Ch), 608 "The word original does not in this connection mean that the work must be the expression of original or inventive thought. Copyright Acts are not concerned with the originality of ideas, but with the expression of thought (...) The Act [requires] that the work not be copied from another work – that it should originate from the author".

2025 Daniel Gervais, 'Feist Goes Global: A Comparative Analysis Of The Notion Of Originality In Copyright Law' [2002] 49 LJ of the Copyright Society of the USA 948, 958.

2026 *Feist Publ'ns, Inc. v. Rural Tel. Serv. Co.*499 U.S. 340, 352-354 (1991).

2027 *Feist Publ'ns, Inc. v. Rural Tel. Serv. Co.*499 U.S. 340, 348 (1991).

reflection of his personality.[2028] This principle was introduced within the acquis communautaire by virtue of the Software Directive,[2029] the Database Directive[2030] and the Term of Protection Directive,[2031] which set out that a work is original if it results from an "author's own intellectual creation". However, in recent years, the CJEU seems to have expanded this definition of originality to any copyright subject matter by means of judicial interpretation, beyond computer programs, photographs and databases.[2032] This has not been without controversy, particularly in the UK, where the originality bar was traditionally lower and was closely linked to the notion of investment in the creation of a work.[2033]

In the context of fragrances, there has been longstanding debate regarding whether they can be regarded as "original". As hinted at above, a number of French decisions from lower courts have acknowledged the artistic dimension of perfumes as works of art resulting from the "intellectual research of a composer, who resorts to his imagination and knowledge to create a bouquet of odorant materials with aesthetic purposes, which constitutes an "*ouvre d'esperit*" perceptible individually and which merits copyright protection".[2034] Notwithstanding this, in 2008, the French Supreme Court regarded that the elaboration of a perfume results from the mere implementation of a set of skills that do not result in the creation of a form of

2028 Eleonora Rosati, *Originality in EU Copyright* (Edward Elgar 2013) 69; according to Andreas Rahmatian, *Copyright and Creativity* (Edward Elgar 2011) 47 "While the Common law copyright systems focus on the work and its potential economic value, the author's right systems concentrate on the author and protect his work because it bears traces of the author's personality. It is not the work that protects (indirectly) the author/maker and his economic interests, but the author's protection as a person which extends to works emanating from that person".

2029 See Article 1 (3) Software Directive.

2030 See Article 3(1) Database Directive.

2031 See Article 6 Term of Protection Directive.

2032 As examined in footnote 1889; in this regard see for instance Eleonora Rosati 2013 (n 2028) 97-119.

2033 See Estelle Derclaye, 'The Court of Justice copyright case law: quo vadis?' [2014] 36 EIPR 716 -723.

2034 *Beauté Prestige International v. Belure et Eva France,* T. com., 4 June 2004, *Propr. Intell.* 2004, pp. 907.900; see also *L'Oréal v. Bellure, TGI Paris, 3rd ch., 26 May 2004,* D 2004, pp. 2641-2645.

expression that merits copyright protection[2035] and restated this position in 2013.[2036]

Outside of France, the Court of Appeals in Hertogenbosch (the Netherlands) in *Lancôme Parfums et Beauté S.N.C., v. Kecofa B.V* held that the perfume Trêsor had its own original character and bore the personal stamp of its author. It was developed from a particular creative path by choosing a limited number of olfactory elements among all of those available in order to create a unique and distinct work of art.[2037] This decision was upheld in 2006 by the Supreme Court, which, despite highlighting that the concept of work of art under the Copyright Act did not encompass those aspects necessary to achieve a technical effect, concluded that perfumes were not only concerned with technical aspects and thus could be protected under authors' rights.[2038]

In a similar vein, some German commentators have suggested that the "*kleine Münze*" doctrine, which affords copyright protection to works of "minor art", could be applied to fragrances.[2039] In this regard, the German Federal Supreme Court has held that works of minor art are simple but nonetheless protectable intellectual creations, such as musical works or non-scientific texts.[2040] Indeed, many have drawn parallels between the processes of composing a musical piece and creating a fragrance.[2041]

Even if in abstract it could be accepted that perfumes may be original for the purposes of copyright law, proving their originality remains prob-

---

2035 *Beauté Prestige International v. Senteur Mazal*, Cass. 1st ch. 1 July 2008 [2009] GRUR Int 622.

2036 Cour de Cassation, *Tresor-Armani-Mania* (10 December 2013) Case No. 11-19.872, IIC 2014, 829-831: "The fragrance of a perfume results from the implementation of know-how and thus cannot be considered a creation of a form of expression that could enjoy the protection granted to works by copyright law".

2037 Dutch Court of Appeal's in Hertogenbosch, *Lancôme Parfums et Beauté et Cie S.N.C., v. Kecofab B.V.*, C0200726/MA (8 June 2004) 4.12.1.

2038 *Kecofa B.V. v. Lancôme parfumes et beauté. Et cie* S.N.C, No. C04/327HR, (16 June 2006): "it is true that the concept of a work in the Copyright Act meets its limit where the work's own original character concerns only what is necessary to obtain a technical effect, but given that, in the case of a perfume, there is no question of a purely technical effect, the latter condition does not prevent copyright protection from being granted to the fragrance of a perfume".

2039 Stefan Fröhlich 2008 (n 2005) 52.

2040 BGH GRUR 1981, 267, 268 – *Dirlada*; for an overview of the "kleine Münze" doctrine see further Ulrich Loewenheim, 'Der Schutz der kleinen Münze im Urheberrecht' [1987] GRUR 761-769.

2041 André Bassard 1979 (n 2016) 463; Stefan Fröhlich 2008(n 2005) 53.

lematic. Odours can only be perceived through the sense of smell, which is highly subjective. Or to be more precise, their description remains very problematic.[2042] Courts in EU jurisdictions have followed mainly two criteria to assess it: (i) the labour and effort invested in creating it and (ii) the novelty of the fragrance.[2043] The first benchmark bears certain similarities to the English interpretation of originality, which is frequently identified with the "skill, judgement and labour" invested in the creation of the work.[2044] As applied to fragrances, it purports that the more difficult it is to create a perfume, the harder it will be to develop it independently, and thus it should be regarded as more original.[2045] This rationale was followed in the Netherlands by the Court of Appeals in Hertogenbosch in the *Lancôme Parfums et Beauté S.N.C., v. Kecofa B.V* decision, where the fact that the plaintiff's perfumist had selected 25 out of hundreds of available olfactory elements to make a distinctive and unique perfume was deemed essential to regard the fragrance as original.[2046]

In contrast, some argue that the originality of a perfume should be understood in terms of the novelty of the aromatic impression it conveys. This approach was adopted by a French court in *Thierry Mugler Parfums v. GLB Molinard* (1999)[2047] and the famous perfumist Edmond Roudniska, who equates originality with novelty and further states that a new form may result from the combination of known materials.[2048]

2042 Claire Guillemin, *Law & Odeur* (Nomos 2016) 56.

2043 Sergio Balañá Vicente 2005 (n 2008) 54-61.

2044 *Ladbroke v William Hill* [1964] 1 WLR 273, 282; for a more detailed account of the originality requirement in the English jurisdiction see Eleonora Rosati, 'Originality in U.S. and UK Copyright Experiences as a Springboard for an EU-Wide Reform Debate' [2010] IIC 524, 537.

2045 This is argued among others by Sergio Balañá Vicente 2005 (n 2008) 54-57.

2046 Court of Appeal's in Hertogenbosch, *Lancôme Parfums et Beauté et Cie S.N.C., v. Kecofab B.V.*, C0200726/MA (8 June 2004) 4.12.1-4.13.

2047 *Thierry Mugler Parfums v. SA GLB Molinard* , T.com. Paris, 15th ch., 24 Septembre 1999, *LPA* 3 March 2000, pp 13-16; such an approach was specifically rejected by the Ducht Court in Court of Appeal in Hertogenbosch in the aforementioned decision *Lancôme Parfums et Beauté et Cie S.N.C., v. Kecofab B.V.*, C0200726/MA (8 June 2004) 4.12.4, where it was noted that "for the granting of copyright law protection it is not required that the work is new in an objective sense, but only that it is original in a subjective sense (i.e. from the author's viewpoint)".

2048 Edmond Roudnitska, *Une vie au service du parfum* (Thérèse Vian Editions1991) 87 highlighting that: "La forme d'un parfum découle d'une combinaison esthétique, choisie, voulue et non du simple voisinage des matériaux dans leur mélange physique. Cette forme sera originale si la pensée que l'a fait naître a

Comparing two specific perfumes and assessing their similarities is ultimately guided by a subjective perception that varies from person to person.[2049] This stands as a major barrier to any originality claim.

### 3. Fixation

Article 2(2) BC provides that Member States are free to require works to be fixated in some material support in order to be protected under copyright rules. Consequently, most common law jurisdictions have established that fixation is a prerequisite to find an infringement,[2050] while civil law jurisdictions merely demand that the work is capable of being perceived by the senses.[2051]

Once a perfume is sprayed on the skin, it vanishes. It also reacts differently to skin types upon application and its perception differs from one individual to another.[2052] Consequently, the volatile and instable nature of fragrances is regarded as a major obstacle to protection in some countries. The French Supreme Court, in its most recent decision regarding the protection of perfumes as artistic works, echoed this argument and established that copyright affords protection to works perceivable by the senses so long as that form "may be identifiable with sufficient precision in order to make possible its communication".[2053] Accordingly, the court concluded that fragrances do not meet this requirement and thus cannot be protected under copyright law.[2054]

---

été elle-même originale. Des matériaux originaux ne sont évidemment pas contre-indiqués pour réaliser une forme originale mais il n'est tout de même pas inconcevable qu'avec des matériaux connus on puisse inventer une forme nouvelle, c'est-à-fire un "arrangement" nouveau, une "combinaison" nouvelle. "

2049 Claire Guillemin, *Law & Odeur* (Nomos 2016) 54-56.

2050 See for instance in the U.S. 17 U.S.C. § 102 (a) U.S. and in the UK Article (1) of the Copyright, Designs and Patents Act 1988.

2051 This is the case in Germany, see Dreier/*Schulze*, *Urheberrechtsgesetz* (5th edn, C.H. Beck 2015) § 2 Rn 13.

2052 Antoon Quaedvlieg,'Copyright and Perfume: Nose, Intellect and Industry' (2011) 6, 9 (English translation by Margaret Platt-Homme) <http://www.klosmorel.com/en/our-people/antoon-quaedvlieg/publications/copyright-and-perfume-nose-intellect-and-industry/> accessed 15 September 2018.

2053 Cour de Cassation, *Tresor-Armani-Mania* (10 December 2013) Case No. 11-19.872 [2014] IIC 829-831.

2054 Cour de Cassation, *Tresor-Armani-Mania* (10 December 2013) Case No. 11-19.872 [2014] IIC 829-831.

In view of the above, some commentators have argued that affording copyright protection to perfumes is not in line with the minimum standards of protection set forth in international treaties (i.e. the BC and TRIPs). In particular, it has been suggested that, pursuant to the wording of Articles 2(2) BC, works that cannot be perceived through the senses of sight and hearing do not fall under the scope of the BC, and therefore perfumes should be deemed subject matter outside the scope of copyright protection.[2055]

However, those in favour of the protection of fragrances through copyright law claim that the possibility of reproducing them is a clear indication that they constitute a "form" and that, for the purposes of copyright protection, the relevant issue is the expression, not the manner in which it is perceived.[2056] Similarly, the Dutch Supreme Court in its famous ruling noted that the definition of "work" laid down in Article 10 of the Copyright Act does not exclude scents so long as they can be identified through human perception.[2057] Along these lines, some suggest that the fixation or perception requirement was originally envisaged to prevent the protection of ideas, following the expression-idea dichotomy and that the use of perfumes is eminently a sensorial experience, beyond the realm of intellectual creations and thus the protection of perfumes cannot be equated to the protection of ideas.[2058]

In light of the above, it is submitted that owing to the volatile and instable nature of scents, it does not seem plausible that perfumes meet the fixation threshold in jurisdictions where such a requirement is mandatory. In

2055 Herman Cohen Jehoram, 'The Dutch Supreme Court Recognises Copyright in the Scent of a Perfume. The Flying Dutchman: All Sails, no Anchor' [2006] 28 EIPR 629, 630; also Antoon Quaedvlieg,'Copyright and Perfume: Nose, Intellect and Industry' (2011) 6, 10 (English translation by Margaret Platt-Homme) <http://www.klosmorel.com/en/our-people/antoon-quaedvlieg/publications/copyright-and-perfume-nose-intellect-and-industry/> accessed 15 September 2018; Claire Guillemin, *Law & Odeur* (Nomos 2016) 203.

2056 Interview with Perfumist Rosendo Mateu (see Annex 2); also also Antoon Quaedvlieg,'Copyright and Perfume: Nose, Intellect and Industry' (2011) 6, 10 (English translation by Margaret Platt-Homme) <http://www.klosmorel.com/en/our-people/antoon-quaedvlieg/publications/copyright-and-perfume-nose-intellect-and-industry/> accessed 15 September 2018.

2057 Translation of the relevant passage of the decision provided by P. Bernt Hugenholtz, 'Chronicle of the Netherlands Dutch copyright law 2001-2010' [2010] RIDA 226, text accompanying footnote 31.

2058 Sergio Balañá Vicente 2005 (n 2008) 63-64.

addition, the subjective nature of the perception of smells also presents a hurdle in civil law jurisdictions that require sensorial perception.

## III. Evaluation

To be sure, protecting perfumes through copyright law would entail a number of advantages for their creators and for scent manufacturers. To begin with, the term of protection is longer than for most IPRs (seventy years after the death of the author).[2059] Furthermore, it is obtained by the mere fact of creation, without the need to fulfil any costly formalities, such as applying for its registration. This, in turn, would facilitate concluding licensing agreements and fighting so-called perfume "knock-offs".[2060] As a whole, protecting the overall impression conveyed by the aromatic message of a fragrance would allow for more comprehensive protection than resorting to simultaneous design and trade mark protection for the perfume's packaging, bottle and name.[2061]

Yet, copyright does not protect against the independent creation of the same scent, unlike patents or design rights, even though in practice cases where this may occur are rather exceptional.[2062] What appears more problematic is the enforcement of copyright against imitations. There has been a longstanding debate as to whether it is possible to set an objective standard that allows for comparing an original perfume with an alleged copy. Olfactory perception is always guided by personal appraisal, which renders judicial decisions on that matter highly subjective.[2063] This has been one of the most disputed aspects in cases concerning the protection of perfumes through copyright law.[2064]

Finally, a number of policy concerns have been raised regarding the protection of fragrances through authors' rights. Indeed, affording copyright protection to olfactory messages may hinder the free movement of per-

2059 See Article 1 of the Term of Protection Directive.

2060 Stefan Fröhlich 2008 (n 2005) 108.

2061 Stefan Fröhlich 2008 (n 2005) 108-109.

2062 Stefan Fröhlich 2008 (n 2005) 109.

2063 Sergio Balañá Vicente 2005 (n 2008) 52-53.

2064 This was particularly the case in *Thierry Mugler Parfums v. SA GLB Molinard* , T.com. Paris, 15th ch., 24 Septembre 1999, *LPA* 3 March 2000 pp 13-16.

fumery products within the common market.[2065] More generally, a number of Dutch commentators have expressed scepticism about the effects that extending protection for seventy years after the death of the author may have on free competition and the legal uncertainty surrounding the contours of the protected subject matter.[2066] For the time being, the Dutch Supreme Court's decision in *Kecofa v. Lancôme* is an isolated one within the EU landscape and it seems unlikely that in the near future other jurisdictions will follow its lead.

## B) Patent Law

The protection of perfumes through patents has garnered much attention from scent manufacturers in recent years. The possibility of resorting to patent rights to protect the products and processes applied in the fragrance industry is examined following the structure implemented with respect to copyright law. Therefore, section I looks into the actual object of protection, while section II studies the requirements for protection. Finally, the advantages and drawbacks of resorting to patent protection are outlined in section III.

### I. Object of protection

Patent rights, regarded by some to be the most robust of all IPRs, can be deployed to protect the technical aspects of a fragrance. Indeed, there is an increasing tendency among companies in the perfume industry to rely on patent protection.[2067] Yet, as with any other invention, they must fall within the eligible subject matter and fulfil the patentability requirements set

---

2065 As noted by Herman Cohen Jehoram, 'The Dutch Supreme Court Recognises Copyright in the Scent of a Perfume. The Flying Dutchman: All Sails, no Anchor' [2006] 28 EIPR 629, 631; contrary, Charles Gielen, 'Netherlands: copyright – blend of ingredients in a perfume constituting a copyright work' [2006] 28 EIPR 174.

2066 Quaedvlieg A,'Copyright and Perfume: Nose, Intellect and Industry' (2011) 6, 7 (English translation by Margaret Platt-Homme) <http://www.klosmorel.com/en/our-people/antoon-quaedvlieg/publications/copyright-and-perfume-nose-intellect-and-industry/> accessed 15 September 2018 (citing *Ars Aequi* [2006] 821-824, note by P. Bernt Hugenholtz).

2067 Stefan Fröhlich 2008 (n 2005) 126-129.

forth in Article 52 EPC, namely they must be new, inventive and capable of industrial applicability. Of particular relevance for the perfume industry is that Article 52(2)(b) EPC prevents the patentability of aesthetic creations. This is further clarified in the Guidelines of Examination, where it is stated that an "aesthetic effect itself is not patentable, neither in product nor in a process claim".[2068] However, technical processes are not excluded from patentability by the mere fact of being applied in the production of an aesthetic creation.[2069] The aroma conveyed by a perfume cannot be the object of a patent due to its non-technical nature, even though indirect protection can be sought for its (i) aromatic compounds (chemical compounds) and (ii) compositions (the perfume's formula), as analysed in the following sections.[2070]

### 1. Aromatic compounds

Traditionally, perfumes were made up of absolute scents and essential oils of natural origin, which are very costly to obtain.[2071] In the XIX century, the advancement of chemistry allowed for the synthesis of odorous substances, which have been used alongside natural ones in the creation of fragrances ever since.[2072] Indeed, a multi-million dollar industry has emerged around the manufacturing of synthetic scents, technically known as "odorants" or "aromatic compounds".[2073] Before turning to their patentability, some background information is provided for a better understanding of the underlying technology.[2074]

2068 Guidelines of Examination in the EPO. Part G. Chapter II. Section 3.4.

2069 Guidelines of Examination in the EPO. Part G. Chapter II. Secction 3.4. explicitly provide that the proteciton of "a substance or composition defined by technical features serving to produce a special effect with regard to scent or flavour, e.g. to maintain a scent or flavour for a prolonged period or to accentuate it, is not excluded".

2070 Stefan Fröhlich 2008 (n 2005) 128.

2071 Thomas G. Field, 'Copyright protection for Perfumes' [2004] 45 IDEA 19, where the author provides an insightful example, whereby he notes that "800 pounds of jasmine blossoms yield only a pound of an essence".

2072 Pierre Laszlo and Sylvie Rivière 2001 (n 1992) 24-28.

2073 Biggest market player include Givaudan in Switzerland; Takasago Int, Corp. in Japan; International Flavors & Fragrances Inc. in the United States and Symrisew AG in Germany.

2074 Pursuant to Francis A. Carey, 'Aromatic Compound', *Encyclopaedia Britannica*, <http://www.britannica.com/science/aromatic-compound> accessed 15

In the first place, any aromatic compound is a type of chemical compound.[2075] As such, it can be the object of a product patent, process patent or use patent like any other chemical compound that meets the aforementioned patentability requirements.[2076] For the purposes of the present research and following the classification laid down by Fröhlich, the term aromatic compound is used to refer to both single odorous substances and individual elements of odorous mixtures.[2077]

A product patent on a new chemical substance will define the way in which its technical structure is construed.[2078] It confers absolute protection on the right to make, dispose of, offer to dispose of, use, import or keep the aromatic compound, whether for disposal or otherwise.[2079] Thus, any subsequent use of the patented odorant without the consent of the patent holder results in a patent infringement, irrespective of whether it is used in isolation or as part of a composition.[2080] Similarly, protection extends to the product per se, regardless of the process applied to manufacture it.[2081] An example of this is the patent obtained by one of the world's leading producers of synthetic scents, Guivaudan, for an odorant molecule known as Florymoss, which adds a fruity note to a fragrance.[2082]

---

September 2018, an aromatic compound is: "a class of unsaturated chemical compounds characterized by one or more planar rings of atoms joined by covalent bonds of two different kinds. The unique stability of these compounds is referred to as aromaticity. Although the term aromatic originally concerned odour, today its use in chemistry is restricted to compounds that have particular electronic, structural, or chemical properties. Aromaticity results from particular bonding arrangements that cause certain π (pi) electrons within a molecule to be strongly held".

2075 A chemical compound is defined by Cal R. Noller, 'Chemical Comound', *Encyclopaedia Britannica;* <http://www.britannica.com/science/chemical-compound> accessed 15 September 2018 as: "any substance composed of identical molecules consisting of atoms of two or more chemical elements".

2076 Stefan Fröhlich 2008 (n 2005) 148.

2077 Stefan Fröhlich 2008 (n 2005) 148.

2078 Gerald Paterson, 'The Novelty of Use Claims' [1996] IIC 179, 181.

2079 See Article 28 (1)(a) TRIPs Lionel Bently and Brad Sherman 2014 (n 125) 541; Rudolf Kraßer and Christoph Ann 2009 (n 120) § 11.III.c) aa). (criticism in§ 11.III.d)d)); Franz Lederer, 'Equivalence of Chemical Product Patents' [1999] IIC 275, 282; absolute patent protection for chemicals was established by the Federal Supreme Court in BGH GRUR 1972, 541 – *Imidazolines.*

2080 Stefan Fröhlich 2008 (n 2005) 161.

2081 Bernhard Jestaedt and Georg Benkard, 'Art. 64' Rdn 20 in Thomas Adams and others (eds) *Europäisches Patentübereinkommen* (4th edn, C.H. Beck 2012).

2082 PCT/EP2011/072590.

Pursuant to Article 64(2) EPC, the process of manufacturing an individual compound of a fragrance formula is also eligible for patent protection.[2083] In this case, protection only extends to the claimed process and the products obtained directly from it. Consequently, the patent can only be asserted against third parties who make use of the claimed process.

Of particular relevance for the perfume industry is that a new use of an already known compound may be eligible for patent protection in the form of use claims. This is best explained with an example. The use of a mixture containing Cis- and Trans-3-Methyl-y-Decalactone as a jasmine mixture was first claimed in 2004 by Symrise Gmbh & Co. Kg.[2084] Both individual compounds and the mixture were known, but its use as a jasmine odorant was deemed new under Article 54(1) EPC.

### 2. Aromatic compositions

Complex aromatic compositions, under certain circumstances, may be eligible for patent protection. For the purposes of the current research and following Fröhlich, they are deemed to consist of multiple, interconnected, single (raw) substances that may be of natural or synthetic origin. The most paradigmatic examples of aromatic compositions are perfume compositions.[2085]

The patentability of aromatic compositions and compounds is examined in the following sections.

## II. Requirements for protection

This section provides a brief overview of the main issues that arise in connection to the patentability of compounds and compositions used in the perfume industry. Article 52(1) EPC lays down the three cumulative requirements that any invention must overcome to merit patent protection, namely it must be new, involve an inventive step and be susceptible of industrial applicability.[2086] Therefore, the patentability of aromatic com-

---

2083 See Article 64 (2) EPC and Article 28 (1)(b) TRIPs.

2084 See DE502005005342D1, EP1761618A1, EP1761618B1, US8034761, US20080194455, WO2005123889A1.

2085 Stefan Fröhlich 2008 (n 2005) 153.

2086 This is examined further in chapter 6 below.

pounds and compositions is governed by the same rules that regulate the protection of chemical substances. Their specificities in the fragrance context are outlined in the following paragraphs.

Turning first to perfume compositions, in theory, they are eligible for patent protection just like any other chemical composition. Nevertheless, in practice, it has been noted that most of them lack inventive character.[2087] In the perfume industry, there are well-established principles for mixing substances. As a result, and following the case law of the Boards of Appeal of the EPO, if a person having ordinary skills in the art could have developed the same composition, it should not to be regarded as inventive.[2088] Similarly, and by virtue of the doctrine of equivalence,[2089] the substitution of one element of the composition with an analogous one does not merit patent protection. Of particular relevance for the perfume industry is the fact that a combination of known materials, with known features, in a known manner to achieve a known result lacks inventiveness. This is typically the case of Eau de Cologne, which is a scented solution containing alcohol, water and between 2% and 6% perfume concentrate.[2090] The selection of the ingredients and its formulation is a standard and routine practice for perfumists and chemists, thus lacking inventive character.[2091]

Finally, in connection to the patentability of aromatic compounds it should be highlighted that these follow the same rules of patentability as any other chemical compounds. In particular, scent manufacturers are individual compounds that when are subject to patent protection are referred to as "captive odorants", which can be used exclusively by the patent

---

2087 Stefan Fröhlich 2008 (n 2005) 138.

2088 See for instance T 426/88 [1992] OJ EP 427; see further Albert Ballester Rodes and others, *Case Law of the Boards of Appeal* (8th edn, 2016 EPO) § 8.1.1., where the person having ordinary skills in the art is defined as: "(…) an experienced practitioner who has average knowledge and abilities and is aware of what was common general knowledge in the relevant art concerned at a particular time (average skilled person). He should also be presumed to have had access to everything in the state of the art, in particular the documents cited in the search report, and to have had at his disposal the normal means and capacity for routine work and experimentation".

2089 See Article 2 of the Protocol on the interpretation of Article 69 EPC: "For the purpose of determining the extent of protection conferred by a European patent, due account shall be taken of any element which is equivalent to an element specified in the claims".

2090 'Compound' *Encyclopaedia Britannica* <http://www.britannica.com/art/cologne > accessed 15 September 2018.

2091 Stefan Fröhlich 2008 (n 2005) 139.

owners and against imitators. Yet again, overcoming the inventive step requirement is problematic in practice.

### III. Evaluation

Based on the foregoing analysis, it is possible to conclude that the protection of perfumes through patent rights, as regards both the individual compounds and the fragrance compositions has advantages and limitations. Regarding the advantages, a patent on a composition or a compound confers upon its holder the right to exploit it exclusively on the market and thus prevents third parties from using the invention.[2092] Patent rights can also be assigned and licensed.[2093] As noted above, relying on patent protection provides greater legal certainty than secrecy does.[2094] The exclusivity conferred by the former lasts for twenty years as of filing, irrespective of whether the invention later becomes public, in contrast to what happens to trade secrets, where protection is lost upon disclosure. In addition, patent rights also afford protection against independent creation and reverse engineering, which is particularly problematic in the case of perfume formulas.

In contrast, every patent application is published eighteen months after it is filed at the latest, even if it turns out not to be granted.[2095] Of particular relevance is that pursuant to Article 83 EPC the content of European patent applications must be enabling, that is, sufficiently clear and complete so that a person having ordinary skill in the art is capable of carrying it out. The upshot of this is that even if the patent is not granted, competitors are able to learn the formula, the compound or the process to manufacture them. What is more, in the event that it is granted, it is likely that the disclosure will instruct competitors on how to invent around. Additionally, resorting to patent protection involves high costs regarding both the application and the annual renewal fees.[2096] According to the EPO, in 2015 the cost of taking a patent through the grant stage alone was estimated to be of around 5.655 €.[2097] The high cost of the patent system was iden-

2092 Stefan Fröhlich 2008 (n 2005) 166.
2093 See Article 72 EPC.
2094 Chapter 1 § 3 A) I. 2. c).
2095 Article 93(1) EPC.
2096 Stefan Fröhlich 2008 (n 2005) 167.
2097 As reported by the EPO <http://www.epo.org/service-support/faq/own-file.html#faq-199> accessed 15 September 2018.

tified by the head of IP of Perfume Company 1 as the main hurdle in seeking patent protection for their innovations.

Finally, it should be stressed that perfume manufacturers are wary of relying on patent protection for their formulas because the marketing of a perfume can extend beyond the twenty year term, after which a given patent falls into the public domain.[2098] Nevertheless, it is also true that since gas-chromatographs devices were developed in 1980, allowing to dissect the composition of a fragrance with an accuracy of 90% after the first chromatographic approach, it is now very easy get a precise picture of the formula of a perfume and produce a replica that can convey a similar olfactory message.[2099] With these considerations in mind, the following section explores the strengths of the protection conferred by trade mark rights to perfumery products.

## C) Trade mark law

### I. Object of protection

Trade mark rights can be applied to protect several aspects of perfumery goods, both individually and in connection to unfair competition provisions. In particular, they can cover their names (through verbal mark), the shapes of their bottles (through three-dimensional marks) and the packaging under which they are marketed (also through three-dimensional marks).[2100] For instance, four different EU trade marks protect the fragrance "1 million" by Paco Rabanne, one of the world's best-selling perfumes.[2101] The verbal marks "1 million"[2102] and "one million"[2103] have

2098 Agnieszka A. Machnicka 2012 (n 1995) 125; see further André Bassard 1979 ( n 2016) 461.

2099 Pierre Laszlo and Sylvie Rivière 2001 (n 1992) 90-91; IFRA, 'Valuable yet vulnerable: Trade Secrets in the fragrance industry' (2013) IFRA Position Paper, 13 <www.ifraorg.org/view_document.aspx?docId=23107> accessed 15 September 2018; Claire Guillemin, *Law & Odeur* (Nomos 2016) 58-61; this was also discussed during the course of an interview with maître parfumaire Rosendo Mateu (see Annex 2).

2100 Agnieszka A. Machnicka 2012 (n 1995) 124-125.

2101 As reported by Sephora France <http://www.sephora.fr/Toutes-les-meilleures-ventes/Parfum/Parfum-Homme/Rimppag0000017/SC310;jsessionid=022FF75A3011336DACD557F8CE516DDE.wfr1n> accessed 15 September 2018.

2102 EUTM Number: 005682141.

2103 EUTM Number 005738489.

been registered in connection to the fragrance's name. A figurative trade mark protects the logo under which the perfume is marketed (see image 1 below).[2104] Also, a three-dimensional mark has been granted for the perfume's bottle, which represents a golden bar (as seen in image 2 below).[2105]

Image 1

Image 2

Then, there is the issue of smell marks' eligibility for protection, which is discussed in section II.2 in connection to the representation requirement.

## II. Requirements for protection

Pursuant to Article 4 EUTMR[2106] (and Article 3 TMD) a trade mark may consist of a (i) sign (ii) capable of being represented. Furthermore, (iii) it must allow consumers to distinguish the goods or services of one undertaking from those of other undertakings. The three limbs of the trade mark definition and the issues they pose in connection to fragrances are discussed in the following sections.

2104 EUTM Number: 006601091.

2105 EUTM Number: 006826556.

2106 Regulation (EU) 2017/1001 of the European Parliament and of the Council of 14 June 2017 on the European Union trade mark [2017] OJ L154/1 ( European Union Trade Mark Regulation or EUTMR).

### 1. Signs

Neither the EUTMR nor the TMD define the term "sign". They merely spell out a list of non-exhaustive examples of what may be deemed a sign for the purposes of trade mark law.[2107] The Encyclopaedia Britannica adopts the definition provided by the American semiotics philosopher Charles Sanders Pierce, who describes them as "something which stands to somebody for something".[2108] In line with this approach and following the literal wording of the EUTMR and the TMD, it seems that no restrictions have been placed on the eligibility of any potential sign as long as it is able to signal the origin of the goods to which it is applied.[2109] Indeed, in the latest reform of the EU Trade mark system, for the first time specific reference was made to non-conventional trade marks such as colours and sounds.[2110]

Regarding fragrances, it is clear that brand names, bottle shapes and packaging can act as signs that consumers associate with a given perfume, as illustrated by Paco Rabanne's "1 million" marks. With respect to the olfactory message, in a decision from 2002 (*Sieckmann v. DPMA*),[2111] the CJEU in abstract opened the door to the protection of signs that cannot be perceived visually (non-conventional trade marks), as would be the case of odours, but still restated the importance of the representation requirement. The following section explores this condition in the wake of the *Sieckmann v. DPMA* case.

### 2. Representation

Until the last reform of the EU trade mark system, the eligibility of a sign for trade mark protection was subject to the possibility of representing it in *a graphical manner.*[2112]

---

2107 That is, "words, including personal names, or designs, letters, numerals, colours, the shape of goods or of the packaging of goods, or sounds".

2108 'Semiotics', *Encyclopaedia Britannica* <https://www.britannica.com/science/semiotics> accessed 15 September 2018.

2109 Annette Kur and Thomas Dreier 2013 (n 506) 170.

2110 See Article 4 EUTMR and Article 3 TMD.

2111 Case C–273/00 *Sieckmann v DPMA* [2002] ECR I-11737.

2112 See Article 4 Council Regulation (EC) No 207/2009 of 26 February 2009 on the Community trade mark [2009] OJ L78/1 and Article 2 of Directive 2008/95/EC of the European Parliament and of the Council of 22 October

The scope of this requirement was interpreted by the CJEU in *Sieckmann v. DPMA*, following a referral by the German Federal Patent Court ("*Bundespatentgericht*"). The CJEU was confronted with the issue of graphical representation after the German Patent and Trade Mark Office ("DPMA") refused to register an olfactory mark on the grounds that it was not possible to represent it in a graphical manner.[2113] Mr Sieckmann had filed a trade mark application for a scent and had described it as "balsamically fruity with a slight hint of cinnamon".[2114] Along with the application, he deposited a sample of the relevant odour, provided a list of laboratories where additional samples could be obtained and submitted the fragrance's chemical formula.[2115] Against this background, the German Federal Patent Court stayed the proceedings and referred a question for a preliminary ruling to the CJEU to clarify two issues: (i) whether a trade mark may consist of a sign that is not perceived visually and (ii) whether the graphic representation requirement in the case of smell marks is satisfied by providing a written verbal description, or its chemical formula or by depositing samples of the scent (or a combination thereof).

Regarding the first question, the CJEU ruled that signs that cannot be perceived visually shall only be eligible for protection if it is possible to represent them graphically in a manner that "is clear, precise, self-contained, easily accessible, intelligible, durable and objective".[2116] The court shed further light on the accepted means of representing a smell mark in

2008 to approximate the laws of the Member States relating to trade marks [2008] OJ L299/25; by virtue of Regulation (EU) 2015/2424 of the European Parliament and of the Council of 16 December 2015 amending Council Regulation (EC) No 207/2009 on the Community trade mark and Commission Regulation (EC) No 2868/95 implementing Council Regulation (EC) No 40/94 on the Community trade mark, and repealing Commission Regulation (EC) No 2869/95 on the fees payable to the Office for Harmonization in the Internal Market (Trade Marks and Designs) [2015] OJ L341/21 as of October 1, 2017 (second phase of implementation) the "graphical representation requirement" has been deleted and it suffices that the subject matter of protection is represented in a manner which enables to identify it in a clear and precise manner.

2113 As laid down in Article 8 (1) of the German Trade Mark Act of 1994 (Markengesetz vom 25. Oktober 1994 (BGBl. I S. 3082; 1995 I S. 156; 1996 I S. 682), das zuletzt durch Artikel 11 des Gesetzes vom 17. Juli 2017 (BGBl. I S. 2541) geändert worden ist).

2114 Case C–273/00 *Sieckmann v DPMA* [2002] ECR I-11737, para13.

2115 The chemical formula was C6H5-CH = CHCOOCH3.'

2116 Case C–273/00 *Sieckmann v DPMA* [2002] ECR I-11737 para 545; this interpretation was anticipated by Advocate General Ruiz-Jarabo Colomer in his opin-

its answer to the second question by noting that chemical formulas were not regarded as "sufficiently intelligible". Furthermore, it was held that chemical formulas did not represent the scent of a composition, but rather represent the composition itself.[2117] The written description of the smell for which protection was sought was also deemed not "sufficiently clear and precise", despite its graphical nature.[2118] Likewise, the deposit of a sample lacked stability and durability and was not of a graphical nature.[2119] Finally, it was held that the combination of the above-enumerated elements did not comply with the requirements of graphical representation.[2120]

After *Sieckman*, it seemed that the graphical representation requirement was an insurmountable obstacle for olfactory signs, at least until new and more precise graphical representation methods were developed,[2121] or this requirement was removed from the acquis communautaire. In fact, the absence of pertinent representation means was confirmed by the GCEU of the European Union in 2005 with respect to the "smell of ripe strawberries".[2122]

---

ion, where he noted that "In any case, I believe that the abstract ability of a sign, capable of perception by the sense of smell, to fulfil an identification function is completely beyond question. If the intention is to symbolise goods or services of a particular origin in order to distinguish them from those of a different origin, or if it is a question of evoking specific source, a quality or the reputation of an undertaking, the best thing is to fall back upon a sense that, like the sense of smell, is undoubtedly, even persuasively, evocative". Case C–273/00 *Sieckmann v DPMA* [2002] ECR I-11737, Opinion of Ruiz-Jarabo Colomer, para 29.

2117 Case C–273/00 *Sieckmann v DPMA* [2002] ECR I-11737, para 69.

2118 Case C–273/00 *Sieckmann v DPMA* [2002] ECR I-11737, para 70.

2119 Case C–273/00 *Sieckmann v DPMA* [2002] ECR I-11737, para 71.

2120 Case C–273/00 *Sieckmann v DPMA* [2002] ECR I-11737, para 72.

2121 In this regard, it is worth noting that prior to *Sieckmann* "the smell of fresh cut grass" was registered in connection to tennis balls Case R 156/1998-2 *Vennootschap onder Firma Senta Aromatic* [1992] OHIM OJ 1239 paras 14-15; thus far, this is the only smell mark registered with EUIPO and according to Advocate General Ruiz-Jarabo Colomer "this seems to be a 'pearl in the desert', however, an individual decision which is unlikely to be repeated" Case C–273/00 *Sieckmann v DPMA* [2002] ECR I-11737, Opinion of Ruiz-Jarabo Colomer para 32; Cristina Hernánder-Martí, 'The possibility of IP protection for smell' [2014] 36 EIPR 665, 668.

2122 Case T–305/04 *Eden SARL v OHIM* [2005] ECR II-04705, para 34 "It is, moreover, common ground that, at the present time, there is no generally accepted international classification of smells which would make it possible, as with international colour codes or musical notation, to identify an olfactory sign ob-

A number of scholarly works purported that the graphical representation requirement was an anachronism in the digital era, and that legal certainty no longer calls for a paper registry system.[2123] Thus, some suggested that it should not be considered when assessing the eligibility of a sign for protection.[2124] Instead, the focus should be placed on the capability of the sign to distinguish the goods and services of one undertaking from another.[2125]

Ultimately, this rationale has crystallised in the new wording of Article 4(b) EUTMR, by virtue of which the relevant criterion is that the signs are capable of "being represented on the Register of European Union trade marks, ("the Register"), in a manner which enables the competent authorities and the public to determine the clear and precise subject matter of the protection afforded to its proprietor".[2126] Consequently, the representation of the sign (not necessarily in a graphical manner) is still a relevant condition to access the registry, even though the new wording shows the EU legislature's clear preference for broadening the scope of protection for non-conventional signs and considering alternative means of representation.[2127] However, despite some isolated interpretations, it appears that the EU legislature when drafting this provision had in mind the registration of musical tunes, 3D marks or colours as such, not smell marks.

---

jectively and precisely through the attribution of a name or a precise code specific to each smell".

2123 Max Planck Institute for Intellectual Property and Competition, 'Study on the Overall Functioning of the European Trade Mark System' (2011) 65-67 <http://ec.europa.eu/internal_market/indprop/docs/tm/20110308_allensbach-study_en.pdf> accessed 15 September 2018; Sergio Balañá Vicente, 'El entorno digital, ¿segunda oportunidad para la marca olfativa?: estudio acerca de la capacidad del signo olfativo' [2005-2006] 26 Actas de Derecho Industrial y Derecho de Autor 18, 24-27.

2124 Max Planck Institute for Intellectual Property and Competition 2011 (n 2123) 67-68; Sergio Balañá Vicente 2005-2006 (n 2123) 24-27; see Nadia Ianeva, *Registration of Non-conventional Signs Under the Community Trademark Regime* (Wissenschaftlicher Verlag Berlin 2008) 146-14.

2125 Max Planck Institute for Intellectual Property and Competition 2011 (n 2123) 67-68.

2126 Article 4(b) EUTMR.

2127 See Recital 10 EUTMR: "A sign should be permitted to be represented in any appropriate form using generally available technology, and thus not necessarily by graphic means, as long as the representation is clear, precise, self-contained, easily accessible, intelligible, durable and objective".

Indeed, the EUIPO Guidelines of Examination unequivocally state that: "Smell/olfactory or taste marks are currently not acceptable".[2128] According to the Office, the current state of technology does not allow for the representation of smells and taste in a manner that is "clear, precise, self-contained, easily accessible, intelligible, durable and objective", in line with the criteria laid down in *Sieckmann*.[2129] Pursuant to the Guidelines, any such application will be regarded as "not filed".[2130] However, even if new technological means allow for the representation of a scent, it is questionable whether odours can meet the third requirement of protection, i.e.whether they can be regarded as distinctive, as examined in the following section.

### 3. Distinctiveness

The raison d'être of trade mark law is to afford protection to signs provided that they are able to distinguish the goods and services offered by one competitor from those offered by another competitor (essential origin function of trade marks).[2131] Such a requirement is indispensable in order to ensure that the policy objectives that justify trade mark law are accomplished and has been codified as an absolute ground for refusal in Article 7(1)(b) EUTMR, which corresponds to Article 4(1)(b) TMD. In the assessment of the distinctive nature of a trade mark the following two parameters are considered: (i) the goods and services object of the registration and (ii) the perception of the sign by the relevant pubic.[2132]

---

2128 EUIPO Guidelines for Examination in the Office, Part B, Section 2, page 3.

2129 See Annette Kur and Martin Senftleben, *European Trade Mark Law* (OUP 2017) para 4.24 noting that "The situation is not expected to change soon. In particular, it is unlikely that courts and offices will in the future accept the deposit of samples in lieu of graphic representation. Such samples as well are not "easily accessible" and may also not be durable".

2130 EUIPO Guidelines for Examination in the Office, Part B, Section 2, page 33.

2131 See Case C–329/02 P *SAT.1 SatellitenFernsehen GmbH v European Union Intellectual Property Office* [2004] ECR II-08317, para 23; see further Case C–299/99 *Koninklijke Philips Electronics NV v Remington Consumer Products Ltd* [2002] ECR I-05475, para 30; the legal discussion surrounding the trade mark functions theories in Europe is discussed in more detail in chapter 5 § 3 C) II. 4 below in connection to the *L'Oréal v. Bellure* case.

2132 See Joined Cases C–468/01 P to C-472/01 P *Procter & Gamble Companyv. OHIM* [2004] ECR I-05141 para 33.

The general principle in the appraisal of the distinctive character of a trade mark, according to the case law from the CJEU, is that no distinction should be made as to the category of trade marks when considering their capacity to distinguish goods and services from different undertakings.[2133] Nonetheless, the court has stated that in the case of non-conventional marks, the average consumer is less prone to make assumptions about the origin of goods.[2134] In the context of fragrances, the distinctiveness requirement poses issues with respect to smell marks and the three-dimensional shapes used to protect perfume bottles. In particular, regarding bottles, the CJEU has pointed out that the shape for which protection is sought should go beyond a mere combination of common elements; to a certain extent, it must be striking.[2135] Following this premise, only those perfume recipients that "depart significantly from the norm or usages of the sector"[2136] are deemed distinctive. Continuing with the "1 million" example, using the shape of a golden bar seems to depart substantially from the other perfume bottles in the market.

The same rationale applies to smell marks. Even if the representation requirement could be overcome, it is not clear that odours could function as trade marks due to their lack of distinctiveness. It is less likely that a scent can convey information about the commercial origin of the goods in connection to which it is registered, because it does not suffice that the consumer identifies the scent as being familiar; he should be able to recognise it as an indicator of the source (the producer).[2137] The EUIPO Board of Appeals confirmed this in the *Myles* case, which was decided in 2001, prior to *Sieckmann*.[2138] There, the registration of the "scent of raspberries" was refused in connection to class 4 goods, "Fuels, including motor fuels, particularly diesel as heating fuel, fuel and engine fuel", owing to its lack of distinctiveness and not because of the impossibility of representing it graphically. The Board held that the average consumer would perceive the scent of raspberries as an attempt to convey a more pleasant smell, not as an in-

---

2133 Case T–194/01 *Unilever NV v OHIM* [2006] ECR II-00383 para 44; Guidelines for Examination in the Office, Part B, page 18.

2134 Case C–136/02 P *Mag Instrument Inc v OHIM* [2004] ECR I-09165 para 30.

2135 Case T–129/04 *Develey Holding GmbH & Co. Beteiligungs KG v OHIM* [2006] II-0811 paras 50-53.

2136 Case T–129/04 *Develey Holding GmbH & Co. Beteiligungs KG v OHIM* [2006] II-0811 para 53.

2137 Bettina Elias, 'Do scents signify origin? - An argument against trademark protection for fragrances' [1992] 82 TMR 475, 480.

2138 Case R 711/1999-3 *Myles Limited* (OHIM Boards of Appeal, 5 December 2001).

dicator of origin. The overall impression conveyed by the mark would not allow for distinguishing the goods at the time of purchase.[2139] In addition, it was contested that the olfactory sign for which protection was sought was not stable and durable, thus precluding registration.[2140]

### 4. Functionality

Drawing on the above analysis, it should be noted that functionality concerns have been raised in connection to smell marks. Before turning to them, some general remarks as to the functionality doctrine should be made.

The general principle underlying the exclusion of functionality from trade mark protection is to avoid that a single manufacturer can monopolize (potentially with no end in sight) the commercial use of the shape (or any other characteristic of a product) that results from its nature, technical features or that confers substantial value to the product in question. In line with this, the European legislature has laid down three categories of functionality as absolute grounds for refusal in Article 7(1)(e) EUTMR.[2141] The first one (paragraph i) prevents the registration of signs that result from the nature of the shape or other characteristics of the goods in question, such as the registration of the shape of a car for a vehicle.[2142] Next, paragraph (ii) refers to the so-called "technical functionality" and precludes the registration of the technical aspects of those signs that exclusively comprise the shape or other characteristics of the goods required to achieve a technical result. This ground of refusal has been applied to deny the registration of the "Red Lego Brick" as a three-dimensional trade mark in relation to "construction toys".[2143] Finally, pursuant to the ornamental functionality provision laid down in Article 7(1)(e)(iii) EUTMR, a sign that essentially

2139 Case R 711/1999-3 *Myles Limited* (OHIM Boards of Appeal, 5 December 2001) paras 43-44.

2140 Case R 711/1999-3 *Myles Limited* (OHIM Boards of Appeal, 5 December 2001) para 40.

2141 Which corresponds to Article 4(1)(e) TMD.

2142 This is the example provided by the EUIPO Guidelines for Examination in the Office, Part B, Section 4, Chapter 6, page 5; see further Annetted Kur, 'UMV 2017 Art. 7 Absolute Eintragungshindernisse' Rdn 117-118 on Annette Kur, Verena von Bomhard and Friedrich Albrecht, *BeckOK Markenrecht* (14th edn, C.H. Beck 2015).

2143 Case C–48/09 P *Lego Juris v OHIM* [2010] ECR I-08403.

consists of the shape or other characteristics that confers substantial value to a specific good is not eligible for trade mark protection. Following the EUIPO Guidelines, such a provision applies when "the aesthetic value of a shape (or by analogy other characteristic) can in its own right, determine the commercial value of the product and the consumers choice to a large extent".[2144] However, the fact that the relevant analysis does not take into account the long-term effects on competition of monopolising a given shape or characteristic of a product has not been without criticism.[2145]

At this point, it should be recalled that until the entry into force of the first phase of the Amending Regulation on 23 March 2016,[2146] the refusal to register a trade mark by the EUIPO was limited to "signs which consist exclusively of the *shape*" of certain functional features of products. This may have led some to think that the functionality exception was not applicable to smell signs, as they do not constitute a shape as such. However, the amended wording of this provision now also refers to other *"characteristics of goods"*, thereby ensuring their scope of application to smell marks.[2147]

The first and third types of functionality described above stand as major barriers to the protection of smell marks. For instance, the application of a

2144 EUIPO Guidelines for Examination in the Office, Part B, Section 4, Chapter 6 , page 9; the leading case on the issue of aesthetic functionality is T–508/08 *Bang & Olufsen A/S v OHIM* [2011] ECR II-06975.

2145 For a critical analysis of the "aesthetic functionality" requirement see Annette Kur, 'Too pretty to protect? '139, 139-140 in Josef Drexl and others *Technology and Competition, Contributions in honour of Hanns Ullrich* (Editions Larcier 2009) alerting of the effects of such an approach for competition law: "(…), the focus should not only rest on how the public, at a given point in time, perceives and evaluates a certain shape. The crucial test should consist of an analysis of the competitive potential of the form at stake, considering to what extent its assignment to one particular right holder would be liable to impede, or even exclude, efficient and meaningful competition. This means that a sign's rising potential to constitute a source identifier is only one factor in the assessment- it does not however, automatically lead to a proportionate decrease in the weight given to competition.

2146 Regulation (EU) 2015/2424 of the Europan Parliament and of the Council of 16 December 2015 amending Council Regulation (EC) No 207/2009 on the Community trade mark and Commission Regulation (EC) No 2868/95 implementing Council Regulation (EC) No 40/94 on the Community trade mark, and repealing Commission Regulation (EC) No 2869/95 on the fees payable to the Office for Harmonization in the Internal Market (Trade Marks and Designs) [2015] OJ L341/21 (Amending Regulation).

2147 Annette Kur and Martin Senftleben 2017 (n 2129) paras 4.175-4.176.

smell mark covering the scent of pineapple in connection to juices or yoghurts should be rejected on the grounds that it results from the nature of the good itself (as per Article 7(1)(i) EUTMR). Otherwise, the trade mark holder could prevent competitors from entering the yoghurt market. The same provision prevents the registration of smell marks for perfumes, as the scent results from the nature of the goods themselves. Additionally, the ornamental functionality doctrine is a major obstacle in the protection of the olfactory message conveyed by fragrances, pursuant to Article 7(1)(e)(iii) EUTMR. Indeed, the aesthetic message of a perfume or any other primary scent determines the commercial value of the product and, largely, the consumer's choice. Following the above-mentioned example, Paco Rabanne's "One Million" value lies mainly in its aromatic appeal to consumers, despite the importance of other factors, such as marketing campaigns and selective distribution agreements. As a final note on technical functionality (Article 7(1)(ii) EUTMR), it has been suggested that smell marks in connection to so-called "product scents" (those used to manufacture soaps, detergents or shampoos) are of a functional nature, as their main objective is to neutralise or mask the smell of the main component. However, the application of this provision appears less straightforward than the two previous cases.[2148]

## III. Evaluation

As is apparent from the above, the use of a trade mark in connection to a fragrance's name and packaging provides strong protection against the marketing of counterfeit products, which is further enhanced by the application of the Customs Regulation.[2149] Crucially, relying on trade marks also facilitates concluding licensing and selective distribution agreements, which are of paramount importance to the luxury perfume industry. Another remarkable advantage is that trade marks are the only IPR that is not subject to time limitations. As long as they are used in trade and the appro-

2148 Sergio Balañá Vicente 2005-2006 (n 2123) 45-46.

2149 Regulation of the European Parliament and of the Council E 608/2013 of 12 June 2013 concerning customs enforcement of intellectual property rights and repealing Council Regulation (EC) No 1383/2003 concerning customs enforcement of intellectual property rights [2013] OJ L181/15 (Customs Regulation).

priate renewal fees are paid, the protection of the registered signs could extend perpetually.

Notwithstanding this, trade mark rights are subject to a number of limitations. For the time being, the representation requirement remains an essential condition of protection in the EU, and it seems unlikely that odours can overcome this hurdle in the near future. Furthermore, even if new technological means allow for the representation of smells in a "clear, precise, self-contained, easily accessible, intelligible, durable and objective" manner, functionality and lack of distinctiveness may be invoked against the registration of scents. Crucially, trade mark rights do not confer protection against imitations that do not have a sign attached, as in the case of "smell-alikes". Instead, this is achieved through the joint protection of trade marks and unfair competition law. Indeed, de lege lata the most effective means of enjoining the distribution of smell-alikes is provided by the MCAD, by virtue of which the presentation of advertied products as replicas is deemed unlawful, as analysed in the following section.

### D) Unfair competition – Comparative advertisement

The present section delves into the protection of perfumes through unfair competition law. In particular, and owing to the broad scope of application of unfair competition rules, it is confined to the study of the legal framework for comparative advertisement and trade mark law regarding smell-alikes. Over the last decade, the national courts of a number of Member States have rendered multiple decisions on this topic, and even more so since the CJEU decided on the famous *L'Oréal v Bellure* case. Following the structure implemented in the previous sections, the object of protection, together with the requirements and the advantages and disadvantages of resorting to comparative advertisement by fragrance manufacturers are examined. In this context, the CJEU's decision *L'Oréal v Bellure* is used as the guiding authority.

#### I. Object of protection

Article 2(c) MCAD defines the concept of "comparative advertisement" as "any advertising which explicitly or by implication identifies a competitor or goods or services offered by a competitor".[2150] The provisions regulating such a marketing practice attempt to strike a balance between three conflicting interests: (i) the advertiser's interests in referring to a leading brand (referential function), (ii) the consumer's need for reliable information ("assisting rational consumers' choice")[2151] and (iii) the competitor's interest in protecting his goodwill from tarnishing and blurring practices.[2152] In line with this three-fold approach, but at a more abstract level, the EU legislation on comparative advertisement aims at achieving the appropriate equilibrium between the "rights of privacy and commercial personality and the freedom of commercial speech and competition".[2153] However, from a competition law perspective, opinions are divided among those who purport that such a practice strengthens competition in the market by increasing transparency and consumer attention and those who are wary of the distortion it generates.[2154]

Comparative advertising as a marketing practice is particularly relevant in the high-end fragrance sector because the number of stores from which perfume smell-alikes can be purchased has steadily increased in recent years.[2155] The analysis conducted throughout this chapter has shown that perfumes "as such" are not the object of protection of any IPR, unless their packaging and bottles bear a protected trade mark or contain a patented compound. Thus, manufacturing and putting in the market perfumes that convey the same olfactory message as other well-known fragrances is lawful according to intellectual property law. Notwithstanding this, following the CJEU's famous *L'Oréal v Bellure* ruling, comparing an original fine perfume with an imitation for marketing purposes shall be deemed unfair. Hereafter, the necessary conditions to regard an act of comparative adver-

---

2150 Another widely cited definition is provided by William L. Wilkie and Paul W. Farris, 'Comparison Advertising: Problems and Potential, Source' [1975] 39 J of Marketing 7, 7 where comparative advertisement is defined as advertising that: "1. Compares two or more specifically named or recognizably presented brands of the same generic product or service class, and 2. Makes such a comparison in terms of one or more specific product or service attributes".

2151 See Recitals 6 and 8 of MCAD.

2152 Ansgar Ohly and Michael Spence, *The Law of Comparative Advertising* (Hart Publishing 2000) 57-59.

2153 Jochen Glöckner, 'The Regulatory Framework for Comparative Advertisement in Europe- Time for a new Round of Harmonisation' [2012] IIC 35, 39.

2154 Jochen Glöckner 2012 (n 2153) 39.

2155 Cristina Fontgivell, 'Equivalenza proyecta 20 aperturas en Estados Unidos' *Diario Expansión* (Barcelona, 20 April 2015) <http://www.expansion.com/catalunya/2015/04/20/5534b784268e3ee1648b4576.html> accessed 15 September 2018.

tisement as lawful are outlined in the wake of the *L'Oréal v Bellure* decision.

## II. Requirements for protection in the wake of L'Oréal v Bellure

The EU legislature has laid down a two-step test to assess the lawfulness of acts of comparative advertisement, which consists of the appraisal of (i) whether there is an actual act of comparative advertisement and (ii) if pursuant to the criteria of fairness spelt out in Article 4 of the Directive, the relevant conduct is permitted.[2156] Each of these is analysed in turn and particular emphasis is given to one of the cumulative conditions in Article 4 MCAD: the presentation of products as imitations.

### 1. Two-step test: Definition of comparative advertisement and the appraisal of fairness

According to the case law from the CJEU, the MCAD applies to direct acts of representation as well as representation by implication to a competitor and the goods and services offered by him.[2157] Furthermore, there must be a competitive relation between the advertiser and the undertaking identified in the advertisement in question. Such an assessment should take into account the state of the market and consumer habits together with the territory in which the advertisement is released. According to the CJEU, attention should be paid to the relevant features of the promoted product.[2158]

The second benchmark of the test assesses whether the reference enshrined in the advertisement is fair. To this end, Article 4 of the Directive

2156 Ansgar Ohly and Michael Spence, *The Law of Comparative Advertising* (Hart Publishing 2000) 44.

2157 Case C–112/99 *Toshiba Europe GmbH v Katun Germany GmbH* [2001] ECR I-07945 para 29 "The test for determining whether an advertisement is comparative in nature is this where it identifies, explicitly or by implication, a competitor of the advertiser or goods or services which the competitors offers".

2158 Case C–381/05 *De Landtsheer Emmanuel SA v Comité interprofessional du Vin de Champagne and Veuve Clicquot Ponsardin SA* [2007] ECR I-03115 paras 20-23; Ansgar Ohly, 'Vergleichende Werbung für Zubehör und Warensortimente - Anmerkungen zu den EuGH-Urteilen 'Siemens/VIPA' und 'LIDL Belgium/ Colruyt'' [2007] GRUR 3, 4-5.

spells out eight cumulative conditions to be satisfied by any comparative advertisement in order to be deemed fair and thus permitted. Such a marketing practice shall only be allowed when it is not misleading (Article 4(a)); it compares products intended for the same purpose (Article 4(b)); it objectively compares one or more material, relevant, verifiable and representative features of those products (Article 4(c)); it does not discredit or denigrate the trade marks and the like of a competitor (Article 4(d)); it refers to products with the same designation of origin (Article 4(e)); it does not take unfair advantage of the reputation of a trade mark, trade name or other distinguishing marks of a competitor (Article 4(f)); it does not present goods as imitations (Article 4(g)); and it does not cause confusion (Article 4(h)).

2. Presentation of products as imitations in the wake of L'Oréal v Bellure

Of particular relevance for the perfume industry is Article 4(g) MCAD, which provides that products that are presented as imitations of those they refer to shall never benefit from comparative advertisement protection. The extent of this provision and its implications for the smell-alike industry were discussed by the CJEU in *L'Oréal v Bellure*. The main facts and findings of the court are summarised below.

Bellure, one of the three defendants, produced a number of fragrances imitating some of L'Oréal's best-selling perfumes. In particular, the perfumes marketed under the names "La Valeur" and "Coffret d'Or" aimed at imitating the "Trésor" brand, whereas "Pink Wonder" imitated "Miracle". In all three cases, the bottles and packaging under which they were marketed were similar in appearance to those of the original perfumes, although "Coffret d'Or" was deemed only "slightly" similar. Notably, for marketing purposes, Malaika and Starion (the distributing companies and the two other defendants) provided retailers with a comparison list, which essentially indicated the correlation between the word mark of the original fragrance and the name under which the smell-alike was marketed. Under this fact pattern, L'Oréal brought proceedings seeking to enjoin the sale of the imitating perfumes on two grounds. In the first place, the French company claimed that the comparison list amounted to trade mark infringement under section 10(1) of the UK Trade marks Act 1994 (which corresponds to Article 10(2)(a) TMD). Secondly, it argued that "Trésor's" word mark, bottle word and figurative marks and packaging marks together with "Miracle's" word mark, packaging mark and bottle mark amounted to trade mark infringement under section 10(3) of the Trade Marks Act 1994 (which corresponds to 10(2)(c) TMD and deals with the protection afforded to trade marks having a reputation). Upon appeal, the referring court submitted five questions for a preliminary ruling to the CJEU, which mostly revolved around the issue of whether the use of a trade mark that does not mislead consumers and does not have an adverse effect on the reputation and distinctive nature of the mark, but provides an advantage to the trader, should be deemed unlawful. The court structured its legal reasoning in three sections, which are outlined below.

The first one dealt with the scope of the protection of Article 10(2)(c) TMD vis-à-vis marks with a reputation, where there was no likelihood of confusion and neither the repute nor distinctiveness of the mark were affected. According to the decision, the packaging the defendants used allowed consumers to establish a link with some of the trade marks used by L'Oréal for the packaging and bottles of its fine fragrances, which was perceived as conferring a commercial advantage to the plaintiffs.[2159] The CJEU famously held that "riding on the coat-tails" of a mark with a reputation in order to take advantage of its power of attraction, reputation and prestige and without providing any compensation should be deemed unlawful and amounts to trade mark infringement.[2160] In its assessment, the court gave particular relevance to the investment and marketing efforts the proprietor of the trade mark took to create and maintain the mark's image.

The remaining enquiries touched upon comparative advertisement. In particular, the first and second questions posed by the referring court attempted to clarify whether the double identity prohibition laid down in Article 10(2)(a) TMD and the prohibition to use in the course of trade signs that are similar or identical to the registered trade mark and to the goods or services it covers, where there is likelihood of confusion between the signs and the trade marks (as set forth in Article 10(2)(b) TMD) is also applicable in the context of comparative advertisement when the essential origin function is not adversely affected. The CJEU premised its decision

---

2159 Case C–487/07 *L'Oréal v Bellure* [2009] ECR I-05185, para 47.

2160 The view expressed by the CJEU has been criticized, among many others by Dev S. Gangjee and Robert Burrell, 'Because You're Worth It: L'Oréal and the Prohibition on Free Riding' [2010] 73 MLR 282-295 who suggest that the fact that taking advantage of the reputation of a mark as such is deemed unlawful amounts to an unjustified expansion of trade mark law. The general prohibition on free riding laid down in *L'Oréal v Bellure* impedes referential function and "building on the efforts of others, which may ultimately negatively affect the competitiveness of the Single Market".

on the fact that comparison lists fall under the scope of the definition of comparative advertisement laid down in Article 2(c) MCAD and that the provision at issue was Article 10(2)(a) TMD (the double identity clause). Indeed, in the case under review the signs were identical (the fragrance's brand name) and they were applied to identical goods (i.e. perfumes). Against this backdrop, it was ruled that the holder of a registered trade mark can enjoin the use of a sign identical to its trade mark in connection to identical goods, provided that the conditions spelt out in Article 4 MCAD are not cumulatively met and that one of the trade mark functions is affected.[2161] Crucially, the court concluded that the essential origin function does not necessarily have to be jeopardised so long as "one of the other functions of the mark is affected".[2162]

With this statement, the CJEU clarified that the "essential origin function" is not the only function protected by trade mark law, thereby broadening the scope of protection afforded under the EU trade mark regime.[2163] In particular, reference was made to the "communication, investment or advertising functions".[2164] This was later confirmed in a number of decisions[2165] and has given rise to vehement criticism from legal scholars, who have mostly raised concerns regarding the expansion of trade mark rights to benefit large undertakings and against the interests of con-

2161 As pointed out by Annette Kur, Lionel Bently and Ansgar Ohly, 'Sweet Smells and a Sour Taste - The ECJ's L'Oréal decision' (2010) Max Planck Institute for Intellectual Property, Competition & Tax Law Research Paper Series No. 09-12 2, Paper No. 10/01, 3, footnote 4 <https://papers.ssrn.com/sol3/papers.cfm?abstract_id=1492032> accessed 15 September 2018 noting that the French and German translations of the decisions use the terms of "porter atteinte" and "beeinträchtigen"; and that these terms have a negative connotation, because they imply that the function of the mark has to be jeopardised to some extent. The English version of the decision makes a similar statement in para 60, referring to the "detriment to any of the functions".

2162 Case C–487/07 *L'Oréal v Bellure* [2009] ECR I-05185, para 58.

2163 Case C–487/07 *L'Oréal v Bellure* [2009] ECR I-05185, para 58: "These functions include not only the essential function of the trade mark, which is to guarantee to consumers the origin of the goods and services, but also its other functions, in particular that of guaranteeing the quality of the goods and services in question and those of communication, investment or advertising".

2164 Case C–487/07 *L'Oréal v Bellure* [2009] ECR I-05185, para 63.

2165 See among others: Case C–323/09 *Interflora Inc. and others v Marks & Spencer and others* [2011] ECR I-08625, para 48; Case C–236/08 *Google France SARL and Google Inc. v Louis Vuitton Malletier SA* [2010] ECR I-02417, paras 75-79; Case C–206/01 *Arsenal Football Club plc v Matthew Reed* [2002 ] ECR I-10273, para 48.

sumers and third parties and, more generally, competition in the market.[2166] Yet, a deeper study of the trade mark function theory in the EU falls outside the scope of the present research.[2167]

Third, the CJEU held that any explicit or implicit statement in a comparative advertisement that presents goods or services as imitations or replicas of a mark having a reputation shall be regarded as infringing for the purposes of Article 4(g) MCAD. More specifically, the court ruled, following the opinion of Advocate General Mengozzi, that it is irrelevant whether an advertisement shows that the product bearing the protected marks is imitated as a whole or for one of its essential characteristics (in the case under review, the smell of the products).[2168] Finally, it was concluded that any act of comparative advertisement where the product is presented as an imitation of a product bearing a well-known trade mark shall be considered to have taken "unfair advantage" of the reputation of said mark, as per Article 4(f) MCAD.[2169] The doctrine followed by the CJEU in *L'Oréal v Bellure* regarding the intersection between comparative advertisement and trade mark law has crystalised in the new wording of Article 10(3)(f) TMD, by virtue of which the use of a sign in comparative advertisement in a manner that is contrary to MCAD is proscribed and therefore leads to dual infringement: unfair competition and trade mark law.

To be sure, *L'Oréal v Bellure* is one of the most contested decisions on the interplay between unfair competition and trade mark law the CJEU has rendered. It has spurred criticism among several authors, who argue that its findings substantially limit one of the pillars upon which modern intellectual property systems are built: the freedom to imitate principle. According to said principle, products that are not specifically covered by

2166 Mats Björkenfeldt, 'The Genie is out of the Bottle: the ECJ's Decision in L'Oréal v Bellure' [2010] 5 JIPLP 105, 106.

2167 Academic works that study this topic include among others: Annette Kur, 'Trade Marks Function, Don't They? CJEU Jurisprudence and Unfair Competition Principles' [2014] IIC 434 -454 and Martin Senftleben, 'Function Theory and International Exhaustion – Why It Is Wise to Confine the Double Identity Rule to Cases Affecting the Origin Function' [2014] 36 EIPR 518; see also Nicole Van der Laan, 'The use of trade marks in keyword advertising: Developments in CJEU and national jurisprudence' 231, 253-256 in Nari Lee, Ansgar Ohly, Annette Kur, Guido Westkamp (eds), *Intellectual Property, Unfair Competition and Publicity* (Edward Elgar 2014).

2168 Case C–487/07 *L'Oréal v Bellure* [2009] ECR I-05185, para 75 but also, Opinion of Mengozzi, para 88.

2169 Case C–487/07 *L'Oréal v Bellure* [2009] ECR I-05185, para 80.

any IPR should be free to imitate,[2170] as famously noted by the U.S. Supreme Court in *Bonito Boats*, "imitation and refinement through imitation are both necessary to invention itself, and the very lifeblood of a competitive economy".[2171]

From the analysis conducted throughout this chapter, it appears that no single IPR affords protection to perfumes as such. Indeed, the possibility of imitating perfumes was not disputed throughout the proceedings. The salient question was whether the defendants could inform consumers that the products being sold were imitations of well-known fragrances. Against this background, some suggest that the CJEU favoured the interest of trade mark holders in preserving the exclusivity of their products through the application of rules preventing comparative advertisement of lawful products where no likelihood of confusion arises, rather than the general interest of consumers in knowing relevant information that may assist them in their rational choice.[2172]

This gave rise to numerous reactions from both academia and national courts, which mostly revolved around the implications of the CJEU's decision on the unlawfulness of marketing products that are not protected by any IPR. One of the most vehement criticisms was expressed by Jacob J, the referring Judge in England, when delivering his judgement after the CJEU's decision. He stressed that "I do not agree with or welcome this conclusion -it amounts to pointless monopoly. But my duty is to apply it".[2173] The judge argued that the ruling of the CJEU negatively affects

---

2170 Ansgar Ohly 2010 (n 1102) 506-524 concluding that imitation should not be deemed unfair, but may be subject to limitations.

2171 *Bonito Boats, Inc. v. Thunder Craft Boats, Inc.*, 489 U.S. 141, 146 (1989).

2172 Annette Kur, Lionel Bently and Ansgar Ohly, 'Sweet Smells and a Sour Taste - The ECJ's L'Oréal decision' (2010) Max Planck Institute for Intellectual Property, Competition & Tax Law Research Paper Series No. 09-12 2, Paper No. 10/01, 3, footnote 4 <https://papers.ssrn.com/sol3/papers.cfm?abstract_id=1492032> accessed 15 September 2018.

2173 *L'Oréal SA v Bellure NV* [2010] EWCA Civ 535 [50].

commercial freedom of speech[2174] and hinders market competition.[2175] He further noted that comparison lists play a central role in ensuring that consumers are informed about the characteristics of competitors' products, thus allowing proper competition.[2176] This is crucial for spare parts manufacturers and generic drug producers and, more generally, to allow consumers to make an informed decision.[2177] Along these lines, Ohly submitted that the legal reasoning developed by the CJEU limits the freedom of imitation and the possibility of informing consumers through the referential use of a mark.[2178] In the same vein, he argued that the interpretation of Article 10(2)(c) TMD the CJEU followed applies the French rationale of "parasitic competition" and seems to regard any act that takes advantage of another trader's reputation as prohibited, without assessing the fairness of the act. In his view, this contravenes the spirit of Article 10(2)(c) TMD and Article 4(f) of the MCAD, which were not drafted to protect the skill, labour and economic resources invested in the creation of a "product im-

2174 *L'Oréal SA v Bellure NV* [2010] EWCA Civ 535 [9]-[14] noting that "poor consumers are the losers. Only poor would dream of the defendant's products. The real thing is beyond their wildest dreams. Yet they are denied their right to receive information which would give them a little bit of pleasure; the ability to buy a product for a euro or so which they know smells like a famous perfume"; this view is also supported by Annette Kur, Lionel Bently and Ansgar Ohly, 'Sweet Smells and a Sour Taste – The ECJ's L'Oréal decision' (2010) Max Planck Institute for Intellectual Property, Competition & Tax Law Research Paper Series No. 09-12 2, Paper No. 10/01, 4 <https://papers.ssrn.com/sol3/papers.cfm?abstract_id=1492032> accessed 15 September 2018, who note that "Freedom of expression and information are enshrined in Art. 11 of the Charter of Fundamental Rights of the European Union (2007/C 303/01), and also figure in Art. 10 of the European Convention of Fundamental Rights (ECHR), to which all EU Member States have adhered". The authors also remind readers that the ECtHR regards commercial speech as falling within the scope of Article 10.

2175 *L'Oréal SA v Bellure NV.* [2010] EWCA Civ 535; [15].

2176 In the words of Jacob J "If a trader cannot (when it is truly the case) say. "my goods are the same as Brand X (a famous registered mark) but half the price", I think there is a real danger that important areas of trade will not be open to proper competition"; *L'Oréal SA v. Bellure NV.* [2010] EWCA Civ 535, [16].

2177 Annette Kur, Lionel Bently and Ansgar Ohly, 'Sweet Smells and a Sour Taste - The ECJ's L'Oréal decision' (2010) Max Planck Institute for Intellectual Property, Competition & Tax Law Research Paper Series No. 09-12 2, Paper No. 10/01, 3-4 footnote 9 <https://papers.ssrn.com/sol3/papers.cfm?abstract_id=1492032> accessed 15 September 2018.

2178 Ansgar Ohly 2010 (n 1102) 135-139.

age".[2179] In sum, critics have argued that the legal reasoning applied by the CJEU limits commercial speech to the detriment of consumers' choices.

However, one crucial distinction should be made. Unlike generic drugs or spare parts, which may be protected under patent rights, utility models and design rights for the features of appearance that do not enable mechanical parts to be connected,[2180] perfumes as such are not the object of IPRs. Most notably, perfumery goods are particularly vulnerable to reverse engineering practices.[2181] Consequently, some commentators have taken a more conservative approach to the protection of marks with a reputation in the context of well-known fragrances and have suggested that products imitating them should not be considered "lawful products", as noted by Jacob J. In this respect, Machinka[2182] underscores that the notion of "quality of a product" was construed in a wide sense by the CJEU in *Copad SA v Christian Dior couture SA* in the context of a trade mark license to include "the allure and prestige image which bestows on them an aura of luxury".[2183] This, in turn, was considered to contribute to the "image of the product", which constitutes an important part of the product itself. Consequently, the CJEU held that an "impairment to that aura of luxury is likely to affect the actual quality of those goods".[2184] In this context, she concludes that, to the extent that comparison lists hinder the quality of products by negatively affecting their image, the protection of fragrances against comparison lists appears justified, as it ultimately results from the wider protection conferred to marks with a reputation.[2185]

While the CJEU's interpretation may appear suitable to ensure that incentives to create new perfumes do not disappear, it cannot be overlooked that it ultimately sets general interpretative principles both for trade mark and comparative advertisement law across all industry sectors, beyond per-

---

2179 Ansgar Ohly 2010 (n 1102) 521-522.

2180 Article 7(2) Directive 98/71/EC of the European Parliament and of the Council of 13 October 1998 on the legal protection of designs [1998] OJ L289/28 (Design Directive).

2181 See chapter 5 § 4 B) I.

2182 Agnieszka A. Machnicka 2012 (n 1995) 136.

2183 Case C–59/08 *Copad SA v Christian Dior couture SA*, ECR [2009] I-03421 para 24.

2184 Case C–59/08 *Copad SA v Christian Dior couture SA*, ECR [2009] I-03421 para 26; the CJEU has confirmed this interpretation in the context of selective distribution agreements of luxury cosmetic and perfume products in Case C–236/2016 *Coty Germany GmbH and Parfümerie Akzente GmbH* (6 December 2017).

2185 Agnieszka A. Machnicka 2012 (n 1995) 136-138.

fumery goods. For this reason, it is concluded that the doctrine enshrined in *L'Oréal v Bellure* undoubtedly limits the possibility of making referential use of trade marks, thereby substantially limiting consumers' choices and hindering competition in the market.

## III. Evaluation

The broad interpretation of the imitation clause in Article 4(g) MCAD has become a powerful tool for manufacturers of fine perfumes to prevent the placing on the market of smell-alikes of their fragrances. In the wake of *L'Oréal v Bellure*, many national courts have ruled against undertakings that implement Bellure's business model.

In Spain, the EU Trade mark Court in Alicante decided in favour of the Puig Group, owner of EUTMs having a reputation, such as "Carolina Herrera", "Ultraviolet", "Paco Rabanne", "Black XS", "One Million", "Nina Ricci" and "J Paul Gaultier" and against four undertakings that offered, marketed and promoted smell-alikes of these perfumes using comparison lists.[2186] Puig launched proceedings against Caravan Fragrancias SL, Grupo del Árbol Distribución y Supermecados SA, Industria Aragonesa del perfume SL and Laboratorios Saphir SA for an infringement of the above listed marks having a reputation pursuant to the three types of conduct set out in Article 9 EUTMR (and 34 of the Spanish Trade Mark Act)[2187] and for carrying out acts of unfair competition.

In its judgement, the court applied the same line of argument as the CJEU in *L'Oréal v Bellure* and ruled that the defendants' conduct amounted to a violation of the double identity clause laid down in Article 34(2)(a) of the Spanish Trade mark Act (Article 9(2)(a) EUTMR), but also of Article 34(2)(c) of the Spanish Trade Mark Act (Article 9(2)(c) EUTMR), which provides enhanced protection to marks with a reputation when the use of the sign without due cause takes unfair advantage of, or is detrimental to, the distinctive character or the repute of the mark. Furthermore, it was noted that the marketing of smell-alikes through comparison lists might

---

2186 See SJMer n° 2 de Alicante n°3/15, de 14 de enero de 2015 (Acting as the Community Trade mark Court of First Instance). This decision that was subsequently upheld by the Court of Appeals in Alicante (SAP Alicante nº 1536/2015, de 14 de septiembre de 2015) and the Spanish Supreme Court in STS 3115/2015, de 16 de noviembre de 2016.

2187 Ley 17/2001, de 7 de diciembre, de Marcas (Spanish Trade Mark Act).

have a negative impact on other trade mark functions recognised by the CJEU. The decision under review expressly refers to functions such as guaranteeing the quality of the product or service, communication, investment and advertising. Secondly, the court found that a number of unfair competition provisions were infringed. In particular, it was held that the conduct of the respondents amounted to acts of unfair comparison (pursuant to Article 10(d) of the Spanish Unfair Competition Act, which corresponds to Article 4(g) MCAD) and taking unlawful advantage of a competitor's reputation (pursuant to Article 12 of the Spanish Unfair Competition Act). Finally, it was held that the promotion of smell-alike perfumes through comparison lists fell within the scope of Article 18 of the Spanish Unfair Competition Act, which prohibits unlawful publicity.

The previous analysis shows that the CJEU in *L'Oréal v Bellure* set a powerful precedent to enjoin the commercial activity of smell-alike manufacturers and retailers, as they are not allowed to advertise the equivalence of their fragrances with fine perfumes marketed by high-end brands. This is particularly important for the perfume industry, as there is no single IPR that protects perfumes as such and because their formulas can be easily unveiled through cheap reverse engineering techniques.

## *§ 4 The role of trade secrets in the protection of perfumes*

### A) Importance of trade secrets for the perfume industry

From the foregoing analysis, it can be concluded that odours are not the object of any specific IPR. Patents, copyright and trade marks, alongside unfair competition, only afford protection to some of the intangible assets involved in the creation, development and marketing of fragrances and new scents. Beyond traditional IPRs, in practice trade secrets play a central role in ensuring the appropriation of returns from innovation and the creation of new products in the perfume industry, as seen in Table 3 below.

| TABLE 3: IRPs APPLICABLE BY THE FRAGRANCE INDUSTRY IN THE PROTECTION OF THEIR INTANGIBLE ASSETS[2188] | | | | |
|---|---|---|---|---|
| IPR | Patents | Copyright | Trade marks | Trade Secrets |
| Molecules | ✓ | | ✓[2189] | ✓ |
| Processes | ✓ | | | ✓ |
| Client lists | | | | ✓ |
| Suppliers list | | | | ✓ |
| Raw materials (stabilisation, processing and sourcing) | ✓ | | | ✓ |
| Know-how / Institutional knowledge | | | | ✓ |
| Client product knowledge | | | | ✓ |
| Market knowledge and surveys | | | | ✓ |
| Logos, Brands and images | | | ✓ | |

As is apparent from the above table, trade secrets are key to ensuring the competitiveness of the perfume industry, as they afford overarching protection at every stage of the creation, manufacture and marketing phases. They are used along with patents to protect molecules, production processes and raw materials (stabilisation, processing and sourcing). Despite their

2188 This table is mostly based on the table included in IFRA, 'Valuable yet vulnerable: Trade Secrets in the fragrance industry' (2013) IFRA Position Paper, 11 <www.ifraorg.org/view_document.aspx?docId=23107> accessed 15 September 2018.

2189 See Guivaudan's U.S. Trademark 79038147 "Florymoss" under which one of its molecules is marketed.

non-exclusive nature, from a practical perspective they are often preferred over patent rights, as the maintenance and enforcement costs of the latter are higher than those for informal means of protection are.[2190] Resorting to trade secrets protection also avoids the risk of disclosing an invention in a patent application that may eventually not be granted and thereafter fall into the public domain. Furthermore, trade secret law provides incentives in areas that are not covered by traditional IPRs, such as small incremental innovations developed over time that are not eligible for patent protection but are nonetheless central to the sector's economic growth.

In recent decades, traditionally small and family-owned perfume companies have substantially grown to become SMEs or even large multinational companies, such as the Esteé Lauder Group, which now employs more than 42.000 people.[2191] Thus, the number of employees, suppliers and retailers has risen accordingly. Ultimately, this has led to a substantial increase in the leakage of confidential information. The following section identifies the main factors responsible for such an escalation and the measures perfume companies have adopted to prevent it.

## B) Increasing vulnerability of trade secrets in the perfume sector

The fragrance industry has traditionally relied strongly on trade secrets protection. As examined in § 2, this is mainly caused by the fact that there is no IPR that affords protection to perfumes as such. However, following an international trend, keeping information secret within the sector has become increasingly problematic.[2192] This section surveys the main factors behind the difficulties in concealing information.

From the existing literature and the interviews conducted, four factors have been identified as the main causes behind the leakage of trade secrets within the perfume sector: (i) reverse engineering practices; (ii) demands for disclosure and transparency; (iii) new means of electronic storage and transmission and (iv) employee mobility. Each of these are analysed in turn. Finally, (v) the main measures to prevent the unauthorised acquisition, use and disclosure of confidential information are examined.

2190 As disclosed by Perfume Company 1 (see Annex 1).

2191 See <https://en.wikipedia.org/wiki/Est%C3%A9e_Lauder_Companies> accessed 15 September 2018.

2192 Conversation with the Head of IP of Perfume Company 1 (see Annex 1).

### I. Reverse engineering

The development of gas chromatography-mass spectrometry techniques in the 1980s allowed competitors to identify the main compounds in a fragrance and their proportions at a relatively low cost.[2193] This only requires an inexpensive device (known as an "artificial nose") which provides an accurate analysis of the mixture after introducing a small sample of the analysed perfume.[2194] A skilled chemist can interpret the results of such an analysis and develop a similar or identical perfume. In fact, some commentators note that after the first chromatograph approach, 90% of the perfume components are revealed, which can increase to 99% with olfactory adjustment.[2195]

In this regard, perfumist Roseando Mateu indicates that to achieve an identical olfactory message, the formula alone does not suffice, as the supplier's identity in the case of organic compounds and mixtures is also relevant. He uses the case of lemon scent as an example. The one supplied by Italian producers is more intense than the one manufactured in Spain due to the technology applied to obtain it. In Italy, the technique is more artisanal, as only the outer layers of the lemon rind (the ones with a more intense smell) are used. This results from the fact that old machines are deployed. In contrast, Spanish manufacturers use modern equipment that uses the entire lemon rind. Hence, the smell of odorous compounds manufactured in Spain is less intense, but also cheaper.[2196]

In the same vein, the head of IP of Perfume Company 1 argues that there is not an exact answer to the question of whether it is possible to reverse engineer perfumes to find out their formulas, as an array of factors come into play. In particular, it is noted that to avoid imitations, very expensive ingredients are included in high-end fragrances. Consequently, exclusivity is achieved through the use of highly priced compounds.[2197]

The policy arguments underlying reverse engineering are examined in greater detail in chapter 6.[2198]

---

2193 IFRA, 'Valuable yet vulnerable: Trade Secrets in the fragrance industry' (2013) IFRA Position Paper, 14 <www.ifraorg.org/view_document.aspx?docId=23107 > accessed 15 September 2018.

2194 Pierre Pierre Laszlo and Sylvie Rivière 2001 (n 1992) 23.

2195 Claire Guillemin, *Law & Odeur* (Nomos 2016) 60.

2196 Interview with Rosendo Mateu (see Annex 2).

2197 Interview with the Head of IP of Perfume Company 1 (see Annex 1).

2198 Chapter 6 § 2 B) II.

## II. Demands for disclosure and transparency

Due to safety and environmental concerns, scent and perfume producers are compelled to disclose their fragrance formulas and the ingredients, following the obligations laid down in the EU legislation that regulates the cosmetic sector.[2199] For the same reasons, clients frequently want to know the formula and ingredients used, thus increasing the likelihood of subsequent trade secret disclosure. Ultimately, this may enable them to produce the secret product or ask a competing firm to do it at a lower price.[2200]

Notwithstanding the aforementioned, the Head of IP of Perfume Company 1 considers that the disclosure to business partners is a "controlled risk", since cooperation with third parties is based on a long-term relationship of trust. Thus, prior to disclosing any sensitive information, the company builds up a stable relationship in order to ensure that adequate measures to protect secret information are adopted.

## III. Electronic information storage and transmission

The advent of new technologies has enabled the dissemination of information faster than ever before. In addition, new storage mechanisms like USB sticks and cloud computing allow potential infringers to collect large amounts of data within a few seconds. From the perspective of trade se-

2199 See Article 21 of the Regulation (EC) of the European Parliament and of the Council (EC) No 1223/2009 of 30 November 2009 on cosmetic products [2009] OJ L342/59, which provides the disclosure of the composition, with limitations as to the quantity: "Without prejudice to the protection, in particular, of *commercial secrecy* and of *intellectual property* rights, the responsible person shall ensure that the *qualitative and quantitative composition* of the cosmetic product and, in the case of perfume and aromatic compositions, the name and code number of the composition and the identity of the supplier, as well as existing data on undesirable effects and serious undesirable effects resulting from use of the cosmetic product are made easily accessible to the public by any appropriate means. The quantitative information regarding composition of the cosmetic product required to be made publicly accessible shall be limited to hazardous substances in accordance with Article 3 of Regulation (EC) No 1272/2008" (emphasis added).

2200 IFRA, 'Valuable yet vulnerable: Trade Secrets in the fragrance industry' (2013) IFRA Position Paper, 15 <www.ifraorg.org/view_document.aspx?docId=23107 > accessed 15 September 2018.

crets holders, this poses high risks.[2201] Indeed, the empirical analysis shows that some undertakings in the fragrance sector have restricted the use of e-mail communications to share information with a view to minimising the likelihood of leakage.[2202] Likewise, the use of so-called "data loss prevention software" is becoming widespread among companies that place great value on their confidential information. In essence, this type of software gives notice to the legal department of an unusual download and sharing of information within the company, thereby allowing the company to take action before the information concerned is actually made public.[2203] In practice, this has proven extremely useful to prevent the spill-over of secret information.

## IV. Employment mobility

The assessment of post-employment non-disclosure obligations is one of the most contested aspects of the law of trade secrets. In this regard, perfume and scent manufacturers have expressed concerns as to the increasing employee mobility within the sector and the loss of confidential information it entails.[2204] To avoid such a situation, the Head of IP of Perfume Company 1 states that creating a working environment where loyalty among employees is promoted is essential and is a very important part of the values of the company. Particularly, owing to the fact that under the applicable law of the Member State where the country is based, non-compete covenants are allowed for a maximum of two years and subject to very high consideration.[2205]

---

2201 IFRA, 'Valuable yet vulnerable: Trade Secrets in the fragrance industry' (2013) IFRA Position Paper, 15 <www.ifraorg.org/view_document.aspx?docId=23107 > accessed 15 September 2018.

2202 Interview with the Head of IP of Perfume Company 1 (see Annex 1).

2203 John Hull, 'Information Matters: Telecoms Business – employee misuse of business information and database' (23 March 2015) <http://www.farrer.co.uk/News/Briefings/Telecoms-Business–Employee-misuse-of-business-information-and-database/> accessed 15 September 2018.

2204 IFRA, 'Valuable yet vulnerable: Trade Secrets in the fragrance industry' (2013) IFRA Position Paper, 15 <www.ifraorg.org/view_document.aspx?docId=23107 > accessed 15 September 2018.

2205 Interview with the Head of IP of Perfume Company 1 (see Annex 1); the issues raised by employment mobility are analysed further in chapter 6 § 1 A).

### V. Measures adopted to protect the company's trade secrets

This section provides an overview of the measures adopted by manufacturers of scents and perfumes to prevent the unlawful acquisition, use and disclosure of their trade secrets. The analysis is based on the responses provided by the Head of IP of Perfume Company 1.

In the first place, a distinction is made between the two types of measures: physical and legal.[2206] Physical measures in the fragrance industry include limiting the number of employees who have access to trade secrets, which results in information being fragmented within a company. Only those employees who need to have actual knowledge of the information are allowed to access it (access on a "need-to-know" basis). For instance, a perfumist can only examine the formulas of the fragrances that he develops. Furthermore, the use of email is also restricted to the sharing of certain information. Likewise, sometimes each employee receives a personalised copy of a document, which he signs, undertaking an obligation not to share it. Finally, in the case of more valuable secrets, the information is deposited within a notaire office.

Surprisingly, Perfume Company 1 does not resort to specific legal measures (typically confidentiality agreements). It is believed that otherwise employees would regard as secret only the information covered by specific agreements.

## *§ 5 Conclusion*

In chapter 5 the perfume industry has been used as an example case to illustrate the increasing challenges that the holders of valuable information face in keeping it undisclosed. From a research perspective, the fragrance sector is particularly interesting because there is no single IPR that affords protection to perfumes as a whole and their formulas can be reversed engineered at a very low cost by competitors.

In the EU, copyright on olfactory messages has only been accepted in the Netherlands in what so far seems an isolated decision. The analysis conducted above also underscores that odorous compounds and fragrance compositions seldom meet the patentability conditions of novelty and inventive step. Likewise, despite the recent legislative amendments at the EU

2206 See chapter 2 § 2 B) II. 3. a).

level, smells, unlike other unconventional signs, are not eligible for protection under the trade mark legal regime in force.

In this context, the empirical research conducted highlights that trade secrets play a central role in allowing scent and perfume producers to appropriate returns from their creations and small incremental innovations. However, it also reveals that over time it is becoming increasingly difficult to conceal sensitive information. This has a number of implications from the standpoint of the complementary relationship between trade secrets and IPRs, but also from a competition law perspective. On the one hand, secrecy is necessary to encourage competition among market participants. If every market participant had access to a competitor's information, competitive pressure would decline, which may in extreme cases lead to a market failure within the fragrance industry. On the other, concealing information can also result in a de facto monopoly and the elimination of effective competition in the market.

Notwithstanding this, chapter 5 has also highlighted that trade mark rights, along with unfair competition provisions that regulate comparative advertisement may provide additional incentives to create information by conferring an aura of luxury and exclusivity to the products that incorporate secret information, thereby allowing their manufacturers to internalize the cost of creation and development of said products. Yet, following the CJEU's *L'Oréal v Bellure* doctrine, this is often achieved at the expense of free speech and limiting consumers' choices.

In sum, the study of the perfume industry has underscored that the increasingly vulnerability of concealed information has reduced the lead time conferred by secrecy, which in turn limits the possibility of the trade secret holder of recouping the investment made in the development of the goods. It has furthermore revealed that secrecy presents a dual dimension: (i) internal within a given company and (ii) external with respect to third parties. The challenges posed by these two distinct spheres are further studied in chapter 6 with a view of finding the optimal balance between openness and secrecy.

# Chapter 6. The internal and external spheres of secrecy and their limitations

## § 1 *The two shperes of secrecy*

This dissertation started in chapter 1 by highlighting that the intrinsic significance of trade secrets revolves around two conflicting forces: the principles of openness, freedom of discourse and communications, which clash with the principles of privacy, secrecy and a restrictive flow of information.[2207] Ultimately, such a dichotomy has guided the dissertation so far, as it has surfaced in each of the jurisdictions studied and the empirical analysis conducted by reference to the perfume industry. As argued in chapter 1, it appears justified and necessary to protect undisclosed information. However, overprotecting secrecy may have negative effects on freedom of speech and innovative and creative activities.

To be sure, secrecy is the cornerstone upon which the law of trade secrets is built: "so long as a secret remains unrevealed, its cloak is everlasting".[2208] Crucially, the secret nature of information is largely a matter of fact and degree. Once a piece of information becomes generally known, even in the event of misappropriation, it ceases to be protected. It is for this reason that trade secrets are said to be of an inherently perishable nature.[2209] To a certain extent, this results from the underpinning strong public policy that encourages the dissemination of information and is wary of the protection of ideas by law.[2210] In the same vein, the factual nature of secrecy imposes a duty of care on the side of the trade secret holder: protection is conditioned upon the adoption of reasonable measures.[2211]

---

2207 William van Caenegem 2014 (n 7) 11.

2208 Jeanne C. Fromer, 'Trade Secrecy in Willy Wonka's Chocolate Factory' 3, 13 in Rochelle C. Dreyfuss and Katherine J. Strandburg (eds), *The Law and Theory of Trade Secrecy: A Handbook of Contemporary Research* (Edward Elgar 2011).

2209 *Attorney General v Newspaper Publishing Plc and Others* [1989] 2 FSR 27 (Ch), 48.

2210 *INS v. Associated Press*, 248 U.S. 215, 250 (1918).

2211 Such a requirement has been criticised by Robert G. Bone, 'Trade Secrecy, Innovation and the Requirement of Reasonable Secrecy Precautions' 46-76 in Rochelle C. Dreyfuss and Katherine J. Strandburg (eds), *The Law and Theory of Trade Secrecy: A Handbook of Contemporary Research* (Edward Elgar 2011).

As examined above,[2212] it is not possible to extract a normative standard that allows for delineating the contours of secrecy in a precise manner. Instead, secrecy is best conceptualised by reference to its negative aspects, i.e. when information enters the public domain.[2213] However, it cannot be overlooked that trade secrets are most frequently ascribed to companies, which usually adopt physical and legal measures to protect them. In particular, in the adoption of these measures two distinct spheres can be identified. The first is the internal sphere of secrecy, which refers to the preservation of confidential information within the company and mostly concerns employees, because they are the ones that regularly have access to valuable secret information in the performance of their duties. Secondly, the external sphere of secrecy refers to the adoption of legal and physical measures in order to avoid the unauthorised use and disclosure of trade secrets by third parties such as suppliers, service providers, licensees or R&D partners that may have accessed the information with authorisation, but for a specific purpose. More generally, it also intends to preserve trade secrets from the interference of third parties.

Considering the previous distinction, this chapter delves into the understanding of secrecy by analysing first, its internal sphere (intra company) and, second, its external sphere (extra company) and the role that contractual provisions play in ensuring confidentiality. Then, the limitations of secrecy are examined with a view to ensuring a homogeneous interpretation within the EU after the implementation of the TSD. Ultimately, in line with the research questions that inform the dissertation, it seeks to propose a balanced solution to the secrecy-openness dichotomy. To that end, § 1 explores the two spheres of secrecy, and § 2 is devoted to the study of the limitations of secrecy. Finally, some conclusions regarding the optimal scope and duration of protection are presented in § 3.

2212 Chapter 4 § 4 B) I.
2213 Chapter 4 § 4 C) II.

## A) The internal sphere of secrecy: confidentiality and employees[2214]

### I. Implied duty of confidentiality during the course of the employment relationship

The survey of the three jurisdictions that has guided the comparative analysis of this dissertation reveals that in all three the relationship between an employer and their employee is premised on the observance of an implied duty of confidentiality.

In the U.S:, this principle has been construed as meaning that the employee must not use or reveal confidential information if it may be detrimental to the employer.[2215] Such a duty governs the relationship with both ordinary employees[2216] and high level employees, which nevertheless have often been considered to be subject to a higher level of fidelity due to the relevance of their position.[2217]

Similar principles are followed in England, where the employer-employee relationship is based on an implied duty of good faith and fidelity.[2218] According to the English courts, such a duty includes: (i) the obligation not to reveal information to unauthorised third parties; (ii) the obligation not to copy confidential information or use any other materials for personal use after the termination of employment; (iii) the obligation not to compete with the employer during the effective term of employment; (iv) the obligation not to work for another employer outside working hours if this

2214 For a recent in-depth analysis of trade secrets protection and departing employees see Magdalena Kolasa, *Trade Secrets and Employee Mobility* (CUP 2018).

2215 Roger M. Milgrim 2014 (n 160) § 5.02[1][a] 7.

2216 However, in some cases, it has been held that when the compensation is very low, no obligation of confidence exists, unless expressly indicated by the employer, such as in *Shatterproof Glass Corp. v. Guardian Glass Co.*, 322 F. Supp. 854, 864-865 (E.D. Mich. 1970).

2217 Roger M. Milgrim 2014 (n 160) § 5.02[1][c] 14-17; William van Caenegem 2014 (n 7) 197, footnote 29; Elizabeth A. Rowe, 'When Trade Secrets become Shackles: Fairness and the Inevitable Disclosure Doctrine' [2005] 7 Tulane J of Technology & IP 167, 186; *E.I. DuPont de Nemours Powder Co. v. Masland*, 244 U.S. 100, 102 (1917).

2218 John Hull 1998 (1016) paras 6.06-6.10; Roger M. Toulson and Charles M. Phipps 2012 (n 326) paras 14-005- 14-007; the two most notable decisions in this regard are *Lamb v Evans* [1893] 1 Ch 218 (CA), 226 and *Robb v Green* [1895] 2 QB 1 (QB).

may result in a conflict of interests; and (v) the obligation to promote the best interests of the employer's business.[2219]

Likewise, in Germany, § 17(1) UWG generally proscribes the unauthorised disclosure of trade secrets entrusted to an employee during the course of the employment relationship.[2220] German courts have held that such an obligation is ultimately rooted in a general duty of loyalty towards the employer and, consequently, it does not need to be expressly included in the terms of the employment agreement to be enforced.[2221] The Federal Labour Court has resorted to the same general duty in order to infer an obligation not to compete with the trade secret holder before the end of the employment relationship, which includes the actions involved in preparing to set up a competing business that may directly affect the interests of the employer.[2222]

Crucially, the TSD does not establish whether, or under which circumstances a confidentiality duty towards the employer should arise; this is left for Member States to regulate. Notwithstanding this, the disclosure of a trade secret is deemed unlawful if it results from a "breach of a confidentiality agreement or any other duty not to disclose the trade secret" and its use is also proscribed if it arises from "a contractual or any other duty to limit the use of the trade secret". Consequently, if national legal regimes provide for the existence of such a general confidentiality duty, employees may be held liable for the unlawful use and disclosure of a trade secret (Article 4(3) TSD). More generally, liability may also arise if, during the term of employment, employees access, appropriate or copy any documents containing trade secrets without authorisation (pursuant to Article 4(2) TSD). This is typically the case of employees during the final stages of their employment relationship who are preparing for the departure.[2223]

2219 See John Hull 1998 (1016) paras 6.12- 6.32 with further references.

2220 Chapter 3 § 2 B) II. 1. a).

2221 Rudolf Kraßer 1977 (n 1327) 186; Christopher Heath, 'Employees, Trade Secrets and Restrictive Covenants in Germany' 85, 90 in Christopher Heath and Anslem Kamperman Sanders (eds), *Employees, Trade Secrets and Restrictive Covenants* (Wolters Kluwer 2017).

2222 BAG BeckRS 2013, 67444, Rdn 17.

2223 John Hull 1998 (1016) para 7.08.

## II. Secrecy obligations of departing employees

One of the most contested areas of the law of trade secrets, which in practice triggers the most litigation, is the problem of concurrent interests between employers and employees after the termination of the employment relationship. There is an inherent tension between the employer's interest in protecting their confidential business information and the employee's need to use the general skills, knowledge and experience that they have accumulated in their new position.[2224] In such a context, the essential underlying problem is that departing employees will apply this information to compete with the original employer. Although at first glance this may seem unfair, it is also the lifeblood of competition in the market. Indeed, labour mobility is essential to the competitive process and a company's productivity.[2225] In the words of Laddie J in *Occular Sciences Ltd v Aspect Vision Care Ltd:*

> For public policy reasons, an employee is entitled to use and put at the disposal of new employers all his acquired skill and knowledge. That is so, no matter where he acquired that skill and knowledge and whether it is secret or was at the time he acquired it. Where the employer's right to restrain the misuse of his confidential information collides with the public policy, it is the latter which prevails.[2226]

As outlined in chapter 3,[2227] employment mobility is one of the principles that inform the TSD. However, it has also been identified as one of the main factors behind the increasing vulnerability of trade secrets.[2228] Against this backdrop, two scenarios are differentiated: post-contractual obligations and implied obligations after the termination of the employment relationship. Both of them pose a number of legal problems from a

2224 Melvin F. Jager, *Trade Secrets Law* (Thomsons Reuters 2015) § 8:6; Miles J. Feldman, 'Toward a Clearer Standard of Protectable Information: Trade Secrets and Employment Relationship' [1994] 9 Berkeley Tech LJ 151, 155; William van Caenegem 2014 (n 7) 11.

2225 William van Caenegem 2014 (n 7) 11; for an economic overview of the benefits triggered by employee mobility see Karin Hoisl, 'Tracing Mobile Inventors – The Causality between Inventor Mobility and Inventor Productivity' [2007] 36 Research Policy 619-636.

2226 *Occular Sciences Ltd v Aspect Vision Care Ltd* [1994] RPC 289, 370-371.

2227 Chapter 3 § 5 C) II. 1.

2228 Impact Assessment (n 385) 15-16.

trade secrets perspective and, in particular, with regard to the maintenance of confidentiality, as is examined in the following sections.

First, section 1 starts by analysing the existence and scope of the implied duty of confidentiality of departing employees in the United States, England and Germany. Then it examines the relevant provisions of the TSD that refer to the skills, knowledge and experience acquired honestly by employees in the performance of their duties. Drawing on the comparative analysis and in view of the harmonisation goals pursued by the TSD, a number of factors are proposed in order to aid national courts to differentiate between unprotected skills, knowledge and experience and protected trade secrets. Thereafter, section 2 presents some considerations regarding contractual provisions that attempt to limit the use of trade secrets by departing employees considering the emerging harmonised framework.

## 1. Employees general skills, knowledge and experience and the implied obligation of secrecy after the termination of the employment relationship

### a) Comparative law analysis

#### aa) U.S.

In the U.S., it is generally accepted by case law that the general duty not to disclose a trade secret extends beyond the termination of the employment relationship.[2229] The finding of such an implied duty requires that the departing employee reasonably believes that the information is of a confidential nature.[2230] This will depend on a number of factors, such as: (i) the circumstances under which the trade secret was disclosed; (ii) the employee's state of mind; and (iii) the "reasonableness" of the conduct of the employer and, in particular, the measures adopted by the employer to signal its

2229 Restatement (Third) of Unfair Competition § 42 (Am. Law Inst. 1995) comment c; by way of illustration see *L.M. Rabinowitz & Co. v. Dasher*, 82 N.Y.S. 2d 431, 435 (1948): "It is implied in every contract of employment that the employee will hold sacred any trade secrets or other confidential information which he acquires in the course of his employment".

2230 James Pooley 2002 (n 66) 6-24.

secret nature, for instance limiting its access or identifying a specific piece of information as confidential.[2231]

If such a duty is established, the UTSA,[2232] the Restatement (Third) of Unfair Competition[2233] and the DTSA[2234] set out general liability for the acquisition, use and disclosure of a trade secret as a result of the breach or the inducement to breach a secrecy obligation.[2235] Consequently, the disclosure and use of a trade secret after the termination of an employment relationship may trigger liability for the former employee under both the state and federal trade secrets legal regimes. Similarly, liability may arise with respect to the new employer if they knew or had reason to know that the information was acquired as a result of such a breach.[2236]

Notwithstanding the above considerations, courts have also acknowledged the right of individuals to carry out their profession and the importance of preventing employers from privatising the skills, knowledge and experiences necessary to that end.[2237] Along this line, in the seminal article 'The legal infrastructure of high technology industrial districts: Silicon Valley, Route 128, and Covenants not to Compete,' Gilson distinguished between mere information and tacit knowledge.[2238] The former includes "easily codifiable information",[2239] while the latter refers to the "skill and expertise" of employees that is necessary for "effectively creating, developing, and implementing" innovations, which is "embedded in the human

2231 See Elisabeth A. Rowe and Sharon K. Sandeen, *Trade Secrecy and International Transactions: Law and Practice* (Edward Elgar 2015) paras 5.13-5.17 with further references.

2232 See § 1(1) and (2) UTSA.

2233 Restatement (Third) of Unfair Competition § 42 (Am. Law Inst. 1995) comment b.

2234 18 U.S.C. § 1839 (6) (A).

2235 Miles J. Feldman 1994 (n 2224) 163-164.

2236 Ronald J. Gilson, 'The Legal Infrastructure of High Technology Industrial Districts: Silicon Valley, Route 128, and Covenants Not to Compete' [1999] 74 NYULR 575, 597 highlighting the difficulties that the former employer faces in providing evidence.

2237 *CVD, Inc. v. Raytheon Co.*, 769 F2d 842, 852 (1st Cir. 1985): "It is also 'well settled that an employee upon terminating his employment may carry away and use the general skill or knowledge acquired during the course of the employment.' This principle effectuates the public interest in labor mobility, promotes the employee's freedom to practice a profession, and freedom of competition".

2238 Ronald J. Gilson 1999 (n 2236) 582.

2239 Ronald J. Gilson 1999 (n 2236) 577, footnote 10.

capital" of the employer.[2240] In turn, tacit information may consist of trade secrets, the disclosure of which can be prevented by employers, and general and industry-specific knowledge, which departing employees are free to use.[2241] Following Gilson's approach, such a division allows for involuntary knowledge spill-overs, when workers move from one employer to another. These are crucial to the development of new technologies that ultimately result in new industrial life cycles, as illustrated by the success of Silicon Valley.[2242]

The most important source of law that regulates the problem of the skills, knowledge and experience that departing employees are free to use is the Restatement (Third) of Unfair Competition (and more recently the DTSA).[2243] Prior to its adoption, the legislative landscape was seemingly uncertain. The relevant provisions of the Restatement (First) of Torts and the UTSA did not address, in a clear manner, the issue of the information that departing employees could use after the termination of their employment relationship.[2244] This normative vacuum was overcome by the Restatement (Third) of Unfair Competition, which provides that information that is part of the skills, knowledge, training and experience of an employee cannot be claimed as constituting a trade secret by the former employer. Such a principle applies even if there is a direct causal link between the acquisition of information and skills by the departing worker and an investment made by the employer.[2245] Yet, in the U.S. there is no universal legal standard that allows for drawing a clear line between protected trade secrets and skills and knowledge that employees are free to use after the termination of their employment relationship. Indeed, in many fields, but particularly in the technological sector, the knowledge and experience gained by an employee in the performance of his duties are inextricably embedded in the trade secrets of the former employer.[2246] Consequently, courts have to balance a number of factors against each other in the event of litigation.

2240 Ronald J. Gilson 1999 (n 2236) 582.
2241 Ronald J. Gilson 1999 (n 2236) 599.
2242 Ronald J. Gilson 1999 (n 2236) 586.
2243 18 U.S.C. § 1836 (b)(3)(A)(i)(I)-(II).
2244 Miles J. Feldman 1994 (n 2224) 155.
2245 Restatement (Third) of Unfair Competition § 42 (Am. Law Inst. 1995) comment d.
2246 Miles J. Feldman 1994 (n 2224) 153.

The five most salient principles developed by the Restatement (Third) of Unfair Competition, legal commentators[2247] and case law to draw the dividing line are: (i) whether the information is specialised or unique to the employer or is common knowledge among a specific industry;[2248] (ii) the contribution of the employer and of the employee in generating the information; (iii) whether competitors had previously failed in developing the same product or process;[2249] (iv) if the employee, shortly before the termination of his contractual relationship, took some physical embodiment of the information such as written formulas, blueprints, plans, or lists of customers;[2250] and (v) whether preventing the employee from using the information would hinder him from finding a new job, taking into account his overall experience.[2251]

The above reproduced multifactor test operates as a default rule when the parties cannot reach an agreement. Its main advantage lies in the fact that it provides greater legal certainty to those considering litigation, since it gives notice of the elements that courts will take into account in rendering their judgement.[2252]

Although the courts in the U.S. have long acknowledged the welfare benefits of employee mobility, the doctrine of "inevitable disclosure" is still applied in a number of states.[2253] Such a doctrine allows courts to enjoin a departing employee from working for a competitor based on the assumption that he will not be able to separate the former employer's trade secrets from his own knowledge, in such a way that the acquisition, use and disclosure of the information during the new employment is unavoid-

---

2247 Miles J. Feldman 1994 (n 2224) 117 proposes a multi-factor test based on the factors mentioned in the Restatement (Third) of Unfair Competition § 42 (Am. Law Inst. 1995).

2248 *GTI Corporation v. Calhoon*; 309 F. Supp. 762, 770-772 (S.D. Ohio 1969).

2249 *Head Ski Co. v. Kam Ski Co.*, 158 F. Supp. 919, 923-924 (D. Md. 1958).

2250 *AMP Inc. v. Fleischhacker*, 823 F.2d 1199, 1204-1205 (7th Cir. 1987).

2251 Restatement (Third) of Unfair Competition § 42 (Am. Law Inst. 1995) comment d.

2252 As noted by Miles J. Feldman 1994 (n 2224) 117.

2253 For an overview of the practice in each state see Ryan M. Wiesner, 'A State-By-State Analysis of Inevitable Disclosure: A Need for Uniformity and a Workable Standard' [2012] 16 Marquette IPLR 211, 217-228; Robert P. Merges, 'The Law and Economics of Employee Inventions' [1999] 13 Harvard Journal of Law & Technology 1, footnote 179; William van Caenegem 2014 (n 7) 118 (citing David W Quito and Stuart H Singer, *Trade Secrets: Law and Practice* (OUP 2009) 91-101) noting that the theory has been disregarded in six states, accepted in thirteen, and received mixed reviews in the rest.

able.[2254] This rationale was expressed in *Lumey Inc. v. Highsmith*, where the court noted that: "Even assuming the best of good faith, it is doubtful whether the defendant could completely divorce his knowledge of the trade secrets from any...work he might engage with the new employer".[2255]

Many authors have criticised this doctrine as being particularly unfair. The employee is prevented from working in his field of expertise without agreeing to such a "garden leave" (unlike the case of non-compete agreements) and without any compensation, thereby by-passing the minimum guarantees provided for under employment law.[2256] As suggested by Milgrim: "It potentially converts into a potential injunctive relief situation virtually any competitive employment taken by an individual who had held any kind of position –technological or commercial- or responsibility with plaintiff but had not entered into a restrictive covenant and accordingly not been given any consideration for restricting his post-employment obligations".[2257] In addition, from a policy perspective, the broad scope of these injunctions may hinder the positive spill-overs derived from employee mobility.[2258] The five main factors that have most often been invoked in the application of the inevitable disclosure doctrine were laid down by the

2254 Melvin F. Jager, *Trade Secrets Law* (Thomsons Reuters 2015) § 7:6; *Dayton Superior Corp. v. Yan et al*, No. 3:2012cv00380 (S.D. Ohio 2012).

2255 *Lumey Inc. v. Highsmith*, 919 F Supp. 624, 633 (E.D.N.Y. 1996).

2256 Elizabeth A. Rowe and Sharon K. Sandeen, *Trade Secrecy and International Transactions* (Edward Elgar 2015) para 5,46 further note that it is a well-established principle under employment law in the U.S. that any employee may decide to resign from his position, unless the parties have contractually agreed to the contratry, as per *McCrady v. Oklahoma Department of Public Safety*, 122 P.3d 473, 474-475 (Okla. 2005).

2257 Roger M. Milgrim 2014 (n 160) § 5.02[3][d] 74.

2258 Ronald J. Gilson 1999 (n 2236) 624; William van Caenegem 2014 (n 7) 203; similar concerns were raised by the District Court of the Southern District of New York in *EarthWeb, Inc. v Schlack*, 71 F. Supp.2d 299, 310-311 (S.D.N.Y. 1999): "While the inevitable disclosure doctrine may serve the salutary purpose of protecting a company's investment in its trade secrets, its application is fraught with hazards. Among these risks is the imperceptible shift in bargaining power that necessarily occurs upon the commencement of an employment relationship marked by the execution of a confidentiality 26 agreement. When that relationship eventually ends, the partie' confidentiality agreement may be wielded as a restrictive covenant, depending on how the employer views the new job its former employee has accepted. This can be a powerful weapon in the hands of an employer; the risk of litigation alone may have a chilling effect on the employee. Such constraints should be the product of open negotiation".

Court of Appeals of the Seventh Circuit in *PepsiCo v. Redmond*[2259] and they are: (i) the intensity of the competition between the companies; (ii) the similarities between the tasks assigned to the departing employee, (iii) the level of responsibility that the employee will take on; and (iv) the value of the secret information and (v) its time-sensitive nature.[2260]

With the above in mind and taking into consideration the sound socio-economic policies underlying employment mobility, the Federal legislator has set forth certain limitations to the doctrine of inevitable disclosure. In effect, section 18 U.S.C. § 1836 (b)(3)(A)(i) (as amended by the DTSA) stipulates that injunction shall not be granted if (i) it would prevent a person from entering into an employment relationship under conditions that result in actual or threatened misappropriation (based not only on the information that the person knows), or (ii) if it conflicts with state law that prohibits restraints on the exercise of a lawful profession, trade or business.

A literal interpretation of the DTSA allows for enjoining a departing employee from entering into a new employment relationship before the Federal Courts if, according to the employment conditions (and not just the information that he knows), he is likely to disclose a former employer's trade secret. The inclusion of this provision has been vehemently criticised by some, as it implicitly recognises the doctrine of inevitable disclosure and incorporates it into Federal Law, despite the positive spill-overs derived from employee mobility and the fact that many state laws reject it.[2261] It is for this reason that its application has been excluded when it conflicts with state law, as would be the case with California state law.[2262] However, in those states that do apply such a doctrine, the requisite that the plaintiff provides evidence of threatened misappropriation has been interpreted as limiting its applicability.[2263]

In the light of the above considerations, it seems that in the near feature a new body of federal jurisprudence regulating post-contractual obligations will emerge, thus shedding further light on the relationship between

---

2259 *Pepsi Co, Inc. v. Redmond*, 54 F3d 1262 (7th Cir. 1995).

2260 A more detailed account of these factors is provided by Elizabeth A. Rowe and Sharon K. Sandeen, *Trade Secrecy and International Transactions* (Edward Elgar 2015) para 5.46.

2261 Eric Godman and others, 'Professors' Letter in Opposition to the Defend Trade Secrets Act of 2015' (November 17, 2015), 5 <https://cyberlaw.stanford.edu/files/blogs/2015%20Professors%20Letter%20in%20Opposition%20to%20DTSA%20FINAL.pdf> accessed 15 September 2018.

2262 Victoria A. Cundiff and others 2016 (n 789) 742.

2263 Sharon K. Sandeen and Christopher B. Seaman 2017 (n 673) 900-901.

trade secrets protection and the skills and knowledge that former employees are free to use, as well the applicability of the restraints of trade doctrine.

### bb) England

In England, the general principle is that employees owe a duty of fidelity and good faith to their employer, which transcends the end of the employment relationship.[2264] This consideration has been criticised by recent academic work, where it is suggested that the duty of fidelity comes to an end with the termination of the employment contract.[2265] Consequently, the better view is to conceptualise the nature of the obligation between the employer and the employee as an implied contract subsisting between the two parties.[2266] Accordingly, the scope of this obligation can only extend to the information that the employee retains and that he knew (or it was obvious from the circumstances) constituted a trade secret.[2267] In a similar vein, the Law Commission Report held that in England the breach of confidence action could not be used to prevent a departing employee from using the skills, knowledge and experience "acquired at work and which is personal to the acquirer".[2268] This principle was subsequently restated in a number of decisions.[2269] However, just like in the U.S., courts have struggled to draw a dividing line between protectable trade secrets and skills,

2264 John Hull 1998 (1016) paras 7.01-7-07 however notes that the "ex-employee's duty to his employer is however narrower than the corresponding duty of good faith which was effective during employment".

2265 Tanya Aplin and others 2012 (n 22) para 12.150.

2266 Tanya Aplin and others 2012 (n 22) para 12.155 also argue that equity could also be invoked as a valid cause of action.

2267 Tanya Aplin and others 2012 (n 22) para 12.164.

2268 Law Commission 1981 (n 327) para 4.33.

2269 For instance, *Generics (UK) Ltd v Yeda Research and Development Co Ltd & Anor* [2012] EWCA Civ 726, [82]: "There is a long-established line of authority that, if an employer wishes to restrict the activities of an employee after termination of the employment, that should be done by a legally valid restrictive covenant. This is because the employee must know with certainty what it is that the employee will be able to undertake for any new employer or otherwise in furtherance of the employee's career; and any new employer will want to know the same; the *employee is entitled to deploy in furtherance of his or her career the general experience, skill and knowledge acquired in the course of it; and it may be, and probably will be, difficult to disentangle in relation to any new employment or other career activity protected confidential information, on the one hand, and other infor-*

knowledge and experience that employees are free to use in their new position.

Hitherto, the leading authority on the issue of implied obligations after the termination of an employment relationship is *Faccenda Chicken v Fowler*.[2270] The facts of the case are as follows: Faccenda Chicken's business model comprised the breeding, rearing, slaughtering and selling of chicken. The defendant, Mr Fowler, was employed by the plaintiff for more than twenty years, during which time he proposed and developed a so-called van sales operation model. In essence, the model involved offering daily fresh chickens to customers (butchers, supermarkets, etc.) using refrigerated vehicles. After resigning, Mr Fowler set up a company consisting of the same business activities and hired nine of the plaintiff's employees. Subsequently, Faccenda Chicken Ltd brought an action for an alleged breach of the implied terms of the contracts of employment of the nine departing workers.

When delivering its judgement, the Court of Appeal differentiated between protectable "trade secrets" and "mere confidential information", a distinction that has garnered substantial criticism from legal commentators[2271] and subsequent decisions.[2272] Most notably, it identified four elements that should guide the decision on whether specific information should be deemed as a trade secret or, instead, as mere confidential information that a departing employee should be free to use, which partially coincide with those followed in the U.S. They are: (i) the nature of the employment; (ii) the nature of the information; (iii) whether the employer impressed on the employee the confidentiality of the obligation; and, (iv) whether the information can be easily isolated from other information that the employee is free to use or disclose.[2273] Each of these is analysed in turn.

The first factor, the nature of the employment, was construed as referring to the circle of people to whom the information is imparted. If it is shared with employees who usually deal with confidential information, it is more likely that the courts will consider it a trade secret. By way of ex-

---

*mation which it is lawful for the former employee to use or disclose, on the other hand*" (emphasis added).

2270 *Faccenda Chicken Ltd v Fowler* [1987] Ch 117 (CA); Roger M. Toulson and Charles M. Phipps 2012 (n 326) [14-008].

2271 Tanya Aplin and others (n 22) para 12.175.

2272 *Lancashire Fires Limited v SA Lyons & Company Limited and Others* [1996] FSR 629 (CA), 655.

2273 *Faccenda Chicken Ltd v Fowler* [1987] Ch 117 (CA), 137-139.

ample, a member of the board is more likely to learn trade secrets in the performance of his duty than a facilities manager.[2274] As regards the nature of the information, the court was of the opinion that in order to merit protection, it is crucial that the information can be defined with some degree of precision.[2275] Next, it went on to highlight that the attitude of the employer towards the information for which protection is sought is of utmost importance, since he must signal its confidential nature to employees. Finally, it was held that it is essential that the information concerned can be separated from other information that the employee is free to use and disclose,[2276] and the skills and knowledge that he acquired during the course of the employment relationship.[2277] The latter principle is in line with the argument that a person should not be restricted from using his skills for his own benefit and that of the general public.[2278]

In *Faccenda Chicken v Fowler* the English Court of Appeal concluded that there had not been a breach of the implied terms, as neither the sales data, nor the price information could be deemed a trade secret.[2279]

#### cc) Germany

In Germany, the Federal Supreme Court and the Federal Labour Court have taken divergent views on the information that employees may use after the termination of a labour contract. The Federal Supreme Court is of the opinion that departing employees may use all of the information that they have acquired *honestly* during the course of their employment relationship, including trade secrets.[2280] Conversely, the Federal Labour Court holds that former employees are bound not to disclose trade secrets even after the termination of an employment relationship on the basis of a duty

---

2274 Tanya Aplin and others (n 22) para 12.196.

2275 Lionel Bently and Brad Sherman 2014 (n 125) 1170-1171.

2276 *Faccenda Chicken Ltd v Fowler* [1987] Ch 117 (CA), 136.

2277 Lionel Bently and Brad Sherman 2014 (n 125) 1170-1171.

2278 Roger M. Toulson and Charles M. Phipps 2012 (n 326) 14-010.

2279 *Faccenda Chicken Ltd v Fowler* [1987] Ch 117 (CA), 140 A-B; Tanya Aplin and others 2012 (n 22) para 12.172;

2280 RGZ 1907 65, 333, 337 – *Pomril*; BGH GRUR 1983, 179, 181 – *Stapel-Automat*; *Harte-Bavendamm*/Henning-Bodewig (n 376) § 17 Rdn 45; Rudolf Kraßer 1977 (n 1327) 187; Richard Schlötter 1997 (n 828) 182.

of loyalty ("*Treuepflicht*"),[2281] and there is no need to refer to them specifically in a labour agreement, in line with the interpretation followed by the courts in England and the U.S.[2282] This presumption applies irrespective of the manner (whether lawful or not) in which the trade secrets were acquired.[2283] Such conflicting views reflect the competing policies embedded in the German Constitution: on the one hand, Article 14 GG mandates the protection of immaterial property; on the other, Article 12 GG endorses employment mobility through occupational freedom.

Ultimately, the view held by the Federal Labour Court assumes that it is possible to distinguish between trade secrets and the skills, knowledge and experience lawfully acquired by employees in the normal performance of their duties (doctrine of separability or "*Trennbarkeitsthese*"), contrary to the proposition supported by the Federal Supreme Court[2284] and several German commentators,[2285] who understand that trade secrets may be intrinsically embedded within the personal experience lawfully acquired by employees (doctrine of inseparability). Considering such divergent perspectives, Ohly argues that neither position is absolute because in practice, their application is relativised by a number of legal provisions.[2286] The general view supported by the Federal Supreme Court is subject to the limitations imposed by the Law on Employee Inventions,[2287] which stipulates that an employee making a service invention must report the invention to the employer immediately (§ 5) and must keep it secret (§ 24) even after the termination of the employment relationship (§ 26). In addition, the Federal Supreme Court has held that the use of materials acquired in an unlawful manner during an employment relationship after its termination is proscribed by virtue of § 17(2)(1) and § 17(2)(2) UWG.[2288] The same

2281 Ansgar Ohly 2014 (n 100) 9; Swantje Richters and Carolina Wodtke, 'Schutz von Betriebsgeheimnissen aus Unternehmenssicht "Verhinderung von Know-how Abluss durch eigene Mitarbeiter"' [2003] NZA-RR 281, 285.

2282 Christopher Heath 2017 (n 2221 ) 101.

2283 Clemens Heusch and others, 'Trade secrets: overlap with restrains of trade, aspects of enforcement' [2015] GRUR Int 932, 934.

2284 BGH GRUR 1983, 179, 181 – *Stapel-Automat*; BGH IIC 2004, 449, 451 – *Spritzgießwerkzeuge.*

2285 Rudolf Kraßer 1977 (n 1327) 186.

2286 Ansgar Ohly 2014 (n 100) 9.

2287 Gesetz über Arbeitnehmererfindungen in der im Bundesgesetzblatt Teil III, Gliederungsnummer 422-1, veröffentlichten bereinigten Fassung, das zuletzt durch Artikel 7 des Gesetzes vom 31. Juli 2009 (BGBl. I S. 2521) geändert worden ist (Law on Employee Inventions).

2288 Ansgar Ohly 2014 (n 100) 9.

court has also ruled that the use of a customer list that was copied into the personal computer of the employee with authorisation during the course of employment is unlawful once the contract is terminated and triggers liability under § 17(2)(2) UWG.[2289] Yet, if the departing employee memorised the information, its use in the new position should be deemed lawful.[2290] Consequently, Ohly argues that in practice the theoretical freedom of the departing employee will be limited to a large extent to the information that he can memorise.[2291] In addition, the condition that the information is acquired in an honest manner ultimately requires courts to conduct a balancing exercise considering all of the circumstances of each specific case and weighing up the competing interests.[2292] Indeed, under the doctrine of inseparability, the appraisal of "honesty" on the side of the departing employee is essential to assess his potential liability, unlike the prevailing approaches in the U.S. and England, where the enquiry is instead centred on the existence of a protectable trade secret.[2293]

By the same token, the protection of trade secrets after the termination of an employment relationship supported by the Federal Labour Court is also subject to certain limitations, in particular, with respect to the imposition of de facto non-competition covenants that do not fulfil the statutory requirements set out in §§ 74 – 74c HGB.[2294]

In view of these considerations, the cardinal problem is distinguishing between the skills, knowledge and experience that a former employee can use in his new position and a protected trade secret.[2295] In this respect, the Federal Supreme Court has noted that in the assessment of competitive conduct pursuant to § 3 UWG, deciding courts should consider, on the one hand, the interests of departing employees in their professional advancement, which are protected by constitutional law (Article 12 GG), and on the other, the interest of former employers in keeping their secrets

---

2289 BGH GRUR 1999, 934, 935 – *Weinberater*.

2290 Clemens Heusch and others, 'Trade secrets: overlap with restrains of trade, aspects of enforcement' GRUR Int [2015] 932, 933; BGH GRUR 1999, 934, 935 – *Weinberater*.

2291 Ansgar Ohly 2014 (n 100) 10.

2292 Ansgar Ohly 2014 (n 100) 10.

2293 Magdalena Kolasa, *Trade Secrets and Employee Mobility* (CUP 2018) 95 onwards.

2294 Handelsgesetzbuch in der im Bundesgesetzblatt Teil III, Gliederungsnummer 4100-1, veröffentlichten bereinigten Fassung, das zuletzt durch Artikel 3 des Gesetzes vom 10. Juli 2018 (BGBl. I S. 1102) geändert worden ist (HGB or German Commercial Code); as noted by Ansgar Ohly 2014 (n 100) 10.

2295 Richard Schlötter 1997 (n 828) 179.

undisclosed (according to Article 2(1) and 14 GG). Consequently, it does not appear likely that one absolute formula would allow for drawing the boundaries between the two, because as a matter of principle "the overall balance must relate to the individual case".[2296] To that end, a number of criteria have been formulated by German courts and legal commentators.[2297]

In the first place, it has been suggested that the more relevant information is for the competitiveness of a company, the more likely it is to be treated as a trade secret.[2298] Also, it is crucial that the employee could not have acquired that knowledge if he had worked in the same or a similar position.[2299] Otherwise, it would not qualify as a trade secret. Additional criteria refer to the nature of the information and its importance for the advancement of the employee's career.[2300] Significantly, if the information is of a technical nature, it is similar to a service invention and when it is embodied in a physical support (like a written document) it will be easier to distinguish it from the skills and knowledge that every employee has acquired.[2301] Similarly, if the employee needs the information in order to be able to perform the tasks inherent to his profession, the likelihood that the information concerned will be regarded as skills, knowledge and experience that he is free to use increases. Otherwise, prohibiting the employee from using such knowledge would amount to a non-compete covenant, which under German law is only accepted under the specific conditions set forth in §§ 74- 74c HGB. Likewise, it has been purported that the position of the departing employee within the former company is also relevant. As already noted, if the information was acquired in a dishonest manner during the course of employment, departing employees should not be free to use it. Indeed, such conduct should trigger liability.[2302] As a final remark, legal scholars have held that courts should also take into consideration the

---

2296 BGH IIC 2004, 449, 452-453– *Spritzgießwerkzeuge*; Rudolf Kraßer 1977 (n 1327) 186.

2297 Richard Schlötter 1997 (n 828) 180.

2298 Richard Schlötter 1997 (n828) 180; Ansgar Ohly 2014 (n 100) 10 noting that the relevance of this criterion should not be overstated.

2299 Richard Schlötter 1997 (n 828) 180.

2300 BGH GRUR 1963, 367, 370 – *Industrieböden*; Ansgar Ohly 2014 (n 100) 10.

2301 Ansgar Ohly 2014 (n 100) 10.

2302 BGH GRUR 1963, 367, 370 – *Industrieböden*; BGH GRUR 1983, 179, 181 – *Stapel-Automat*; Ansgar Ohly 2014 (n 100) 10; Christopher Heath 2017 (n 2221 ) 102.

contribution of the employee in creating the information. If it is substantial, it is more likely that he will be free to use it.[2303]

In sum, an analysis of the German statutory provisions and case law reveals that there is no universally accepted principle that allows for drawing a clear line. It is again a matter of balancing interests.[2304] However, from the comparative analysis conducted, it seems that in Germany the assessment of the lawfulness and honesty of the conduct of a former employee acquires more relevance in the German Courts than in England and the U.S., at least under the doctrine of separability.

### b) Implied secrecy obligation of departing employees under the TSD

In line with the balancing exercise that the courts and legislatures of the studied jurisdictions conduct in order to weigh up the competing interests of trade secret holders and departing employees, Recital 3 TSD states that employee mobility is essential for employment growth and improving the competitiveness of the EU economy. In this context, Article 1(3) TSD clarifies, with respect to the definition of the subject matter and the scope of application of the Directive, that:

> Nothing in this Directive shall be understood to offer any ground for restricting the mobility of employees. In particular, in relation to the exercise of such mobility, this Directive shall not offer any ground for:
> (a) limiting employees' use of information not constituting a trade secret as defined in point (1) of Article 2;
> (b) limiting employees' use of the experience and skills honestly acquired in the normal course of their employment; (…)

As is apparent from the above, firstly the Directive shall not provide a legal basis to prevent employees from using information that falls outside the scope of the definition of trade secrets. In addition, paragraph (b) specifies that the TSD should not be construed as restricting the use of the skills, experience and knowledge that an employee acquired *honestly* during the course of their employment, which furthermore, according to Recital 14, do not constitute a trade secret either.

Such a legislative technique has been criticised for a number of reasons. Firstly, it has been questioned whether including the balancing test of the

2303 Christopher Heath 2017 (n 2221) 90.
2304 Ansgar Ohly 2014 (n 100) 10.

information that employees are free to take into their new positions in the overall assessment of the subject matter protected (Article 2 TSD) rather than in the liability assessment (Article 4(3) TSD) diverts attention away from the real enquiry, i.e. whether employees are free to use the trade secret.[2305] Indeed, the establishment of additional limitations to the subject matter protected adds confusion with respect to the definition of trade secrets, as in some cases the skills, knowledge and experience acquired by an employee may constitute a trade secret according to the statutory definition established in Article 2(1) TSD.[2306] Consequently, the EU legislator should have included the prohibition to limit the use of "experience and skills honestly acquired" within the framework of the exceptions established in Article 5 TSD. This provision does not exclude liability ex ante and in all circumstances, but rather calls upon national judicial authorities to balance the competing interests at stake on a case-by-case basis. Indeed, the application of the legitimate interest exception established in Article 5(d) TSD would allow courts to weigh up whether an employee should be free to use the information acquired as part of their freedom to choose an occupation and the right to engage in work enshrined in Article 15 ChFREU and the interests of the employer in preserving secrecy.[2307] Such an approach is also more in line with the unfair competition principles that inform the appraisal of liability in the TSD and ultimately seek to proscribe only those market practices that are contrary to honest commercial practices.

Secondly, pursuant to the wording of the TSD it is unclear whether it is a matter of EU law or of national courts to establish the relevant criteria to assess whether an employee should be allowed to use a specific piece of information in his new position.[2308] While the existence of an implied duty of confidentiality that may trigger liability under Article 4(3)(b) and 4(4) TSD is left to Member States to regulate, Article 1(3) is ultimately subject to interpretation by the CJEU.[2309] Nevertheless, if the competence of the CJEU is affirmed to regulate post-contractual secrecy obligations, the complex doctrines developed by national courts will be overridden and will have to filled in by means of judicial interpretation on the basis of the

2305 Tanya Aplin 2014 (n 384) 270.

2306 Aurea Suñol, *El Secreto Empresarial* (Thomson Reuters 2009) 252.

2307 See chapter 3 § 5 C) III. 3; see Annette Kur, Reto Hilty and Roland Knaak 2014 (n 383) para 35 and para 38.

2308 Tanya Aplin 2014 (n 384) 271.

2309 Magdalena Kolasa, *Trade Secrets and Employee Mobility* (CUP 2018) 156.

scarce guidance provided in Article 1(3) and Recital 14 TSD. This seems an undesirable result considering that contractual obligations have been excluded from the scope of the harmonised framework established in TSD and the inherent complexity of this topic. Harmonisation should be achieved by means of a legislative proposal rather than judicial interpretation.[2310] Ultimately, such an approach may conflict with the rules that govern the ownership of employee creations, which are governed by national provisions and differ substantially on the topic of secret inventions.[2311]

### c) Guiding principles

Drawing from the comparative analysis above, it appears that it is not possible to extract a normative test that allows for delineating in a precise manner when a specific piece of information constitutes a trade secret that merits protection or when it is part of the skills, knowledge and experience that employees are free to use in their new position. Indeed, the case law and legal doctrines in the three studied jurisdictions have acknowledged that the information, skills and knowledge acquired by employees may in fact also meet the standards of protection of trade secrets laws. Consequently, competent national judicial authorities will have to conduct a balancing exercise in which a number of factors will have be weighed against each other in other to find the most appropriate equilibrium between employers' right to protect their valuable information and employees' right to pursue their professional career. In the following paragraphs the eight main factors that should inform such an analysis are formulated.

In the first place, courts should start by looking into whether the information was obtained by the departing employee outside the normal performance of his duties, for instance, by entering into areas of limited access within the company or memorising and printing out documents and taking them outside the premises of the firm, or in any other dishonest manner. This is a clear indicator the information should be deemed as constituting a trade secret and ultimately reflects the requirement established in Article 1(3) TSD that the employee must have acquired the disputed information, skills and knowledge in an *honest* manner (factor 1).[2312] In particu-

2310 For a more detailed argument see Magdalena Kolasa, *Trade Secrets and Employee Mobility* (CUP 2018) 156.

2311 Tanya Aplin 2014 (n 384) 271.

2312 Tanya Aplin and others 2012 (n 22) para 12.192.

lar, due attention should be paid to whether the departing employee acquired the information pursuant to any of the types of conduct deemed unlawful under Article 4(2)(a) TSD.

Next, competent national judicial authorities should consider whether the information concerned is unique to the employer or common ground among a specific industry. In the latter case, it will not meet the secrecy requirement and, as a result, it should not be afforded protection under the trade secrets liability rules (factor 2). Similarly, courts should ponder whether the departing employee could not have acquired the information if he had not been working for the employer (factor 3). This should be construed as signalling the existence of a trade secret worthy of protection, as it provides evidence that the information was not generally known among or readily accessible to persons within the circles that normally deal with similar information. In effect, the new employer would be saving the cost of creating the information concerned.[2313]

Following the principle of employment mobility that informs the Directive, it should also be considered whether precluding the departing employee from using and (or) disclosing certain information would prevent him from working in the field in which he specialises, performing the tasks inherent to his profession or advancing in his career (factor 4). In such a case, the information should not trigger liability under the trade secrets legal regime. To hold otherwise would run counter to the freedom to choose an occupation and the right to engage in work enshrined in Article 15 ChFREU.[2314]

In a similar vein, courts should look into the nature of the information and the difficulties experienced by competitors in duplicating it.[2315] If the information provides a clear competitive advantage to its holder, or competitors have attempted to reverse engineer it (without success) or find a similar technical solution, the information concerned should merit protection (factor 5). In effect, any third party trying to find it out would have to invest time and effort in developing the secret, which in turn suggests that the information concerned is a valuable secret worthy of protection. By the same token, some commentators have suggested that information that can

2313 But see William van Caenegem (n 7) 199 noting that the importance of this principle should not be overstated becasuse its unique nature may be “coincidental”, “irrelevant” and “unidentified” by the employer. Hence, the author argues that courts should not enforce trade secrets that the employers decided after the termination of the contract that constituted valuable trade secrets.

2314 See Article 15 ChFREU.

2315 Tanya Aplin and others 2012 (n 22) para 12.184.

be acquired through mechanical processes (such as Internet searches) lacks the necessary quality of secrecy.[2316] By contrast, high expenditure on the development of the information concerned (particularly Research and Development) should be viewed as a sign that it is eligible for trade secrets protection.[2317] After all, the law of trade secrets protects investment in the creation of information.[2318]

An additional factor that is taken into consideration in jurisdictions such as the U.S. and Germany and seems pertinent in the assessment of protection is whether the contribution of the employee in the development of the secret is substantial (factor 6). In such a case, it should be deemed as part of the experience and skills that he should be able to use and develop in his new position. However, defining when the contribution is in fact substantial in relation to the employer or other employees appears to be a grey area and is very difficult to assess in terms of evidence due to the high mobility and collaborative environment within companies. In addition, it also contravenes the ownership presumptions applicable under some intellectual property national laws, which provide that if an invention (patentable or not) is developed in the normal course of employment, the ownership should be vested on the employer, irrespective of the employee's contribution.[2319] As a result, this factor seems weak not only from a practical standpoint, but also taking into consideration the harmonisation goals pursued by the Directive, and should only be considered secondary evidence.

On the contrary, the attitude of the employer towards the information is essential (factor 7). In line with the third prong of the definition of trade secrets laid down in Article 2(1)(c) TSD and the prevailing doctrine in the English jurisdictions, the holder of the information must take measures to protect its secret nature. That is, the employer must impart the necessary quality of confidence and treat the information as confidential under the general standard of due diligence within the company sphere.

Finally, the more identifiable the information is, the more likely it is to be regarded as a trade secret (factor 8). In effect, information about specific products or processes, and the best way and skills necessary to implement them is acquired during the course of the employee's development and, as

---

2316 Tanya Aplin and others 2012 (n 22) para 12.184.

2317 Tanya Aplin and others 2012 (n 22) para 12.183.

2318 As argued in chapter 1 § 2 B) I.

2319 For instance Articles 15, 16 and 17 of the Spanish Patent Act refer to inventions in general, thereby including both trade secrets and patents.

a result, integrates the so-called "mental equipment" or "professional expertise" inherent to the position that he occupies within his company.[2320] This set of skills and knowledge is linked to his professional development and therefore he should be free to use them in any new position that he takes on. In this context, the fact that the information can be easily isolated from his professional expertise, for instance, because it is embodied in a physical support, will be a factor pointing towards the existence of a trade secret. Indeed, if the information is of a mixed nature, and includes skills and knowledge that do not qualify for trade secrets protection and valuable trade secrets that are not precisely identified, the courts will tend to deny injunctions and favour the freedom to work.[2321]

### 2. Some considerations regarding post contractual non-disclosure and non-competition clauses

The foregoing analysis has delved into the non-contractual secrecy obligations after the termination of an employment relationship. Nonetheless, due to the lack of uniform standards in the enforcement of the implied terms after the termination of an employment relationship, post-contractual obligations play a central role in preventing former employees from using secret information that they acquired in their previous positions.[2322] The two most important contractual devices deployed to that end are confidentiality clauses and non-compete agreements.

The former seek to "identify, clarify or extend the information classified as a trade secret, and introduce express legal obligations in relation to them during employment, but more relevantly, after the termination".[2323] Yet, the courts have long since acknowledged the shortcomings of confidentiality clauses. Indeed, it is very difficult to monitor the use and disclosure of information by a departing employee in his new position; the employer will only learn ex post facto about it and, thus, will not be able to prevent it. In addition, the enforcement of confidentiality clauses is seemingly problematic, as it requires that the alleged secret information is precisely

2320 Tanya Aplin and others 2012 (n 22) para 12.186.

2321 William van Caenegem (n 7) 199.

2322 Charlotte Sander, 'Schutz nicht offenbarter betrieblicher Informationen nach der Beendigung des Arbeitsverhältnisses im deutschen und amerikanishcen Rect' [2013] GRUR Int 217, 225.

2323 William van Caenegem (n 7) 202.

defined and usually courts tend to take into account specific aspects on a case-by-case basis.[2324]

In view of the hurdles posed by NDAs, non-competes are usually perceived as a more efficient tool to prevent the dissemination of confidential information.[2325] As such, these preclude the departing employee from working in a specific field, subject to geographical and time limitations.[2326] In this context, it is much easier for the former employer to identify the field in which the employee will work and to seek ex ante remedies to prevent disclosure. Notwithstanding this, the effects of such contractual devices on employee mobility and competition have been the object of extensive scholarly debate and have given rise to substantial economic literature on the potential negative impact on innovation.[2327]

### a) Comparative law analysis

#### aa) U.S.

Under U.S. law, the validity of non-disclosure agreements is assessed according to the applicable state law. In general, these types of agreements seem to be accepted in all states and they are not subject to additional consideration, as it is regarded that they expressly establish an obligation that is implicitly provided for by law.[2328] They mostly take two forms: they can be regulated in a separate confidentiality agreement (also known as a non-disclosure agreement or NDA) or they can be included as a contractual

2324 Tanya Aplin and others 2012 (n 22) para 12.04.

2325 Yuval Feldman, 'Behavioral And Social Mechanisms that Undermine Legality in The Workplace: Examining The Efficacy of Trade-Secrets Laws Among Knowledge Workers in Silicon Valley' (2005) Bar Ilan University Public: Law Working Paper No. 1-05, 24 <https://papers.ssrn.com/sol3/papers.cfm?abstract_id=714481> accessed 15 September 2018.

2326 Tanya Aplin and others 2012 (n 22) para 12.04.

2327 William van Caenegem 2014 (n 7) 203; White House, 'Non-Compete Agreements: Analysis of the Usage, Potential Issues, and State Responses' (2016); Elisabeth A. Rowe. 'When Trade Secrets become Shackles: Fairness and the Inevitable Dis- closure Doctrine' [2005] 7 Tulane J of Technology & IP 167.<https://obamawhitehouse.archives.gov/sites/default/files/non-competes_report_final2.pdf> accessed 15 September 2018.

2328 Elizabeth A. Rowe 2005 (n 2327) 189; James Pooley 2002 (n 66) 8-4.

clause within the employment contract.[2329] From a practical perspective, the inclusion of these types of clauses is important in order to define the obligations regarding secrecy of the employee and to show the adoption of reasonable measures to protect the secret nature of information by the trade secret holder.[2330]

Unlike in the case of non-competes, the employee can move on to work for a competitor, but he cannot disclose (or use) the information that he acquired while working for the former employee.[2331] However, in the event that a specific NDA may have a negative impact on the career development of departing employees, courts will proceed to examine the reasonability of its terms in their assessment of its enforceability.[2332] In effect, most state courts require that NDAs are reasonable in scope and protect a legitimate business interest, such as a trade secret.[2333] Accordingly, an NDA covering an obligation not to disclose or use information that is part of the skills, knowledge, training and experience of an employee will generally be considered null and void.[2334] By the same token, non-disclosure agreements that cover information that is publicly available will also be considered non-enforceable.[2335] Consequently, courts have stated that it is of utmost importance that the employer identifies the information in a precise manner. Indeed, some courts in the U.S. have rejected the enforcement of NDAs drafted in a very general and vague manner.[2336] As a final note, it should be stressed that courts have given divergent interpretations in regard to the question of whether NDAs need to be geographically and temporally limited.[2337] While some take a very strict approach, others seem

2329 Elizabeth A. Rowe and Sharon K. Sandeen, 'Trade Secrecy and International Transactions: Law and Practice' (Edward Elgar 2015) para 5.19.

2330 Elizabeth A. Rowe 2005 (n 2327) 190.

2331 Norman D. Bishara, Kenneth J. Martin, Randall S. Thomas, 'An Empirical Analysis of Noncompetition Clauses and Other Restrictive Postemployment Covenants' [2015] 68 Vandervilt LR 1, 20.

2332 Elizabeth A. Rowe and Sharon K. Sandeen, 'Trade Secrecy and International Transactions: Law and Practice' (Edward Elgar 2015) para 5.18.

2333 Norman D. Bishara, Kenneth J. Martin, Randall S. Thomas, 'An Empirical Analysis of Noncompetition Clauses and Other Restrictive Postemployment Covenants' [2015] 68 Vandervilt LR 1, 21.

2334 Jodi L. Short, 'Killing the Messenger The Use of Nondisclosure Agreements to Silence Whistleblowers' [1999] 60 University of Pittsburgh LR 1207, 1226.

2335 Jodi L. Short 1999 (n 2334) 1227.

2336 *Disher v. Fulgoni*, 464 N.E.2d 639, 643 -644(Ill. App. Ct. 1984).

2337 Jodi L. Short 1999 (n 2334) 1223.

more flexible in their assessment of the "reasonableness" of the terms of a contract.[2338]

With respect to non-competition agreements, it should be noted that the assessment of their validity should also be conducted according to the applicable state law.[2339] In some of them, these types of covenants are considered non-enforceable, while others only accept them under very limited circumstances.[2340] Most notably, the California Business and Professions Code stipulates that "every contract by which anyone is restrained from engaging in a lawful profession, trade, or business" is void.[2341] This provision aims at fostering open competition and employees' right to pursue employment and enterprise and has been interpreted in a very restrictive manner by the California Supreme Court.[2342] In effect, in *Edwards v Arthur Andersen*, the court concluded that any restriction on the employee's ability to work in his profession (even if limited or narrow) was void under § 16600 of the California Business and Professions Code.[2343] With time, the Californian approach has become increasingly popular among a minority of States, such as Hawaii, North Dakota, and Oklahoma, where non-competes are also considered generally non-enforceable.[2344] Similarly, in Colorado and Oregon, non-competes are not enforceable against managers and professional workers.[2345] Some commentators have suggested that this tendency results from the establishment of a causality link between the economic success of Silicon Valley and the invalidity of non-competes under California law, which other state legislatures are trying to replicate by proscribing the enforcement of non-competes.[2346] In this respect, it should

2338 *Papa John's International, Inc. v. Pizza Magia International, LLC*, No. 00-10071 (5th Cir. 2001).

2339 Viva R. Moffat, 'Making Non-Competes Unenforceable' [2012] 54 Arizona LR 939, 943.

2340 Elizabeth A. Rowe 2005 (n 2327) 190.

2341 Cal. Bus. & Prof. Code § 16600 (West. 2010).

2342 On Amir and Orly Lobel, 'Driving Performance: A Growth Theory on Non-compete Law' [2013] 16 Stanford Technology LR 833, 842.

2343 *Edwards v. Arthur Andersen LLP*, 189 P.3d 285, 296 (Cal. 2008).

2344 Robert W. Gomulkiewicz, 'Leaky Covenants-Not-to-Compete' [2015] 49 University of California Davis LR 251, 265.

2345 On Amir and Orly Lobel, 'Driving Performance: A Growth Theory on Non-compete Law' [2013] 16 Stanford Technology LR 833, 843.

2346 Robert W. Gomulkiewicz, 'Leaky Covenants-Not-to-Compete' [2015] 49 University of California Davis LR 251, 255 referring to the impact of Ronald J. Gilson 1999 (n 2236) 575.

be noted that the Congress has recently proposed a bill to prohibit employers from entering into covenants not to compete.[2347]

Notwithstanding the aforementioned, according to the prevailing legal doctrine, in most states where non-competes are deemed enforceable, courts examine their validity through strict lenses and on a case-by-case basis. Generally, the employer is required to provide evidence that the agreement is *reasonably* ("rule of reason"): (i) necessary to protect a trade legitimate interest of the employer (for example, trade secrets and goodwill); (ii) limited in duration (according to the prevailing views, two years seems to be the maximum allowed);[2348] (iii) limited in geographical scope; and (iv) limited in the scope of the proscribed activity.[2349] In addition, their validity is subject to receiving adequate compensation, which is usually considered to be satisfied by the salary agreed. However, in the event that the non-compete is executed after the employment relationship has commenced, states' case law is divided among those states that require additional compensation (in the form of a salary increase or a mere lump sum) and those that consider that no increase is required.[2350] In sum, it appears that different states have developed different tests to apply the rule of reason, which has led to a general lack of uniformity and predictability with regard to the enforceability of non-competes.[2351]

### bb) England

In England, post-contractual non-disclosure and non-competition agreements are assessed under the general contractual restraints of trade doctrine. According to Diplock LJ:

> A contract in restraint of trade is one in which a party (the covenantor) agrees with another party (the covenantee) to restrict his liberty in the

---

2347 See H. R. 5631 To prohibit employers from requiring employees to enter into covenants not to compete, and for other purposes <https://www.congress.gov/115/bills/hr5631/BILLS-115hr5631ih.pdf> accessed 15 September 2018.

2348 James Pooley 2002 (n 66) 8-36.

2349 Elizabeth A. Rowe 2005 (n 2327) 190; Roger M. Milgrim 2014 (n 160) § 6.01[3][d] 12; Viva R. Moffat, 'Making Non-Competes Unenforceable' [2012] 54 Arizona LR 939, 948.

2350 Elizabeth A. Rowe and Sharon K. Sandeen, 'Trade Secrecy and International Transactions: Law and Practice' (Edward Elgar 2015) para 5.39.

2351 Viva R. Moffat, 'Making Non-Competes Unenforceable' [2012] 54 Arizona LR 939, 948.

> future to carry on trade with other persons not parties to the contract in such a manner as he chooses.[2352]

As is apparent from the above, the restraint of trade doctrine applies when a person is contractually "bound for the future, and with respect to third parties".[2353] From the outset it should be noted that its applicability is not limited to employment contracts; it also applies to agreements between suppliers of goods and services that restrict competition; exclusive dealing agreements; and also covenants affecting the use of land, to name some.[2354] However, it is generally accepted that post-employment agreements are scrutinised under more strict lenses than other types of covenants.[2355]

The foundation of the modern restraints of trade doctrine was formulated by the House of Lords in *Nordenfelt v Maxim Nordenfelt Guns and Ammunition Co Ltd*[2356] and it essentially provides that contracts that result in a restraint of trade are void, unless such a restraint is reasonable in the interests of the parties and the general public. This doctrine is ultimately built on the public interest in allowing citizens to use their skills to develop the means to make a living and the right of individuals to work,[2357] which collide with the principle of freedom of contract and the right of corporations to protect their secrets.[2358] Recent academic work has identified five sequential steps to be used in order to assess whether an agreement affecting a departing employee is void under the restraint of trade doctrine, which will guide the present discussion.[2359]

First, the competent court should delineate with precision the obligations imposed upon the departing employee by the agreement. Secondly, it should be established whether the contractual provisions restrain the

---

2352 *Petrofina (Great Britain) Ltd v Martin* [1966] Ch 146, 180 (CA).

2353 John D. Heydon, *The restraint of trade doctrine* (2nd edn, Butterworths 1999) 43.

2354 Edwin Peel, *The Law of Contract* (14th edn, Sweet&Maxwell 2015) para 11-065.

2355 John D. Heydon, *The restraint of trade doctrine* (2nd edn, Butterworths 1999) 66-67.

2356 *Nordenfelt v Maxim Nordenfelt Guns and Ammunition Co Ltd* [1984] AC 535 (HL).

2357 Tanya Aplin and others 2012 (n 22) 12.09

2358 Guy Tritton, 'Employees, Trade Secrets and Restrictive Covenants in the United Kingdom' 61, 69 in Christopher Heath and Anselm Kamperman Sanders (eds), *Employees Trade Secrets and Restrictive Covenants* (Wolters Kluwer 2017).

2359 Tanya Aplin and others 2012 (n 22) para 12.12.

employee, for instance, by preventing him from working in a particular field.[2360]

Thirdly, courts should interrogate whether the restraint falls within one of the interests that case law has identified as *legitimate*. The imposition of a restraint of trade may only be justified if it protects a proprietary interest of the employer.[2361] In particular, the House of Lords identified as legitimate interests that may justify a restraint: (i) trade secrets and confidential information, and (ii) customer connections and goodwill.[2362] The scope of the former category was famously addressed in *Faccenda Chicken v Fowler,*[2363] where the Court of Appeal held that a departing employee's implied obligations were confined to "trade secrets, or the equivalent of trade secrets", which was a distinctly narrower notion than that of confidential information.[2364] In addition, it was held that restrictive covenants would only be enforceable if they protected a trade secret as opposed to confidential information in general.[2365] Such a limited interpretation of trade secrets with respect to restrictive covenants has been the object of vehement criticism.[2366] Consequently, more recent decisions have ruled that a legitimate interest may include both trade secrets and confidential information.[2367]

Fourthly, after identifying the concurrence of a legitimate interest, courts must assess if the restraint is reasonable considering the employer's and the employee's interests and the temporal, geographic, and material scope of the covenant. In particular, in one of the leading decisions on the subject, *Herbert Morris Ltd v Saxelby*, it was noted that the restraint "must afford no more than adequate protection to the benefit of the party in whose favour it is imposed".[2368] In effect, the assessment of reasonableness is usually conducted from the perspective of the employer and the protec-

---

2360 Tanya Aplin and others 2012 (n 22) para 12.20.

2361 John Hull 1998 (1016) para 8.13

2362 *Herbert Morris Ltd v Saxelby* [1916] AC 688 (HL), 702.

2363 *Faccenda Chicken Ltd v Fowler* [1987] Ch 117 (CA); a summary of the facts of the case is provided in chapter 6 § 1 A) II. 1. a) bb).

2364 *Faccenda Chicken Ltd v Fowler* [1987] Ch 117 (CA), 127.

2365 *Faccenda Chicken Ltd v Fowler* [1987] Ch 117 (CA), 127.

2366 John Hull 1998 (1016) para 8.79; Tanya Aplin and others 2012 (n 22) paras 12.72 -12.76.

2367 Guy Tritton 2017 (n 2358) 76 72; *Lancashire Fires Limited v S.A. Lyons & Company Limited and Others* [1996] FSR 629 (CA), 666.

2368 *Herbert Morris Ltd v Saxelby* [1916] AC 688 (HL), 707.

tion of his legitimate interests, rather than that of the employee.[2369] Ultimately, the assessment of reasonableness will depend on the specific circumstances of the case and the specific industry practices.[2370] Additional factors that courts have taken into consideration are the amount of time during which the employee worked for the employer, the negotiation process of the contract or how the employment relationship was terminated.[2371] Interestingly, in England, the compensation received by the employee is not taken into consideration in the assessment of the reasonableness of the restraint.[2372] This contrasts with the prevailing view in most U.S. states and Germany, where adequate consideration is a precondition of validity for non-competition agreements. Finally, if a court considers that a contract imposes an unreasonable restraint, it will strike out the void parts by application of the doctrine of severance.[2373]

Having regard to the above, a number of considerations should be presented with respect to the applicability of the restraints of trade doctrine to non-disclosure and non-competition agreements.

Firstly, considering NDAs, it should be noted that courts seem inclined to enforce them provided that they do not include information that is in the public domain or that constitutes part of the skills, knowledge and experience that employees should be free to use.[2374] This mostly favourable tendency results from the fact that the scope of these agreements mostly coincides with the scope of the implied obligation not to disclose trade secrets. However, limitations regarding use (non-use clauses) are typically assessed under more strict parameters and courts usually proceed to evaluate whether the time, scope and geographical limitations are reasonable.[2375]

Secondly, in the assessment of the reasonableness of non-compete clauses, English courts are especially strict due to the inherent anticompetitive effects triggered by these kinds of provisions. In particular, their duration must be short. There are several cases where restrictions that extended beyond twelve months after the termination of the employment relationship

2369 Dan Prentice, 'Illegality and Public Policy' para 16-106 in Hugh Beale (ed) *Chitty on contracts* (32th edn, Sweet&Maxwell 2017).
2370 John Hull 1998 (1016) para 8.57.
2371 Tanya Aplin and others 2012 (n 22) para 12.95.
2372 Tanya Aplin and others 2012 (n 22) para 12.46.
2373 Guy Tritton 2017 (n 2358) 76 ; Tanya Aplin and others 2012 (n 22) para 12.135
2374 Tanya Aplin and others 2012 (n 22) para 12.99.
2375 Tanya Aplin and others 2012 (n 22) para 12.101.

were declared unreasonable.[2376] Another crucial aspect is the establishment of the scope of the restricted field of activity. English courts tend to demand that the sector and the role that the departing employee is prevented from taking are defined in a very specific manner. Otherwise, it is regarded that the covenant extends beyond the mere prohibition of competition with another business, thereby unreasonably affecting the ability of the employee to develop his professional career.[2377] With respect to the geographical scope, recent decisions seem to support a flexible approach when the legitimate interest invoked is the protection of a trade secret. In such cases, due to the inherently perishable nature of trade secrets, courts seem more inclined to enforce covenants that include a world-wide non-competition clause.[2378] However, if the legitimate interest aims at protecting customer connections, the geographical scope should be limited to the area in which the company had customers on the date on which the employment contract was entered into.[2379]

As a whole, it appears that the restraints of trade doctrine provides great flexibility to courts in their assessment of the validity of NDAs and non-competes, which furthermore are not subject to additional consideration. Notwithstanding this flexibility, the negative effect of non-competes on innovation was acknowledged by the UK Government in 2016 in the context of a consultation regarding the assessment of the need to pass a specific regulation on this subject. However, due to the fact that the vast majority of the respondents argued that non-competes were useful tools to protect their business interests, the consultation was dropped.[2380]

---

2376 In *Polymasc Pharmaceuticals plc v Charles* [1999] FSR 711 (Pat), 720 and *Dyson Technoloy Ltd v Strutt* [2005] EWHC 2814 (Ch), [66] a one year restrain was not considered problematic.

2377 Tanya Aplin and others 2012 (n 22) paras 12.116 - 12.121.

2378 *Dyson Technology Ltd v Strutt* [2005] EWHC 2814 (Ch), [66].

2379 *Spencer v Marchington* [1988] IRLR 392 (Ch), 395.

2380 Department for Business Innovation & Skills, 'Non-compete clauses – Call for Evidence' (2016) <https://assets.publishing.service.gov.uk/government/uploads/system/uploads/attachment_data/file/525293/bis-16-270-non-compete-clause-call-for-evidence.pdf> accessed 15 September 2018.

cc) Germany

In German law, NDAs are usually considered permissible under §§ 134[2381] and 138[2382] BGB and are not subject to additional consideration and time limitations.[2383] These types of agreements can include trade secrets and information that does not constitute a trade secret but that was expressly identified as confidential by the employer.[2384] However, pursuant to § 138 BGB, an NDA that provides that the employer must keep secret all the information related to the business will be considered void.[2385] The cardinal problem in the assessment of the validity of NDAs is differentiating them from non-competition agreements that are subject to the fulfilment of the statutory requirements set out in §§ 74- 74c HGB.[2386]

By way of illustration, the Federal Labour Court held that an NDA that prevented the manager of a laboratory from disclosing a specific secret formula developed by the employer after the termination of the contract was enforceable, because the development of his professional career would not be hindered by such a prohibition and, furthermore, it did not affect the possibility of the departing employee competing with the former employer.[2387] In contrast, in a later decision, the same court concluded that an NDA that precluded a sales representative from using the names and addresses of clients that the employee had learned during the course of his employment relation for his own benefit (or a third party) was not enforceable because it would prevent him from working in his field of specialisation. Such a non-disclosure agreement would amount to a non-competition covenant that did not meet the statutory requirements.[2388] However, the Federal Labour Court did affirm that the sale of the customers' data would contravene the terms of the NDA.[2389] This position was clari-

2381 § 134 BGB: "A legal transaction that violates a statutory prohibition is void, unless the statute leads to a different conclusion".

2382 § 138 (1) BGB: "A legal transaction which is contrary to public policy is void".

2383 Charlotte Sander 2013 (n 2322) 225.

2384 Martin Brock, 'Know-how im Arbeitsrecht' Rdn 56 in Christop Ann, Michael Loschelder and Markus Grosch (eds), *Praxishandbuch Know-how-Schutz* (Carl Heymanns Verlag 2011).

2385 Martin Brock 2011 (n 2384) Rdn 56; Swantje Richters and Carolina Wodtke 2003 (n 2281) 281.

2386 Wolf Hunold, 'Rechtsprechung zum nachvertraglichen Wettbewerbsverbot' [2007] NZA-RR 617, 619.

2387 BAG NJW 1983, 134, 135 – *Thrombosol.*

2388 BAG NZA 1988, 502, 503 – *Weinhändler.*

2389 BAG NZA 1988, 502, 504 – *Weinhändler.*

fied in a ruling in 1993, regarding the validity of a post-contractual non-disclosure clause of an employee that had been working for forty years for a company in the chemical sector that manufactured a chemical compound known as titandioxid. After the termination of his contract he went on to work for a competitor that also manufactured titandioxid, and consequently, the former employer sought to enforce the NDA in court. The Federal Labour Court generally ruled that an NDA could not prevent a departing employee from using the experience-based knowledge ("*Erfahrungswissens*") that he had acquired while working for the former employer.[2390] It further noted that the use of such information could only be prevented through the conclusion of a valid non-competition agreement.[2391]

The principle that emerges from the analysis of the decisions referred to above is that according to the case law from the Federal Labour Court, in practice NDAs do not provide solid ground to protect trade secrets against use and disclosure by departing employees when such information is embedded in the general skills, knowledge and experience acquired during the course of service.[2392] Ultimately, courts should assess this on a case-by-case basis considering the particularities of the case at hand and whether the NDA concerned in fact covers *Erfahrungswissens* or whether such a provision can de facto be equated to a non-competition agreement.[2393]

Under German law, once the employee has terminated his employment relationship with the principal, he is free to compete with his former employer either by joining a competitor or by setting up his own business.[2394] Such a general principle may only be limited by the conclusion of an express non-competition agreement, which is subject to the fulfilment of the statuary requirements set out in §§ 74-74c HGB, unlike the common law jurisdictions studied, where no statutory provisions in this regard have been enacted. As a preliminary remark, it should be noted that until 2003, these requirements were only applicable to shop clerks. However, by virtue

2390 BAG NZA 1994, 502, 505 – *Titandioxid.*
2391 BAG NZA 1994, 502, 504 – *Titandioxid.*
2392 Martin Brock 2011 (n 2384) Rdn 60-62.
2393 Swantje Richters and Carolina Wodtke 2003 (n 2281) 285.
2394 Wolf Hunold 2007 (n 2386) 617; Dirk Helge Laskawy, 'Die Tücken des nachvertraglichen Wettbewerbsverbots im Arbeitsrecht' [2012] NZA 1011, 1012.

of § 110 of the Industry Regulation Act,[2395] their scope of application was extended to all types of employees.[2396] To be enforceable, non-competition covenants (i) must be in writing and (ii) must be executed by the employee in a separate agreement where the exact terms are specified; (iii) must be subject to the appropriate consideration, which shall be at least 50% of the last gross salary of the employee; and (iv) must not extend beyond two years. Furthermore, pursuant to § 74a HGB, a non-competition agreement is unenforceable if, considering the subject matter, geographical and time scope, it constitutes an unreasonable obstacle to the employee's career development.[2397]

Additionally, just like in the U.S. and England, the validity of non-competes is subject to the protection of the *legitimate interest* of the principal (§ 74a HGB).[2398] The Federal Labour Court has interpreted such a requirement in a rather restrictive manner; it does not suffice that the former employer imposes such a clause with the intention of restraining competition. Consequently, there must be a causal relationship between the activities developed by the former employer and the prohibited act of competition.[2399] In particular, the Federal Labour Court has identified two legitimate interests: (i) the safeguarding of trade secrets (so long as the requirements for protection are still met), and (ii) the protection of a customer base,[2400] which partially coincide with the legitimate interest identified in England under the restraints of trade doctrine. Regarding the question of whether the advancement of an employee's career is unduly affected, the Federal Labour Court has stated that this must be decided on a case-by-case basis taking into consideration a number of factors, such as the age of the employee, the consideration received, the actual scope of the covenant and the mobility within the specific industry.[2401]

2395 See Gewerbeordnung in der Fassung der Bekanntmachung vom 22. Februar 1999 (BGBl. I S. 202), die zuletzt durch Artikel 1 des Gesetzes vom 17. Oktober 2017 (BGBl. I S. 3562) geändert worden ist (Industry Regulation Act).

2396 Martin Brock 2011 (n 2384) Rdn 77.

2397 William van Caenegem (n 7) 191; Wolf Hunold 2007 (n 2386) 617; Charlotte Sander 2013 (n 2322) 225.

2398 Martin Brock 2011 (n 2384) Rdn 87.

2399 Dirk Helge Laskawy, 'Die Tücken des nachvertraglichen Wettbewerbsverbots im Arbeitsrecht' [2012] NZA 1011, 1013.

2400 BAG NZA 1996, 310, 310 – *Nachvertragliches Wettbewerbsverbot.*

2401 BAG NZA 2010, 1175, 1176 – *Anspruch auf KarenzentschÄdigung nur bei verbindlichem Wettbewerbsverbot.*

In sum, it appears that in Germany the conclusion of NDAs after the termination of an employment agreement does not protect the employer against the use and disclosure of the skills, knowledge and experience acquired by the departing employee, which may inextricably include trade secrets. This can only be limited by a non-competition agreement, the validity of which is subject to the fulfilment of the conditions set out in the HGB. In particular, appropriate consideration should be paid and a maximum duration of two years is established. Crucially, this includes the assessment of whether a legitimate interest exists and whether, in view of its territorial, temporal and material scope, it will unduly affect the employee's professional advancement. Hence, the assessment of reasonableness of NDAs and non-competes is ultimately carried out by means of judicial interpretation considering all of the circumstances at stake.[2402]

b) Post-contractual obligations under the TSD

Following a systematic interpretation of the TSD, it can be concluded that the establishment of post-employment contractual obligations is excluded from its scope of application. Pursuant to Recital 13, the possibility of concluding non-compete agreements is governed by the relevant statues of EU and national law. Similarly, Recital 39 sets forth that contract law should not be affected by the norms enshrined in the Directive, which clearly indicates that the regulation of NDAs is also governed by national law. This rationale has further crystallised in Article 1(3)(c) TSD, which lays down that the validity of any contractual restrictions on employee mobility should be assessed in accordance with the relevant national or EU provisions in force.[2403]

However, it is likely that when interpreting the validity of these clauses, national courts across the EU will take into consideration the policy advantages triggered by employee mobility, as one of the principles that inform the TSD and which is therefore part of the acquis communautaire, along with the freedom of movement principle. Indeed, in all of the jurisdictions

2402 William van Caenegem (n 7) 191-192.

2403 Article 1(3) TSD: "Nothing in this Directive shall be understood to offer any ground for restricting the mobility of employees. In particular, in relation to the exercise of such mobility, this Directive shall not offer any ground for (c) imposing any additional restrictions on employees in their employment contracts other than in accordance with Union or national law".

studied, the enforcement of NDAs and non-competes is ultimately based on the assessment of the reasonableness of their terms, considering, among other factors, the impact on the career prospects of the employee. Without doubt, post-contractual secrecy obligations are central to preverseving the secret nature of the innovations created intracompany. Yet, they are also subject to a number of limitations to foster competition and safeguard the right of employees to advance in the development of their career.

## B) The external sphere of secrecy

The external sphere of secrecy refers to the preservation of confidentiality against the unlawful use and disclosure of trade secrets by third parties that may have accessed the information with authorisation from the holder but only for a limited time, or in order to achieve a specific purpose. This is typically the case for licensing agreements, where the trade secret holder grants the licensee the right to use the secret information in exchange for the payment of an agreed fee. In effect, in order to exploit trade secrets, their holders are required to carefully balance a number of competing interests. On the one hand, they should attempt to share the information with as few people as possible in order to limit the risk of disclosure and the resulting loss of the competitive advantage conferred by its secrecy. Indeed, once the information has left the internal sphere of the company, it cannot be reintroduced due to the inherently irreversible nature of cognitive processes: what has been learnt cannot be unlearnt.[2404]

On the other, to maximise the economic potential of trade secrets, their holder may have to share the information with a substantial number of parties, particularly in the absence of funding resources or manufacturing capabilities that allow for developing the final product.[2405] Similar considerations apply in the conclusion of R&D agreements, by virtue of which a number of parties (including both private and public entities) may decide to cooperate in the generation of technical innovations. Against this background, in order to minimise unauthorised disclosures that may result in the loss of secrecy, it is of utmost importance that the contractual clauses

2404 Stefan Maaßen and Tobias Wuttke, 'Know-how-Verwertung (Veräußerung und Lizenz)' Rdn 38-40 in Christoph Ann, Michael Loschelder and Marcus Grosch (eds), *Praxishandbuch Know-how-Schutz* (Carl Heymanns Verlag 2011).

2405 Stefan Maaßen and Tobias Wuttke 2011 (n 2404) Rdn 40.

that regulate the use and subsequent revelation of secret information are carefully drafted.

More generally, the external sphere of secrecy also refers to the adoption of measures to prevent the unlawful acquisition of trade secrets by any third parties through industrial espionage, as mandated by Article 2(1)(c) TSD. The standard of "reasonableness" has already been examined in previous chapters,[2406] and some examples of the types of measures adopted have been mentioned during the study of the perfume industry.[2407] Consequently, no further reference will be made to the need for companies to implement physical and IT measures.[2408] Instead, the following sections will delve into the study of the regulation of confidentiality obligations in two types of contracts entered into between trade secret holders and third parties in order to maximise the returns from their valuable secret information: licensing agreements (section I) and R&D agreements (section II).

## I. Licensing agreements

### 1. Object and legal nature

Licensing agreements are often conceptualised in contrast to the rights conferred by assignment agreements. Licences, as opposed to assignment agreements, convey no "proprietary interest" in the IPRs that are the object of the contract.[2409] By virtue of such a covenant, the licensee is essentially authorised by the licensor to carry out acts that would otherwise amount to an infringement of IPRs, which would usually be subject to the payment of an agreed consideration.[2410] Consequently, it has been suggested that the licence is "a contractual right rather than an interest in property".[2411]

---

2406 See chapter 4 § 3 E).
2407 See chapter 5 § 4 B) V.
2408 For an overview of potential measures see Victoria A. Cundiff 2009 (n 739) 364-377.
2409 Noel Byrne and Amanda McBratney, *Licensing Technology* (3rd edn, Jordans 2005) 20-21.
2410 John Hull 2013 (n 934) 170.
2411 Mark Anderson, *Technology Transfer* (3rd edn, Haywards Heath 2010) para 13.5.

In the context of trade secrets,[2412] despite the fact that licensing is one of the main paths by which technology is transferred and commercially exploited, in England and Germany there has been a longstanding debate regarding the legal nature of know-how licences.[2413] This mostly stems from the uncertainty surrounding the legal nature of trade secrets and the fact that they do not confer erga omnes exclusivity on their holders.[2414] In England, case law and commentators have argued that these types of contracts do not confer the right to carry out acts that otherwise are exclusively vested in the owners, as in the case of formal IPR licences. Their essence lies in the disclosure of information between the parties to the contract under specific conditions.[2415]

Similar considerations have been raised in Germany, where, unlike the English jurisdiction, it is generally accepted that know-how licences do confer the licensee the right to use the information imparted.[2416] However, unlike patent or trade mark licences, their existence is not statutorily foreseen. Nevertheless, their validity is inferred from the freedom of contract principle (§§ 134 and 138 BGB), the right to claim the performance of an obligation (§ 241(2) BGB) and the need to conclude a contract in order to create valid contractual obligations (§ 311(1) BGB).[2417] According to the prevailing view, know-how licences are considered to be a sui generis type of contract that should be governed by the rules of legal usufruct ("*Rechtspacht*") as per §§ 581 to 584b BGB for as long as a licensing fee is

2412 Hereafter the term "know-how" will be used in accordance with the definition provided in Article 1(1)(i) TTBER. While this provision requires information to be secret, some German commentators have noted that know-how licences do not require that the information object of the contract is secret, see for instance Kurt Bartenbach, *Patentlizenz-und Know-how-Vertrag* (Verlag Dr. Otto Schmidt 2013) Rdn 2548: "Das nicht geheime Erfahrungswissen ist dagegen das in der jeweiligen Branche bekannte (Grund-) Wissen, das sich jeder Interessent unter Aufwand vo Zeit und Geld auch selbst erarbeitetn könnte"

2413 Recital 4 TTBER highlights the pro-competitive effects of licensing agreements concerning technology because they avoid the duplication of research efforts and spur incremental innovation.

2414 Tanya Aplin and others 2012 (n 22) paras 8.120-8.121.

2415 This was the position supported by the House of Lords in *Rolls-Royce Ltd v Jeffrey (Inspector of Taxes)* [1962] 1 WLR 425 (HL) and Aplin and others 2012 (n) para 8.121.

2416 Kurt Bartenbach 2013 (n 2412) Rdn 2655.

2417 Stefan Maaßen and Tobias Wuttke 2011 (n 2404) Rdn 41-43.

paid.[2418] Notwithstanding this consideration, some commentators have suggested that when the licensor conveys the information without further secrecy or assistance obligations and in exchange for the payment of a lump sum, the rules regulating purchase agreements should apply.[2419]

Likewise, in the U.S., where trade secrets have predominantly been considered a type of IPR by the courts[2420] and know-how licenses are generally accepted, some judicial decisions have also differentiated between the legal nature of formal IPR licences and know-how licences because the latter only bind the licensee, whereas all other competitors are entitled to reverse engineer the product and use it in a lawful manner.[2421]

Finally, it is important to note that based on the object of the contract, know-how licences are generally divided into two categories: (i) pure trade secrets licences, and (ii) technical assistance licences.[2422] The former provide for the use of know-how,[2423] while the latter include the impartment of the secret information along with the supply of technical assistance by the licensor.[2424] Some commentators also distinguish between licences that only provide for the use of know-how and those that foresee a hybrid licence, which includes the conveyance of know-how along with the right to use other IPRs, typically patent rights.[2425] Similarly, a distinction is drawn between exclusive and non-exclusive licences, considering whether the terms of the agreement provide that the licensor undertakes not to share the know-how with any third party (sometimes limited within a specific territory) and not to exploit it himself (exclusive licence) or whether the possibility of granting multiple licences is established (non-exclusive licences).[2426]

---

2418 Michael Groß, *Der Lizenzvertrag* (Deutsche Fachverlag 2015) Rdn 24; Stefan Maaßen and Tobias Wuttke 2011 (n 2404) Rdn 45; Kurt Bartenbach 2013 (n 2412) Rdn 2660.

2419 Eike Ullman and Hermann Deichfuß, '§ 15 Übertragbarkeit des Rechts; Lizenzen' Rdn 241 in Georg Benkard (ed), *Patentgesetz* (11th edn, C.H. Beck 2015).

2420 See chapter 1 § 3 B) I. 2. b).

2421 See for instance *Painton Company v. Bourns Inc.*, 442 F2d 216, 223 (2d. Cir. 1971).

2422 John Hull 2013 (n 934) 175.

2423 Stefan Maaßen and Tobias Wuttke 2011 (n 2404) Rdn 51

2424 John Hull 2013 (n 934) 175.

2425 Wolfgang Winzer, *Der Lizenzvertrag* (C.H. Beck 2014) Kap. 4, Rdn 17.

2426 Noel Byrne and Amanda McBraty, *Licensing Technology* (3rd edn, 2005 Jordans) 22-24.

### 2. Secrecy obligations

The legal issues raised by know-how licensing agreements are manifold. However, providing an in-depth analysis of all of them exceeds the scope of the present investigation. In line with the research questions that inform the dissertation, the following sections are devoted to the study of the secrecy obligations of the parties to a licensing agreement in three scenarios: during the pre-contractual negotiations, during the term of the licence, and after its termination. In particular, this thesis does not look into the competition law issues raised by licensing practices and the application of the TTBER, which are only considered insofar as they affect the confidentiality obligations of the parties.

#### a) Pre-contractual obligations of secrecy

As argued in chapter 1, one of the utilitarian rationales that justifies trade secrets protection is that it provides a legal solution to Arrow's Information Paradox, whereby licensors are wary of disclosing their secret information to potential licensees before concluding an agreement because it puts their information at risk[2427] and, most importantly, the potential licensee may gain knowledge of the information without the need to effectively conclude the agreement and pay any consideration in return.[2428] At the same time, licensors may be sceptical about executing a licensing agreement that binds them for the future without knowledge of the licensed information, because the information may in fact be known to them or it may already be part of the public domain.[2429]

Against this background, it appears that building a relationship of trust with licensees to minimise the risk inherent to such negotiations is of paramount importance, in line with the arguments suggested by the representatives of the perfume industry.[2430] For legal certainty purposes, the conclusion of NDAs also appears particularly advisable,[2431] even though in some jurisdictions an implied duty of secrecy may be established and trig-

2427 Stefan Maaßen and Tobias Wuttke 2011 (n 2404) Rdn 48.
2428 See chapter 1 § 2 B) II.
2429 Robert G. Bone 1998 (n 15) 280.
2430 See chapter 5 § 4 B) V.
2431 John Hull 2013 (n 934) 174.

ger liability in the event of a breach.[2432] In any case, the entering into of such a pre-contractual agreement provides solid evidence that an obligation of secrecy existed. In order to effectively protect the licensor, its scope should be confined to the regulation of the conditions under which the information is disclosed for the sole purpose of allowing the licensee to assess his interest in taking a full licence, without granting the right to make use of the information concerned.[2433] Consequently, such a contract should identify in a precise manner the secret materials and delineate the pre-acquired knowledge of the potential licensee and the knowledge submitted for consideration. Furthermore, in order to ensure the enforceability of secrecy against departing employees, a clause should be included, whereby the licensee undertakes to obtain an express confidentiality obligation from its employees.[2434]

#### b) During the term of the contract

One of the main objectives of licensing agreements is to regulate the obligations of the parties during the term of the contract. In the context of know-how agreements, confidentiality obligations play a central role both for the licensor and the licensee, as examined in the following sections.

##### aa) Secrecy obligations of the licensor

The main obligation of the licensor is to supply the licensee with the information that constitutes the know-how object of the contract,[2435] along with the necessary documents to provide the necessary technical assistance and support to the licensee.[2436] In addition, know-how licences frequently include clauses regulating the warranties and representations of the licensor, in particular regarding the transmission of the know-how, the accura-

2432 If such a duty is established, it triggers liability according to Article 4(3)(b) TSD.

2433 John Hull 2013 (n 934) 174-175; *Pagenberg*/Beier, *License Agreements* (Carl Heymanns Verlag 2008) Sample 3, Rdn 4.

2434 *Pagenberg*/Beier (n 2433) Sample 3, Rdn 5-6.

2435 Kurt Bartenbach 2013 (n 2412) Rdn 2776.

2436 Stefan Maaßen and Tobias Wuttke 2011 (n 2404) Rdn 54 highlighting that the scope of this obligation should be assessed on a case-by-case basis considering the specifc circumstances of each case.

cy and completeness of the documents, and even the instruction of the licensee (and his employees).[2437] The obligation to share any further developments and improvements over the licensed information is also usually included in these types of agreements, although in the absence of any specific provision, such an obligation should not be implied, at least under German law.[2438]

As regards secrecy, the licensor is obliged to keep the information secret during the term of the agreement. Otherwise, the information would become generally known and the contract would be deprived of its object. Ultimately, the licensee would not be able to recover the investment made in the preparations for the exploitation of the technology.[2439] Consequently, under German law, if the secret nature of the information is lost for reasons attributable to the licensor, the licensee is entitled to claim damages.[2440]

#### bb) Secrecy obligations of the licensee

The main obligations of the licensee include, among others, the payment of the agreed licensing fee and keeping the licensed information secret.[2441] The observance of the secrecy obligation is essential to maintain the competitive advantage conferred by the information. Hence, if a breach occurs as a result of a disclosure to a third party by the licensee, liability may arise and accordingly the licensor may claim damages, at least under German law.[2442] Therefore, in the interest of legal certainty, it is highly advisable to specify the terms that will govern such an obligation in the body of the agreement.

Express confidentiality clauses should first identify in a precise manner the information that is the subject of the licensing agreement that should be kept secret. Secondly, the parties should regulate the content and scope of the secrecy obligation and in particular the possibility of disclosing the licensed information to third parties. Specifically, it should be established

2437 Stefan Maaßen and Tobias Wuttke 2011 (n 2404) Rdn 58.
2438 Stefan Maaßen and Tobias Wuttke 2011 (n 2404) Rdn 60.
2439 Stefan Maaßen and Tobias Wuttke 2011 (n 2404) Rdn 60.
2440 According to § 581(1) BGB and §§ 535 and 536a BGB; see further Stefan Maaßen and Tobias Wuttke 2011 (n 2404) Rdn 61.
2441 Kurt Bartenbach 2013 (n 2412) Rdn 2800; Michael Groß, *Der Lizenzvertrag* (Deutsche Fachverlag 2015) Rdn 98-99.
2442 Stefan Maaßen and Tobias Wuttke 2011 (n 2404) 64.

under which conditions the information can be imparted to third parties in order to allow for its commercial exploitation. These obligations should be equally demanding as those imposed upon the licensee, considering that once the information is generally known, the subject of the contract is lost.[2443] Similarly, it is also advisable that the licensing agreement regulates the possibility of taking copies (in electronic, paper or any other form) and the number of copies that can be made, which furthermore should always be labelled as confidential.[2444] Another aspect that should be included in the agreement is the duration of the confidentiality obligation, particularly after the termination of the contract, and the exceptions thereto. Crucially, the prohibition of disclosing information that constitutes a trade secret but does not meet all of the requirements of the definition of know-how established in the TTBER may not benefit from the block exemption and may be enforceable as a restraint of competition, pursuant to Article 101 TFEU.[2445] In addition, the block exemption will only apply for as long as the information is secret.[2446] Consequently, the exceptions to the obligation of confidentiality should exclude the information that was already known to the licensee at the time that the agreement was concluded; the information that was acquired in a lawful manner from third parties; the information that was developed independently by the licensee; and the information that it is generally known or readily accessible.[2447] Finally, it is advisable that the licensing agreement includes a clause that establishes that the licensed information can only be used for the purpose agreed in the contract,[2448] along with a penal clause in the event that the licensee breaches the secrecy obligation.[2449]

2443 Stefan Maaßen and Tobias Wuttke 2011 (n 2404) 70.

2444 *Pagenberg*/Beier (n 2433) Sample 3, Rdn 10.

2445 Hinrich Mummenthey, 'Vertraulichkeitsvereinbarungen' [1999] CR 651, 655.

2446 See Article 2(2) TTBER.

2447 Stefan Maaßen and Tobias Wuttke 2011 (n 2404) Rdn 73; the legal questions raised by the interplay between know-how licensing agreements and competition are manifold. However, providing a more detailed analysis falls outside the scope of the present analysis.

2448 Kurt Bartenbach 2013 (n 2412) Rdn 2237; Hinrich Mummenthey 1999 (n 2445) 656.

2449 For an overview of the scope and limits of penal clauses under German law see Stefan Maaßen and Tobias Wuttke 2011 (n 2404) Rdn 75-77.

c) After the termination of the contract

A comparative analysis reveals that the existence of an implied post-contractual secrecy obligation is a highly controversial issue. In Germany, the non-disclosure obligation continues after the termination of the contract on the basis of a post-contractual duty of loyalty ("*Treuepflicht*").[2450] However, in the interest of legal certainty, it is suggested that the licensing agreement should establish such a possibility in an express manner, in particular with regard to the duration of the non-disclosure obligation.[2451] Some German commentators have suggested that the duration of the post-contractual obligation should be between three and five years, even though a clause that provides that the obligation should remain in force for as long as the information remains secret should also be considered valid.[2452] Similarly, the German competition authority considers that the imposition of a fixed term (of 15 years) is questionable and that confidentiality obligations should rather extend for as long as the information remains secret, in accordance with Article 2(2) TTBER.[2453] From a practical perspective, it is extremely difficult to assess whether the licensee has disclosed or used the information concerned. Hence, due to the difficulty in monitoring the return of the documents and the use of the licensed information, it is recommended that the contract foresees the possibility of establishing penalty clauses in the event of early termination of the contract by the licensee.[2454]

In England, the courts have mostly addressed the existence of post-contractual secrecy obligations from the perspective of the information that the licensee is entitled to use after the termination of the contract, which has to be assessed pursuant to the specific terms of the agreement. A review of the main decisions on this topic reveals that once the contract is terminated, the right of the licensee to use the information also comes to an end.[2455] However, there are a number of decisions where such a principle

2450 Kurt Bartenbach 2013 (n 2412) Rdn 2871.
2451 Kurt Bartenbach 2013 (n 2412) Rdn 2871.
2452 Stefan Maaßen and Tobias Wuttke 2011 (n 2404) Rdn 72; Hinrich Mummenthey 1999 (n 2445) 656.
2453 *Pagenberg*/Beier (n 2433) Sample 1, Rdn 128, Rudolf Kraßer 1970 (n 831) 590; BKartA 1977 TB 94.
2454 Michael Groß, *Der Lizenzvertrag* (Deutsche Fachverlag 2015) Rdn 490; Kurt Bartenbach 2013 (n 2412) Rdn 2873.
2455 John Hull 2013 (n 934) 176-177 with further references.

is not followed.[2456] For instance, in *Regina Glass Fibre v Werner Schuller*, the Court of Appeal interpreted that the licensee was entitled to use the licensed confidential information, which concerned the manufacture of glass fibre, along with any improvements thereto, after the termination of the contract.[2457] Most commentators understand that this is an isolated decision and that the rationale for such an interpretation is that in the absence of such a use right, the viability of the licensee's business would have been dubious.[2458] Ultimately, the outcome of *Regina Glass Fibre v Werner Schuller* highlights that in the assessment of the possibility of using licensed secret information after the termination of the agreement, the English Courts will decide considering the terms of the licensing agreement.[2459]

In sum, from a comparative law perspective, it appears that there is no uniform interpretation regarding the admissibility of implied post-contractual secrecy obligations on the licensee and their duration. This issue will be addressed further in § 3 B) in the context of the study of the legal application of the Nordhaus Model.

### II. R&D agreements

#### 1. Object and legal nature

The EU legislature in the Preamble of the TSD underscored the importance of collaborative research and development activities in order to foster employment and innovation growth within the single market in the context of the TSD.[2460] Indeed, R&D agreements are central to allowing for the exchange of information between companies (both in the public and private sectors) particularly in innovative environments. A number of definitions have been proposed by lawmakers and commentators to conceptualise these types of agreements.[2461] For the purpose of the current analysis,

2456 Tanya Aplin and others 2012 (n 22) para 8.140 noting that "there is no general principle that governs this situation, rather it is a matter of interpretation of the licence agreement".

2457 *Regina Glass Fibre v Werner Schuller* [1972] RPC 229 (CA), 235.

2458 John Hull 2013 (n 934) 177.

2459 Tanya Aplin and others 2012 (n 22) paras 8.146 - 8.147.

2460 Recital 3 TSD.

2461 See Commission Regulation (EU) No 1217/2010 of 14 December 2010 on the application of Article 101(3) of the Treaty on the Functioning of the European

the following working definition will be referenced: by virtue of R&D agreements two or more parties "agree to conduct research activities as a service (contract research) or in collaboration (research cooperation) to gain new scientific know-how or related IP".[2462] Under the first category, one party undertakes to provide specific research and development activities for the other. In contrast, in research cooperations, all of the parties share their knowledge and competences and agree on an R&D plan.[2463] As regards the object of the agreement, it can comprise anything that is developed, manufactured and distributed and that requires a production method or any device to that end, such as individual products, systems, software and any kind of procedures.[2464]

In general, R&D agreements can be divided into three stages.[2465] First, in the initial phase, the parties examine their pre-existing IP and trade secrets under strict confidentiality obligations and establish the objectives of the cooperation.[2466] In the second stage (the development phase), the parties collaborate to achieve the joint goals established in the initial phase. Finally, in the third stage (the utilization phase), the parties exploit the results of the research on an individual basis or jointly, in accordance with the terms of the R&D agreement.[2467]

In order to cooperate effectively, it is essential that the parties expressly specify the terms that govern the transfer of background IP (i.e. the pre-existing formal IPRs and trade secrets owned by each party).[2468] In contract research agreements, usually the background IP is licensed to the execut-

---

Union to certain categories of research and development agreements [2010] OJ L335/36 (R&DBER), Article 1(1)(a); Wolfgang Winzer, *Forschungs- und Entwicklungsverträge* (2nd edn, C.H. Beck 2011) Rdn 3-18.

2462 Melanie Graf and Herbert Zech, 'IP in Research and Development Agreements: object and legal qualification' 293, 293 in Duncan Matthews and Herbert Zech (eds), *Research Handbook on Intellectual Property and the Life Sciences* (Edward Elgar 2017).

2463 Claudia Milbradt and Marco Stief, 'Forschungs- und Entwicklungsvertrag'126, 126 in Marco Stief and Boris Bromm (eds), *Vertragshandbuch Pharma und Life Sciences* (C.H. Beck 2015).

2464 Wolfgang Winzer 2011 (n 2461) Rdn 1-3.

2465 Philipp Maume,'Know-how in Kooperationen (Entwicklung und Outsourcing)' Rdn 12 in Christoph Ann, Michael Loschelder and Marcus Grosch (eds), *Praxishandbuch Know-how-Schutz* (Carl Heymanns Verlag 2011).

2466 Melanie Graf and Herbert Zech 2017 (n 2462) 293.

2467 Philipp Maume 2011 (n 2465) Rdn 12.

2468 Christoph Bertsch,'Research Agreement' 38, 55-56 in Wolfgang Weitnauer and others (eds), *Life Sciences Agreements in Germany* (C.H. Beck 2014).

ing parties, while in research cooperation agreements, the parties establish a cross license for their respective background IP.[2469]

From the above considerations it follows that the crucial provisions of R&D agreements concern the regulation of the assignment and the licensing of the resulting R&D efforts, the so-called "foreground IP"[2470] or "project technology",[2471] which includes all of the formal IPR developed as a result of the implementation of the R&D plan, as well as trade secrets.[2472] The parties are free to regulate the assignment and licensing of the trade secrets created as a result of the execution of the R&D plan, provided that the competition law limitations imposed by the R&DBER and the applicable national law on employee creations are complied with.

As regards their legal nature, contract research agreements are usually entered into between a private entity and a public entity, such as universities and basic research centres. The latter party usually carries out the research activities according to the research plan designed by the financing party. Consequently, the agreement takes the form of a service contract or an agency contract depending on the certainty of the research outcome.[2473] Indeed, it has been suggested that the more certain the result is, the more likely it is to be qualified as a service contract. In contrast, in research cooperation agreements, the parties may create a partnership to exploit the foreground IP.[2474] Furthermore, in some instances, if the exploitation of the project technology requires the creation of new distribution or manufacturing structures, it may even be advisable to establish a joint venture.[2475]

## 2. Secrecy obligations

In the context of R&D agreements, secrecy plays a central role in ensuring the success of the common efforts of the parties. However, confidentiality obligations cannot be inferred from the nature of these types of contracts

---

2469 Claudia Milbradt and Marco Stief, 'Forschungs- und Entwicklungsvertrag' 126, 145 in Marco Stief and Boris Bromm (eds), *Vertragshandbuch Pharma und Life Sciences* (C.H. Beck 2015).

2470 Melanie Graf and Herbert Zech 2017 (n 2462) 293.

2471 Christoph Bertsch 2014 (n 2468) 55-56.

2472 Melanie Graf and Herbert Zech 2017 (n 2462) 293.

2473 Melanie Graf and Herbert Zech 2017 (n 2462) 293.

2474 In Germany it is governed by §§ 705-740 BGB.

2475 Philipp Maume 2011 (n 2465) Rdn 13-14.

and, therefore, it is of utmost importance that the content and scope of such obligations is expressly regulated in the body of the agreement, particularly after the termination of the contract.[2476] From a competition law perspective, it should be noted that the admissibility of confidentiality clauses is not expressly addressed in the R&DBER, even though they are generally considered valid if they are necessary for the implementation of the R&D agreements, to the extent that such clauses do not circumvent the safeguards established in Article 3 R&DBER.[2477] In addition, in order to ensure the adequacy of secrecy obligations in regard to the limitations imposed by competition law, most agreements include so-called "escape clauses", whereby it is established that the duty of secrecy terminates once the information becomes generally known.[2478] Indeed, if one of the parties to the agreement obtains the information lawfully from a third party, confidentiality obligations persist until the information becomes generally known among the relevant circles, because in such a case the common interest in keeping the information from other market participants also continues.[2479]

In pre-contractual negotiations, it is of utmost importance that confidentiality clauses are agreed upon before the R&D agreement is concluded, to ensure that the information disclosed during the negotiations is only used for the purposes of assessing the background IP and the viability of the R&D agreement. As argued in the context of licensing agreements, such a clause should include a prohibition on taking copies and the obligation to return the documents if the negotiations break off, or after the agreement is terminated.[2480]

Most importantly, the implementation of an R&D research plan can lead to the development of numerous trade secrets, such as data and labbooks, that are included in the foreground IP. In contract research agreements, usually the financing party acquires the resulting trade secrets, whereas in research collaboration agreements, this will depend on the national rules governing partnerships.[2481] Ultimately, in both instances, the

2476 Philipp Maume 2011 (n 2465) Rdn 5.
2477 Philipp Maume 2011 (n 2465) Rdn 53.
2478 Lorenz Kaiser, 'Vetragsmanagement' 257, 268 Alexander Wurzer and Lorenz Kaiser (eds), *Handbuch Internationaler Know-how-Schutz* (Bundesanzeiger Verlag 2011); *Pagenberg*/Beier (n 2433) Sample 8, Rdn 33; Wolfgang Winzer 2011 (n 2461) Rdn 199.
2479 Philipp Maume 2011 (n 2465) Rdn 55.
2480 Melanie Graf and Herbert Zech 2017 (n 2462) 295
2481 Melanie Graf and Herbert Zech 2017 (n 2462) 295.

national provisions regulating employee creation will have to be observed. Against this background, secrecy obligations concerning the foreground IP and the necessary background IP to exploit the results of the R&D Agreement are desirable for both parties during the term of the agreement and do not give rise to competition law concerns.[2482] However, in post-contractual scenarios, from a competition law perspective, they will only be admissible to the extent that they do not preclude disclosure to third parties during the exploitation of the foreground technology or have a negative impact on the ability of any of the parties to conduct further research.[2483]

In line with the above, several commentators submit that post-contractual secrecy obligations should be limited to a specific term to be able to benefit from the R&DBER. In effect, a duration of two to five years has been suggested by some authors,[2484] even though most commentators indicate that a general clause that provides that confidentiality obligations persist until the information becomes generally known should also be considered admissible, because the common interest of the parties in keeping the information undisclosed persists.[2485]

The foregoing analysis underscores that confidentiality clauses are key to safeguarding the exploitation of the trade secrets developed in the context of R&D agreements to allow for a return on joint innovative efforts. Notwithstanding this consideration, they are also subject to a number of limitations regarding their scope and duration to avoid restraints of competition law.

## § 2 *The limitations of secrecy*

The legal regime for the protection of trade secrets must strike a delicate balance between, on the one hand, the interest of the holder in concealing his valuable information from competitors, in order to recoup the cost of its development, and on the other, the access of third parties, which is necessary to foster competition and follow-on innovation. Much of this debate has been channelled through the discussion of whether trade secrets should be protected as a form of IPRs or under the unfair competition

2482 Christoph Bertsch 2014 (n 2468) 63-64.
2483 Philipp Maume 2011 (n 2465) Rdn 62.
2484 Wolfgang Winzer 2011 (n 2461) Rdn 197.
2485 *Pagenberg*/Beier (n 2433) Sample 8, Rdn 3; Wolfgang Winzer 2011 (n 2461) Rdn 197.

regime. As examined in the first chapter of this dissertation, many commentators and judicial decisions understand that in order to prevent a trade secret holder from being able to reap the fruits of his endeavours indefinitely, thus circumventing the trade-off imposed by the IPRs system, it is crucial that the property approach is abandoned in connection to trade secrets.[2486] However, this dissertation posits that trade secrets have an inherently hybrid nature and that even if formally they are regarded as a species of IPRs, this should not necessarily entail enhancing the level of protection, but rather allows for focusing on the limitations to the rights conferred.[2487]

In line with the latter argument, the TSD has adopted an open-ended approach to the legal nature issue and has expressly included a number of limitations in order to ensure the complementarity between trade secrets and formal IPRs and to safeguard the fundamental freedoms enshrined in the ChFREU. Consequently, Article 3 TSD refers to lawful means of acquiring, using and disclosing a trade secret and Article 5 TSD spells out a number of exceptions to the rights conferred on the trade secret holder. From a legislative technique perspective, the types of lawful conduct specified under Article 3 exclude liability ex ante by limiting the scope of application of the TSD, whereas the exceptions mentioned in Article 5 call upon national judicial authorities to conduct a balancing exercise to determine whether liability arises.

The present analysis looks into the most important statutory limitations that may lead to a disclosure of information in order to understand the optimal scope of secrecy. These are independent discovery (section A), reverse engineering (section B), and competition law (section C), and they are examined in the following sections.

## A) Independent discovery and creation

The protection of trade secrets is premised on the fact that any competitor can, in an independent manner, come up with the same information as that covered by an already existing secret. Such a limitation is essential to prevent a trade secret holder from having an exclusive absolute right over the unrevealed information. This is also of paramount importance to en-

2486 Josef Drexl 2009 (n 369) 449; Gintare Surblyte 2011 (n 182) 90.

2487 Mark A. Lemley 2008 (n 15) 352; Lionel Bently 2013 (n 307) 91-92 and chapter 1 § 3 B).

sure the complementarity between the legal regime for the protection of trade secrets and the IPRs system in place, particularly regarding patents.[2488] Otherwise, if protection were accorded even in the case of independent discovery, the rationale underlying the protection of IPRs would be by-passed. Inventors would opt for informal means of protection, as this would allow them to benefit from their innovative endeavours (potentially) indefinitely without disclosing the information to competitors and without bearing the costs of the patent system.[2489] This would hinder the information function pursued by the publication of patent specifications. As a whole, if trade secret holders were protected against independent discovery or creation, the incentives to apply for patent protection would practically disappear. Consequently, the secrecy requirement compels inventors to choose the form of IP protection that better serves the objectives of society.[2490]

The importance of independent discovery has crystallised in Article 3(1)(a) TSD as a lawful form of acquiring a trade secret and mirrors a well-established practice among EU jurisdictions.[2491] It constitutes a defence against misappropriation claims, and should be construed as meaning that certain information that the plaintiff regards as his own trade secret has not been derived either directly or indirectly from knowledge gained in confidence from the holder or as a result of espionage activities.[2492] In sum, there cannot be a causal link between the information acquired from the trade secret holder and the information independently generated.[2493]

Against this background, it is noteworthy that innovations rarely occur in isolation.[2494] Areas of technology such as biotechnology and computer

---

2488 See chapter 1 § 3 A).

2489 *Kewanee Oil Co. v. Bicron Corp.*, 416 U.S. 470, 476 (1974) "a trade secret law, however, does not offer protection against discovery by fair and honest means, such as by independent invention, accidental disclosure, or by so-called reverse engineering".

2490 Mark A. Lemley 2008 (n 15) 339-341 arguing that the secrecy requirement compels inventors to choose the form of IP protection that better serves the objectives of society.

2491 For instance, in England see Law Commission 1981 (n 327) para 4.71-4.72; in Germany see Rudolf Kraßer 1977 (n 1327) 191.

2492 James Pooley 2002 (n 66) § 5.01[1] 5-3.

2493 Lionel Bently 2012 (n 114) para 3.23; see also *Seager Limited v Copydex Limited* [1967] 2 All ER 415 (CA).

2494 Vincent Chiappetta 1999 (n 24) 88 arguing that such a restriction on the trade secret holder's right to exclude third parties offers the right counterbalance to the incentives to invest in secrecy.

software are to a large extent cumulative. In those fields, inventions are mostly based on prior innovations.[2495] Thus, it is likely that a large percentage of the trade secrets end up being independently created by competitors working in the same industry.[2496] Indeed, "the original owner's risk is another's opportunity.[2497]

In view of this consideration, if a second inventor generates the information independently and applies for a patent covering such information, the grant process will inevitably lead to the publication of the application, and consequently the information will no longer be regarded as secret.[2498] In this particular scenario, under the EPC, the first inventor will not be able to destroy the novelty of the patent on the basis of its use, unless it is proved that the prior use made the information available to the public.[2499] In addition, if the patent is granted, except if the specific national regime provides for a "prior user's right", the trade secret holder will have to enter into a licensing agreement with the patentee in order to avoid the risk of patent infringement.[2500]

### B) Reverse engineering

#### I. Conceptual introductory remarks

In the design of every trade secrets legal regime, the legislature should consider whether reverse engineering practices should be regarded as a lawful (or unlawful) form of acquiring undisclosed information and under which conditions, in order to strike the most appropriate balance between the conflicting interests of trade secret holders and their competitors, as well as the general public. Reverse engineering is central to the assessment of se-

---

2495 Suzanne Scotchmer 2004 (n 41) 125-126.

2496 Samson Vermont, 'Independent Invention as a Defense to Patent Infringement' [2006] 105 Michigan LR 475, 478-479.

2497 James Pooley 2002 (n 66) § 5.01[1] 5-3; this principle was famously acknowledged by the U.S. Supreme Court in *Kewanee Oil Co. v. Bicron Corp.*, 416 U.S. 470, 490 (1974), where it was noted that an invention is likely to be discovered by competitors and that therefore, what was once secret may become common knowledge within a given industry.

2498 Lionel Bently 2012 (n 114) para 3.37.

2499 According to consistent case law from the Boards of Appeal of the EPO, such as G 1/95 [2006] OJ EPO 615.

2500 Lionel Bently 2012 (n 114) para 3.38; on the prior user's right defence, see chapter 1 § 3 A) I. 2. c).

crecy, because the need to undergo such a process to obtain a specific piece of information signals that it is secret and that therefore, a priori, it is eligible for protection. In addition, it is also essential to ensure the erosion of concealed information so that with time it eventually enters the public domain. However, the subsequent use and disclosure of information obtained from the said process and its interplay with other areas of law, in particular contract law, formal IPRs and unfair competition, remains controversial. Consequently, the inclusion of reverse engineering as a lawful form of obtaining information, subject to certain limitations, constitutes one of the milestones of the TSD.[2501]

It is the first time that such an overarching provision has been included within the acquis communautaire, thus bringing greater legal certainty to one of the pillars upon which the regime for the protection of trade secrets and its limitations is articulated. In effect, as surprising as it may seem, no right to reverse engineering (a so-called "reverse engineering defence") has been positively codified into patent law, even though it is a well-established practice among competitors across all industries.[2502] Before the adoption of the TSD, only Article 6 of the Software Directive allowed for "decompilation", a specific form of reverse engineering used in computer programming, but only for the purposes of achieving interoperability of independently created programs,[2503] along with Article 5(3) of the same directive, which enshrined the right to observe, study or test the functioning of a program in order to determine the underlying ideas and principles.[2504] Similarly, Article 5 of the Directive on the protection of topographies of semiconductor products provided that reproduction for private purposes or for the purposes of evaluation, analysis, research or teaching is permitted, but the sale of identical chips is proscribed.[2505]

---

2501 See Article 3(1)(b) TSD.

2502 Pamela Samuelson and Suzanne Scotchmer 2002 (n 226) 1582; but note that Article 27 of the Agreement on a Unified Patent Court [2013] OJ C–175/01 stipulates that the effects of a patent do not extend to (a) acts done privately and for non-commercial purposes, and (b) acts done for experimental purposes, which to a certain extent preserves the right to reverse engineer.

2503 See Article 6 Software Directive, which is examined below in chapter 6 § 2 B) IV. 2).

2504 Thomas Dreier, 'The Council Directive of 14 May 1991 on the Legal Protection of Computer Programs' [1991] 13 EIPR 319, 322.

2505 Council Directive 87/54/EEC of 16 December 1986 on the legal protection of topographies of semiconductor products [1987] OJ L24/36.

From a conceptual perspective, the TSD defines reverse engineering as the "observation, study, disassembly or testing of a product or object that has been made available to the public or that is lawfully in the possession of the acquirer of the information".[2506] A similar interpretation has been followed by the courts in the U.S., where the Supreme Court in *Kewanee Oil Co. v. Bicron Corp* defined it as "starting with the known product and working backward to divine the process which aided in its development or manufacture".[2507] Both explanations reveal that ultimately reverse engineering is an intellectual process that aims at "extracting know-how or knowledge from a human-made artifact".[2508] It can be applied in every field of technology, even though the amount of time, effort and costs required will largely depend on the specific characteristics of the product.[2509]

The reasons that may lead someone to engage in reverse engineering activities beyond the manufacturing of a replacement (or a clone) of a competitor's product are manifold. These include learning, repairing a product, providing related services, creating a compatible product or improving an existing one, to name some.[2510] Thus, from a dogmatic perspective, reverse engineering comprises the act of discovering the concealed information and, more extensively, the use of the resulting knowledge, even if it leads to the dissemination of information and the loss of secrecy.[2511] The root of the discrepancies with regard to the permissibility of reverse engineering in EU jurisdictions lies in the multiple ends to which it is applied. While innovative activities seem to provide legitimate grounds, creating replacements (or clones) has raised fairness concerns in some jurisdic-

2506 Recital 16 TSD: "Reverse engineering of a lawfully acquired product should be considered as a lawful means of acquiring information, except when otherwise contractually agreed. The freedom to enter into such contractual arrangements can, however, be limited by law".

2507 *Kewanee Oil Co. v. Bicron Co.*, 416 U.S. 470, 476 (1974).

2508 Pamela Samuelson and Suzanne Scotchmer 2002 (n 226) 1577; in the same vein, Henning Harte-Bavendamm 1990 (n1502) 658 has defined it as "any process by which a product manufactured by a third party is analysed in detail with the aim of gaining actual knowledge of the underlying structure and function" (translation by the author).

2509 Pamela Samuelson and Suzanne Scotchmer 2002 (n 226) 1587.

2510 James Pooley 2002 (n 66) § 5.02[2] 17; see more generaly Ansgar Ohly 2009 (n 98) 537 distinguising between (i) "the innovative analyst"; (ii) "the copycat analyst" and (iii) "the right-owner analyst"; further reasons for engaging in reverse engineering practices are examined by Henning Harte-Bavendamm 1990 (n1502) 659-660.

2511 Tanya Aplin 2013 (n1600) 343.

tions.[2512] In the latter instance, drawing the boundaries between the simplest act of reverse engineering and copying activities appears to be a grey area.[2513] As a result, Member States' practices in this field have differed greatly.

In the light of the above considerations, the following section looks into the rationales underlying reverse engineering (section II). Next, the thesis goes on to examine the regulation of reverse engineering from a comparative law perspective (section III). First, it starts by analysing the legal framework of these practices (or its absence) in the TRIPs Agreement. Then, it compares the approach adopted with regard to this specific subject in the U.S., where it has long been accepted as a lawful way of acquiring a trade secret, with the one followed in England and Germany before the implementation of the TSD. Drawing on this comparative analysis, some interpretative considerations with respect to secrecy and the optimal scope of protection are presented in the light of Article 3(1)(b) TSD (section IV).

## II. Rationales underlying reverse engineering

The deontological and utilitarian justifications for trade secrets protection examined in chapter 1 do not appear suitable to justify a limitation on the right to extract secret information from a marketed product in all instances.[2514] These inconsistencies can be best explained by two factors. First, the finished product has left the internal sphere of the company and therefore there is no need to deter an over-investment in self-help measures (the limit to the arms race doctrine) and protect the trial and error process inherent to its development (the privacy doctrine).[2515] In addition, a limitation on reverse engineering does not help to lower transaction costs because the contract that regulates the transaction has already been concluded before the item is placed on the market or delivered to the counterparty (incentives to disclose doctrine). In fact, agreeing on a limitation on reverse engineering seems most appropriate during pre-contractual negotia-

2512 Ansgar Ohly 2009 (n 98) 537; see in this regard the analysis in chapter 1 § 2 A).

2513 William Landes and Richard Posner 2003 (n 38) 370; Ansgar Ohly 2009 (n 98) 538 "it emerges that there is a wide range of possible motives for reverse engineering. In some cases reverse engineering is a necessary or at least useful step in the process of further innovation, in other cases it may only enable imitation".

2514 Chapter 1 § 2.

2515 Ansgar Ohly 2009 (n 98) 548.

tions, for instance in the exchange of prototypes before concluding the final agreement. Second, there is no universal commercial morality standard that allows for establishing whether devising secret information should be considered contrary to "honest commercial practices".[2516]

In contrast, the most intuitive justification for reverse engineering is that such a right stems from the ownership of the product in which the secret is embedded.[2517] In the words of Jacob J in *Mars UK Ltd v Teknowledge Ltd*: "what the owner has is the full right of ownership. With that goes an *entitlement to dismantle the machine* and tell anyone he pleases" (emphasis added).[2518]

From a legal perspective, reverse engineering is regarded as an essential element in maintaining the equilibrium with the IPRs system and particularly with respect to patent rights.[2519] Ultimately, it is also central to find a balanced solution to the secrecy-openness dichotomy: if secret innovations could not be subject to reverse engineering activities, the incentives to apply for patents and participate in the trade-off imposed by the patent system would disappear, along with the knowledge externalities derived from it.[2520] The fact that competitors may take apart a product to find out the underlying functioning and principles imposes a factual time limitation on the exclusivity conferred by secrecy. As a result, when informal means of protection are the preferred option to appropriate returns from innovation, it is likely that the duration of the exclusivity will be limited until the product is reverse engineered. To avoid such a risk, the innovator will apply for a patent in order to secure exclusivity for a finite period (the patent term).[2521]

From an economic perspective, Samuelson and Scotchmer, in their seminal article, "The Law and Economics of Reverse Engineering", conclude that a general prohibition on reverse engineering would amount to granting perpetual rights without publicising the knowledge of the invention. In this context, they suggest that in traditional manufacturing industries the *cost* and *time* necessary to reverse engineer a product allow innovators to recoup the investment made in its generation through the lead-time

2516 Ansgar Ohly 2009 (n 98) 548.
2517 Tanya Aplin 2013 (n 2511) 341-377.
2518 *Mars UK Ltd v Teknowledge Ltd* [2000] FSR 138 (Pat), 149.
2519 Ansgar Ohly 2009 (n 98) 546-547.
2520 Chapter 1 § 3 A); Pamela Samuelson and Suzanne Scotchmer 2002 (n 226) 1583.
2521 Pamela Samuelson and Suzanne Scotchmer 2002 (n 226) 1583-1584.

conferred by secrecy.[2522] Therefore, the innovator is sufficiently protected against the reverse engineer.[2523] Indeed, the investment of *time* and *cost* strikes the balance between the interests of the trade secret holder, and those of their competitors.[2524] In sum, reverse engineering practices foster market competition, decrease prices and enhance follow-on innovation.[2525] In the same vein, Landes, Posner and Friedman suggest that one of the most important aspects of reverse engineering practices is that they allow competitors to gain knowledge of inventions and creations, thus fostering follow-on innovation.[2526] Consequently, the cost of subsequent innovations is shared between the originator's initial research and development expenditure and the second-comer's investment in reverse engineering the product and developing the improvements.[2527]

Notwithstanding this consideration, reverse engineering is not always costly and time consuming.[2528] As examined in the context of perfumes, finding out the composition of a fragrance can be carried out fast and at a low price. It only requires that a small portion of a perfume is introduced into a gas-chromatograph. In a matter of minutes, the composition of the formula will be revealed to the skilled chemist, who may produce an identical product.[2529] In this regard, it has been argued that when reverse engi-

2522 Pamela Samuelson and Suzanne Scotchmer 2002 (n 226) 1590; a similar view is expressed by Jerome H. Reichman 1994 (n 102) 2521 where the author notes that "reverse engineering provides originators with an indispensable period of lead time in which to recoup their initial investment and to establish footholds in the market".

2523 Tanya Aplin 2013 (n 2511) 372.

2524 Pamela Samuelson and Suzanne Scotchmer 2002 (n 226) 1590; see comment to § 1 UTSA, which provides that: "Often, the nature of a product lends itself to being readily copied as soon as it is available on the market. On the other hand, if reverse engineering is lengthy and expensive, a person who discovers the trade secret through reverse engineering can have a trade secret in the information obtained from reverse engineering";; similarly Gintare Surblyte, 'Enhancing TRIPS: Trade Secrets and Reverse Engineering' 725, 742-743 in Hanns Ullrich and others (eds), *TRIPS plus 20 – From Trade Rules to Market Principles* (Springer 2016).

2525 Pamela Samuelson and Suzanne Scotchmer 2002 (n 226) 1590.

2526 David D. Friedman, William M. Landes and Richard A. Posner, 'Some Economics of Trade Secret Law' [1991] 5 JEP 61, 70 noting that "Reverse engineering will often generate knowledge about the product being reverse engineered that will make it possible to improve on it".

2527 Jerome H. Reichman 1994 (n 102) 2521.

2528 Jerome H. Reichman 1994 (n 102) 2527.

2529 See chapter 5 § 4 B) 1.

neering practices are "cheap" and "rapid" and allow for creating identical copies, they may ultimately have "*market destructive consequences*" as innovators will not be able to recoup the investment in their creation, which in turn may lead to a market failure.[2530] In such a context, and in line with the incentives to innovate doctrine previously analysed,[2531] an intervention by the legislator to prevent such market destroying practices by limiting reverse engineering may be justified.[2532] In fact, this is the justification underpinning the limitations on reverse engineering in the semiconductor industry and Article 6 of the Software Directive, which provides that acts of decompilation shall only be permissible to the extent that they are necessary to achieve interoperability.[2533]

Furthermore, this rationale has also crystallised in Recital 17 TSD, in which the EU legislature has acknowledged that in those industries where creators and innovators cannot resort to IPRs protection and reverse engineering can be carried out at a very low cost, these activities may amount to parasitic copying or slavish imitation that free ride on the reputation and innovation efforts of the trade secret holder. Against this background, the TSD indicates that this specific area may be the object of harmonisation in the near future.[2534] Yet, such an approach does not take into consideration the different practices among EU Member States regarding parasitic competition and that market economies operate under the principle of freedom to imitate.

With the above arguments in mind, the following section delves into the regulation of reverse engineering from a comparative law perspective. First, it starts by analysing the regulation of this conduct (or rather its absence) in the TRIPs Agreement. Next, it compares the regulatory approach adopted on this specific practice in the U.S., where it has long been accepted as a lawful form of acquiring a trade secret, with the ones followed in England and Germany before the implementation of the TSD. Finally,

2530 Pamela Samuelson and Suzanne Scotchmer 2002 (n 226) 1594.

2531 Chapter 1 § 2 B) I.

2532 Pamela Samuelson and Suzanne Scotchmer 2002 (n 226) identify five potential options to regulate reverse engineering: (i) restricting destructive means of reverse engineering; (ii) introducing a breadth requirement for products obtained through reverse engineering; (iii) establishing purpose-and necessity-based criteria for determining the legitimacy of reverse engineering; (iv) regulating the use of reverse engineering tools; and (v) restricting the publication of information discovered by a reverse engineer.

2533 Thomas Dreier 1991 (n 2504) 324.

2534 See Recital 17 TSD.

some policy considerations regarding the interplay between secrecy and reverse engineered products are presented in the light of Article 3(1)(b) TSD.

## III. Comparative law analysis

### 1. TRIPs

Article 39 TRIPs is silent on the permissibility of reverse engineering.[2535] Even though the wording of this provision to a large extent mirrors § 1(2) UTSA, the drafters of TRIPs failed to establish a reverse engineering defence and define its contours vis-à-vis misappropriation.[2536] Therefore, the approaches adopted by the WTO Member States on this specific issue differ greatly, as no minimum standards of protection are laid down in this regard. In essence, the root of the discrepancies is whether information that can be acquired through reverse engineering is to be deemed readily ascertainable and whether such a practice may be considered contrary to honest commercial practices according to Article 10bis PC.[2537]

2535 Pamela Samuelson and Suzanne Scotchmer 2002 (n 226) 1577: "It neither requires nor sanctions a reverse engineering privilege".

2536 Jerome Reichman, 'How trade secrecy law generates a natural semicommons of innovative know-how' 185, 186 in Rochelle C. Dreyfuss and Katherine J. Strandburg (eds), *The Law and Theory of Trade Secrecy: A Handbook of Contemporary Research* (Edward Elgar 2011); in this regard, François Dessemontet 2008 (n 601) 275 uses this argument to note that "The function of Article 39 TRIPs is to protect trade secrets, not to allow reverse engineering - which may be allowed under some legal orders, but might also have been outlawed by Article 39 TRIPs – since, as Professor Reichman points out, the definition of trade secrets embedded in Article 39 TRIPs closely follows Sec . 38 et seq. of the Restatement (Third) of Unfair Competition §39 (Am. Law Inst. 1995), but does not mention reverse engineering contrary to the restatement"; it is submitted here that this interpretation of the wording of Article 39 TRIPs is too simplistic.

2537 Markus Peter and Andreas Wiebe 2007 (n 304) Art. 39 Rdn 21.

## 2. U.S.

In the U.S., reverse engineering has long been accepted as a lawful form of acquiring a trade secret.[2538] This is statutorily recognised in the four most relevant sources of law that regulate trade secrets, namely the Restatement (First) of Torts,[2539] the Restatement (Third) of Unfair Competition,[2540] the UTSA[2541] and, more recently, the DTSA.[2542] Crucially, the UTSA subjects the lawfulness of reverse engineering to the acquisition of the product in which the trade secret is embodied by lawful and fair means, such as purchasing it on the open market.[2543] Accordingly, if the access to the item was gained in an illegal way, for instance, by resorting to trespass or theft, the acquisition of the information embodied therein will be considered illegal.[2544] For the same reason, information that is obtained through reverse engineering because of the breach of an explicit or implicit agreement is also deemed to have been obtained through improper means.[2545]

The policy justifications underlying the right to reverse engineer were examined by the U.S. Supreme Court in the famous case *Kewanee Oil Co. v. Bicron Corp*.[2546] This ruling concerned a classic case of trade secrets misappropriation in the chemical industry by departing employees who went on to work for a competing firm after the termination of their contracts. This decision is particularly notable because the Supreme Court clearly stated for the first time after the *Sears, Roebuck & Co. v. Stiffel Co.* judgement[2547] that there is no conflict between the objectives pursued by federal patent law and the goals of state trade secrecy law and that therefore the law of trade secrecy is not pre-empted by federal patent law.[2548]

In particular, the court argued that if a trade secret did not meet the patentability requirements, according trade secret protection would not have an adverse impact on the disclosure of information, one of the main

2538 *Kewanee Oil Co. v. Bicron Corp.*, 416 U.S. 470, 476 (1974); similarly, *Sinclair v. Aquarius Electronics, Inc.*, 42 Cal. App.3d 216, 226 (Cal. Ct. App.1974).

2539 Restatement (First) of Torts § 757 (Am. Law Inst. 1939).

2540 Restatement (Third) of Unfair Competition §43 (Am. Law Inst. 1995) comment b.

2541 Comment to § 1 UTSA.

2542 18 U.S.C. § 1839 (6)(B).

2543 Comment to § 1 UTSA.

2544 Gale R. Peterson 1995 (n 1602) 451.

2545 Pamela Samuelson and Suzanne Scotchmer 2002 (n 226) 1582.

2546 *Kewanee Oil Co. v. Bicron Corp.*, 416 U.S. 470 (1974).

2547 *Sears, Roebuck & Co. v. Stiffel Co.*, 376 U.S. 225 (1964).

2548 *Kewanee Oil Co. v. Bicron Corp.*, 416 U.S. 470, 485 (1974).

objectives pursued by the patent system. Under such circumstances, the trade secret holder would not risk disseminating his valuable information (inter alia in a licensing context) if he could not protect it against unlawful acquisition, use and disclosure.[2549]

More notably, as regards trade secrets where there is doubt about their compliance with the standards of patentability, the Supreme Court held that the holder of information would most likely opt for patent protection because of its "superior benefits" compared to trade secrecy law. Along the same lines, it was argued that even if the invention were clearly patentable, no tension would arise as to the protection of undisclosed information. The Supreme Court strikingly held that the holder would always apply for a patent, given that trade secrets law provides weaker protection than patent law. In this context, the court enshrined reverse engineering (together with independent discovery) as a fair means of discovering a trade secret.[2550] Consequently, a specific state law prohibiting reverse engineering would be pre-empted by federal law.[2551] Yet, this reasoning seems to disregard the fact that, in many industries, secrecy is the preferred means of appropriating returns from innovation, particularly when the patent system is too costly considering the value of the invention, or it is envisaged that the returns obtained will be higher than if a patent were applied for.[2552]

This consideration was restated in another landmark case decided by the U.S. Supreme Court some years later: *Bonito Boats, Inc. v. Thunder Craft Boats, Inc.*[2553] This case dealt with the lawfulness of manufacturing fiber-

---

2549 *Kewanee Oil Co. v. Bicron Corp.*, 416 U.S. 470, 485 (1974).

2550 See *Kewanee Oil Co. v. Bicron Corp.*, 416 U.S. 470, 476 (1974) "trade secret law, however, does not offer protection against discovery by fair and honest means, such as by independent invention, accidental disclosure, or by so-called reverse engineering"; this was later emphasised in *Chicago Lock Co. v. Fanberg*, 676 F.2d 400 (9th Cir. 1982).

2551 *Chicago Lock Co. v. Fanberg*, 676 F.2d 400, 405 (9th Cir. 1982) noting that "such an implied obligation upon the lock owner (obligation not to reverse engineer) in this case would, in effect, convert the Company's trade secret into a state-conferred monopoly akin to the absolute protection that a federal patent affords. Such an extension of California trade secrets law would certainly be preempted by the federal scheme of patent regulation"; see also Ansgar Ohly 2009 (n 98) 539.

2552 As explored in chapter 1 § 3 A) I. 2. a); see in particular David D. Friedman, William M. Landes and Richard A. Posner, 'Some Economics of Trade Secret Law' [1991] 5 JEP 61, 63-64.

2553 *Bonito Boats, Inc. v. Thunder Craft Boats, Inc.*, 489 U.S. 141 (1989).

glass hulls through a direct moulding process, for which no patent had been applied, in order to produce imitations of the boat hulls produced by the plaintiff, Bonito Boats. The petitioner sought an injunction on the basis of a state law enacted in Florida, which prohibited the use of a direct melding process to duplicate the vessel hull made by a third party without the consent of the original manufacturer. The fact pattern reveals that this case falls between a reverse engineering case and a mere copying case.[2554]

In its legal reasoning, the Supreme Court started by noting that reverse engineering forms an essential part of innovation and that variations in the original product may in fact result in progress in the specific field.[2555] Furthermore, it argued that, "the competitive reality of reverse engineering may act as a spur to the inventor, creating incentives to develop inventions that meet the rigorous requirements of patentability".[2556] While highlighting the importance of reverse engineering for market competition, the court also emphasised the significance of imitation for innovation by stating that:

> From their inception, the federal patent laws have embodied a careful balance between the need to promote innovation and the recognition that imitation and refinement through imitation are both necessary to invention itself and the very lifeblood of a competitive economy.[2557]

As is apparent from the above, allowing for reverse engineering was deemed an essential element not only to spur innovative practices, but also to ensure complementarity with the patent system.[2558] In view of these arguments, the Supreme Court concluded that the Florida Statute was preempted by federal patent law.[2559]

---

2554 Ansgar Ohly 2009 (n 98) 537.

2555 *Bonito Boats, Inc. v. Thunder Craft Boats, Inc.*, 489 U.S. 141, 160 (1989); Pamela Samuelson and Suzanne Scotchmer 2002 (n 226) 1583.

2556 *Bonito Boats, Inc. v. Thunder Craft Boats, Inc.*, 489 U.S. 141, 160 (1989).

2557 *Bonito Boats, Inc. v. Thunder Craft Boats, Inc.*, 489 U.S. 141, 160 (1989).

2558 *Bonito Boats, Inc. v. Thunder Craft Boats, Inc.*, 489 U.S. 141, 142 (1989) noting that: "(...), the threat of reverse engineering of unpatented articles creates a significant spur to the achievement of the rigorous standards of patentability established by Congress. By substantially altering this competitive reality, the Florida statute and similar state laws may erect themselves as substantial competitors to the federal patent scheme".

2559 *Bonito Boats, Inc. v. Thunder Craft Boats, Inc.*, 489 U.S. 141, 168 (1989).

### 3. England before the implementation of the TSD

The reverse engineering exception in England has been underexplored both by case law and by legal commentators.[2560] So far, only one appellate decision has expressly recognised the freedom to reverse engineer, and only in a very succinct manner, without analysing the actual scope of this defence.[2561] However, the proposal to implement the TSD in the UK noted that such a principle has in fact been implemented by UK common law.[2562] Indeed, several rulings from lower courts have accepted it as the necessary corollary to the patent system.

The starting point of the analysis of the legal framework that governs reverse engineering in England draws from the principles spelt out in chapter 4 in the context of placing an item on the open market in which a trade secret is embodied.[2563] In a nutshell, when a product is marketed in a manner that discloses the commercial secret so that little or no intellectual skill is necessary to obtain it, such information loses its confidential nature and can be freely used by anyone.[2564] This is in line with the first of the five principles articulated by Aplin after reviewing the limited English case law that addresses the issue of reverse engineering.[2565]

The second principle suggested by the author considers that "*commercial secrets that may be ascertained by reverse engineering retain limited confidentiality*".[2566] This is particularly relevant when the trade secret embodied in a

---

2560 Tanya Aplin 2013 (n1600) 346.

2561 *Force India Formula One Team Ltd v 1 Malaysia Racing Team SDN BHD* [2013] EWCA civ 780 (CA), [72] commenting on the fact pattern of *Saltman Engineering v Campell Engineering* [1948] 65 RPC 203 (CA): "In that case, the plaintiffs instructed the defendant to make tools for the manufacture of leather punches in accordance with drawings which the plaintiffs provided to the defendant for this purpose. The defendant used the drawings to make tools, and the tools to make leather punches, on their own account. The finished product (i.e. the leather punches) were readily available to buy in the shops; and the defendants could have bought one and reverse engineered it".

2562 See United Kingdom Intellectual Property Office, 'Consultation on draft regulations concerning trade secrets' (18 February 2018) 28 <https://www.gov.uk/government/uploads/system/uploads/attachment_data/file/682184/Consultation_Trade_Secrets_Directive.pdf> accessed 15 September 2018.

2563 Chapter 4 § 4 C) II. 3.b)

2564 See for instance *Force India Formula One Team Limited v 1 Malaysia Racing Team SDN BHD* [2012] EWHC 616 (Pat), [222].

2565 The principles proposed by Tanya Aplin 2013 (n 2511) 346-363 will guide the present discussion.

2566 Tanya Aplin 2013 (n 2511) 349-355.

marketed product is not readily apparent, but it is possible to acquire it through reverse engineering i.e. with the investment of time, labour and particularly cost and intellectual skill. Under such circumstances, the Chancery division in *Terrapin Ltd v. Builders' Supply Co (Hayes) Ltd*[2567] suggested that the mere marketing of the good does not necessarily imply that the commercial secrets embodied therein lose their confidential nature. Instead, this should be determined on the basis of (i) whether the good was reverse engineered, and (ii) the use of the information ascertained via reverse engineering, in line with the arguments already suggested.[2568]

In *Terrapin Ltd v. Builder's Supply Co (Hayes) Ltd*, the plaintiff, a producer of prefabricated portable buildings, had concluded a manufacturing agreement with the defendant. To that end, drawings, technical information and know-how were conveyed in confidence to the respondent. Several months after the termination of the contract, the defendant started to sell portable buildings with essentially the same features as the buildings produced during the manufacturing agreements. In the ratio decidendi, the Court of Chancery held that: "springboard it remains even when all the features have been published or can be ascertained by actual inspection by any member of the public". According to Aplin, this should be understood as meaning that the "information obtained via reverse engineering retains limited confidentiality".[2569] In other words, the information is not deprived of its confidential nature because the amount of time and intellectual skill necessary to obtain it prevents it from being generally known or easily accessible to the relevant circles and the general public.[2570] In addition, associated secrets that cannot be obtained through reverse engineering also remain concealed.[2571] In *Terrapin Ltd v Builders' Supply Co (Hayes) Ltd* the information was considered confidential because the defendants had by-passed the trial and error process inherent to reverse engineering practices and instead had developed the improved model on the basis of information conveyed in confidence.

In line with the second principle, the third principle states that "*commercial secrets that have been obtained via reverse engineering do not necessary lose their confidentiality*".[2572] The assessment of whether reverse engineering de-

2567 *Terrapin Ltd v Builders' Supply Co (Hayes) Ltd* [1962] RPC 375 (Ch).
2568 Chapter 4 § 4 C) II. 3. b).
2569 Tanya Aplin 2013 (n 2511) 352.
2570 Chapter 4 § 4 C) II. 3. b); Jacob J holds the opposite view in in *Mars UK Ltd v Teknowledge Ltd* [2000] FSR 138 (Pat), 149.
2571 Tanya Aplin 2013 (n 2511) 354.
2572 Tanya Aplin 2013 (n 2511) 355-356.

stroys secrecy will depend on two factors, namely (i) whether the information acquired through reverse engineering has been further disseminated, and (ii) the number of people that have succeeded in reverse engineering the secret. If the number is substantial, the information will be deemed to fall into the public domain,[2573] consistent with the doctrine of relevant circles examined above.[2574] Indeed, with time, most trade secrets erode because more competitors are able to reverse engineer them. Consequently, the secret progressively loses its commercial value (it no longer provides a competitive advantage) and also its concealed nature.

The fourth principle provides that "*a person seeking to reverse engineer will not usually come under an obligation of confidence*".[2575] Several cases have drawn attention to this point, but it was most notably elaborated by Jacob J in *Mars UK v Teknowledge Ltd*,[2576] the leading authority to date on reverse engineering.[2577]

Mars UK Ltd was a British manufacturer of coin receiving and changing mechanisms. Their machines incorporated discriminators whose function was to control the authenticity and value of the coins introduced into the machine. Modern discriminators operate through sensors that take a series of electrical measurements. The disputed discriminator was known as the "Cashflow" and its main feature, as opposed to the existing models, was that it could be reprogrammed for new coin data. The recalibration function of the Cashflow was protected through several mechanisms, and in particular, the encryption of information. Furthermore, the re-programmation function was outsourced by Mars to several independent authorised companies. The defendant succeeded in reverse engineering the Cashflow discriminator and consequently Mars launched proceedings for copyright and database rights infringement, as well as breach of confidence.

2573 By way of illustration Lionel Bently 2012 (n 114) para 3.44 suggests that: "it is conceivable that someone (Z) who reverse engineered "E" and thereby worked out how to make it may simply take advantage of that knowledge himself. If that occurred, X could not object to Z's activities, but X might retain an enforceable secret itself. This is because confidentiality only requires that information remain relatively secret. Thus, X might continue to be able to enforce of confidentiality against those to whom he disclosed the information about the process of making "E" in confidence (such as its employees); " Jacob J holds the opposite view in *Mars UK Ltd v Teknowledge Ltd* [2000] FSR 138 (Pat), 149.

2574 See chapter 4 § 4 D) II. and IV.

2575 Tanya Aplin 2013(n 2511) 356-362.

2576 *Mars UK Ltd v Teknowledge Ltd* [2000] FSR 138 (Pat).

2577 Tanya Aplin and others 2012 (n 22) para 671.

With respect to the breach of confidence claim, in the legal arguments Jacob J started by noting that "encrypted information is to be regarded in law as a trade secret and treated as such".[2578] Next, he went on to analyse whether the three requirements set forth in *Coco v A.N. Clark* had been met. With regard to the first requirement, whether the information possessed the "necessary quality of confidence", it was held that the owner of encrypted information was entitled to take apart the machine by virtue of its ownership right. In this particular aspect, the decision seemed to indicate that whenever a piece of information has been acquired through reverse engineering it automatically loses its quality of confidence.[2579] This proposition has been the object of vehement criticism by some commentators, because the information had only been reverse engineered by the defendant and had not been circulated further. By holding that the information was no longer secret, Jacob J was equating the confidence requirement with the objective novelty test under patent law, and disregarding the factual nature of such a condition.[2580]

With respect to the second and third liability requirements, by virtue of which the information must have been communicated in circumstances importing an obligation of confidence and subsequently misused, Jacob J held that the mere fact of receiving encrypted information does not give rise to a duty of confidence and that "there is nothing surreptitious in taking a thing apart to find out how it is made". .[2581] Thus, it was concluded that the information incorporated in the machine was obviously not confidential and that finding out information from a product purchased on the

2578 *Mars UK Ltd v Teknowledge Ltd* [2000] FSR 138 (Pat), 150, [29]; later on he further notes that "mere difficulty in doing the job is not enough - there must be some element of deliberate difficulty put in the way. Mars make no bones about the far-reaching nature of their case. In the words of their closing submissions "the issue is whether it is possible to impose confidentiality upon someone who receives information by purchasing an article in the open market".

2579 *Mars UK Ltd v Teknowledge Ltd* [2000] FSR 138 (Pat), 149 "(…) starting with the first requirement, does the encrypted information in the Cashflow, have the "necessary quality of confidence"? I think the answer is clearly "no". The Cashflow is on the market. Anyone can buy it. And anyone with the skills to de-encrypt has access to the information. The fact that only a few have those skills is, as it seems to me, neither here nor there. Anyone can acquire the skills and anyway, a buyer is free to go to a man who has them. Mars suggest that the owner, although he owns the machine, does not own the information within it. That is too glib".

2580 Tanya Aplin 2013 (n 2511) 355.

2581 *Mars UK Ltd v Teknowledge Ltd* [2000] FSR 138 (Pat), 149 [33].

open market was part of the fair game for competitors.[2582] In sum, the legal reasoning in *Mars v. Teknowledge* underscores that under the breach of confidence action the general principle is the freedom to reverse engineer, which can be limited by contractual provisions and IPRs, but not based on an implied equitable duty of confidence. In particular, the inclusion of technical measures in the product to prevent the acquisition of the information does not give rise to a duty of confidence.[2583]

Finally, the fifth principle suggested by Aplin states that, "*it is no defence to a breach of confidence claim to say that a product could have been –or has been– reverse engineered.*[2584] In essence, this should be construed as meaning that even if it had been possible to reverse engineer the disputed product, if the defendants did not do so and instead used confidential information they would still be liable for a breach of confidence. This was clarified, among others, in *Saltman*[2585] and *Force India,*[2586] where the deciding courts held that by-passing independent research and using confidential information instead should amount to a breach of confidence. In essence, this principle purports that whoever wants to benefit from the reverse engineering defence must show that he has gone through the trial and error process necessary to devise the secret information.

The previous analysis reveals that despite the absence of an express reverse engineering defence, in England courts mostly understand that the acquisition of a trade secret through reverse engineering constitutes a lawful form of acquiring secret information and therefore it cannot give rise to liability under the breach of confidence action provided that the item is acquired on the open market and unless a limitation on these types of practices is agreed upon contractually.

---

2582 Lionel Bently 2012 (n 114) para 3.42.

2583 Tanya Aplin 2013(n 2511) 357.

2584 Tanya Aplin 2013 (n 2511) 362-363.

2585 *Saltman Engineering v Campell Engineering* [1948] 65 RPC 203 (CA) 215: "What the Defendants did in this case was to dispense in certain material respects with the necessity of going through the process which had been gone through in compiling these drawing, and thereby to save themselves a great deal of labour and calculation and careful draughtsmanship. (...) They have saved themselves that trouble by obtaining the necessary information either from the original drawings or from the tools made in accordance with them. That, in my opinion, was a breach of confidence".

2586 *Force India Formula One Team Limited v 1 Malaysia Racing Team SDN BHD* [2012] EWHC 616 (Pat), [22].

## 4. Germany before the implementation of the TSD

In Germany, reverse engineering is predominantly regarded as unfair, as opposed to in the U.S. and England, where it is considered as a lawful form of acquiring a trade secret. Under German law, such practices may be captured under paragraph 1 of § 17(2) UWG and, in particular, by litera (a), which proscribes the acquisition or securement of a trade secret through any technical means that enable it, and by litera (b), which renders unlawful the physical reproduction of the secret information.[2587] The general test of fairness that governs the UWG is not applicable to §§ 17 and 18 UWG and, therefore, it is irrelevant whether the trade secret is effectively used or disclosed because the mere acquisition or securement of the information triggers both criminal and civil liability.[2588] Accordingly, a person that engages in reverse engineering practices will be held liable unless a specific ground of justification exists, such as consent, a statutory duty or contractual claim to disclose, or a state of emergency.[2589]

The cornerstone of the reverse engineering doctrine followed by the German courts was first developed in 1935 by the Supreme Court of the German Reich ("*Reichsgericht*") in the *Stiefeleisenpresse* decision.[2590] In essence, the facts of the case are as follows: the plaintiff was the sole producer of a complex machine used to manufacture metal fittings ("*Spiefeleisen*"), which were necessary in order to strengthen the soles of boots and shoes. A Polish manufacturer of metal fittings ("*Stiefeleisen*"), which in the past had purchased one of the plaintiff's machines, sought to acquire a second unit after some time, but at a lower price. In view of their refusal to negotiate the price, the Polish company contacted the defendant, an undertaking which also produced metal fittings machines ("*Stiefeleisenpresse*"), but using a different technology. Following the Polish company's

2587 Andreas Wiebe, 'Reverse Engineering und Geheimnisschutz von Computerprogrammen' [1992] CR 134, 135; Gintare Surblyte, 'Enhancing TRIPS: Trade Secrets and Reverse Engineering' 725, 750-753 in Hanns Ullrich and others (eds), *TRIPS plus 20 – From Trade Rules to Market Principles* (Springer 2016); Henning Harte-Bavendamm 1990 (n1502) 662 noting that in the context of reverse engineering the acquisition of the physical support in which a trade secret is embodied may trigger liability according to litera (c) of paragraph 1 of § 17(2) UWG as a preparatory means of acquiring the secret prior to conducting reverse engineering.

2588 Henning Harte-Bavendamm 1990 (n1502) 662.

2589 Ansgar Ohly 2009 (n 98) 541.

2590 RGZ 1935 149, 329 – *Stiefeleisenpresse*.

request, the defendant agreed to manufacture and deliver a machine that fitted the tools used for the machine that they already owned, which had been purchased from the plaintiff some time before. Accordingly, one of the defendant's experts disassembled the machine, took measurements and made drawings of the different parts and finally copied the tools used to repair it. As a result, the defendant ended up supplying a replica of the plaintiff's machine to the Polish company. When the plaintiff learnt about this fact he brought an action for a violation of § 17(2) of the UWG, under the doctrine of slavish imitation, despite the fact that a patent covering the invention had expired thirty years before. Both claims were upheld by the Supreme Court of the German Reich. With respect to the trade secrets claim, in the legal reasoning the court first assessed whether the requirements for protection were met.[2591] Secondly, the ruling deemed that in order to dissemble the *Stiefeleisenpresse* machine, substantial effort (in the sense of great difficulty and cost) was required to devise the secret and, in view of that, the defendant's conduct was unfair and violated § 17(2) UWG. In particular, the court specifically noted that tearing apart the machine was not the normal way of acquiring information.[2592]

The "great difficulty and cost" ("*große Schwierigkeit und Opfer*") benchmark has been adopted in subsequent judicial decisions as the prevailing criteria to assess whether the acquisition of confidential information through reverse engineering is lawful.[2593] If substantial effort is required in order to devise secret information, its acquisition will be deemed an act of unfair competition. However, this has not been without criticism. Some commentators consider that this doctrine is inherently vague and leads to much legal uncertainty, because it poses the additional question of elucidating from a quantitative perspective when the degree of difficulty and cost is such that triggers liability.[2594] Most notably, it has been questioned because by protecting the investment made, the trade secret holder is conferred a type of exclusivity akin to that granted by formal IPRs, thereby disregarding the salutary effects of reverse engineering on price competition

2591 Chapter 4 § 2 A).

2592 Andreas Wiebe, 'Reverse Engineering und Geheimnisschutz von Computerprogrammen' [1992] CR 134, 135.

2593 Ansgar Ohly 2009 (n 98) 542 noting that most subsequent cases have followed this decision and only a minority have deviated from it, based on the argument that the information seems to be available without substantial effort, in this regard see for instance OLG Hamburg GRUR-RR 2001, 137, 139 – *Nachbau einer technischen Vorrichtung nach Ablauf des Patentschutzes.*

2594 Florian Schweyer 2012 (n 99) 466.

and follow-on innovation.[2595] In addition, such an approach overlooks the relative nature of secrecy, which is necessary to reconcile the interests protected, on the one hand, by the law of trade secrets and, on the other, under formal IPRs and patents in particular. Devising the internal structure or composition of a product purchased on the open market is a well-established practice in most industries and is considered an important part of the competitive process. Thus it should not be considered an unlawful form of acquiring information. In this regard, Ohly states that not enough attention has been paid to the policy arguments that speak in favour of the allowance of reverse engineering and against the establishment of such a high threshold for trade secrets protection.[2596]

Notwithstanding this restrictive interpretation, with the implementation of the TSD the reverse engineering doctrine will have to be reconsidered in Germany, as is examined in the following section.

## IV. Reverse engineering under the TSD

### 1) Scope of the reverse engineering pursuant to Article 3(1)(b) TSD

One of the critical aspects of the TSD is the inclusion of a general reverse engineering defence (Article 3(1)(b) TSD), which constitutes a maximum standard of protection.[2597] The provision reads as follows:

> The observation, study, disassembly or testing of a product or object that has been made available to the public or that is lawfully in the possession of the acquirer of the information who is free from any legal valid duty to limit the acquisition of the trade secret.

Further clarification is provided in Recital 16, which states:

> (…) Reverse engineering of a lawfully acquired product should be considered as a lawful means of acquiring information, except when otherwise contractually agreed. The freedom to enter into such contractual arrangements can, however, be limited by law.

---

2595 Ansgar Ohly 2009 (n 98) 542 noting that "The court point out that thedefendant by taking apart a machine'which was not meant to be taken aprt,' had strengthened its own competitive position at the plaintiff's cost. In other words: the defendant had reaped where it had not sown".

2596 Ansgar Ohly 2009 (n 98) 543.

2597 Article 1 TSD.

Pursuant to Article 3(1)(b) TSD, reverse engineering will be deemed a lawful form of acquiring a trade secret as long as either of the two following alternative pre-conditions is met: (i) the product or object in which the trade secret is embodied has been made available to the public, or (ii) the product or object in which the trade secret is embodied is possessed lawfully by someone under no legal obligation to limit the acquisition of the information. In this regard, the relevant provision also foresees the possibility of limiting by contract reverse engineering practices, which allows the holder to keep the information secret for a longer period and thereby prolong the exclusivity conferred by secrecy. Yet, pursuant to the wording of Recital 16, such a possibility may be excluded by law.[2598]

The first condition stipulates that the product or object must have been *made available to the public*. By analogy with patent law, a product will be regarded as available if it can be accessed or acquired on the open market free from any legal duty of confidence or non-disclosure.[2599] This includes the production, offering, marketing or otherwise exploiting of the product or object concerned.[2600]

The second condition provides that the product has to be *lawfully* possessed by someone "who is free from any legal valid duty to limit the acquisition of the trade secret". This wording seems more problematic insofar as it raises a number of interpretative questions. First, uncertainty arises regarding how to assess when a good is possessed *lawfully*. From a systematic perspective, it seems that lawfulness should be evaluated by reference to the types of conduct listed in Article 4(2)(a) TSD, which spells out a number of examples of when the acquisition of trade secrets is to be considered contrary to honest commercial practices, such as the unauthorised appropriation of objects, materials, substances or electronic files. However, the latter provision refers to the acquisition of the information as such and not the item in which it is embodied, which may include a broader spectrum of behaviours. The protection of possession has not been harmonised

2598 Gintare Surblyte, 'Enhancing TRIPS: Trade Secrets and Reverse Engineering' 725, 742 in Hanns Ullrich and others (eds), *TRIPS plus 20 – From Trade Rules to Market Principles* (Springer 2016).

2599 Guidelines for Examination in the EPO, Part G, Patentability, Chapter IV. Section 7.2.1: "Subject-matter should be regarded as made available to the public by use or in any other way if, at the relevant date, it was possible for members of the public to gain knowledge of the subject-matter and there was *no bar of confidentiality restricting the use or dissemination of such knowledge*"(citation omitted, emphasis added).

2600 Guidelines for examination in the EPO, Part G, Chapter IV. Section 7.1.

across the EU and therefore the relevant national civil provisions in each jurisdiction should govern the assessment of lawfulness. Consequently, in line with the escape clause included in Article 4(2)(b) TSD, national courts may also consider unfair other forms of obtaining the products subject to a reverse engineering proceedings, such as theft, misrepresentation, bribery or espionage, despite the fact that these were excluded from the scope of the TSD due to their criminal law nature. Similarly, in those borderline cases where it may be unclear whether the item has been acquired in an unlawful manner, for instance, if the seller concealed its identity at the time of purchase, national rules apply.[2601]

Second, an additional interpretative question refers to whether the *acquirer of the information* refers only to the purchaser (the owner) or also to those that have hired or licensed the object. From the wording of the provision, it seems that if the product is lawfully under the sphere of control of the acquirer (factual possession), either because it has been sold, licensed or hired, it should be possible to conduct reverse engineering activities, even if this leads to the revelation of the secret and the production of a competing product, unless agreed otherwise contractually or proscribed by law.[2602]

Furthermore, Article 3(1)(b) TSD provides that the acquirer must be "free from any *legal valid duty* to limit the acquisition of the trade secret". Pursuant to Recital 16, the expression "legal valid duty" refers to the possibility of limiting reverse engineering practices by contract.[2603] However, the inclusion of contractual clauses appears problematic because it upsets the equilibrium between the trade secrets legal regime and formal IPRs, particularly in the case of software licences. This is analysed in the following section.

---

2601 Tanya Aplin 2013 (n 2511) 375.

2602 Tanya Aplin 2013 (n 2511) 372.

2603 Article 3(1)(b) TSD refers to "any legal valid duty to limit the acquisition of the trade secret", whereas Recital 16 TSD refers to contractual provisions. Hence, the term "legal valid duty" is understood to refer to contractual provisions. However, one could also argue that it includes statutory limitations that restrict the possibility of conducting reverse engineering practices, such as the prohibition of decompilation enshrined in Article 6 of the Software Directive. In addition, by virtue of the principle of primacy law of EU law, it may be debatable whether national statutory limitations on reverse engineering should be effective.

2) Contractual limitations on the possibility of reverse engineering and in particular the interplay with the Software Directive

Contractual relationships between private parties are governed by the freedom of contract principle, which may nevertheless stand as an obstacle to the safeguards established by law. This problem is particularly acute in the context of trade secrets because if the parties agree not to reverse engineer a licensed product, the balance struck by the EU legislator may tip in favour of the trade secret holder.[2604] To be sure, contractual clauses proscribing reverse engineering enhance secrecy because they defer the entrance of information into the public domain. An illustrative example of this is mass-distribution software licensing agreements that include clauses preventing the licensee from reverse engineering the licensed program. This type of provisions raises concerns not only from a trade secrets perspective, but also in terms of a conflict with the safeguards enshrined in the Software Directive. Before turning to them, it is important to introduce a number of considerations regarding the protection of software and its interface with the law of trade secrets.

Both the object code and the source code of a computer program can be protected under copyright rules.[2605] However, in order to capture the market, frequently software manufacturers resort to trade secrets protection for the source code, which is in human-readable programming language, and to copyright protection for the object code, which needs to undergo a process of decompilation in order to be translated into source code. Thereby, competitors are prevented from copying the program or creating compatible or even competing programs because the object code prevents access to the principles and ideas and its translation into source code amounts to an act of reproduction, which is subject to the right holder's authorisation under Article 4 of the Software Directive.[2606]

In view of such a broad scope of protection, the EU legislature included a number of safeguards in the Software Directive that allow for reverse engineering a computer program, subject to several conditions, in order to foster competition and follow-on innovation within the software market.[2607] First, Article 5(3) of the Software Directive provides that the li-

2604 Mark A. Lemley 1995 (n 1617) 1246.

2605 See chapter 1 § 3 A) II.

2606 Thomas Dreier 1991 (n 2504) 323-324.

2607 See Commision, 'Proposal for a Council Directive on the legal protection of computer programs' COM (88) 816 final, paras 3.10-3.15; Robert J. Hart, 'In-

censee is entitled without prior authorisation from the licensor "to observe, study or test the functioning of the program in order to determine the ideas and principles which underlie any element of the program if he does so while performing any of the acts of loading, displaying, running, transmitting or storing the program which he is entitled to do".[2608] This purpose-based safeguard allows for the analysis of a computer program to devise the underlying ideas and principles, but only in the performance of the acts inherent to its use.[2609] Hence, such practices fall within the definition of reverse engineering laid down in Article 3(1)(b) TSD, which also includes the observance, testing and analysis of products.

Second, Article 6 of the Software Directive lays down that the restricted acts established in Articles 4(1)(a) and 4(1)(b) of the Software Directive do not require prior authorisation if they are necessary to achieve the interoperability of an independently created computer program with other programs, provided that: (i) they are carried out by the licensee or any third party entitled to use a copy of the program; (ii) the information has not been previously readily available to them; and (iii) the acts of decompilation are limited to those parts that are indispensable to achieve interoperability.[2610] Therefore, Article 6 permits a specific form of reverse engineering known as decompilation, but only for the purposes of achieving interoperability (purpose-based norm).[2611]

---

teroperability information and the Microsoft decision' [2006] 28 EIPR 361, 363.

2608 Article 5(3) Software Directive.

2609 Gintare Surblyte, 'Enhancing TRIPS: Trade Secrets and Reverse Engineering' 725, 743 in Hanns Ullrich and others (eds), *TRIPS plus 20 – From Trade Rules to Market Principles* (Springer 2016).

2610 Thomas Dreier 1991 (n 2504) 324; furthermore, pursuant to Article 4 the use of information acquired through decompilation activities is also restricted to (i) any uses other than achieving interoperability; (ii) sharing it with others except for the purposes of achieving interoperability; and (iii) for the creation of a computer program substantially similar in its expression; on the importance of interoperability for innovation see Urs Gasser and John Palfrey, 'Breaking Down Digital Barriers: How and When Interoperability Leads to Innovation, plus three companion case studies on DRM, Digital Identity, and Web Services' (2007) Berkman Center Publications Series <http://nrs.harvard.edu/urn-3:HUL.InstRepos:2710237> accessed 15 September 2018.

2611 Julie E. Cohen, 'Reverse Engineering and the Rise of Electronic Vigilantism: Intellectual Property Implications of "Lock-Out" Programs' [1995] 68 Southern California LR 1091, 1094 defines decompilation as a specific form of reverse engineering that "parses the binary object code in which computer programs are distributed into higher-level, human-readable commands".

As regards the interplay between the two provisions, a systematic analysis reveals that the acts of decompilation (Article 6 Software Directive) constitute a specific form of reverse engineering and that therefore they do not fall within the scope of the acts of analysis laid down in Article 5(3) of the Software Directive. Consequently, if a party performs an act of decompilation that does not meet the statutory requirements set out in Article 6 (such as achieving interoperability), it will not be possible to claim that the conduct falls under the exception set out in Article 5(3) of the Software Directive.[2612]

Most importantly, in order to ensure that parties do not circumvent these exceptions by means of a contract, the second paragraph of Article 8 of the Software Directive stipulates that contractual provisions that contravene the safeguard established in Article 5(3) and Article 6 will be null and void. At first glance, the application of this principle appears rather straightforward. However, upon closer examination, a number of questions arise regarding the actual scope of such a prohibition and its intersection with the law of trade secrets.

The correlation between the exception established in Article 5(3) and Article 8 of the Software Directive was examined by CJEU in the highly contested decision, *SAS Institute Inc. v World Programming Ltd.*[2613] Among other questions, the CJEU was asked whether, pursuant to Article 5(3) of the Software Directive, the licensee of a computer program is entitled to observe, study or test the functioning of that program in order to determine the underlying ideas and principles with a purpose that goes *beyond* the framework established by the licence. According to the decision, the terms of the disputed licence provided that the defendant, World Programming Ltd, was only allowed to carry out acts for non-commercial purposes, but in fact had performed the said acts for purposes that fell outside the scope of the licence.[2614] In the judgement the court came to two apparently conflicting conclusions. First, it held that the software holder could not ban a licensee from determining the ideas and principles underlying the program provided that: (i) the licensee had carried out *acts that the licence had permitted him to perform*; (ii) the said acts were necessary to conduct loading and running acts to use the program; and, (iii) the licensee had not

2612 Ansgar Ohly 2009 (n 98) 545; Thomas Dreier 1991 (n 2504) 323.
2613 Case C–406/10 *SAS Institute Inc. v World Programming Ltd* (CJEU, 2 May 2012).
2614 Case C–406/10 *SAS Institute Inc. v World Programming Ltd* (CJEU, 2 May 2012), para 47.

infringed the rights of the software holder.[2615] This general statement was later qualified by the CJEU in the same decision, where it was noted that "*copyright* in a computer program *cannot be infringed* where, as in the present case, the lawful acquirer of the licence did *not have access to the source code of the computer program* to which that licence relates, but merely studied, observed and tested that program in order to reproduce its functionality in a second program". (emphasis added).[2616] Hence, the first statement indicates that acts of study are lawful as long as they do not exceed the terms of licence, whereas the second statement suggests that the discovery of the ideas and principles of a program should be deemed lawful because there is no copyright infringement if the lawful acquirer did not access the source code, regardless of the purpose indicated in the terms of the licence.

The ambiguity of this conclusion has been highlighted by several commentators[2617] and also by the referring judge,[2618] who interpreted the acts "permitted by the licence" as "the acts of loading, displaying, running, transmitting or storing" the program.[2619] Consequently, the defendant was still entitled to invoke the protection conferred by Article 5(3) of the Software Directive to extract the underlying principles and ideas through the said acts, irrespective of whether or not these were for a licensed purpose. The interpretation followed by the English Court of Appeal seems to be the most pertinent one, particularly in the light of the confusing reasoning followed by the CJEU in the decision. It prevents the software holder from availing himself of rights that were expressly excluded from the scope of application by the EU legislator and it is also in line with the expression-idea dichotomy enshrined in Recital 11 of the Software Directive. Otherwise, the safeguards established in the second paragraph of Article 8 would be devoid of meaning and purpose.

---

2615 Case C–406/10 *SAS Institute Inc. v World Programming Ltd* (CJEU, 2 May 2012), para 59.

2616 Case C–406/10 *SAS Institute Inc. v World Programming Ltd* (CJEU, 2 May 2012), para 61.

2617 Daniel Gervais and Estelle Derclaye, 'The scope of computer program protection after SAS: are we closer to answers?' [2012] 34 EIPR 562, 571; Gintare Surblyte, 'Enhancing TRIPS: Trade Secrets and Reverse Engineering' 725, 746 in Hanns Ullrich and others (eds), *TRIPS plus 20 - From Trade Rules to Market Principles* (Springer 2016).

2618 *SAS Institute Inc. v World Programming Limited* [2013] RPC 17 (Ch), [64].

2619 *SAS Institute Inc. v World Programming Limited* [2013] RPC 17 (Ch), [68]-[69].

In line with the previous argument, the interplay between the contractual limitations and the trade secrets legal regime has been questioned on the basis of the first paragraph of Article 8 of the Software Directive, which stipulates that the scope of application of the said Directive shall not affect other legal provisions that regulate "patent rights, trade-marks, unfair competition, *trade secrets*, protection of semi-conductor products or the law of contract". Thus, this leads to the question of whether contractual provisions that ban decompilation or the analysis of the ideas and principles underlying a computer program may be deemed null and void under the Software Directive but enforceable under Article 3(1)(b) TSD and thereby trigger liability as a breach of contract leading to the unauthorised use or disclosure of a trade secret (Article 4(3)(c) TSD).[2620]

A combined reading of Article 6 and Article 8 (second paragraph) of the Software Directive reveals that if a licensing agreement stipulates that the licensee is proscribed from decompiling a program for the purposes of achieving interoperability, such a clause will not be considered enforceable by courts under copyright rules. Therefore, considering that such a clause may nonetheless be valid and trigger liability under Article 3(1)(b) TSD if it is breached does not seem sound because it would circumvent one of the main goals of the Software Directive: to allow access to interfaces in order to ensure interoperability and avoid consumers being locked-in with a specific software manufacturer.[2621] The same is true for clauses that contract out the possibility of observing, studying or testing the functioning of the program to extract the underlying ideas or principles during the acts of loading, displaying, running, transmitting or storing the program (Article 5(3) of the Software Directive). As a result, the second paragraph of Article 8 of the Software Directive should be considered to take percent as lex specialis because it specifically regulates software contracts and the rights of the parties and, therefore, any contractual provision that would undermine the objectives pursued by the said Article should be considered null and void.[2622] This proposition is reinforced by Recital 39 TSD, which provides that the scope of application of the TSD shall not affect other regimes in

2620 Gintare Surblyte, 'Enhancing TRIPS: Trade Secrets and Reverse Engineering' 725, 750-753 in Hanns Ullrich and others (eds), *TRIPS plus 20 - From Trade Rules to Market Principles* (Springer 2016).

2621 Case T–201/04 *Microsoft v Commission* [2007] ECR II-03601, para 650.

2622 This is also the view supported by Tanya Aplin 2013 (n 2511) 373; Pamela Samuelson and Suzanne Scotchmer 2002 (n 226) 1660 and Thomas Dreier 1991 (n 2504) 325, who notes with respect to Article 6 of the Software Directive that "such a conclusion, which in essence would mean that a legitimate

place, and in particular IPRs. Notwithstanding this consideration, ultimately the interplay between the TSD and the Software Directive will be subject to the interpretation of the CJEU.

Having regard to the above legal framework, from a policy perspective, it should be noted that, in general, contractual restrictions may have an adverse effect on competition and innovation.[2623] In essence, one of the policy rationales that justifies trade secrets protection is that it is the necessary counterbalance to the patent system. In the words of the U.S. Supreme Court in *Kewanee Oil Co. v. Bicron Corp.*: "where patent law acts as a barrier, trade secret law functions relatively as a sieve.[2624] Reverse engineering promotes follow-on innovation by disseminating knowledge, even if not as directly as a patent specification, and gradually diminishes the market power of the first-comer. Thus, if customers contract out reverse engineering, information may never enter the public domain.[2625] In turn, this enhances the position of the trade secret holder, who may retain exclusivity in the market, to the detriment of their competitors. As noted by Samuelson and Scotchmer, the possibility of excluding reverse engineering is particularly problematic in markets that depend on IPRs, as these were established in order to regulate the scope of exclusive rights and their limitations and provide for the most adequate balance.[2626]

Consequently, the possibility that the legislator is allowed to establish that contractual clauses that offset this balance shall be null and void (Recital 16) appears sound from a policy perspective. It ensures that secrecy progressively erodes and that new competitors can enter the market, con-

---

program user could obtain information within the limits prescribed by the directive but that he could not use it, would run counter to the directive's very purpose of guaranteeing a certain minimum access to interface information in order to ensure interoperability. Therefore, Article 9(1) (now 8(1)) must be understood as meaning that the interface information which may mandatorily be obtained without infringement of exclusives right, may not be retained by contractual restrictions based on trade-secret protection".

2623 Gintare Surblyte, 'Enhancing TRIPS: Trade Secrets and Reverse Engineering' 725, 750-753 in Hanns Ullrich and others (eds), *TRIPS plus 20 - From Trade Rules to Market Principles* (Springer 2016).
Case T–201/04 *Microsoft v Commission* [2007] ECR II-03601, para 650.

2624 *Kewanee Oil Co.v. Bicron Corp*, 416 U.S. 470, 490 (1974).

2625 However, Michael Risch, 'Hidden in Plain Sight' [2017] 31 Berkeley Technology LJ 1635, 1652 argues in favour of applying such clauses to non-visible aspects of software, as well as to visible aspects regardless of whether they constitute trade secrets.

2626 Pamela Samuelson and Suzanne Scotchmer 2002 (n 226) 1660.

sidering its specific characteristics.[2627] Indeed, an absolute bar on such clauses without considering the specific circumstances of each market seems too far reaching and disregards their importance in pre-contractual negotiations. However, the validity of such clauses will have to be assessed in accordance with national civil law and, in particular, the provisions that regulate standard business terms.[2628]

### 3) Guiding principles

The analysis conducted reveals that the reverse engineering limitation is central to striking the optimal balance between the interests of trade secrets holders, competitors and third parties because it allows for the erosion of secrecy, which leads to the incorporation of information in the public domain. Therefore, to ensure that such a limitation is construed in a uniform manner across the EU the following interpretive remarks are presented.

First, drawing from the principles presented in chapter 4, and in order to delineate the boundaries of secrecy, the mere placing on the market of a product in which a trade secret is embodied does not automatically reveal all of the trade secrets associated with it. To hold otherwise would substantially limit the subject matter protected by the law of trade secrets.[2629] Instead, only those features (i) that are readily apparent upon inspection of the product, or (ii) that can be devised with little time and cost shall be deemed to have been made available. Secrecy remains with regard to the intrinsic features or processes that can only be devised after the investment of substantial time, effort and, in particular, cost and intellectual skill. In addition, if a secret is unveiled after a costly process of reverse engineering it shall not be automatically regarded as publicly available for the purposes of trade secrets law. The deciding factor is whether the information has been so widely disseminated within an industry that the competitive advantage conferred by it has disappeared.

Second, it should be noted that the wording of Article 3(1)(b) TSD does not allude to the actions of *use* and *disclosure*. Indeed, during the negotiation process, representatives from certain sectors (such as the perfume in-

2627 Pamela Samuelson and Suzanne Scotchmer 2002 (n 226) 1653.
2628 Christian Alexander 2017 (n 1091) 1041 referring to the test of reasonableness of content enshrined in § 307 BGB.
2629 Tanya Aplin 2014 (n 384) 271.

dustry) raised concerns as to the lawfulness of the subsequent use and disclosure of information acquired through reverse engineering, as well as regulatory disclosure. They claimed that allowing any subsequent use or disclosure would affect the "the functioning of the internal market and the commercial interests of the trade secret holder if it occurs without his permission and/or in a way contrary to fair commercial practices".[2630] Notwithstanding this consideration, following a systematic interpretation of the Directive, the subsequent use and disclosure of confidential information lawfully acquired through a process of reverse engineering should be a priori be permitted, unless contracted out. From a practical point of view, it does not always seem feasible to differentiate between the acquisition and subsequent use or disclosure of a trade secret.[2631] Also, from a policymaking perspective, it seems unsound to allow for the acquisition of secret information through reverse engineering and to prevent its subsequent use and disclosure: the economic justifications that apply to the acquisition of reverse engineered products also apply to any use and disclosure that follow, even if competing products are created.[2632] This fosters knowledge dissemination and ultimately strengthens competition in the market.[2633] Otherwise, the trade secret holder would be in a position similar to the patent holder, where the relevant technology is disclosed in the patent specification but competitors are not allowed to use it for commercial purposes.

However, when reverse engineering is so cheap, easy and rapid that it may have market destructive consequences, because it could undermine the incentive to invest in the creation of new products, there may be a case for prohibiting specific forms of reverse engineering or limiting the use of the products manufactured with the information obtained, for instance, by introducing a breath requirement with respect to the products obtained through a process of reverse engineering .[2634] Consequently, the products created as a result of the said process should meet a certain threshold of in-

---

2630 IFRA, 'Comments on the Proposal for a Directive on the Protection of Undisclosed Know-How and Business Information (Trade Secrets)' (2014) 2 <http://www.ifraorg.org/en-us/library/tag/21005/s0> accessed 15 September 2018.

2631 This is the view expressed by Annette Kur, Reto Hilty and Roland Knaak 2014 (n 383) para 35, who note that it is not always possible to differentiate between acquisition and use.

2632 Tanya Aplin 2013 (n 2511) 373.

2633 Tanya Aplin 2013 (n 2511) 372-373.

2634 Pamela Samuelson and Suzanne Scotchmer 2002 (n 226) 1653; Ansgar Ohly 2009 (n 98) 550.

novation; they cannot be mere replicas. This was the approach followed by the EU legislator with respect to semiconductor chip layout. Ultimately, by virtue of the principle of precedence of EU law over national legal regimes and considering that Article 3(1)(b) TSD constitutes a maximum standard of protection,[2635] the introduction of limitations that ban specific forms of reverse engineering or demand forward programming should be assessed and proposed by the EU legislator (not national lawmakers).[2636]

As a final note, it should not be overlooked that reverse engineering practices are also subject to the limitations imposed by IPRs and unfair competition regimes. If in the process of reverse engineering an IPR is infringed, the said act will trigger liability under the specific IPR regime, unless an exception is expressly included to that end, such as in the case of the reproduction right under copyright law to achieve the interoperability of a computer program. It should not constitute a defence to argue that the product has been reverse engineered.[2637] The admissibility of creating identical products is also subject to the scrutiny of national unfair competition rules and doctrines that regulate unfair copying.[2638] The scope of the freedom to imitate principle runs as a common threat in all jurisdictions, and the limitations to such a doctrine are applicable not only vis-à-vis formal IPRs, but also trade secrets.[2639]

### C) Competition law as an inherent limitation to the protection conferred by a trade secret

Competition law operates as the third limitation to the rights conferred by a trade secret, even though it is not expressly set out in the body of the TSD, only in Recital 38.[2640] In this regard, it should be noted that the relationship between trade secrets and competition law is of a two-fold nature. On the one hand, secrecy is essential to ensuring competition in the market. If every market participant had access to competitors' information, no

---

2635 This principle is enshrined in Case 6/64 *Flaminio Costa v ENEL* [1964] ECR 585, 593-594.

2636 Pamela Samuelson and Suzanne Scotchmer 2002 (n 226) 1653.

2637 Tanya Aplin 2013(n 2511) 376.

2638 Ansgar Ohly 2009 (n 98) 550; see § 4(3) UWG and Article 11 of the Spanish Unfair Competition Act.

2639 See chapter 1 § 3 B) III.

2640 See Recital 38 TSD.

competitive pressure in innovation would exist.[2641] Such a rationale is embedded within the policy goals that inform the TSD. In the Impact Assessment prepared by the Commission, it was noted that restrictions on the use of misappropriated secret information are justified "in order to promote an economically efficient and competitive process".[2642] Indeed, as argued in chapter 1, secrecy provides incentives to innovate, as it allows its holders to internalise the benefits of innovations. Yet, this should not be viewed as an absolute statement.[2643] An array of factors should be weighed up to assess whether trade secrets protection will in fact lead to innovation within the market, namely the degree of market power or the specific features of the industry.[2644] To be sure, as already noted, "in the case of trade secrets the law does not guarantee that the protected information contains innovation".[2645]

On the other hand, secrecy may lead to de facto exclusivity, even if trade secrets are not exclusive absolute rights by nature like other formal IPRs, such as patents or copyright.[2646] Indeed, the fact that a market participant is able to withhold information from the rest of his competitors may confer on him exclusivity, which may ultimately result in an abuse of market dominance pursuant to Article 102 TFEU. This is best illustrated by refer-

2641 Gordon L. Doerfer, 'The Limits on Trade Secret Law Imposed by Federal Patent and Antitrust Supremacy' [1967] 80 Harvard LR 1432, 1462: "Trade secret law serves a positive function in the promotion of competition by providing a needed lead time within which development costs can be at least partially recovered. On balance, because of the relatively small and speculative harm to competition and because the of the probable benefits to competition through the basic incentive of lead time, trade secret law does not seem inimical to free competition".

2642 See in this regard the Explanatory Memorandum attached to the Commission, 'Proposal for a Directive of the European Parliament and of the Council on the protection of undisclosed know-how and business information (trade secrets) against their unlawful acquisition, use and disclosure' COM (2013) 813 final, 2.

2643 See chapter 1 § 2 B) I.

2644 Gintare Surblyte, 'Enhancing TRIPS: Trade Secrets and Reverse Engineering' 725, 735 in Hanns Ullrich and others (eds), *TRIPS plus 20 – From Trade Rules to Market Principles* (Springer 2016).

2645 See also Josef Drexl 2011 (n 50) 182.

2646 See Recital 16 TSD: "In the interest of innovation and to foster competition, the provisions of this Directive should not create any exclusive right on the know-how or information protected as trade secrets"; see further Gintare Surblyte, 'Enhancing TRIPS: Trade Secrets and Reverse Engineering' 725, 735 in Hanns Ullrich and others (eds), *TRIPS plus 20 – From Trade Rules to Market Principles* (Springer 2016).

ence to the *Microsoft* case decided in 2007 by the GCEU (then CFI), following an appeal from a previous decision rendered by the Commission.[2647] The main facts and legal reasoning are summarised below.

In the 1990s, Microsoft was dominant in the EU market for PC operating systems through its Windows platform.[2648] In 1998, Sun Microsystems, Inc., a competing firm that supplies servers and server operating systems, lodged a complaint before the Commission, arguing that Microsoft's refusal to disclose information necessary to achieve interoperability amounted to an abuse of market dominance pursuant to Article 102 TFEU, as it prevented the plaintiff and other competitors from working as a group server operating system supplier.[2649] At this point, it should be recalled that both the Commission and the GCEU held that it was not commercially viable to reverse engineer Microsoft's interoperability information owing to its high cost and the fast moving nature of the software market.[2650] In its response, *Microsoft* argued that "the Interoperability information requested by Sun constitutes valuable intellectual property protected by copyright, trade secret laws and patents".[2651]

Against this factual pattern, the Commission and the GCEU applied the "exceptional facilities" test developed in connection with the refusal to license IPRs (*Volvo*,[2652] *Magill*,[2653] *IMS Health*)[2654] and deemed that Microsoft's conduct amounted to an abuse of market dominance. Notwithstanding this, the GCEU reshaped the test, considering the fast-moving na-

---

2647 *Microsoft* (Case COMP/C-3/37.792) Commission Decision 2007/53/EC [2007] OJ L32/23 and Case T–201/04 *Microsoft v Commission* [2007] ECR II-03601; for an in-depth analysis of trade secrets and their impact on competition law see: Gintare Surblyte 2011 (n 182); see also Josef Drexl 2011 (n 50) 185.

2648 *Microsoft* (Case COMP/C-3/37.792) Commission Decision 2007/53/EC [2007] OJ L32/23, para 15.

2649 At that time Article 82 EC Treaty.

2650 *Microsoft* (Case COMP/C-3/37.792) Commission Decision 2007/53/EC [2007] OJ L32/23, paras 685-687; see Case T–201/04 *Microsoft v Commission* [2007] ECR II-03601 para 362.

2651 *Microsoft* (Case COMP/C-3/37.792) Commission Decision 2007/53/EC [2007] OJ L32/23, footnote 249.

2652 Case 238/87 *AB Volvo v Erik Veng (UK) Ltd* [1988] ECR I- 6211.

2653 Joined Cases C-241/91 P and C-242/91 *Radio Telefis Eireann (RTE) and Independent Television Publications (ITP) v Commission of the European Communities* [1995] ECR I-00743.

2654 Case C–418/01 *IMS Health v NDC* [2004] ECR I-5039.

ture of the software industry and the legal nature of trade secrets.[2655] The latter are not formally IPRs, but may in fact confer exclusivity in the market on their holders.[2656] The test, as envisaged by the CJEU in *IMS Health*, takes into account four cumulative elements.[2657] In the first place, the supply of the product must be indispensable for conducting the specific business. Secondly, the refusal to license must prevent the emergence of a new product. Thirdly, such a refusal cannot be justified on objective grounds. Finally, it excludes competition in a secondary market.[2658]

In *Microsoft* the cardinal question was whether the new product requirement, as laid down in *IMS Health*, would mean that Sun could develop a new product other than a group serving operating system, which was already offered by Microsoft. It was against this specific background that the Commission and the GCEU departed from the CJEU's case law and turned to the wording of Article 102(b) TFEU.[2659] The GCEU noted that the appearance of a new product should not be the only criterion:[2660]

> The circumstances relating to the appearance of a new product, as envisaged in Magill and IMS Health, cited in paragraph 107 above, cannot be the only parameter which determines whether a refusal to license an intellectual property right is capable of causing prejudice to consumers within the meaning of Article 82(b) EC. As that provision states, such prejudice may arise where there is a limitation only of production or markets, but also of technical development.

In the case of *Microsoft*, the value of the information did not lie in its technological superiority but rather in its secret nature, which prevented other

---

2655 Gintare Surblyte 2011 (n 182) 129; *Microsoft* (Case COMP/C-3/37.792) Commission Decision 2007/53/EC [2007] OJ L32/23, para 118 and Case T–201/04 *Microsoft v Commission* [2007] ECR II-03601, para 635.

2656 A new standard of intervention is proposed by Surblyte Gintare Surblyte 2011 (n 182) 213-217, who argues that owing to the fundamental differences in the legal nature of trade screts and formal IPRs, the legal test applied should be a different one.

2657 As clarified by the CJEU in Case C–418/01 *IMS Health v NDC* [2004] ECR I-5039, para 38.

2658 Beatriz Conde Gallego, 'Unilateral refusal to license indispensable intellectual property rights – US and EU approaches'215-238 in Josef Drexl (ed), *Research Handbook on Intellectual Property and Competition Law* (Edward Elgar, 2008).

2659 See Gintare Surblyte 2011 (n 182) 128-133, T-201/04 *Microsoft v Commission* [2007] ECR II-03601, para 128-133.

2660 Case T–201/04 *Microsoft v Commission* [2007] ECR II-03601, para 647.

potential competitors from entering the market.[2661] This poses a number of questions vis-à-vis the complementarity theory that governs the relationship between IPRs and competition law. In effect, the prevailing approach is that IPRs and competition law strive to achieve the same objective, namely, to foster competition and innovation.[2662] [2663] However, in the case of trade secrets, protection is afforded without taking into consideration whether the information covered is in fact innovative.[2664] Furthermore, where access to information is key to enter a specific market, the likelihood of monopolisation is high if the law affords protection to trade secrets (or access to information in general).[2665]

In addition, as already noted,[2666] contractual agreements between the parties that limit the use of trade secrets may result in a restrain of competition and therefore are also subject to the scrutiny of competition law under Article 101 TFEU and the corresponding block exemption regulations approved to improve the production or distribution of goods and to promote technical or economic progress, such as the TTBER and the R&DBER.

In sum, it seems that secrecy is necessary to foster competition in the market. Yet, as seen in the example of *Microsoft*, under certain circumstances it may lead to an abuse of dominant position prohibited under to Article 102 TFEU or a restrain of competition proscribed under Article 101 TFEU. In such a context, competition law may arise as a necessary limitation to secrecy. Such a rationale has been incorporated as part of the TSD in Recital 38, which lays down the prevalence of Articles 101 and 102

---

2661 Josef Drexl 2011 (n 50) 182-183.

2662 Josef Drexl, 'Intellectual Property and Antitrust Law – IMS Health and Trinko – Antitrust Placebo for Consumers Instead of Sound Economics in Refusal-to-Deal Cases' [2004] IIC 788, 792.

2663 Commission, 'Guidelines on the application of Article 81 of the EC Treaty to technology transfer agreements' [2004] OJ C101/2, para 7: "Indeed, both bodies of law share the same basic objective of promoting consumer welfare and an efficient allocation of resources. Innovation constitutes an essential and dynamic component of an open and competitive market economy. Intellectual property rights promote dynamic competition by encouraging undertakings to invest in developing new or improved products and processes. So does competition by putting pressure on undertakings to innovate. Therefore, both intellectual property rights and competition are necessary to promote innovation and ensure a competitive exploitation thereof".

2664 Josef Drexl 2011 (n 50) 181.

2665 Josef Drexl 2011 (n 50) 183.

2666 Chapter 6 § 1 B).

TFEU and sets out that the provisions of the Directive should not provide legal grounds to restrict competition in a manner contrary to the TFEU.

## *§ 3 The optimal scope of secrecy: a balanced approach in the light of the TSD*

Trade secrets play a central role in many industries, where they are deemed essential assets to appropriate returns from innovation, particularly when no formal IPR protection applies, such as in the perfume industry. Their strategic importance for economic growth and competitiveness prompted the Commission to harmonise this area of law among the EU Member States. Yet, during the negotiation process concerns were raised regarding the optimal scope of secrecy and its effect on creative and innovative industries. In fact, the analysis conducted throughout this thesis underscores the difficulties in finding the appropriate strength of trade secrets protection. To be sure, if the scope is too broad, follow-on innovation and free speech may be hindered. Conversely, if the protection of secret information is tailored in a manner that is too narrow, the incentives to create valuable information will be substantially diminished, which in turn may lead to market failure in certain industries where formal intellectual property protection falls short, such as the cosmetics industry. Considering the above, this section explores potential solutions to define the optimal scope of secrecy.

### A) The Nordhaus model and trade secrets protection

First, it should be recalled that trade secrets may last for as long as the information that they cover remains undisclosed. This is a well-established principle among EU jurisdictions as well as in the U.S., and results from the interplay between the patent system and the trade secrets legal framework.[2667] In fact, the duration of trade secrets may exceed that of patents or copyright.[2668] Pursuant to TRIPs, the patent term of protection is twenty years from filing.[2669] Similarly, copyright protection lasts for at least fifty

2667 Accordingly, the TSD does not set forth any term of protection.

2668 But note that for trade marks the term of protection extends for as long as the mark is used in commerce and the appropriate fees are paid.

2669 See Article 33 TRIPs.

years after the death of the author.[2670] It is generally regarded that misappropriation, reverse engineering and independent creation limit the duration of secrets and make them more vulnerable than any other IPR.[2671] However, in some instances this may not be possible and the holders of undisclosed information may be able to exploit it in an exclusive manner with no end in sight, which may ultimately affect the possibility of competitors to innovate.

A prime example of the potentially perpetual duration of trade secrets is the Coca-Cola formula, which was developed over one hundred and twenty-five years ago and remains one of the most valuable secrets of all time.[2672] In the same vein, in the software industry, the practical difficulties of reverse engineering Microsoft's interoperability information were one of the main hurdles that competitors faced in entering the operating systems market. As highlighted both by the Commission and the GCEU (then CFI), it was not commercially viable to reverse engineer Microsoft's interoperability information owing to its high cost and the fast moving nature of the software market.[2673] In this regard, Scotchmer noted that, "unlike other forms of intellectual property, trade secret allow owners to supress knowledge".[2674] Such a statement is at odds with the need to reconcile the need to provide incentives to innovate for trade secret holders and the interests of the public at large in using such information.[2675]

When reverse engineering is too costly and lengthy, the holder of the secret will be able to reap the fruits of his innovation perpetually (or after the patent term) without complying with the disclosure obligations imposed by the patent system and the knowledge spill-over derived from it.

From a law and economics perspective, the optimal strength of trade secrets protection has been analysed from four different, yet not necessarily

---

2670 See Article 12 TRIPs; but note that in many jursidictions, such as the EU and the U.S., the term has been extended to seventy years.

2671 Mark A Lemley 2008 (n 15) 352-353.

2672 See 'Coca-Cola Moves Its Secret Formula to The World of Coca-Cola' (The Coca-Cola Company, 8 December 2011) <http://www.coca-colacompany.com/press-center/press-releases/coca-cola-moves-its-secret-formula-to-the-world-of-coca-cola/> accessed 15 September 2018.

2673 *Microsoft* (Case COMP/C-3/37.792) Commission Decision 2007/53/EC [2007] OJ L32/23, paras 685-687; Case T–201/04 *Microsoft v Commission* [2007] ECR II-03601, para 362.

2674 Suzanne Scotchmer 2004 (n 41) 81. However, the author further notes that "the law encourages the sharing and sale of ideas"; see also Robert G. Bone 1998 (n 15) 281.

2675 Mark A. Lemley 2008 (n 15) 353.

mutually exclusive, angles. The most prominent theory, purported by Friedman, Landes and Posner, is that the optimal scope of secrecy should be determined by reference to the liable conduct i.e. the lawful ways of acquiring, using and disclosing secret information and the costs and benefits associated with it.[2676] For instance, as has already been examined, allowing competitors to obtain a secret through reverse engineering off-sets the cost of preventing such conduct, due to the benefits triggered by follow-on innovation. However, if no trade secrets protection were afforded against theft, the expenditure on self-help measures by trade secrets owners would be very high, which in turn would increase the expenditure of competitors and consequently lead to a wasteful arms race.[2677] This approach seems to be the one followed by the EU legislator in view of the broad array of exceptions and lawful conducts laid down in the TSD. Other scholars propose that the optimal scope of protection should be modulated during the enforcement phase, i.e. through establishing the amount of damages.[2678] In a similar vein, it would be possible to limit the subject matter eligible for trade secrets protection.[2679] This seems to be one of the principles applied to foster employee mobility: the skills and knowledge acquired during the normal course of the employee's work do not constitute a protectable trade secret.[2680] Finally, a fourth possibility would be to limit the duration of protection, which is a major theme of discussion in the field of patent law, but has garnered little attention with regard to trade secrets.

To study the optimal scope of trade secrecy, this thesis focuses on duration as a key parameter and looks into the inherent trade-off between static and dynamic efficiency, particularly in the context of technical inventions. To do so, it applies the Nordhaus model, which was developed to analyse the optimal length of patent rights.[2681] Nordhaus' concept has been at the centre of the patent policy discussion for the last fifty years, not least be-

2676 David D. Friedman, William M. Landes and Richard A. Posner, 'Some Economics of Trade S–et Law' [1991] 5 J Econ Perspectives 61, 67-70.

2677 David D. Friedman, William M. Landes and Richard A. Posner, 'Some Economics of Trade Secret Law' [1991] 5 JEP 61, 69; see more generally chapter 1 § 2 B) III.

2678 Thomas Rønde, 'Trade secrets and information sharing' [2001] 10 J of Economics & Management Strategy 391-417.

2679 Luigi A. Franzoni and Arun Kaushik, 'The optimal scope of trade secrets law' [2016] 45 International Review of Law and Economics 45, 45.

2680 This issue has been analysed under chapter 6 § 1 A) II.

2681 William D. Nordhaus, *Invention Growth, and Welfare: A Theoretical Treatment of Technological Change* (The MIT Press 1969) 10.

cause duration arguably represents the most direct way in which legislators can control the scope of rights.[2682]

As examined in chapter 1, patents equip the innovator with exclusionary rights so that he can reap the benefits of his invention.[2683] These benefits are necessary to incentivise the inventor to conduct costly and uncertain R&D investments. However, the innovator's monopoly rents come at a cost for society, because the profit maximising product price in a monopoly is higher than in a competitive environment. This excludes some consumers who are not able pay the monopoly price. This so-called "deadweight loss" reduces the benefits for society coming from the invention. Limiting the exclusionary rights to a specific duration, such as is the case for patents with a maximum length of twenty years, seeks to achieve a compromise between the costs in static efficiency,[2684] due to the exclusion of consumers, and the costs in dynamic efficiency,[2685] due to insufficient incentives for innovators.

In sum, there is a social cost in extending IPR induced monopolies beyond the duration necessary to incentivise the innovator. This is also true in the case of secrecy induced monopolies. However, the investment necessary for invention differs greatly between industries. For instance, pharmaceutical inventions are particularly investment-intensive, but also come with potentially large benefits for society.[2686] By setting the duration of protection to a very long period or even making it infinite, these kinds of investment-intensive inventions become worthwhile; however, inventors in other fields are provided with unnecessarily long monopolies. Nordhaus, for the first time, analysed this trade-off and argued for a finite duration of patents. He theoretically concluded that after a certain patent duration, the social benefits generated by more costly new innovations no longer compensated for the dead-weight loss from the prolongation of monopolies.[2687] Hence, a socially optimal patent duration cannot be infinite.

In the light of the above argument, this thesis posits that following the Nordhaus Model by analogy, trade secrets protection should also be finite. Yet, it does not seem advisable to impose a fixed term duration as it exists

2682 François Lévêque and Yann Ménière, *The Economics of Patents and Copyright* (The Berkeley Electronic Press 2004) 25.
2683 The following arguments draw from the synthesis of the Nordhaus model provided in Lévêque and Ménière 2004 (n 2682).
2684 François Lévêque and Yann Ménière 2004 (n 2682) 26.
2685 François Lévêque and Yann Ménière 2004 (n 2682) 19.
2686 François Lévêque and Yann Ménière 2004 (n 2682) 46.
2687 François Lévêque and Yann Ménière 2004 (n 2682) 32.

for formal IPRs.[2688] Protection should cease when the additional incentive from the prospect of secrecy is marginal, while the social costs of maintaining an artificial monopoly rather remain constant. In such a case, the social benefits generated by the innovation would no longer compensate for the dead-weight loss from the prolongation of a monopoly.[2689] Consequently, from a legal perspective the duration of trade secrets would be best modulated by the inclusion of an exception to infringement claims. Here, the alleged infringer could counterclaim that trade secrets protection should not be enforceable if the dead-weight loss prevails in the above mentioned welfare trade-off. The problem, however, is that the information necessary to conduct such an assessment is, if at all, only in the possession of the trade secret holder. Third parties hence cannot evaluate in a reliable manner the point in time when the investment devoted to the development of the secret has been recouped and ultimately, from a welfare perspective, when they should be free to use the information.

Notwithstanding this, the final chapter of the dissertation has highlighted the relevance of contractual agreements in maintaining secrecy intra companies (with employees), but also extra companies (with regards to suppliers, licensees or R&D partners). Consequently, a manner of modulating the finite duration of secrecy protection would be to introduce a general presumption in the context of business-to-business agreements, by virtue of which the duration of secrecy and non-use obligations is limited to four years after the termination of the contract, unless the parties expressly agree otherwise. The contours of such a presumption are analysed in the following section.

### B) Legal application of the Nordhaus model to trade secrets protection: introduction of a presumption regarding post-contractual duration in business-to-business relationships

Contractual provisions that regulate non-disclosure obligations play a central role in deferring the entrance of information into the public domain both with regard to the internal and external spheres of secrecy of a company. Therefore, a potential legal application of the Nordhaus model

2688 Mark A. Lemley 2008 (n 15); Michael P. Simpson, 'The Future of Innovation: Trade Secrets, Property Rights, and Protectionism—An Age-Old Tale' [2005] 70 Brooklyn LR 1121, 1156-1158.

2689 Mark A. Lemley 2008 (n 15) 353.

would be to introduce a general presumption within the TSD that limits the duration of non-disclosure and non-use obligations in business-to-business contracts (including non-business entities, such as universities and research institutions) to four years after the termination of the agreement, unless the parties expressly agree for another term of duration. The wording of the proposed clause reads as follows:

> *In business-to-business agreements (including non-business entities) that regulate the acquisition, use and disclosure of trade secrets by virtue of which the parties undertake not to disclose and not to use the information that constitutes the object of the agreement after its termination, failure to mention the term of such obligations shall limit their duration to four years after the termination of the contract. In any case, these obligations will cease to exist once the information no longer meets the requirements for protection established in Article 2(1) of the present Directive for reasons not attributed directly or indirectly to the parties to the agreement to which the trade secrets have been disclosed.*

The introduction of the above reproduced contractual presumption is in line with the principle supported in many civil law jurisdictions by virtue of which obligations of an indefinite duration are considered non-enforceable by courts,[2690] which has also been questioned by the German competition authority in the context of licensing agreements that establish long post-contractual obligations of confidentiality (15 years).[2691] Consequently, the introduction of such a limited duration presumption in the absence of an express agreement between the parties would enhance legal certainty in post-contractual scenarios across the EU and would allow to strike a balance between the conflicting interests of trade secret holders and their commercial partners.

In effect, on the one hand, trade secret holders would be protected against unauthorised disclosure and use for four years after the termination of the contract. This would allow them to recoup the investment made in the creation of the information while ensuring that the recipient is prevented from taking advantage of the knowledge gained on the basis

2690 In Spain the invalidity of obligatons without a finite term is enshrined in Article 1583 of the Civil Code and has been the object of numeros judicial decisions such as STS de 14 de marzo de 2013. It has also been acknowledged by the most relevant civil law commentaries, such as Luis Díez-Picazo, *Fundamentos del derecho civil patrimonial*, vol II (5th edn, Tecnos 1996) 323.

2691 See BKartA 1977 TB 94.

of an extinct contractual relationship. On the other hand, the applicability of this presumption would ensure that the recipient of the information is not unreasonably burdened with secrecy and non-use obligations, the duration and scope of which were not clearly identified during the negotiation of the agreement. Indeed, the duty of loyalty invoked in many jurisdictions to justify secrecy obligations, which is inherent to the very nature of the employment relationship, is applied with more difficulty in business-to-business relationships among competitors. It is for this reason that the scope of such a presumption should only be applicable in business-to-business contractual agreements, such as R&D agreements, licensing agreements and agreements with suppliers concluded between legal entities and not in business-to-consumer or employment contracts. However, considering that one of the main goals of the Directive is to foster research and innovative efforts, such a presumption should also apply with respect to contractual agreements in which at least one of the parties is a non-business entity, such as a university or research institution.

Crucially, the duration of the non-disclosure and non-use obligation is first and foremost dictated by the will of the parties, in line with the principle of party autonomy that governs civil law. Only in the absence of a specific agreement regarding the duration, the four year post-contractual presumption becomes relevant. The fact that the proposed provision states that non-disclosure and non-use obligations cease once the information no longer meets the requirements of protection for a trade secret stipulated in Article 2(1) TSD ensures that the parties that receive the information are not bound to keep it secret and not use it after it has become generally known among the relevant circles, which would seem unreasonable considering that the object of the contract has ceased to exist. Yet, if the secret is lost for reasons attributable to one of the parties to which the trade secret was disclosed, the secrecy and non-use obligations should remain enforceable with respect to that party, in line with Article 13(2) TSD. By way of contrast, clauses that provide that confidentiality and non-use obligations last until the information becomes generally known should be considered valid, because such a wording provides sufficient legal certainty to the parties at the time that the contract is concluded regarding the temporal scope of the obligations undertaken. It is also in line with the view expressed by competition authorities and the TTBER, which consider that no competition law issues arise with respect to the agreements that regulate the non-use and disclosure of the licensed technology rights after the expiry of the agreement, provided that the rights remain valid and in force.[2692]

Following the line of reasoning suggested by English courts in the context of licensing agreements, the reference to non-disclosure obligations is understood to include also the non-use of the information object of the contract, unless the terms of the agreement provide otherwise.[2693] Indeed, from a systematic perspective it does not always appear feasible to differentiate between use and disclosure because often the use of the information leads to its disclosure. Consequently, in post-contractual scenarios non-disclosure obligations also entail non-use of the information. According to the proposed presumption, in the absence of a specific term of duration, such obligations will be limited to four years after the termination of the agreement.

The recourse to contractual presumptions to balance the interests of the contracting parties is not alien to the IRPs legal system and is frequently included in copyright laws to safeguard the rights of authors, who are deemed to be in a weaker bargaining position than their counterparties. For instance, Article 43(2) of the Spanish Copyright Act provides that in an inter vivos assignment, failure to mention the time limits the assignment to five years.[2694] In the case of non-disclosure and non-use obligations, the four year duration term has been proposed as the default rule as a compromise between the various terms suggested by the different authors.[2695] In effect, in innovation-driven economies, the innovation race renders most technology known among competitors within a few years. Thus, the four years term seems to provide the optimal balance between the interests of all contracting parties.

Ultimately, it should be noted that the relevant provisions of the TRIPs Agreement that regulate undisclosed information do not require that any exceptions to the right conferred comply with the three-step test envisaged for copyright (Article 13 and Article 17 TRIPs), patent rights (Article 30 TRIPs), trade mark rights (Article 17 TRIPs) and design rights (Article

---

2692 Commission, 'Guidelines on the application of Article 101 of the Treaty on the Functioning of the European Union to technology transfer agreements' [2014] OJ C89/3, para 183 (c).

2693 See chapter 6 § 1 B) I. 2. c).

2694 See María del Carmen Gete-Alonso Valero, 'Artículo 43' 756, 784 in Rodrigo Bercovitz Rodríguez-Cano (ed), *Comentarios a la Ley de Propiedad Intelectual* (3rd edn, Tecnos 2007).

2695 See chapter 6 § 1 B) I. 2.c) and chapter 6 § 1 B) II.2.

26(2) TRIPs). Consequently, the implementation of the proposed presumption would not result in a breach of the TRIPs Agreement.

# Conclusion

The so-called "Digital Revolution" has allowed companies and individuals to generate and share information faster than ever before. This has entailed radical shift in the traditional paradigm of creating, accessing, and transmitting information. Indeed, information has become a good few would still associate with scarcity and a lack of conveyance. Hence, it is no coincidence that in 2016 two major jurisdictions on both sides of the Atlantic sought to harmonise and strength the law of trade secrets. In May of 2016, the U.S. Congress passed the DTSA, while a month later, the Council adopted the TSD, following the approval by the EU Parliament. Such a legislative convergence evidences the strategic role that valuable confidential information plays for the competitiveness and growth of companies. However, as underscored throughout this dissertation, if trade secret legislation affords excessively wide protection, free speech and follow-on innovation might be set back. In light of the harmonisation goals pursued by the EU legislature, the primary aim of this study has been to examine the circumstances under which information loses its secret nature, with a view of finding a balanced solution to the optimal scope of secrecy.

The point of departure in such an appraisal is to understand the extent to which valuable information merits protection for the mere fact of being kept secret. As outlined in chapter 1, protection is justified both from a deontological and utilitarian perspective. However, utilitarian arguments appear to provide more solid grounds. To be sure, the law of trade secrets generates incentives to create information, even if not necessarily innovative. According to Duffy and Merges, it spurs market experimentation that allows undertakings to generate data. It also fosters cooperation and the sharing of information among market participants, even if such information is not ultimately disclosed to the general public. Furthermore, it allows companies to strike the optimal balance between the measures adopted to protect their secret information. Most importantly, it provides a Laboratory Zone in which companies can develop their innovations and market strategies without the interference of competitors. This is essential to ensure that patentable inventions are deemed novel and therefore eligible for protection. As noted by the Commission, "every IPR starts with a secret".[2696]

Ultimately, such a statement begs the question of whether trade secrets should be considered as a form of property (or intellectual property) or instead as falling under the realm of unfair competition. In fact, a certain overlap may occur between the subject matter protected under the law of trade secrets and the patentable subject matter (and to a lesser extent copyright and the sui generis database right). Numerous studies show that when patents and trade secrets are mutually exclusive to each other, secrecy is the preferred method to appropriate returns from innovation. In this particular scenario, resorting to trade secret protection may undermine the disclosure function on which the patent system is built and may lead to a wasteful duplication of efforts, impairing competitive processes and follow-on innovation.

The dissertation has looked into the consequences of characterising trade secrets as a pure IPR or rather as falling under the realm of unfair competition rules and the implications that this may have on the scope of secrecy. Against this background, it has been submitted that the legal system for the protection of trade secrets presents an inherent hybrid legal nature. The relevant liability rules resemble unfair competition norms, whereas their enforcement seems very close to formal IPRs. Hence, in chapter 1 it has been argued that no legal consequences should derive from considering trade secrets as a form of intellectual property or as the object of unfair competition rules, i.e. the scope of protection should not be enhanced if trade secrets are regarded as IPRs. This is also the approach followed by the EU legislator in the TSD. Recital 16 merely sets out that the provisions of the Directive should not create any exclusive right on the information protected as a trade secret. Therefore, it seems that Member States are free to adopt either approach, as long as no absolute proprietary erga omnes rights are conferred upon the holder. The lawfulness of the conduct should remain at the centre of the assessment.

At the international level, Article 39 TRIPs laid down the minimum standards of protection, which created common ground across the EU jurisdictions, even though substantial differences in their implementation and the scope of protection persisted. Indeed, the requirements for protec-

2696 Commission 'Explanatory Memorandum, Proposal for a Directive of the European Parliament and of the Council on the protection of undisclosed know-how and business information (trade secrets) against their unlawful acquisition, use and disclosure' 2.

tion set out in Article 39(2) have been included as the normative definition in Article 2(1) TSD. Hence, to merit protection information must be (i) secret; (ii) derive economic value from its secret nature and (iii) the holder must adopt reasonable measures under the circumstances to keep it secret. These are closely interconnected and ultimately reveal that the law of trade secrecy is concerned with the protection of the investment made in creating valuable information, but only against specific conducts that do not comply with the accepted market practices. Information is protected by the mere fact of being kept secret and providing its holder a competitive advantage. No additional qualitative threshold beyond secrecy has to be met. As a result, if the information is disclosed, the competitive advantage disappears. However, only if the acquisition, use or disclosure is carried out in a manner contrary to honest commercial practices, the holder of the information concerned will be able to seek legal redress.

The comparative analysis conducted in chapter 3 has underscored that despite the existence of common ground, prior to the implementation of the Directive, there were substantial differences in the regulation of trade secret protection across the Single Market and consequently, the level of protection varied substantially from one Member State to the other. For instance, regarding the liability of third parties, under German law conditional intent was required, whereas in England the threshold was much lower and referred to the observance of the standard of care followed by a honest person placed under the same circumstances. In addition, in Germany, it was unclear what remedies courts may award. Similarly, the assessment of the information that departing employees were free to use in their new positions and under which circumstances reverse engineering should be deemed lawful remained unsettled in both jurisdictions.

Against this background, in order to ensure the good functioning of the Single Market and to create a level playing field for the holders of valuable confidential information, the European Parliament passed the TSD, which was adopted by the Council on 8 June 8 2016, and which should be implemented in all EU jurisdictions before 9 June 2018. The Directive has managed to find a reasonable equilibrium between the interests of trade secrets holders in keeping their information concealed and the interest of third parties in accessing such information. To this end, the Directive sets out of a number of flexible and open-ended clauses, by virtue of which the appraisal of the lawfulness of a conduct is carried out by reference to the general standard of honest commercial practices enshrined in Article 10bis PC. The establishment of independent discovery and reverse engineering as lawful forms of acquiring a trade secret is crucial to strike such a balance and to preserve the complementarity between the patent system and the trade secrets regime. In this context, the EU legislator has further laid down an array of exceptions to the rights conferred by a trade secret that safeguard the fundamental freedoms of expression and information and deem whistle-blowing lawful. Wisely, the applicability of these exceptions will ultimately depend on the balance of interests conducted by the competent national authorities. As a whole, the flexibility principle that informs the Directive, together with the minimum standards of protection, allows for considering all the relevant interests in each individual case and for adapting to future technological developments. However, it may result in divergent interpretations among Member States, thus hindering the ultimate harmonisation goals pursued by the EU lawmaker.

With regard to the secrecy standard, the TSD provides little interpretative guidance as to when information should be regarded as secret or as part of the public domain. This is mostly because the assessment of secrecy is of a factual nature and should be carried out on case-by-case basis. It is not possible to extract a normative test from the secrecy prong, unlike the novelty or inventive step requirements in patent law. Notwithstanding this, construing and defining the contours of private rights and the intangible objects to which they refer is of utmost importance in every legal regime.

Drawing on the foregoing conclusion, the dissertation has delved into the notion of secrecy by application of the methodology of comparative law, which has revealed that this standard is of a relative nature. Consequently, it is possible to share the information with a limited number of recipients, as long as the holder retains control and can prevent unwanted disclosures to third parties. According to Article 2(1)(a) if information is readily or accessible, it is automatically deemed part of the public domain. Ultimately, such an analysis is of an economic nature. If third parties with an interest can gain knowledge of the information concerned without incurring in great labour, intellectual skill or cost, the information should be regarded as readily ascertainable and thus, as being automatically part of the public domain. Conversely, secrecy is preserved if the interested third parties cannot acquire the information without that substantial amount of resources (i.e. undergoing the same intellectual development process as the trade secret holder). To hold otherwise would equate the secrecy standard to the absolute novelty standard followed in patent law and would render the secrets embodied in a product automatically part of the public domain upon their first sale. Instead, secrecy remains with regard to the intrinsic features or processes that can only be devised after the investment of substantial time, effort and cost. In particular, following the English case law, it has been submitted that the need to invest intellectual skill should be considered as the decisive factor that indicates that the information is secret. Ultimately, this is consistent with the utilitarian rationales analysed in chapter 1, by virtue of which, the law of trade secrets attempts to preserve the investment made in the creation of information.

The research has further attempted to conceptualise the notion of secrecy by reference to its negative dimension, i.e. when information enters the public domain. Taking a case-oriented approach, the effects of specific disclosures have been examined following the methodology of comparative law and a number of guiding principles have been proposed to ensure a homogeneous interpretation across the EU once the Directive is implemented. In view of the increasing vulnerability of information in the last decade, particular emphasis has been placed on the effects of disclosure in the digital age, such as disclosures to the state and its authorities, Internet disclosures, the protectability of combination secrets and cloud computing. In all of these instances, a dedicated analytical framework has been proposed to assess whether the information merits protection under the trade secrets liability regime. In this context, the suitability of resorting to trade secrets protection for Big Data sets has also been examined and an analytical framework to assess whether large streams of raw data may be legible for protection under the TSD has been suggested in order to avoid privatising information in the public domain.

In chapter 5 the perfume industry has been used as a study case to illustrate the increasing challenges that the holders of valuable information face in keeping it undisclosed. From a legal perspective the investigation has revealed that there is no single IPR that affords protection to perfumes as such. In addition, the empirical research conducted highlights that trade secrets play a central role in allowing scent manufacturers to appropriate returns from their creations an small incremental innovations. However, it has also revealed that their formulas can be reverse engineered at a very low cost by competitors, which reduces the incentives to create such products

The empirical analysis has further shown that secrets are most frequently ascribed to companies, which usually adopt physical and legal measures to protect them. In particular, in the adoption of these measures two distinct spheres can be identified. First, the internal sphere of secrecy, which refers to the preservation of confidential information within the company and mostly concerns employees, because they are the ones that regularly have access to valuable secret information in the performance of their duties.

Secondly, the external sphere of secrecy refers to the adoption of legal and physical measures in order to avoid the unauthorised use and disclosure of trade secrets by third parties such as suppliers, service providers, licensees or R&D partners that may have accessed the information with authorisation, but for a specific purpose. More generally, it also intends to preserve trade secrets from the interference of third parties. Consequently, chapter 6 has examined the relevance of contractual provisions (legal measures) to ensure secrecy in the two spheres identified.

During the course of the employment relationship, employees are bound not to disclosed trade secrets on the basis of a duty of loyalty. However, the application of such a duty in post-contractual scenarios appears more complex, particularly considering that the TSD provides that employees should not be prevented from using the skills, knowledge and experienced gained in the normal course of their employment in their new position. Hence, resorting to NDAs and non-competes appears to be the best way to conceal trade secrets from competitors. However, these agreements may negatively affect the career development of employees and stifle follow-on innovation. Consequently, the admissibility of such contractual provision is subject to different requirements in different Member States, as it has not been harmonised across the EU by the TSD.

The external sphere of secrecy refers to the preservation of confidentiality against the unlawful use and disclosure of trade secrets by third parties that may have accessed the information with authorisation from the holder but only for a limited time, or in order to achieve a specific purpose. This is typically the case of licensing agreements, where the trade secret holder grants the licensee the right to use the secret information in exchange for the payment of an agreed fee. In effect, in order to exploit trade secrets, their holders are required to carefully balance a number of competing interests. On the one hand, they should attempt to share the information with as few people as possible in order to limit the risk of disclosure and the resulting loss of the competitive advantage conferred by its secrecy. Indeed, once the information has left the internal sphere of the company, it cannot be reintroduced due to the inherently irreversible nature of cognitive processes: what has been learnt cannot be unlearnt.[2697] On the other, to maximise the economic potential of trade secrets, their holder may have to share the information with a substantial number of parties, particularly in the absence of funding resources, manufacturing capabilities or technical knowledge that allow for the development of the final product. Conse-

2697 Stefan Maaßen and Tobias Wuttke 2011 (n 2404) Rdn 38-40.

quently, the contractual clauses that regulate the use and subsequent revelation of trade secrets are in licensing and R&D agreements should be carefully drafted.

After examining the internal and external spheres of secrecy and its limitations, this dissertation has considered the possibility that secret information might never be unveiled, as some secrets are after all impenetrable. Therefore, it has been submitted that under specific circumstances, trade secrets protection should be finite, following the rationale applied in the Nordhaus model to justify limits in patent duration. However, it does not seem sound to set a fixed term of duration, such as for formal IPRs. In view of the casuistic nature of trade secret protection, it is argued that after some time protection should cease, even if the object of protection remains concealed. This would be best articulated by means of an exception in an infringement claim. The alleged infringer could counterclaim that trade secrets protection should not be enforceable if the dead-weight loss prevails in the above mentioned welfare trade-off. The problem, however, is that the information necessary to conduct such an assessment is, if at all, only in the possession of the trade secret holder. Third parties hence cannot evaluate in a reliable manner the point in time when the investment devoted to the development of the secret has been recouped and ultimately, from a welfare perspective, when they should be free to use the information.

Notwithstanding this, the dissertation has highlighted the relevance of contractual agreements in maintaining secrecy intra companies (with employees), but also extra companies (with regards to suppliers, licensees or R&D partners). Consequently, the thesis has propose to modulate the finite duration of secrecy protection by introducing a general presumption in the context of business-to-business agreements, by virtue of which the duration of secrecy and non-use obligations is limited to four years after the termination of the contract, unless the parties expressly agree otherwise.

# Annex 1: Transcript of the Interview with head of IP Perfume Company 1

The interview was held on July 10, 2015.

1. **Do you regard trade secrets (both of commercial and technical nature) as an important asset for your company? Do you prefer other alternative methods of protection such as patents?**
   Trade secrets are very important assets for the Company. The protection that they confer is used alongside patent rights, even though the latter are perceived as being too costly, both as regards the cost of maintenance and enforcement.
2. **What is the IP strategy followed by your company against fragrance imitations?**
   We implement a multiple strategy.
   In the first place, the formulas are always kept secret. In addition, we keep a close relationship with our suppliers and employees to avoid dissemination of confidential information.
   As regards trade mark rights, for every registered trade mark we keep a file with evidence of its reputation.
   Finally, we try to use very expensive ingredients in order to avoid that low-cost manufacturers can come up with an imitation of our perfumes. The exclusivity of a perfume, to a certain extent, is achieved through the price of its components.
3. **Is it possible to obtain the formula of a perfume through reverse engineering?**
   It is not possible to give a straightforward answer to this question, as there are many nuances that come into play.
4. **Could you please provide an example of some legal or physical measures that are adopted in the company to protect valuable trade secrets?**
   <u>Physical measures</u>
   1. Limit the number of people who have access to the information on a need-to-know basis. Only people that need to work with the information concerned have access to it.
   2. Limited use of email to share information.

3. Sometimes, personalized copies of a document are handed in to specific recipients, who must sign them. The signatory thereby undertakes an obligation to guard and not to disclose the information contained in its copy.

Legal measures

1. The company considered the possibility of requiring employees and third parties to sign NDA. Yet, this was ultimately rejected, as it was considered that it would convey the idea that only specific information is confidential and the rest is free to use by employees.

**5. Is information fragmented within the Company?**

Yes. For instance, each perfumist can only access the formulas that he is developing.

**6. Does the Company foresee specific measures to prevent departing employees from using secret information in their new position?**

We believe that this topic is closely connected with the values of the Company, We try to limit as much as possible employee mobility and want our employees to stay with for as long as possible.

**7. Do you believe that trade secrets have become increasingly vulnerable in the last decade?**

Yes. In addition, we have also noticed that imitations come to the market much faster, in some instances, even before the original product.

**8. Do you take into account the risk of losing confidential information during judicial proceedings before taking legal action in the event of misappropriation?**

We have not litigated any case of misappropriation, but the likelihood of leakage would certainly be one of our main concerns if we decided to take legal action.

**9. Do you believe that the risk of losing confidential information has a negative impact on the possibility of establishing cooperation agreements with other companies?**

It is a controlled risk. We only collaborate with companies that we know that are diligent in the protection of our trade secrets. In these cases, it is of utmost importance for us to build a relationship based on mutual trust.

**10. How do you assess the Directive ?**

We do not have an official corporate view on the Directive.

# Annex 2: Transcript of the interview with Perfumist Rosendo Mateu

The interview was held on June 20, 2015.

1. **Is it important to disclose the content of perfumes?**
   Some years ago, dermatologist in the Scandinavian countries published a number of studies warning about the toxicity of some components that were regularly used by perfume manufacturers in small quantities, such as musketone. As a result, the EU legislator has imposed strict disclosure obligations. However, few cases have been documented where an adverse reaction has actually occurred. Nonetheless, the legislation in the EU is more restrictive than in other jurisdictions. ,
2. **How is the process of creating a formula?**
   The creation of a perfume has both a creative and a technical dimension. It is a very complex process. It takes me months, even years to create a perfume. The process is as follows: usually, a brand (such as fashion designer) and its marketing team get in touch with scent manufacturers (or providers). In turn, the scent manufacturers have an in-house team of perfumists, who are commissioned the creation of a perfume, under the aesthetic guidance of the marketing team of the fashion company.
   Only a few fashion brands like Chanel and Hermes have their own in-house perfumist. Nowadays, this is very rare.
3. **Could you clarify if imitations of perfumes, such as the ones sold through comparison lists, have the same quality as the original ones?**
   From my experience, perfumes sold through comparison list are usually of lower quality than the original perfume.
4. **This is leads as to the question of whether a perfume can actually be reverse engineered.**
   This is a very complex question. Nowadays, there is technology that allows finding a formula that is very similar to the original one. It works as follows: a small amount of the original perfume is introduced into a chromatograph. The machine heats the perfume up to 250°C. During the stationary phase, the mass spectrum identifies each of the components of the formula. The technology has improved, so that the formu-

la can be reproduced in a very precise manner. However, high-end perfumes are more expensive because they have very expensive components. Imitations and lower-end perfumes have less quantity of organic compounds and higher amounts of dissolvent, which is cheaper. For instance, a kilogram of concentrate of rose scent of good quality costs around 600 euros. In this regard, it should be noted that higher end perfumes now have lower quality than some years ago. A lot of expenditure goes into the marketing.

It is very important to identify the provider of a perfume. For example, the lemon scent in Spain is cheaper than the Italian one. The key lies in the machines used. The Italian ones only peel a very thin layer of the lemon, where scent is more intense. Spanish manufacturers, peel a thicker layer, so that the scent is less intense and cheaper.

5. **How are formulas best protected against misappropriation or imitation?**

   If one of the synthetic compounds of the formula is patented, this provides a very strong protection against competitor's imitations. However, please note that RD is usually carried out by scent manufactures. Fashion labels do not deem it important. The problem lies in meeting the inventiveness hurdle.

   What I do is to divide the formula into several parts. Usually, each of the scents providers had a part of the formula. Only preparators of a specific formula had access to the entire formula, but only of a specific perfume.

# Zusammenfassung

Im digitalen Zeitalter sind Informationen zu einem zunehmend wertvollen, aber gleichzeitig gefährdeten Gut geworden. Unternehmen, welche in der wissensbasierten Wirtschaft weltweit tätig sind, lagern ihre Forschungs- und Produktionstätigkeiten auf der Suche nach Kostenoptimierung und dem am besten qualifizierten Personal vermehrt in andere Länder aus. In einem solchen globalisierten Kontext bewirkte die EU-Kommission aufgrund der strategischen Rolle, die Geschäftsgeheimnisse für die Wirtschaft des Binnenmarktes spielen, und des uneinheitlichen rechtlichen Rahmens für Geschäftsgeheimnisse in den EU-Rechtssystemen eine Angleichung dieses Rechtsrahmens. Dies führte zur Verabschiedung der Geschäftsgeheimnisse-Richtlinie[2698] (GGR), die bis zum 9. Juni 2018 in allen EU-Mitgliedstaaten hätte umgesetzt werden sollen. Diese Dissertation untersucht die Grundlagen des Gesetzes für das GGR. Insbesondere wird die Grundlage des Schutzes von Geschäftsgeheimnissen analysiert: die Geheimnisvoraussetzung. Das Hauptziel der Dissertation ist die Analyse der Bedingungen, unter denen Informationen ihren geheimen Charakter verlieren, öffentlich zugänglich sind und den Wettbewerbern unter Berücksichtigung der durch die GGR geschaffenen rechtlichen Rahmenbedingungen zur Verfügung stehen. Zwar sind die Anforderungen zum Schutz von formellen geistigen Eigentumsrechten wie Urheberrechten oder Patenten seit Jahren Gegenstand akademischer Studien. Den Anforderungen zum Schutz von Geschäftsgeheimnissen und den Implikationen ihrer Definition im engeren oder weiteren Sinne wurde jedoch wenig Aufmerksamkeit gewidmet.

Vor diesem Hintergrund geht die Dissertation den folgenden Forschungsfragen nach. Zunächst wird untersucht, ob der Schutz von Geschäftsgeheimnissen allein dadurch schon gerechtfertigt ist, dass jene Wettbewerbern unbekannt sind. Zweitens soll im Verhältnis zwischen formellen Schutzrechten des geistigen Eigentums und Geschäftsgeheimnissen untersucht werden, ob Gesetze über Geschäftsgeheimnisse in den Rechtsbe-

2698 Richtlinie (EU) 2016/943 des Europäischen Parlaments und des Rates vom 8. Juni 2016 über den Schutz vertraulichen Know-hows und vertraulicher Geschäftsinformationen (Geschäftsgeheimnisse) vor rechtswidrigem Erwerb sowie rechtswidriger Nutzung und Offenlegung [2016] OJ L157/1.

reich des geistigen Eigentums oder des unlauteren Wettbewerbs fallen. Anschließend wird analysiert, wie die Geheimhaltungsvoraussetzung in Deutschland und England bis zur Umsetzung der Richtlinie ausgelegt wurde. Diese Länder wurden ausgewählt, weil sie vor der Harmonisierung zwei der offenbar wirksamsten Modelle zum Schutz von Geschäftsgeheimnissen in der EU verwenden. Basierend auf dieser vergleichenden Studie werden in der Dissertation Gemeinsamkeiten identifiziert, die eine weitere Harmonisierung der Anforderungen ermöglichen würden. Des Weiteren prüft die Dissertation die strategische Bedeutung der Geheimhaltung als Mittel zur Aneignung von Erträgen aus Innovationen im Vergleich zu formalen Rechten des geistigen Eigentums und untersucht die Auswirkungen neuer Technologien auf die durch Geheimhaltung gewährte Vorlaufzeit. Letztendlich zielt die Dissertation darauf ab, in diesem Kontext eine ausgewogene rechtliche Lösung für den optimalen Umfang des Schutzes der Geheimhaltung vorzuschlagen.

Zur Beantwortung der oben genannten Forschungsfragen werden in Kapitel 1 zunächst die potenziellen Gründe für den Schutz von Geschäftsgeheimnissen nach der Klassifizierung in deontologische und utilitaristische Ansätze im Zusammenhang mit Theorien des geistigen Eigentums untersucht. Erstere umfassen (i) die Notwendigkeit, den Standard der Wirtschaftsethik-Theorie aufrechtzuerhalten, (ii) die Arbeitswerttheorie, nach der die Person, die Informationen erstellt, ein Recht auf diese Informationen und den Ausschluss Dritter hat, und (iii) die von John Rawls entwickelte Vertragstheorie, die die Notwendigkeit eines Schutzes von Geschäftsgeheimnissen rechtfertigt, basierend auf der Annahme, dass rationale Individuen sich unter dem sogenannten ‚Schleier des Nichtwissens' auf einen solchen Schutz einigen würden. Der inhärente offene Charakter des Standards für Handelsethik bietet keine soliden Gründe, um die Verwendung von Informationen durch ausscheidende Angestellte oder das Erhalten von Informationen durch Rekonstruktion, also Reverse Engineering, anzugehen. In ähnlicher Weise rechtfertigt die Arbeitswerttheorie die Ausnahmen und Beschränkungen des Schutzes von Geschäftsgeheimnissen nicht, da der Schutz unabhängig von den Mitteln zur Erlangung der Informationen gewährt werden sollte. In Bezug auf die Vertragstheorie ist es schließlich fraglich, ob die Stakeholder in der realen Welt dieselbe Vereinbarung erzielen würden.

Diese Arbeit macht daher geltend, dass utilitaristische Argumente besser geeignet sind, um die Verabschiedung von Vorschriften zu rechtfertigen, die den Schutz von Geschäftsgeheimnissen vor Unterschlagung regeln. Solche Regeln schützen das tatsächliche Geheimnis und ermöglichen es dem Ersteller von Informationen, sich die Vorteile seiner (inkrementellen) Innovation anzueignen. Hierdurch wird potenzielles Marktversagen bei der Entwicklung von Informationen verhindert, die nicht unter den allgemeinen Schutz der Rechte des geistigen Eigentums fallen. Entscheidend ist, dass der Schutz von Geschäftsgeheimnissen in seiner Funktion als Innovationsanreiz Marktexperimente und die Entwicklung des Geschäfts an sich fördert. Entsprechend den Anreizen, die Begründung offenzulegen, werden auch die Transaktionskosten für die kommerzielle Nutzung vertraulicher Informationen gesenkt, es wird die Zusammenarbeit zwischen den Marktteilnehmern gefördert und die Fragmentierung von Informationen im internen Bereich des Unternehmens verhindert. Vor allem verhindern Geschäftsgeheimnisgesetze verschwenderisches Wettrüsten zwischen Unternehmen bei der Einführung von Schutzmaßnahmen und bieten Unternehmen eine sogenannte ‚Laboratory-Zone', in der sie ihre Innovationen ohne Einmischung Dritter entwickeln können.

Während einige der oben untersuchten Doktrinen, wie etwa die Vertragstheorie und die Anreize zur Erneuerung von Grundsätzen, für andere geistige Eigentumsrechte (Patente und Urheberrechte) üblich sind, dienen andere entgegengesetzten Interessen. Beispielsweise verfolgen die Anreize zur Offenlegung von Doktrinen, die im Zusammenhang mit Geschäftsgeheimnissen entwickelt wurden, andere Ziele als die patentrechtliche Offenlegungsfunktion. Ein solches Spannungsfeld führt unweigerlich zu der Frage, inwiefern Geschäftsgeheimnisse mit anderen geistigen Eigentumsrechten zusammenhängen und ob sie als eine Art von ihnen hätten konzeptioniert werden oder ausschließlich unter das Paradigma des unlauteren Wettbewerbs fallen sollen.

Um diese hervorstechende Frage zu beantworten, untersucht die Dissertation die Beziehung und die Überlappung zwischen Geschäftsgeheimnissen und anderen geistigen Eigentumsrechten und beginnt mit den drei Szenarien, in denen Geschäftsgeheimnisse und Patente zusammenwirken können: (i) Geschäftsgeheimnisse vor dem Patentieren; (ii) Bevorzugung des Geschäftsgeheimnisses gegenüber Patenten und (iii) Kombination des Patentschutzes mit dem Schutz von Geschäftsgeheimnissen. In Bezug auf das erste Szenario ist zu beachten, dass Unternehmen vor dem Erreichen der Patentierbarkeitsstufe in der Regel kostspielige und langwierige Entwicklungsbemühungen vornehmen müssen, insbesondere um eine Erfindung mit einem gewissen Grad an gewerblicher Anwendbarkeit zu entwickeln. Dieses Verfahren sollte in einem Arbeitsumfeld durchgeführt werden, in dem die Geheimhaltung gewährleistet ist, um sicherzustellen, dass

Erfindungen die Neuheitsanforderung erfüllen, wie in Artikel 54 EPÜ[2699] festgelegt, und die sich letztendlich auf die oben erwähnte Laborzone bezieht. Andernfalls würde die Erfindung in den öffentlichen Bereich fallen und wäre nicht patentrechtlich geschützt. In der Praxis nehmen sich Interessenvertreter die Zeit, um aus betriebswirtschaftlicher Sicht zu beurteilen, ob sie ein Patent beantragen oder sich für einen informellen Schutz entscheiden. Tatsächlich bietet der durch das EPÜ geschaffene rechtliche Rahmen dem Erfinder, der vor der Patentierung auf Geheimhaltung angewiesen ist, einen gewissen Schutz, so dass die Erfindung genutzt werden kann, sofern sie nicht vor dem maßgeblichen Prioritätstag der Öffentlichkeit zugänglich gemacht wird. In ähnlicher Weise werden vertraulich offengelegte geheime Informationen für die Zwecke der Prüfung der patentrechtlichen Neuheit nicht als verfügbar betrachtet. Dieser Ansatz steht im Einklang mit dem Argument der Kommission, dass jedes geistige Eigentumsrecht mit einem Geheimnis beginnt, und unterstreicht die Komplementarität von Patenten und Geschäftsgeheimnissen, deren Schutz für das reibungslose Funktionieren des Patentsystems unerlässlich ist.

Ungeachtet der oben angeführten Punkte, zeigt eine Überprüfung der verfügbaren Wirtschaftsdaten, dass die Wahl zwischen Patentschutz und Geschäftsgeheimnissen, wenn sich beide ausschließen (zweites Szenario), vom Zusammenspiel einer Reihe von Faktoren abhängt. In erster Linie bevorzugen die Inhaber von Informationen den Schutz von Geschäftsgeheimnissen, wenn die Kosten des Patentsystems im Vergleich zum Wert der Erfindung zu hoch sind oder der erwartete Gewinn unter ihrem Wert liegt. Dies wäre der Fall, wenn die Erfindung in kürzerer Zeit als der Patentdauer von 20 Jahren entschlüsselt werden kann (‚reverse engineering'). In einem solchen Fall scheinen die mit dem Patentsystem verfolgten Ziele und die gesetzlichen Bestimmungen über Geschäftsgeheimnisse unvereinbar zu sein, da der Inhaber des Geschäftsgeheimnisses die Früchte seiner Bemühungen möglicherweise unbegrenzt ernten kann. Geschäftsgeheimnisse sind jedoch nicht nur bei Erfindungen im Frühstadium entscheidend, sondern auch dann, wenn Innovationen gleichzeitig durch Geschäftsgeheimnisse und Patente geschützt werden können (drittes Szenario). In diesem Fall werden die Unternehmen von beiden Aneignungsmechanismen Gebrauch machen. Einerseits werden Verfahren oder Produkte, die die Patentierbarkeitskriterien erfüllen, durch das Patentgesetz geschützt, während spezifischere Informationen, die nicht zwingend in der

2699 Übereinkommen vom 5. Oktober 1973 über die Erteilung Europäischer Patente (Europäisches Patentübereinkommen) (EPC).

Patentanmeldung offengelegt werden müssen, durch Geheimhaltung geschützt werden. In Anbetracht der Tatsache, dass der Gegenstand, der unter Geschäftsgeheimnissen geschützt werden kann, breiter ist als bei Patenten, kommt die Arbeit zu der Schlussfolgerung, dass das gleichzeitige Vertrauen auf den Schutz der Rechte an geistigem Eigentum und Geschäftsgeheimnisse die Exklusivität erhöht und eine Rückfallposition darstellt, wenn die anderen Rechte am geistigen Eigentum nicht durchsetzbar sind.

Obwohl die offensichtlichste Wechselwirkung zwischen Geschäftsgeheimnissen und formellen geistigen Eigentumsrechten auf Patente Bezug nimmt, kann es auch zu Überschneidungen hinsichtlich des durch das Urheberrecht geschützten Gegenstands kommen, insbesondere im Hinblick auf den Schutz von Computerprogrammen. Sowohl der Objektcode als auch der Quellcode sind gemäß den urheberrechtlichen Bestimmungen geschützt, obwohl Software-Hersteller in der Regel auf den Schutz von Geschäftsgeheimnissen für den Objektcode und das Urheberrecht für den Quellcode zurückgreifen. Dadurch können sie den Marktzugang anderer Softwareentwickler behindern, die mit einem neuen Programm konkurrieren möchten. Im Markenbereich besteht dagegen praktisch keine Möglichkeit, dass sich der Schutzgegenstand mit Geschäftsgeheimnissen überschneidet. Marken sind zwar wertvoll, weil sie den Verbrauchern Informationen vermitteln, jedoch liegt der Wert von Geschäftsgeheimnissen in ihrer verborgenen Natur. Dennoch ist es möglich, dass die gleichzeitige Verfügbarkeit von Geschäftsgeheimnissen und Marken weitere Anreize für die Erstellung beider Arten von Informationen bietet. Dies wird am besten durch die Parfümindustrie veranschaulicht, in der die Formeln leicht durch Reverse Engineering enthüllt werden können und kein geistiges Eigentumsrecht einen absoluten Schutz für Duftstoffe als solche bietet. In diesem Zusammenhang bieten die Markenrechte zusätzliche Anreize, indem sie den Parfümen eine Aura der Exklusivität und des Luxus verleihen, so dass ihre Hersteller die Kosten für die Entwicklung dieser Art von Feinprodukten tragen können, wie dies in der vom EuGH getroffenen Entscheidung *L'Oréal v Bellure*[2700] verdeutlicht wird. Abschließend wird auch die Wechselwirkung zwischen dem Schutzgegenstand der des Datenbankregimes der Geschäftsgeheimnisse-Richtlinie untersucht. Im Rahmen der harmonisierten Regelung kann (i) die Struktur einer Datenbank urheberrechtlich geschützt sein, während (ii) ihr Inhalt durch das Datenbankrecht *sui generis* vor erheblicher Entnahme und Wiederverwendung geschützt werden kann und (iii) gegen unrechtmäßigen Erwerb, Verwendung und

2700 Case C–487/07 *L'Oréal v Bellure* [2009] ECR I-05185.

Offenlegung nach dem Gesetz der Geschäftsgeheimnisse, sofern der Inhalt nicht allgemein bekannt ist. Vor diesem Hintergrund wird geltend gemacht, dass die Einbeziehung von Geheimhaltungsvereinbarungen, die den Zugang, die spätere Verwendung und die Offenlegung von Informationen in einer Datenbank regeln, insbesondere für den Schutz von Geschäftsgeheimnissen relevant ist. Dies ist ausdrücklich der Fall für ausschließliche Quellendatenbanken, die nicht betroffen sind von den in der Datenbankrichtlinie festgelegten obligatorischen Ausnahmen.

In Anbetracht der obenstehenden Überlegungen analysiert die Dissertation die Rechtsnatur von Geschäftsgeheimnissen nach der Rechtsvergleichungsmethodik. Auf internationaler Ebene definiert das Übereinkommen über handelsbezogene Aspekte der Rechte des geistigen Eigentums (TRIPs-Abkommen)[2701] nicht offenbarte Informationen als „Arten des geistigen Eigentums", während der Schutz nicht offenbarter Information im Gesetz gegen den unlauteren Wettbewerb durch Verweis auf Artikel 10bis der Pariser Verbandsübereinkunft verankert ist.[2702] In England haben die Gerichte traditionell den Gedanken abgelehnt, dass Informationen durch ein Eigentumsrecht geschützt werden können, auch wenn in einer kürzlich ergangenen Entscheidung im Fall *Vestergaard v Bestnet*[2703] darauf hingewiesen wurde, dass Geschäftsgeheimnisse im Rahmen der Durchsetzungsrichtlinie als Gegenstand geistigen Eigentums betrachtet werden sollten. In den USA weist der Defend Trade Secrets Act (DTSA) darauf hin, dass Geschäftsgeheimnisse „kein geistiges Eigentum" sind, „wenn auf andere Bundesgesetze (‚Act of Congress') Bezug genommen wird", obwohl der Oberste Gerichtshof der USA im Fall *Ruckelshaus v. Monsanto Co*[2704] die Rechtsnatur von Geschäftsgeheimnissen als geistiges Eigentum bestätigt hatte. Folglich wird der Wortlaut in der DTSA dahingehend ausgelegt, dass eine Normenhierarchie festgelegt und die Anwendbarkeit der Safe-Harbour-Bestimmung für Online-Intermediäre im Sinne des § 230 des Communications Decency Act sichergestellt wird. Unterschiede zwischen Ländern bestehen auch im Zivilrecht. Beispielsweise werden gemäß Artikel 1 des italienischen Gesetzes über das gewerbliche Eigentum von 2005 Geschäftsgeheimnisse als eine Art von geistigen Eigentumsrechten betrach-

2701 Übereinkommen über handelsbezogene Aspekte der Rechte des geistigen Eigentums (unterzeichnet am 15. April 1994) (TRIPs-Abkommen).

2702 Pariser Verbandsübereinkunft zum Schutz des gewerblichen Eigentums, (Beschluss am 29. März 1883, abgeändert in Stockholm am 14. Juli 1967 und erneut abgeändert am 28. September 1979) 21 UST 1583, 828 UNTS 305 (PC) .

2703 *Vestergaard Frandsen A/S v Bestnet Europe Ltd* [2011] EWCA Civ 424 (CA).

2704 *Ruckelshaus v. Monsanto Co.*, 467 U.S. 986 (1984).

tet. Dies wurde von einer Reihe von Rechtswissenschaftlern vehement kritisiert, welche der Auffassung sind, dass dies zur Schaffung eines neuen Schutzrechts mit erga omnes Effekt führt. In Deutschland scheint die Rechtsprechung ebenfalls keine eindeutige Lösung zu bieten. Kommentatoren sind sich jedoch einig, dass die Einstufung von Geschäftsgeheimnissen als geistige Eigentumsrechte praktische rechtliche Auswirkungen hat. Wenn sie tatsächlich als Eigentumsrechte betrachtet werden, sollte ihr Schutz durch die Eigentumsklausel des deutschen Grundgesetzes (Artikel 14) sowie der §§ 823 I, 812 I und 687 des Bürgerlichen Gesetzbuchs (BGB) gewährleistet werden.

In Bezug auf die GGR kommt die Arbeit zu der Schlussfolgerung, dass die Richtlinie die Mitgliedstaaten nicht zwingend verpflichtet, Geschäftsgeheimnisse als Rechte am geistigen Eigentum zu schützen. Folglich wird geltend gemacht, dass das in der Richtlinie eingeführte Rechtssystem zum Schutz von Geschäftsgeheimnissen eine inhärente hybride Rechtsnatur hat. Die einschlägigen Haftungsregeln scheinen als unlautere Wettbewerbsnormen zu gelten, während ihre Durchsetzung der von Rechten am geistigen Eigentum ähnelt. Aus diesem Grund wird der Schluss gezogen, dass keine rechtlichen Konsequenzen daraus resultieren sollten, dass Geschäftsgeheimnisse als Rechte am geistigen Eigentum betrachtet werden, d. h., der Schutzbereich sollte bei der Umsetzung der Richtlinie in nationale Rechtsvorschriften nicht erweitert werden. Folglich sollte die Beurteilung der Rechtmäßigkeit des Verhaltens im Mittelpunkt der Beurteilung stehen, ob eine Verletzung vorliegt.

In Anbetracht dessen, dass die Konturen der Geheimnisvoraussetzung in der EU im Hinblick auf die auf internationaler Ebene festgelegten Verpflichtungen und Flexibilitäten gestaltet werden sollten, prüft Kapitel 2 die im TRIPS-Abkommen festgelegten Mindeststandards für den Schutz und das geltende Rechtssystem in den USA, welches als Ausgangspunkt für die Verhandlungen der Uruguay-Runde genommen wurde. In Übereinstimmung mit dem zuvor geprüften hybriden Naturargument verankert Artikel 39(1) TRIPS den Schutz von Geschäftsgeheimnissen in den Regeln des unlauteren Wettbewerbs, indem er auf Artikel 10bis PC Bezug nimmt. In Artikel 39 Absatz 2 TRIPS werden wiederum die drei miteinander verbundenen Anforderungen festgelegt, die Informationen erfüllen müssen, um Schutz zu verdienen: (i) Sie müssen geheim sein; (ii) wirtschaftlichen Wert haben, weil sie geheim sind, und (iii) Gegenstand von den Umständen nach angemessenen Geheimhaltungsmaßnahmen seitens der Person sein, unter deren Kontrolle sie rechtmäßig stehen. Diese drei kumulativen Anforderungen stellen Mindestschutzstandards dar, die für alle Mitgliedstaaten der Welthandelsorganisation (WTO) verbindlich sind. Letztendlich ergibt sich aus der gemeinsamen Betrachtung von Absatz 1 und Absatz 2 von Artikel 39 TRIPS, dass das Gesetz zum Schutz von Geschäftsgeheimnissen den Schutz von Investitionen zur Schaffung wertvoller Informationen zum Ziel hat; dies jedoch nur gegen bestimmte, vom Markt nicht akzeptierte Verhaltensweisen: die unbefugte Erfassung, Nutzung und Weitergabe wertvoller geheimer Informationen.

Die drei im TRIPs-Abkommen festgelegten Voraussetzungen für den Schutz beruhten auf den in den Hauptquellen des Gesetzes zum Schutz von Geschäftsgeheimnissen in den USA festgelegten Bestimmungen. In der Tat hat diese Rechtsprechung eines der am weitesten entwickelten Systeme zum Schutz von Geschäftsgeheimnissen entwickelt, das zu einer umfangreichen Rechtsprechung geführt hat. Bis zum Erlass der DTSA im Mai 2016 beruhten Zivilrechtsmittel im Falle einer Unterschlagung jedoch auf staatlichen Gesetzen, die dem Uniform Trade Secrets Act (UTSA) nachempfunden waren, und den Common-Law-Grundsätzen, die in den entsprechenden Abschnitten der Restatement (First) of Torts und der Restatement (Third) of Unfair Competition hinterlegt sind. Die erste Klage auf Bundesebene wurde 1996 im Rahmen des Economic Espionage Act erhoben und war strafrechtlicher Natur. Die Mängel einer derart zerstreuten Gesetzgebung wurden von der DTSA im Jahr 2016 überwunden, die im Falle einer Veruntreuung eine Zivilklage des Bundes einleitete und, ähnlich wie die UTSA, sechs potenzielle Arten von Verstößen gegen das Verhalten feststellte: (i) den Erwerb mit Wissen (oder Grund zu wissen), dass die Informationen auf unzulässige Weise erlangt wurden; (ii) die unbefugte Nutzung und Weitergabe von Informationen durch eine Person, die zum Erwerb unrechtmäßige Mittel verwendet hat; (iii) die Nutzung oder Weitergabe des Geschäftsgeheimnisses eines anderen mit Wissen (oder Grund zu wissen), dass es auf unzulässige Weise erworben wurde; (iv) die Offenlegung oder Nutzung eines Geschäftsgeheimnisses, wenn die Informationen unter Wahrung der Geheimhaltung oder der Einschränkung ihrer Nutzung erworben wurden; (v) die Offenlegung oder Nutzung eines Geschäftsgeheimnisses, das von einer Person stammt oder durch eine Person erlangt wurde, die der ersuchenden Person die Pflicht zur Aufrechterhaltung seiner Geheimhaltung oder Nutzungsbeschränkung geschuldet hat, und (vi) die Offenlegung und Nutzung eines Geschäftsgeheimnisses in Kenntnis dessen, dass dieses aus Versehen oder Irrtum erworben worden. Im Gegensatz dazu wurden Reverse Engineering und unabhängige Ableitung als rechtmäßige Mittel zum Erwerb eines Geschäftsgeheimnisses etabliert.

Vor dem Hintergrund der obigen Überlegungen untersucht Kapitel 3 die uneinheitliche Regulierung des Schutzes von Geschäftsgeheimnissen in den EU-Mitgliedstaaten, die zur Angleichung der nationalen Rechtssysteme in diesem Rechtsbereich geführt hat. Bislang unterschieden sich die Geschäftsgeheimnisregime erheblich, so dass das Schutzniveau von Land zu Land als ungleich anzusehen war. Trotz dieser Unterschiede identifizierten Kommentatoren sechs herausragende Modelle in Europa. Das erste ist das Modell Schwedens, des einzigen EU-Mitgliedstaats, in dem ein spezielles Gesetz zum Schutz von Geschäftsgeheimnissen erlassen wurde. Das zweite Modell ist das ‚IP-Modell', in dem Geschäftsgeheimnisse als geistiges Eigentumsrecht betrachtet wurden, wie dies durch das italienische Regime veranschaulicht wird. Drittens folgte Frankreich einem sogenannten ‚Hybridmodell', wobei *secrets de fabrique* in den *code* des gewerblichen Eigentums aufgenommen wurden, während *secret d'affaires* im weitesten Sinne auf der Grundlage allgemeiner unerlaubter Handlungen, unlauteren Wettbewerbs und strafrechtlicher Sanktionen geschützt wurden. Im Gegensatz dazu bauten die Länder, die dem vierten Modell folgten, wie Spanien und die Schweiz, ihre Geschäftsgeheimnisregelungen auf zivilrechtliche Bestimmungen auf, die in den Gesetzen zum unlauteren Wettbewerb verankert sind. Im fünften Modell, dem Länder wie Deutschland, Polen und Österreich folgten, beruhte der Schutz auf strafrechtlichen Bestimmungen, die Teil ihrer jeweiligen Gesetze zum unlauteren Wettbewerb waren. Schließlich hatten die Länder des sechsten Modells keine Bestimmungen zum Umgang mit Geschäftsgeheimnissen erlassen, der Schutz wurde jedoch auf die sogenannte *breach of confidence action* aufgebaut.

Vor dem Hintergrund einer derart fragmentierten Rechtslandschaft untersucht die Dissertation die letzten beiden Modelle, wobei die deutschen und englischen Rechtsordnungen als Studienfälle herangezogen werden. Die Methodik des Rechtsvergleichs wird angewendet, um erstens die beiden Rechtssysteme zu analysieren, welche zu zwei verschiedenen Rechtstraditionen gehören (Zivilrecht und Common Law), und zweitens die verschiedenen Mechanismen zu verstehen, durch die ein wirksamer Schutz erreicht wird. Darüber hinaus hatten beide rechtlichen Regelungen bei den Verhandlungen und der Konfiguration des harmonisierten Systems einen großen Einfluss und bilden daher den Ausgangspunkt für die kritische Analyse des entstehenden gemeinsamen Rahmens, der von der GGR eingeführt wurde und die Konturen der Nichtoffenkundigkeits-Voraussetzung umreißt. Aus methodologischer Sicht ist zu beachten, dass die Recherche für diese Dissertation vor der Implementierung der GGR in beiden Ländern abgeschlossen wurde und daher kein Hinweis auf den sich daraus ergebenden harmonisierten nationalen Rahmen gegeben wird. Trotz des Austritts des Vereinigten Königreichs aus der EU im März 2019 wird ferner darauf hingewiesen, dass die Untersuchung der englischen Rechtsprechung nach wie vor von großer Bedeutung ist, da die englischen Gerichte eine reiche und vielfältige Rechtsprechung haben, die es den Beteiligten ermöglicht, wirksame Rechtsmittel im Fall einer Verletzung in Anspruch zu nehmen.

Deutschland folgt dem fünften Modell. Daher sind die wichtigsten Bestimmungen zum Schutz von Geschäftsgeheimnissen in den §§ 17 bis 19 UWG enthalten, die sowohl zivilrechtlicher als auch strafrechtlicher Natur sind. Demgemäß ist zumindest ein bedingter Vorsatz erforderlich, um nicht nur eine strafrechtliche, sondern auch eine zivilrechtliche Haftung zu finden. In § 17 UWG werden drei Verhalten als Straftaten bezeichnet, die ebenfalls zivilrechtliche Schritte einleiten. Erstens verbietet § 17(1) UWG die unerlaubte Mitteilung von Geschäftsgeheimnissen im Rahmen der Beschäftigung. Das wesentliche Merkmal des in dieser Bestimmung beschriebenen Verhaltens ist, dass es ausschließlich von einer Person ausgeübt werden kann, die sich in einem Arbeitsverhältnis mit dem Unternehmen befindet. Der Geltungsbereich umfasst die unbefugte Übermittlung des Geschäftsgeheimnisses an alle Personen mit mindestens einem der folgenden Zwecke (‚Absicht'): (i) zu Zwecken des Wettbewerbs, (ii) aus Eigennutz, (iii) zugunsten eines Dritten oder (iv) in der Absicht, dem Inhaber des Unternehmens Schaden zuzufügen. Um eine Haftung auszulösen, muss die Mitteilung während der Dauer des Beschäftigungsverhältnisses des Verletzers abgeschlossen sein. Dementsprechend kann die Offenlegung geheimer Informationen nach Beendigung des Arbeitsverhältnisses nur zu einer Klage wegen Verletzung vertraglicher Verpflichtungen oder einer Straftat nach § 17 Abs. 2 UWG führen.

Zweitens verbietet Absatz 1 von § 17(2) UWG die unerlaubte Verschaffung oder Sicherung eines Geschäftsgeheimnisses, jedoch nur, wenn diese durch eines der folgenden unzulässigen Mittel ausgeführt wird: (i) die Anwendung technischer Mittel; (ii) Herstellung einer verkörperten Wiedergabe des Geheimnisses; oder (iii) die Wegnahme einer Sache, in der das Geheimnis verkörpert ist. Im Gegensatz zum Verhalten, das in § 17 Abs. 1 UWG beschrieben ist, kann es jedoch von jeder Person, nicht nur von Mitarbeitern, ausgeführt werden. Wieder müssen die relevanten Handlungen mit mindestens einem der folgenden Zwecke (‚Absicht') durchgeführt werden: (i) zu Zwecken des Wettbewerbs, (ii) aus Eigennutz, (iii) zugunsten eines Dritten oder (iv) in der Absicht, dem Inhaber des Unternehmens Schaden zuzufügen.

Drittens sieht Nummer 2 von § 17(2) UWG ein weitergehendes Verbot vor, wonach jemand aufgrund der Verwendung oder Weitergabe eines Geheimnisses bestraft wird, wenn er (i) das Geheimnis durch eine Mitteilung von einem Beschäftigten gemäß § 17(1) UWG erlangt hat oder (ii) durch eine eigene oder fremde Handlung das Geschäftsgeheimnis durch einen der in § 17(2) UWG Nummer 1 genannten Wege erlangt hat oder (iii) sich das Geheimnis anderweitig unbefugt verschafft oder gesichert hat. Aus praktischer Sicht macht ein derart breites Verbot den unbefugten Erwerb eines Geschäftsgeheimnisses rechtswidrig, wenn er von einem Arbeitnehmer oder einem Dritten ausgeübt wird. Diese Bestimmung ist besonders relevant, weil sie die rechtswidrige Nutzung von Geheimnissen erfasst, von denen ehemalige Angestellte während ihres Arbeitsverhältnisses mit dem Inhaber des Geschäftsgeheimnisses Kenntnis erhalten haben. Wie in den beiden vorigen Fällen müssen die relevanten Handlungen zu einer der folgenden Absichten durchgeführt werden: (i) zu Zwecken des Wettbewerbs, (ii) aus Eigennutz, (iii) zugunsten eines Dritten oder (iv) in der Absicht, dem Inhaber des Unternehmens Schaden zuzufügen.

§ 18 UWG wurde 1909 nach Beschwerden von Stickerei- und Spitzenherstellern eingeführt, um diese gegen die sogenannte ‚Vorlagenfreibeuterei' zu schützen. Heute beschränkt sich seine Verwendung auf den Schutz von technischen Anweisungen und Modellen, die im Rahmen von Know-how-Vereinbarungen bereitgestellt werden. In ihrer strafrechtlichen Dimension erfordert es zumindest wieder einen bedingten Vorsatz und die Durchführung des *actus reus* (unbefugte Verwertung oder Mitteilung) zu Zwecken des Wettbewerbs oder aus Eigennutz. In Anbetracht der vorangehenden Erwägungen scheint der Haftungsstandard nach deutschem Recht gegenüber Dritten höher zu sein als nach dem TRIPS-Abkommen und Artikel 4(4) GGR, wobei grobe Fahrlässigkeit ausreicht. Als letzte Anmerkung ist hervorzuheben, dass das UWG strafrechtliche Sanktionen für den Fall der Verletzung der §§ 17 und 18 vorsieht, jedoch keinen Hinweis auf die unter diesen Umständen verfügbaren Zivilklagen enthält, die auf der Grundlage der strafrechtsakzessorischen und zivilrechtsautonomen Ansprüche nach den einschlägigen Bestimmungen des BGB gewährt werden.

Ferner wird das sechste Modell untersucht, wobei die englische Gerichtsbarkeit als Fallstudie dient, in der der Schutz von Geschäftsgeheimnissen durch die *breach of confidence action* artikuliert wird. Diese Action wird auch verwendet, um andere Arten vertraulicher Informationen, wie künstlerische und literarische Informationen, Staatsgeheimnisse und private Informationen, zu schützen, und zwar unabhängig von dem Gegenstand. In England wurden im Gegensatz zu den USA und den meisten *civil law* Ländern keine speziellen rechtlichen Bestimmungen zum Schutz von Geschäftsgeheimnissen in Kraft gesetzt. Stattdessen wurden zunächst die Voraussetzungen geschaffen, um eine Haftung bei Verletzung des *breach of confidence* zu ermitteln, und zwar im wegweisenden Fall *Coco v A.N. Clark (Engineers) Ltd*[2705] und wiederholt in der nachfolgenden Rechtsprechung, wonach ein vierstufiger Test entwickelt wurde, um zu beurteilen, ob Informationen geschützt werden sollen. Das erste Element des Tests fragt, ob der Gegenstand der Informationen schutzfähig ist. Die zweite Haftungspflicht prüft, ob die Informationen die erforderliche Vertrauensqualität besitzen. Das dritte Haftungserfordernis verlangt, dass die Informationen unter Umständen übermittelt werden, die eine Vertrauenspflicht darstellen. Schließlich prüft das vierte Element, ob die Informationen auf unautorisierte Weise nachteilig für die Parteiquelle der Informationen angegeben wurden. In Bezug auf die Haftung Dritter hat die Rechtsprechung traditionell zwischen zwei möglichen Szenarien unterschieden. Das erste bezieht sich auf die Offenlegung von Informationen durch einen Dritten, der wusste, dass sie aufgrund eines Vertrauensbruchs erworben wurden. In einem solchen Fall ist der Dritte verpflichtet, sie nicht zu dem Zeitpunkt offenzulegen, an dem er sie erhält. Im zweiten Szenario erwirbt der Empfänger Informationen, ohne sich deren vertraulichen Charakters bewusst zu sein, und die Haftung entsteht ab dem Zeitpunkt, an dem er darüber informiert wird, dass die Informationen aufgrund eines *breach of confidence* erlangt wurden.

Aus den vergleichenden Analysen schlussfolgert die Arbeit, dass trotz einiger Gemeinsamkeiten bei bestimmten Aspekten des Schutzes von Geschäftsgeheimnissen erhebliche Unterschiede zwischen den englischen und deutschen Regelungen bestehen. Diese reichen von der mangelnden Klarheit über den Klagegrund, den die Parteien in England geltend machen können, bis hin zum zweifachen Schutz des Geschäftsgeheimnisses nach dem deutschen UWG. Unstimmigkeiten bestehen auch hinsichtlich der in Deutschland verfügbaren Rechtsbehelfe und der Anwendbarkeit der Durchsetzungsrichtlinie in England sowie hinsichtlich der Bedingungen, unter denen Reverse Engineering als rechtmäßig angesehen wird. In Anbetracht dieser Unterschiede und zur Förderung des Binnenmarktes ohne Hindernisse hat der Unionsgesetzgeber beschlossen, rechtliche Schritte zur Harmonisierung dieses Rechtsraums zu unternehmen. Daher hat das Europäische Parlament nach einem dreijährigen Verhandlungsprozess am 14. April 2016 die GGR verabschiedet.

2705 *Coco v A.N.Clark (Engineers) Ltd* [1969] RPC 41 (Ch).

Die Richtlinie ist in eine Präambel und vier Kapitel unterteilt, von denen die ersten drei den drei Hauptbereichen des Gesetzes über Geschäftsgeheimnisse entsprechen, die harmonisiert sind: (i) Gegenstand und Anwendungsbereich; (ii) Schutzumfang und (iii) Ansprüche. Aus legislativer Sicht ist zu beachten, dass in der Richtlinie Mindeststandards für den Schutz festgelegt sind und ausdrücklich erwähnt wird, dass die Mitgliedstaaten einen stärkeren Schutz als den im harmonisierten Text vorgesehenen einführen können, der kritisiert wurde, weil er die von den EU-Gesetzgebern verfolgten Harmonisierungsziele behindert. Es wurden jedoch einige Einschränkungen festgelegt, um die Einhaltung bestimmter Verpflichtungen sicherzustellen, beispielsweise im Zusammenhang mit der Definition des rechtswidrigen Erwerbs und der rechtswidrigen Nutzung und Offenlegung von Geschäftsgeheimnissen und der Ausnahmen von den durch ein Geschäftsgeheimnis gewährten Rechten.

In Bezug auf den Gegenstand unterliegt die GGR der gleichen Definition eines Geschäftsgeheimnisses wie das TRIPS-Abkommen (Artikel 2(1) GGR). Darüber hinaus wird klargestellt, dass der ‚Inhaber eines Geschäftsgeheimnisses' jede natürliche oder juristische Person ist, die die rechtmäßige Kontrolle über ein Geschäftsgeheimnis besitzt (Artikel 2(2) GGR). Im Gegensatz dazu wird der ‚Rechtsverletzer' als jede natürliche oder juristische Person betrachtet, die auf rechtswidrige Weise Geschäftsgeheimnisse erworben, genutzt oder offengelegt hat (Artikel 2(3) GGR). Der Begriff ‚rechtsverletzende Produkte' bezieht sich auf die Produkte, deren Konzeption, Merkmale, Funktionsweise, Herstellungsprozess oder Marketing in erheblichem Umfang auf rechtswidrig erworbenen, genutzten oder offengelegten Geschäftsgeheimnissen beruhen (Artikel 2(4) GGR). Diese Bestimmung wurde kritisiert, da zwar die Feststellung der Kausalität zwischen Konzeption und Herstellungsprozess eines Produkts unkompliziert sein kann, dies jedoch in anderen Fällen problematisch sein kann, insbesondere im Zusammenhang mit der Erbringung von Dienstleistungen, die auf einem verletzten Geschäftsgeheimnis oder der Marketingstrategie zur Vermarktung bestimmter Produkte beruht.

Das zweite Kapitel des GGR beginnt mit der Aufzählung einer Reihe von Arten von Verhalten, die als rechtmäßig angesehen werden sollen (Artikel 3). Dazu gehören der Erwerb von Informationen (i) durch unabhängige Entdeckung oder Schöpfung von Informationen, (ii) durch Reverse Engineering, (iii) durch Inanspruchnahme des Rechts der Arbeitnehmer oder Arbeitnehmervertreter auf Information und Anhörung und (iv) jede andere Vorgehensweise, die unter den gegebenen Umständen mit einer seriösen Geschäftspraxis vereinbar ist. Darüber hinaus sind der Erwerb, die

Nutzung und die Offenlegung durch EU- und nationale Regelungen vorgeben. Die Handlungsarten, welche in dieser Bestimmung geregelt sind, scheinen *ex ante*-Haftung für Verletzung auszuschließen, während die in Artikel 5 dargelegten Ausnahmen verlangen, dass die zuständige Justiz, unter Berücksichtigung der besonderen Umstände des Falls, eine Abwägungsprüfung durchführt.

Im Einklang mit den in Artikel 39(2) TRIPS festgelegten Mindeststandards hat der EU-Gesetzgeber festgelegt, dass der rechtswidrige Erwerb, die Verwendung und die Offenlegung von Geschäftsgeheimnissen Arten von Verstößen darstellen. Gemäß Artikel 4(2) wird der Erwerb eines Geschäftsgeheimnisses nur dann als rechtswidrig angesehen, wenn er ohne Zustimmung des Geschäftsgeheimnisinhabers erfolgt. Die Richtlinie definiert jedoch nicht das Konzept des ‚rechtswidrigen Erwerbs'. Stattdessen enthält sie eine Reihe von Beispielen von Handlungen, die als unrechtmäßiger Erwerb angesehen werden (unbefugter Zugang zu, unbefugte Aneignung oder unbefugtes Kopieren von Dokumenten, Gegenständen, Materialien, Stoffen oder elektronischen Dateien) und erklärt jedes sonstige Verhalten, das unter den jeweiligen Umständen als mit einer seriösen Geschäftspraxis nicht vereinbar gilt, als rechtswidrig. Sodann regelt Artikel 4(3) die rechtswidrige Nutzung und Offenlegung, welche auch aus der mangelnden Zustimmung des Geschäftsgeheimnisinhabers hervorgeht. Darüber hinaus muss der Verletzer das Geschäftsgeheimnis auf unrechtmäßige Weise gemäß Artikel 4(2) GGR erworben haben oder gegen eine Geheimhaltungsvereinbarung, eine Geheimhaltungspflicht, einen Vertrag oder eine andere Verpflichtung zur Beschränkung der Verwendung eines Geschäftsgeheimnisses verstoßen haben. Danach regelt Artikel 4(4) die Haftung Dritter, die ein Verschuldenselement in die Beurteilung einbringen. Er erweitert im Wesentlichen den Umfang der rechtswidrigen Nutzung oder Offenlegung auf einen Dritten, der unter den Umständen wusste oder hätte wissen müssen, dass die Informationen durch eine rechtswidrige Offenlegung erworben wurde. Folglich ist der Haftungsumfang bei grober Fahrlässigkeit im Einklang mit Fußnote 10 des TRIPS-Abkommens.

Schließlich enthält Artikel 5 GGR eine Liste mit vier Ausnahmen von den durch Artikel 4 eingeräumten Rechten, die versuchen, die Interessen der Inhaber von Geschäftsgeheimnissen an der Offenlegung ihrer Informationen und die Bedenken Dritter hinsichtlich des Zugriffs auf diese Informationen und deren Verwendung zu vereinbaren. Im Gegensatz zu den in Artikel 3 GGR genannten Verhaltensweisen werden die Ausnahmen als spezifische Einschränkungen der Rechte hinsichtlich eines Geschäftsgeheimnisses verstanden, die von Fall zu Fall unter Berücksichtigung der jeweiligen konkurrierenden Interessen zu bewerten sind. Diese Ausnahmen wurden offen formuliert: (i) die Ausübung des Rechts der freien Meinungsäußerung und der Informationsfreiheit gemäß der Charta, einschließlich der Achtung der Freiheit und der Pluralität der Medien; (ii) Whistleblowing; (iii) die Offenlegung durch Arbeitnehmer gegenüber ihren Vertretern während rechtmäßigen Erfüllung der Aufgaben dieser Vertreter und (iv) der Schutz des legitimen Interesses, das nach Unionsrecht oder nationalem Recht anerkannt ist.

Schließlich regelt Kapitel 3 der Richtlinie die Durchsetzung von Geschäftsgeheimnissen bei Verletzung in ähnlicher Weise wie die Bestimmungen der Durchsetzungsrichtlinie. Zu den im Falle einer Verletzung verfügbaren Rechtsmitteln gehören vorläufige und vorsorgliche Maßnahmen (Artikel 10), gerichtliche Anordnungen und Abhilfemaßnahmen (Artikel 12), Schadensersatz (Artikel 14) und die Veröffentlichung von Gerichtsentscheidungen (Artikel 15). Es gibt jedoch einige auffällige Unterschiede. Die GGR harmonisiert nicht die Maßnahmen zur Bereitstellung und Bewahrung von Nachweisen oder des Rechts auf Auskunft, die den Mitgliedstaaten bei der Umsetzung überlassen werden. Darüber hinaus wurden spezifische Bestimmungen zur Wahrung der Vertraulichkeit im Verlauf von Gerichtsverfahren aufgenommen (Artikel 9 GGR).

Insgesamt scheint es, dass die Richtlinie ein Gleichgewicht zwischen dem Interesse der Inhaber von Geschäftsgeheimnissen an der Geheimhaltung ihrer Informationen und dem Interesse Dritter am Zugriff auf solche Informationen schafft. Dies wird vor allem durch die Festlegung einer Reihe flexibler und offener Klauseln in den Bestimmungen erreicht, die die Rechtmäßigkeit der Verletzung regeln, indem auf den Standard seriöser Geschäftspraktiken in Artikel 10bis PC Bezug genommen wird sowie der Standard der Haftung Dritter aufgenommen wird, welcher zumindest grobe Fahrlässigkeit des Verletzers erfordert.

Im digitalen Zeitalter ist es immer schwieriger geworden, Datensicherheit und Datenschutz zu gewährleisten. Vor diesem Hintergrund werden in Kapitel 4 die Konturen der Nichtoffenkundigkeits-Anforderung in Anbetracht der zunehmenden Anfälligkeit von Informationen dargelegt. Zu diesem Zweck werden zunächst die Definitionen des Geschäftsgeheimnisses untersucht, die vor der Einführung der GGR in der deutschen und englischen Rechtsordnung verwendet wurden. In Deutschland gibt es keine gesetzliche Definition von Geschäftsgeheimnissen, obwohl § 17 UWG zwischen zwei Kategorien unterscheidet: ‚Geschäftsgeheimnisse' und ‚Betriebsgeheimnisse'. Die erstere bezieht sich auf geschäftsbezogene Informationen eines Unternehmens, während die letztere technische Informationen umfasst. Die vom Bundesgerichtshof entwickelte und von Vorinstanzen weitergeführte Definition sieht vor, dass „ein Geschäfts- oder Betriebsgeheimnis […] jede im Zusammenhang mit einem Betrieb stehende Tatsache [ist], die nicht offenkundig, sondern nur einem eng begrenzten Personenkreis bekannt ist und nach dem bekundeten, auf wirtschaftlichen Interessen beruhenden Willen des Betriebsinhabers geheim gehalten werden soll". In Deutschland können somit vier Schutzanforderungen identifiziert werden. Erstens können Informationen gemäß der Anforderung der Geschäftsbezogenheit nur dann als Geschäftsgeheimnis geschützt werden, wenn sie einem bestimmten Geschäft zugeordnet werden können. Private Geheimnisse oder Informationen, die von Universitäten oder Forschungseinrichtungen stammen, fallen nicht in den Schutzbereich der §§ 17 und 18 UWG. Die zweite Anforderung, die Nichtoffenkundigkeit, sieht vor, dass Informationen weder allgemein bekannt noch leicht zugänglich sind. Zahlreichen Entscheidungen zufolge gilt: „Informationen, die in bestimmten Ausprägungen nur unter großen Schwierigkeiten und Kosten erlangt werden können (‚große Schwierigkeit und Opfer'), gelten als geheim." Diese Anforderung umfasst sowohl den tatsächlichen Zugang als auch die Möglichkeit des Zugriffs auf die betreffenden Informationen. Die Schwelle für die Beurteilung dieser Anforderung sind die Fachkreise, aber auch die Wettbewerber, deren Handlungen letztlich Gegenstand der UWG-Verordnung sind. Die dritte Voraussetzung, der Geheimhaltungswille, verlangt, dass Informationen aufgrund des Willens des Geschäftsgeheimnisinhabers nicht offengelegt werden. Hinter einer solchen subjektiven Voraussetzung steht die Unterscheidung von lediglich unbekannten Informationen von Informationen, die absichtlich geheim gehalten werden. Diese Forderung wurde stark kritisiert, weil sie eine überflüssige Schutzbedingung darstelle. Sie hängt letztlich mit der letzten durch die Rechtsprechung aufgestellten Anforderung zusammen: dem Interesse an der Geheimhaltung der Informationen (Geheimhaltungsinteresse). Dies wurde größtenteils dahingehend ausgelegt, dass der Inhaber eines Geschäftsgeheimnisses ein berechtigtes wirtschaftliches Interesse daran hat, die Informationen geheim zu halten, da die bloße Absicht als unzulänglicher Parameter betrachtet wird.

In England hingegen hat die Einbeziehung von Geschäftsgeheimnissen in die *breach of confidence action* dazu geführt, dass ein komplexes System geschaffen wurde, in dem die Grenzen zwischen Privatsphäre und Nichtoffenkundigkeit schrittweise unscharfer geworden sind. So wird davon ausgegangen, dass der Ausdruck ‚confidential information' der allgemeine Begriff ist, der sich auf Informationen bezieht, die unter der *breach of confi-*

*dence action* geschützt werden, während ‚trade secret' verwendet wird, um eine der Informationskategorien zu kennzeichnen, die unter diese Handlung fallen, auch wenn keine gesetzliche Definition existiert. Triviale und unmoralische Informationen werden insbesondere nicht durch die *breach of confidence action* geschützt, obwohl Gerichte solche Beschränkungen in der Praxis nur ungern anwenden, da konzeptionelle Schwierigkeiten bei der Einstufung von Informationen als trivial oder unmoralisch bestehen. In ähnlicher Weise müssen Informationen, um geschützt zu werden, spezifisch sein, d. h. klar und identifizierbar. Um die Vertraulichkeit von Informationen zu beurteilen, wenden die Gerichte den allgemeinen Test der Unzugänglichkeit an, nach dem ‚besondere intellektuelle Fähigkeiten und Arbeit' für die Wiedergabe der betreffenden Informationen unerlässlich sind. Dies wird dahingehend interpretiert, dass der mutmaßliche Verletzer denselben belastenden mentalen Prozess durchlaufen musste wie die Vertrauensperson, um die geschützten Informationen zu erhalten.

Ein Vergleich der Definitionen eines Geschäftsgeheimnisses unter deutscher und englischer Rechtsprechung zeigt, dass beide Rechtssysteme wertvolle, nicht offengelegte Informationen wirksam schützen. Die rechtlichen Definitionen entsprechen jedoch nicht vollständig der Definition eines Geschäftsgeheimnisses in Artikel 2(1) GGR, wonach Informationen (i) geheim sein, (ii) aufgrund ihres geheimen Charakters kommerziellen Wert haben und (iii) Gegenstand von den Umständen angemessenen Geheimhaltungsmaßnahmen durch die Person sein müssen, die die rechtmäßige Kontrolle über die Informationen besitzt, im Einklang mit den Mindestverpflichtungen gemäß Artikel 39 Absatz 2 TRIPS. Um die Einheitlichkeit in allen Mitgliedstaaten sicherzustellen, enthält die vorliegende Arbeit die Empfehlung, dass die nationalen Gerichte die Notwendigkeit betonen sollten, eine Kausalität zwischen dem Wert der Informationen und ihrer geheimen Natur herzustellen. In der Arbeit wird daher argumentiert, dass der Begriff des kommerziellen Werts dahingehend interpretiert werden sollte, dass er sich auf die Wettbewerbsfähigkeit des Inhabers des Geschäftsgeheimnisses bezieht und nicht nur Unternehmen, sondern auch Universitäten und Forschungseinrichtungen umfasst. Außerdem wird in der Arbeit befürwortet, dass die Voraussetzung von angemessenen Geheimhaltungsmaßnahmen, die weder in Deutschland noch in England als normativer Standard enthalten sind, flexibel ausgelegt werden sollte, um verschwenderisches Wettrüsten zu vermeiden und den Informationsfluss zwischen den Marktteilnehmern zu fördern.

Unter Berücksichtigung der obigen konzeptionellen Überlegungen wird in der vorliegenden Arbeit die Rechtsprechung aus den USA, England und

Deutschland geprüft, in der die Geheimnisanforderung erörtert wird. Diese vergleichende Analyse lässt den Schluss zu, dass es nicht möglich ist, einen normativen Standard zu extrahieren, der unter allen Umständen anwendbar ist, um die Konturen schützbarer Informationen, die tatsächlich geheim sind, von öffentlich zugänglichen Informationen abzugrenzen. Letztendlich hängt eine solche Beurteilung von einer Reihe von Faktoren ab, beispielsweise davon, ob besondere intellektuelle Fähigkeiten und Arbeit erforderlich sind, um das Geheimnis zu erlangen, ob der Inhaber des Geschäftsgeheimnisses die Kontrolle über die spätere Nutzung und Offenlegung dieser Informationen behält oder ob die Informationen anderen Mitgliedern der Industrie bereits bekannt sind. Demnach wird die relative Natur des Geheimnisses am besten fallweise mit Bezug auf seine Abgrenzung zur Gemeinfreiheit beurteilt, was für die Ermittlung der Auswirkungen von Offenlegungen im digitalen Zeitalter von größter Bedeutung ist.

Nach diesem fallorientierten Ansatz analysiert die Arbeit das Spannungsfeld zwischen behördlichen Offenlegungspflichten und dem Interesse der Inhaber von Geschäftsgeheimnissen an der Geheimhaltung wertvoller Informationen. Die Arbeit kommt zu der Schlussfolgerung, dass die Offenlegung eines Geschäftsgeheimnisses bei Behörden, welches gemäß den nationalen oder EU-Rechtsvorschriften vorgeschrieben oder zulässig ist und aufgrund von geschäftlichen Interessen oder aufgrund gewerblicher Schutzrechte des Inhabers Beschränkungen unterliegen kann, wie in der entsprechenden Satzung dargelegt, von Fall zu Fall beurteilt werden sollte. Insbesondere wird vorgeschlagen, dass, wenn die Offenlegung der Informationen dem Inhaber einen nicht wiedergutzumachenden Schaden zufügen könnte, die öffentlichen Behörden in Erwägung ziehen sollten, ob die Angabe von Teiloffenlegungen oder überarbeiteten Fassungen auch der öffentlichen Transparenz dienen und das Geschäftsinteresse der Parteien schützen könnte.

Die Dissertation untersucht anschließend aus vergleichender rechtlicher Sicht (USA, England und Deutschland) die Auswirkungen der Vermarktung eines Produkts, in dem ein Geschäftsgeheimnis enthalten ist. Sie schließt daraus, dass das Inverkehrbringen eines Produkts als solches keine der Erfindungen und der Geschäftsgeheimnisse preisgibt, es sei denn, sie werden nach Prüfung und Analyse ersichtlich. Es wird jedoch darauf hingewiesen, dass nach dem Patentrecht die bloße Möglichkeit, auf die Informationen zuzugreifen, sie zur Bewertung ihres neuartigen Charakters zur Verfügung stellt, selbst wenn die Informationen einem Reverse-Engineering-Prozess unterliegen. Im Falle von Geschäftsgeheimnissen hängt eine solche Beurteilung dagegen davon ab, ob Dritte (d. h. die betroffenen Kreise) tatsächlich das vermarktete Produkt untersucht und das Geheimnis erlangt haben oder ob die Informationen mit so wenig Arbeitsaufwand und intellektuellen Fähigkeiten zugänglich oder offensichtlich sind, dass es nicht angemessen erscheint, dem Erwerber des Produkts eine Vertraulichkeitsverpflichtung aufzuerlegen. Folglich bleiben Informationen, die nach einem Reverse Engineering eines Wettbewerbers erhalten werden, für den Schutz von Geschäftsgeheimnissen berechtigt, solange sie in der betreffenden Industrie nicht allgemein bekannt werden. Nach beiden Rechtssystemen werden die extrinsischen Eigenschaften des Produkts nicht sofort bekannt gegeben und sind daher sowohl für den Patent- als auch für den Geschäftsgeheimnisschutz geeignet.

Als Nächstes wird die Überlegung, dass Offenlegungen im Internet und Offenlegungen in der Cloud Informationen automatisch ihrer geheimen Natur berauben, auch aus vergleichender rechtlicher Sicht beleuchtet. In Bezug auf Internet-Offenlegungen argumentiert die Arbeit, dass die Beurteilung, ob Informationen ihren geheimen Charakter behalten, unter Berücksichtigung der individuellen Umstände jedes Einzelfalls durchgeführt werden sollte, wobei zu beachten ist, wie wahrscheinlich es ist, dass Verkehrskreise auf die Informationen zugegriffen haben. Ausschlaggebende Faktoren sind die Dauer der Online-Veröffentlichung der Informationen und die bei der Entdeckung der Veröffentlichung ergriffenen Maßnahmen sowie der Website-Verkehr zwischen den relevanten Kreisen. In diesem Zusammenhang wird die Schlussfolgerung gezogen, dass die Weitergabe von Informationen an einen Cloud-Diensteanbieter nicht als automatisch Geheimnis preisgebend gilt. Nur die Offenlegung von Informationen, die die Weitergabe von Wissen durch Parteien beinhaltet, die nicht an eine Geheimhaltungsverpflichtung gebunden sind, sollte relevant sein. Darüber hinaus hindern Haftungsausschlüsse von Cloud-Diensteanbietern bei unberechtigtem Zugriff nicht die Durchsetzung von Geschäftsgeheimnissen hinsichtlich der unrechtmäßig von Dritten erworbenen Informationen.

Die fallorientierte Analyse wird durch den Schutz sogenannter ‚Kombinationsgeheimnisse' vervollständigt. Dabei handelt es sich um einen Mehrelementeanspruch, der nicht geheime Informationen auf einzigartige Weise zu einem Geschäftsgeheimnis zusammenfügt. Ihre Schutzberechtigung wurde auf beiden Seiten des Atlantiks (in den USA, in England und in Deutschland) akzeptiert und steht im Einklang mit Artikel 39(2) TRIPS. Wenn Gerichte jedoch den Schutz von Geschäftsgeheimnissen für bereits öffentlich zugängliche Informationen durch Anklagen gegen ehemalige Angestellte oder Durchsetzung von Wettbewerbsverboten bestätigen, können die wirtschaftlichen und sozialen Vorteile, die mit der Verbreitung und Wiederverwendung von Informationen verbunden sind, möglicherweise behindert werden und zu missbräuchlichen Rechtsstreitigkeiten führen. Um dies zu vermeiden, schlägt die Dissertation einen analytischen Rahmen vor, den die Gerichte in der EU einhalten sollten, um die Relevanz des Schutzes von Geschäftsgeheimnissen zu prüfen, die Informationen im öffentlichen Bereich enthalten. Dementsprechend werden fünf Prinzipien vorgeschlagen: (i) Es muss ein funktionaler Zusammenhang zwischen den Elementen des beanspruchten Kombinationsgeheimnisses bestehen; (ii) das Kombinationsgeheimnis als diskrete Entität sollte mehr Wert haben als die einzelnen Elemente, die isoliert betrachtet werden; (iii) die Kombination muss aus der Investition intellektueller Fähigkeiten resultieren; (iv) die Gerichte sollten prüfen, ob der Beklagte einige der Elemente der Kombination unabhängig erstellt hat, und (v) der Kläger muss immer die einzelnen Elemente der Kombination identifizieren, aus denen die diskrete Einheit besteht. Letztendlich spricht sich die Arbeit für die Anwendung des analytischen Rahmens aus, der im Zusammenhang mit Kombinationsgeheimnissen zum Schutz von Big-Data-Sets entwickelt wurde, deren Wert in der Aggregation reiner Datenmengen liegt, die einzeln nicht wertvoll sind und die möglicherweise auch durch Wettbewerber generiert werden.

Entsprechend den wirtschaftlichen Zielen, die der Unionsgesetzgeber letztendlich mit der Verabschiedung der GGR erreichen wollte, konzentriert sich Kapitel 5 auf die Untersuchung der strategischen Bedeutung von Geschäftsgeheimnissen für bestimmte Industrien und deren zunehmende Anfälligkeit durch die Anwendung qualitativer empirischer Forschung. Die Parfümindustrie wird insbesondere als Beispiel für die Veranschaulichung der wachsenden Herausforderungen dargestellt, denen sich die Inhaber wertvoller Informationen stellen müssen, wenn sie nicht offengelegt werden. Aus rechtswissenschaftlicher Sicht ist der Duftstoffsektor besonders interessant, da es kein besonderes gewerbliches Schutzrecht für Parfüme gibt und ihre Formeln von den Wettbewerbern zu niedrigen Kosten rekonstruiert werden können.

In der EU wurde das Urheberrecht an Düften nur in den Niederlanden in einer isolierten Entscheidung anerkannt. Die Patentierbarkeitsanforderungen werden selten von Duftverbindungen und Duftzusammensetzungen erfüllt. Trotz der jüngsten Gesetzesänderungen auf EU-Ebene können Gerüche im Gegensatz zu anderen unkonventionellen Anzeichen im Rahmen der geltenden Markenregelung nicht geschützt werden. Nach dem derzeitigen Stand der Technik ist es nicht möglich, Gerüche und Geschmack auf eine Weise zu repräsentieren, die „klar, eindeutig, in sich abgeschlossen, leicht zugänglich, verständlich, dauerhaft und objektiv ist" ist, wie vom EuGH im Fall *Sieckmann*[2706] festgelegt.

In diesem Zusammenhang unterstreichen die Schlussfolgerungen der qualitativen empirischen Untersuchung in Form von zwei halbstrukturierten Interviews mit dem Rechtsberater eines multinationalen Unternehmens und dem *maître parfumaire* Rosendo Mateu, dass Geschäftsgeheimnisse eine zentrale Rolle bei der Zulassung von Duft- und Parfümherstellern spielen und angemessene Erträge aus neuen Kreationen und kleinen inkrementellen Innovationen ermöglichen. Sie zeigen jedoch auch, dass es im Laufe der Zeit immer schwieriger wird, sensible Informationen zu verbergen. In der Studie wurden vier Faktoren für das Durchsickern von Geschäftsgeheimnissen im Parfümsektor ermittelt: (i) Reverse-Engineering-Praktiken; (ii) regulatorische Forderungen nach Offenlegung und Transparenz; (iii) neue Arten der elektronischen Speicherung und Übertragung und (iv) Mobilität der Arbeitnehmer. Dies hat eine Reihe von Auswirkungen aus der Perspektive der sich ergänzenden Beziehung zwischen Geschäftsgeheimnissen und geistigen Eigentumsrechten, aber auch aus wettbewerbsrechtlicher Sicht. Einerseits ist Geheimhaltung erforderlich, um den Wettbewerb zwischen Marktteilnehmern zu fördern. Wenn jeder Marktteilnehmer Zugang zu den Informationen eines Mitbewerbers hätte, nähme der Wettbewerbsdruck ab, was im Extremfall zu einem Marktversagen in der Parfümindustrie führen könnte. Andererseits kann das Verschweigen von Informationen auch zu einem De-facto-Monopol und der Beseitigung eines wirksamen Wettbewerbs auf dem Markt führen.

Ungeachtet dieser Überlegungen hat Kapitel 5 zum Schluss geführt, dass Markenrechte zusammen mit Bestimmungen über unlauteren Wettbewerb, die vergleichende Werbung regeln, zusätzliche Anreize schaffen können, indem sie den Produkten, die geheime Informationen enthalten, eine Aura der Exklusivität und des Luxus verleihen, die es den Herstellern ermöglichen, Kosten für die Erstellung, Entwicklung und Vermarktung dieser Produkte zu verinnerlichen. Nach der Doktrin *L'Oréal v Bellure*[2707] des EuGH wird dies jedoch häufig auf Kosten der Meinungsfreiheit und der Einschränkung der Wahlmöglichkeiten der Verbraucher erreicht.

Die empirische Analyse hat auch gezeigt, dass Geheimnisse am häufigsten Unternehmen zugeschrieben werden, die zum Schutz physische und rechtliche Maßnahmen ergreifen. Bei der Annahme dieser Maßnahmen können insbesondere zwei unterschiedliche Bereiche identifiziert werden.

2706 Case C–273/00 *Sieckmann v DPMA* [2002] ECR I-11737, para 55.
2707 Case C–487/07 *L'Oréal v Bellure* [2009] ECR I-05185.

Erstens handelt es sich um die interne Sphäre des Geheimnisses, die sich auf die Aufbewahrung vertraulicher Informationen im Unternehmen bezieht und hauptsächlich die Mitarbeitenden betrifft, da diese Personen regelmäßig Zugang zu wertvollen geheimen Informationen zur Erfüllung ihrer Pflichten haben. Zweitens bezieht sich die äußerliche Sphäre des Geheimnisses auf die Verabschiedung rechtlicher und physischer Maßnahmen, um der rechtswidrigen Nutzung und Offenlegung von Geschäftsgeheimnissen durch Dritte wie Lieferanten, Diensteanbieter, Lizenznehmer oder Partner im Bereich Forschung und Entwicklung (F&E), die auf die Informationen mit Genehmigung zu einem bestimmten Zweck Zugriff haben, entgegenzuwirken. Generell beabsichtigt diese auch, Geschäftsgeheimnisse vor dem Eingreifen Dritter zu bewahren. Daher untersucht Kapitel 6 die Relevanz der vertraglichen Bestimmungen (rechtliche Maßnahmen), um die Geheimhaltung in den beiden ermittelten Bereichen zu gewährleisten.

Während des Arbeitsverhältnisses sind die Mitarbeiter aufgrund einer Loyalitätspflicht verpflichtet, Geschäftsgeheimnisse nicht preiszugeben. In nachvertraglichen Szenarien erscheint die Anwendung einer solchen Verpflichtung komplexer, zumal die GGR vorsieht, dass „die Definition eines Geschäftsgeheimnisses [...] die Erfahrungen und Qualifikationen, die Beschäftigte im Zuge der Ausübung ihrer üblichen Tätigkeiten erwerben, [ausschließt]“. Deswegen dürfen Mitarbeiter nicht daran gehindert werden, die im normalen Verlauf ihrer Beschäftigung erworbenen Fähigkeiten, Kenntnisse und Erfahrungen in ihrer neuen Position einzusetzen. Daher scheint der Rückgriff auf Geheimhaltungsvereinbarungen und Wettbewerbsverbotsvereinbarungen die beste Möglichkeit, um Geschäftsgeheimnisse vor Wettbewerbern zu verbergen. Diese Vereinbarungen können sich jedoch negativ auf die Karriereentwicklung von Mitarbeitern auswirken und Folgeinnovationen behindern. Folglich unterliegt die Zulässigkeit solcher Vertragsbestimmungen in verschiedenen Mitgliedstaaten unterschiedlichen Anforderungen, da sie nicht durch die GGR EU-weit harmonisiert wurde. In England werden nachvertragliche Vertraulichkeitsvereinbarungen und Wettbewerbsverbotsvereinbarungen allgemein akzeptiert, sofern sie keine sogenannten ‚restraints of trade‘ darstellen. Englische Gerichte scheinen generell dazu geneigt zu sein, Vertraulichkeitsvereinbarungen durchzusetzen, sofern sie keine Informationen enthalten, die öffentlich zugänglich sind oder einen Teil der Fähigkeiten, Kenntnisse und Erfahrungen bilden, die die Mitarbeiter nutzen sollten. Diese meist günstige Tendenz resultiert aus der Tatsache, dass der Geltungsbereich dieser Vereinbarungen größtenteils mit dem Umfang der implizierten Verpflichtung übereinstimmt, Geschäftsgeheimnisse nicht offenzulegen. Nutzungsbeschränkungen (durch Nichtverwendungsklauseln) werden jedoch in der Regel unter strengeren Gesichtspunkten bewertet, und die Gerichte beurteilen meist, ob Zeit, Umfang und geografische Einschränkungen angemessen sind. Die Beurteilung der Angemessenheit von Wettbewerbsverbotsvereinbarungen ist problematischer. Englische Gerichte sind aufgrund der damit verbundenen wettbewerbswidrigen Wirkungen, die durch solche Bestimmungen ausgelöst werden, besonders streng. Sie müssen ein berechtigtes Interesse des Arbeitgebers wie Geschäftsgeheimnisse und vertrauliche Informationen (‚confidential information') oder Kundenbeziehungen und Firmenwert (‚goodwill') schützen. Ihre Dauer muss kurz sein (nicht länger als zwölf Monate), und die Industrie und die Rolle, die der ausscheidende Angestellte nicht mehr einnimmt, müssen ebenfalls spezifisch definiert werden.

In Deutschland schützt der Abschluss von Geheimhaltungsvereinbarungen nach Beendigung eines Arbeitsvertrags den Arbeitgeber auch nicht vor der Nutzung und Offenlegung der Fähigkeiten, Kenntnisse und Erfahrungen des ausscheidenden Arbeitnehmers, die untrennbar mit Geschäftsgeheimnissen einhergehen können. Dies kann nur durch ein Wettbewerbsverbot begrenzt werden, dessen Gültigkeit von der Erfüllung der Voraussetzungen des §§ 74-74c des Handelsgesetzbuchs[2708] abhängig ist. Insbesondere sollte eine angemessene Entschädigung gezahlt und eine Höchstdauer von zwei Jahren festgelegt werden. Deutsche Gerichte prüfen insbesondere, ob ein berechtigtes Interesse besteht und ob dies aufgrund seines territorialen, zeitlichen und materiellen Umfangs den beruflichen Aufstieg des Arbeitnehmers unangemessen beeinträchtigt. Insgesamt ergibt sich aus der vergleichenden Analyse, dass die Bewertung der Angemessenheit von Geheimhaltungsvereinbarungen und Wettbewerbsverbotsvereinbarungen letztendlich durch gerichtliche Auslegung erfolgt, wobei alle vorliegenden Umstände berücksichtigt werden.

Die äußerliche Sphäre des Geheimnisses bezieht sich auf die Wahrung der Vertraulichkeit gegen die rechtswidrige Nutzung und Offenlegung von Geschäftsgeheimnissen durch Dritte, die möglicherweise die Informationen mit Genehmigung des Inhabers abgerufen haben, jedoch nur für einen begrenzten Zeitraum oder um einen bestimmten Zweck zu erreichen. Dies ist typischerweise der Fall bei Lizenzvereinbarungen und F&E-

2708 Handelsgesetzbuch in der im Bundesgesetzblatt Teil III, Gliederungsnummer 4100-1, veröffentlichten bereinigten Fassung, das zuletzt durch Artikel 3 des Gesetzes vom 10. Juli 2018 (BGBl. I S. 1102) geändert worden ist (HGB).

Vereinbarungen. Um Geschäftsgeheimnisse auszunutzen, müssen die Inhaber eine Reihe konkurrierender Interessen sorgfältig abwägen. Zum einen sollten sie versuchen, die Informationen mit möglichst wenigen Personen zu teilen, um das Offenlegungsrisiko und den daraus resultierenden Verlust des Wettbewerbsvorteils zu begrenzen, der durch ihre Geheimhaltung entsteht. Sobald die Informationen die interne Sphäre des Unternehmens verlassen haben, können sie aufgrund der inhärent irreversiblen Natur der kognitiven Prozesse nicht wieder eingeführt werden: Das Erlernte kann nicht verlernt werden. Andererseits müssen die Inhaber der Informationen zur Maximierung des wirtschaftlichen Potenzials von Geschäftsgeheimnissen die Informationen möglicherweise mit einer großen Anzahl von Parteien teilen, insbesondere wenn keine Finanzierungsmittel, Fertigungskapazitäten oder technisches Wissen vorhanden sind, die die Entwicklung des Endprodukts ermöglichen. Daher sollten die Vertragsklauseln, die die Verwendung und spätere Offenlegung von Geschäftsgeheimnissen in Lizenz- und F&E-Vereinbarungen regeln, sorgfältig ausgearbeitet werden. Die Arbeit untersucht anschließend die Zulässigkeit von nachvertraglichen Geheimhaltungspflichten im Rahmen von Lizenzverträgen aus vergleichender rechtlicher Sicht (England und Deutschland) und kommt zu dem Schluss, dass, während in Deutschland eine Loyalitätspflicht des Lizenznehmers impliziert wird, die Auferlegung von langen Zeiträumen (15 Jahren) aus wettbewerbsrechtlicher Sicht nicht durchsetzbar sein kann. Die englische Rechtsprechung ist weniger klar und geht meistens davon aus, dass das Vorliegen einer Geheimhaltungsverpflichtung aus dem Wortlaut der Vereinbarung abgeleitet werden sollte. In F&E-Vereinbarungen ist aus Wettbewerbssicht die Durchsetzung der nachvertraglichen Geheimhaltungsverpflichtungen nur zulässig, wenn diese Verpflichtungen nicht die Weitergabe der entwickelten Technologie an Dritte oder die Fähigkeit Dritter zum Wettbewerb ausschließen.

Nach der Untersuchung der inneren und äußerlichen Sphären des Geheimnisses und ihrer Grenzen wird in der Dissertation die Möglichkeit in Betracht gezogen, dass geheim gehaltene Informationen niemals aufgedeckt werden, da manche Geheimnisse undurchschaubar bzw. unzugänglich bleiben. Daher wird vorgebracht, dass der Schutz von Geschäftsgeheimnissen unter bestimmten Umständen begrenzt sein sollte, und zwar im Einklang mit den im Nordhaus-Modell verwendeten Gründen, um die Begrenzung der Patentlaufzeit zu begründen. Es scheint jedoch nicht sinnvoll zu sein, eine feste Dauer festzulegen, beispielsweise für formale Rechte des geistigen Eigentums. In Anbetracht der Kasuistik des Schutzes von Geschäftsgeheimnissen wird argumentiert, dass der Schutz nach einiger Zeit eingestellt werden sollte, selbst wenn der Schutzgegenstand verborgen bleibt. Dies lässt sich am besten durch eine Ausnahme in einem Vertragsverletzungsanspruch artikulieren. Der mutmaßliche Verletzer könnte widersprechen, dass der Schutz von Geschäftsgeheimnissen nicht durchsetzbar sein sollte, wenn der statische Wohlfahrtsverlust in der im Nordhaus-Modell geschilderten Abwägung zwischen Innovationsanreizen und höheren Preisen überwiegt. Das Problem ist jedoch, dass die zur Durchführung einer solchen Beurteilung erforderlichen Informationen, wenn überhaupt, nur im Besitz des Geschäftsgeheimnisinhabers sind. Dritte können daher den Zeitpunkt, zu dem die für die Entwicklung des Geheimnisses aufgewendete Investition wiedererlangt wurde, nicht zuverlässig einschätzen und somit nur schwer argumentieren, wann aus Wohlfahrtsgesichtspunkten die Informationen frei verwendet sollte.

Ungeachtet dieser Überlegung unterstreicht die Dissertation die Bedeutung vertraglicher Vereinbarungen für die Aufrechterhaltung der Geheimhaltung innerhalb von Unternehmen (zwischen Mitarbeitern), aber auch außerhalb von Unternehmen (hinsichtlich Lieferanten, Lizenznehmern oder F&E-Partnern). In der vorliegenden Arbeit wird daher vorgeschlagen, die endliche Dauer des Geheimhaltungsschutzes durch die Einführung einer allgemeinen Annahme im Rahmen von Business-to-Business-Vereinbarungen im GGR zu modulieren, wodurch die Dauer der Geheimhaltung und der Nichtbenutzungsverpflichtungen auf vier Jahre nach der Kündigung des Vertrages beschränkt wäre, sofern die Parteien nicht ausdrücklich etwas anderes vereinbaren. Die vorgeschlagene Einschränkung lautet wie folgt:

> *Im Rahmen von Business-to-Business-Vereinbarungen (einschließlich Vereinbarungen zwischen nichtgewerblichen Einheiten) wird der Erwerb, die Nutzung und die Offenlegung von Geschäftsgeheimnissen geregelt, aufgrund derer sich die Parteien verpflichten, die Informationen, die den Vertragsgegenstand bilden, nach ihrem Abschluss nicht offenzulegen und nicht zu verwenden. Die Nichtangabe der Laufzeit solcher Verpflichtungen beschränkt ihre Wirksamkeit auf vier Jahre nach Vertragsbeendigung. In jedem Fall erlöschen diese Verpflichtungen, wenn die geheimen Informationen aus Gründen, die den Vertragspartnern nicht direkt oder indirekt zugerechnet werden können, nicht länger die in Artikel 2(1) dieser Richtlinie festgelegten Schutzanforderungen erfüllen.*

Die Einführung der oben wiedergegebenen vertraglichen Annahme steht im Einklang mit dem Grundsatz, der in vielen zivilrechtlichen Gerichtsbarkeiten gilt, wonach Verpflichtungen auf unbestimmte Zeit von Gerichten als nicht durchsetzbar angesehen werden. Infolgedessen würde die Einführung einer solchen Annahme ohne ausdrückliche Vereinbarung zwischen den Parteien die Rechtssicherheit in nachvertraglichen Szenarien EU-weit verbessern und ein Gleichgewicht zwischen den gegensätzlichen Interessen der Inhaber von Geschäftsgeheimnissen und ihren Geschäftspartnern herstellen.

Tatsächlich wären die Inhaber von Geschäftsgeheimnissen vier Jahre nach Vertragsbeendigung gegen unbefugte Nutzung und Offenlegung geschützt. Dies würde es ihnen ermöglichen, die in die Erstellung der Informationen getätigten Investitionen wiederzuerlangen und gleichzeitig zu gewährleisten, dass der Empfänger die Erkenntnisse nicht nutzen kann, die er aufgrund einer abgelaufenen Vertragsbeziehung gewonnen hat. Andererseits würde die Anwendbarkeit dieser Annahme sicherstellen, dass der Empfänger der Informationen nicht unangemessen mit Geheimnispflichten und Nichtnutzungspflichten belastet wird, deren Dauer und Umfang während der Verhandlung der Vereinbarung nicht eindeutig festgelegt wurden. In der Tat ist die Treuepflicht, die in vielen Rechtsordnungen zur Rechtfertigung von Geheimhaltungspflichten besteht, die dem Wesen des Arbeitsverhältnisses innewohnen, in Business-to-Business-Beziehungen zwischen Wettbewerbern schwieriger anzuwenden. Aus diesem Grund sollte der Geltungsbereich einer solchen Vermutung nur in Business-to-Business-Vertragsvereinbarungen gelten, z. B. F&E-Vereinbarungen, Lizenzvereinbarungen und Vereinbarungen mit Lieferanten, die zwischen juristischen Personen geschlossen werden, und nicht in Business-to-Consumer- oder Arbeitsverträgen. In Anbetracht dessen, dass eines der Hauptziele der Richtlinie die Förderung von Forschungs- und Innovationsanstrengungen ist, sollte eine solche Annahme auch in Bezug auf vertragliche Vereinbarungen gelten, bei denen mindestens eine der Parteien eine nicht geschäftliche Einheit ist, beispielsweise eine Universität oder Forschungseinrichtung.

Entscheidend ist, dass die Dauer der Geheimhaltungsverpflichtung und der Nichtgebrauchsverpflichtung in erster Linie vom Willen der Parteien bestimmt wird, und zwar in Übereinstimmung mit dem Grundsatz der Parteienautonomie, die das Zivilrecht leitet. Nur wenn keine besondere Vereinbarung hinsichtlich der Dauer besteht, wird die vierjährige vertragliche Annahmerelevant. Der Umstand, dass die vorgeschlagene Bestimmung besagt, dass die Geheimnispflicht und die Nichtnutzungspflicht entfallen, sobald die Informationen die Schutzanforderungen für ein Geschäftsgeheimnis gemäß Artikel 2(1) GGR nicht erfüllen, stellt sicher, dass die Parteien, die die Informationen erhalten, nicht gebunden sind, diese geheim zu halten und nicht zu verwenden, nachdem es in den einschlägigen Kreisen allgemein bekannt geworden ist. Dies erscheint angesichts des Wegfalls des Vertragsgegenstands jedoch unvernünftig. Wenn jedoch das Geheimnis aus Gründen verloren geht, die einer der Parteien zuzuschreiben sind, an die das Geschäftsgeheimnis weitergegeben wurde, sollten die Geheimhaltungspflichten und die Nichtbenutzungspflichten gegenüber dieser Partei gemäß Artikel 13(2) GGR durchsetzbar bleiben. Im Gegensatz dazu sollten Klauseln, die vorsehen, dass Vertraulichkeits- und Nichtnutzungspflichten bestehen bleiben bis die Informationen allgemein bekannt sind, als gültig angesehen werden, da eine solche Formulierung den Parteien zum Zeitpunkt des Vertragsschlusses ausreichende Rechtssicherheit hinsichtlich des zeitlichen Umfangs der eingegangenen Verpflichtungen bietet. Sie steht auch im Einklang mit der Gruppenfreistellungs-Verordnung für Technologietransfer-Vereinbarungen und der Auffassung der Wettbewerbsbehörden,[2709] dass keine wettbewerbsrechtlichen Fragen in Bezug auf die Vereinbarungen bestehen, die die Nichtnutzung und Offenlegung der lizenzierten Technologierechte nach Ablauf der Vereinbarung regeln, gegeben dass die Rechte gültig und in Kraft bleiben.[2710]

Unter dem Hinweis auf Geheimhaltungsverpflichtungen wird auch die Nichtnutzung des Informationsgegenstandes des Vertrags verstanden, sofern sich aus den Vertragsbedingungen nichts anderes ergibt. Aus systematischer Sicht erscheint es in der Tat nicht immer möglich, zwischen Nutzung und Offenlegung zu unterscheiden, da die Verwendung der Informationen häufig zu ihrer Offenlegung führt. In nachvertraglichen Szenarien beinhalten die Geheimhaltungspflichten auch die Nichtnutzung der Informationen. Nach der vorgeschlagenen Annahme sind diese Verpflichtungen auf vier Jahre nach Beendigung des Vertrages befristet, sofern keine bestimmte Laufzeit festgelegt ist.

---

2709 Verordnung (EU) Nr. 316/2014 der Kommission vom 21. März 2014 über die Anwendung von Artikel 101 Absatz 3 des Vertrags über die Arbeitsweise der Europäischen Union auf Gruppen von Technologietransfer-Vereinbarungen [2014] OJ L97/17.

2710 Kommission, 'Leitlinien zur Anwendung von Artikel 101 des Vertrags über die Arbeitsweise der Europäischen Union auf Technologietransfer-Vereinbarungen' [2014 ] OJ C89/3, para 183 (c).

# Bibliography

## *§ 1 Legislation*

### *A) International legislative sources*

Agreement on Trade-Related Aspects of Intellectual Property Rights (TRIPs) (adopted 15 April 1994) (Annex 1C to the Agreement establishing the World Trade Organization) 1869 UNTS 183.

Berne Convention for the Protection of Literary and Artistic Works (adopted 9 September 1886) 828 UNTS 221 (BC).

Convention Establishing the World Intellectual Property Organisation (signed on 14 July 1967 and amended on 28 September 1979).

Convention for the Protection of Human Rights and Fundamental Freedoms (European Convention on Human Rights, as amended on 1 June 2010) (ECHR).

Convention on the Grant of European Patents (European Patent Convention) of 5 October 1973 (as revised by the Act revising Article 63 EPC of 17 December 1991 and the Act revising the EPC of 29 November 2000) (EPC).

Euro-Mediterranean Agreement establishing an Association between the European Communities and their Member States, of the one part, and the Arab Republic of Egypt, of the other part [2004] OJ L304.

Free Trade Agreement between the European Union and its Member States, of the one part, and the Republic of Korea, of the other part [2010] OJ L127/6.

General Agreement on Tariffs and Trade (adopted 30 October 1947) 55 UNTS 194 (GATT Agreement).

Marrakesh Agreement Establishing the World Trade Organization (adopted 15 April 1994) 1867 UNTS 154 (WTO Agreement).

North American Free Trade Agreement (United States-Canada-Mexico) (adopted 17 December 1992, entered into force 1 January 1994) ILM 289 (NAFTA).

Paris Convention for the Protection of Industrial Property (adopted 29 March 1883, as revised at Stockholm on 14 July 1967 and as amended on 28 September 1979) 21 UST 1583, 828 UNTS 305 (PC).

Universal Declaration of Human Rights (adopted 10 December 1948) UNGAs 217 A (III) (UDHR).

Vienna Convention on the Law of Treaties (adopted 23 May 1969) 1155 UNTS 331 (VCLT).

Washington Act (adopted 2 June 1911, entered into force 1 May 1913) TRT PARIS 006.

WIPO Copyright Treaty (adopted 20 December 1996, entered into force 6 March 2002) 2186 UNTS 121 (WCT).

*B) U.S. legislation*

*I. Federal legislation*

Communications Decency Act of 1996, Pub. L. No. 104-104, 110 Stat. 133-145 (1996) (codified in scattered sections of U.S.C. § 223 et seq.).

Copyright Act, Public Law 94-553, 90 Stat. 2541 (1976) (codified as amended at 17 U.S.C. §§ 101-1332) (U.S. Copyright Act).

Defend Trade Secrets Act of 2016, Pub. L. No. 114-153, 130 Stat. 376 (2016) (codified at 18 U.S.C. §§ 1831 et seq) (DTSA).

Patent Act of 1952, Public Law 593, 66 Stat. 792 (1952) (codified as amended at 35 U.S.C. §§ 1 et seq) (U.S. Patent Act).

The Economic Espionage Act Pub. L. No. 104-294, 110 Stat. 3488 (1996) (codified as amended at 18 U.S.C.§§ 1831 -1839) (EEA).

The Leahy-Smith America Invents Act, Pub. L. No. 112-29, 125 Stat. 284 (2011) (codified in scattered sections of 35 U.S.C.)(America Invents Act of 2011 or AIA).

*II. State Statutes*

Cal. Bus. & Prof. Code § 16600 (West. 2010).

Uniform Trade Secrets Act (Am. Law Inst. 1979, as amended in 1985).

*III. Restatements of the Law*

Restatement (First) of Torts (Am. Law Inst. 1939).

Restatement (Third) of Unfair Competition (Am. Law Inst. 1995).

*C) English legislation*

Atomic Energy Authority Act 1986.

Copyright, Designs and Patents Act 1988.

European Union Notification of Withrawal Bill 2017.

European Union Referendum Act 2015.

Human Rights Act 1998 (HRA).

Patents Act 1977.

The Building Societies Act 1997.

The Corporation Tax Act 2009.

*D) German legislation*

Bundesgesetz gegen den unlauteren Wettbewerb (UWG) vom 19. Dezember 1986 (Stand am 1. Juli 2016) (UWG).

Gesetz über Arbeitnehmererfindungen in der im Bundesgesetzblatt Teil III, Gliederungsnummer 422-1, veröffentlichten bereinigten Fassung, das zuletzt durch Artikel 7 des Gesetzes vom 31. Juli 2009 (BGBl. I S. 2521) geändert worden ist (Act on Employee Inventions).

Gewerbeordnung in der Fassung der Bekanntmachung vom 22. Februar 1999 (BGBl. I S. 202), die zuletzt durch Artikel 1 des Gesetzes vom 17. Oktober 2017 (BGBl. I S. 3562) geändert worden ist.

Grundgesetz für die Bundesrepublik Deutschland in der im Bundesgesetzblatt Teil III, Gliederungsnummer 1001, veröffentlichten bereinigten Fassung, das zuletzt durch Artikel 1 des Gesetzes vom 13. Juli 2017 (BGBl. I S. 2347) geändert worden ist (German Constitution or GG).

Handelsgesetzbuch in der im Bundesgesetzblatt Teil III, Gliederungsnummer 4100-1, veröffentlichten bereinigten Fassung, das zuletzt durch Artikel 3 des Gesetzes vom 10. Juli 2018 (BGBl. I S. 1102) geändert worden ist (HGB or German Commercial Code).

Markengesetz vom 25. Oktober 1994 (BGBl. I S. 3082; 1995 I S. 156; 1996 I S. 682), das zuletzt durch Artikel 11 des Gesetzes vom 17. Juli 2017 (BGBl. I S. 2541) geändert worden ist.

Patentgesetz in der Fassung der Bekanntmachung vom 16. Dezember 1980 (BGBl. 1981 I S. 1), das zuletzt durch Artikel 4 des Gesetzes vom 8. Oktober 2017 (BGBl. I S. 3546) geändert worden ist (German Patent Act).

Strafgesetzbuch in der Fassung der Bekanntmachung vom 13. November 1998 (BGBl. I S. 3322), das zuletzt durch Artikel 1 des Gesetzes vom 30. Oktober 2017 (BGBl. I S. 3618) geändert worden ist (StGB or German Criminal Code).

Urheberrechtsgesetz vom 9. September 1965 (BGBl. I S. 1273), das zuletzt durch Artikel 1 des Gesetzes vom 1. September 2017 (BGBl. I S. 3346) geändert worden ist.

*E) Spanish legislation*

Ley 3/1991, de 10 de enero, de Competencia Desleal (Spanish Unfair Competition Act).

Ley Orgánica 10/1995, de 23 de noviembre, del Código Penal (Spanish Criminal Code).

Ley 17/2001, de 7 de diciembre, de Marcas (Spanish Trade Mark Act).

Real Decreto Legislativo 1/1996, de 12 de abril, por el que se aprueba el texto refundido de la Ley de Propiedad Intelectual, regularizando, aclarando y armonizando las disposiciones legales vigentes sobre la materia (Spanish Copyright Act).

*F) Italian Legislation*

Decreto legisltaivo 10 febbraio 2005, n. 30 1 Codice della proprietà industriale, a norma dell'articolo 15 della legge 12 dicembre 2002, n. 273, aggiornato a seguito del decreto legislativo di correzione 13 agosto 2010, n. 13 (Italian Industrial Property Code).

*G) French Legislation*

Code de la propriété intellectuelle (version consolidée au 25 avril 2016) (French Intellectual Property Code).

*H) Swiss Legislation*

Bundesgesetz gegen den unlauteren Wettbewerb (UWG) vom 19. Dezember 1986 (Stand am 1. Juli 2016).

*I) EU legislation*

Agreement on a Unified Patent Court [2013] OJ C–175/01.

Charter of Fundamental Rights of the European Union [2012] OJ C326/391 (ChFREU).

Commission Regulation (EC) No 772/2004 of 27 April 2004 on the application of Article 81 (3) of the Treaty to categories of technology transfer agreements [2004] OJ L123/11.

Commission Regulation (EU) No 1217/2010 of 14 December 2010 on the application of Article 101(3) of the Treaty on the Functioning of the European Union to certain categories of research and development agreements [2010] OJ L335/36 (R&DBER).

Commission Regulation (EU) No 316/2014 of 21 March on the application of Article 101 (3) of the Treaty on the Functioning of the European Union to categories of technology transfer agreements [2014] OJ L93/17 (TTBER).

Council Directive (EC) 2001/29 on the harmonisation of certain aspects of copyright and related rights in the information society [2001] OJ L167/10 (Information Society Directive).

Council Directive 87/54/EEC of 16 December 1986 on the legal protection of topographies of semiconductor products [1987] OJ L24/36.

Council Regulation (EC) No 1/2003 of 16 December 2002 on the implementation of the rules on competition laid down in Articles 81 and 82 of the Treaty [2003] *OJ L 1/1*.

Council Regulation (EC) No 1383/2003 [2013] OJ L181/1 (Customs Regulation).

Council Regulation (EC) No 207/2009 of 26 February 2009 on the Community trade mark [2009] OJ L 78/1 and Article 2 of Directive 2008/95/EC of the European Parliament and of the Council of 22 October 2008 to approximate the laws of the Member States relating to trade marks [2008] OJ L299/25.

Directive (EU) 2015/2436 of the European Parliament and of the Council of 16 December 2015 to approximate the laws of the Member States relating to trade marks [2015] OJ L336/1 (Trade Mark Directive or TMD).

Directive (EU) 2016/943 of 8 June 2016 on the protection of undisclosed know-how and business information (trade secrets) against their unlawful acquisition, use and disclosure [2016] OJ L157/1 (Trade Secrets Directive or TSD).

Directive 2000/31/EC of the European Parliament and of the Council of 8 June 2000 on certain legal aspects of information society services, in particular electronic commerce, in the Internal Market [2000] OJ *L178* (Directive on Electronic Commerce).

Directive 2005/29/EC of the European Parliament and of the Council of 11 May 2005 concerning unfair business-to-consumer commercial practices in the internal market and amending Council Directive 84/450/EEC, Directives 97/7/EC, 98/27/EC and 2002/65/EC of the European Parliament and of the Council and Regulation (EC) No 2006/2004 of the European Parliament and of the Council [2005] OJ L149/22 (Unfair Commercial Practices Directive).

Directive 2006/116/EC of the European Parliament and of the Council of 12 December 2006 on the term of protection of copyright and certain related rights (codified version) [2006] OJ L372/12 (Term of Protection Directive).

Directive 96/9 on the legal protection of databases [1996] OJ L77/20 (Database Directive).

Directive 98/71/EC of the European Parliament and of the Council of 13 October 1998 on the legal protection of designs [1998] OJ L289/28 (Design Directive).

Directive of the European Parliament and of the Council 2006/114/EC of 12 December 2006 concerning misleading and comparative advertising [2006] OJ L376/21 (Misleading and Comparative Advertisement Directive).

Directive of the European Parliament and of the Council 2009/24/EC of 23 April 2009 on the legal protection of computer programs [2009] OJ L122/9 (Software Directive).

Directive of the European Parliament and of the Council 95/46/EC of 24 October 1995 on the protection of individuals with regard to the processing of personal data and on the free movement of such data [1995] OJ L281/0031 (Data Protection Directive).

Directive of the European Parliament and the Council 2004/48/EC of 29 April 2004 on the enforcement of intellectual property rights [2004].OJ L195/16 (Enforcement Directive).

European Parliament and of the Council (EC) No 1223/2009 of 30 November 2009 on cosmetic products [2009] OJ L342/59.

Regulation (EC) of the European Parliament and of the Council (EC) No 1223/2009 of 30 November 2009 on cosmetic products [2009] OJ L342/59.

Regulation (EU) 2015/2424 of the European Parliament and of the Council of 16 December 2015 amending Council Regulation (EC) No 207/2009 on the Community trade mark and Commission Regulation (EC) No 2868/95 implementing Council Regulation (EC) No 40/94 on the Community trade mark, and repealing Commission Regulation (EC) No 2869/95 on the fees payable to the Office for Harmonization in the Internal Market (Trade Marks and Designs) [2015] OJ L341/21 (Amending Regulation).

Regulation (EU) 2016/679 of the European Parliament and of the Council of 27 April 2016 on the protection of natural persons with regard to the processing of personal data and on the free movement of such data, and repealing Directive 95/46/EC (General Data Protection Regulation) [2016] OJ L119/01 (GDPR).

Regulation (EU) 2017/1001 of the European Parliament and of the Council of 14 June 2017 on the European Union trade mark [2017] OJ L154/1 (European Union Trade Mark Regulation or EUTMR).

Regulation of the European Parliament and of the Council (EC) 1049/2001 of 30 May 2001 regarding public access to European Parliament, Council and Commission documents [2001] OJ L145/43.

Regulation of the European Parliament and of the Council E 608/2013 of 12 June 2013 concerning customs enforcement of intellectual property rights and repealing Council Regulation (EC) No 1383/2003 concerning customs enforcement of intellectual property rights [2013] OJ L 181/15 (Customs Regulation).

*J) EU Commission Documents*

Commision, 'Proposal for a Council Directive on the legal protection of computer programs' COM (88) 816 final.

Commission, 'Building a European Data Economy Initiative' COM(2017) 9 final.

Commission, 'Commission Staff Working Document on the free flow of data and emerging issues of the European data economy' SWD(2017) 2 final.

Commission, 'Commission Statement concerning Article 2 of Directive 2004/48/EC of the European Parliament and of the Council on the enforcement of intellectual property rights' [2005] OJ L 94/37.

Commission, 'Commission Statement on Directive 2004/48/EC' [2005] OJ L94/3.

Commission, 'Communication from the Commission to the European Parliament, the Council, the European and economic and social committee and the committee of the regions. A Single Market for Intellectual Property Rights. Boosting creativity and innovation to provide economic growth, high quality jobs and first class products and services in Europe' COM (2011) 287 final, 3.

Commission, 'Europe 2020: a strategy for smart, sustainable and inclusive growth' COM(2010) 2020 final.

Commission, 'Explanatory Memorandum, Proposal for a Directive of the European Parliament and of the Council on the protection of undisclosed know-how and business information (trade secrets) against their unlawful acquisition, use and disclosure'.

Commission, 'Final report on the E-commerce Sector Inquiry' COM(2017) 229 final <http://ec.europa.eu/competition/antitrust/sector_inquiry_final_report_en.pdf> accessed 15 September 2018.

Commission, 'First evaluation of Directive 96/9/EC on the legal protection of databases' (2005) DG Internal Market and Services Working Paper.

Commission, 'Green Paper on Copyright and Challenge of Technology – Copyright Issues Requiring Immediate Action COM (88) 172, final' [1988] OJ C71.

Commission, 'Guidelines on the application of Article 101 of the Treaty on the Functioning of the European Union to technology transfer agreements' [2014] OJ C89/3.

Commission, 'Impact Assessment accompanying the document proposal for a Directive of the European Parliament and of the Council on the protection of undisclosed know-how and business information (trade secrets) against their unlawful acquisition, use and disclosure' SWD(2013) 471 final.

Commission, 'Proposal for a Directive of the European Parliament and of the Council on the protection of undisclosed know-how and business information (trade secrets) against their unlawful acquisition, use and disclosure' COM (2013) 813 final.

Commission, 'Proposal for a Regulation of the European Parliament and the Council on the Law Applicable to non-contractual obligations ("ROME II")' COM (2003) 427 final.

Commission, 'Public Consultation On The Protection Against Misappropriation Of Trade Secrets And Confidential Business Information, Summary Of Responses' (2013) 11 <http://ec.europa.eu/growth/industry/intellectual-property/trade-secrets/index_en.htm> accessed 15 September 2018.

Commission, 'Synopsis Report on the Consultation on the Building a European Data Economy Initiative.' 2018 <https://ec.europa.eu/digital-single-market/en/news/synopsis-report-public-consultation-building-european-data-economy> accessed 15 September 2018.

Commission, 'Synopsis Report on the Consultation on the Building a European Data Economy Initiative'.

Commission, 'Towards a common European data space' COM(2018) 232 final.

Commission, 'Unleashing the Potential of Cloud Computing in Europe' COM(2012) 529 final.

Commission, 'Guidelines on the application of Article 81 of the EC Treaty to technology transfer agreements' [2004] OJ C101/2.

DG Internal Market and Services Working Paper. First evaluation of Directive 96/9/EC on the legal protection of databases.

*K) Council Documents*

Council, 'General Approach on the Proposal for a Directive of the European Parliament and of the Council on the protection of undisclosed know-how and business information (trade secrets) against their unlawful acquisition, use and disclosure' 2013/0402 (COD) <http://register.consilium.europa.eu/doc/srv?l=EN&f=ST%209870%202014%20INIT> accessed 15 September 2018.

Council, 'Council Decision 94/800/EC of 22 December 1994 concerning the conclusion on behalf of the European Community as regards matters within its competence, of the agreements reached in the Uruguay Round multilateral negotiations (1986-1994)' [1994] OJ L336.

*§ 2 **Books***

Ahrens HJ and McGuire MR, *Modellgesetz für Geistiges Eigentum, Normtext und Begründung* (GRUR 2012).

Anderson M, *Technology Transfer* (3rd edn, Haywards Heath 2010).

Aplin T and others, *Gurry on Breach of Confidence* (2nd edn, OUP 2012).

Ballester Rodes A and others, *Case Law of the Boards of Appeal* (8th edn, 2016 EPO).

Bartenbach K and Volz F, *Arbeitnehmererfindungen* (6 edn, Carl Heynemanns Verlag 2014).

Bartenbach K, *Patentlizenz-und Know-how-Vertrag* (Verlag Dr. Otto Schmidt 2013).

Beater A, *Unlauterer Wettbewerb* (2nd edn, C.H. Beck 2011).

Benkler Y, *The Wealth of Networks* (Yale University Press 2006).

Bentham J, *An Introduction to the Principles of Morals and Legislation* (first published 1781, Batoche Books 2000).

Bently L and Sherman B, *Intellectual Property Law* (4th edn, OUP 2014).

Beyerbach H, *Die geheime Unternehmensinformation* (Mohr Siebeck 2012).

Blayn JF and others, *Questions de Parfumerie* (Corpman Editions 1988).

Bodenhausen G H C, *Guide to the application of the Paris Convention* (BIRPI 1967).

Brearley K and Bloch S, *Employment covenants and confidential information* (Butterworths1993).

Burrows A and Feldman D, *Oxford Principles of English Law* (2nd edn, OUP 2009).

Byrne N and McBratney A, *Licensing Technology* (3rd edn, Jordans 2005).

Coleman A, *The Legal Protection of Trade Secrets* (Sweet&Maxwell 1992).

Cornish W, Llewellyn D and Aplin T, *Intellectual Property: Patents, Copyright, Trade Marks and Allied Rights* (8th edn, Sweet&Maxwell 2013).

Correa C, *Trade Related Aspects of Intellectual Property Rights, A commentary on the TRIPs Agreement* (OUP 2007).

Craig P and de Búrca G, *EU Law, Text, Cases, and Materials* (5th edition OUP 2011).

Derclaye E and Leistner M, *Intellectual Property Overlaps* (Hart 2011).

Derclaye E, *The legal protection of Databases* (Edward Elgar 2008).

Dorner M, *Know-how Schutz im Umbruch* (Carls Heymanns 2013).

Dreier T and Hugenholtz P B, *Concise European copyright law* (2nd ed, Kluwer Law International 2016).

Floridia G and others, *Diritto Industriale Proprietà Intellettuale e concorrenza* (4th edn, Giappichelli Editore 2012).

François Lévêque and Yann Ménière, *The Economics of Patents and Copyright* (The Berkeley Electronic Press 2004).

Frenz W, *Handbuch Europa-Recht*, vol 6 (1st edn, Springer 2011).

Fröhlich S, *Düfte als geistiges Eigentum* (Mohr Siebeck 2008).

Gervais D, *The TRIPs Agreement* (4th edn, Sweet&Maxwell 2012).

Gintare S *The Refusal to Disclose Trade Secrets as an Abuse of Market Dominance – Microsoft and Beyond* (Stämpfli 2011).

Gordon R, *EC Law in judicial review* (1st edn, OUP 2007).

Groß M, *Der Lizenzvertrag* (Deutsche Fachverlag 2015).

Grosse Ruse-Kahn H, 'The Protection of Intellectual Property in International Law' (OUP 2016).

Guillemin C, *Law & Odeur* (Nomos 2016).

Harguth A and Carlsson S, *Patents in Germany and Europe* (2nd edn, Wolters Kluwer 2017).

Harte-Bavendamm H and Henning-Bodewig F, *Gesetz gegen den unlauteren Wettbewerb* (4th edn, C.H. Beck 2016).

Henning-Bodewig F and Ruijsenaars H E, *Protection against Unfair competition* (WIPO 1994).

Henning-Bodewig F, *International Handbook on Unfair Competition* (C.H. Beck 2013).

Heydon J D, *The restraint of trade doctrine* (2nd edn, Butterworths 1999).

Hillenbrand S, *Der Begriff des Betriebs- und Geschäftsgeheimnisses* (Herbert Utz Verlag 2017).

Hirsch G and others, *Münchener Kommentar zum Lauterkeitsrecht* (2nd edn, C.H. Beck 2014).

Hull J, *Commercial Secrecy* (1st edn, Sweet&Maxwell 1998).

Ianeva I, *Registration of Non-conventional Signs Under the Community Trademark Regime* (Wissenchaftlicher Verlag Berlin 2008).

Jager M F, *Trade Secrets Law* (Thompsons Reuters 2015).

Kalbfus B, *Know-how Schutz in Deutschland zwischen Strafrecht und Zivilrecht-welcher Reformbedarf besteht?* (1st edn, Carl Heymanns Verlag 2011).

Kamperman Sanders A, *Unfair Competition Law* (1st edn, OUP 1997).

Kant I, *Groundwork for the Metaphysics of Morals* (first published 1785, CUP 2011).

Köhler H, Bornkamm J and Feddersen J, *Gesetz gegen den unlauteren Wettbewerb* (36 edn, C. H. Beck 2018).

Kolasa M, *Trade Secrets and Employee Mobility* (CUP 2018).

Kraßer R and Ann C, *Patentrecht* (6th edn, C.H. Beck 2009).

Kur A and Dreier T, *European Intellectual Property Law* (Edward Elgar 2013).

Kur A and Senftleben M, *European Trade Mark Law* (OUP 2017).

Ladas S P, *Patents; Trademarks, and Related Rights – National and International Protection* (HUP 1975).

Landes W and Posner R, *The Economic Structure of Intellectual Property Law* (Belknap Press 2003).

Laszlo P and Rivière S, *Perfume, Arte y Ciencia* (Omega 2001).

Lehmer L, *UWG: Kommentar zum Wettbewerbsrecht* (Luchterhand 2007).

Lessig L, *Free Culture* (The Penguin Press 2004).

Locke L, *The Selected Political Writings of John Locke* (Paul E. Sigmund ed, Norton& Company 2005).

Melvin F. Jager, *Trade Secrets Law* (Thomsons Reuters 2015).

Merges R P and Duffy J F, *Patent Law and Policy, Cases and Materials* (6th edn, Lexis Nexis 2013).

Merges R P, *Justiffying Intellectual Property Law* (HUP 2011).

Milgrim R G, *Milgrim on Trade Secrets* (Matthew Bender 2014).

Nordhaus W D, *Invention Growth, and Welfare: A Theoretical Treatment of Technological Change*. (The MIT Press 1969).

Ohly A and Lucas-Schloetter A, *Privacy, Property and Personality* (CUP 2005).

Ohly A and Sosnitza O, *Gesetz gegen den unlauteren Wettbewerb* (7th edn, C.H. Beck 2016).

Ohly A and Spence M, *The Law of Comparative Advertising* (Hart Publishing 2000).

Peel E, *The Law of Contract* (14th edn, Sweet&Maxwell 2015).

Pires de Carvalho N, *The TRIPs Regime of Antitrust and Undisclosed Information* (Wolters Kluwer 2007).

Pires de Carvalho N, *The TRIPS Regime of Antitrust and Undisclosed Information* (Kluwer Law International 2008).

Pooley L, *Trade Secrets* (Law Journal Press 2002).

Rahmatian A, *Copyright and Creativity* (Edward Elgar 2011).

Rawls J, *A Theory of Justice* (OUP 1972).

Reger G, *Der internationale Schutz gegen unlauteren Wettbewerb und das TRIPS-Übereinkommen* (Carl Heymanns Verlag 1999).

Rosati E, *Originality in EU Copyright* (Edward Elgar 2013).

Roudnitska E, *Une vie au service du parfum* (Thérèse Vian Editions1991).

Rowe E A and Sandeen S K, *Trade Secrecy and International Transactions: Law and Practice* (Edward Elgar 2015).

Scheppele K M, *Legal Secrets: Equality and Efficiency in the Common Law* (The University of Chicago Press 1992).

Schlötter R, *Der Schutz von Betriebs- und Geschäftsgeheimnissen und die Abwerbung von Arbeitnehmern* (Carl Heymanns Verlag 1997).

Schweyer F, *Die rechtliche Bewertung des Reverse Engineering in Deutschland und den USA* (Mohr Siebeck 2012).

Scotchmer S, *Innovation and Incentives* (1st edn, The MIT Press 2004).

Sundbo J, *The Theory of Innovation: Entrepreneurs, Technology and Strategy* (Edward Elgar 2009).

Suñol A, *El Secreto Empresarial* (Thomson Reuters 2009).

Thomas M. Cooley on Torts, *A Treatise on the Law of Torts, Or, The Wrongs which Arise Independent of Contract* (2nd edn, Callaghan 1879).

Toulson R M and Phipps C M, *Confidentiality* (3rd edn, Sweet&Maxwell 2012).

UNCTAD-ICTSD, *Resource Book on TRIPS and Development* (CUP 2005).

van Caenegem W, *Trade Secrets and Intellectual Property* (Kluwer Law International 2014).

van den Bossche P and Zdouc W, *The Law and Policy of The World Trade Organization* (3rd edn, CUP 2013).

van Eechoud M and others, *Harmonizing European Copyright Law* (Kluwer Law International 2009).

Wadlow C, *The Law of Passing-off* (4th edn, Swett&Maxwell 2011).

Westerman I, *Handbuch Know-how-Schutz* (C.H. Beck 2007).

Winzer W, *Forschungs- und Entwicklungsverträge* (2nd edn, C.H. Beck 2001)

WIPO, *Guide to the Berne Convention for the Protection of Literary and Artistic Works* (WIPO Publications 1978).

### *§ 3 Book Chapters*

Aplin T, 'A right of privacy for corporations?' 475 in Torremans P LC (ed), *Intellectual Property and Human Rights* (Kluwer Law International 2008).

Aplin T, 'Right to Property and Trade Secrets' 421 in Geiger C (ed), *Research Handbook on Human Rights and Intellectual Property* (Edward Elgar 2015).

Aplin T, 'Subject Matter' 49 in Derclaye E (ed), *Research Handbook on the Future of EU Copyright Law* (Edward Elgar 2009).

Arrow K J, 'Allocation of Resources for invention' 609 in Universities-National Bureau Committee for Economic Research and Committee on Economic Growth of the Social Science Research Council (ed), *The Rate and Direction of Inventive Activity: Economic and Social Factors* (Princeton University Press 1962).

Bently L, 'Patents and trade secrets' 57 in Wilkof N and Basheer S (eds), *Overlapping Intellectual Property Rights* (OUP 2012).

Bently L, 'Trade Secrets Intellectual Property but not property?' 60 in Howe H R and Griffiths J (eds), *Concepts of property in Intellectual Property Law* (CUP 2013).

Bertsch C, 'Research Agreement' 38 in Weitnauer W and others (eds), *Life Sciences Agreements in Germany* (C.H. Beck 2014).

Bone R G, 'Trade Secrecy, Innovation and the Requirement of Reasonable Secrecy Precautions' 46 in Dreyfuss R C and Strandburg K J (eds), *The Law and Theory of Trade Secrecy: A Handbook of Contemporary Research* (Edward Elgar 2011).

Bukow J W, 'Defences' in Maximilian Haedicke and Henrik Timmann (eds), *Patent Law Handbook* (C.H. Beck 2013).

Conde Gallego B, 'Unilateral refusal to license indispensable intellectual property rights – US and EU approaches' 215 in Drexl J (ed), *Research Handbook on Intellectual Property and Competition Law* (Edward Elgar, 2008).

Cornish W, 'The Expansion of Intellectual Property Rights' 9 in Schricker G, Dreier T and Kur A (eds), Geistiges Eigentum im Dienst der Innovation (Nomos 2001).

Denicola R, 'The Restatements, the Uniform Act and the status of American trade secret law' 18 in Dreyfuss R C and Strandburg K J (eds), *The Law and Theory of Trade Secrecy: A Handbook of Contemporary Research* (Edward Elgar 2011).

Dessemontet F, 'Protection of Trade Secrets and Confidential information' 271 in Correa C and Yusuf A (eds), *Intellectual Property and International Trade* (2nd edn, Wolters Kluwer 2008).

Dreier T, 'How much 'property' is there in intellectual property?' 116 in H R and Griffiths J (eds), *Concepts of Property in Intellectual Property Law* (CUP 2013).

Dreier T, 'Regulating information: Some thoughts on a perhaps not quite so new way of looking to intellectual property' 35 in Drexl J and others (eds), *Technology and Competition, Contributions in Honour of Hanns Ullrich* (Larcier 2009).

Drexl J, 'Die Verweigerung der Offenlegung von Unternehmensgeheimnissen als Missbrauch marktbeherrschender Stellung' 437 in Hilty R and others (eds), *Schutz von Kreativität und Wettbewerb* (C.H. Beck 2009).

Drexl J, 'Refusal to grant access to trade secrets as an abuse of market dominance'165 in Anderman S and Ezrachi A (eds), *Intellectual Property and Competition Law* (OUP 2011).

Dusollier S, 'Pruning the European intellectual property tree: in search of common principles and roots' 24 in Geiger C (ed), *Constructing European intellectual property* (Edward Elgar 2013).

Dusollier S, 'The commons as a reverse intellectual property-from exclusivity to inclusivity' 258 in Howe H R and Griffiths J (eds), *Concepts of Property in Intellectual Property Law* (CUP 2013).

Fisher W, 'Theories of Intellectual Property' 168 in Munzer S R (ed), *New Essays in the Legal and Political Theory of Property* (CUP 2001).

Foucault M, 'The Order of Discourse' 52 in Young R (ed), *Untying the Text: A Post-Structuralist Reader* (1st edn, Routledge & Kegan Paul 1981).

Fromer J C, 'Trade Secrecy in Willy Wonka's Chocolate Factory' 3 in Dreyfuss R C and Strandburg K J (eds), *The Law and Theory of Trade Secrecy: A Handbook of Contemporary Research* (Edward Elgar 2011).

Gete-Alonso Valero M C, 'Artículo 43' 756 in Bercovitz Rodríguez-Cano R (ed), *Comentarios a la Ley de Propiedad Intelectual* (3rd edn, Tecnos 2007).

Ghidini G and Falce V, 'Trade secrets as intellectual property rights: a disgraceful upgrading – Notes on an Italian reform' 140 in Dreyfuss R C and Strandburg K J (eds), *The Law and Theory of Trade Secrecy: A Handbook of Contemporary Research* (Edward Elgar 2011).

Graf M and Zech H, 'IP in Research and Development Agreements: object and legal qualification' 293 in Matthews D and Zech H (eds), *Research Handbook on Intellectual Property and the Life Sciences* (Edward Elgar 2017).

Graves C T, 'Trade Secrecy and Common Law Confidentiality: The Problem of Multiple Regimes' 77 in Dreyfuss R C and Strandburg K J (eds), *The Law and Theory of Trade Secrecy: A Handbook of Contemporary Research* (Edward Elgar 2011).

Harte-Bavendamm H, '§ 77 Schutz von Geschäfts- und Betriebsgeheimnissen (§§ 17-19 UWG)' in Loschelderr M and Erdmann W (eds), *Wettbewerbsrecht* (4th edn, C.H. Beck 2010).

Heath C, 'Employees, Trade Secrets and Restrictive Covenants in Germany' 85 in Heath C and Kamperman Sanders A (eds), *Employees, Trade Secrets and Restrictive Covenants* (Wolters Kluwer 2017).

Henning-Bodewig F, 'International Unfair Competition Law' 53 in Hilty R and Henning-Bodewig F (eds), *Law Against Unfair Competition* (Springer 2007).

Hon W K and Millard C, 'Control, Security, and Risk in the Cloud' 18 in Millard C (ed), *Cloud Computing Law* (OUP 2013).

Hon W K and Millard C, 'What is Regulated as Personal Data in Clouds' 165 in Millard C (ed), *Cloud Computing Law* (OUP 2013).

Höpperger M and Senftleben M, 'Protection Against Unfair Competition at the International Level – The Paris Convention, the 1996 Model Provisions and the Current Work of the World Intellectual Property Organisation' 61 in Hilty R and Henning-Bodewig F (eds), *Law Against Unfair Competition* (Springer 2007).

Hugenholtz P B 'Something Completely Different: Europe's Sui Generis Database Right' 205 in Frankel S and Gervais D (eds), *The Internet and the Emerging Importance of New Forms of Intellectual Property* (Wolters Kluwer 2016).

Janssen G and Maluga G, '§ 17 Verrat von Geschäfts- und Betriebsgeheimnissen' in *Joecks W and Miebach K (eds), Münchener Kommentar zum StGB* (1st edn, C.H. Beck 2010).

Jestaedt B and Benkard G, 'Art. 64' in Adams T and others (eds) Europäisches Patentübereinkommen (4th edn, C.H. Beck 2012).

Kaiser L, 'Vetragsmanagement' 257, 268 Wurzer A and Kaiser L (eds), *Handbuch Internationaler Know-how-Schutz* (Bundesanzeiger Verlag 2011).

Kämmerer J A, 'European Commission', *The Max Planck Encyclopedia of European Private Law* (OUP 2012).

Kamperman Sanders A, 'The Actio Servi Corrupti" from the Roman Empire to the Globalised Economy' 3 in Heath C and Kamperman Sanders A (eds), *Employees, Trade Secrets and Restrictive Covenants* (Wolter Kluwer 2016).

Katzenberger P and Kur A, 'TRIPs and Intellectual Property' 10 in Beier FK and Schricker G (eds), *IIC Studies, Studies in Industrial Property and Copyright Law, From GATT to TRIPs – The Agreement on Trade-Related Aspects of Intellectual Property Rights* (Weinheim 1996).

Knospe M, 'Germany' 62 in Melvine F. Jager (ed), *Trade secrets throught the world* (2012 Thomsom West).

Kraßer R, 'The Protection of Trade Secrets in the TRIPs Agreement' 216 in Beier FK and Schricker G (eds), *IIC Studies, Studies in Industrial Property and Copyright Law, From GATT to TRIPs – The Agreement on Trade-Related Aspects of Intellectual Property Rights* (Weinheim 1996).

Kur A, 'What to Protect, and How? Unfair Competition, Intellectual Property, or Protection Sui Generis' 11 in Lee N and others (eds), *Intellectual Property, Unfair Competition and Publicity* (Edward 2014).

Kur A, 'Too pretty to protect? '139 in Drexl J and others *Technology and Competition, Contributions in honour of Hanns Ullrich* (Editions Larcier 2009).

Landry F, 'The proceedings for grant' 338 in Haedicke M and Timmann H (eds), *Patent Law Handbook* (C.H. Beck 2013).

Lee KD and von Lewinski S, 'The Settlement of International Disputes in the field of Intellectual Property' 278 in Beier FK and Schricker G (eds), *IIC Studies, Studies in Industrial Property and Copyright Law, From GATT to TRIPs – The Agreement on Trade-Related Aspects of Intellectual Property Rights* (Weinheim 1996).

Lee N, 'Public domain at the interface of trade mark and unfair competition law: The case of referential use of trade marks' 309 in Lee N and others (eds), *Intellectual Property, Unfair Competition and Publicity* (Edward Elgar 2014).

Lehmann M, 'European Market for Digital Goods' 111 in de Franceschi A (ed), *European Contract Law and the Digital Single Market – the Implications of the Digital Revolution* (Intersentia 2016).

Leistner M, 'The Legacy of International News Service v Associated Press (USA)' 33 in Heath C and Kamperman Sanders A (eds), *Landmark Intellectual Property Cases and Their Legacy* (Kluwer Law International 2010).

Leistner M, 'The Protection of Databases' 427 in Derclaye E (ed), *Research handbook on the future of EU Copyright* (Edward Elgar 2009).

Leistner M, 'Unfair Competition and Freedoms of Movement', *Max Planck Encyclopaedia of European Private Law* (OUP 2012).

Lemley M A, 'The surprising virtues of treating trade secrets as IP rights' 109 in Dreyfuss R C and Strandburg K J (eds), *The Law and Theory of Trade Secrecy: A Handbook of Contemporary Research* (Edward Elgar 2011).

Levin M, 'Trade Secret Protection and the Computation of Damages under Swedish Law' 735 in Dreier T, Götting HP, Haedicke M, Macdonald J and Crail R, *John Macdonald on the Law of Freedom of Information* (3rd edn, OUP 2016).

Mayring P, 'Qualitative content analysis' 266 in Uwe Flick, Ernst von Kardoff and Ines Steinke (eds), *A companion to qualitative research* (Sage 2004).

Menell P S and Scotchmer S, 'Intellectual Property' 1473 in Polinsky A M and Shave S (eds), *Handbook of Law and Economics*, vol 2 (Elsevier 2007).

Michaels R, 'Property', *The Max Planck Encyclopaedia of European Private Law* (OUP 2012).

Milbradt C and Stief M, 'Forschungs- und Entwicklungsvertrag' 126 in Marco Stief and Boris Bromm (eds), Vertragshandbuch Pharma und Life Sciences (C.H. Beck 2015).

Nägerl J and Walder-Hartmann L, 'Differentiation from the state of the art' 129 in Haedicke M and Timmann H (eds), *Patent Law A Handbook on European and German Patent Law* (C.H. Beck 2014).

Ohly A, 'Gibt es einen Numerus clausus der Immaterialgüterrechte?' 105 in Ohly A and others (eds), *Perspektiven des Geistiges Eigentums und Wettbewerbsrechts* (C.H. Beck 2005).

Ohly A, 'Harmonising the Protection of Trade Secrets' 2 in de Werra J (ed), *La protection des secrets d'affaires* (Schulthess 2013).

Ohly A, 'Unfair Competition', *Max Planck Encyclopaedia of European Private Law* (OUP 2012).

Ohly A, 'Reverse Engineering: Unfair Competition or Catalyst for Innovation?' 540 in Drexl J and others (eds), *Patents and Technological Progress in a Globalized World* (Springer 2009).

Passa J, 'La protection des secrets d'affaires en droit français' 47 in de Werra J (ed), *La protection des secrets d'affaires* (Schulthess 2013).

Peter M and Wiebe A, 'Art. 39' in Busche J and Stoll T (eds), *TRIPs* (Carl Heymanns 2013).

Prentice D, 'Illegality and Public Policy' in Beale H (ed), *Chitty on contracts* (32th edn, Sweet&Maxwell 2017).

Reichman J, 'How trade secrecy law generates a natural semicommons of innovative know-how' 185 in Dreyfuss R C and Strandburg K J (eds), *The Law and Theory of Trade Secrecy: A Handbook of Contemporary Research* (Edward Elgar 2011).

Samuelson P, 'Challenges in Mapping the Public Domain' 7 in Hugenholtz P B and Guibault L (eds), *The Public Domain of Information* (Kluwer International Law 2006).

Sandeen S K, 'The limits of trade secret law: Article 39 of the TRIPs Agreement and the Uniform Trade Secrets Act on which it is based' 537 in Dreyfuss R C and Strandburg K J (eds), *The Law and Theory of Trade Secrecy: A Handbook of Contemporary Research* (Edward Elgar 2011).

Schaffert W, '4 Nr 11' Rdn 68 in Heermann P W and others (eds), *Münchener Kommentar zum Lauterkeitsrecht* (1st edn, C.H. Beck 2006).

Straus J, 'Implications of the TRIPs Agreement in the Field of Patent Law' 160 Beier FK and Schricker G (eds), *IIC Studies, Studies in Industrial Property and Copyright Law, From GATT to TRIPs – The Agreement on Trade-Related Aspects of Intellectual Property Rights* (Weinheim 1996).

Suñol A, 'Trade Secrets vs Skill and knowledge' 197 in Cafaggi F and others (eds), *The Organizational Contract, From Exchange to Long-term network Cooperation in European Contract Law* (Ashgate 2013).

Surblyte G, 'Enhancing TRIPS: Trade Secrets and Reverse Engineering' 725 in Ullrich H and others (eds), *TRIPS plus 20 – From Trade Rules to Market Principles* (Springer 2016).

Ullman E and Deichfuß H, '§ 15 Übertragbarkeit des Rechts; Lizenzen' in Benkard G (ed), *Patentgesetz* (11th edn, C.H. Beck 2015).

van der Laan N, 'The use of trade marks in keyword advertising: Developments in CJEU and national jurisprudence' 231 in Lee N and others (eds), *Intellectual Property, Unfair Competition and Publicity* (Edward Elgar 2014).

Zech H, 'Data as a Tradable Commodity' 51 in De Franceschi A (ed), *European Contract Law and the Digital Single Market – The Implications of the Digital Revolution* (Insertia 2016).

Zech H, 'Data as Tradeable Commodity – Implications for Contract Law' 2 in Drexl J (ed), *Proceedings of the 18th EIPIN Congress: The New Data Economy between Data Ownership, Privacy and Safeguarding Competition* (Edward Elgar forthcoming).

Zimmerman D L, 'Trade secrets and the "philosophy" of copyright: a case of culture crash' 299 in Dreyfuss R C and Strandburg K J (eds), *The Law and Theory of Trade Secrecy: A Handbook of Contemporary Research* (Edward Elgar 2011).

### *§ 4 Journal Articles*

Abramowicz M and Duffy J F, 'Intellectual Property for Market Experimentation' [2008] 83 NYULR 337.

Ackermann-Blome N and Rindell J, 'Should trade secrets be protected by private and/or criminal law? A comparison between Finnish and German laws' [2018] 13 JIPLP 78.

Adams K D, 'Blaming the Mirror: The Restatements and the Common Law' [2007] 40 Indiana LR 205.

Alexander C, 'Gegenstand, Inhalt und Umfang des Schutzes von Geschäftsgeheimnissen nach der Richtlinie (EU) 2016/943 1034' [2017] WRP 1034.

Almeling D S, 'Seven Reasons Why Trade Secrets are Increasingly Important' [2012] 27 Berkeley Technology LJ 1091.

Amir O and Lobel O, 'Driving Performance: A Growth Theory on Noncompete Law' [2013] 16 Stanford Technology LR 833.

Ann C, 'Know-how- Stiefkind des Geistiges Eigentums?'[2007] GRUR 39.

Aplin T, 'A critical evaluation of the proposed Trade Secrets Directive' [2014] IPQ 257.

Aplin T, 'Reverse Engineering and Commercial Secrets' [2013] 66 Current Legal Problems 341.

Aplin T, 'The future of the breach of confidence action and the protection of privacy' [2007] Oxford University Commonwealth J 137.

Aplin T,'Confidential Information as property?' [2013] 24 King's LJ 172.

Arundel A V, 'The relative effectiveness of patents and secrecy for appropriation' [2001] 30 Research Policy 611.

Balañá S, 'El entorno digital, ¿segunda oportunidad para la marca olfativa?: estudio acerca de la capacidad del signo olfativo' [2005-2006] 26 Actas de Derecho Industrial y Derecho de Autor 18.

Balañá S, 'La perfumería toma posiciones en torno al derecho de autor "¿...fumus boni iuris?"' [2005] 19 Pe.i. 37.

Balasubramanian N and Sivadasan J, 'What happens when firms patent? New evidence from U.S. economic census data' [2011] 93 The Review of Economics and Statistics 126.

Barrett M, 'The "Law of Ideas" Reconsidered' [1989] 71 J Patent & Trademark Office Society 691.

Bassard A, 'La composition d'une formule de parfum est-elle une (oeuvre de l'esprito au sens de la loi du 11 mars 1957?' [1979] 118 RIPIA 461.

Beier FK and Straus J, 'The Patent System and Its Informational Function - Yesterday and Today' [1977] IIC 387.

Beier FK, 'Traditional and Socialist Concepts of Protecting Inventions' [1970] IIC 328.

Beier FK, 'Die Bedeutung des Patentsystems für den technischen, wirtschaftlichen und sozialen Fortschritt' [1979] GRUR Int 227.

Benkler Y, 'Free As the Air to Common Use: First Amendment Constraints on Enclosure of the Public Domain' [1997] 74 NYULR 354.

Bishara N D, Martin K J, Thomas R S, 'An Empirical Analysis of Noncompetition Clauses and Other Restrictive Postemployment Covenants' [2015] 68 Vandervilt LR 1.

Björkenfeldt M, 'The Genie is out of the Bottle: the ECJ's Decision in L'Oréal v Bellure' [2010] 5 JIPLP 105.

Blind K, Edler J, Frietsch R and Schmoch U, 'Motives to patent: Empirical evidence from Germany'[2006] 35 Research Policy 655.

Bone R G, 'A New Look at Trade Secret Law: Doctrine in Search of Justification' [1998] 86 California LR 241.

Bone R G, 'The Still Shaky Foundations of Trade Secret Law' [2014] 92 Texas LR 1803.

Boyle J, 'Foreword: The Opposite of Property?' [2003] 66 Law and Contemporary Problems 1.

Bronckers M and McNelis N, 'Is the EU Obliged to improve the Protection of Trade Secrets? An Inquiry into TRIPS, the European Convention on Human Rights and the EU Charter of Fundamental Rights' [2013] 34 EIPR 673.

Bronckers M, 'The Impact of TRIPs: Intellectual Property Protection in Developing Countries' [1994] 31 Common Market LR 1245.

Cannan J, 'A [Mostly] Legislative History of the Defend Trade Secrets Act of 2016' [2017-2019] 109 Law Library Journal 363.

Chally J R, 'The Law of Trade Secrets: Toward a More Efficient Approach' [2004] 57 Vanderbilt LR 1269.

Chiappetta V, 'Myth, Chameleon or Intellectual Property Olympian?' [1999] 8 George Mason LR 69.

Claeys ER, 'Private Law Theory and Corrective Justice in Trade Secrecy' [2011] 4 J of Tort Law 1.

Cohen J E, 'Reverse Engineering and the Rise of Electronic Vigilantism: Intellectual Property Implications of "Lock-Out" Programs' [1995] 68 Southern California LR 1091.

Cornish W 'Genevan Bootstraps' [1997] 19 EIPR 336.

Cornish W, 'The Essential Criteria for Patentability of European Inventions: Novelty and Inventive Step' [1983] IIC 765.

Cornish W, 'The International Relations of Intellectual Property' [1993] 52 Cambridge LJ 46.

Cundiff V A, 'Reasonable Measures to Protect Trade Secrets in a Digital Environment' [2009] 49 IDEA 359.

Cundiff V A and others, 'The Global Harmonisationof Trade Secret Law: The Convergence of Protection for Trade Secrets in the US and EU' [2016] 38 EIPR 738.

Davison M J and Hugenholtz P B, 'Football fixtures, horse races and spin-offs: the ECJ domesticates the database right' [2005] 27 EIPR 113.

Denicola R, 'The New Law of Ideas' [2014] 28 Harvard Journal of Law & Technology 195.

Derclaye E, 'Databases sui generis right: what is a substantial investment?' [2005] IIC 2.

Derclaye E, 'Intellectual Property Rights on Information and Market Power- Comparing European and American Protection of Databases' [2007] IIC 275.

Derclaye E, 'The Court of Justice copyright case law: quo vadis?' [2014] 36 EIPR 716.

Determann L, 'What Happens in the Cloud: Software as a Service and Copyrights' [2015] 29 Berkeley Tech LJ 1095.

DiCicco-Bloom B and Crabtree B F, 'The qualitative research interview' [2006] 40 Medical Education J 314.

Dinwoodie GB, 'The International intellectual property law system: new actors, new institutions, new sources' [2006] 10 Marquette IPLR 206.

Doerfer G L, 'The Limits on Trade Secret Law Imposed by Federal Patent and Antitrust Supremacy' [1967] 80 Harvard LR 1432.

Dorner M, 'Big Data und "Dateneigentum"' [2014] CR 617.

Dreier T, 'The Council Directive of 14 May 1991 on the Legal Protection of Computer Programs' [1991] 13 EIPR 319.

Drexl J, 'Intellectual Property and Antitrust Law – IMS Health and Trinko – Antitrust Placebo for Consumers Instead of Sound Economics in Refusal-to-Deal Cases' [2004] IIC 788.

Drexl J, 'Nach "GATT und WIPO": Das TRIPs-Abkommen und seine Anwendung in der Europäischen Gemeinschaft' [1994] 43 GRUR Int 777.

Dreyfuss R C, 'Trade Secrets: How Well Should We Be Allowed to Hide them? The Economic Espionage Act of 1996' [1998] 9 Fordham IP Media & Entertainment LJ.

Elias B, 'Do scents signify origin? - An argument against trademark protection for fragrances' [1992] 82 TMR 475.

Falce V, 'Trade Secrets – Looking for (Full) Harmonization in the Innovation Union' [2015] IIC 940.

Feldman M J, 'Toward a Clearer Standard of Protectable Information: Trade Secrets and Employment Relationship' [1994] 9 Berkeley Technology LJ 151.

Field T G, 'Copyright protection for Perfumes' [2004] 45 IDEA 19.

Finger P, 'Die Offenkundigkeit des mitgeteilten Fachwissens bei Know-how-Verträgen' [1970] GRUR 3.

Fisk C, 'Working Knowledge: Trade Secrets, Restrictive Covenants in Employment, and the Rise of Intellectual Property' [2001] 52 Hastings LJ 441.

Former J C, 'Expressive Incentives in Intellectual Property' [2012] 98 Virginia LR 1745.

Franzoni L A and Kaushik A, 'The optimal scope of trade secrets law' [2016] 45 International Review of Law and Economics 45.

Galloux JCH, 'Profumo di diritto – Le principe de la protection des fragrances par le droit d'auteur, note sous TGI Paris, 26 mai 2004' [2004] 36 Recueil Dalloz 2641.

Gandomi A and Haider M, 'Beyond the hype: Big data concepts, methods, and analytics' [2015] 35 International J of Information Management 137.

Gangjee D S and Burrell R, 'Because You're Worth It: L'Oréal and the Prohibition on Free Riding' [2010] 73 Modern LR 282.

Gervais D and Derclaye E, 'The scope of computer program protection after SAS: are we closer to answers?' [2012] 34 EIPR 562.

Gervais D, 'Feist Goes Global: A Comparative Analysis Of The Notion Of Originality In Copyright Law' [2002] 49 LJ of the Copyright Society of the USA 948.

Gervais D, 'The compatibility of the skill and labour standard with the Berne Convention and the TRIPs Agreement' [2004] 26 EIPR 75.

Gielen C, 'Netherlands: copyright - blend of ingredients in a perfume constituting a copyright work' [2006] 28 EIPR 174.

Gielen C,'WIPO and Unfair Competition' [1997] 19 EIPR 78.

Gilburne M R and Johnston R L, 'Trade Secret Protection for Software Generally and in the Mass Market' [1981] 3 Computer LJ 211.

Gilson R J, 'The Legal Infrastructure of High Technology Industrial Districts: Silicon Valley, Route 128, and Covenants Not to Compete' [1999] 74 NYULR 575.

Glöckner J, 'The Regulatory Framework for Comparative Advertisement in Europe - Time for a new Round of Harmonisation' [2012] IIC 35.

Goldman E, 'The Defend Trade Secrets Act Isn't an "Intellectual Property " Law' [2017] 33 Santa Clara High Technology LJ 541.

Gomulkiewicz R W, 'Leaky Covenants-Not-to-Compete' [2015] 49 University of California Davis LR 251.

Gordon S, 'The Very Idea! Why Copyright Law is an Inappropriate Way to Protect Computer Programs' [1998] 1 *EIPR* 10.

Gordon W J, 'On Owning Information: Intellectual Property and the Restitutionary Impulse' [1992] 78 Vanderbilt LR 149.

Graves C T and Macgillivray A, 'Combination Trade Secrets and the Logic of Intellectual Property' [2004] 20 Santa Clara High Technology LJ 261.

Graves C T and Range B D, 'Identification of Trade Secret Claims in Litigation: Solutions for a Ubiquitous Dispute' [2006] 5 New JTechnology IP 68.

Graves C T, 'Trade Secrets as property: Theory and Consequences' [2007] 15 JIPL 39.

Hall B H, Helmers C, Rogers M and Sena V, 'The Choice between Formal and Informal Intellectual Property: A Review' [2014] 52 Journal of Economic Literature 1.

Harabi N, 'Appropiability of Technichal Innovations an Empirical Analysis' [1995] 24 Research Policy 981.

Harold Demsetz, 'The Private Production of Public Goods' [1970] 13 Journal of Law and Economics 293.

Hart RJ, 'Interoperability information and the Microsoft decision' [2006] 28 EIPR 361.

Harte-Bavendamm H, 'Wettbewerbsrechtliche Aspekte des Reverse Engineering von Computerprogrammen' [1990] GRUR 657.

Henning-Bodewig F, 'A New Act Against Unfair Competition' IIC [2005] 421.

Henning-Bodewig F, 'Internationale Standards gegen unlauteren Wettbewerb' [2013] GRUR Int 1.

Hernández-Martí C, 'The possibility of IP protection for smell' [2014] 36 EIPR 665.

Heusch C and others, 'Trade secrets: overlap with restrains of trade, aspects of enforcement' [2015] GRUR Int 932.

Hilton W E, 'What sort of improper conduct constitutes misappropriation of a trade secret' [1990] 30 IDEA 287.

Hoeren T, 'Zur Einführung: Informationsrecht' [2002] JuS 947.

Hofmann F, '"Equity" im deutschen Lauterkeitsrecht? Der "Unterlassungsanspruch" nach der Geschäftsgeheimnis-RL' [2018] WRP 1.

Hoisl K, 'Tracing Mobile Inventors – The Causality between Inventor Mobility and Inventor Productivity' [2007] 36 Research Policy 619.

Holder N and Schmidt J, 'Indirect patent infringement – latest developments in Germany' [2006] 28 EIPR 480.

Hon W K, Millard C and Walden I, 'Negotiating Cloud Contracts: Looking at clouds from both sides now' [2012] 16 Stanford Technology LR 79.

Höpner M, 'Der Europäische Gerichtshof als Motor der Integration' [2011] 21 Berlin J Soziol 203.

Hören T and Müncker R, 'Die EU-RL für den Schutz von Geschäftsgeheimnissen und ihre Umsetzug' [2018] WRP 150.

Hören T und Münkner R, 'Die neue EU-Richtlinie zum Schutz von Betriebsgeheimnissen und die Haftung Dritter' [2018] CCZ 85.

Hughes J, 'The Philosophy of Intellectual Property' [1988] 77 George Mason LJ 287.

Hull L, 'Trade Secret Licensing: the art of the possible' [2009] 14 JIPLP 203.

Hunold W, '*Rechtsprechung zum nachvertraglichen Wettbewerbsverbot*' [2007] NZA-RR 617.

Hunt C, 'Rethinking Surreptitious Takings in the Law of Confidence' [2011] IPQ 66.

Jehoram H C, 'The Dutch Supreme Court Recognises Copyright in the Scent of a Perfume. The Flying Dutchman: All Sails, no Anchor' [2006] 28 EIPR 629.

Joachim B, McGuire MR, Künzel J and Weber N, 'Der Schutz von Geschäftsgeheimnissen durch Rechte des Geistigen Eigentums und durch das Recht des unlauteren Wettbewerbs' [2010] GRUR Int 829.

Jones G, 'Restitution of Benefits Obtained in breach of another's Confidence' [1970] 86 LQR 463.

Judge E F and Gervais D, 'Of Silos and Constellations: Comparing notions of Originality in Copyright Law' [2009] 27 Cardozo Arts and Entertainment LJ 375.

Kalbfus B, 'Die EU-Geschäftsgeheimnis-Richtlinie - Welcher Umsetzungsbedarf besteht in Deutschland?' [2016] GRUR 1009.

Kambatla K, Kollias G, Kumar V and Grama A, 'Trends in big data analytics' [2014] 74 J of Parallel and Distributed Computing 2561.

Kerber W, 'A New (Intellectual) Property Right for Non-Personal Data? An Economic Analysis' [2016] GRUR Int 989.

Kitch E, 'The Nature and the Function of the Patent System' [1977] 20 Journal of Law and Economics 265.

Kokott J and Sobotta C, 'The distinction between privacy and data protection in the jurisprudence of the CJEU and the ECtHR' [2013] IDPL 222.

Koós C, 'Die europäische Geschäftsgeheimnis-Richtlinie - ein gelungener Wurf? Schutz von Know-How und Geschäftsinformationen - Änderungen im deutschen Wettbewerbsrecht' [2016] MMR 224.

Kraßer R, 'Der Schutz des Know-how nach deutschem Recht' [1970] GRUR 587.

Kraßer R, 'Grundlagen des zivilrechtlichen Schutz von Geschäfts- und Betriebsgeheimnissen sowie von Know-how' [1977] GRUR 177.

Kur A, 'The Enforcement Directive - Rough Start, Happy Landing?' [2004] IIC 821.

Kur A, 'Trade Marks Function, Don't They? CJEU Jurisprudence and Unfair Competition Principles' [2014] IIC 434.

Kur A, Hilty R and Knaak R, 'Comments of the Max Planck Institute for Innovation and Competition of 3 June 214 on the Proposal of the European Commission for a Directive on the Protection of Undisclosed Know-How and Business Information (Trade Secrets) Against Their Unlawful Acquisition, Use and Disclosure of 28 November 2013, COM(2013) 813 Final' [2014] IIC 45.

Landes WM and Posner RA, 'Some Economics of Trade Secret Law' [1991] 5 JEP 61.

Laskawy D H, 'Die Tücken des nachvertraglichen Wettbewerbsverbots im Arbeitsrecht' [2012] NZA 1011.

Lavery P, 'Secrecy, Springboards and the Public Domain' [1998] 20 EIPR 93

Lederer F, 'Equivalence of Chemical Product Patents' [1999] IIC 275.

Lehmann M, 'The Theory of Property Rights and the Protection of Intellectual and Industrial Property'[1985] IIC 525.

Lejeune M, 'Die neue EU Richtlinie zum Schutz von Know-How und Geschäftsgeheimnissen' [2016] CR 330.

Lemley M A, 'Does "Public Use" Mean the Same Thing It Did Last year?' [2014] 93 Texas LR 1119.

Lemley M A, 'Intellectual Property and the Shrinkwrap Licenses' [1995] 68 Southern California LR 1239.

Lemley M A, 'Property, Intellectual Property, and Free Riding' [2004] 83 Texas LR 1031.

Lemley M A, 'The Surprising Virtues of Treating Trade Secrets as IP Rights' [2008] 61 Stanford LR 311.

Levin R C, Klevorick A K, Nelson R R and. Winter S G 'Appropriating the Returns from Industrial Research and Development' [1987] 18 Brookings Papers on Economic Activity 783.

Lieberman M B, 'First-Mover Advantage' [1988] 9 Strategic Management J 41.

Loewenheim U, 'Der Schutz der kleinen Münze im Urheberrecht' [1987] GRUR 761.

Machnicka A A, 'The Perfume Industry and Intellectual Property Law in the Jurisprudence of the Court of Justice of the European Union and National Courts' [2012] IIC 123.

Malgieri G, 'Trade Secrets v Personal Data: a possible solution for balancing rights' [2016] 6 International Data Privacy LR 1.

Mansfield E 'Patents and Innovation: An Empirical Study' [1986] 32 Management Science 173.

McCullagh K, 'A tangled web of access to information: reflections on R (on the application of Evans) and another v Her Majesty's Attorney General' [2015] 21 European J of Current Legal Issues.

McGuire M, 'Der Schutz von Know-how im System des Immaterialgüterrechts' [2016] GRUR 1000.

Mcguire MR, 'Know-how:Stiefkind, Störenfried oder Sorgenkind?' [2015] GRUR 424.

Merges R P, 'Priority and Novelty Under the AIA' [2012] 27 Berkeley Technology LJ 1023.

Merges R P, 'The Law and Economics of Employee Inventions' [1999] 13 Harvard Journal of Law & Technology 1.

Mes P, 'Indirect Patent Infringement' [1999] IIC 531.

Moffat V R, 'Making Non-Competes Unenforceable' [2012] 54 Arizona LR 939.

Montville C, 'Reforming the Law of Proprietary Information' [2007] 56 Duke LJ 1159.

Mummenthey H, 'Vertraulichkeitsvereinbarungen' [1999] CR 651.

Nimmer M B, 'The Law of Ideas' [1954] 27 Southern California LR 119.

Ohly A, 'Der Geheimnisschutz im deutschen Recht: heutiger Stand und Perspektiven' [2014] GRUR 1.

Ohly A, 'The Freedom of Imitation and Its Limits – A European Perspective' [2010] IIC 506.

Ohly A, 'Vergleichende Werbung für Zubehör und Warensortimente - Anmerkungen zu den EuGH-Urteilen 'Siemens/VIPA' und 'LIDL Belgium/Colruyt'' [2007] GRUR 3.

Ottoz E and Cugno F, 'Patent-Secret Mix in Complex Product Firms' [2008] 10 American Law & Economics R 142.

Pace C R J, 'The Case for a Federal Trade Secrets Act' [1995] 8 Harvard Journal of Law & Technology 427.

Pajak S, 'Do innovative firms rely on big secrets? An analysis of IP protection strategies with the CIS 4 survey' [2016] 25 Economics of Innovation and New Technology 516.

Paterson G, 'The Novelty of Use Claims' [1996] IIC 179.

Peterson G R, 'Trade Secrets in an Information Age' [1995] 32 Houston LR 385.

Pooley J, 'The Uniform Trade Secrets Act: California Civil Code 3426' [1985] 1 Santa Clara High Technology LJ 193.

Posner R, 'Trade Secret Misappropriation: A Cost-Benefit Response to the Fourth Amendment Analogy' [1992] 106 Harvard LR 461.

Psaroudakis G, 'Trade Secrets in the Cloud' [2016] 38 EIPR 344.

Reichman J H, 'Computer Programs as applied scientific know-how: implications of copyright' [1989] 42 Vanderbilt LR 639.

Reichman J H, 'Legal Hybrids Between the Patent and Copyright Paradigm' [1994] 94 Columbia LR 2432.

Reimann T,'Einige Überlegungen zur Offenkundigkeit im Rahmen von §§ 17 ff. UWG und von § 3 PatG' [1998] GRUR 298.

Risch M, 'Hidden in Plain Sight' [2016] 31 Berkeley Technology LJ 1635.

Risch M, 'Why Do We Have Trade Secrets?' [2007] 11 Marquette IPLR.

Robert P. Merges and Richard R. Nelson, 'On the complete economics of patent scope' [1990] 90 Columbia LR 839.

Rønde T, 'Trade secrets and information sharing' [2001] 10 J of Economics & Management Strategy 391.

Rosati E, 'Originality in a work, or a work of originality: the effects of the Infopaq decision' [2011] 33 EIPR 746.

Rosati E, 'Originality in U.S. and UK Copyright Experiences as a Springboard for an EU-Wide Reform Debate' [2010] IIC 524.

Rowe E A, 'Contributory Negligence, Technology, and Trade Secrets' [2009] 17 George Mason LR 1.

Rowe E A, 'When Trade Secrets become Shackles: Fairness and the Inevitable Disclosure Doctrine' [2005] 7 Tulane J of Technology & IP 167.

Samuelson P and others, 'A Manifesto Concerning the Legal Protection of Computer Programs [1994] 94 Columbia LR 2308.

Samuelson P and Scotchmer S, 'The law and economics of reverse Engineering' [2002] 111 Yale LJ 1575.

Samuelson P, 'Information as Property: Do Ruckelshaus and Monsanto Carpenter Signal a Changing Direction in Intellectual Property Law' [1988] 38 Catholic University LR 365.

Samuelson P, 'Principles for Resolving Conflicts Between Trade Secrets and the First Amendment' [2007] 58 Hastings LJ 777.

Sandeen S K and Seaman C B, 'Toward a Federal Jurisprudence of Trade Secret Law' [2017] 32 Berkeley Technology LJ 829.

Sandeen S K, 'A Contract by Another Name is Still a Contract: Examining the Effectiveness of Trade Secrets Clauses to Protect Databases' [2005] 45 IDEA 119.

Sandeen S K, 'Lost in the Cloud: Information Flows and the Implications of Cloud Computing for Trade Secrets Protection' [2014] 19 Virginia Journal of Law & Technology 2.

Sandeen S K, 'The Evolution of Trade Secret Law and why courts commit error when they do not follow the Uniform Trade Secrets Act' [2010] 33 Hamline LR 493.

Sander C, 'Schutz nicht offenbarter betrieblicher Informationen nach der Beendigung des Arbeitsverhältnisses im deutschen und amerikanishchen Recht' [2013] GRUR Int 217.

Schulze G, 'Schleichende Harmonisierung des urheberrechtlichen Werkbegriffs? - Anmerkung zu EuGH "Infopaq/DDF"' [2009] GRUR 1019.

Scotchmer S, 'Standing on the Shoulders of Giants: Cumulative Research and the Patent Law' [1991] 5 JEP 29.

Senftleben M, 'Function Theory and International Exhaustion – Why It Is Wise to Confine the Double Identity Rule to Cases Affecting the Origin Function' [2014] 36 EIPR 518.

Shmueli G, 'To Explain or to Predict?' [2010] 25 Statistical Science 289.

Short J L, 'Killing the Messenger The Use of Nondisclosure Agreements to Silence Whistleblowers' [1999] 60 University of Pittsburgh LR 1207.

Simpson M P, 'The Future of Innovation: Trade Secrets, Property Rights, and Protectionism—An Age-Old Tale' [2005] 70 Brooklyn LR 1121.

Sobel L S, 'The Law of Ideas, Revisited' [1994] 1 UCLA Entertainment LR 9.

Sołtysiński S, 'Are Trade Secrets Property?' [1986] IIC 331.

Sousa e Silva N, 'What exactly is a trade secret under the proposed Directive?' [2014 ] 9 JIPLP 923.

Steele C and Trenton A, 'Trade secrets: the need for criminal liability' [1998] 20 EIPR 188.

Strandburg K J, 'What does the public get? Experimental use and the patent bargain?' [2004] 57 Wisconsin LR 81.

Surblyte G, '6th GRUR Int / JIPLP Joint Seminar: Internet search engines in the focus of EU competition law – a closer look at the broader picture' [2015] GRUR 127.

Ullrich H, 'Technologieschutz nach TRIPS: Prinzipien und Probleme' [1995] GRUR Int 623.

Unikel R, 'Bridging the "Trade Secret" Gap: Protecting "Confidential Information" Not Rising to the Level of Trade Secrets' [1998] 29 Loyola University Chicago LJ 841.

van der Sloot B and van Schendel S, 'Ten Questions for Future Regulation of Big Data: A comparative and Empirical Legal Study' [2016] 7 JIPITEC 110.

Vermont S, 'Independent Invention as a Defense to Patent Infringement' [2006] 105 Michigan LR 475.

von Lewinski S, 'Introduction: The Notion of Work under EU Law' [2014] GRUR Int 1098.

Wadlow C, 'Trade secrets and the Rome II Regulation on the law applicable to non-contractual obligations' 30 EIPR [2008] 309.

Warren S and Brandeis L, 'The Right to Privacy' [1980] 4 Harvard LR 193.

Wiebe A, 'Protection of industrial data – a new property right for the digital economy?' [2016] GRUR Int 877.

Wiebe A, 'Reverse Engineering und Geheimnisschutz von Computerprogrammen' [1992] CR 134.

Wiesner R M, 'A State-By-State Analysis of Inevitable Disclosure: A Need for Uniformity and a Workable Standard' [2012] 16 Marquette IPLR 211, 217-228.

Wilkie W L and Farris P W, 'Comparison Advertising: Problems and Potential, Source' [1975] 39 J of Marketing 7.

Zech H, 'Information as Property' [2015] 6 JIPITEC 192.

Zypries B, 'Hypertrophie der Schutzrechte?' [2004] GRUR 977.

### *§ 5 Studies and Reports*

Baker McKenzie, 'Study on Trade Secrets and Confidential Business Information in the Internal Market' (MARKT/2011/128/D) (2013) <http://ec.europa.eu/growth/tools-databases/newsroom/cf/itemdetail.cfm?item_id=8269> accessed 15 September 2018> accessed 15 September 2018.

Federal Trade Commission, 'Big Data: A Tool for Inclusion or Exclusion, Understanding the issues' (2016) FTC Report, 1 <https://www.ftc.gov/reports/big-data-tool-inclusion-or-exclusion-understanding-issues-ftc-report> accessed 15 September 2018.

Grosse Ruse-Khan H, 'The International Legal Framework for the protection of Utility Models' (2012) WIPO Regional Seminar on the Legislative, Economic and Policy Aspects of the Utility Model System, Kuala Lumpur <http://www.wipo.int/edocs/mdocs/aspac/en/wipo_ip_kul_12/wipo_ip_kul_12_ref_t2b.pdf> accessed 15 September 2018.

Hogan Lovells, 'Study on Trade Secrets and Parasitic Copying (Look-alikes) – Report on Parasitic Copying' (MARKT/2010/20/D) (2012) <https://www.google.com/url?sa=t&rct=j&q=&esrc=s&source=web&cd=1&cad=rja&uact=8&ved=2ahUKEwiy8tzludndAhWDaFAKHfYHC3UQFjAAegQICRAC&url=http%3A%2F%2Fec.europa.eu%2Finternal_market%2Fiprenforcement%2Fdocs%2Fparasitic%2F201201-study_en.pdf&usg=AOvVaw2Ws2o9bYEnYOj5RM9bFb8y> accessed 15 September 2018.

Hogan Lovells, 'Study on Trade Secrets and Parasitic Copying (Look-alikes) – Report on Trade Secrets' (MARKT/2010/20/D) (2012) <https://www.google.com/url?sa=t&rct=j&q=&esrc=s&source=web&cd=3&cad=rja&uact=8&ved=2ahUKEwiz8ZrYt9ndAhVEiRoKHUfLBxsQFjACegQIBxAC&url=http%3A%2F%2Fec.europa.eu%2Finternal_market%2Fiprenforcement%2Fdocs%2Fparasitic%2F201201-study_en.pdf&usg=AOvVaw2Ws2o9bYEnYOj5RM9bFb8y> accessed 15 September 2018.> accessed 15 September 2018.

Law Commission, *Law Commission Report on Breach of Confidence* (Law Com No 110, 1981).

Law Commission, *Legislating the Criminal Code: Misuse of Trade Secrets* (Law Com No 150, 1997).

Machlup F 'Economic Review of the Patent System' (1958) Study No. 15 of the subcommittee on the Judiciary-United States Senate 85th Congress, 2nd session, Washington.

Max Planck Institute for Intellectual Property and Competition, 'Study on the Overall Functioning of the European Trade Mark System' (2011) 65-67 <http://ec.europa.eu/internal_market/indprop/docs/tm/20110308_allensbach-study_en.pdf> accessed 15 September 2018.

McGuire MR, Joachim J, Künzel J and Weber N,'Protection of Trade Secrets through IPR and Unfair Competition Law' (2010) AIPPI Report Question Q215, 10 <http://aippi.org/wp-content/uploads/committees/215/GR215germany_en.pdf> accessed 15 September 2018.

OECD, 'Data-Driven Innovation: Big Data for Growth and Well-Being' (OECD Publishing 2015) 11-15 <http://dx.doi.org/10.1787/9789264229358-en> accessed 15 September 2018.

OECD, 'Digital Economy Outlook' (OECD Publishing 2015) 61 <http://dx.doi.org/10.1787/9789264232440-en> accessed 15 September 2018.

Suthersanen U, 'Utility Models and Innovation in Developing Countries' (2006) ICTSD Issue Paper No. 13 <http://unctad.org/en/docs/iteipc20066_en.pdf> accessed 15 September 2018.

The Tegernsee Group 'Consolidated Report on the Tegernsee user consultation on substantive Patent Law Harmonization (Tegernsee V)' (2014) <http://www.epo.org/news-issues/issues/harmonisation_de.html> accessed 15 September 2018.

The Tegernsee Group 'Report on Prior User Right (Tegernsee III)' (2012) <http://www.epo.org/news-issues/issues/harmonisation_de.html> accessed 15 September 2018.

### § 6 *Newspaper Articles*

'Data, data everywhere' *The Economist* (London, 25 February 2010) <http://www.economist.com/node/15557443> accessed 15 September 2018.

'Huge volumes of data make real time insurance a possibility – Pay per risk' *The Economist* (21 September 2017) <https://www.economist.com/finance-and-economics/2017/09/21/huge-volumes-of-data-make-real-time-insurance-a-possibility> accessed 15 September 2018.

'News Pirating Case in Supreme Court' *The New York Times* (New York, 3 May 1918) 1.

'Where the smart is' *The Economist* (San Francisco, 11 June 2016) <https://www.economist.com/news/business/21700380-connected-homes-will-take-longer-materialise-expected-where-smart> accessed 15 September 2018.

Chartrand S, 'Patents; Many companies will forgo patents in an effort to safeguard their trade secrets' *New York Times* (New York, 5 February 2001) C00005.

Fontgivell C, 'Equivalenza proyecta 20 aperturas en Estados Unidos' *Diario Expansión* (Barcelona, 20 April 2015) <http://www.expansion.com/catalunya/2015/04/20/5534b784268e3ee1648b4576.html> accessed 15 September 2018.

Rand B and Severson K, 'Recipe for Coke? One More to Add to the File' *New York Times* (New York, 19 February 2011) WK3.

### § 7 *Internet sources*

'Amazon Web Service User Agreement', para 3.1 <https://d1.awsstatic.com/legal/awsamendedCAterms/AWS%20Amended%20CA%20Terms_es.pdf> accessed 15 September 2018.

'Coca-Cola Moves Its Secret Formula to The World of Coca-Cola' (The Coca-Cola Company, 8 December 2011) <http://www.coca-colacompany.com/press-center/press-releases/coca-cola-moves-its-secret-formula-to-the-world-of-coca-cola/> accessed 15 September 2018.

'Obama Administration unveils "Big Data" Initiative: Announces $ 200 million in new R&D investments' (29 March 2012) <https://www.whitehouse.gov/sites/default/files/microsites/ostp/big_data_press_release.pdf> accessed 15 September 2018.

Bradshaw S and others, 'Contracts for Clouds: Comparison and Analysis of the Terms and Conditions of Cloud Computing Services' (2010) Queen Mary School of Law Legal Studies Research Paper No. 63/2010, 21-22 <http://dx.doi.org/10.2139/ssrn.1662374> accessed 15 September 2018.

Carey F A, 'Aromatic Compound' *The Encyclopaedia Britannica*, <http://www.britannica.com/science/aromatic-compound> accessed 15 September 2018.

Cohen W, Nelson R R, Walsh J P, 'Protecting Their Intellectual Assets: Appropriability Conditions and Why U.S. Manufacturing Firms Patent (or Not)' (2000) National Bureau of Economic Research Working Paper 7552 <http://www.nber.org/papers/w7552> accessed 15 September 2018.

Department for Business Innovation & Skills, 'Non-compete clauses – Call for Evidence' (2016) <https://assets.publishing.service.gov.uk/government/uploads/system/uploads/attachment_data/file/525293/bis-16-270-non-compete-clause-call-for-evidence.pdf> accessed 15 September 2018.

Drexl J and others, 'Position Statement of the Max Planck Institute for Innovation and Competition of 26 April 2017 on the European Commission's Public consultation on Building the European Data Economy' (2017) Max Planck Institute for Innovation & Competition Research Paper No. 17-08 <https://ssrn.com/abstract=2959924> accessed 15 September 2018.

Drexl J, 'Designing Competitive Markets for Industrial Data – Between Propertisation and Access' ( 2016) Max Planck Institute for Innovation & Competition Research Paper No. 16-13 <https://ssrn.com/abstract=2862975> accessed 15 September 2018.

European Copyright Society, 'Opinion on the pending reference before the CJEU in Case 310/17 (copyright protection of tastes)' (19 February 2018) para 17 <https://europeancopyrightsocietydotorg.files.wordpress.com/2018/03/ecs-opinion-on-protection-for-tastes-final1.pdf> accessed 15 September 2018.

Feldman Y, 'Behavioral And Social Mechanisms that Undermine Legality in The Workplace: Examining The Efficacy of Trade-Secrets Laws Among Knowledge Workers in Silicon Valley' (2005) Bar Ilan University Public: Law Working Paper No. 1-05, 24 <https://papers.ssrn.com/sol3/papers.cfm?abstract_id=714481> accssed 15 September 2018.

Gasser U and Palfrey J, '*Breaking Down Digital Barriers: How and When Interoperability Leads to Innovation*, plus three companion case studies on DRM, Digital Identity, and Web Services' (2007) Berkman Center Publications Series <http://nrs.harvard.edu/urn-3:HUL.InstRepos:2710237> accessed 15 September 2018.

Gintare S, 'Data Mobility in the Digital Economy' (2016) Max Planck Institute for Innovation & Competition Research Paper No. 16-03, 15 <https://papers.ssrn.com/sol3/papers.cfm?abstract_id=2752989> accessed 15 September 2018.

Godman E and others, 'Professors' Letter in Opposition to the Defend Trade Secrets Act of 2015' (November 17, 2015), 5 <https://cyberlaw.stanford.edu/files/blogs/2015%20Professors%20Letter%20in%20Opposition%20to%20DTSA%20FINAL.pdf> accessed 15 September 2018.

GRUR, 'Opinion on the proposal for a Directive on the protection of undisclosed know-how and business information (trade secrets) against their unlawful acquisition, use and disclosure, COM (2013) 813 final' (2014) <http://www.grur.org/uploads/tx_gstatement/2014-03-19_GRUR_Stellungnahme_zum_Know-how-Schutz_EN.pdf> accessed 15 September 2018.

Hall B H, Helmers C, Rogers M and Sena V, 'The importance (or not) of patents to UK Firms' (2013) NBER Working Paper No. 19089 <http://www.nber.org/papers/w19089> accessed 15 September 2018.

Hoss E, 'Delays in Patent Examination and their Implications under the TRIPS Agreement' (Master Thesis, MIPLC 2010/11) <http://ssrn.com/abstract=2166853 > accessed 15 September 2018.

Hugenholtz P B, 'Data Property: Unwelcome Guest in the House of IP' (2017) <https://www.ivir.nl/publicaties/download/Data_property_Muenster.pdf> accessed 15 September 2018.

Hughes A and Mina A, 'The Impact of the Patent System on SMEs' (2010) Centre for Business Research, University of Cambridge Working Paper No.411 Working Papers <https://www.uspto.gov/sites/default/files/aia_implementation/ipp-2011nov08-ukipo-1.pdf> accessed 15 September 2018.

Hussinger K, 'Is Silence golden? Patent versus secrecy at the firm level, Governance and the Efficiency of Economic Systems' (2005) ZEW Discussion Papers 04-78 <https://ideas.repec.org/p/zbw/zewdip/2883.html> accessed 15 September 2018.

IFRA, 'Comments on the Proposal for a Directive on the Protection of Undisclosed Know-How and Business Information (Trade Secrets)' (2014) 2 <http://www.ifra org.org/en-us/library/tag/21005/s0> accessed 15 September 2018.

IFRA, 'Valuable yet vulnerable: Trade Secrets in the fragrance industry' (2013) IFRA Position Paper <www.ifraorg.org/view_document.aspx?docId=23107> accessed 15 September 2018.

IP Federation, 'The EU Trade Secrets Directive' (2014) Policy Paper PP04/15 <https://www.ipfederation.com/news/ip-federation-comments-on-the-compromise-text-for-the-eu-trade-secrets-directive/> 15 September 2018.

Kur A, Bently L and Ohly A, 'Sweet Smells and a Sour Taste – The ECJ's L'Oréal decision' (2010) Max Planck Institute for Intellectual Property, Competition & Tax Law Research Paper Series No. 09-12 2, Paper No. 10/01, 2 <https://papers.ssrn.com/sol3/papers.cfm?abstract_id=1492032> accessed 15 September 2018.

Lapousterle J, Geiger C, Olszak N and Desaunettes L, 'What protection for trade secrets in the European Union?' (2015) Centre for International Intellectual Property Studies (CEIPI) Research Paper No. 2015-02 <https://ssrn.com/abstract=2970461> accessed 15 September 2018.

Lichtman D G, 'How the Law Responds to Self-Help' (2004) John M. Olin Program in Law and economics Working Paper 232 <http://www.law.uchicago.edu/Lawecon/index.html> accessed 15 September 2018.

Loukides M, 'What is Data Science?' (2010) <https://www.oreilly.com/ideas/what-is-data-science> accessed 15 September 2018.

Mell P and Grance T, 'The NIST Definition of Cloud Computing' (2011) The National Institute of Standards and Technology Special Publication 800-145, 2 <https://www.nist.gov/publications/nist-definition-cloud-computing> accessed 15 September 2018.

Noller C R, 'Chemical Comound' *The Encyclopaedia Britannica;* <http://www.britannica.com/science/chemical-compound> accessed 15 September 2018.

Quaedvlieg A, 'Copyright and Perfume: Nose, Intellect and Industry' (2011) 6, 7 (English translation by Margaret Platt-Homme) <http://www.klosmorel.com/en/our-people/antoon-quaedvlieg/publications/copyright-and-perfume-nose-intellect-and-industry/> accessed 15 September 2018.

Risch M, 'An Empirical Look at Trade Secret Law's Shift from Common to Statutory Law' (2013) Working Paper No. 2012-2008, 11-12 <http://ssrn.com/abstract=1982209> accessed 15 September 2018.

Surblyte G, 'Data as a Digital Resource' (2016) Max Planck Institute for Innovation and Competition Research Paper No. 16-12 <https://dx.doi.org/10.2139/ssrn.2849303> accessed 15 September 2018.

The European Corporate Observatory, 'A New Right To Secrecy For Companies, And A Dangerous EU Legislative Proposal Which Must Be Rejected' (30 March 2016) <https://corporateeurope.org/power-lobbies/2016/03/trade-secrets-protection> accessed 15 September 2018.

United Kingdom Intellectual Property Office, 'Consultation on draft regulations concerning trade secrets' (18 February 2018) 28 <https://www.gov.uk/government/uploads/system/uploads/attachment_data/file/682184/Consultation_Trade_Secrets_Directive.pdf> accessed 15 September 2018.

Volkswagen, 'With the aim of increasing safety in road traffic, Volkswagen will enable vehicles to communicate with each other as from 2019' (28 June 2017) <https://www.volkswagen-media-services.com/en/detailpage/-/detail/With-the-aim-of-increasing-safety-in-road-traffic-Volkswagen-will-enable-vehicles-to-communicate-with-each-other-as-from-2019/view/5234247/7a5bbec13158edd433c6630f5ac445da> accessed 15 September 2018.

White House, 'Non-Compete Agreements: Analysis of the Usage, Potential Issues, and State Responses' (2016) <https://obamawhitehouse.archives.gov/sites/default/files/non-competes_report_final2.pdf> accessed 15 September 2018.

Winter R, 'Big Data: Business Opportunities, Requirements and Oracle's Approach' (2011) Executive Report <http://www.oracle.com/us/corporate/analystreports/infrastructure/winter-big-data-1438533.pdf.> accessed 15 September 2018.

Zaby AK, 'Losing the lead: Patents and the disclosure requirement' (2005) Tübinger Diskussionsbeitrag No. 296 <http://nbn.resolving.de/urn:nbn:de:bsz:21-opus-20528> accessed 15 September 2018.

### *§ 8 Multilateral Trade Negotiations*

Multilateral Trade Negotiations: the Uruguay Round, Communication from Brazil (MTN.GNG/NG11/W/57).

Multilateral Trade Negotiations: the Uruguay Round, Draft Agreement on Trade-Related Aspect of Intellectual Property Right – Communication from the European Communities (MTN.GNG/NG11/W/68).

Multilateral Trade Negotiations: the Uruguay Round, Draft Agreement on the Trade-Related Aspects of Intellectual Property Rights – Communication from the United States (MTN.GNG/NG11/W/70).

Multilateral Trade Negotiations: the Uruguay Round, Draft Agreement on the Trade-Related Aspects of Intellectual Property Rights – Communication form Switzerland (MTN.GNG/NG11/W/73).

Multilateral Trade Negotiations: the Uruguay Round, Draft Agreement on the Trade-Related Aspects of Intellectual Property Rights – Chairman's Report to the Group of Negotiations on Goods (MTN.GNG/NG11/W/76).

Multilateral Trade Negotiations: the Uruguay Round, Draft Agreement on the Trade-Related Aspects of Intellectual Property Rights – Draft Final Act Embodying the Results of the Uruguay Round of Multilateral Trade Negotiations submitted by the Group of Negotiation on Goods (MTN.TNC/W/35/Rev. 1).

Multilateral Trade Negotiations: the Uruguay Round, Draft Agreement on the Trade-Related Aspects of Intellectual Property Rights – Draft Final Act Embodying the Results of the Uruguay Round of Multilateral Trade Negotiations (MTN.TNC/W/FA).

Multilateral Trade Negotiations: the Uruguay Round, Guidelines for Negotiations that strike a Balance Between Intellectual Property Rights and Development Objectives – Communication from Peru (MTN.GNG/NG11/W/45).

Multilateral Trade Negotiations: the Uruguay Round, Meeting of 30 October - 2 November 1989 – Note by the Secretariat (MTN.GNG/NG11/16).

Multilateral Trade Negotiations: the Uruguay Round, Meeting of the Negotiating Group dated 12 September 1989 (MTN.GNG/NG11/14).

Multilateral Trade Negotiations: the Uruguay Round, Note of the Secretariat on the Meeting of Negotiating Group on 2, 4 And 5 April 1990, dated 24 April 1990 (MTN.GNG/NG11/20).

Multilateral Trade Negotiations: the Uruguay Round, Standards and Principles Concerning the Availability, Scope and Use of Trade-Related Intellectual Property Rights – Communication from Switzerland – Addendum on Proprietary Information (MTN.GNG/NG11/W/38/Add.1).

Multilateral Trade Negotiations: the Uruguay Round, Standards and Principles concerning the Availability Scope and Use of Trade-Related Intellectual Property Rights – Communication from India (MTN.GNG/NG11/W/37).

### *§ 9 Case law*

*A) U.S. case law*

*I. Supreme Court*

Bonito Boats, Inc. v. Thunder Craft Boats, Inc., 489 U.S. 141 (1989).

E.I. DuPont de Nemours Powder Co. v. Masland, 244 U.S. 100 (1917).

Feist Publ'ns, Inc. v. Rural Tel. Serv. Co., 499 U.S. 340 (1991).

INS v. Associated Press, 248 U.S. 215 (1918).

Kewanee Oil Co. v. Bicron Corp., 416 U.S. 470 (1974).

Ruckelshaus v. Monsanto Co., 467 U.S. 986 (1984).

Sears, Roebuck & Co. v. Stiffel Co., 376 U.S. 225 (1964).

*II. Federal cases*

A.L. Labs., Inc. v Philips Roxane, Inc., 803 F.2d 378 (8th Cir. 1986).

American Can Co. v. Mansukhami, 728 F.2d 818 (7th Cir. 1982).

AMP Inc. v. Fleischhacker, 823 F.2d 1199 (7th Cir. 1987).

Anaconda Company v. Metric Tool & Die Company, 485 F. Supp. 410 (E.D. Pa 1980).

Cataphote Corporation v. Hudson, 444 F.2F 1313 (5th Cir. 1971).

Conmar Products Corp. v. Universal Slide Fastener Co., 172 F.2d 150 (2d Cir.1949).

CVD, Inc. v. Raytheon Co., 769 F2d 842 (1st Cir. 1985).

Data General Corp. v. Grumman Systems Support Corp., 36 F.3d 1147 (1st Cir. 1994).

Epic Systems Corporation v. Tata Consultancy Services Limited et al, No. 3:2014cv00748 - Document 243 (W.D. Wis. 2015).

Gates Rubber Co. v. Bando Chemical Industries, Ltd. et al., *9 F.3d 823* (10th Cir. 1991).

Head Ski Co. v. Kam Ski Co., 158 F. Supp. 919 (D. Md. 1958).

Julie Research Laboratories, Inc. v. Select Photographic Engineering Inc., 998 F.2d 65 (2d Cir. 1993).

Learning Curve Toys Incorporated v. Playwood Toys Inc., 342 F. 3d 714 (7th Cir. 2003).

Leo M. Hall, 781 F.2d 897 (Fed. Cir. 1986).

Lumey Inc. v. Highsmith, 919 F Supp. 624 (E.D.N.Y. 1996).

Matter of Innovative Construction Systems, Inc., 793 F.2d 875 (7th Cir. 1986).

Metallurgical Industries v. Fourtek Inc., 790 F.2d 1195 (5th Cir. 1986).

Murray v. National Broadcasting Co., Inc., 844 F.2.d 988 (2d Cir. 1988).

National Basketball Association (BA) v. Motorola Inc., 105 F.3d 841 (2d Cir. 1997).

Nickelson v. General Motors Corporation, 361 F.2d 196 (7th Cir. 1966).

Northern Petrochemical Co. v. Tomlinson, 484 F.2d 1057 (7th Cir. 1973).

On-Line Technologies, Inc. v. Bodenseewerk Perkin-Elmer GmbH, 386 F.3d 1133 (Fed. Cir. 2004).

Painton Company v. Bourns Inc., 442 F2d 216 (2d Cir. 1971).

Papa John's International, Inc. v Pizza Magia International, LLC, No. 00-10071 (5th Cir. 2001).

Penalty Kick Management, Ltd. v. Coca-Cola Co, 318 F. 3d 1284 (11th Cir. 2003).

Pepsi Co, Inc. v. Redmond, 54 F3d 1262 (7th Cir. 1995).

Q-CO Industries, Inc. v. Hoffman, 625 F.Supp. 608 (S.D.N.Y. 1985).

Religious Technology Center v. Lerma 908 F.Supp. 1362 (E.D. Va. *1995*).

Religious Technology Center v. Netcom On-Line Commc'n Servs., Inc., 923 F.Supp. 1231 (N.D. Cal. 1995).

Richter v. Westab, Inc., 529 F.2d 896 (6th Cir. 1976).

Rockwell Graphic Systems, Inc. v. DEV Industries, Inc., 925 F.2d 174 (7th Cir. 1991).

Servo Corp. of Am. v. General Electric Co., 393 F.2d 551 (4th Cir. 1968).

Shatterproof Glass Corp. v. Guardian Glass Co., 322 F. Supp. 854 (E.D. Mich. 1970).

Storage Tech. Corp. v. Custom Hardware Eng'g & Consulting Inc., 421 F.3d 1307 (Fed Cir. 2005).

Timely Products Corp v. Arron 523 F 2d 288 (2d Cir. 1975).

VD, Inc. v. Raytheon Co., 769 F.2d 842 (1st Cir. 1985).

*III. State cases*

Abba Rubber Co. v. Seaquist, 286 Cal.Rptr. 2d 518 (Cal. Ct. App. 1991).

Anadarko Petroleum Corp. v. Davis, 2006 WL 3837518 (S.D. Tex. 2006).

Colony Corp. of America v. Crown Glass Corp., 430 N.E.2d 225(Ill. App. Ct.1981).

Data Gene Corp. v. Digital Computer Controls Inc., 297 A.2d 437, 439 (Del. 1972).

Dayton Superior Corp. v. Yan et al, No. 3:2012cv00380 (S.D. Ohio 2012).

Disher v. Fulgoni, 464 N.E.2d 639 (Ill. App. Ct. 1984).

DVD Copy Control Association Inc. v. Andrew Bunner, 75 P.3d 1 (Cal. 2003).

Eastman Co. v. Reichenbach, 20 N.Y.S. 110 (1892).

Edwards v. Arthur Andersen LLP, 189 P.3d 285 (Cal. 2008).

Furr's Inc. v. United Speciality Advertising Co., 338 S.W.2d 762 (Tex. App. 1960).

Hamer Holding Group, Inc. v. Elmore, 560 N.E.2d 907 (Ill. App. Ct. 1990).

Hyde Corporation v. Huffines, 314 S.W.2d 763 (1958).

L.M. Rabinowitz & Co. v. Dasher, 82 N.Y.S. 2d 431 (1948).

McCrady v. Oklahoma Department of Public Safety, 122 P.3d 473 (Okla. 2005).

Merck v. Smithkline Beecham Pharm Co., No. C.A. 15443-NC (Del. Ch 1999).

Peabody v. Norfolk, 98 Mass. 452 (1868).

Sinclair v. Aquarius Electronics, Inc., 116 Cal.Rptr. 654 (Cal. Ct. App. 1974).

Smith v. Recrion Corporation, 541 P.2d 663 (Nev. 1975).

Smithkline Beecham Pharmaceuticals Co. v. Merck & Co., Inc., 766 A.2d 442 (Del. 2000).

Tan-Line Studios Inc. v. Bradley, 1 U.S.P.Q.2d 2032 (E.D. Pa. 1986).

Teller v. Teller, 53 P.3d 240 (Haw. 2002).

TGC Corp. v. HTM Sports, B.V., 896 F. Supp. 751 (E.D. Tenn. 1995).

U.S. West Communications, Inc. v. Office of Consumer Advocate, 498 N.W.2d 711 (Iowa 1993).

Vacco Indus., Inc. v. Van Den Berg, 5 Cal. App. 4th 34 (Cal. Ct. App.1992).

Wal-Mart Stores, Inc. v. The P.O. Market Inc., 66 S.W.3d 620 (Ark. 2002).
Wilson. v. Barton & Ludwig Inc., 296 S.E.2d 74 (Ga. Ct. App. 1982).
Wissman v. Boucher, 240 S.W.2d 278 (Tex. 1951).

*B) German case law*

BAG NJW 1983, 134, 135 – Thrombosol.
BAG NZA 1988, 502 – Weinhändler.
BAG NZA 1994, 502 – Titandioxid.
BAG NZA 1996, 310 – Nachvertragliches Wettbewerbsverbot.
BAG NZA 2010, 1175 – Anspruch auf KarenzentschÄdigung nur bei verbindlichem Wettbewerbsverbot.
*BAG* BeckRS 2013, 67444.
BayObLG GRUR 1991, 694 – Geldspielautomat.
BGH GRUR 1955, 388 – Dücko.
BGH GRUR 1955, 468 – Schwermetall-Kokillenguß.
BGH GRUR 1962, 207 – Kieselsäure.
BGH GRUR 1963, 367 – Industrieböden.
BGH GRUR 1964, 31 – Petromax II.
BGH GRUR 1966, 576 – Zimcofot.
BGH GRUR 1972, 541 – Imidazolines.
BGH GRUR 1975, 206 – Kunststoffschaum-Bahnen.
BGH GRUR 1977, 539 – Prozessrechner.
BGH GRUR 1980, 750 – Pankreaplex.
BGH GRUR 1981, 267 – Dirlada.
BGH GRUR 1983, 179 – Stapel-Automat.
BGH GRUR 1999, 934 – Weinberater.
BGH GRUR 2003, 356 – Präzisionsmessgeräte.
BGH GRUR 2009, 603 – Versicherungsvertreter.
BGH GRUR 2010, 47 – Füllstoff.
BGH GRUR 2012, 1048 – Movicol.
BGH IIC 2004, 449 – Spritzgießwerkzeuge.
BGH MMR 2006, 815 – Kundendatenprogramm.
OLG Hamburg GRUR-RR 2001, 137, 139 – Nachbau einer technischen Vorrichtung nach Ablauf des Patentschutzes.
OLG Karlsruhe MMR 2016, 562.
RGZ 1907 65, 333 – Pomril.
RGZ 1935 149, 329– Stiefeleisenpresse.

*C) English case law*


Ackroyds (London) Ltd v Islington Plastics Ltd [1962] RPC 97 (Ch).

Alfa Laval Cheese Systems Ltd and Another v Wincanton Engineering Ltd [1990] FSR 583 (Ch).

Attorney General v Guardian Newspapers Ltd (No2) [1990] 1 AC 109 (HL).

Attorney General v Newspaper Publishing Plc and Others [1989] 2 FSR 27 (Ch).

Barclays Bank Plc v Guardian News and Media Ltd [2009] EWHC 591 (QB).

Boardman v Phipps [1967] 2 AC 46 (HL).

Campbell v MGN Ltd [2004] 2 AC 457 (HL).

Carflow Products (UK) Ltd v Linwood Securities [1996] FSR 424 (Ch).

Coco v A.N.Clark (Engineers) Ltd [1969] RPC 41 (Ch).

Coulthard v Disco Mix Club Ltd [2000] 1 WLR 707 (Ch).

Cray Valley Ltd v Deltech Europe Ltd [2003] EWHC 728 (Ch).

Creations Records Ltd v News Group Newspaper Ltd [1997] EWHC Ch 370 (Ch).

De Maudsley v Palumbo [1996] FSR 447 (Ch).

Department of Health v Information Commissioner, (EA/2008/0018, 18 November 2018).

Douglas v Hello! Ltd and others [2007] UKHL 21.

DWP v IC (EA/2010/0073, 20 September 2010).

Dyson Technoloy Ltd v Strutt [2005] EWHC 2814 (Ch).

English & American Insurance Co Ltd v Herbert Smith 2 [1988] FSR 232 (Ch).

Faccenda Chicken Ltd v Fowler [1987] Ch 117 (CA).

Financial Times Ltd & Ors v Interbrew SA [2002] EWCA Civ 274 (CA).

Football Dataco & Others v Stan James Plc & Others and Sportradar GmbH & Other [2013] EWCA Civ 27 (CA).

Force India Formula One Team Ltd v 1 Malaysia Racing Team SDN BHD [2012] EWHC 616 (Pat).

Force India Formula One Team Ltd v 1 Malaysia Racing Team SDN BHD [2013] EWCA civ 780 (CA).

Franchi v Franchi [1967] RPC 149 (Ch).

Fraser v Thames Television Ltd [1984] QB 44 (QB).

Gartside v Outram [1857] 26 LJ Ch 113.

HEFCE v Information Commissioner and the Guardian News and Media Ltd (EA/2009/0036, 10 January 2010).

Helmet Integrated Systems Ltd v Tunnard [2007] FSR 385 (CA).

Herbert Morris Ltd v Saxelby [1916] AC 688 (HL).

International Scientific Communications Inc v Pattinson and Others [1979] FSR 429 (Ch).

L'Oréal SA v Bellure NV [2007] EWCA Civ 968 (CA).

L'Oréal SA v Bellure NV [2010] EWCA Civ 535 (CA).

Lamb v Evans [1893] 1 Ch 218 (CA).
Lancashire Fires Limited v S.A. Lyons & Company Limited and Others [1996] FSR 629 (CA).
Malone v Commissioner of Police of the Metropolis (No 2) [1979] 2 All ER 620 (Ch).
Marcel v Commissioner of Police of the Metropolis [1992] Ch 225 (CA).
Mars UK Ltd v Teknowledge Ltd [2000] FSR 138 (Pat).
McKennitt v Ash [2006] EWCA Civ 1714 (CA).
Morison v Moat (1851) 9 Hare 241.
Mustad v Son v Dosen and another [1964] 1 WRL 109 (HL).
Nichrotherm Electrical Co Ltd v Percy [1956] RPC 272 (Ch).
Nordenfelt v Maxim Nordenfelt Guns and Ammunition Co Ltd [1984] AC 535 (HL).
Ocular Sciences Ltd v Aspect Vision Care Ltd [1997] RPC 289 (Pat).
Petrofina (Great Britain) Ltd v Martin [1966] Ch 146 (CA).
Polymasc Pharmaceuticals plc v Charles [1999] FSR 711 (Pat).
Prince Albert v Strange [1849] 2 De G & Sm 652.
Re Smith Kline & French Laboratories Ltd [1990] 1 AC 64 (HL).
Regina Glass Fibre v Werner Schuller [1972] RPC 229 (CA).
Robb v Green [1895] 2 QB 1 (QB).
Rolls-Royce Ltd v Jeffrey (Inspector of Taxes) [1962] 1 WLR 425 (HL).
Royal Brunei Airlines Sdn Bhd v Philip Tan Kok Ming [1995] 2 AC 378 (PC).
Sales v Stromberg [2006] FSR 7 (Ch).
Saltman Engineering v Campbell Engineering [1948] 65 RPC 203 (CA).
SAS Institute Inc v World Programming Limited [2013] RPC 17 (Ch).
Schering Chemicals Ltd v Falkman Ltd [1982] QB 1 (CA).
Seager Limited v Copydex Limited [1967] 2 All ER 415 (CA).
Shelley Films Limited v Rex Features Limited [1994] EMLR 134 (Ch).
Spencer v Marchington [1988] IRLR 392 (Ch).
Stephens v Avery [1988] FSR 510 (Ch).
Sun Valley Foods Ltd v Vincent [2000] FSR 825 (Ch).
Susan Thomas v Elizabeth Pearce and Another [2000] FSR 718.
Terrapin Ltd v Builders' Supply Co (Hayes) Ltd [1962] RPC 375 (Ch).
Thomas Marshall (Exports) Limited v Guinle [1979] FSR 208 (Ch).
Under Water Welders & Repairers Ltd v Street and Longthorne [1968] RPC 498 (QB).
University of London Press v University Tutorial Press [1916] 2 Ch 601 (Ch).
Vestergaard Frandsen A/S v Bestnet Europe Ltd [2011] EWCA Civ 424 (CA).
Vestergaard Frandsen A/S v Bestnet Europe Ltd [2013] UKSC 31.

Voila ES Nottinghamshire Ltd and Nottinghamshire County Council v Dowen [2010] EWCA Civ 1214 (CA).

Wainwright v Home Office [2003] 3 WLR 1137 (HL).

*D) Australian case law*

Moorgate Tobacco Co, Ltd v Philip Morris Ltd (No 2) [1984] 156 CLR 414.

Tablot v General Television Corp [1981] RPC 1.

*E) Dutch case law*

Kecofa B.V. v. Lancôme parfumes et beauté. Et cie S.N.C, No. C04/327 Hoge Raad (16 June 2006).

Lancôme Parfums et Beauté et Cie S.N.C., v. Kecofab B.V., C0200726/MA (8 June 2004).

*F) French case law*

Fabrique de Produits de Chimie Organique de Laire v. Societé de parfums Marcel Rocha, Tribunal Commercial de Paris (7 Januar 1974); unpublished.

Thierry Mugler Parfums v. SA GLB Molinard, T.com. Paris, 15th ch., 24 Septembre 1999, LPA 3 March 2000, pp 13-16.

*Beauté Prestige International v. Bellure*, CA Paris, 4th ch., (17 September 2004) unpublished.

Beauté Prestige International v. Senteur Mazal, Cass. 1st Civ (1 July 2008) 07-13952

Bsiri-Babur v. Haarmann &Reimer et al, Cass. 1st Civ.(13 June 2006).

Rochas v. de Laire, CA Paris, 4th ch., 3 July 1975, Gaz. Pal.21-22 January 1976, pp. 43-45.

L'Oréal v. Bellure, TGI Paris, 3rd ch., 26 May 2004, D. 2004; 2641-2645.

Cour de Cassation, Tresor-Armani-Mania (10 December 2013) Case No. 11-19.872, IIC 2014, 829-831.

*G) European case law*

*I. Court of Justice of the EU*

6/64 Flaminio Costa v ENEL [1964] ECR 585.

8/74 Procureur du Roi v Dassonville [1974] ECR I-837.

120/78 Rewe-Zentrale AG v Bundesmonopolverwaltung für Branntwein (Cassis de Dijon) [1979] ECR I-649.

238/87 AB Volvo v Erik Veng (UK) Ltd [1988] ECR I-6211.

C–267/91 and C-268/91 Keck and Mithurard [1993] ECR I-6097.

C-241/91 P and C-242/91 Radio Telefis Eireann (RTE) and Independent Television Publications (ITP) v Commission of the European Communities [1995] ECR I-00743.

C–112/99 Toshiba Europe GmbH v Katun Germany GmbH [2001] ECR I-07945.

C–2/00 Hölterhoff v Freiesleben [2002] ECR I-4187.

C–273/00 Sieckmann v DPMA [2002] ECR I-1173.

C–299/99 Koninklijke Philips Electronics NV v Remington Consumer Products Ltd [2002] ECR I-05475.

C–46/02 Fixtures Marketing Ltd v Oy Veikkaus Ab [2004] ECR I-10396.

C–136/02 P Mag Instrument Inc v OHIM [2004] ECR I-09165.

C–203/02 The British Horseracing Board Ltd v William Hill Organization Ltd [2004] ECR I-10415.

C–338/02 Fixtures Marketing v Svenska Spel AB [2004] ECR I-10497.

C–418/01 IMS Health v NDC [2004] ECR I-05039.

C–444/02 Fixtures Marketing Ltd v Organismos prognostikon agonon podosfairou AE (OPAP) 1 [2004] ECR I-10549.

C–468/01 P to C-472/01 P Procter & Gamble Companyv. OHIM [2004] ECR I-05141.

C–321/03 Dyson Ltd v Registrar of Trademarks [2007] ECR I-687.

C–381/05 De Landtsheer Emmanuel SA v Comité interprofessional du Vin de Champagne and Veuve Clicquot Ponsardin SA [2007] ECR I-03115.

C–450/06 Varec SA v Belgium [2008] ECR I-581.

C–5/08 *Infopaq International v Danske Dagblades Forening* [2009] ECR I-6569.

C–487/07 L'Oréal v Bellure [2009] ECR I-05185.

C–48/09 P Lego Juris v OHIM [2010] ECR I-08403.

C–92/09 and C–93/09 Volker und Markus Schecke and Eifert [2010] ECR I-11063.

C-393/09 Bezpečnostní softwarová asociace v Ministerstvo kultury [2010] ECR I-13971.

C-145/10 Eva-Maria Painer v Standard VerlagsGmbH and Others [2011] ECR I-12533.

C–323/09 Interflora Inc and others v Marks & Spencer and others [2011] ECR I-08625.

C-403/08 and C-429/08 Football Association Premier League and Others [2011] ECR I-9083.

C–404-10 P Lagardère SCA v Éditions Odile Jacob SAS (CJEU, 29 June 2012).

C–406/10 SAS Institute Inc. v World Programming Ltd (CJEU, 2 May 2012).

C–477/10 P European Commission v Agrofert Holding a.s. (CJEU, 28 June 2012).

C-604/10 F*ootball Dataco Ltd and others v Yahoo! UK Ltd and others (CJEU, 1 March 2012).*

C–30/14 Ryanair Ltd v PR Aviation BV (CJEU, 15 January 2015).

C–481/14 Jørn Hansson v Jungpflanzen Grünewald GmbH [2016] (CJEU, 9 June 2016).

*II. General Court*

T–76/98 Independent Television Publications Ltd v Commission [1991] ECR II-575.

T–305/04 Eden SARL v OHIM [2005] ECR II-04705.

T–129/04 Develey Holding GmbH & Co. Beteiligungs KG v OHIM [2006] II-0811.

T–194/01 Unilever NV v OHIM [2006] ECR II-00383.

T–201/04 Microsoft v Commission [2007] ECR II-03601.

T–508/08 Bang & Olufsen A/S v OHIM [2011] ECR II-06975.

T–189/14 Deza v ECHA (13 January 2017).

T–718/15 PTC Therapeutics International Ltd v EMEA (GC, 5 February 2018).

*III. Commission*

Microsoft (Case COMP/C-3/37.792) Commission Decision 2007/53/EC [2007] OJ L32/23.

*H) EPO case law*

EPO T 381/87 [1990] OJ EPO 213.

EPO T 931/92 (10 August 1993).

T 426/88 [1992] OJ EPO 427.

G 1/92 [1993] OJ EPO 277.

T 830/90 [1994] OJ EPO 713.

T 472/92 [1998] OJ EPO 161.

G 2/99 [2001] OJ EPO 83.

G 3/98 [2001] OJ EPO 62.

T 681/01 (28 November 2006).

T 355/07 (28 November 2008).

EPO T1553/06 (12 March 2012).

*I) OHIM Boards of Appeal case law*

Case R 156/1998-2 Vennootschap onder Firma Senta Aromatic [1999] OHIM OJ 1239.

*Case R 711/1999-3* Myles Limited (OHIM Boards of Appeal, 5 December 2001).

*J) EctHR case law*

Hertel v Switzerland (1998) 28 EHHR 534.

Société Colás Est v France (2004) 39 EHRR 17.

Von Hannover v Germany (2005) 40 EHHR 1.

Ashby Donald and Others v France App no 36769/08 (ECtHR, 10 January 2013).

*K) WTO case law*

WTO, Argentina – Footwear (EC), WTO Appellate Body Report, WT/DS121/AB/R (14 December 1999) .

WTO, United States –Upland Cotton, WTO Appellate Body Report, WT/DS267/AB/ (2 March 2005).